THE ENCYCLOPEDIA OF

American Food & Drink

Also by John F. Mariani

The Dictionary of Italian Food and Drink

Eating Out

Mariani's Coast-to-Coast Dining

America Eats Out

Vincent's Cookbook

The Four Seasons

THE ENCYCLOPEDIA OF

American Food & Drink

JOHN F. MARIANI

Lebhar-Friedman Books

New York Chicago Los Angeles London Paris Tokyo

Lebhar-Friedman Books
425 Park Avenue
New York, NY 10022

© 1999 John F. Mariani
Published by Lebhar-Friedman Books
First copyright © 1983 by John F. Mariani, published by Ticknor & Fields
Revised and updated edition copyright © 1994 by John F. Mariani,
    published by Hearst Books

Published by Lebhar-Friedman Books
Lebhar-Friedman Books is a company of Lebhar-Friedman, Inc.

Printed in the United States of America

Library of Congress Cataloging-in-Publication Data

Mariani, John F.
    The encyclopedia of American food and drink / by John Mariani.
        p. cm.
    Includes bibliographical references
    ISBN 0–86730–784–6
    1. Cookery. American Dictionaries.   2. Food Dictionaries.
3. Beverages Dictionaries.   I. Title
641.5973'03—dc21
                                                    99-23630
                                                    CIP

COVER DESIGN BY KEVIN HANEK
COMPOSITION BY MILLER WILLIAMS DESIGN ASSOCIATES

Visit our Web site at lfbooks.com

Volume Discounts

This book makes a great gift and incentive. Call (212) 756-5240
for information on volume discounts.

For Galina

PREFACE: IN SEARCH OF
AMERICAN FOOD

In 1977 my wife and I drove crosscountry for eleven weeks, with no firmer commitment than to see what we had not seen, learn what we did not know, and savor what we had not tasted. We began in New York, went south, then west across Texas and over the mountains to California. Our return took us through the Grand Canyon, the flatlands of Kansas, and the snowy hills of the Midwest before ending on the edges of New England.

At that time I had no intention of compiling a gastronomic encyclopedia nor even of writing a book of any kind about American food. In fact, most of our meals on the road were disappointing, consumed in restaurants recommended by friends, editors, and guide books, the most thorough of which was the multivolumed *Mobil Travel Guide,* an oil company's Baedeker with the uncanny ability to choose the most restaurants specializing in steaks, chops, and prime ribs. Depending on such a guide would lead a traveler to believe that Americans live on nothing but steak and potatoes—a prevailing view in most people's minds anyhow, and one the compilers of the *Mobil Travel Guide* took to heart.

One can hardly blame them, since even in the large cities and small towns of the South and West our request for a good meal was usually answered with directions to the nearest steak house. The "best" restaurant in town was invariably the kind of place peripatetic author Calvin Trillin spoke of when he described "some purple palace that serves 'Continental cuisine' and has as its chief creative employee a menuwriter rather than a chef." My wife was almost brought to tears at a penthouse restaurant atop a hotel in Birmingham, Alabama, when a waiter tried to make up for some stale shrimp cocktail with a sweet lime sherbet intended to "clear the palate" before moving on to a tough, burned steak.

What we found difficult to believe was that restaurants serving traditional, fine American cuisine are exceedingly difficult to find. The board members of local chambers of commerce, the businesspeople, and the tourist-information agents may eat in a wonderful little barbecue place on the outskirts of town, but without fail they will send the traveler to one of those hotel dining rooms where decor and situation mean far more than quality or integrity of food. So we'd ply our way through a wretchedly made béarnaise, wilted stringbeans *amandine,* filet mignon topped with canned liver pâté, and *mousse au chocolat* with all the taste and texture of shaving cream.

Only with the greatest and most insistent effort did we ferret out a good American restaurant serving old-fashioned fare or just plain, well-made contemporary cookery. We found that most of the cooking of this sort, as the Time-Life *American Cooking* series indicated, was being done in the homes of Americans who were upholding a long and honorable heritage of baking, roasting, grilling, barbecuing, and mixing—from frosted silver mugs of mint julep to tortillas with a salsa cruda more complex than any Gallic *rouille.*

We sampled excellent corn bread, made without sugar in the South, and crabmeat dishes in Charleston that were creamy and full of the flavor of the Caribbean, and in the Southwest a bowl of fresh, fragrant guacamole.

But it was not only in the homes that we began to find American food: there were cafeterias serving well-made stews and perfect pies; diners where the German chocolate cake was hot out of the oven; a barbecue pit set up in what was once an Army barracks; and pastry shops that served up the best muffins I've ever had.

In New Orleans we had red beans and rice and sampled beignets and chicory coffee in the French Market there. There were walnut waffles in Greensboro, and deep-fried, cornmeal-dusted catfish at a Vicksburg restaurant where we were entertained by an organ player wearing a VFW cap. We couldn't get enough of those succulent Gulf shrimp or pecan pie with peach ice cream, and in Texas a meal of chili and ice-cold beer seemed one of the best things in the world as we listened to a jukebox full of Hank Williams classics. We were introduced to chimichangas in Arizona, enjoyed fresh game in Nevada, burgers of real substance in Los Angeles, and exquisite wines in the Napa and Sonoma valleys. Traveling back across the western plains we had fine roast beefs and sturdy pot roasts, breakfasts with hefty side orders of bacon, ham, grits, hash browns, and the inevitable orange slice. In a ski town in Pennsylvania we warmed up with a white bean soup, and in New England a pot of chowder made with quahog clams and topped with common crackers. Back in New York we threw ourselves into every imaginable ethnic cuisine— from Czech to Greek, from Sichuan to Hunan, from Moroccan to Korean. And there were plenty of prime steaks, black on the outside, pink within, sidled with crisp, golden onion rings and cottage fries. We were soon trying to make up our minds whether to buy a Jewish cheesecake on the Lower East Side or an Italian cheesecake in Little Italy.

In the years since then Americans have become more interested in more kinds of food than anyone might have imagined two decades before. Much of the writing on food and wine continued to praise the products and preparations of chefs in Lyons, Munich, Florence, and Hong Kong, but along with the growth of the delicacy or "gourmet" shops in American cities came a reevaluation of the conclaves of ethnic cooking in our immigrant cities, which in turn led to a reappreciation of regional American dishes. And although the new boom towns like Houston and Atlanta made fast progress in installing deluxe French restaurants in their new hotels, there arose an attendant interest in American cookery. Trendy city magazines might review the new *nouvelle cuisine* dining room downtown, but they would also scour the countryside to find the best pizza, the best cheesecake, the ice cream, the best chili, or the best hamburger in the state. Even Julia Child began demonstrating how to prepare American dishes on her TV show.

Ironically, the very critics who had argued that complexity meant excellence now began to see the virtues of simplicity in a well-grilled piece of fish or a beautifully roasted loin of pork with fresh applesauce. The idea of a clambake on a beach was taking on fashionable social overtones, and no one would argue that a Maine lobster, just boiled and then served with butter, accompanied by a baked Idaho potato and a glass of California Chardonnay could ever be improved upon by any chef in the world.

I thought about all this after that trip in 1977, and I was encouraged to write this book when I could find no gastronomic dictionary or encyclopedia that traced the origins, terminology, slang, and methods of American cookery, except as part of a larger international cuisine. I decided I needed such a book, and so I wrote it.

Since then American gastronomy has gone through enormous changes, and it is arguable that the United States has become the world capital of cuisine, both as an exemplar of the most modern culinary styles and as an influence on world food culture. Not only has the intrusion (some would say invasion) of American fast food eateries like McDonald's and KFC had enormous effect on the way young Europeans, South Americans, and Asians now eat, but the influence of American restaurants at the white tablecloth level have had an equal impact on the way fine dining is now perceived and carried out in cities from Berlin to Singapore.

So much has occurred in American gastronomy that it was necessary to revise my original research to show the extraordinary evolution of the American table, both at home and in restaurants. The availability of new ingredients, the adaptation of new cooking techniques, the increased appetite for eating out among those who have little time left to cook at home, and the resiliency of an American food industry that must constantly create new foods and flavors designed for an international market have all required a more far-reaching look at what is now the subject of American gastronomy.

ACKNOWLEDGMENTS

Without the help of my wife, Galina, in tasting, testing, and criticizing so many recipes and so much good and bad food, this book would not have been conceived in the first place.

My thanks for more than a decade of encouragement and professionalism to Diane Cleaver.

And for help in so many ways, I will always count among my friends and critics Michael and Ariane Batterberry, Anthony Dias Blue, Gene Bourg, Ellen Brown, Craig Claiborne, A. Craig Copetas, Cara Da Silva, Malachy Duffy, Tom Fitzmorris, Pierre Franey, Lila Gault, Marion Gorman, Dotty Griffith, Nika Hazelton, Jack McDavid, Peter Meltzer, Joan Nathan, Warren Picower, Stephen Raichlen, Delbert Runyon, Janice Schindeler, Barbara Seldin, Jane and Michael Stern, Richard David Story, and John Martin Taylor.

Last, I owe a great debt to my mother and father, Renee and Eligio Mariani, who truly believed that setting a good table is an expression of love and one of the highest traditions of culture.

CONTENTS

Preface: In Search of
American Food...vii

Introduction: Toward
a Misunderstanding
of American Food...xiii

A Guide to the Encyclopedia......................................xxiii

The Encyclopedia of
American Food and Drink 1

A Bibliographic Guide..359

Index..365

INTRODUCTION: TOWARD A MISUNDERSTANDING OF AMERICAN FOOD

In 1947 expatriate American author Henry Miller wrote, "Americans can eat garbage, provided you sprinkle it liberally with ketchup, mustard, chili sauce, cayenne pepper, or any other condiment which destroys the original flavor of the dish."

Miller might have gone on with such hyperbolic scorn by noting that the French will eat anything with a cream sauce, Italians anything with tomato and garlic, Indians anything with curry powder, and Chinese anything with soy sauce—all to cover up the original flavor of the dish.

None of these assertions holds true, but such facile and offhanded criticism of American food, wine, and drink has become almost a tradition; by now it is a gastronomic cliché to identify American food as hamburgers, hot dogs, Coca-Cola, and ice cream—a list that would not even adequately describe the offerings at a summer baseball game. More than once, back in 1982, the response of friends to the news that I was preparing the first edition of this book was "But what is American food? Fried chicken and pizza?"—as if to suggest that all American food is prepared at fast-food outlets and dispensed by young people wearing silly hats.

Others would argue that there is no such thing as American food (except, perhaps, whatever it was the Indians ate before the coming of the white man) because everything was brought over by Europeans, Africans, and Asians; or that, even if "created" here, an American dish is merely an adaption of or variation on a foreign dish—as evidenced by America's distressing fondness for chop suey, spaghetti and meatballs, and "Chablis" made in the hills of California. Jambalaya, these critics will assert, is little more than a Louisiana version of Spain's paella; New England clam chowder derives from French seafood soups cooked in a copper pot called a *chaudière*; even a quintessentially American cocktail like the Harvey Wallbanger depends for its effectiveness on Galliano, an Italian liqueur.

Such allegations completely and conveniently ignore how every culture in the world has borrowed, absorbed, and been changed by the food and drink of other cultures, whether through conquest, assimilation, or mere emulation. It has long been debated whether Marco Polo brought noodles back from the Orient, but we do know he returned with recipes for frozen milk desserts that may have been the first European sherbets. Had India not been dominated by the Persian Moguls, the cuisine of Punjab, Kashmir, and Uttar Pradesh would be utterly different from what it is, and Japan would not have its tempura dishes had Portuguese traders not introduced the idea there three hundred years ago. Italians will always be delighted to remind their French neighbors that Gallic cookery was forever transformed after Caterina de' Medici (who became Catherine de Médicis) brought her Italian chefs with her in 1547 when she set up her French court.

So, too, the influence of the American cornucopia on the rest of the world has been enormous, from the time the tomato was first introduced to Italy in the sixteenth century, through the era of triangular trade between England, Africa, and New England, based on American cod and West Indies sugar, and up to the modern age, when American food-processing technology and agricultural surpluses have not only saved nations from starvation but altered the diets of their people. Even the American-inspired "Japanese steak house" has become popular in Tokyo, while the McDonald's hamburger stand on the Champs-Élysées is crowded with young Parisians who undoubtedly douse their burgers with ketchup, mustard, and the rest of the condiments Henry Miller deplored. Nor shall the *vignerons* of Bordeaux and Burgundy ever forget that it was roots from American vines that salvaged the French wine industry after the phylloxera blight of the nineteenth century.

The simple truth is that no nation's cuisine has ever sprung entirely and ingenuously from its own kitchens. Thus, the United States—a stewpot of cultures—has developed a gastronomy more varied, more distinctive, and more colloquially fascinating than that of any other country in the world, all based on an astounding bounty of meat, fruit, vegetables, grains, dairy products, and fish, as well as an incomparable system of transportation that makes finding Pacific salmon on a New York dinner plate an unremarkable occurrence. In any major American city one will find restaurants representing a dozen national cuisines, including northern Italian trattorias, bourgeois French bistros, Portuguese seafood houses, Vietnamese and Thai eateries, Chinese dim sum parlors, Japanese sushi bars, and German rathskellers. Add to these an endless array of regional delicacies—Creole gumbo, Philadelphia scrapple, Texas chili, Maryland she-crab soup, the Detroit bullshot, Florida Key Lime pie, Napa Valley Zinfandel, North Carolina pork barbecue, the Arizona chimichanga, Rhode Island johnnycake, Long Island duckling, Boston scrod, the New Orleans Sazerac, Kentucky bourbon, Minnesota blue cheese, and thousands of others—and one must marvel at the diversity and breadth of American food and drink. And in the decade since this *Encyclopedia* first appeared, the style and cuisine created by young Americans have begun to affect the way gastronomy has developed around the world, from the appearance and popularity of fast-food outlets in Paris, Rome, Moscow, and Peking to the look and taste of so-called California grill restaurants in London, Peking, and Melbourne.

"In nothing is there more evolution than the American mind," wrote Walt Whitman, and this is as true of an American's food as it is of his politics, his art, or his treasured mobility, which allowed him to maintain his immigrant heritage while assimilating a new one. The apple may have been brought to America by the Pilgrims, but it was a gentle Swedenborgian named John Chapman, better known as Johnny Appleseed, who extended the fruit into the western territories and helped turn the United States into the world's largest grower of apples. An ex-slave named George Washington Carver revived the depleted economy of the South through his experiments in and promotion of peanut farming. A movement of men and beasts from Texas to Kansas after the Civil War resulted in a cattle industry that determined the social, political, and even literary character of the Midwest. In 1840 a German-American Philadelphian named John Wagner produced a light lager that immediately became the dominant style of beer in America and led to the establishment of the great brewery families that shaped the destinies of cities like Milwaukee and Portland, Oregon.

For all this, however, American gastronomy has been chronically underrated, constantly satirized, and continuously characterized as unimaginative, unsophisticated, and unredeemably bland, depending more on portion size than preparation time for its effect. Such bias began early in our history, coming from both European and native gastronomes who found the American way of eating all at odds with civilized behavior. It became fashionable for French travelers to shudder at the barbaric table manners and eating habits of Americans. Constantin François de Chasseboef, Count de Volney, showed his disdain for American palates in a report published in 1804 in London:

> *In the morning at breakfast they deluge their stomach with a quart of hot water, impregnated with tea, or so slightly with coffee that it is more colored water, and they swallow, almost without chewing, hot bread, half baked, toast soaked in butter, cheese of the fattest kind, slices of salt or hung beef, ham, etc., all of which is nearly insoluble. At dinner they have boiled pastes under the name of puddings, and their sauces, even for roast beef, are melted butter; their turnips and potatoes swim in hog's lard, butter, or fat; under the name of pie or pumpkin, their pastry is nothing but a greasy paste, never sufficiently baked. To digest these viscous substances they take tea almost instantly after dinner, making it so strong that it is absolutely bitter to the taste, in which state it affects the nerves so powerfully that even the English find it brings on more obstinate restlessness than coffee.*

Europeans gasped at the amount of salt pork, lard, oysters, and pastries Americans consumed, and in much of the criticism there is a strong hint of envy, for Americans, on the whole, ate far better than any other people on the face of the earth. After the initial years of starvation faced by the earliest settlers, the American land gave up its bounty, as the forests and lakes and seas had done immediately. There seems no exaggeration in the reports of the first Europeans on these shores about hundred-pound cod, forty-pound wild turkeys, six-foot lobsters, and game birds so numerous as to blacken the sky when they flew. In his first dispatch to England in 1606 Captain John Smith asked, with a proud immigrant's exuberance, was it not wonderful to be in a land "where man, woman and childe, with a small hooke and line, by angling, may take divers sorts of excellent fish, at their pleasures? And is it not a pretty sport, to pull up two pence, six pence, and twelve pence, as fast as you can haule and were a line?" This was written at a time when the great majority of Europeans lived on nothing but bread or porridge, when they could get it at all.

Certainly deprivations persisted, but not for lack of abundance. The diets of African slaves on Southern plantations were severely restricted by their owners, usually insufficient for good nutrition and rarely augmented by foraging in the fields and forests. The diet of the indentured servant was little, if at all, better. But for others the American larder was full and fully utilized. Hogs, brought to the West Indies by Columbus and introduced to Jamestown by the English, proliferated so well that by the end of the seventeenth century Virginia and Maryland were exporting pork back to Europe. Corn, a native grain, became the most important crop in the States; molasses fueled the economies of several nations; and oysters were so plentiful that by the late eighteenth century they had become the staple of the urban poor's diet.

With the establishment of strong, well-governed colonies came wealth, and with wealth came refinement both in the arts and at the dinner table. For the most part food remained plain-fried or roasted meats and game, boiled fish, cider to drink, and hot breads. Involved sauces were frowned upon as Gallic kickshaws and the food of fops. Yet there were large numbers of "cookery books" (most of them British until the publication in 1796 of *American Cookery*, a forty-seven-page volume by "An American Orphan" named Amelia Simmons), which gave complicated, though less than detailed, recipes for stewed carp in a sauce of claret, anchovies, and shallots thickened with butter and egg yolks; ice creams and purees of fruits; and all manner of pastries. Few Americans of the eighteenth century ever made or even came across such dishes, but, it must be stated forcefully, neither did most Europeans. The fallacy of European taste and elegance lies in its microcosmic scope; it involved no more than a small percentage of the population and focused on only two classes of people the gentry and the nouveau riche. Nevertheless, tables set by Americans like Thomas Jefferson easily rivaled in gastronomic interest those presented at the finest dining salons of France or England.

Jefferson's passion for good food was merely an extension of his voracious appetite for knowledge in every form. His experiments in farming and gardening were directly involved with his experiments in cooking, and he was forever fascinated by foreign foods, methods of preparation, and botanical distinctions that affected the flavors of things. He even installed a French chef in the White House, then brought in two African-American women to apprentice with the master and learn his techniques. Jefferson brought back a waffle iron from Holland as well as a pasta machine from Italy, and imported all sorts of plants, fruits, and even olives from Europe. Though criticized by Patrick Henry for renouncing American victuals, Jefferson was not at all interested in turning Monticello into a Virginian Petit Trianon or in turning his back on American food; indeed, he was, in Evan Jones's words, "determined to surround the best of Virginia food with the best from European cuisine." As Jefferson told his friend Lafayette, if a man wishes to learn about French food he must "ferret people out of their hovels, as I have done, look into their kettles, eat their bread."

By the nineteenth century American cooking had developed quite naturally along regional lines and European traditions, always modified by the exigencies of the land. Foods that were major items in one region's diet may have been marginal in another's, but Americans did share a certain manner of cooking and eating by the middle of the nineteenth century. The cuisine of New Orleans was easily the most distinctive of all the gathered strains of American cookery, but there were dishes to be found in New England— Joe Froggers, Deacon Porter's hat, rum tum tiddy, Harvard beets, and Parker House tripe, to name a few—unlikely to be encountered in the South, while a South Carolinian spending a week in Vermont would be hard put to find a kitchen serving cooter stew, Lady Baltimore cake, mint juleps, hopping john, or benne brittle.

The farther west settlers trekked, the more culinary cohesion Americans took on, for although the Midwest was settled largely by people of German extraction who continued making many dishes from the Old Country, the new territories and broad farms provided such a wealth of grain, fruits, vegetables, and livestock that the whole country began eating much the same diet, still buoyed by copious portions of meat. Barbecue grew out of the South and Southwest, and there was considerable Mexican influence along the Rio Grande. The food of the pioneers was often horrifying, meant only to keep body and soul, though not appetite, together during the push across the wilderness. The stories of these settlers are harsh, full of tales of starvation and revulsion for a diet that never varied from St. Louis to Oregon. Mostly they ate preserved foods, salt pork, jerky, dried corn, and dried-apple pies. Trappers might make a "butter" from buffalo marrow, blood, and boiling water, while others survived on insects, vultures, and reptiles.

After the Civil War beef asserted itself as a most desirable alternative to pork, and by the twentieth century "steak and potatoes" had become synonymous with the American diet; at the same time the American sweet tooth developed with the drop in sugar prices. There were by the end of the nineteenth century lavish restaurants serving the most extravagant meals and bars serving all manner of beers and cocktails to a public that never lacked for ice, while everyone ate at chowder houses, delicatessens, coffeehouses, and tamale stands. Even as far west as Denver, in 1892 a hotel like the Brown Palace could put up a spread that included littleneck clams, consommé renaissance, trout ravigote, Maryland terrapin, German wines, and French champagne. This was as nothing compared to the meals created in New York's Delmonico's, Boston's Parker House, or Chicago's Sherman House, where ten-course meals were everyday suppers.

In fact, it was the virtue of such restaurants to bring America into gastronomic repute. They impressed even European visitors who previously had expected the kind of disastrous dining experiences noted by Charles Dickens, who described dinner, supper, and breakfast aboard a Pennsylvania canal boat as identical to one another—tea, coffee, bread, butter, salmon, shad, liver, steak, potatoes, pickles, ham, chops, black puddings, and sausages, all consumed by gentlemen who "thrust the broad-bladed knives and the two-pronged forks farther down their throats than I ever saw the same weapons go before except in the hands of a skillful juggler."

By the same token the opulent restaurants and grand hotels of the Gilded Age focused attention on the gluttonous nature of dining among the newly rich, which led quite naturally to a general criticism of all Americans' eating habits. And the menus of such establishments—fussed up with French dishes and French terminology for American dishes scorned the food of the common man in an attempt to elevate the status and palate of the American trying desperately to appear civilized.

As a result, regional American cuisine became a subject of homely virtues, expressive of the gracious and genteel traditions of Victorian womanhood. Old recipes for local delicacies were not so much forgotten as ignored, so that the first edition in 1896 of Fannie Merritt Farmer's extraordinarily successful *Boston Cooking-School Cook Book* contained sensible, well-tested recipes for *potage à la reine, maître d'hôtel* butter, charlotte russe, and cutlets *à la Maintenon* (along with hints on how to clean mirrors, remove wine stains, and sweep carpets) and had a three-page glossary composed almost entirely of French terms.

Nothing so relegates a culture to mediocrity as to be thought quaint, and by the beginning of the twentieth century American cookery had entered just such a phase, largely as a reaction to the ways in which the populace had come to enjoy its meals—at beer halls, at ball parks, at county fairs, on boardwalks, at roadside stands, at soda fountains, at lunch counters, at pizzerias, at hash houses, at saloons, at spaghetti joints, at barbecue pits. Food was taken on the run, eaten on park benches, wolfed down at taverns, consumed at beach parties, and all of it was ingested too quickly. Concerns about the health of the population not only led to a reassessment of the nutritive values of foods, but also resulted in federal regulations to combat corrupt and sickening practices in the meat and agriculture industries. These concerns ultimately led, with a strident moralism, to Prohibition, which radically altered the manner in which people cooked, ate, and dined out for more than a decade.

The so-called "ladies' books" had long imitated Victorian hesitancy when describing food in print—rice would be called "farinaceous dishes" and a meal was "a simple repast"—and this tradition continued well into the present century. There was an attempt to ban the use of the term "hot dog" from all vendors' signs in Coney Island, lest people think their frankfurters really contained dog meat. And the vitality of lunch-counter speech—"cat's eyes" for tapioca, "baby" for a glass of milk, "Jerk" for ice cream soda, and "Adam and Eve on a raft" for fried eggs on toast—had a raciness about it that many people sought to put an end to in the 1930s.

More profound than any other factor affecting the image of American cookery in this century was the pervasive influence of immigrants on the culture. The waves of new settlers driven to the American shore were inspired not by a belief that the streets were paved with gold but by sheer, basic hunger. What the Poles, Jews, Italians, Irish, Germans, Armenians, and others found in America was far more valuable than gold: It was a constantly available supply of fruits, fresh water, good grains, green vegetables, annual harvests of plenty, and safe, healthful milk.

The immigrants immediately set about adapting their native cookery to what was available in the American marketplace. Certain vegetables were not readily found here, and the water was different, as were the flour, the butter, the meat, and the wonderful cookstoves (by the 1930s, gas and electric stoves too). These differences altered traditional cooking methods and changed the tastes and textures of their foods.

Lox, so closely associated with Jewish Americans, was unknown to European Jews; the Italian pizza, once a staple of the Neapolitan poor, became an American snack food; *gulyás*, in Hungary a dried meat carried by shepherds, became in America goulash, a kind of peppery stew; chop suey and chow mein came out of the makeshift kitchens of Oriental workers on the western railroads; and wines from native American grapes were labeled "Green Hungarian," "Chianti," and "Sauterne."

The culture was immeasurably enriched by the influx of the immigrants, as was the language of our gastronomy: Americans spoke with evident familiarity about beerfests, wieners, bagels, tutti-frutti, hamburgers, Swedish meatballs, ravioli, smörgasbörds, Danish pastries, liverwurst, vichyssoise, chow-chow, lager, curry, matzo ball soup, halvah, tortillas, paprika, baklava, moussaka, and sukiyaki, and they visited bodegas, delicatessens, trattorias, sushi bars, taco stands, Greek coffee shops, dim sum parlors, pizzerias, rathskellers, and bistros. All these foods and all these places were transformed into American institutions, for better or for worse. Add to these the extraordinary growth of the processed-food and confections industries, with items like Coca-Cola, Crisco, Sugar Daddy, Eskimo Pie, Cheerios, Grape-Nuts, Pork & Beans, Niblets, and thousands of others, and one begins to sense the dimensions of American gastronomy.

It is, of course, legitimate to suggest that many of these items fall far short of the culinary sublime, or that much of the "ethnic" food on this side of the Atlantic bears scant resemblance to that in the Old Countries. But such a criticism accepts three erroneous claims:

First, that people in France, Germany, Italy, or China at the turn of the century were eating splendid meals on a daily basis—that a citizen of Bordeaux sat down each evening to a fine *coq au vin* made with a bottle of excellent claret; that a Sicilian peasant each afternoon enjoyed a steaming plate of macaroni with a rich tomato-and-garlic sauce, followed by fresh mussels and a glass of Marsala with dessert; or that a worker in Canton province regaled his neighbors with a meal of lobster steamed with ground pork or chicken with wild mushrooms.

Second, that the transformation of a dish, especially by Americanized immigrants, is always inferior to the original. Yet, except for certain classic and mannered dishes in French and other gastronomies, there are really very few dishes in the world that have not been modified or radically altered by inventive cooks. In northern Italy the cooks look down with dyspepsia on the olive-oil-and-garlic-rich cuisine of the south, while the people from one province to another regard the butter and wines of their direct neighbors with disdain. A French *cassoulet* will have as many variants as there are households in Toulouse, and every Moroccan will argue vociferously that her *couscous* is the only "authentic" one in her village. (This same form of debate rages among American cooks who consider the alteration of a single ingredient in a southern fried chicken recipe or the use of the wrong kind of cornmeal in a johnnycake as tantamount to bona fide heresy and sacrilege.)

Third, that American cuisine is nothing more than the cookery of peasants, dispossessed people, and uneducated amateurs whose foods may taste wholesome, even delicious, but rarely sublime. Such a position is not only snobbish but misses the whole thrust of American cookery—or any nation's cookery, for that matter. The cuisine of the royal courts, the gentry's manors, and the entrepreneur's town houses is never the cuisine of a country. Fabled dishes—from excesses like tournedos Rossini to glories like *poularde à la périgourdine*—are not to be found simmering in the kettles of French kitchens, but hearty *choucroute*, aromatic *bouillabaisse*, and oxtail stew are. For every Carême or Escoffier in France there are a million unheralded home cooks whose cuisine truly carries on the reputation of France over the centuries.

Yet French deluxe cuisine—meaning that prepared only in the greatest, most expensive, and most socially exclusive restaurants—continues as the measure of a country's culinary culture and sophistication, a criterion rigidly promoted by those who own, cook, and dine in such places. The notable restaurants of the nineteenth and early twentieth centuries in America were designed not for an appreciative mass of middle-class eaters—and certainly not for the new immigrant class—but for the wealthy, who did not expect to find on the menu homely dishes like peanut soup, barbecued spareribs, spoon bread, ham with redeye gravy, and fudge cake, much less Polish sausage, manicotti, and Irish soda bread. (To be fair, restaurants like Delmonico's, Rector's, and others offered a wide variety of American game, pies, and desserts, though usually described on the bill of fare as "*à la*" this or "*au*" that.) By the turn of the century, hotel restaurants like the Waldorf's Palm Garden had hired tyrannical maître d'hôtels like Oscar Tschirky, an ex-busboy who rose to near royalty in New York society by decreeing who was and was not fashionable in his dining room, which served a menu rife with Gallicisms. A menu of 1904 served to William Howard Taft, then secretary of war, read as follows:

Cocktail aux Huîtres, Consommé de Volaille, Printanière, Tortue Verte Claire, Radis Olives Céleri Amandes Salées, Coquilles de Bass à la Virchow, Concombres Marines, Couronne de Ris de Veau avec Champignons Frais, Mignons de Filet de Boeuf à la Cardinalice, Pommes de Terre Sautées en Quartiers, Petits Pois à la Française, Fond d'Artichauts Frais à la Dubarry, Sorbet de Fantasie, Pluviers d'Herbes Rôtis, Gelée de Groseilles Salade Chiffonade, Glaces à la Grenadine, Petits Fours, Fruits, Cigars, Café. [The wines were all French.]

Ironically, the Waldorf could turn out some very "American" meals—dishes like colombine of chicken California style, ruddy duck, and the famous Waldorf salad. Even in the French dishes the chefs used excellent-quality American ingredients, a fact that should not be lost on those current-day practitioners of what is called the New American Cuisine, which uses American ingredients and French techniques.

But reputations were not built on serving the kind of food that might just as easily be turned out by immigrant housewives or African-American cooks. Interestingly enough, it was the African-American cooks who maintained, even in restaurants, the great traditions of southern cuisine in cities like New Orleans, Charleston, Richmond, and Savannah and who kept up the strain of northern cookery in Boston, Philadelphia, and Chicago. None of these cooks, however, was known to anyone except steady customers, who might have called them by their first names. Professional American cooks were known only as "Jimmy" or "Thomas" or "Henry" to their public, and the fame of ethnic cooks in the northern cities was enshrined in the names of the restaurants themselves—Tony's, Haussner's, or O'Brien's, for example. Memoirs of the first half of this century speak of ethnic restaurants with believable affection, but rarely with high regard for the food, except to say that it was cheap, belly-filling, and honestly prepared.

It is significant that of the more than fifty volumes in the American Guide series published under the Federal Writers' Project during the Depression, only a handful mention the food of a region, and fewer still mention restaurants at all. American cooking was simply not considered worthy of critical scrutiny, even though a work like Irma S. Rombauer's *Joy of Cooking*, which first appeared in 1931 and has gone through several revisions, remains a thorough and authoritative collection of American recipes and kitchen techniques.

American food was looked upon as rib-sticking, plain, sometimes wholesome, sometimes not, fun to eat, fast to eat, and never anything to be fussed with or over. Writers took true delight in exalting the lowliest of sandwiches, the greasiest of meats, the hottest of preparations, and the gloppiest of desserts with a kind of deliberate thumb-to-the-nose attitude that only hardened the opinions of gastronomic critics who believed all along that Americans reveled in bad taste. Or, as Henry Miller wrote, Americans would eat garbage if you put ketchup on it. We Americans prided ourselves on the number of hot dogs we could eat, the amount of candy we could consume, the intensity of hot peppers we could abide, and the time in which we could devour all of it. None of these achievements was likely to build a national reputation for gastronomic excellence.

At the same time Americans were being taunted by one of the most unreasonable and baffling forms of temperance, which sprang not from a nutritional argument but, for the most part, from a religious one. We are the only people in the world who, possibly because of our abundance, have been made to feel guilty about our good fortune. In a mild form this self-recrimination is evident in the pangs of conscience a person feels when he goes off his diet, and in the ridiculous way chocolate is described as "devil's food," especially considering that other cultures call chocolate the "food of the gods" (*Theobroma* in the Linnaean system) and describe rich desserts as "sinfully delicious." Clearly it was the duty of American religious crusaders to point out the sins of dissolution that result from too much wine, spirits, and extravagant food, but this was far more a position of the established English and German religions than of the new immigrant faiths.

Nevertheless, the passage of the Volstead Act in 1919 only ostensibly cut off most Americans from the enjoyment of wine and spirits (and actually led to more crime, corruption, and "sin") while severely crippling an already struggling wine industry in California, New York, and other states. To survive such a blow, vineyard owners turned to raisin production and selling grape juice for jams and jellies.

Prohibition also destroyed any possibility that American restaurants would develop a reputation for fine dining, much less a distinctive cuisine based on American fare. Even the first-class speakeasies of the era were not places one went to for great food. As Michael and Ariane Batterberry note in their book *On the Town in New York* (1973), "The depressing truth was that New Yorkers could not be enticed into a dry restaurant, no matter how superior the food; on the other hand, they seemed perfectly content to eat sawdust as long as it came with a drink."

The era of the grand banquets and twelve-course meals had vanished too, as did Delmonico's and Louis Sherry, two of the outstanding restaurants of pre-World War I days. Ethnic restaurants—tellingly referred to as "joints"—provided the cities with considerable liveliness, and the speakeasies provided gossipmongers with a new "Café Society" to write about.

After Prohibition ended in 1933, there was no scramble to restore the opulent dining of the past, though the enjoyment of good food was considerably more enjoyable now that wine and spirits were again available. Major cities began to nurture truly fine restaurants, like New York's Le Pavillon, which opened in 1941, but again, most of these were French or described by a new word—*Continental*. Continental restaurants aimed to please everyone's palate, serving up a mélange of dishes that ranged from filet mignon and clams casino to striped bass *à la meunière*, beef Wellington, and Baked Alaska, usually with an emphasis on French and Italian items. This approach to menu planning was precisely what gourmets might have expected from inferior kitchens, and too often the results were as expected.

If a restaurant was not dishing out such international approximations of authentic classics, it was busy gearing everything, including the food and service, to a "theme," created so that people who felt uneasy about ordering a meal at a fancy, formal restaurant, where one had to dress and act in a certain way, could casually enter dining rooms that were decorated like pirates' coves, Wild West saloons, Colonial taverns, or Roman temples, where all the waiters were dressed appropriately to the idea and where the food was described in the most expressive prose since *Euphues*. The most extravagant of such eateries were run by New York's Restaurant Associates, which could certainly turn out good meals on occasion but did so according to a "concept." Thus, at the Forum of the Twelve Caesars the menu was in Latin (with English subtitles), dishes were named after Cleopatra and Nero, and there were even barbaric puns on notable American dishes, like Caesar salad ("The Noblest Caesar of Them All").

The theme concept was quickly adopted throughout the country, and one never quite knew what to expect when one walked through the swinging doors of a restaurant called the Auto Pub or Long John Silver's; certainly one's gustatory expectations were not very high.

Restaurants with a superb view of the city became faddish by the 1970s; some dining rooms even revolved atop bank buildings as customers wolfed down plates of "Mile-High Pie." Waiters themselves were encouraged to become so friendly as to announce their first name to customers, whether or not the customer wanted to know it. This practice expressed a democratic spirit of such insecurity that implicit in the act was the common understanding that having a swell time was more important than having a great meal. What did it matter if the fish had been frozen and cooked by microwave, or that the entire entrée had been packaged in a New Jersey processing plant and merely needed to be heated up in order to serve a customer a perfectly proportioned meal, complete with bright green beans and bright orange carrots and a rim of powdered mashed potatoes caressing the veal Parmesan?

The advent of frozen foods in the 1940s and 1950s made life easier and to be sure, offered a new diversity of food items to a large number of people. The labor involved in cooking was reduced, and the guesswork and worry over a poorly wrought meal were removed. Another advance was "instant" foods—powdered puddings, potatoes, and cereals, prepackaged pancake batter, vegetables sealed in plastic pouches, and other less than delectable but wholly efficient preparations that seized the American imagination and made convenience a virtue far outweighing matters of taste and flavor.

Yet for all the criticism of such foods (and of an agricultural industry that propagated fewer varieties but hardier breeds of fruits and vegetables), the next phase of frozen, instant, and packaged foods was even worse—"gourmet dishes," such as fettuccine Alfredo, asparagus with hollandaise sauce, and "Oriental" vegetables. The final blow to American taste came with the plethora of diet foods, which were either traditional processed foods made with less sugar, oil, or syrup or smaller portions of the same old stuff. In recent years, nutritional terrorists have tried to sting Americans into believing that most of what they consume on an everyday basis is going to kill them—sooner or later.

It is no wonder, then, that American food deserved the hard knocks it has taken in the last twenty years. Indeed, Americans seemed proud of their so-called junk food, which at first meant snacks, candies, and other less than nutritious items but came to encompass "fast foods" sold at roadside stands usually run by nationwide chains. Several such operations have specialized in some of the more obvious items in the American kitchen—hamburgers, hot dogs, fried chicken, french-fried potatoes, apple pie, and ice cream—serving them lickety-split from assembly lines of griddles and deep fryers at the hands of patently chummy young people in standardized uniforms. Cheap, casual, and geared for ingestion of product rather than the pleasure of dining, these places reduced the flavor of such foods to the point where Henry Miller's comment about drowning the original taste with sweet-and-sour condiments began to make sense.

More disturbing was the fact that small, family-owned restaurants, where such food was traditionally made according to old recipes, were being nudged aside in favor of the fast-food eateries, so that even American institutions like the diner and the cafeteria, where excellent American fare could be had, found it difficult if not impossible to compete with the fast-food places' prices and "fun atmosphere."

The reaction to all this was the development of a culinary elitism that once again pronounced the excellence of French, Italian, and Oriental cuisines and the horrid state of American gastronomy. Even a charming Boston woman named Julia Child enjoyed a long run on public television showing Americans how to cook, not turkey with stuffing, clam chowders, or scrod, but *rôti de porc poêle*, *canard à l'orange*, and *choux de Bruxelles*. Credit must be given to such a television program and to Mrs. Child for relieving the inferiority complex American cooks had about French food and complex cooking processes in general. Her tone was typically Yankee and refreshingly reassuring, and she taught a generation how to care about excellent ingredients and attention to detail. And in her TV series in the 1980s, Child did feature American cooking and championed California wines.

There also appeared in the 1970s a number of works by authors who began seriously to restore traditional American fare to its proper perspective. James Beard, Craig Claiborne, James Villas, and Waverley Root spoke with authority and great affection of their childhood memories of catfish, Dungeness crab, pork barbecue, grits, blueberry bread, hot chilies, New England boiled dinner, Pacific oysters, potato salad, and scores of other delectables that many people had forgotten could be so very good when prepared with care and love and served with those same homely virtues.

At the same time, food magazines like *Gourmet, Cuisine, Food & Wine,* and others began devoting more space to American cookery, and even the Culinary Institute of America, a cooking school in Hyde Park, New York, long devoted to Continental cuisine, opened a separate course of study on American food.

The publication in 1970 of Time-Life's beautifully produced *Foods of the World* included seven volumes on regional American cookery, which gave the food a legitimacy of the kind afforded French, Italian, and Japanese cuisines. Well written, gorgeously illustrated, and full of well-tested, explicit recipes, these volumes on New England, Creole and Acadian, Northwest, Eastern Heartland, Southern Style, Great

West, and Melting Pot regional cooking showed just how diverse this nation's cookery is. They revealed the wealth of tradition and history behind each dish and a people's pride in every preparation.

Scores of other authoritative regional cookbooks have appeared since then, ranging from specific books on a single item like chili or cheesecake to thick volumes of recipes compiled by women's organizations throughout the United States. Several excellent histories of American food and drink have appeared within the last decade, along with delightful compendiums of lore and anecdotes on everything from candy bars and ice cream to North American fish. American wines, which in the 1970s became internationally respected, have been boosted by wine writers and recorded in narratives and encyclopedias with the same care and devotion to accuracy given the vineyards of Bordeaux and Burgundy. Things seem to be on the right track again.

Since the first edition of this book appeared in 1983, American restaurants have garnered worldwide reputations, the American marketplace has absorbed thousands of new foods from every corner of the globe, the American farmer is now raising everything from kiwifruit to foie gras, and the American consumer has become far more sophisticated and demanding about the quality, availability, and safety of his or her food. And finally, the FDA has put some meaning and muscle into monitoring and defining what goes into our processed foods.

As ever, but even more so now, American food is diversified, modified, substantial, complex, heterogeneous, subtle, humdrum, exciting, excessive, embracing, soul-warming and stomach-filling, hot, cold, prepared with honesty, concocted with audacity, promoted with passion, consumed with courage, debated with conviction, tossed in a pot, simmered in a kettle, fried in a skillet, chilled in a bowl, shaken in a canister, brewed in an urn, topped off, tossed out, shoved down, pushed aside, got through, held up, jiggled at the end of a pole, brought down with an arrow, skinned with a knife, tested with a finger, squeezed with a hand, sniffed at, cursed at, argued over, and beloved by a people who will try anything once.

What is American food?

It is this—

A GUIDE
TO THE ENCYCLOPEDIA

No one ever starts writing an encyclopedia of anything believing it will be a complete record of its subject. Even a compiler of known facts on Etruscan art hopes that tomorrow a new shard of pottery will be unearthed that will add to or alter his work in small but important ways. The subject of a country's food, more than most others, is as inexhaustible as language itself, for each generation renames, reworks, and reevaluates the culture that produced it, discarding some prejudices and reinforcing others. Two of the most American of American animals—the buffalo and the turkey—were misnamed from the start (the American buffalo is really a bison, and the turkey was confused with a guinea fowl brought from Turkey), yet we retain their appellations proudly. Other foods go through so many mutations that they bear scant resemblance to the original.

No county worth its salt has fewer than six different names for the same kind of regional fish, all of which differ from the next locality's names for the same creature. And what Yankees refer to as a "Partridge" is really a ruffed grouse, while a southerner who points out a "partridge" is really indicating a quail. The American who calls a sweet potato a "yam" has never seen a true yam.

Language is consistent only in its mutability, as is the food and drink we eat, celebrate, and argue over. A Texan would never dream of letting a kidney bean near the chili, but a midwesterner couldn't imagine chili without a whole mess of beans. (A "mess," incidentally, may mean a lot of food sloppily thrown together, but an older usage denotes nothing more than an assemblage of people eating together or a portion of food.)

Etymologists will argue forever as to the true origins of "martini" (indeed, the word "cocktail" itself is still under linguistic scrutiny), the exact derivation of "Harvard beets," the root of the name "calas" for the deep-fried rice cakes of New Orleans, and the way "doughboys" got their nickname. Who can say just when the old usage of "truck farm," meaning a fresh-produce market, took on the contemporary usage of the farm on which the produce sold at market is grown? Why and when did Americans show a preference for "hot dogs" over "weenies," or "bar" over "saloon"?

My aim in this encyclopedia is to demonstrate both the array of American food, wine, and drink and the way Americans speak of it, consume it, and have changed it over the centuries. In each case I have tried to answer the questions I myself would ask were I looking for information on an apple or a tamale, a brief history of Prohibition, or a slang term for a "bartender." I have endeavored to include as much as possible about American gastronomy, and, thanks to the input of so many readers of the first edition, this third edition is far more comprehensive.

More important than all-inclusiveness is accuracy, and I hope that my research has been fruitful enough to turn up the best information and the most reliable anecdote on a particular subject, although I have been quick to point out when this or that story is mere legend. Sometimes a story is so enjoyable it begs for inclusion, even with my strong reservations about its veracity.

While I regret any errors or omissions, I welcome corrections and addenda from the reader, and I fully expect to hear what I hope will be sympathetic words from people all over the country who can enlighten me as to the precise origin of a dish or the only correct way to mix a drink.

This volume is not a history of gastronomy or of the American language, nor is it a cookbook. It assuredly is not a book to tell the reader the best way to skin a rabbit or skim a broth. There are several books available on each of these subjects. This book contains elements of all of them, gathered into a survey, from *A* to *Z*, of the origins, changes, and current status of food and drink items, terms of culinary interest, and slang.

Although my own background is academic and journalistic, my approach has been to inform the general reader in as readable and entertaining a way as possible. I have, therefore, kept abbreviations to a minimum and discarded footnotes in favor of giving full credit in the body of the text or in the Bibliographic and Guide acknowledgments. While I hope every sentence makes a good point, I sometimes cannot resist an anecdote that I believe the reader will enjoy.

My dependence on the work of others who have labored for a lifetime in the fields of etymology and linguistics has been enormous, and I take scant credit for illuminating dark corners where others' lights have failed to find a convincing explanation. I merely suggest what seems to me plausible, and then throw it open for discussion with the reader. I stand humbly in the shadow of H. L. Mencken, who wrote in the preface to his second supplement to *The American Language* (1948), "I am not trained in linguistic science, and can thus claim no profundity for my book. It represents gatherings, not of an expert in linguistics, but simply of a journalist interested in language, and if there appears in it any virtue at all it is with the homely virtue of diligence. Someone had to bring together the widely scattered field material and try to get some order and coherence into it, and I fell into the job."

Main Entries

Main entries are listed alphabetically, sometimes as a general heading for a type of food or drink. Under the more general topics—for example, APPLE, BEER, PANCAKE—there may very well be dozens of more specific terms, types, species, regional variants, slang phrases, or ancillary items within the body of the entry. The reader is urged to check the index for an item not found as a main entry. Within the main entries, a subitem may be printed in SMALL CAPITAL LETTERS, indicating that there is further information on that subject as a main entry.

Recipes

The recipes that follow a main entry's description of an item are chosen in most cases to be *representative* of a dish or item; the directions have deliberately been kept simple and brief. In some cases the source of a recipe is cited, especially if it is of historical importance or if it is the original source of the dish or drink. Recipes from an original source are always thus credited, as, for example, those for the Parker House roll or Trader Vic's mai tai. I have also included recipes from historical sources, either to give a sense of a food's original form or because such dishes are rarely, if ever, made anymore. Hartshorn jelly, for instance, was a well-known eighteenth-century confection, but as it is unlikely to be found today, I have provided an eighteenth-century recipe and noted the origin.

By a "representative" recipe I mean one that seems close to the way in which such a dish is usually made. I am well aware that there may be hundreds of variations on a "classic" recipe, but I have tried to choose the one that represents the principal ingredients and method of preparation that would be used by a wide range of cooks. I have not tried to choose the *best* recipe I've ever found for a specific dish, for the reason that it may very well *not* be representative of the way Americans cook. (Recipes for some of the finest desserts, pastries, and cookies I know come from several cookbooks written by

Maida Heatter, but they often do not represent the way most American cooks would prepare an item; they represent the unique and imaginative talents of this singularly remarkable woman.)

Many readers may find the recipes stingy with details and not specific enough in comparison with many cookbooks that lead the reader by the apron strings, explaining everything from how to peel a carrot to how to beat an egg. I have assumed that the user of this book possesses a certain culinary acumen—as did his or her ancestors, who cooked by very simple directions—and I simply did not have the space to include instructions on how to whip an egg white to "soft, glistening peaks" every time such a preparation was called for. So, too, if a cooked-sugar recipe calls for bringing the caramel to a "hard-ball" or "soft-ball" stage, the reader is assumed to be familiar with such terms, but is nevertheless provided with a temperature to test for on a candy thermometer. The details of making a dough and letting it rise in bulk are kept to a minimum, and often I will instruct the reader only to "make a pastry crust," rather than tell again how to make one.

This is not a book on nutrition, and I have tried to keep clear of arguments for or against the "healthfulness" of this or that dish or spirit. Nor is this an industry manual meant to contain hints on how best to cut, package, and store meat, fish, or fowl.

One rule I do advise the reader to follow with these recipes is to pay attention to the order in which ingredients are listed, for the order indicates at what point they should be added to a preparation. Although in many cases the addition of several spices or seasonings at once is justified, I have attempted to indicate the moment at which the next ingredient should be added, and it is best to blend each new addition thoroughly before putting in the next one. Cooks more or less familiar with the routine of such matters will know when this is important or not.

As for the terminology of cooking, I have conservatively adhered to level teaspoons and standard measurements in ounces and pounds, and avoided old-fashioned instructions like "add a wineglass of" such and such. On the other hand, I see no reason to be stringently specific about what constitutes a dash or a pinch, long-honored terms that make sense to anyone who cooks regularly. (There is an apocryphal story about Fannie Merritt Farmer giving instructions on making a martini that go, "To one cup gin, add . . .")

The recipes themselves come from a wide variety of sources from three centuries of American cookery, but the bulk come from cookbooks of the last thirty years for the reason that it is impossible to gauge the success factor of a recipe from an era when flour, yeast, molasses, baking powder (which came along only in the 1850s), wine, spirits, and even ovens were very different from what they have become in the past quarter century. Despite the prejudice of those who believe that cookbooks of the eighteenth and nineteenth centuries represent American culinary arts at their highest, there is really no way to reproduce recipes that call for ingredients like isinglass, pearl ash, and sack. Others would shudder at the thought of my including recipes from "ladies' magazines," because such journals often try to oversimplify or change recipes to suit some imaginary housewife who has access only to processed and packaged foods. The point is well taken, especially since many of these magazines depend on the advertising of the very products they recommend in a recipe. But if one is to compile an encyclopedia of gastronomy that tells the reader how Americans actually do cook and eat, such recipes play an important part. I have, for the record, never recommended margarine where butter is preferred, but it may be argued that Americans cook with far more margarine and shortening than butter. So, too, I have avoided brand names of products, except where they seem an intrinsic part of a recipe— Tabasco sauce, for example.

I claim no originality for any of these recipes—that would defeat the whole point of the book—and I have tried to cull workable recipes from reliable sources and to stay clear of arguments as to the "correct" method of preparing a dish. "Correct methods" are usually those that an individual believes to be the best method or those derived from a recipe of antique interest. American cookery has very few "classic" recipes; even those that originated at a specific place and time have been changed, sometimes for the worse, often for the better. That is the role of a good cook, for absolute imitation is the drudgery of the slave or the pedant.

What Is and Is Not Included

As I have indicated, there is no workable definition of what constitutes American cuisine. Most American dishes are essentially variations or derivatives, which is true of almost every dish in the world. "The discovery of a new dish is more beneficial to humanity than the discovery of a new star," wrote Brillat-Savarin (who rather liked American food when he visited here in 1794), but every new dish is really a variation on an old one. Anyone who has ever paged through Escoffier's *Le Guide Culinaire* will immediately be struck by the minor modifications of one dish that allow it to be called something entirely different; the same is true of *Larousse Gastronomique*, in which one finds that the addition of one standard sauce or another to poached chicken deserves a new appellation and brief cooking instructions.

Certain dishes or drinks indisputably originated in America: Key Lime pie, corn bread, bourbon, fudge, and hundreds of others. Other dishes, like jambalaya, gumbo, beignets, and much of the cuisine of the Creoles and Cajuns, were derived from European, Caribbean, Indian, and African sources, but were then turned into distinctive American foods. Beverages like shrubs, flips, grogs, and punches became popular in Great Britain and America at the same time, while turkey, buffalo, and numerous species of fish were exported to Europe, where they became delicacies.

I have been liberal in my choice of what to include, but I believe I have good reasons to keep many items out. While it may be true that the Bloody Mary cocktail was "created" in Paris in the 1920s (when it was called the "Bucket of Blood"), the drink caught on here, not there, and has remained a standard American bar item ever since the 1930s. On the other hand, even though Americans drink more scotch than any other people outside Britain, the fact is that by law scotch is produced only in Scotland and has no business being in an encyclopedia of American gastronomy.

The real problem develops when one deals with the foods brought over by the immigrants of the late nineteenth and early twentieth centuries. (Fifty years from now it will be interesting to see how many Korean, Vietnamese, and Thai dishes have become standard menu items here.) What is the rationale for including dishes like veal parmigiana or chili con carne or vichyssoise? These three are easily defensible: There is no dish in Italy by the name "veal parmigiana" (much less "veal Parmesan"); chili con carne is a Texas dish, frowned upon by most Mexicans; and vichyssoise was created at New York's Ritz-Carlton Hotel dining room by chef Louis Diat, who named it after a French spa. Such dishes are simply inspired by Italian, Mexican, or French notions.

Other ethnic foods have been so transformed over the years that they bear scant resemblance to their ancestral origins. Read, for example, the bewildering difference between the recipe given for *filets de sole Marguery* in *Larousse Gastronomique*, supposedly provided by the original chef, and that attributed to George Rector, Jr., who brought the recipe back from France for the delectation of "Diamond Jim" Brady and, afterward, for the approval of generations of American cooks (see SOLE MARGUERY). The original recipe for fettuccine Alfredo—ubiquitous here, rarely found in Italy by this name—contains no cream at all, which in America is the main ingredient. English muffins are never called by that name in England. And "french fries" refers not to potatoes as invented by some Frenchman, but to the way in which they are sliced, or "frenched."

My rule of thumb, then, with regard to such transformed dishes has been to include them if they have really been changed over the years by American cooks, or if they have become so popular here as to be immediately identifiable by the majority of Americans. Certain items, like Cornish pasties, are so associated with the miners of Michigan that to exclude them would be to omit one of the dishes that help define the region's gastronomic character. The same would be true of many Pennsylvania Dutch or Moravian items, delicacies of New Orleans, or dishes of New York's Jews.

By the same token I cannot in good conscience include foreign dishes that may still be prepared in the traditional way for special feasts among a certain group of people. My wife, for instance, prepares traditional Russian foods at Easter, but none of them—such as the tall cake called *kulich* or the pot cheese dessert called *paskha*—has been Americanized, nor are they known outside of the Russian families that still make them in this country. So, too, Czech families in this country may still make *brnenský rízek*, Greeks their *entrada*, Austrians their *Haussulz*, and Japanese their *kyogashi*, but these foods are still uncommon, especially among second- or third-generation ethnic Americans.

As for drinks and cocktails, I have tried to list those that are well known today or that have some historic interest. These would include everything from Coca-Cola and Gatorade to the numerous slang terms for coffee and the various kinds of beer and alcoholic beverages enjoyed both regionally and nationally, such as mint juleps, screwdrivers, and Manhattans. I have avoided listing alcoholic concoctions that seem to have been invented and forgotten almost in the same night. As far as I have been able, I have traced the origins of these drinks and provided recipes according to current tastes, with notes on how such beverages may have changed through the decades.

Last, I have no intention of declaring my own fondness or antipathy for certain dishes or terms, nor do I ever want to get in between two southerners debating the right way to make hush puppies. Even though I will never understand all the fuss about chicken-fried steak or grits, I happily include them here. As someone who grew up on Bronx egg creams, I can understand others' astonishment that such a confection could have inspired so many New Yorkers to praise it.

If it's true—and it is—that we are what we eat, then what is included here is all about what we are.

A

abalone (genus *Haliotis*). Any of a variety of univalve gastropods having an ear-shaped shell. The name is from the Spanish *abulón*, was introduced into English in 1850, and in 1883 appeared in George Brown Goode's *Fisheries and Fishery Industries of the United States*. There are about a hundred species of abalone in the world, eight of which inhabit the waters of the Pacific coast; they are pried from the rocks they attach themselves to and commercially harvested in California and to a lesser extent in Washington. All species are edible, but the flesh is rubbery and must be pounded. Abalone is usually dredged with flour and sautéed in butter. The main American species are "black abalone" (*Haliotis cracherodi*), "green abalone" (*H. fulgens*), "pink abalone" (*H. corrugata*), "red abalone" (*H. rufescens*), "white abalone" (*H. sorenseni*), "flat abalone" (*H. walallensis*), "threaded abalone" (*H. assimilis*), and "pinto abalone" (*H. kamtschatkana*). Only 45,000 pounds of abalone was landed commercially in 1997.

Aberdeen angus. Also "angus" or "black angus." A breed of black hornless steer originally bred in Scotland, this variety was brought to the United States in 1873 and quickly replaced the longhorn as a beef steer. The name comes from two counties in northeastern Scotland, Aberdeen and Angus.

absinthe. A green cordial derived from wormwood (*Artemisia absinthium*). Absinthe is anise-flavored and rather bitter, and has a proof of 136. It was originally promoted as a stomach tonic by French doctor Pierre Ordinaire in Switzerland in 1792 and popularized by Henri-Louis Pernod about 1797.

The drink was reputed to have aphrodisiacal qualities and became extremely popular in New Orleans, which came to be known as the absinthe capital of the world and where the liqueur was known under brand names such as Green Opal, Herbsaint, and Milky Way. It became a standard ingredient in many of New Orleans COCKTAILS such as the SAZERAC. One of the city's most famous restaurants was called the Old Absinthe House, opened in 1874.

Absinthe was usually diluted by dripping it through a perforated spoon containing a sugar cube and then dripping water through the absinthe, which turned the liqueur cloudy.

At the turn of the century wormwood was discovered to have harmful effects on people's health and to be habit-forming. Belgium banned the sale of absinthe in 1905, and after a celebrated trial in 1906 of a Swiss farmer, Jean Lanfray, who was said to have murdered his wife and children under the influence of absinthe, the Swiss legislature banned the drink in 1910. The United States followed with its own ban in 1912. Absinthe was replaced in cocktails by anise-flavored liqueurs like Ojen, from Spain, or Herbsaint, made by a New Orleans pharmacist named J. Marion Legendre in 1934.

OLD ABSINTHE HOUSE FRAPPÉ

Mix 1 T. Herbsaint or Pernod with a dash of anisette and pour into a small, thin glass filled with crushed ice and water; let the mixture get very cold and serve. (The absinthe frappé may be served without the anisette. Some add the white of an egg.)

ABSINTHE SUISSESSE

Combine 1½ oz. Herbsaint or Pernod with 2 T. cream, 1 T. orgeat syrup, 1 egg white, and crushed ice and shake (or mix in an electric blender) until completely blended. Pour the unstrained liquid into a chilled glass.

achiote. The hard seed of the annatto tree (*Bixa orellana*), it is pounded into a powder or made into a paste for its mild, earthy flavor. It is also used as a coloring for butter.

acorn. A hard-shelled nut, the fruit of an oak tree, that in some varieties can be poisonous. The word is from Old English *aecern*.

Acorns are rarely eaten today, but they were once an important food of Native Americans. Of the sixty species of oak in America, twenty-seven yielded acorns that were eaten by about half the Indians in North America and that provided California Indians with a staple of their diet. Because of their bitter, sometimes poisonous character, the acorns were cracked with a hammer, ground up with a mortar and pestle, and then leached in a stream by rinsing with several changes of water. They were then often boiled or roasted.

acorn squash. An acorn-shaped SQUASH weighing between one and two pounds, measuring four to seven inches in length, with a dark green-and-orange-streaked fluted rind. Sometimes called a "Des Moines squash," this American winter fruit was long favored by Native Americans. The name first appears in American print in 1937.

Adam's ale. Slang for water. A colloquialism based on the biblical assumption that the only drink Adam had was water; this term is often heard in soda fountains and at LUNCH COUNTERS.

additive. Any substance added either directly or indirectly to a food product. About twenty-eight hundred substances, ranging from vitamins to preservatives, are added directly, while more than ten thousand—including pesticides used on growing plants, drugs added to animals' diets, and chemicals from wrapping materials—enter indirectly.

Most of the time, the term refers to those substances added directly and intentionally for a wide variety of reasons that include: **1.** Maintaining freshness by adding nitrites and sodium nitrates to protect cured foods from bacterial toxins such as botulin. Antioxidants such as butylated hydroxyanisole (BHA) help prevent discoloration; vitamin C keeps peaches from turning brown. **2.** Maintaining or improving nutritional value by adding vitamins, iodine to salt, and other minerals. Often this is done after processing has already removed many of the same nutrients from a food item like bread. **3.** Making food more appealing to the eye by adding coloring agents. **4.** Making food tastier by adding natural or synthetic flavors, enhancers such as MONOSODIUM GLUTAMATE (MSG), various sweetening agents such as SUGAR, CORN SYRUP, and SACCHARIN, or just plain salt and pepper. **5.** Aiding processing and preparation by adding emulsifiers to give consistent texture, thickeners to prevent the formation of ice crystals, and humectants to retain moisture. Yeasts and BAKING POWDER are leavening additives essential in baked goods.

In recent years there has been a great deal of con-

cern over food additives, and health-food zealots damn them all without considering the virtues of or necessity for some. Many harmless additives add immeasurably to the appearance, freshness, and edibility of food items, and the availability of certain foods year-round is due to the preserving additives that have revolutionized the marketplace throughout the world and made scarcity far less severe than it might be. The first governmental attempts to oversee food additives came with the 1906 Food and Drugs Act, followed by the Food, Drug and Cosmetic Act of 1938, which helped remove some dangerous and poisonous elements from processed food. In 1958 the Food Additives Amendment established specific laws, bolstered two years later by the color-additive amendments, authorizing the FOOD AND DRUG ADMINISTRATION (FDA) to monitor and regulate additives for safety, although no power was given the FDA to limit the number of additives in a food or the reasons for their being added. Approval of a new additive comes after a long, thorough process of experimentation, and there is a "100-fold margin of safety" rule that dictates that only $\frac{1}{100}$ of the maximum amount of an additive that has been found *not* to produce any harmful effects in test animals may be used by a manufacturer of a food item. Under the Delaney Clause, no substance that has been shown to cause cancer in man or animal may be added to food in any amount.

Exempt from such tests are what are known as "generally recognized as safe" substances (GRAS) in use before the passage of the amendments, and "prior sanctioned substances" that had already been approved before 1958, although substances in both of these categories are under constant review. Currently thirty-one color additives are fully approved.

Listed below are the most commonly used additives. The reader is encouraged to look under main entries for many of the following.

1. Substances to maintain or improve nutritional quality: ASCORBIC ACID, beta carotene, iodine, iron, niacinamide, potassium iodide, riboflavin, thiamine tocopherols (vitamin E), vitamin A, and vitamin D.

2. Substances to maintain product quality: ascorbic acid, butylated hydroxyanisole (BHA), butylated hydroxytoluene (BHT), butylparaben, calcium lactate, calcium propionate, calcium sorbate, citric acid, ethylenediaminetetraaceticacid (EDTA), heptylparaben, lactic acid, methylparaben, potassium

propionate, potassium sorbate, propionic acid, propyl gallate, propylparaben, sodium benzoate, sodium diacetate, sodium erythorbate, sodium nitrate, sodium nitrite, sodium propionate, sodium sorbate, tertiary butyl hydroquinone (TBHQ), and tocopherols (vitamin E).

3. Substances to aid in processing and preparation: acetic acid, acetone peroxide, adipic acid, ammonium alginate, arabinogalactan, azodicarbonamide, benzoyl peroxide, calcium alginate, calcium bromate, calcium phosphate, CALCIUM PROPIONATE, calcium silicate, carobbean gum, CARRAGEENAN, cellulose, citric acid, diglycerides, dioctyl sodium sulfosuccinate, gelatin, glycerine, glycerol monostearate, guar gum, gum arabic, gum ghatti, hydrogen peroxide, iron-ammonium citrate, karaya gum, lactic acid, larch gum, lecithin, locust-bean gum, mannitol, modified food starch, monoglycerides, pectin, phosphates, phosphoric acid, polysorbates, potassium alginate, potassium bromate, propylene glycol, sodium acetate, silicon dioxide, sodium aluminum sulfate, sodium bicarbonate, sodium calcium alginate, sodium citrate, sodium stearyl fumarate, sorbitan monostearate, sorbitol, tartaric acid, tragacanth gum, and yellow prussiate of soda.

4. Substances that affect appeal characteristics: annatto extract, beta carotene, canthaxanthin, caramel, citrus Red No. 2, cochineal extract, corn endosperm, corn syrup, dehydrated beets, dextrose, disodium guanylate, disodium inosinate, dried algae meal, Blue No. 1, Red No. 3, Red No. 40, Yellow No. 5, fructose, glucose, grape-skin extract, hydrolyzed vegetable protein, invert sugar, iron oxide, mannitol, monosodium glutamate (MSG), paprika, riboflavin, saccharin, saffron, sorbitol, spices, sucrose, tagetes (Aztec Marigold), titanium dioxide, toasted partially defatted cooked cottonseed flour, turmeric, ultramarine blue, vanilla, vanillin, yeast-malt sprout extract.

5. Outlawed substances: dulcin, safrole, Green No. 1, cobalt sulfate, cyclamate, Violet No. 1, Red No. 2.

adobe bread. A bread made by the Pueblo Indians in a beehive-shaped adobe oven called a *horno.* Often meat, vegetables, nuts, or seeds were mixed into the dough, and the bread was frequently shaped like animals indigenous to the Southwest.

ADOBE BREAD

In a small bowl dissolve 1 pkg. yeast in ½ c. warm water to proof. In a large bowl mix 1 c. flour, 2 T. shortening, 1½ c. hot water, 2 t. salt, and 2 t. sugar. Mix until well blended, then add the yeast mixture. Blend well, then add 3 c. more flour to make a dough. Knead well. On a pastry board spread out 1 c. flour, place dough on it, and incorporate the flour into the dough. Knead for 10 min. Place in a greased bowl, turn over to grease entire dough, and cover with a towel. Let rise until double in bulk. Divide into 2 portions and form into round loaves. Cover again and let rise until doubled in bulk. Bake in an adobe oven or at 350° for 1 hr.

---

agave. Any of a more than three hundred different species of plants in the genus *Agave.* It is also called " mescal" and "century plant," so named because it may live thirty or forty years. *Agave,* in New Latin, means "noble," because of the plant's tallness. Its first appearance in English print was circa 1797.

Edible species of this fast-growing goldenflowered plant thrive in Arizona, New Mexico, southeastern California, southern Utah, and northern Mexico. The plant was extremely important to the Indians of the Southwest, especially the Mescalero Apache, who held to a lengthy ritual in cooking the agave. The crowns of the plant were carefully placed in a deep pit covered with bear grass and a thick layer of earth, then roasted for about two days, during which the tribe refrained from both drinking and sexual activity. When fully cooked, the centers of the crowns could be eaten immediately or dried in the sun. The leaves were consumed like artichokes or boiled into a syrup. Ground agave would be mixed into a drink.

The Chiricahua Apache referred to blooming agaves as "woman" plants and nonblooming ones as "man" plants.

The agave also makes an alcoholic drink known to both the Indians and the Mexicans, who call the drink *maquey, mexca,* or *mescal.* (*Mezcal* is also a name for a candy made from a piece of the barbecued leaf of the agave.)

The fermented pulp of the agave is made into a liquid called "aquamiel," which is similar to, but not the same as, sotol and TEQUILA made from the "blue agave" (*A. Rigidae tequiliana weber, var. azul*), although "mescal" is a general term that covers tequila. In her book *American Indian Food and Lore* (1974), Carolyn Niethammer wrote that the plant has a "pleasant, sweet flavor," but that it is poisonous if eaten raw. It is best baked or made into a nut butter or syrup.

aguardiente. A form of Spanish or Mexican brandy, though in the Southwest the term may refer to any strong alcoholic beverage. The word is from the Spanish for brandy and first appeared in English in 1818.

ahi. Also, "skipjack" and "shore bonito." A Hawaiian word for any large TUNA (1933), but especially the "yellow fin" (*Thunnus albacares*) and "bigeye" (*T. obesus*), whose fatty flesh is prized for making sushi and sashimi.

ahole (*Kuhlia sandvicensis*). A silvery large-eyed Hawaiian fish whose name derives from the Hawaiian, "to strip away," because the fish was used to drive away evil spirits. The young ahole is called "ahole-hole," which first saw print in 1926.

airline food. The American airline industry has since its earliest days provided some form of food service for passengers. The first airplane to have an actual onboard galley was an American Airlines Douglas DC-3 in 1936. The service of alcohol beverages onboard was inaugurated in October 1949 by Northwest Airlines.

Today airlines must provide hundreds of thousands of meals each day to their customers and must serve them under less-than-ideal circumstances at thirty-five thousand feet in the air. United Airlines alone serves 1.2 million meals per week, prepared in seventeen kitchens in the United States and Tokyo. Most of the food is prepared and usually precooked in large airport kitchens or purchased in frozen form from food-service companies. In regular coach class, the food is usually prepackaged in plastic containers and heated in onboard ovens, although in first class the food may well be cooked and prepared on board. Service can become quite lavish, with linen, fresh flowers, fresh cheeses, and premium wines.

Most airlines offer breakfast, lunch, and dinner, or, depending on the duration of the flight, a snack item such as a sandwich or pastry. Airlines also offer "special meals," which must be ordered prior to boarding, for vegetarians and those who keep kosher. Only 5 percent of passengers order such meals.

Given the difficulties involved in such mass feeding, airline food has been the consistent butt of many jokes, and, in a survey of one hundred thousand frequent fliers, food service was ranked eleventh out of fourteen concerns when people booked a flight. As a result, different airlines spend widely varying amounts of money on their food service. The average amount spent for food was $5.86 per passenger in 1992 and only $3.03 in 1997, with one airline spending only 20 cents per passenger on domestic travel. Average spending for food per passenger on overseas travel is $18.26.

aku. Hawaiian name for the red-fleshed "skipjack tuna" (*Katsuwonus pelamis*), considered the region's most important commercial fish (1933).

akule (*Selar crumenophthalmus*). A food fish of Hawaii, known on the mainland as "bigeye scad." Hawaiians usually salt and dry the fish. The word first appeared in print in 1902.

Alabama slammer. A cocktail popularized at the University of Alabama made with sloe gin, amaretto, Southern Comfort, and orange juice.

Albany beef. A nineteenth-century slang term for sturgeon, so called because the specimens taken from the Hudson River near Albany, New York, could weigh up to two hundred pounds. The term was used at least as early as 1779.

albóndiga. A meatball flavored with vegetables and served with a sauce. Albóndiga (the name is the same in Spanish) is a popular dish in the Southwest and comes from Mexico. The name dates in English print to a 1923 menu at the Sonora Cafe in Los Angeles as "Spanish meatball soup" and as "albondigas" at its offshoot, El Cholo in 1927; it is almost always used in the plural, "albóndigas."

ALBÓNDIGA

Combine ½ lb. each of ground pork, beef, and veal, add ½ c. bread crumbs, 1 chopped onion, ½ t. cumin, salt and pepper, and 1 beaten egg. Form into 1½-in. balls, roll in flour, and sauté in a skillet until browned. Remove from skillet. Puree 3 chili peppers with ½ c. warm water. In skillet sauté 1 clove minced garlic, 1 chopped onion, and then the chili puree. Add 2 c. peeled, seeded, chopped tomatoes and sauté for 5 min. Add 1 c. beef stock, season with salt and pepper and ¼ t. sugar, simmer, add meatballs, cook for about 20 min. Serve with rice. Serves 6.

algin. A thickening agent derived from seaweed and used in processed foods to maintain desired texture (1883). Propylene glycol alginate thickens soda pop, ice cream, candy, yogurt, and stabilizes the foam in beer.

alligator (*Alligator mississippiensis*). A large, lizardlike reptile that may grow up to nineteen feet in length. It is a dangerous denizen of the Louisiana and Gulf states swamplands, and was introduced into the Rio Grande in Texas. The name is from the Spanish *el lagarto,* and ultimately from the Latin *lacertus,* "lizard." As "lagarto" the name appears in English print first in 1568. The alligator in American waters, along with the crocodile (from the Greek *krokodilus,* "worm of the pebbles," for its habit of lying on pebbles to absorb the sun's heat), has long been a favorite meat of Cajuns and is considered a delicacy by others. But, more for its hide than its meat, the alligator was brought dangerously close to extinction by the early 1960s, when state game officials began protection of the animal and restocking of nesting areas. By the late 1960s the alligator was once again abundant and today is more widely available as meat than ever before. In 1997 Florida alligator farms sold 112,822 pounds of alligator meat. The tail of the alligator is particularly relished and usually cooked in a form of stew or fried in nuggets.

alligator bread. A round loaf of bread with a bumpy top like an alligator's skin, first recorded in 1968.

alligator corn. Colloquial name for the edible seed of the American lotus known as "water chinquapin" (*Nelumbo lutea*), first in print in 1841.

almond (*Prunus amygdalus*). A tree native to the Mediterranean and a member of the rose family whose nut is widely used in desserts, candy, and garnishes and as a SNACK. The name is from the Greek *amygdalē,* and is first found in English print about 1300.

Almonds were introduced to California in the mid-1800s, and that state now produces half the world's crop. American almonds are often roasted and ground as a topping for ice cream or cakes, made into a marzipan paste, or coated with candy or chocolate. After peanuts, almonds are American's favorite nut, with per capita consumption in 1997 about half a pound.

alphabet soup. A soup, usually tomato or chicken based, containing pasta cut into the shapes of alphabet letters. The term saw print in 1934.

amaretto. A cordial with the flavor of almonds, though it may contain no almonds at all and is often made from apricot pits. The original formula, called "Amaretto di Saronno," comes from the Italian town of Saronno. (*Amaretto* in Italian means "a little bitter.") A wholly unsubstantiated legend, promoted by the producers' American distributor, Glenmore Distilleries of Lexington, Kentucky, tells of how Renaissance artist Bernardino Luini came to the town of Saronno in 1525 to paint a fresco in the sanctuary of Santa Maria delle Grazie. One of his models was a widow who gave him the liqueur that came to be called amaretto.

The drink was imported into the United States in the 1960s, and by 1980 it had become the second best-selling cordial here (after Kahlúa), causing several American producers to make their own amarettos in American distilleries.

Amaretto is sometimes used as a topping for ice-cream desserts, and used as a flavoring for cakes and pies or coffee.

ambrosia. A cocktail reputedly first concocted at Arnaud's restaurant in New Orleans immediately following the end of Prohibition. The name, from the Greek *ambrotos,* "immortal," refers to the food of the Roman and Greek gods, thought to bestow immortality.

AMBROSIA COCKTAIL

Shake together the juice of 1 lemon, 1 oz. apple-jack, 1 oz. brandy, ½ oz. Cointreau, and top with champagne.

ambrosia. A dessert made from fruits, sugar and grated coconut, most popular in the South (1932).

AMBROSIA DESSERT

Peel and slice 3 oranges into ¼-in. wedges and layer in a bowl. Sprinkle with confectioners' sugar and about 1 T. grated coconut. Make another layer the same way, and another, until the oranges are used up. Chill before serving. Serves 4.

Amish preaching soup. A thick bean soup served in large quantities before or after Amish church services (circa 1965).

ammonia cookies. Any of a variety of cookies made with a leavening agent called ammonium carbonate, or baking ammonia. They are most commonly found in Scandinavian-American communities. In their book *Farm Recipes and Food Secrets from the Norske Nook* (1993), Helen Myhre and Mona Vold wrote, "Talk about Old Faithful, this was one of those basic standbys every farm lady made."

Anadama bread. A bread made from cornmeal and molasses. The term dates in print to 1915, but is probably somewhat older. If it were not for the frequency of their citation, it would be difficult to believe the stories of how this New England bread got its name. The story most often cited is of a Gloucester, Massachusetts, fisherman's wife named Anna, who gave her husband nothing but cornmeal and molasses to eat every day. One night the fisherman got so angry, he tossed the ingredients in with some yeast and flour and made a bread in the oven while muttering to himself, "Anna, damn her!"

A more affectionate story has a New England sea captain referring to his wife with the same expletive as a phrase of endearment. This Anna was apparently adept at bread baking, and she became well known for her cornmeal-and-molasses loaf among the fishing crews who appreciated this long-lasting, hearty bread. There was, supposedly, a gravestone to this legendary woman that read, ANNA WAS A LOVELY BRIDE, BUT ANNA, DAMN 'ER, UP AND DIED.

One source contends that a commercial bakery called its product "Annadammer" or "Annadama" bread.

ANADAMA BREAD

Combine 3 c. all-purpose flour, 1 c. cornmeal, 2 pkgs. dry yeast, and 1 T. salt together in a bowl. In another bowl mix 2 c. hot water, 4 T. butter, and ½ c. molasses, then add to flour mixture. Beat and knead to form a stiff dough. Place in greased bowl and let rise until doubled. Punch down, shape into two balls, and place in greased 8-in. cake tins. Let rise until doubled. Bake at 375° for about 1 hr., until deep brown in color.

---

anchovy (family Engraulidae). A small, herringlike fish that travels in large schools. Anchovies are generally packed in oil and canned for the American market, even though there are sixteen species in United States waters, and they are abundant on both coasts. The word is from the Spanish *anchova* and was first printed in English in Shakespeare's *Henry IV, Part I* (circa 1597). Anchovies are often used as an ingredient on pizza or as a part of several salad preparations. In 1997 U.S. landings for anchovies totaled 12.7 million pounds, though 94 percent were used for animal food, reduction, or bait.

andouille. A highly seasoned smoked-pork sausage commonly made from neck and stomach meat. The word dates in English print to 1605. This specialty of CAJUN cookery is traditionally made in only three parishes in Louisiana and takes its name from a French word meaning "sausage." It is commonly used to flavor GUMBOS and JAMBALAYAS, though it is eaten on its own. La Place, Louisiana, calls itself the "Andouille Capital of the World" and each year holds an Andouille Festival.

angel-food cake. Also, "angel cake." A very light, puffy cake, perhaps of Pennsylvania-Dutch heritage, made without yeast and with several beaten egg whites. The egg whites give it a texture so airy that the confection supposedly has the sublimity of angels. Angel-food cake was known by the 1870s in America (the word appeared in print in the 1880s) and served as a sensible usage of leftover egg whites.

angelliquor. Also, "angel liquor." An African American term (dating in print to 1942) for a wine made from the angelica plant.

angel's tit. Also, "King Alphonse." A cocktail made by floating heavy cream on crème de cacao and topping it with a cherry (1984).

antelope (*Antilocapra americana*). Also, "pronghorn." A North American deerlike horned animal with a white rump and two white throat bands. They inhabit the plains and prairies of the United States. The word "antelope" derives from Middle English and dates in print to the fifteenth century.

Antelope are most commonly cut into steaks and then roasted, fried, or stewed.

antifogmatick. A Colonial era term for a drink of alcohol taken in the morning to counteract the effects of dampness or fog, dating in print to 1789.

apee. Also, "apea" and, in the plural, "eepies." A spiced butter cookie or form of gingerbread. Legend has it that the word derives from the name of Ann Page, a Philadelphia cook who carved her initials into the tops of the confection. This was first noted in print in J. F. Watson's *Annals of Philadelphia* (1830) to the effect that Ann Page, then still alive, "first made [the cookies] many years ago, under the common name of cakes." But William Woys Weaver, in *America Eats* (1989), wrote, "The origin of the name is a bit confusing. Essentially, [apeas] were a form of *Anis Plätchen* (anise cookies) and stamped *A.P.* to distinguish them from cookies with carraway, which were known as 'seed cakes.' A great many bakers hawked Apeas to children on the streets. One of those bakers in Philadelphia was Ann Page. The *A.P.* became associated with her, if only because *Anis Plätchen* were extremely popular."

APEE

Cream 1 c. butter with 1 t. vanilla and 1⅓ c. sugar until very smooth. Add 2 eggs. Sift 2⅓ c. flour, ¼ t. cream of tartar, and ¼ t. salt, then stir into mixture with ⅔ c. sour cream. Drop by spoonfuls onto buttered cookie sheet, bake for 10 min. at 375°. Cool on rack. Makes about 70 cookies.

aplet. A confection made with boiled-down apple juice, gelatin, and nuts. If made with apricots, it is called a "cotlet." The confection was first produced by Armenian immigrants. Armen Tertsagian and Mark Balaban in 1920, who based it on a Middle Eastern sweet called *rahat locum* made with orange-blossom or rosewater and nuts.

apple (genus *Malus,* family Rosaceae). A sweet fruit with a firm flesh and thin skin found in temperate regions. The apple is native to Europe and Asia, though the United States now produces about one quarter of the world's crop. There are probably tens of thousands of apple varieties, and more than seven thousand are classified in the United States alone, but most apples sold at market come from no more than fifty varieties, and the consumer is unlikely to encounter more than a half-dozen of the most successfully propagated varieties.

About 2500 varieties are grown in the U.S., with 100 varieties grown commercially, and 15 of those representing 90 percent of U.S. production. The most popular varieties are Red Delicious, Golden Delicious, Fuji, Granny Smith, Rome, Gala, and MacIntosh.

The largest producing states are Washington, New York, California, Michigan, and Pennsylvania. In 1998 the U.S. produced 269.7 million bushels of apples, and Americans per capita consumption was 18.4 pounds fresh and 27.1 pounds processed.

The apple (the word is from the Old English *aeppel*) has been a favorite fruit for millennia; it was known to the people of the Iron Age and cultivated four thousand years ago in Egypt. The Roman Pliny the Elder listed thirty-six varieties in the first century A.D., and the fruit has mythological associations in many different civilizations.

There were no native American apples when the first settlers arrived on these shores. (The "custard apple" [*Annona reticulata*] of the American tropics and the "mayapple" or "mandrake" [*Podophyllum peltatum*] of eastern North America are not true apples.) The first apple seeds were brought by the Pilgrims in 1620, and there were plantings in New Jersey as of 1632. Governor John Endecott of the Plymouth Colony traded five hundred three-year-old apple trees for two hundred acres of land in 1649, and in 1647 Governor Peter Stuyvesant brought to New Amsterdam a Dutch apple tree that flourished until it was accidentally knocked down in 1866.

The French brought the apple to Canada, and the fruit was grown up and down the thirteen colonies. In 1730 the first commercial apple nursery was opened on New York's Long Island, and by 1741 apples were being shipped to the West Indies.

The proliferation of the fruit into the western territories came by the hand of an eccentric but gentle man named John Chapman, affectionately known as "Johnny Appleseed." Born in Leominster, Massachusetts, in 1774, Chapman left his father's carpentry shop to explore the new territories and to preach a Swedenborgian philosophy of life. Beginning in Pennsylvania in 1791—barefoot, wearing a saucepan for a hat, and subsisting on a vegetarian diet of buttermilk and "beebread" (pollen)—Chapman planted apple trees and started nurseries over ten thousand square miles of American frontier. (He did not, as folklore would have it, merely toss apple seeds to the ground in the faith that they would grow true.) He got as far as Fort Wayne, Indiana, where he died at the age of seventy-one in 1845.

Apples were introduced in the Northwest by Captain Aemilius Simmons, who planted seeds at Fort Vancouver in Washington in 1824. His first tree grew but one apple, but the seeds of that single fruit bore future generations of hardier stock. Commercial growing of apples in the Northwest began with two Idahoans, Henderson Luelling and William Meek, who became the fathers of Washington's major crop and made the state the top producer of apples in the United States.

Apples were among the most versatile and long-lasting of fruits for the early settlers, and they have long been stored for the winter in "dry houses" or made into CIDER. By the year 1800 there were a hundred American-bred varieties, and *Downing's Fruits and Fruit Trees in America* (1872) listed more than a thousand varieties of apples bred in America. Most of these have been forgotten or are grown only in "collectors' orchards," where varieties such as the "Roxbury Russet," "Golden Russet," "Black Gillflower," "Chenango," "Black Esopus Spitzenburg," "Sweet Bough," and "Winter Banana" are still sustained. But the majority of the most important varieties still marketed date from before 1850, and only one, the "Cortland," is the result of experiments by a scientific plant breeder; the rest come from seedlings.

The early apple storage cellars, called "common storages," lasted well into the nineteenth century. One of the first commercial cold-storage plants for apples was established in 1870 in Niagara County, New York, but not until 1915 was a refrigerated storage facility possible. A method of slowing apple maturation by what is called "controlled atmosphere storage" (pioneered by Frenchman Jacques Bérard in the early 1800s) extended the life of apples so that they have become available year-round. Increasingly this method is being used throughout the United States to preserve apples.

Almost half of the American apple crop is turned into products such as cider, or juice, applesauce, canned slices, apple butter, and other packaged items. See CANDY APPLE.

"Apple-harvest time" is a festive and social occasion in America, and "apple bees" used to be held to core apples to be dried for the winter. At Halloween children "bob for apples," that is, they attempt to pick up apples floating in a large tub of water with their teeth, a pastime that may derive from druidic or Roman harvest rites.

The following list of American apple varieties includes the most popular and most important ones sold and cultivated. In addition to these common varieties, some newer apples that show promise for the future include "Kendall" (a cross between McIntosh and Zusoff); "Spartan" (McIntosh and Yellow Newtown); "Idared" (Jonathan and Wagener); and "Jondel" (Jonathan and Delicious).

Baldwin. Red-skinned; harvested in autumn. An all-purpose apple not easily found anymore except in New England and New York retail outlets in the autumn months. The Baldwin appeared around 1740 as a seedling on the farm of John Ball in Wilmington, Massachusetts. For a long while the apple was called "Butters' apple," after the name of the next farmer who owned the land. Butters himself called it "Woodpecker." The variety was publicized by Colonel Baldwin of Woburn, Massachusetts, who gave his name to the apple, and after 1850 it was introduced into New York, where it was the major variety for years. Since 1945 the Baldwin has declined in popularity, though it is still used by commercial processors.

Cortland. Red-skinned; September to April. An all-purpose apple that stores well. The only major variety that is the result of scientific breeding, the Cortland was first propagated at the New York State Agricultural Experiment Station at Geneva, New York, and introduced in 1915 as a cross between the McIntosh and the Ben Davis.

crab. Red-skinned. Used primarily in cooking, the crab apple is small and deep-hued. It is a wild species and goes by the names "American sweet" or "garland" (*Malus coronaria*) and "prairie crab apple" (*Malus ioensis*).

Delicious. Red-skinned; mid-September to August. A heart-shaped eating apple also called the "Red Delicious," this variety is the largest apple crop in the United States, with several sports, strains, and tree types. It was discovered by a farmer named Hesse Hiatt at Peru, Iowa, in 1872 near an old Yellow Bellflower apple tree. Hiatt cut it down twice because of its irregular growing pattern, but it grew back, and, finally, Hiatt -named it the "Hawkeye." In 1895 rights to the variety were bought by a commercial nursery, Stark Brothers, that renamed it the "Delicious." Today the eastern variety of Red Delicious is often possessed of better flavor than the western variety of the same name.

Golden Delicious. Gold-skinned; late September to August. An eating apple with a long peak season, the Golden Delicious bruises less readily than other varieties and is preferred for eating rather than cooking. It was discovered in 1914 on the Anderson Mullens farm in West Virginia, possibly from a Grimes Golden variety pollinated by the Golden Reinette. First called "Mullens' Yellow Seedlings," the variety was purchased by, the Stark Brothers Nursery as a companion to its Red Delicious and is now the second-largest apple crop in the United States.

Granny Smith. Green-skinned; August to November. An eating apple now gaining popularity in the United States, where it is widely grown in California. The apple was discovered in Ryde, Australia, about 1850 by Mary Anne Smith, who lent the fruit her name, and it was within a decade widely propagated in Australia and New Zealand, not coming to the United States for a century. Commercial plantings in California's San Joaquin Valley began in the 1970s at H. P. Metzler and Sons Orchards.

Gravenstein. Yellow-skinned; early fall. An all-purpose apple of uncertain origins. Some authorities hold that the variety came from the eighteenth-century garden of the duke of Augustinberg, in Gravenstein, Germany, but others cite the Grafenstein garden in Sleswick, Germany. Still others trace the variety to Italy. No one knows who first introduced the breed to the United States, but Russians planted the variety in Bodega, north of San Francisco, by 1820, and the apple was apparently grown in New York prior to 1826. Today the Gravenstein is still better known as a California breed, where it is a major variety for applesauce.

Jonathan. Red-skinned; mid-September to March. A highly aromatic, spicy apple good for eating, pies, and applesauce. Discovered in 1800 in Woodstock, New York, where it was originally called the "Rick," after farmer Philip Rick, who found it among his trees, the variety was popularized by Jonathan Hasbrouk and Judge J. Buel of Albany, New York, and took the former's first name. The Jonathan may be a seedling of the Esopus Spitzenburg variety. The Jonathan grew better in Michigan and the Ohio Valley than in the East and became a major variety in the Midwest and as far as Idaho and Colorado.

McIntosh. Red-skinned; mid-September to July. A round, all-purpose apple, the McIntosh is excellent for crossbreeding and has given us varieties such as the Cortland, Spartan, Melba, Macoun, Niagara, Puritan, and others. A plaque in Dundas County, Ontario, across the Lawrence River from Massena, reads, THE ORIGINAL MCINTOSH RED APPLE TREE STOOD 20 RODS NORTH OF THIS SPOT. IT WAS ONE OF A NUMBER OF SEEDLINGS TAKEN FROM THE BORDER OF THE CLEARINGS AND TRANSPLANTED BY JOHN MCINTOSH IN THE YEAR 1796. John McIntosh took seedlings from the brush near his home near Dundela, Ontario, and planted them in his garden. By 1830 only one tree had survived, and this was the original tree that, with some grafting assistance given by an itinerant peddler five years later, resulted in a nursery of identical trees that gave excellent, sweet fruit. McIntosh's wife, Hannah, took care of the nursery, and neighbors took to calling the apple "Granny's apple" after her, though a son, Allan, gave the family name to the variety, and other relatives began propagating it in New York and Vermont. It became the predominant variety of the Northeast (the original Ontario tree was burned in a fire and died in 1910), especially in New York State, where it is grown in the Hudson Valley, the Champlain Valley, and near Lake Ontario.

Newtown Pippin. Greenish-yellow-skinned; mid-September to April. An all-purpose apple of uncertain origins, the Newtown Pippin is also called the "Albemarle." The original seedling may have come from Gershon Moore's estate in Newtown, Long Island, though it is not certain whether the fruit of the original tree, which died in 1805, was yellow or green. Both varieties go by the name "Newtown Pippin," with the yellow primarily grown in the West and in Virginia (where Albemarle County lent its name to the variety, brought from Philadelphia in 1755 by Dr. Thomas Walker). It was the first variety sent to England, in 1759, when Benjamin Franklin gave some to the court of England.

Northern Spy. Red-skinned, with some blush; mid-October to February. A robust eating and cooking variety produced mainly in New York, Michigan, and Ontario, the Northern Spy is not widely available. It originated as a seedling in an orchard planted in 1800 by Herman Chapin in East Bloomfield, New York, from Salisbury, Connecticut, seeds. The origin of the name, however, is obscure. Some say it may derive from the fact that Bloomfield was a site of activity for the Underground Railroad, a secret system by which slaves were brought North to freedom.

The original seedling died, but the first apple from the seedling's transplanted suckers came from the farm of Roswell Humphrey, and it became an important apple throughout the northern states. Owing to its tendency to appear only in alternate years, the variety has declined in popularity, but many people consider Northern Spy apples among the very best in America.

Rhode Island Greening. Yellow-green-skinned. A baking or cooking apple considered best for apple pie, the Rhode Island Greening is produced mainly in New York and is commercially processed for applesauce and frozen pies, and, therefore, rarely seen in the market. The variety began in Green's End, Rhode Island, about 1748 through the efforts of a tavern keeper named Green. It was carried from Newport to Plymouth, Massachusetts, then to Ohio by 1796, where it was established in a nursery at Marietta.

Rome Beauty. Red-skinned; late September to July. An excellent baking apple, originally propagated by Alanson Gillett from a discarded tree given to him by his brother Joel, of Proctorville, Ohio, the variety was named by George Walton about 1832 for the township of Rome, where the Gillett farm was located. The Rome Beauty has given us hybrids like the "Gallia Beauty," "Monroe," and "Ruby." The Rome Beauty is produced in all the apple-growing regions of the United States.

Stayman. Red-skinned; early October to May. An eating apple grown throughout Appalachia with some uses for cooking, the variety came from a Winesap seedling, discovered in Leavenworth, Kansas, in 1866 by Dr. J. Stayman. It is sometimes called "Stayman's Winesap" or "Stayman Winesap." After 1900 extensive plantings took place in the East and Midwest.

Winesap. Red-skinned; late October to June. A tart, crisp apple for eating, the Winesap is of obscure origins, possibly of New Jersey stock before 1800. Its long keeping time made it popular until controlled atmosphere storage made other varieties even more so. It is now produced mainly in Washington, Virginia, and West Virginia.

York Imperial. Red-skinned; mid-September to May. A good baking apple, the York Imperial was first discovered near York, Pennsylvania, about 1830 by a man named Johnson. He took it to nursery owner Jonathan Jessup, who in turn produced the variety and called it "Johnson's Fine Winter Apple," but had little success with it. Other farmers planted the discarded variety, and it took on its noble name from horticulturist Charles Downing, who promoted its long keeping qualities in the mid-1800s. It is now a processing apple.

Apple Annie. A term for any vendor who sold apples on city street corners during the Great Depression of the 1930s. Most were very poor people with no other trade and no other wares to sell at regular markets.

apple brown betty. A layered dessert of apples and buttered crumbs. The origin of the name is unknown, but the dish was first mentioned in print in 1864. It is also called "apple crisp" and "apple crust."

APPLE BROWN BETTY

Mix together 1½ c. dry bread crumbs with ¼ c. melted butter and place one third of the mixture in a buttered baking pan. Slice 4 pared and cored apples into ¼-in.-thick slices and place a layer on top of the crumbs. Cover with part of a mixture of 1 t. cinnamon, ¼ t. ground cloves, ¼ t. nutmeg, and 1 t. grated lemon rind. Repeat layers of bread crumbs, apples, and spice mixture, then sprinkle the top with a mixture of the juice of 1 lemon and ¼ c. water. Bake at 400° for 10 to 15 min. Serve with whipped cream or ice cream.

---

apple butter. A Pennsylvania-Dutch cooked fruit puree, dating at least to 1765, made by cooking and pureeing apples with cider.

apple charlotte. A dessert of French origins made of cooked apples and bread slices. Apple charlotte is distinguished from CHARLOTTE RUSSE, a creamy pudding placed in a deep mold lined with lady fingers, a dessert generally credited to Frenchman Antonin Carême, who first called it *"Charlotte parisienne."* But apple charlotte predated charlotte russe. In France it was called a "Fruit Charlotte," and, according to André Simon's *A Concise Encyclopedia of Gastronomy* (1952), named after Charlotte Buff, on whom the heroine of Johann Wolfgang von Goethe's *Die Leiden des Jungen Werthers* (1774), a tremendously popular epistolary novel of the time, was based. Apple charlotte became a fashionable dessert in America soon afterward, as a rather fancy version of APPLE BROWN BETTY.

APPLE CHARLOTTE

Line the bottom and sides of a charlotte mold with thin bread slices (which may be cut into the shape of hearts) that have been soaked in melted butter. Slice up a dozen apples that have been peeled and cored, and place in a saucepan with 3 T. butter. Add 2 T. powdered sugar, 1/4 t. cinnamon, 1/2 t. grated lemon rind, and 1/4 t. vanilla extract. Cook until apples have broken down, then add 4 T. apricot jam. Stir and blend. Fill the mold, place buttered bread slices on top, trim, then cook in a 350° oven for 40 min. Let rest for a few minutes, then turn out on a plate. Serve with apricot sauce, if desired.

apple dumpling. A baked dessert made of apples wrapped in pastry dough.

apple fritter. An apple slice that has been covered with a batter and fried in hot oil. Apple fritters have been popular since the middle of the eighteenth century.

APPLE FRITTER

Peel and core 4 apples and cut into 1/4-in.-thick slices. Mix together 2 c. flour, 2 beaten eggs, 1 T. dark rum, 1/4 t. salt, and 1 c. milk. Dip apple slices in batter, then deep-fry. Serve with powdered sugar and/or sour cream and maple syrup.

applejack. Also, "jack." Apple CIDER or a BRANDY made from apple cider. Apple brandy was particularly favored in early New England, where any household might have the means to make the spirit.

When produced in the United States, applejack must spend at least two years in wood casks, though most are aged much longer, and the proof is 100, or, if blended with neutral spirits, 80. As a term for cider, "applejack" dates back at least to 1816. Later in the century it was also referred to as "apple john" (which in England is a term for a specific type of apple).

"Applejack" is also a term for sweet apple syrup, dating in print to 1968, or to an apple turnover, as of 1852.

apple knocker. A club used to loosen fruit from trees, or a person who picks apples very fast (in use at least since 1919).

apple pandowdy. A dish of sliced apples covered with a crust, sometimes referred to as "apple grunt" or "apple Jonathan" in the Northeast. First mentioned in print in 1805, apple pandowdy seems to be specifically American by name, and Nathaniel Hawthorne mentions the dish in his *Blithedale Romance* (1852). The name's origins are obscure, but perhaps its homely simplicity connotes a "dowdy," i.e., unstylish, appearance.

APPLE PANDOWDY

Core, peel, and slice 4 apples and place in a buttered dish. Pour 1/2 c. cider over them, sprinkle with 1/2 t. cinnamon, 1/8 t. ground cloves, 1/8 t. nutmeg, 3/4 c. light brown sugar, 1/4 c. maple syrup, and dot with butter. Cover with a biscuit dough about 1/4-in. thick, then slit the top to allow for the escape of steam. Bake in 350° oven until apples are tender. Serve with cream.

apple pie. If something is said to be as "American as apple pie," it is credited with being as American as "The Star-Spangled Banner." In fact, apples were brought from Europe to America, and apple pies (1780) were very popular in Europe, especially in England, before they came to epitomize American food. But Americans popularized the apple pie as the country became the world's largest apple-producing nation.

There are hundreds of apple-pie recipes from every region of the country, some with a top crust, some without, some with a bottom crust, some without, some with raisins or dates or nuts or cranberries, some with buttery crumbs on top. "Deep-dish apple pie" means it is baked in a pie pan of at least 1½ inches in depth.

See also MOCK APPLE PIE.

applesauce. A puree of apples, sugar, and, sometimes, spices. The term dates in print to 1739. In New England it is often called "apple sass."

apple snow. Also, "apple float." A dessert made from apples, sugar, and beaten egg whites, quite popular in the early part of this century. It first appeared in print in 1939.

APPLE SNOW

Beat 3 egg whites, add 1/4 c. sugar and 1 c. applesauce, and serve with whipped cream or custard sauce.

apricot (*Prunus armeniaca*). A tree native to western Asia and Africa that gives a yellow-orange fruit. The word is from the Latin *praecocia,* "early ripening," and first appears in English print in 1551.

The apricot reached North America sometime in the eighteenth century, when Spanish monks brought it to California, which now produces 95 percent of the American crop (with the rest from Oregon, Washington, Utah, and Idaho). The first commercial orchard was started in 1792 in California's Santa Clara Valley. About 56 percent of the crop is canned, 16 percent dried, 12 percent frozen, and only 16 percent sold fresh.

The major cultivated varieties include the "Patterson," "Blenheim," "Tilton," "Castlebrite," "Modesto," and "Katy."

Apricots are called "cots" for short. Americans eat ½ pound of apricots per person annually.

aquaculture. Food cultivated in water (1865). Aquaculture has long been part of man's history, though the term (from the Latin *aqua* [water] + *culture*) dates in print only to 1867. *Hydroponics* (from Greek *hýdōr* [water] and *geo* [earth] plus *pono* [work]) refers more specifically to the cultivation of plant life under water and dates in print to 1937.

Aquaculture grew rapidly in the 1980s, with advances in the cultivation of mussels, crayfish, trout, oysters, catfish, salmon, hybrid striped bass, and tilapia. Currently, more than 3,400 farms in twenty-three states are raising approximately 15 percent of the U.S. seafood supply, with catfish, trout, crayfish, and salmon accounting for 80 percent of all domestic aquaculture products.

Arab. Also "street Arab" and "arabber." A term used in Baltimore for a street peddler of fruits and vegetables. Often they drove through town on a horsecart. The term first appeared in print in 1935, but dates back at least to the turn of the century.

arctic wine. Also, "ar'tic wine." Slang term for straight whiskey, dating in print to 1939.

Arkansas traveler. Also, "Arkansas wedding cake." A dish of sliced corn bread with roast beef and brown gravy, served with french-fried potatoes, pinto beans, and a slice of onion. It is a specialty of the Fort Worth, Texas, area.

Arkansas water. Derogatory slang term for a non-alcoholic beverage served at a picnic, because of the connotation that people from Arkansas are crude and have common taste. The term first appeared in print in 1951.

armadillo. Any of a variety of New World mammals of the family Dasypodidae having bony plates resembling armor, especially the "nine-banded armadillo" (*D. novemcinctus*). The name comes from the Spanish *armado,* "armored" and first appears in English print in 1570. The armadillo is rarely eaten in the United States today, but some westerners consider it an unusual delicacy, usually to be stewed.

army chicken. World War II army slang for frankfurters and beans (1942).

arroz con pollo. A Hispanic-American dish the name of which is Spanish for "rice with chicken." The term was first mentioned in print in 1938.

ARROZ CON POLLO

Brown cut-up pieces of 1 chicken in 4 T. olive oil until browned, add 6 chorizo sausages cut into chunks, and brown with the chicken. Add 2 c. cooked rice to the skillet. In another pan sauté 2 chopped cloves of garlic, 1 chopped onion, 1 chopped green bell pepper, and add to the chicken and rice. Mix 1¼ t. crumbled saffron in 6 c. chicken stock and add to rice. Add 4 peeled and chopped tomatoes and 1 c. peas. Cover and bake at 350° for 1½ hr. Garnish with pimiento strips. Serves 8.

artichoke (*Cynara scolymus*). A tall plant native to the Mediterranean bearing a large, globular flower head with scaly, thistlelike bracts. The artichoke is eaten as a vegetable, usually boiled and served with butter or stuffed with bread crumbs and other seasonings and baked.

The word is from the Italian dialect word *articiocco,* ultimately from the Arabic *al-khurshūf,* first mentioned in English print in 1525.

The Spanish introduced the artichoke to California, but it was almost unknown to most Americans until well into the twentieth century, when its cultivation in the South and, principally, in California (which produces 100 percent of the U.S. commercial crop) gave the vegetable a popularity that today is equaled only in France and Italy. The only commercial kind grown in the United States is the "common" or "globe artichoke." See also JERUSALEM ARTICHOKE.

ascorbic acid. Vitamin C. Ascorbic acid can be used as an antioxidant or a nutrient and color stabilizer; it also prevents the formation of nitrosamines (cancer-causing chemicals).

aseptic packaging. A package of food or drink filled so that almost all the air is driven out, thus preserving the contents from bacteria and spoilage. The word "asceptic" has been in print since 1855. Wines thus stored are commonly called "wine in a box" or "wine in a bag," terms used since the 1980s.

Ashley bread. A southern batter bread, similar to SPOON BREAD, made from rice flour. The name may commemorate Anthony Ashley Cooper, first earl of Shaftesbury (1621–1683), who was one of the first proprietors of the royal colony of Carolina, for which he had John Locke draw up the first constitution. The following recipe is from Panchita Heyward Grimball, of the Wappaoolah Plantation, Cooper River, South Carolina, as printed in *200 Years of Charleston Cooking* (1930).

ASHLEY BREAD

Mix and sift 1 c. rice flour, ½ t. salt, 1½ t. baking powder; beat 1 egg with 1 c. milk and add to the dry ingredients. Stir in 1½ t. melted butter and turn batter into well-greased shallow pan. Bake at 350° for about 45 min. Makes 8 large pieces.

---

asparagus (genus *Asparagus*). Any of 150 species of a Eurasian plant with long branchlets that is a very popular vegetable and is usually boiled or steamed. The name is from the Greek *asparagos,* and first appeared in English print around A.D. 1000. Though it is not known when the vegetable reached America, Swedish naturalist Peter Kalm reported he found them growing both wild and cultivated in New Jersey during his travels in 1740, and asparagus recipes appear in cookery books of the latter eighteenth century.

The common asparagus (*A. plumosus*) has flourished in the United States. A particularly hardy variety, the "Mary Washington" was developed by the United States Department of Agriculture. Most American asparagus is sold fresh.

aspartame. An artificial sweetener of aspartic acid and phenylalanine created accidentally in 1965 by chemist James M. Schlatter of the G. D. Searle & Company of Skokie, Illinois. Aspartame, also known as NutraSweet, is two hundred times sweeter than sugar and is used in processed foods and as a substitute for sugar. The monopoly on the use of the name "aspartame" by the NutraSweet Company in the U.S. market ended on December 14, 1992.

atole. A southwestern drink made from MASA or a form of cornmeal mush often sweetened with honey and frequently served with BUÑUELOS. The term is from Mexican Spanish and dates in English print to 1672.

Automat. An inexpensive and informal restaurant where food was displayed in small compartments whose windows open when the required number of coins were deposited. The term comes from the Greek *automatos,* "self-acting." The first such establishment was Joseph V. Horn and F. Hardart's Automat, opened June 9, 1902, in Philadelphia and using German equipment based on a Swedish patent, but it was in New York City (where they opened their first Automat in Times Square on July 2, 1912) that the concept became an important part of city life, with forty establishments operating by 1939.

So linked to the idea of the Automat were its originators' names that Americans more often than not referred to such places as "Horn and Hardarts." These eateries became representative of Americans' love of economy coupled with a mock grandiosity that resulted in a period of lavish Automats full of white tile and Carrara marble. They were kept spotlessly clean, and it was quite normal to find everyone from unemployed drifters, lingering over a cup of five-cent coffee, to the brightest of Broadway's celebrities there. Silver-ornamented spigots dispensed coffee, tea, and hot chocolate. Stews, desserts, rolls, and sandwiches were offered in profusion.

Robert F. Byrnes wrote of the Horn & Hardart Company in its heyday: "If you were the young man who had escaped from Easton, and you went to Horn & Hardart for Thanksgiving and for company, after you ate your fill you could walk back to your furnished room and write to your sister about the great meal. You could say you went in with a dollar in your pocket, and came out with 50 cents."

After World War II FAST-FOOD restaurants and hamburger stands ascended in popularity while the Automats declined; the last Automat closed its doors in New York City on April 10, 1991.

The facade of glass doors of an original Automat is displayed at the Smithsonian Institution's Museum of American History.

avocado (*Persea gratissima* or *P. americana*). Also, "alligator pear." A tropical tree that bears a globular green fruit with a large seed and tough skin. The name is from the Nahuatl *ahuacati,* "testicle" (because of its shape), and entered English via the Spanish, first appearing in print in the seventeenth century and in America in 1690.

The Aztecs ate avocados, as was noted by the early Spanish explorers, but the avocado was long considered a rather tasteless food, enjoyed only in Central and South America and in the Caribbean, where it acquired its alternative name "alligator pear," possibly because it grew where there were alligators, as in Florida, or because of its alligatorlike skin.

Horticulturist Henry Perrine planted the first avocados in Florida in 1833, but it was not until the turn of the century that the plant took on commercial importance. Even then the avocado was not particularly relished by most Americans, and only in California, Florida, and Hawaii, the major producing states, was it much appreciated until it became popular as a salad item in the 1950s. The major varieties grown include the "Hass," "Fuerte," "Bacon," "Zutano," "Rincón," "Mexican," "Guatemalan," "Booth 8," "Booth 7," "Lula," and "Waldin."

The avocado is the major ingredient of GUACAMOLE.

awa (*Piper methysticum*). The kava shrub with heartshaped leaves traditionally used by Hawaiians as a drink and a medicine. The word is Polynesian, dating in English print to 1930.

"Awa" also is a Hawaiian word for the milkfish (*Chanos chanos*), similar to a herring and at least three feet in length (1960). They are usually baked or steamed

Awenda bread. Also, "Awaendaw." A Carolinas bread made from hominy grits and/or cornmeal, named after an Indian settlement near Charleston, South Carolina. The term dates in print to 1847.

AWENDA BREAD

Push ½ c. cooked hominy grits through a sieve, beat in 1 egg, ½ c. cornmeal, 1 t. sugar, 1 t. salt, 1 t. baking powder, and ¾ c. milk to make a thin batter. Grease a 1-qt. baking pan, pour in batter, and cook 40–50 min. at 350° Serve with butter.

baby beef. Western term since the 1890s for young cattle killed for market. Today the term refers to a calf several months old and weaned from its mother. This is often sold as VEAL, though it is not considered of the highest quality because of its age.

baby food. A general term for any food served to infants, but also a food-industry term for those products developed for feeding infants. Until the twentieth century infant food was a matter of individual families' choice, directed by conventional and inherited wisdom as well as published guidelines for good nutrition. Some pureed infant food might be purchased at pharmacies for special diets, but in 1927 Daniel F. Gerber began marketing a strained baby food under the name Gerber's (now based in Fremont, Michigan); a year later Gerber was issuing five varieties of baby food. By 1935 more than sixty other companies had entered the baby-food market.

baby vegetable. Also, "miniature vegetable." A food marketing term that gained currency in the early 1980s to describe vegetables that are picked very young and small or for hybrids genetically grown to be of a small size. They are prized both for their sweetness and texture and for their appearance on a plate.

Bacardi cocktail. A cocktail made with lime juice, sugar, grenadine, and Bacardi light rum. The name dates in print at least to 1934 and is directly associated with the firm Bacardi Imports, Inc., of Miami, Florida. In 1936 a New York State Supreme Court ruled that to be authentic, a "Bacardi cocktail" had to be made with Bacardi rum, since the name Bacardi was a registered trademark.

BACARDI COCKTAIL

Shake together with ice 2 t. lime juice, ½ t. sugar, 1 t. grenadine, and 1½ oz. Bacardi light rum. Strain into chilled cocktail glasses.

---

bachelor's button. A cookie with a cherry set on top and made to resemble a button (1969). The cookie has nothing to do with the flower called by the same name, except for its similar shape.

backdaag. A Pennsylvania-Dutch word for "Baking Day," which was Friday on Pennsylvania-Dutch farms. One day was set aside for baking because occasional baking of one or two items could not satisfy the needs of the hardworking farmers.

back of the house. Restaurant workers' slang term meaning the kitchen or the kitchen staff itself.

bacon. Salted and/or smoked meat taken from the sides and back of a pig. Bacon is cut in slices and fried, usually as a breakfast item, or used as larding in certain dishes. It is customarily served with broiled or fried calf's liver. "Belly bacon" is taken from the belly of the animal.

The word "bacon" derives from Frankish *bako,* "ham," and Common Germanic *bakkon,* and in Middle English was spelled either *bacon* or *bakoun,* which was also a more general term for pork well into the sixteenth century. In America bacon has long been a staple of most households, largely because of a long history of pork consumption and hog butchering on farms. "Bacon pigs" are animals especially grown for their bacon, often from breeds like the Yorkshire and Tamworth.

Bacon may be cured at home with salt and some sugar, but factory bacon may be either "dry cured" with salt before cooking and smoking or "pickle cured" with brine before being smoked and cooked.

"Regular" bacon is sold at markets cut into slabs or slices. "Thin sliced" (also known as "hotel" or "restaurant" bacon) is sliced approximately $\frac{1}{32}$ of an inch in thickness; "regular" is sliced $\frac{1}{16}$ of an inch; "thick sliced" or "thick-cut" is cut about twice as thick as regular bacon. "Country style" bacon is usually a generously sliced, well-cured bacon. Canned bacon is usually precooked and used where there is little access to kitchen stoves and equipment. "Cracklings" are the fried pieces of fat left in the pan after the bacon is removed. In Mexican-American regions, these are called *chicharrons* (from the Spanish). "Bacon bits" are preserved and dried (though there are also artificial bacon-flavored bits sold in jars), usually for tossing with a salad dressing.

"Canadian-style" bacon (called "back bacon" in Canada) is cut from the loin, strip, or sirloin muscles along the pig's back. It is a leaner, drier, fully-cooked meat usually sold in a packaged hunk. The reason for the name is not clear. "Flitch" is a term used in Pennsylvania for unsmoked slab bacon.

"Lower salt bacon" has decreased levels of salt. "Salt pork" is a very fatty cured pork (also called "white bacon") generally used as a cooking fat or flavoring for other dishes. "Beef bacon" is made from boneless beef short plates cured like regular bacon. "Turkey bacon" is made from turkey that is cured and then molded to look like regular bacon.

"Bac.Os," introduced in 1966 by General Mills, are bits of SOY PROTEIN isolate flavored to taste like bacon.

In the U.S., nearly 70 percent of bacon is consumed at breakfast.

bagel. A round yeast bun with a hole in the middle, which is cooked in boiling water, and then baked. The bagel, once a staple of Jewish immigrants' Sunday breakfasts, has become a reasonable substitute for sandwich bread in many American cities where DELICATESSENS exist. Traditionally the bagel is eaten with such delicacies as LOX, Nova Scotia salmon, and slices of white onions; the most classic match is cream cheese (an American creation) and lox. Bagels are sometimes toasted, and one will find them studded with onion flakes, sesame seeds, poppy seeds, or raisins, or made from dark flours. Because of its heaviness, the bagel is sometimes referred to as a "cement doughnut."

The bagel was first mentioned in American print only in 1932. The first bagels sold in a supermarket were from Lender's Bagel Bakery (the nation's oldest frozen bagel maker) in New Haven, Connecticut, in 1955. The same company was the first to sell frozen bagels, as of 1962, which helped enormously to popularize the item nationally. Lender's also claims credit for the first green bagels, now a common variation baked each year for Saint Patrick's Day.

The origins of the bagel are lost somewhere in the history of the Ashkenazi Jews, who brought Yiddish culture to America. The word "bagel" derives from a Yiddish word, *beygl,* from the German *bügel,* for a round loaf of bread. There is a story that the word may also derive from the German word *Buegel,* meaning "stirrup," referring to a legend that the bakers of Vienna commemorated John III's victory over the Turks in their city in 1683 by molding their bread into the shape of stirrups because the liberated Austrians had clung to the king's stirrups as he rode by. But Leo Rosten in *The Joys of Yiddish* (1968) notes that the first printed mention of the word "bagel" is in the Community Regulations of Cracow for 1610, which stated that the item was given as a gift to women in childbirth.

So associated with New York City folklore and food culture is the bagel, that in 1951 *The New York Times* printed a story on its front page headlined BAGEL FAMINE THREATENS IN CITY/LABOR DISPUTE PUTS HOLE IN SUPPLY.

Bagel sales have soared since the 1980s, now accounting for an $800 million industry. Americans consume about 3.6 pounds of bagels per capita per year.

Bagel Dog. Trademark name for a hot dog boiled and then baked in a bagel dough topped with poppy seed. The item, similar to the cocktail-party item called "pig-in-a-blanket," was created in 1980 by bakery owner Milan R. Burger of Durham, North Carolina.

bagoong. A fermented fish or shrimp condiment used in Hawaii to flavor meats and vegetable dishes. The word derives from the Tagalog and dates in English print to 1940. Bagoong is made by salting the fish or shrimp and allowing it to ferment for several days, after which the liquid is pressed out. The condiment is usually eaten raw.

baked Alaska. A dessert made of sponge cake covered with ice cream and a meringue that is browned in the oven, but the ice cream remains frozen (1905).

The idea of baking ice cream in some kind of crust so as to create a hot-cold blend of textures occurred to Thomas Jefferson, who in 1802 served minister Manasseh Cutler a puddinglike dish that included "ice cream very good, crust wholly dried, crumbled into thin flakes." And a report in the French journal *Liberté* for June 1866 indicates that the master cook of the Chinese mission in Paris imparted a technique for baking pastry over ice cream to the French chef Balzac of the Grand Hotel. But baked Alaska as we know it today may be traced to the experiments in heating and cooking conducted by Benjamin Thompson (1753–1814), born in Woburn, Massachusetts, who became a celebrated scientist both at home and in

England, where he was awarded the title of Count Rumford for his work (the name Rumford came from the town of Rumford [now Concord], New Hampshire, where his wife was born). His studies of the resistance of egg whites to heat resulted in the browned topping that eventually became the crown for what came to be called "Baked Alaska." Patricia M. Tice in *Ice Cream for All* (1990) asserted that Delmonico's chef, Charles Ranhofer, created "Baked Alaska" in 1869 to commemorate the purchase of Alaska by the United States, although in his own cookbook, *The Epicurean* (1893), Ranhofer calls the dish "Alaska, Florida." The term "Baked Alaska" dates in print at least to 1905 and was used by Fannie Merritt Farmer in the 1909 edition of her cookbook.

BAKED ALASKA

Trim a sponge cake to a 1-in. thickness and cover with about 3 in. of ice cream. Freeze until very firm. Beat 5 egg whites until stiff with 1 t. vanilla, ½ t. cream of tartar, and ⅔ c. sugar. Remove the ice-cream cake from freezer and spread the egg whites in swirls around the ice cream in the shape of a dome. Bake in a 500° oven until the top is golden brown, about 3 min. Serve immediately.

---

bake sale. A neighborhood or school social event at which baked goods and confections are sold in order to raise money for a charitable purpose. The idea goes back to Colonial America, when money might be raised to build a church, barn, or other building.

baking powder. A combination of sodium bicarbonate and acid salt that became popular in the 1850s as a leavening agent in baking what came to be called "quick bread," "lightnin' bread," or "aerated bread." By 1854 Americans had self-rising flour, which was baking powder mixed with flour. In 1867 James A. Church introduced Arm & Hammer "baking soda," a new term for the earlier used but less desirable potassium or sodium bicarbonate, also called "saleratus" (an American variant of the Latin *sal* [salt] "+ *aeratus*" [aerated]).

In 1889 William M. Wright developed a "double-acting" baking powder whose leavening action began in the dough and repeated in the oven. Wright and his partner, chemist George C. Rew, marketed the product under the name Calumet Baking Powder ("Calumet" was the name the French gave to the peace pipe Indians offered to Father Jacques Marquette when he explored the territories around Chicago in the 1670s; for Wright the name symbolized "friendliness.")

bald face. Nineteenth-century slang term for inferior whiskey (1836).

balkenbry. A pork loaf that is cooked and cut into slabs and usually served for breakfast. The word is from the Dutch, meaning the rafter from which the meat was hung to cure, dating in English print to 1940.

bamboche. Also, "bambache." A Cajun or Deep South term for a drinking spree, from the French (1944).

bamboo cocktail. A cocktail said to have been invented about 1910 by bartender Charlie Mahoney of the Hoffman House in New York.

BAMBOO COCKTAIL

Drink made with a dash of orange bitters, 1 oz. sherry, and 1 oz. dry vermouth, stirred with ice, strained, and served in a wineglass with a lemon peel.

---

banana. Any of a variety of tropical or subtropical trees of the genus *Musa* bearing clusters of long yellow or reddish fruits. The name is from Portuguese and Spanish, via a West African name, and was first printed in English in the seventeenth century.

The banana, which has been traced to southern Asia and India, may have been cultivated as long ago as 1000 B.C. in Assyria. The Arabs brought the fruit to Egypt in the seventh century, and Portuguese navigators found them in 1482 on Africa's west coast and thereafter transplanted them to the Canary Islands. The early Spanish explorers of the New World remarked on the "bananas" in the West Indies, but actually had seen plantains (*Musa paradisiaca*). In 1516, on the island of Hispaniola, Friar Tomás de Berlanga planted the first banana trees in the West Indies, but propagation of the fruit was limited to the islands until well into the nineteenth century. The first bananas entered the United States only in 1804, when they were brought from Cuba to New York City by Captain John Chester on the schooner *Reynard*. But no further shipments arrived in the city, or anywhere else in North America, until 1830, when Captain John Pearsall brought in fifteen hundred stems on the schooner *Harriet Smith*. By the 1840s New York markets were receiving frequent shipments of bananas, and in 1870 Captain Lorenzo D. Baker of the *Telegraph* brought a cargo of the fruit to Boston from Jamaica, leading to a partnership with a fruit broker named Andrew Pearson. Together they founded the Boston Fruit Company and introduced the banana as an exotic fruit wrapped in foil and sold for a dime at the Philadelphia Centennial Exposition of 1876. The Boston Fruit Company was merged by Samuel Zemurray and Minor Keith into the United Fruit Company (later United Brands) in 1899, which, with the introduction of refrigerated cargo holds, began shipping bananas to new ports and markets in the United States. The success of the banana after the turn of the century led to widespread involvement of American companies and the federal government in the affairs and politics of the Caribbean and Central and South America. Plantations were established in what came to be called "banana republics" run for the benefit and interests of the fruit companies in the United States, often to the detriment of the inhabitants of those countries.

Although Hawaii had long grown bananas (discovered there by Captain James Cook in 1799), the state has never had a significant commercial banana industry. Most bananas eaten in the United States—between 70 million and 80 million bunches a year, making it Americans' most popular fruit—are shipped in from Costa Rica, Guatemala, and other countries, with the majority being the common banana (M. *sapientum*), of which the "Gros Michel" variety (from Jamaica) was the predominant variety until 1944, when the "Valery," "Lacatan," "Williams," "Grand Nain" and other varieties entered the marketplace.

The "red banana" and the plantain varieties are becoming more common in American markets.

Americans eat bananas raw, in salads, in various desserts, and as a flavoring for breads and other confections.

banana bread. Also, "banana cake." A loaf with a cakelike consistency made from flour and mashed bananas. Fannie Merritt Farmer's cookbook makes reference in 1896 to a "banana cake," which was really a cake with sliced bananas on top. But in the 1960s and 1970s, during a period of delight in hearty, fresh-made breads, banana bread took on a certain faddishness.

bananas Foster. A dessert made from sliced bananas cooked with butter, brown sugar, rum, and banana cordial and served with vanilla ice cream. The dish was created by chef Paul Blange in the early 1950s at Brennan's Restaurant in New Orleans as part of a Breakfast at Brennan's promotion that has since become a city tradition (the restaurant was opened in 1946). It was named after a regular customer, Richard Foster, owner of the Foster Awning Company in New Orleans. The recipe below is from Brennan's.

BANANAS FOSTER

Melt 4 T. butter over an alcohol burner in flambé pan. Add 1 c. brown sugar, ½ t. cinnamon, 4 T. banana cordial, and mix well. Heat for a few minutes, then place 4 bananas that have been cut in half lengthwise and then halved widthwise in pan and sauté until soft. Add ¼ c. rum and allow to beat well, then tip pan so that flame from burner ignites alcohol. Allow to burn until flame dies out. Serve over vanilla ice cream by placing 4 pieces of banana on each portion, then spooning hot sauce from the pan onto the bananas and ice cream.

banket. A Dutch-American rolled pastry filled with almond paste. It is commonly shaped into alphabet letters and called "banket letters." The word is from the Dutch, dating in print to 1969.

bannock. Also, "Indian bannock." A nineteenth-century New England cornmeal cake derived from a Scottish barley or wheat pancake of the same name, first in American print in 1806. Sometimes this was called "White Indian bannock," because of the use of white Indian cornmeal.

Baptist cake. A New England deep-fried doughnut-like confection. Baptist cakes are risen dough balls that have been immersed, like Baptists who are immersed in water at their baptism, in hot oil. The term dates in print to 1931. In Connecticut they are called "holy pokes," in Maine "huff juffs," and in other parts "hustlers."

bar. Also, "bar room" or "barroom." A tavern or room where alcoholic beverages are served, or the long counter at which one stands or sits to drink such beverages. The word derives from the more general meaning of a long slab or block of wood or other material used to separate or support, and in this sense derives from Vulgar Latin *barra*. In its usage for a tavern, the word dates from the sixteenth century, when bars would be pulled across the counter at closing time. "Bar room" came into the language in the late eighteenth century, and in America "bartender" (one who tends the bar) was known by 1836; ten years later "bar keep" was also used. "Bar-counter" was used by Dickens in his *American Notes* (1842), and by

1857 there were female hostesses called, with some condescension, "bargirls" (also "B-girls").

By the 1830s "saloon" (from the French *salon,* room) was an alternative word for bar, and there were many other, less savory terms, like "barrel-house," "watering hole," "gin mill," "rum hole," "whiskey joint," and, later, "JUKE joint," to join the more refined, post-Prohibition, "cocktail lounge." "Dram shop" first saw print in 1839. Today the word "bar" suggests an establishment where the principal business is the dispensing of alcoholic drinks, while "tavern" is somewhat quaint and "saloon" a bit dated, except when used as a deliberately nostalgic reference. The idea of the "corner saloon" began in New York City after an 1841 ordinance permitted the sale of meat and vegetables in shops removed from the marketplace. This eventually led to the sale of spirits in these same shops, many of which were located on corners. When the sale of spirits took precedence over the sale of food, a "corner saloon" or "corner bar" was the result.

"Bar and grill" conveys some culinary interest at such a place, while "lounge" refers more to a bar's booths-and-tables section than to its counter, which is usually flanked by "barstools" (first noted in Arthur Koestler's novel *Twilight Bar* in 1945) and a "bar rail," on which to rest one's foot.

A "smart bar" is a 1990s term denoting a bar (often set within a conventional bar) that serves nonalcoholic drinks.

barbecue. Also "Bar-B-Q," "BBQ," " 'cue," and other variations. A method of cooking meat, poultry, or fish over an open pit fire, often with the whole animal skewered on a spit and almost always done out-of-doors. Barbecues are as much a social ritual in America as they are a means of cooking, for they are held as often for large parties, celebrations, and political rallies as for cooking a family's meal. Barbecuing methods go back to the earliest days, when man first used fire to cook his food, but the term "barbecue" comes from the Spanish and Haitian word *barbacoa* ("framework of sticks"), which referred first to a kind of latticework bench but soon after was adapted to mean the grill on which meat was roasted. The *Dictionary of American English* shows that the word was in use in America at least by 1655, when it first appeared in print, and by 1733 it had taken on the implications of a social gathering. By 1836 barbecues were popular in Texas, and in 1850, at a barbecue held in Kansas, the menu included six cattle, twenty hogs, fifty sheep, pigs, and lambs, a hundred hams, and hundreds of baked goods.

Regional distinctions and preferences for various styles of barbecue have long been part of folkloric debate in America, and barbecue contests have proliferated in recent years throughout the United States. In the South barbecue is akin to a religion, and from county to county the preferences for one ratio of tomato to vinegar or sugar to chile peppers are myriad. Even the condiments and side dishes are steeped in tradition. In eastern North Carolina, for instance, vinegar-based barbecue sauce is preferred with coleslaw colored with turmeric. In western North Carolina recipes are more tomato based, and pure white coleslaw is preferred.

Barbecue may be done over an open fire on a spit (as is most common in Texas and the West) or over a "barbecue pit," which may be constructed of anything from a simple outdoor grill to an iron smoker, and barbecue enthusiasts delight in inventing new contraptions in which to cook and smoke their barbecue. In Hawaii KALUA PIG is wrapped in ti leaves and cooked in a pit dug in the ground.

The most basic distinction in barbecue is the meat used, with pork more commonly used east of the Mississippi River and beef preferred west of it, although both meats are used throughout the United States. Sausage is also a very popular meat, and hamburgers, hot dogs, steaks, seafood, and vegetables are barbecued too.

Pork barbecue takes two primary forms, as ribs or as meat that has been sliced, chopped, or "shredded," then served on a hamburger bun or sliced white bread. In St. Louis, Missouri, deep-fried pig's noses called "snoots" are a local SOUL FOOD favorite.

Beef barbecue, especially in Texas, is heavily smoked, usually made from the brisket, and served with white bread and pickles on the side.

Next comes the issue of sauce. Barbecue of various kinds has always been basted with herbs and marinades, but "barbecue sauce" as such is of rather recent vintage. The earliest reference to a sauce by this name was cited by Betty Fussell (in *I Hear America Cooking* [1986]) as a "French brown sauce, spiked with ketchup, onions, mustard, and Worcestershire sauce" that came from Louis De Gouy's *Chefs Cook Book* (1939).

In parts of the South (even within the same city) "wet barbecue" vies with "dry barbecue" for honors. The former is based on a sauce that commonly contains tomato, vinegar, chile, and other seasonings, and sugar that is continuously basted on the meat. Dry barbecue is made by rubbing the meat with dry seasonings like chiles, cumin, black pepper, and herbs, then barbecued slowly.

A third main difference in barbecue styles is in the kind of wood used to smoke and cook the meat, usually dependent upon the wood available in the region. Hardwoods like oak, ash, apple, beech, butternut, chestnut, cherry, and walnut are popular in the South, while mesquite is preferred in the West, and grapevines are often used in viticultural areas.

Americans barbecue 2.3 times a week in summer (steak is the most popular item on the grill), with most of the cooking done by men. The most popular grill was for decades the saucer-shaped "Weber Kettle" grill, invented by George Stephen of Chicago in 1952, now produced by Weber-Stephans Products Company of Palatine, Illinois. Charcoal grills have given way to gas grills in popularity, with 42 percent favoring charcoal and 58 percent gas, as of 1998 (11 percent own both). Sixty-two percent of those who barbecue do so year-round. Small Japanese-style "hibachis" are also commonly used in small spaces. The use of store-bought charcoal and packaged "briquets" of compressed charcoal is widespread. The two principal aromatic woods used to add flavor to barbecue are hickory and mesquite. "Water smoker" cookers utilize a water pan, usually containing wood chips for flavor, set above the coals to generate steam that slow-cooks the ingredients.

SPARERIB BARBECUE

Sauté 3 c. coarsely chopped onions and 1½ T. minced garlic in 4 T. oil until soft but not brown. Add one 1-lb. can drained, chopped tomatoes with liquid, 2 T. dry mustard, 2 T. sugar, 1½ T. vinegar, ¾ c. tomato paste, salt, pepper, and about 6 seeded chilies (or add chilies to taste). Bring to a boil and reduce till thickened. Correct seasoning and remove from heat. Skewer spareribs, baste lavishly with sauce, and grill over hot coals, basting often, for about 30 min. Serve with heated sauce on side. (This same sauce may be used for chicken barbecue.)

PORK BARBECUE

In a large kettle brown 3 lb. pork shoulder in 3 T. fat. Mix together ½ c. ketchup, 1 t. chili powder or cayenne, ½ t. nutmeg, ¼ t. cinnamon, 1 t. celery seed, 1 t. sugar, ½ t. nutmeg, salt and pepper, ⅓ c. vinegar, and 1 cup water. Bring to a boil and cook for 10 min. Pour over pork, cover, and bake at 325°, basting often, for about 1½ hr. or more, until pork is very tender and

comes away easily with knife and fork. Remove all meat from bone and chop into fine pieces or shreds, then add salt, pepper, and hot sauce to taste. Serve with coleslaw and corn bread.

bar chum. Bartender slang for snack foods serve at a bar, usually free with drinks. The term dates in print to 1991.

barfly. A term dating in print to 1906 for someone who stays too long at a saloon, or a drunkard. Harry MacElhone, owner of Harry's New York Bar in Paris, founded a less-than-serious organization called "International Bar Fly" ("IBF") in 1924, which now supposedly has more than eighty thousand members.

bar glasses. Any of the various types of glassware used at a bar. There are dozens of such glasses (*Grossman's Guide to Wines, Beers, and Spirits*, by Harold J. Grossman, revised by Harriet Lembeck [1977], shows thirty-seven different glasses), but few bars or restaurants stock more than a few useful kinds such as those listed below:

> **cocktail glass.** A 2½-oz. stemmed glass with a tapered bowl used to serve cocktails. A larger 4½-oz. cocktail glass with a wider rim is preferred, especially for MARTINIS, and this glass is usually called a "martini glass."

> **Collins glass.** A cylindrical 12-oz. glass for long drinks like the TOM COLLINS.

> **highball glass.** A cylindrical 8-oz. glass for mixed drinks on the rocks.

> **jigger.** A short, squat, thick glass used to hold 1½ oz. of spirits, it is often used as a measuring glass or shot glass.

> **old-fashioned glass.** A short, cylindrical, sometimes stemmed 6-oz. glass with a thick bottom, used for serving short drinks on the rocks, like the OLD-FASHIONED.

> **pilsner glass.** A long, conical glass of at least 10 oz. used to hold beer. Its design helps to maintain a foamy head on the beer.

> **pony or liqueur glass.** A 1-oz. glass that is stemmed and tubular in shape, used for CORDIALS.

saucer glass or champagne glass. Traditionally (though not recommended by connoisseurs) used for serving CHAMPAGNE and sparkling drinks, this stemmed 5-oz. glass has a flat, saucerlike bowl.

sherry glass. A slightly fluted 2-oz. glass used for sherry and cordials.

shot glass. A short, squat, thick-bottomed glass used to serve a "shot" of whiskey or other spirits. It is often called a "cheater" because the customer often does not receive a full ounce.

sour glass. A stemmed 6-oz. glass for serving SOURS.

wineglass. According to the wine served, these glasses may be of various heights, shapes, and stems. The all-purpose wineglass holds between 6½ and 8½ oz. of liquid. White wines are customarily served in long-stemmed glasses with a medium-size bowl; Bordeaux and other red wines are served in glasses with a slightly larger bowl; Burgundy and other red wines are considered best served in a balloon glass with a large bowl; German wines customarily are served in a small-bowled, long, green-stemmed glass; brandies are served in snifters, glasses with short stems and large-bottomed bowls.

barley (genus *Hordeum*). A grain of the grass family that was brought to the United States by early settlers, who ground the seed for use as a cereal, in breads and cakes, and as "barley sugar." The word is from Old English *boerlic*. Today the United States is the second-largest producer of barley, after the Soviet Union. Most barley is used for livestock feed or for making beer, but it is still also used in cakes, breads, and mixed CEREALS. The total U.S. production of barley in 1997 was 7.4 million short tons.

barracuda (genus *Sphyraena*). Any of various long silvery tropical fishes with a row of sharp, long teeth. Barracudas are often poisonous to eat, though the Pacific barracuda has long been a delicacy in California, where it is sold fresh. The fish, which is voracious and feared, may be broiled, grilled, or smoked.

The word is from the Spanish, and its first appearance in English was in 1678.

bass. Any of a variety of salt- or freshwater fish, whose general name derives from Old English *baers*

and has German roots that mean "bristle," which describes the spiny appearance of any number of fish of the perch and other, families. *The American Heritage Dictionary* defines bass, first, as "Any of several North American freshwater fishes of the family Centrarchidae," and, second, as "Any of various marine fishes of the family Serranidae." U.S. commercial landings of sea bass totaled 3.6 million pounds in 1997. The CHILEAN SEA BASS, also known as the "Patagonian toothfish," is not a true bass.

Some sea PERCH, GROUPER, JEWFISH, BLACK BASS, BLACK SEA BASS, STRIPED BASS and others go by the name "bass," but the only fish in Europe by this specific name is what the French call *loup*.

bastard bread. Bread made with a mixture of white flour and cornmeal (1965).

bath towel. Meatpackers' slang for beef tripe.

bathtub gin. Prohibition term for alcohol mixed with herbs for illicit sale (1930). The name derives from the fact that often the liquor was actually mixed in a bathtub.

batter bread. A cornmeal bread often associated with Virginia and first mentioned in print in 1897. The following recipe by Houston Eldredge appeared in *Famous Old Receipts,* published in Philadelphia in 1908.

BATTER BREAD

Scald ½ pt. cornmeal, cool, then beat in ½ pt. CLABBER with 1 t. melted butter, 1 t. salt, and another ½ pt. clabber. Dissolve ½ t. baking soda in ½ c. clabber, beat into mixture, place in buttered pudding dish, and bake at 425° for about 30 min.

---

battery acid. Slang term for poorly made or distasteful coffee (1941). In army slang, "battery acid and armored cow" would be bad coffee with canned milk, but, according to an article in *American Heritage* (August–September 1986), fliers used "battery acid" to describe canned grapefruit juice.

bayou blue. Prohibition term for inferior or illicit whiskey made in the bayou and backwoods country.

beach plum. A northeastern shrub, *Prunus maritima,* that grows along the seashore and has edible berries.

bean. Any of a variety of pods from plants in the genus *Phaseolus,* and, for culinary purposes, especially *P. vulgaris,* of which there are more than a thousand varieties. The word is from the Old English *bēan.*

The oldest domesticated beans in the Americas were found in the Ocampo Caves of Mexico, dating back to 4000 B.C. Beans were often planted in the same fields with corn and were carried to North America from Mexico.

The two main types of beans grown and eaten in the United States are "field" beans, including the pea or NAVY BEAN, the BLACK BEAN, KIDNEY BEAN, and others raised in Michigan, California, Idaho, New York, Colorado, New Mexico, and elsewhere; and "garden" beans, including the STRING BEAN, the "butter" or LIMA BEAN, and the wax bean. SOYBEANS (*Glycine max*), whose seeds are called "soya" or "soyabean," are generally used for fodder, though some oil, soy sauce, and bean curd is made from them too.

bean eater. Since 1881, a slang term for a Bostonian, because of the association with BOSTON BAKED BEANS. Also, a slur word for Mexicans because of their fondness of beans. See also entry under COWBOY SLANG.

beanery. Also, "bean wagon." A small, inexpensive eatery like a diner. The term dates in print to 1887.

bean-hole cookery. A method of baking, originally used by the Indians of the Northwest and adapted by lumber jacks, by which a hole in the ground is filled with very hot stones on which is placed an earthenware pot filled with beans. This is then covered further with hot stones, then earth, and left to bake for hours. The technique was first mentioned in print in 1907.

bean supper. A New England social event, usually held by a local church to raise money. It dates in print only to 1968, but bean suppers have long been part of New England social life.

bear. Any of a variety of large, shaggy-furred mammals in the family Ursidae, especially in North America the black bear (*Ursus americanus*), also called the "brown bear" and "cinnamon bear," the "grizzly bear" (*U. horribilis*), also called the "silver tip," and the polar bear (*U. maritimus*).

Omnivorous and ferocious, bears have been among the most sought-after game, for their fur, their fat, and their meat, all of which the Native Americans used long before the arrival of the European trappers, who hunted the animal mainly for its coat and nearly drove the beast to extinction in the East. Because of bear's gaminess, young bear is the most desirable, and bear meat, needing to be marinated or covered with a strongly seasoned sauce to make it palatable to most tastes, was available in city markets of the nineteenth century.

beef. The meat of a full-grown steer, ox, cow, or bull. Beef, in preparations ranging from steak and stews to HAMBURGERS and BARBECUE, is one of the most important meats in the American diet.

The word is from the Latin *bōs* (ox), which in Middle English became *boef* or *beef.*

Cattle for beef have been domesticated for millennia, all descended from the wild bulls of Europe called "aurochs" (*Bos primienius*). By 3500 B.C. cattle were being raised in Egypt, and the ox is constantly used as a symbolic animal of the Old and New Testaments. By A.D. 500 the aurochs had been brought to England to be bred with the native "shorthorn," and most American breeds are descendants of English cattle, though the Spanish explorer Francisco Vasquez de Coronado brought cattle to the Southwest in 1540. Jamestown had cattle by 1611, but there was no commercial meat-packing in the colonies until William Pynchon set up a slaughterhouse in Boston in 1662. In 1690 cattle were brought to missions in Texas by the Spanish, and once the missions were abandoned, the cattle ran wild, eventually developing into what were called LONGHORNS, the only cattle used for beef production in America for the next 160 years.

PORK was much preferred for meat until well into the nineteenth century, however, because pigs were easier to care for and feed. Still, while beef was not so common as pork, the early settlers had sufficient land on which to raise enough beef for their needs, and the word "beef-steak" was in use since the late seventeenth century. In 1711 a "Beef-Stake Club" was thriving in London and later was imitated in Philadelphia, where a similar organization under the same name met at Tunn Tavern as of 1749. In those days a "beef-steak" was a flattened piece of beef that was usually fried and served with gravy. The English liked it served very rare, and so the American colonists followed suit. By the 1760s some cities had "beef steak houses." Nineteenth-century American cookbook authors insisted that beef should be cooked until very well done.

Most of the beef consumed, however, was salted or corned, and little meat was shipped over long distances. By 1767 the Franciscan friars of California had enlisted Mexicans and Indians to herd cattle, and the French in Louisiana initiated the first cattle drive in 1779 when they brought in cattle from the Spanish in San Antonio. Americans were involved in similar activities in Texas by the 1820s, where the LONGHORN steer became an important breed in the decades to follow. By the 1850s Chicago had already established itself as a meat-packing center, but again, the industry produced mainly salted or corned meat products. After the Civil War the demand for beef increased with the rise in population and the decrease in forage land east of the Mississippi River, and on September 5, 1867, the first cattle were shipped by railroad car out of Abilene, Kansas, a town that livestock trader Joe McCoy bought for $4,250 as a central depot for cattle movements out of Texas. This began the era of the great cattle drives and the expansion of the West's mythos into romance and literature, with the cowboy as the central figure of America's seemingly unending destiny. According to Edwin C. McReynolds in *Oklahoma: A History of the Sooner State* (1954), the total number of cattle driven from Texas to Kansas City between 1866 and 1885 was 6 million head, with a peak of six hundred thousand in 1871. The main cattle drives were from Austin, Texas, to Abilene (the Chisolm Trail), San Antonio to Baxter Springs, Kansas (the Shawnee Trail), and Bandera, Texas, to Ogallala, Nebraska (the Western Trail). But the cattle drives were short-lived for several reasons. The introduction of barbed wire in 1875 and the intrusion of more farm families into the western territories meant an end to free access to land. Then, over the winter of 1886–87, a bitter cold spell wiped out 90 percent of the herds, and the end came quickly.

Americans had developed a great appetite for beef by the turn of the century, and after Detroit meat-packer G. H. Hammond brought out the refrigerated railway car in 1871, chilled carcasses became readily available in the East, though fresh beef was still not common in the outer reaches of the western frontier. Still, by the 1880s beef was being shipped even to England, and "steakhouses" were among the most popular restaurants in large American cities.

A hardy American breed of cattle called the "Santa Gertrudis," developed from shorthorns and Brahmans at the King Ranch in Texas, became an extremely adaptive steer for the beef market, though ABERDEEN ANGUS, Herefords, and Galloways were also important in the late nineteenth century.

Slaughterhouses of this era were primitive and generally unhygienic, leading to frequent campaigns to correct their abuses and to the passage in 1906 of the Pure Food and Drug Law, to a large extent the result of the impression made on the public by Upton Sinclair's accusatory novel about the meatpacking industry, *The Jungle* (1906).

In rural communities where there was little or no refrigeration, as in the South, "beef clubs" were formed by members who acquired shares by bringing in beef to be slaughtered and to take their portion.

By the 1920s beef had become a competitor with pork in terms of consumption, and Europeans began characterizing Americans as a "nation of beefeaters." To be sure, a meal of a two-inch-thick steak and a baked potato or french-fried potatoes became an icon of American gastronomy and remains so to this day, despite the fact that beef consumption has begun to decrease in recent years. In 1952 the average American ate 62 pounds of beef per year; by 1960, 99 pounds; by 1970, 114 pounds. But in 1993 the figure stood at only 61.5 pounds and as of 1999 stands at about 97 pounds per person. The decrease is due both to Americans' desire to cut out excessive fat and cholesterol from their diet and to the high price of beef.

There have in recent years been attempts by meat producers to change the federal regulations on meat quality (based on marbling of intramuscular fat, color, and texture), but for the moment the standards are as follows: "prime," "choice," "good," "standard," "commercial," "utility," "cutter," and "canner." Prime, which has the heaviest marbling, constitutes only about 3 percent of all graded beef and is very expensive to produce because of additional special feed and the time needed to bring the animals to the proper weight and fat consistency. The lowest five grades are generally available only in processed or canned meats.

These standards are enforced by the Department of Agriculture and stamped on the outside of each carcass, but for producers this is a voluntary process and must be requested of the Department of Agriculture.

The terminology of American butchering is often confusing, and many terms are used as synonyms for poorly defined standard cuts. The most commonly used terms are explained below.

primal brisket. The breast section of the animal, just under the first five ribs of the chuck. The brisket, which is usually braised or pot-roasted, is cut into two pieces, the flat half and the point half. See also, CORNED BEEF.

primal chuck. The shoulder and part of the neck. Chuck is usually ground for hamburger or other meat dishes. The "cross-rib roast" (also called "English" or "Boston" cut) is usually pot-roasted, as is the next cut, the arm pot roast (also called "shoulder roast"). The "blade cut," which may be made into a roast or steak, is next. This may be further divided into the "chuck eye" (also called "market" or "Spencer" roast), the "chuck steak" (or "flat iron" steak), and the "mock tenderloin" (or "Scotch tender," "Jewish fillet," and "chuck eye").

primal flank. Meat from the belly section below the loin. It is usually braised or, if marinated, grilled for LONDON BROIL.

primal plate. From the chest in front of the "flank steak," which Jewish Americans call FLANKEN. It is cut into short ribs or braised without the bone. PASTRAMI is often made from this cut, as is the "skirt steak" (also called "Romanian steak"), a diaphragm muscle that is braised or ground. It is the basis for the FAJITA.

primal rib. The meat between the primal chuck and short loin containing seven ribs. "Prime rib," often encountered on menus and considered the most desirable part of the animal, is from this section. A boned rib roast is often called a "Delmonico steak" (after Delmonico's Restaurant in New York, where it was a popular cut of the nineteenth century). A "standing rib roast" includes the seven ribs of this section.

primal round. Meat from the hind leg of the animal, from the end of the primal loin to the hock or ankle. This is divided into several other cuts: the "top round" (often sold as LONDON BROIL), the "bottom round," the "eye of the round," the "sirloin tip," the "heel of the round," and the shin.

primal shank. Meat taken from the shin section of the front leg of the animal. Primal shank requires braising or grinding.

primal short loin. Meat from the hindquarter between the pinbone of the primal sirloin and the small end of the rib. It is considered the best cut for steaks, which include the PORTERHOUSE (containing the top loin, the tenderloin, and the tail and retaining the "T-bone"); the "T-bone steak" (which first appeared as a term in 1916), comprised of meat that is often the same as the "porterhouse"; the "club steak," sometimes called a "Delmonico steak,"

having no tenderloin or flank attached; the TENDERLOIN, also called "filet mignon," "tournedos," and "chateaubriand" (though this last is also the name of a recipe for a porterhouse steak); and the "strip steak" or "strip roast," which contains the top loin muscle and bones and is called in some parts of the country "New York strip," in others "Kansas City strip," and "shell" in others.

primal sirloin. The meat on the animal's hip, which may be cut into "pinhouse sirloin," "flatbone sirloin," "round-bone sirloin," "wedgebone sirloin," "cut-with-the-grain tenderloin," "top butt sirloin" (also called "boneless rump steaks" or "honeymoon steaks"), "cut-with-the-grain bottom sirloin," and "whole sirloin roast." See also SIRLOIN.

The varieties of ground beef recognized by the United States Department of Agriculture include the following:

ground beef. Meat from any part of the animal except "undesirable" parts, such as ears, snout, and innards.

ground sirloin. Meat specifically from the primal sirloin section.

ground round. Meat exclusively from the primal round section.

ground chuck. Meat exclusively from the primal chuck.

hamburger meat. Meat that is intended for use in meat patties; however, this is an ambiguous term. See HAMBURGER.

beef. Slang term for a restaurant check.

beef-on-weck. A Buffalo, New York, specialty, made of thin slices of roast beef topped with its own juices and served on a hard caraway-seeded roll called a "kummelweck" (1952), from German *Kümmel* (caraway), *Weck* (roll). The term beef-on-weck dates to 1969, but is certainly older. The sandwich is usually eaten with horseradish.

beer. A low-alcohol beverage made from fermented barley and other grains and flavored with hops. Beer is easily the most popular of all alcoholic drinks enjoyed by Americans, with a per capita consumption in 1997 of 22 gallons and a total U.S. sales of 175 million barrels (1 barrel = 31 gallons), with another 14.3 million barrels imported.

The word "beer" comes from the Middle English *ber(e),* and, ultimately, from Latin *bibere,* "to drink." The beverage in various forms has been made for at least eight thousand years, evidence having been found in Babylonian records of beer being used in sacrificial rituals. Egypt, China, and India all made beer, as did the Incas in Peru. Beer was well known throughout Europe even before viticulture had developed to any significant degree, with evidence dating back five thousand years, and the addition of hops (the dried flowers of vines of the genus *Humulus*) to give a characteristic bitterness has been traced at least as early as A.D. 768.

The first brewery in America was set up by the Dutch in New Amsterdam in 1612, and Governor Peter Minuit established the first public brewery in 1632. The Pilgrims, who had intended to settle in Virginia in 1620, instead landed at Plymouth Rock, Massachusetts, because, according to a chronicler, "We could not now take time for further search or consideration, our victuals being spent, especially our beer."

Early settlers in America made beer from all sorts of substances, including corn, pumpkins, and persimmons, sometimes flavored with sassafras or pine. Early Colonial breweries generally reflected the preference for English-style beers, strong, lusty, and dark, over the lighter German styles. By 1629 there were breweries in Virginia, and eight years later the first licensed brewhouse was opened in Massachusetts. ("Brewery" entered the language a century later.) During the seventeenth century beer was considered a light, everyday "small drink," consumed by men, women, and children throughout the day. Before that time "ale" (from Old English *ealu*) was distinguished from beer because it contained no barley or hops. When brewers added both to ale in the seventeenth century, the two terms became synonymous, with Englishmen preferring to keep the name "ale" and Americans "beer." Both were "top fermented," meaning the spent yeasts rose to the top of the barrel.

Beer was a perfectly respectable beverage among the Founding Fathers of the country. William Penn (1644–1718) set up Philadelphia's first brewhouse in 1685, and Jefferson, Madison, and Adams all had interests in such establishments, while George Washington maintained his own brewhouse at his Mount Vernon home.

Several kinds of beer were available to the Americans of those days. "Stout," a strong English beer

or ale, was dark in color and bitter in taste; "porter," which originated in England about 1722, was a blend of ale and beer. Its name derived from its popularity among the eighteenth-century porters who carried produce to London's Covent Garden. Porter was heavily malted and had a slightly sweet taste. In America it was purveyed at porterhouses, and the proprietor of one such place, Martin Harrison, became known for his cut of beef, which was called after 1814 a "porterhouse steak." And then there was spruce beer, made with the tops of spruce trees, which became so popular during the Revolutionary War that the Continental Congress in 1775 decreed that the American troops should receive a choice of one quart of either cider or spruce beer daily.

After the turn of the century the arrival of German immigrants in Philadelphia made that city a major brewing center, and German-style beers became increasingly available. Then, about 1840, John Wagner of Philadelphia began making a "lager" from the German *Lager Bier,* storehouse beer, that was "bottom fermented"—that is, the yeast sank to the bottom, making the beer lighter and somewhat weaker than top-fermented beers. Wagner's German contemporaries followed suit, building special facilities to keep the beer cool during fermentation and to age the product for two to three months. Although some immediately dismissed these light lagers (also called "Pilsner" or "pilsener," from the Pilsner Urquell beer of Pilsen, Czechoslovakia, where quality beer had been made since 1292) as a "woman's drink," they caught on rapidly, at first in German communities, where beerhalls and beergardens flourished in midcentury, and afterward in every major city in America. The first outdoor beer garden was opened in St. Louis, Missouri, in 1854 by Franz Josef Uhrig, who cooled the beer in wooded caves called Uhrig's Cave.

"Beerhalls"—some of which could hold up to twelve hundred people—became social centers for the lower and middle classes, and one moralist of the day wrote of their lavish and bawdy atmosphere: "The quantity [of lager] sold in a day is enormous. A four-horse team from the brewery . . . finds it difficult to keep up the supply."

Soon "lager" and "beer" were interchangeable terms, and the golden, effervescent beverage (sometimes called "a bucket of suds") surpassed cider and all others in popularity. The cities of the Midwest—Cincinnati, St. Louis, Chicago, and, particularly, Milwaukee—grew powerful as brewing centers, all following the lead of John Wagner's Philadelphia. One of the first in the new market, however, was a New

York family, Frederick and Maximilian Schaefer, who purchased the Sebastian Sommers Brewery in New York City in 1842 and began making lager there under their own name. Two years later Jacob Best, Sr., and his four sons opened a brewery on Chestnut Street Hill in Milwaukee that later came under the control of Frederick Pabst, who increased output to half a million barrels in 1889 and by 1902 had built the first plant in America equipped to carry the fresh beer from brewery to bottler. Bottled beer was first produced in 1875 by the Joseph Schlitz Brewing Company, which advertised its product as "the Beer That Made Milwaukee Famous." Before then all beer was drawn from a spigot and referred to as "draft beer," also then called "shenkbeer" (from the German *Schenkbier*).

By 1900 the brewery facilities of Anheuser-Busch covered sixty acres of St. Louis. The firm had forty-two branches in other cities and even operated its own railroad. Jacob Schmidt built another great brewery in Minneapolis-St. Paul, while Henry Weinhard and Arnold Blitz merged resources to make Portland, Oregon, a major beer producer. In San Francisco, where the shortage of ice in midcentury was a factor in making decent lager, there developed STEAM BEER, so called because of the high amount of pressure built up in the barrel through a special process of fermentation (see main entry for more information on this beer). By 1870, however, American refrigeration techniques made it possible to make beer year-round without regard to temperature. By 1876 there were more than four thousand breweries in the United States. PROHIBITION in America (1920–33, with some states banning alcoholic beverages, that is, "going dry," as early as 1916) was a disaster for the beer industry, which survived by producing malt and yeast and by providing ice. The Volstead Act defined a forbidden beverage as one containing 0.5 percent alcohol (regular beer varies from 3.2 to 4 percent by weight), so a market developed for "near beer," which had been made since 1909 as a substitute for the real thing and contained 0.4 percent alcohol. If illegal spirits were added to near beer, it was called "needle beer" or "needled beer." On April 7, 1933, President Franklin D. Roosevelt signed the Cullen-Harrison Act, which raised the definition of nonintoxication to 3.2 percent, and people started referring to such brews as "3.2 beer." Of course, illegal beer was made throughout Prohibition, often at home, where it was called "home brew." When Prohibition finally ended in 1933, only 750 breweries reopened, and though new ones opened and demand for beer grew rapidly through the 1930s and 1940s, competition drove many breweries into consolidation or out of business.

One of the greatest boons for the industry was the introduction in 1935 by the Kreuger Brewery Company of Richmond, Virginia, and the Adolph Coors Company of Golden, Colorado, of beer in cans, at first scoffed at by those used to bottles but acquiring popularity during World War II when GIs overseas got used to the idea. The aluminum beer can was introduced in 1958. The nonreturnable bottle became the norm in the early 1950s, further increasing the ease of the consumer to enjoy his beer at home.

With this expansion of the market came increased competitiveness. Price-cutting among the largest breweries drove the small local breweries out of the market, so that today there are only about seventy full-scale breweries left in the United States, still the largest beer-producing country. (Germans, however, are the largest beer drinkers, per capita, in the world; Americans rank twelfth worldwide.)

In the 1980s "microbreweries" (breweries making fifteen thousand or fewer barrels per year) proliferated, swelling from 45 in 1986 to 423 in 1998. During this same period "brewpubs," where beer was both made and served along with food, increased in popularity. There were 184 brewpubs in the United States in 1992 and 910 in 1998. In addition, there are "regional breweries" that have a production capacity of between 15,000 and 2 million barrels, and a sub-category of "regional specialty breweries" whose flagship brand is an all-malt or specialty beer. All these categories fall under the general term "craft breweries," which have sales of over $3 billion annually and represent 12.4 percent of the U.S. market.

Making beer in America is a complex process, beginning with the malting of barley, which is combined with a cereal like corn that has been cooked. The two are mixed and mashed to convert starch to maltose and dextrin. This is called "wort" and is filtered through a "lauter tun," which separates wort from grain (the latter is used for cattle feed). Hops are added to the wort for flavor, and high heat is added until the wort is completely soluble (called the "hot break"), before being run through a "hop strainer" or "hop jack," which removes the hops and leaves "hot wort." This is cooled, yeast is added, and fermentation begins. Beer is usually fermented between 37 and 49 degrees Fahrenheit, whereas ale, which uses a different type of yeast, ferments at temperatures between 50 and 70 degrees. Brewer's yeast is used in beer, and, in lagers, it settles to the bottom. Ale's yeasts settle at the top. The beer ferments for eight to eleven days, ale five to six. The beer is then stored and kept close to the freezing temperature to precipitate out the yeast and solids. As the beer mellows over the next month or two, it takes on its final character before having carbon dioxide (CO_2) added to give it effervescence. This carbon dioxide comes from that thrown off during fermentation or from a process called "kräusening," by which a small amount of still fermenting young beer is added to produce a short second fermentation.

The beer is then refrigerated, filtered, and, if intended for bottling or canning, usually pasteurized. (Beers put in strong aluminum or stainless-steel kegs are usually not pasteurized, because they are likely to be consumed faster and therefore would not undergo any further fermentation, which could cause additional carbon dioxide to burst cans or bottles.) Peak drinking time for canned beer is considered to be about four months; for bottles, six. Some bottled or canned beer that has not been pasteurized goes under the name "draft beer," but "draft brewed" and "draft beer flavor" are phrases used on bottles and cans that may contain pasteurized beer, as long as the pasteurization is noted on the label.

Other beer terms include:

ale. Once a term for a brew of malt and cereal without hops or barley. In the seventeenth century hops and barley were added, and the distinction between ale and beer disappeared for a hundred years, until the lagers of the 1840s became synonymous with beer while ale continued to be made in an older, more flavorful style. Ales average 4.5 percent alcohol by weight, slightly higher than beer.

bock beer. Also, "Bockbier." In Germany bock beer was usually brewed in the spring and was a heavier, darker beer than most lagers. In America its style and taste are a matter of individual companies' definition and marketing.

dry beer. Beer made to have a somewhat less "sweet" flavor, accomplished by allowing the yeast to consume more of the sugar in the fermentation process. Dry beer was introduced in Japan in 1987 by Asahi Breweries, and in the United States in June 1988 by Kirin. Michelob Dry (owned by Anheuser-Busch of St. Louis, Missouri) was the first American-made dry beer introduced in 1988. Dry beer is also somewhat lower in calories than regular beer.

light. Also, "Lite." Beer that is lower in alcohol (averaging 3.1 percent alcohol by weight) and, with

fewer calories than regular beer. The first light beer sold in a bar was Miller Lite in 1973. Light beer has become an enormously popular category among American beerdrinkers. In 1998, the second best-selling brand of beer in the U.S. was Bud Light, made by Anheuser-Busch of St. Louis, Missouri.

low-alcohol beer. Also called "L.A.," this beer has an alcohol content of less than 2 percent.

malt liquor. A malt beverage that is higher in alcohol than beer, up to 8 percent by weight in some states (1693).

nonalcohol. Also, "nonalcoholic." These terms are actually nonlegal under FDA regulations, which categorize such beverages, with less than one-half of one percent of alcohol, as "near beers," "malt beverages," or "nonalcoholic brews." Beverages containing no alcohol whatsoever may include the word "alcohol-free" on their labels, but not the word "beer." Such brews make up less than one percent of all beer sales in the United States. "California beer" is a slang term for nonalcohol beer made from "beer seed," sugar, and water.

The taste of beers in the United States has been mellow and, to some, lacking in distinction from one major brand to another. There has been a great increase in the importation of stronger beers from other countries (currently about 3 percent of the American market). Nevertheless, the same brand of beer may taste different from state to state because the alcoholic content is regulated by each individual state's legislation. Federal law requires a minimum alcohol level for beer of 0.5 percent, but sets no maximum.

beer blast. Also, "beer bust" and "beer bash." Campus or young people's term for a party at which the primary beverage is beer, often served from a keg. It has been used at least since the 1950s, but first appears in print in 1963.

beer up. Colloquialism meaning to drink a good deal of beer.

beet. (*Beta vulgaris*). A dark, reddish-purple fruit of a plant with leafy greens sometimes eaten as a vegetable on their own.

The name is from the Latin *bēta*, which in Middle English became *bete*. The vegetable is a native of the Mediterranean, but it was not of much gastronomic interest until the nineteenth century in France, and, afterward, in America, where most of the beet crop is canned, or sometimes pickled. The most popular varieties are the "Detroit Dark Red," "Egyptian," and "Eclipse." Swiss chard is also known as the "spinach beet."

beggar's purse. An appetizer of caviar and crème fraîche wrapped in a crêpe and tied with thin strips of chives to resemble a little purse. The term was used by Barry and Susan Wine for such a dish served at their restaurant, the Quilted Giraffe, in New York City, in the 1980s after having enjoyed the item at Vieille Fontaine in Maison-Laffitte outside of Paris, where chef François Clerc called it *un aumonière* (an alm's purse).

behind the stick. Bartender slang for working the beer taps. The term first appeared in print in 1990.

beignet. A puffy yeast pastry deep-fried and served with sugar (1835). The beignet, which is French for fritter, is a traditional food item of New Orleans, where they are often just called DOUGHNUTS.

In the French Market in New Orleans's Vieux Carré beignets are served with CHICORY coffee for breakfast and as an afternoon snack.

belt. Colloquialism for a swig of liquor (1922).

bend an elbow. To drink whiskey. The term dates at least to the 1830s.

bender. Slang term for a drunken spree. The term goes back at least to the 1820s.

Benedictine sandwich spread. According to food writer Phyllis Richman, "A Louisville caterer, it is said, invented this vivid green sandwich spread made of cream cheese thinned with mayonnaise, flavored with grated onion and cucumber, tinted green with spinach, parsley or even green food coloring."

beta carotene. A coloring agent added to butter, margarine, and nondairy products used as shortening. The body converts beta carotene to vitamin A.

bialy. A Jewish-American baked roll sprinkled with onion flakes. The name, first mentioned in print in 1960 but certainly older, comes from the Polish city of Bialystok.

bière douce. A Louisiana Creole beer made from

the skin of the pineapple, sugar, rice, and water. The term is from the French for "sweet beer."

billi-bi. A soup made from mussels, cream, and seasonings. Under the name "mouclade" it is a well-known soup of Normandy, where the mussels are left in the final preparation; in a true billi-bi they are removed before straining the soup.

Billi-bi (sometimes spelled "Billy By") is a popular soup in American restaurants, but its origins are French. Some have claimed that the soup was named after William Bateman Leeds, Sr. (1861–1908), president of the American Tin Plate Company, at Maxim's restaurant in Paris. But Jean Mauduit in his book *Maxim's, Soixante Ans de Plaisir et d'Histoire* (1958), wrote, "The recipe was created by chef [Louis] Barthe to please an old regular customer who nourished an exclusive passion for mussels; the success of the dish was so great that they named it, as an honor, with the diminutive and the initial of the customer's name, even though he was not really the creator [my translation]." Mauduit gives the man's name as William Brand. The management of Maxim's, however, says that Barthe created the dish for Brand ("an American client of Maxim's") in 1925, but not at Maxim's; instead Barthe created the dish at Ciro's restaurant in Deauville.

BILLI-BI

Clean 2 lb. mussels, place in kettle with 2 chopped shallots, 2 chopped onions, 2 sprigs parsley, salt and pepper, 1/8 t. cayenne pepper, 1 c. white wine, 2 T. butter, 1 bay leaf, and 1/2 t. dry thyme. Cover, bring to a boil, lower to simmer and cook for 10 min., until mussels have opened (discard those that do not). Strain soup through cheesecloth, reserve mussels for other use. Return soup to kettle, bring to boil, add 2 c. heavy cream, remove from heat, add 1 beaten egg yolk, and return to heat to thicken. Sprinkle with Parmesan cheese. Serves 6.

---

billy-goat date cake. A cookie made with dates and nuts. As noted by Betty Fussell in *I Hear America Cooking* (1986), it is specific to the Pacific states after the Deglet Noor date was introduced from Arabia into the Coachella Valley in California in 1890. The reason for the cookie's name is not known.

binder. Also, "extender." A food additive that binds meat and poultry products together and helps retain moisture. Binders are sometimes used as a supplement for nutrients in the meat or merely to add bulk. A non-meat binder would be SOY PROTEIN.

bird's-nest pudding. Also, "crow's-nest pudding." A very old New England fruit pudding (most commonly made with apples), usually with a crust and some kind of sauce. The finished dish somewhat resembles a bird's nest. It dates in print to 1833.

biscuit. A small leavened and shortened bread served with meals. The word derives from the Latin words *bis*, "twice," plus *coctus*, "cooked." In England, a "biscuit" is what Americans usually call a CRACKER or COOKIE. The American meaning for "biscuit" was first noted by John Palmer in his *Journal of Travels in the United States of North America, and in Lower Canada* (1818), and by 1828 Webster defined the confection as "a composition of flour and butter, made and baked in private families." In general usage such puffy leavened little breads were called "soda biscuits" or "baking-soda biscuits," in contrast to the unleavened cracker type.

The most common form of biscuit is made from dough with baking soda and baking powder and rolled out to the thickness of one-quarter inch or so, cut into the form of a disk, then baked. "Dropped biscuits" are made by simply dropping biscuit dough onto a baking pan rather than cutting them into disks. "Funeral biscuits" were biscuits whose tops were impressed with ornate symbolic and religious designs from specially made molds or stamps and served at funerals.

Recipes for soda biscuits are found in every nineteenth-century cookbook, especially with reference to the cookery of the South, where biscuits with ham remain a specialty. The South is also home of the "beaten biscuit," which was first mentioned in 1853. This curious confection, known in Maryland as a "Maryland biscuit," is rarely made today, but was once common in the South, where the sound of a mallet beating the biscuit dough was a nostalgic morning sound. This process made for a very hard, crisp biscuit that is the antithesis of the soft, puffy biscuits usually encountered. "Angel biscuits" are described by Betty Fussell in *I Hear America Cooking* (1986) as "a double-light biscuit because they use both yeast and baking powder to leaven the dough . . . [and] made of very moist buttermilk dough more easily shaped into biscuit blobs than rolled."

In 1930 General Mills began selling a packaged quick biscuit mix called "Bisquick" that was a great success and spawned many imitators.

Biscuits are usually broken open and buttered or served with slices of ham and gravy.

BISCUIT

Sift together 2 c. flour, 1½ t. salt, and 4 t. baking powder. Cut in 2 T. butter or lard with a fork till it has the texture of coarse meal. Add ¾ c. milk and blend quickly. Knead for about 30 sec., then roll out to ½-in. thickness on floured board. Cut out in 2-in. circles, let stand, bake for 20 min. at 425°.

BEATEN BISCUITS

Combine ½ c. lard with 4 c. flour and 1 t. salt until the texture is like that of coarse meal. Add ½ c. milk and ice water mixed together, then add 1 beaten egg white. Beat with a mallet for 30 min. or more, until dough is blistered and smooth. Roll out on floured board to ½-in. thickness, cut in 2-in. circles, prick with fork, and bake for 25 min. at 350°.

bishop. A drink of mulled wine, sugar, spices, and citrus fruit. The name possibly derives from its red color, as in a bishop's robes. Jonathan Swift was the first to mention the drink in print as of 1738, and James Boswell in his *Life of Johnson* (1791) says that it was a favorite drink of his subject, as it was in America throughout the eighteenth and nineteenth centuries. Often, as in the recipe below, the citrus fruit is first roasted.

BISHOP

Insert about 1 doz. cloves into the rind of an orange and roast it for about 15 min. Cut into quarters, place in a saucepan with 1 qt. port or wine and 1 T. sugar, and simmer on a very low flame for about 30 min.

bishop's bread. A sweet bread made with dried fruit. According to the *Better Homes and Gardens Heritage Cook Book* (1975), it is a bread of the American nineteenth-century frontier, when settlements would be visited by traveling clergymen. Legend has it that "one early Sunday morning a circuit-riding bishop in Kentucky dropped in on one family unexpectedly for breakfast. The resourceful hostess invented a quick fruit bread for the occasion [and] named it Bishop's Bread in honor of her guest."

There is, however, a similar bread traditionally made in Germany by this same name, *bischofbrot*.

bismarck. Also, "Berliner." An oblong cake, usually fried in oil, with a filling of jelly. In bakeries bismarcks are commonly baked, not fried, and often sugared or topped with whipped cream. The item is particularly popular in the Midwest, and the name may refer to Bismarck, North Dakota, although it may refer in some way to Otto von Bismarck, first chancellor of the modern German Empire (1871–1890) or to the fact that the shape of the cake is similar to that of the famous German battleship the *Bismarck*. Earliest references to bismarcks date to the 1930s. Such cakes are also sometimes called "longjohns."

bite-and-stir box. A box used by the New York Dutch with two compartments—one containing sugar lumps that one may bite and chew, and one holding granulated sugar to use in one's tea or coffee.

bitters. Aromatic, bitter blends of various spices, herbs, and alcohol (1705). Bitters are usually sold as a digestive or medicinal aid, but several bottlings of bitters are used specifically as seasonings in foods and alcoholic beverages. "Peychaud's bitters" was an essential ingredient in many Louisiana cocktails, and many recipe books call for angostura bitters as a matter of course.

The herbs most often used would include gentian, orange, quinine, and ginger. Bitters have been spoken of in England since the early eighteenth century.

black and fat. An Alaskan colloquialism, first mentioned in print in 1985, for the skin and fat of the bowhead whale, used in making an Eskimo dish called *muktuk*.

black-and-white. A term used to describe several soda-fountain confections mixing chocolate and vanilla flavors, although it may also refer to black coffee with a container of cream on the side. In the East, "black-and-white" usually refers to a chocolate soda made with vanilla ice cream. Elsewhere it may be a chocolate MILK SHAKE with vanilla ice cream blended in (a "black-and-white float" would have the vanilla ice cream floating on top of the milk shake) or even a sundae made with vanilla ice cream and chocolate sauce.

In and around New York City a "black-and-white" also refers to a circular yellow cookie about five inches wide topped with contrasting frostings of vanilla and chocolate. They are commonly sold in pastry shops and lunch counters.

black bass. (genus *Micropterus*). A member of the SUNFISH family, Centrarchidae, these freshwater fish of North America have been widely introduced throughout the United States. Because of the difficulty in catching black bass, they became popular for consumption only during the nineteenth century, when they were shipped from eastern to western waters for sport fishermen. "Black bass" first saw print in 1815. Black bass are now found in forty-nine states of the Union. The best black bass are those under three pounds; they are prepared in all manner of ways, grilled, poached, fried, or broiled. The principal kinds of black bass for eating are "largemouth bass" (*M. salmoides*), "redeye bass" (*M. coosae*), "smallmouth bass" (*M. dolomieui*), and "spotted bass" (*M. punctulatus*).

black bean. (*Phaseolus vulgaris*). A bean usually cooked in a soup called "black bean soup." The bean, which is known to have been eaten in Mexico as much as seven thousand years ago, is used throughout the Caribbean. Venezuelans refer to the bean as *caviar criollo*, "creole caviar," and Brazilians make it part of their national dish, *feijoada*. In America the black bean has long been part of southern diets, and in Florida it is a favorite dish of the Cuban-American communities. The following recipe is from the Coach House restaurant in New York City, which popularized the dish in the 1970s.

BLACK BEAN SOUP

Brown 3 lb. beef bones, 1 lb. beef shin, and 3 lb. ham shank with rind in a 400° oven for about 20 min. Cut off meat and place in a kettle with 15 c. water, 3 cloves, 1 t. black peppercorns, and ¾ t. celery seed. Bring to a boil, simmer with lid ajar for 8–10 hr. Strain, remove meat for other purposes, and refrigerate stock. Soak 2½ c. black beans overnight in refrigerator. Remove congealed fat from stock, reserving 2 T. Melt fat in skillet and sauté 1 c. chopped onion and ½ c. chopped celery until soft. Drain beans and add to skillet. In a kettle add beans and vegetables, 2 c. water, and 7 c. stock. Add 2 t. chopped garlic, simmer for 2½ hr., stirring occasionally. Coarsely puree the bean mixture through strainer or in blender. Reheat, add salt and pepper. Before serving, add a dash of dry sherry. Top with lemon slice and garnish, if desired, with chopped boiled egg.

---

blackberry. Any of a variety of plants in the genus

Rubus that bear black sweet berries. The berry is often called a "bramble" because it grows on prickly shrubs.

Blackberries have long flourished in North America, where the majority of the crop is produced in Texas, Oklahoma, and Arkansas, with a great amount of wild blackberries growing throughout the Southwest. Americans have always cherished the blackberry, and Wait Whitman wrote in *Song of Myself* (1855) that "the running blackberry would adorn the parlors of heaven."

Two important hybrids of the blackberry were discovered by Americans: the "loganberry" (possibly a cross between the blackberry and the RASPBERRY, found by Judge J. H. Logan of California, in 1881); and the "boysenberry" (a cross of the loganberry and blackberry), developed by horticulturist Rudolph Boysen in 1923. The DEWBERRY is another form of blackberry particularly beloved in the South.

The most important cultivated varieties include the "Marion," "Himalaya," the "Lucretia," the "Black Diamond," the "Agawam," the "Lawton," and the "Snyder."

"Blackberry winter" is the period of cool weather in May when the blackberries are in bloom. The term dates back at least to the turn of the present century.

"Blackberry vinegar" is a drink of blackberries, sugar, and vinegar boiled together, strained, and cooled.

black Betty. A bottle of liquor that is passed among wedding guests. It dates in print to 1737.

black bottom. A term describing either of two confections: a sundae made with chocolate ice cream and chocolate syrup, or a pie made with a chocolate custard topped with rum custard and whipped cream.

The term derives from what the *Oxford English Dictionary* describes as "a low-lying area inhabited by a coloured population," first mentioned in print as of 1915. The black-bottom pie probably derives its name from this usage, and, notes James Beard in his *American Cookery* (1972), recipes for the pie began appearing in cookbooks around the turn of the century, although the first printed reference known for the pie is not until 1951.

The black-bottom sundae, on the other hand, probably gets its name from a popular dance of and following 1926 called the "black bottom," which itself may have come out of African-American culture.

BLACK BOTTOM PIE

Dissolve 1 T. unflavored gelatin in ¼ c. cold water. Scald 2 c. milk over low heat. Mix together ½ c. sugar, ¼ t. salt, 2 T. flour, and 4 beaten egg yolks. Pour in some of the hot milk until blended, then pour this mixture into the rest of the hot milk. Stir over low heat to thicken (about 15 min.), remove from heat, and remove 1 c. of custard. Add 2 oz. unsweetened chocolate and ½ t. vanilla, blend well, then cool. Add gelatin to remaining custard and blend well. Add 2 T. dark rum. Chill. Spread chocolate mixture into chilled baked graham-cracker crust and refrigerate. Beat 3 egg whites with ¼ t. cream of tartar and, gradually, add ⅓ c. sugar. Fold into gelatinized custard and spread over chocolate layer. Top with whipped cream and garnish with shaved chocolate.

black cake. Also, "black fruitcake," "dark fruitcake," "English fruitcake," and "Merry Christmas cake." A nineteenth-century cake made from molasses, spices, and fruit, dating in print to a recipe given in a letter by Emily Dickinson in 1883. The name derives from the dark color of the cake.

black cow. Any of a variety of ice-cream sodas made with a scoop of vanilla ice cream. Usually the soda itself is either chocolate, sarsaparilla, or root beer (called a "Boston cooler"), and the name refers to the mixture of dark soda with the white dairy item floating in it. If made with chocolate soda (that is, seltzer, milk, and chocolate syrup), it might be called a BLACK-AND-WHITE, especially in the East. In the 1930s plain root beer sometimes went by this term, as did chocolate milk as of 1918 in print, especially at lunch counters.

black drink. A drink of the boiled leaves of *Ilex cassine* in water, used by the Gulf State Indians as a purification medicine. The drink sometimes induced a nervous state of mind and was drunk as part of a ritual. The Catawba Indians called it *yaupon,* the Creeks *ássi-lupupútski* ("small leaves"), and the English traders named it the black drink or "Carolina tea."

blackened. A style of cooking fish or meat by searing seasoned food in a black skillet at a very high temperature. The term was first used by Cajun chef Paul Prudhomme to describe a dish of red DRUM (in Louisiana called "redfish") so cooked, and in the 1980s "blackened redfish" became an enormously popular dish, the recipe for which is contained in *Chef Paul*

Prudhomme's Louisiana Kitchen (1984). Indeed, the dish became so popular that the species was in danger of being depleted, and a federal ban on commercial fishing of the species was put into effect in 1987.

Prudhomme said that the dish was created out of necessity at his New Orleans restaurant called K-Paul's Louisiana Kitchen because he had no grill or salamander, so he used the black skillet to give his food its crisp texture.

blackjack. A hard molasses candy with a pronounced burnt flavor. The name dates in print to 1886. The word also refers to rum sweetened with molasses.

black sea bass (*Centropristis striata*). Also, "blackfish" (though different from the true blackfish or TAUTOG), "black harry," "hannahill," "humpback," "tallywag," "rock bass" and "Black Will." A carnivorous fish that ranges from Maine to Florida, though most come from the coast between North Carolina and New York (1835). The black sea bass has always been a highly valued eating and sport fish, and, as A. J. McClane notes in *The Encyclopedia of Fish Cookery* (1977), "Party boats already in vogue [in the early nineteenth century] (the first record is of George Washington chartering a boat to fish the banks off Sandy Hook) became so popular that woodcut posters were distributed around New York depicting men carrying great strings of sea bass." Sea bass usually run between one-and-a-half and five pounds at market, and they are a major fish in Chinese-American recipes. See also BLACK BASS.

blackstrap. Also, "blackstrap molasses." A very dark molasses often used to make cattle feed or industrial alcohol (1915). The term also refers to a mixture of rum and molasses in New England. See also MOLASSES.

black velvet. A cocktail made with equal parts champagne and Guinness Stout. The drink was supposedly concocted in 1861 by the steward of London's Brook's Club on hearing the news of Prince Albert's death, commemorating the event with a "black" champagne drink.

blended whiskey. A whiskey blended from at least 20 percent straight whiskey together with varying amounts of grain spirits, light whiskeys, or neutral spirits (1935). About half the American whiskey consumed in the United States is blended. It is sometimes erroneously called "rye," but a true rye must contain at least 51 percent of that grain. U.S. production of blended whiskey in 1997 totaled 6.4 million 9-liter cases.

blind tiger. Also, "blind pig." A term used to describe an illegal establishment serving alcoholic beverages. It may also mean a cheap or inferior whiskey, though the phrase is no longer used in either sense.

The *Dictionary of Americanisms* cites an 1857 account in a sportsmen's gazette called *Spirit of the Times* as the term's first appearance in print: "I sees a kinder pidgeon-hole cut in the side of the house, and over the hole [a sign,] 'Blind Tiger, ten cents a sight.' Says I to the feller inside, 'here's your ten cents, Walk out your wild-cat.'. . . I'll be dod-busted if he didn't shove out a glass of whiskey. You see that 'blind tiger' was an arrangement to evade the law, which won't let 'em sell licker there, except by the gallon."

An alternate term, "blind pig," appeared in print in 1872.

blintz. A pancake or crepe stuffed with any of several fillings, such as cheese, jam, fish, fruit, or potatoes and then folded. The word is from the Yiddish *blintseh,* via the Russian *blinyets,* and first appeared in English print in 1903. Blintzes are usually served with sour cream.

BLINTZ

Make a batter from 3 beaten eggs, ¾ c. matzo meal, ½ t. salt, and 1½ c. water. Pour a very thin layer of batter into a frying pan brushed with fat and brown on one side. Continue to make pancakes until all batter is used. Mix 1 lb. cottage cheese with 2–3 T. sugar and 2 T. sour cream. Fill pancakes with mixture, fold over three sides, and roll into envelope shape, tucking in the flap to seal. These may be fried or baked. Serve with sour cream. Serves 6.

Bloody Mary. Also, "Bloody" for short. A cocktail made of tomato juice, vodka, and seasonings, by far the most popular mixed alcoholic drink with Americans, especially as part of weekend BRUNCHES. Recipes for the Bloody Mary date in print at least to 1946.

Ernest Hemingway wrote in a letter in 1947 that he had introduced the Bloody Mary to Hong Kong in 1941, an act he said "did more than any other single factor except the Japanese Army to precipitate the Fall of that Crown Colony."

But the drink seems to have originated in Paris, under another name, at Harry's New York Bar.

Bartender Ferdinand "Pete" Petiot was experimenting with vodka, to which he'd been introduced in 1920, and a year later came up with the blend of tomato juice, vodka, and seasonings that American entertainer Roy Barton christened the "Bucket of Blood," after a nightclub in Chicago. The drink did not then become popular in Paris, but in 1933 Petiot was brought to New York by Vincent Astor to man the King Cole Bar at the St. Regis Hotel, where the drink caught on—particularly as a supposed cure for hangovers—under the less sanguine name "Red Snapper."

Just when other bars around town began calling it the "Bloody Mary" (with reference to Mary Tudor, Mary I of England and Ireland, known for her bloody reign against Protestants) is vague, but in an ad campaign for Smirnoff vodka, entertainer George Jessel claimed to have named the drink after a friend, Mary Geraghty, about 1929.

Butch McGuire's Bar in Chicago claims to have added the celery stick as a flavored stirrer, now a common ingredient in Bloody Marys.

Bloody Marys have been made with gin or rum, and replacing vodka with tequila and the lemon juice with lime gives one a Bloody Maria. When Japanese saké is used, the drink becomes a "Bloody Mary Quite Contrary," and when no alcohol at all is used, the drink becomes a "Virgin Mary," which some imbibers have called a "Bloody Shame."

BLOODY MARY

Shake with ice cubes 1½ oz. vodka, 2 oz. thick tomato juice, 1 dash lemon juice, 2 dashes salt, 1 dash black pepper, 2 dashes cayenne pepper, and 3 dashes Worcestershire sauce. The Bloody Mary is often served with a celery stick or a slice of lemon or lime.

---

blow foam. Slang expression meaning to drink beer, known in print since the 1890s.

blueberry. Any of a variety of native North American shrubs of the genus *Vaccinium* bearing deep blue berries (1709), which give the fruit and shrub its name. Blueberries, first noted by Captain James Cook in the late eighteenth century, are often confused with HUCKLEBERRIES, for both grow wild. Blueberries are cultivated in Michigan, Maine, New Jersey, North Carolina, Washington, and elsewhere, with an annual commercial crop of about 280 million pounds; commercially grown varieties account for more of the crop than do the wild ones (98 percent of which are picked

in Maine, largely by Micmac Indians and schoolchildren). The "blueberry rake," invented by Abijah Tabbutt of Columbia Falls, Maine, in 1822 is still used today for gathering wild berries.

The most important variety is the "highbush blueberry" (*V. corymbosum*), while the wild "lowbush berry" (*V. anqustifolium* or *V. pennsylvanicum*) is important as a crop in Maine. Other varieties include the "dryland blueberry" (*V. ashei*) of the South and the "evergreen blueberry" (*V. ovatum*) of the Northwest. Nursery woman Elizabeth White and UDA plant breeder Dr. Frederick V. Coville of Oregon were the first to crossbreed wild blueberries commercially.

Blueberries are eaten raw, with cream, and baked in muffins or pies.

blue blazer. A cocktail made from scotch sweetened with honey and dramatically ignited to form a blue flame that is passed back and forth from one mug to another. The drink was the creation of a famous bartender named "Professor" Jerry Thomas, author of *How to Mix Drinks* (1862) and other recipe books. The story goes that Thomas made the drink for a weary miner whose time away from civilization made him long for something out of the ordinary. Thomas came up with the blue blazer, cautioning the amateur mixer "to practice for some time with cold water." Thomas also considered the drink strictly a cold-weather cocktail and supposedly refused to make one until the thermometer dropped to ten degrees or less above zero.

The name "blue blazer" refers to the blazing blue flame passed between mugs, but it has also come to share its meaning with the men's jacket with brass buttons named after the colorful jackets worn by the crew of the Lady Margaret Boat Club of St. John's College, Cambridge.

BLUE BLAZER

In a silver mug dissolve 1 T. honey in 4 oz. boiling water. Put 4 oz. scotch in another mug and ignite, passing the liquid back and forth between the mugs until the flame dies out. Pour into a glass and garnish with lemon peel and grated nutmeg.

---

bluefish (*Pomatomus saltatrix*). Also, "snapper" (though no relation to the true SNAPPER), "tailor," and other names. A warm-water fish found from Maine to the Gulf of Mexico (1615), the bluefish is ferocious and a great sport fish, nicknamed "bulldog of the ocean" for its tenacity. Early English settlers on

Nantucket caught bluefish in abundance as of 1659, but a hundred years later the schools had vanished and did not reappear until 1800. They became abundant again about 1825, when bluefish sailing parties were organized for both men and women of Connecticut and New York.

Bluefish may have a strong flavor and must be dressed quickly. U.S. commercial landings of bluefish totaled 9.3 million pounds in 1997.

blue lagoon. A cocktail made first at Harry's New York Bar in Paris about 1960 by Andrew MacElhone, son of the original owner, Harry MacElhone.

> ### BLUE LAGOON
>
> *Shake together one part blue curaçao, one part vodka, and one part lemon juice, strain, and pour over an island of ice.*

blue meat. Ranchers' term for the meat of an unweaned calf (1944).

bluff lettuce (*Dudleya farinosa*). A succulent plant in the stonecrop family, it is a native plant of the Pacific coast, first mentioned in print in 1925.

Blush Wine. A trademark term used by Mill Creek Vineyards in Healdsburg, California, for a white wine made from red grapes whose short skin contact imparts a rosy-pink "blush" of color to the wine. The name came about when winery co-owner Bill Kreck discussed the new wine with wine writer Jerry Mead, who commented, "You sure picked up one hell of a blush." The term was registered in 1981, though the trademark was retroactive to 1977, and other wineries must pay a fee to Mill Creek for use of the term on their labels.

boardinghouse meat. Ranchers' term for the meat of an unweaned calf.

boardinghouse potatoes. A southern term for fried potatoes, probably because they were so common at boardinghouse tables (1966).

boardinghouse reach. A nineteenth-century colloquialism referring to the need to reach quickly and decisively across a boardinghouse common dinner table or risk not getting any food (1947). At such establishments the social graces were usually not observed, and grabbing at food was more the norm.

bodega. A Hispanic-American grocery store, but, less commonly, a Hispanic-American wineshop or wine warehouse. The word is American Spanish, derived from the Latin *apotheca*, "storehouse." The word dates in print to 1846, but only gained currency in the United States as of the 1950s.

boeren jongens. A Dutch-American drink (from the Dutch for "peasant boy") made from whiskey and raisins, traditionally served at Christmastime; the name first appeared in print in 1940.

bog. A dish made with rice and meat like chicken ("chicken bog") or squirrel; the name dates in print to 1941.

boilermaker. A shot of straight whiskey followed immediately with a beer, called a "chaser" or "helper." Sometimes the whiskey is poured right into a glass of beer. The term, which dates to 1934, probably refers to the kind of men, called "boilermakers," who make and repair heavy metal items, supposedly the kind of strong, tough fellow who drinks such concoctions.

A "boilermaker's delight" is MOONSHINE or inferior whiskey. In the Montana mining camps of the early part of this century a similar drink, called a "Shawn O'Farrell" or "Shawn O'," referring to the number of Irish immigrants who became miners here, was a popular after-work refresher.

bolichi roast. A beef roast stuffed with hardboiled eggs. The term, dating in English print to 1939, is from Cuban Spanish *boliche*, for roasted round of beef.

bollo. A fritter made from black-eyed peas. The term, first cited in 1966, is from the Spanish for a small loaf.

bologna. Also "baloney" and "boloney." A smoked, seasoned SAUSAGE made from a variety of meats and popular as a sandwich meat or cold cut. The word derives from the Italian city of Bologna, where the sausage was supposedly first produced, an observation first made in print in 1555. In the United States bologna (pronounced "baloney") is usually made of pork and beef and sold in groceries as a sliced meat.

"Lebanon bologna" is a specialty of the Pennsylvania Dutch who live around Lebanon, Pennsylvania, where two versions—"regular" and "sweet"—are produced, mostly made from beef. Most of it is produced by two manufacturers, the Daniel Weaver Company (which claims to be the oldest) and the Palmyra Bologna Company, both established in the late nineteenth century in Lebanon County.

"Bologna" is also a meatpacker's term for an inferior quality animal whose meat is fit only for making sausages.

bolted meal. Corn that has not been homeground.

bombo. Also, "bumbo," which first appears in print in 1848. A North Carolina term for a beverage made from equal parts rum, water, and New England molasses, possibly named after British admiral John Benbow (1653–1702).

bonefish (*Albula vulpes*). Also, "banana fish," "oio" in Hawaii, and "ladyfish." A silver fish with a piglike snout found in the waters of Florida and the Caribbean. It is a popular game fish, though rarely caught for food. "Bonefish" dates in print to 1725.

bongo bongo soup. A soup made with oysters and spinach, created by Victor "Trader Vic" Bergeron, owner of the Trader Vic's restaurants. Bergeron contended that he tasted the soup during World War II in New Zealand, made with "toheroa" clams, for which he substituted oysters at his restaurant in San Francisco.

BONGO BONGO SOUP

In a saucepan heat 2½ c. half-and-half to a simmer. Poach 10 oz. oysters, then puree them in a blender and add ¼ c. spinach puree, 2 T. melted butter, 1½ t. monosodium glutamate, 1 t. A.1 sauce, pepper and salt to taste, a dash of garlic salt, and a dash of cayenne. Place back in saucepan, bring to a simmer, add 2 T. cornstarch dissolved in 2 T. water. Simmer until thickened, top with whipped cream and place under broiler until browned. Serves 8.

bonito. Any fish of the species *Sarda,* especially the "Atlantic bonito" (*S. sarda*), also called the "skipjack" or "horse mackerel," and the "skipjack" (*Euthynnus pelamis*). See also SKIPJACK. The beauty of this steel-blue striped fish gives it its Spanish name, *bonito,* which means "beautiful." The word "bonito" dates to 1884 in American print. U.S. commerical landings of bonito totaled 993,000 pounds in 1997.

bootleg. A term dating back in print to about 1885 for making illegal whiskey, derived from the attempt to conceal something in one's boot. A "bootlegger" is one who makes or sells illegal whiskey. The term was in wide usage during Prohibition.

boova shenkel. A Pennsylvania-Dutch beef stew with potato dumplings. The name means "boys' legs," which may refer to the shape of the dumplings.

BOOVA SHENKEL

In a large kettle cover with water 1½ lb. beef, 1 t. salt, and ⅛ t. pepper. Bring to a boil, lower to a simmer and cook for 2½ hr. Boil 6 potatoes until tender, peel and rice, add 1 T. butter, 1 T. minced onion, 1 beaten egg, and let stand. In a bowl sift 1¼ c. flour, 1 t. baking powder, ½ t. salt, and cut in 2 T. butter to make a coarse, crumbly texture. Add 3 T. water to make a dough. Roll into 10-in. circles and spread potato mixture on top. Fold in half-circles, press together, and place on top of the meat and broth in the kettle. Cover and boil for 25 min. When done, place on large platter and decorate with croutons. Serves 4.

booya. A Minnesota and Wisconsin dish of meats like turtle, oxtail, beef, or chicken, carrots, potatoes and, commonly, rutabagas. Because the dish is usually cooked in enormous batches for a large social gathering and church suppers, "booya" has also come to refer to the outdoor feast itself. Most booyas are held in the fall when the harvest comes in. The origin of the word is unknown, perhaps from the French *bouillir,* or Canadian French *bouillon,* "broth," although it has been suggested the dish is of Belgian or Bohemian origin. It appears in print at least as early as the 1880s. According to Marcia Adams in *Heartland* (1991), the Belgian immigrants in Wisconsin originally used turtle meat in the dish, but later chicken and other ingredients were substituted.

BOOYA

Soak 1 c. navy beans overnight. Cook in salted water for 1 hr. In a very large kettle place beans, a 4–5 lb. stewing chicken and 2 lb. cut-up stewing beef. Add water to cover, bring to a boil, lower to a simmer and cook, covered, for 2 hr. Remove meat, skim fat from surface of liquid, and remove skin from chicken. Separate the meat from the bones, chop coarsely, then add back into kettle. Add 1 lb. chopped carrots, 4 sliced celery ribs, 2 large minced onions, 1 minced garlic clove, ½ c. barley, one 16-oz. can of tomatoes, one 10-oz. package of kernel corn, and 2 large peeled and diced potatoes. Add ⅓ oz. pickling spices wrapped in cheesecloth. Salt, pepper, and allspice to taste. Cover and simmer for about 1 hr.

bop. An old North Carolina confection—the name may describe the puffy appearance of the pastry.

BOP

🔄 *Mix 2 c. milk, 3 beaten eggs, 1 T. butter and 4 T. flour to make a batter, which is then baked in a pan at 450° until brown.*

borscht. Also, "borsch." A beef-and-cabbage soup of Russian and Polish origins, borscht was particularly popular among Jews who emigrated from those countries, so much so that Abel Green, an editor at the show-business industry newspaper *Variety* in the 1930s, used "Borscht Belt" (also "Borscht Circuit") as a synonym for those resorts in New York's Catskill Mountains frequented by Jewish entertainers and patrons.

The Russian *borsch* (*borscht* is Yiddish) actually means "cow parsnips," which originally were the basis of the soup. The term dates in print to 1829.

The soup is traditionally served hot or cold, often with a dollop of sour cream on top.

BORSCHT

🔄 *In a large kettle place 8 scraped, coarsely grated beets, 4 coarsely chopped onions, 2 cloves minced garlic, 1 c. peeled, seeded chopped tomatoes, and 2 lb. beef brisket. Pour in 2 qt. water and bring to a boil. Lower heat to a simmer and cook until meat is tender. Add about 2 T. sugar and lemon juice to taste. Add salt and pepper to taste.*

bosk. Also *"boos-ke-tan."* The so-called "green corn dance," an eight-day ritual of the Gulf State Indians, during which they drank the BLACK DRINK that had the effect of altering their state of mind in ways they believed increased the spirituality of the feast.

Boston baked beans. A dish of navy beans made with molasses and salt pork or bacon. Some argue that baked beans were introduced to the colonists by the Indians, but novelist Kenneth Roberts, in an essay on "The Forgotten Marrowbones," printed in Marjorie

Mosser's *Foods of Old New England* (1957), argues that baked beans had long been a traditional Sabbath dish among North African and Spanish Jews, who called the dish *"skanah."* Roberts also cites *Riley's Narrative* (1816) by James Riley as a source and supposes that New England sea captains brought the idea home with them from Africa.

Nevertheless, the dish clearly became associated with Boston, whose Puritan settlers baked beans on Saturday, served them that night for dinner, for Sunday breakfast with codfish cakes and BOSTON BROWN BREAD, and again for Sunday lunch, because no other cooking was allowed during the Sabbath, which extended to Sunday evening. Sometimes the housewives would hand over their pots of uncooked beans to a community oven, often located within a tavern, to be baked.

Because of the association between Bostonians and beans, the city came to be called "Bean Town." A recipe for baked beans of this type was printed in Lydia Maria Child's *The American Frugal Housewife* in 1832, though the term "Boston baked beans" dates to the 1850s. "Boston strawberries" was a restaurant slang term for the same beans in the late nineteenth century. Baked beans of this kind were first canned in 1875 by the Burnham E. Morrill Company of Portland, Maine, for local fishermen. The first canned beans with tomato sauce were sold by the Van Camp Packing Company of Indianapolis, Indiana, in 1891.

BOSTON BAKED BEANS

🔄 *Rinse 32 oz. of pea (navy) beans in cold water. Heat beans over high heat in large pot, add 4 t. salt, 8 c. boiling water, and boil for 2 min. Cover and let stand for 1 hr. Reboil beans, then turn heat to low and simmer for 1 hr. Mix together ¼ c. dark molasses, ¼ c. dark brown sugar, 1 t. pepper, 1 t. dry mustard, and stir into beans. Alternate layers of beans with slices of browned-salt-pork-and-molasses mixture, adding onion to the middle if desired. On top lay strips of salt pork or bacon, and bake in a covered pot at 250° for about 7 hr., adding more water if necessary to keep the beans moist. Serves 12.*

Boston brown bread. Also, "brown bread" and "Boston bread." A rye-flour bread made with molasses. Boston brown bread was well known among the Puritans, who served it on the Sabbath with BOSTON BAKED BEANS. It is often made with graham flour. "Brown bread" was first mentioned in print in 1831; "Boston bread" in 1889.

BOSTON BROWN BREAD

Sift together ½ c. rye flour, ½ c. whole-wheat or graham flour, ½ t. baking soda, ½ t. baking powder, ½ c. cornmeal, and ½ t. salt. Mix in 1½ c. buttermilk and ½ c. dark molasses, then pour into 1 qt. buttered baking pan or tall pudding mold, and cover tightly. Place in kettle of boiling water until mold is immersed halfway. Cover and steam in 300° oven for about 3 hr., then place bread, uncovered, in oven to dry for a few minutes. Serves 6.

BAKED BOSTON BROWN BREAD

Sift 4½ c. graham flour with ¾ c. sugar, ½ t. salt, and add 1 c. dark molasses, 2 beaten eggs, and 2 c. buttermilk in which 2 t. baking soda have been dissolved. Add 2 c. raisins if desired. Pour into greased pans and let rise for 1 hr. Bake at 300° for 1 hr.

Boston butt. Also, "Boston shoulder." A late-nineteenth-century term for meat cut from the top of the shoulder of a California ham and consisting of about two thirds lean and one third fat. The term was first used in print in 1903.

Boston cracker. A large, thin semisweet biscuit, similar to a COMMON CRACKER and eaten with cheese or other savories. Boston crackers were first mentioned in print in 1818.

Boston cream pie. A pie made of white cake and custard filling or topping. If chocolate icing is added, it is called "Parker House chocolate pie," after the Parker House Hotel in Boston, Massachusetts, where the embellishment was first contrived.

The pie goes back to early American history, when it was sometimes called "pudding-cake pie," or, when made with a raspberry jelly filling, "Mrs. Washington's pie." The first mention of the dessert as "Boston cream pie" was in the New York Herald in 1855.

BOSTON CREAM PIE

Mix together 1 c. cake flour, ¾ c. sugar, 6 T. softened butter, ⅓ c. milk, 1½ t. baking powder, 1½ t. vanilla, ¼ t. baking soda, a dash of salt, and 2 beaten eggs. Pour into greased pan and bake at 375° for 25 min., or until inserted knife comes out clean. Cool on cake rack. In a

saucepan stir 2 c. milk, ¼ c. sugar, 3 T. cornstarch, ¼ t. salt, and 2 beaten egg yolks. Cook until thickened, boil for 1 min., stir in 1 t. vanilla, and remove from heat to cool. Spread thickly onto cake and cool in refrigerator for 30 min.

---

bottle baby. Slang term for an alcoholic (1925).

bottle club. An after-hours social club where liquor may be legally sold. The term dates back at least to the 1940s.

bottled water. Any water sealed in bottles and intended for drinking. This designation would include mineral water, which usually comes from a source of water containing various minerals rather than water to which such minerals have been added.

Because of the relative purity of American drinking water in this century, bottled waters held little allure for most Americans, who never developed the habit of taking mineral waters as a medicinal aid, as Europeans did. There were, in the nineteenth century, spas and resorts where the waters were considered of healthful benefit, and in Saratoga, New York, "Saratoga Vichy" water (later "Saratoga Mineral Water") was bottled and had widespread popularity. Bottled waters took on a certain fashionability after an intensive advertising campaign by Perrier, a French water-bottling company, in 1977, which stressed its purity at a time when Americans began to doubt the merits of their own water-purification systems and began to regard mineral water as an alternative to high-calorie soft drinks.

As a result, the bottled-water business soared in the 1980s, and there are now more than 430 American bottling facilities and 700 brand labels in the market, in addition to more than 75 imported brands (most of which are carbonated mineral waters). The bottled water industry in 1998 had sales of nearly $4 billion dollars, with a total gallonage at 3.6 billion, composed of 148 million gallons of domestic sparkling water, 3.3 billion of domestic non-sparkling, and 160 million of imported waters. In 1997 the U.S. per capita consumption of bottled water was 12.1 gallons. More than 70 percent of all bottled water is sold in five states—California, Florida, Illinois, New York and Texas.

Bottled waters are either "sparkling," with natural or added bubbles, or "nonsparkling" (also called "still"). The various categories of bottled waters are as follows:

drinking water. Bottled water obtained from an approved source that has undergone a minimum of treatment and filtration.

mineral water. Under 1993 FDA regulations, mineral water is defined as bottled water with at least 250 parts per million of total dissolved solids like calcium. Mineral water must also come from a protected underground water source.

natural water. Bottled spring, mineral, or artesian-well or well water not derived from a municipal water supply.

spring water. Bottled water derived from an underground formation from which water flows naturally to the earth's surface.

well water. Bottled water from a hole bored in the ground that taps the water of an aquifer.

purified water. Bottled water produced by distillation, deionization, reverse osmosis, or other suitable process that meets U.S. Pharmacopeia standards for purified water.

bottoms up! A drinking toast, indicating that the entire contents of a glass or bottle should be drunk up quickly.

boudin. A Louisiana sausage of two varieties: *boudin rouge* (French for "red pudding"), which is a blood sausage, and *boudin blanc* (French for "white pudding"), which is made with pork shoulder. Boudin (the name dates in print to 1805) is customarily made and served at hog-butchering parties called "boucheries," still held occasionally in the Cajun country during autumn or winter. The *Dictionary Of American Regional English*, however, gives a primary definition of "boudin" as "the intestines of buffalo esp[ecially] as prepared for food," citing an 1805 report from the journals of Lewis and Clark.

According to Bruce Aidells and Denis Kelly in *Hot Links and Country Flavors* (1990), white boudin often contains rice and onions, and the sausage filling is usually pushed out of the casing after cooking and eaten without the casing.

boula. A green-pea-and-green-turtle soup, flavored with sherry and topped with whipped cream and cheese. The dish is described in *The White House Cookbook* (1964) as "an old favorite which was served

in President Martin van Buren's day. President and Mrs. John F. Kennedy served it at the White House and, as sports enthusiasts, renamed it for the old college song, 'Boula-Boula!'" Theodora FitzGibbon in *The Food of the Western World* (1976) noted that the soup came originally from the Seychelles.

BOULA

Combine 1 can pea soup with 1 can green turtle soup, boil, season with ¾ c. sherry and a dash of ground pepper. Fill bowls and top with whipped cream and a sprinkle of Parmesan cheese. Place under broiler until lightly browned. Serves 4–6.

---

bounce. A fermented beverage popular in Colonial days, made by pouring spirits such as rum or brandy over fruit, adding sugar, citrus fruit, spices, and water. Bounce is similar to, and perhaps interchangeable with, "shrub," which is strained and sweetened with brown sugar. The former's name probably derived from its ability to give the imbiber a bounce, the latter's possibly from the Arabic *shrub,* "drink."

BOUNCE

Pour 1 qt. rum or brandy over 5 pt. pitted cherries or other fruit, and let stand to ferment for a week. (For a shrub, strain the liquid and add brown sugar to taste.) Bottle and let stand another week.

---

bouncer. A person hired by a saloon or restaurant to "bounce" unwanted customers from the premises. The term dates to 1865 in print.

bourbon. A spirit distilled from a fermented mash of grain, at least 51 percent of which must be corn. Bourbon is bottled between 80 and 125 proof (legal minimum is 60 proof) and must be aged at least two years in new, charred white-oak barrels. Only limestone-filtered spring water may be used to lower alcoholic proof.

Bourbon is the only distinctly American spirit, although it was not until May 4, 1964, that the federal government recognized it as such and protected it under law. In the South it has been traditionally synonymous with WHISKEY. It is the essential ingredient of a Kentucky MINT JULEP and finds its way into many sweet confections such as "bourbon ball" and "bourbon cakes."

The name comes from Bourbon County, originally in Virginia but now part of Kentucky. (The Bourbons were a line of European monarchs whose subjects settled colonies in the Americas.) Corn spirits had been made as early as 1746 in America, and Evan Williams established a distillery in Bourbon County as of 1783. But credit for creating the distinctive taste of bourbon goes to a Baptist minister, Reverend Elijah Craig, who began making spirits at Royal Spring, Virginia (presently Georgetown, Kentucky), in 1789. At first this was called merely "corn whiskey" or "corn," but by 1821 an ad appeared in the *Western Citizen* selling a spirit specifically called "BOURBON WHISKEY." By the middle of the nineteenth century the spirit was so associated with Bourbon County, Kentucky, that it was called, simply, "bourbon," and often "Kentucky bourbon." The first bottled bourbon was sold in 1870, all bourbon prior to that being shipped in barrels to taverns.

Most bourbon uses sour mash (introduced in 1823 by Dr. James C. Crow)—that is, a part of the spent beer, or distiller's beer (a residue from a previous mash run), allowed to sour overnight and then added to a new batch of mash. "Sour mash whiskey" or "sippin' whiskey" refers to whiskey made by such a process.

The law requires the use of new, charred, white-oak barrels to give the bourbon its character, part of a tradition whose origins are obscure. In *American Cooking: Southern Style* (1971), Eugene Walter gives three stories of how the distilling method came about:

One story tells of a careless cooper who drowsed while some dampened staves were steaming by the fire. The staves burned but he made the barrels with them anyway, and a new flavor was imparted to the contents. Another tarrydiddle would have it that a thrifty cooper, intending to resell some barrels in which salted fish had been shipped, carefully burned out the interiors to get rid of every trace of fishiness. My own favorite explanation holds that a Kentucky farmer buried several barrels of whiskey under his barn to age. Lightning struck the barn, it burned down and a few years later, digging there, the farmer rediscovered the barrels, charred black but with the honey-red liquid unharmed, and noticeably better than any other whiskey he had made.

There are now thirteen operating distilleries in Kentucky making bourbon—78.6 percent of the world's supply—with the remaining 21.4 percent produced in Tennessee, Virginia, and Missouri. See also, TENNESSEE WHISKEY.

"Single barrel bourbon" is a 1990s marketing term for specially selected barrels of bourbon whose distinctive taste allows them to be sold at a premium price.

"Small batch" bourbons are made in lots of less than 1,000 gallons (about 20 barrels).

Bourbon is drunk STRAIGHT, ON THE ROCKS, ideally with so-called BRANCH WATER, or in SOURS and other mixed drinks. Bourbon makes up about 15 percent of the United States spirits market. In 1997 total U.S. production of bourbon (including Tennessee whiskey) was 12.9 million 9-liter cases.

bowfin (*Amia calva*). Also, "grindle," "jack grindle," "John A. Grindle," "mudfish," "mudjack," "prairie bass," "scaled ling," "speckled cat," "spot-tail," "lake lawyer," "choupique," "blackfish 5," "cypress trout," and "dogfish." A carniverous ganoid freshwater fish of North America. "Bowfin" first saw print about 1845, although "grindle" dates back to the beginning of the eighteenth century and derives from the German *Gründel*, "ground," because it inhabits sluggish waters. They are generally not considered good eating fish, but in Louisiana the roe of the fish (there called "choupique," a word that derives from French and in American print since 1763 as *choupic*) is cultivated as a form of CAVIAR.

bramble jelly. An eighteenth-century jelly made from crab apples and blackberries. It originated in England.

branch water. Supposedly the clearest, purest water from a small stream called a "branch." The term dates in print to 1835. "BOURBON and branch water" is a nostalgic request in the South, but one that can hardly be fulfilled unless the bartender has access to such a stream's water supply.

Brandon puff. A South Carolina muffin of flour and cornmeal. The origin of the name may in some way refer to Charles Brandon, first duke of Suffolk (died 1545).

BRANDON PUFF

Combine 1 qt. flour, ¾ c. melted cooled butter, 4 beaten eggs, 1 yeast cake, and enough milk to make a muffin batter. Let rise overnight. Add 1 t. cornmeal, pour into muffin tins, bake until brown at 425°, about 10–15 min.

brandy. A spirit obtained from distilled wine or the fermented mash of fruit. The word comes from *brandewijn*, a Dutch word meaning to "burn" or "distill." In America most brandy is made in California (about 72 percent) from grapes such as the THOMPSON SEEDLESS and the Flame Tokay, although some is made from fruits such as apples (APPLEJACK), peaches, and others. About 20 percent of the distilleries use a "pot still" (or "alembic") by which the wine is heated in a pot, becomes vaporized, and condenses into a receptacle. The rest of the brandy is produced in a "continuous still," which allows brandy to be produced without pausing between batches and gives off a very clean product.

Brandies are aged in fifty-gallon white-oak barrels that add flavor and slight color. By federal law brandy must have a minimum proof of 60 (30 percent alcohol by volume). In 1997 total U.S. production of brandy was 5.3 million 9-liter cases.

brandy alexander. Also, "alexander." A cocktail made from brandy, cream, and a chocolate cordial. The origin of the name is unknown, as is its date of concoction, though it was first in print in 1925. A recipe appeared in 1939 in *World Famous Chef's Cook Book* by Ford Naylor, who calls it simply "Alexander." For a long time it was considered a "ladies' cocktail"—an alcoholic beverage for those who were not used to drinking strong liquors. If made with gin instead of brandy, the drink is called a "Panama," after the country in Central America.

BRANDY ALEXANDER

Shake with ice cubes 1½ oz. brandy, 1 oz. chocolate cordial, and 1 oz. light or heavy cream. Strain into cocktail glass.

brandy smash. A cocktail of the mid-nineteenth century made from brandy, crushed ice, and mint.

brannigan. Archaic term for a drinking bout, dating back at least to 1927.

brasserie. In France, a small, inexpensive restaurant (usually with Alsatian roots) serving various types of beer, or a brewery itself, although the term has also come to mean a restaurant serving simple neighborhood fare. In America, a brasserie more often approximates this second meaning, usually connoting a place serving inexpensive French food in informal surroundings (1864).

brat. A slang term for Bratwurst sausage, especially in the Midwest (1950). "Double brat" refers to two sausages on a hard roll, which is especially popular in Sheboygan, Wisconsin, which calls itself the "Bratwurst Capital of the World" or the "Wurst City of the World."

bread. One of the world's basic foods, made from flour and water, often with the addition of yeast, salt, and other ingredients. Shaped into loaves, rolls, flat cakes, or rings, and then baked, bread is one of man's earliest foods, dating back more than ten thousand years, soon after man cultivated cereal grains and pounded them to make porridge (which may have been baked as the first breads). The word itself is from the Old English *brēad*.

The bread of the Native Americans was based on cornmeal and included a wide variety of preparations. *Piki* bread was very thin, often made from blue cornmeal batter on a hot stone. This was the bread of the Hopi; the Zunis call it *hewe,* the Tewa call it *mowa,* and those in San Ildefonso call it *bowahejahui* ("Put it on, take it off"). As Carolyn Niethammer notes in *American Indian Food and Lore* (1974), "Piki making is an art and a ritual. . . . Years ago a young woman was required to demonstrate that she had mastered the art of piki-baking before she was considered a suitable bride . . . but today the number of those who excel in this art is dwindling." The TORTILLA, common still in Mexican-American restaurants, was originally a Native American cornmeal bread. Later, after Columbus brought wheat to the New World in 1493, tortillas were also made with wheat flour. Other breads were baked in adobe ovens or in a hole in the earth. Niethammer describes *kinaalda*, a bread measuring eight inches deep and five feet across, as "the traditional food for the Navajo girl's puberty ceremony."

The Native Americans of the East Coast also used corn exclusively for their bread, and as of the 1650s the European settlers called this "Indian bread," as an alternative to the earlier "pone" or "corn pone" (from an Algonquian word *apan*, "baked"). The colonists immediately adapted cornmeal as a flour and made their own "corn bread" (first mentioned in 1750) or combined rye, molasses, cornmeal, and yeast to make RYE 'N' INJUN BREAD.

Yeast was easily obtainable from beer brewers (the yeast-rich foam atop the beer was called "barm"), and there was also a whole range of steamed breads like BOSTON BROWN BREAD. BISCUITS were found throughout the United States, especially after the new leavenings like pearl ash, saleratus, BAKING POWDER, and baking soda came into use during the midnineteenth century, thereby creating a new variety of "quick" or "lightnin'" breads. Home baking was further helped along with a novelty of the 1850s, self-rising flour, and an increase in store-bought and bakery bread was spurred by the invention in 1834 of the Swiss steel roller that processed flour finely and uniformly.

During the Gold Rush in California in 1849 an old-fashioned form of bread was revived—SOURDOUGH—that has since been associated with San Francisco's history.

During a period of deprivation in the Civil War, a wing of the United States Senate in Washington was turned into an enormous oven to bake sixteen thousand loaves of bread a day for the Union troops.

After the Civil War bakeries grew in number, especially in large cities with new immigrant populations, and there was a trend toward purer, whiter bread. Before this time bakers were accused of adulterating their bread with lime. "Whole wheat" bread (also called "middling bread," which referred to the coarse particles of whole wheat in it) came to be considered a coarse, common type of bread, while white bread signified purity and a more refined product. But later in the twentieth century, nutritionists advocated whole-wheat bread as healthier and won the support of those in the HEALTH FOOD movement.

Ready-made, packaged yeast was available for the homemaker by 1868, and for the rest of the century most bread was still made at home. By 1900, 95 percent of the flour produced was sold to home bakers. But in 1911 the National Association of Master Bakers quoted a study showing the percentage had changed radically: 60–65 percent of the city families did not make their own bread any longer. Today only 15 percent of the flour bought is used by home bakers.

The twentieth century also brought innovations in technology that produced a loaf whiter but less nutritious than those previously baked. The whiteness represented purity to those brought up on dark, coarse breads (however full of nutrients they were), but the new loaves were made by extracting 28–30 percent of the wheat kernel's bulk, thereby eliminating the bran and wheat germ. This resulted in 1941 in a federal law requiring that such breads be "enriched" with thiamine, niacin, riboflavin, and iron, an action that seemed to placate nutritionists for two decades until the HEALTH FOOD movement pointed out the contradictory idea of removing nutrients only to replace them in another form.

Today some commercial breads are in fact jammed with vitamins and minerals ordinary breads do not have; but, then, bleached-flour breads lack the other nutrients derived from the bran and wheat germ.

Sliced bread, also called a "sandwich loaf," was introduced in 1930 by the Continental Bakeries under the name "Wonder Bread" (which had been around in an unsliced form since 1920) after Otto Frederick Rohwedder of Battle Creek, Michigan, invented the bread-slicing machine in January 1928. Most American bread is bought sliced.

There has been a trend in the last fifteen years to produce commercial breads of coarser textures and varied grains, ironically often sweetened with sugar, molasses, or honey. At the same time there has been a tremendous growth in packaged mixes for breads, rolls, muffins, and biscuits, as well as frozen breads and pastries or "heat-and-serve" (also, "brown-and-serve") varieties that need no true baking, only warming.

Peak consumption of white bread in the United States was 9 billion pounds in 1963. In 1992 Americans ate 51.2 one-pound loaves of bread per person, and total consumption of bread products, including hot dog and hamburger buns, whole-grain breads, and other forms, has been increasing since the 1980s.

"Italian bread" is a long, cylindrical bread with blunt-pointed tips. It is slightly fatter or wider than "French bread" as sold in American groceries. "Pita bread" (from the Greek *pitta*) is a flat Middle Eastern-style bread often called "pocket bread." "Raisin bread" is a popular sweet variety, while *rye* and PUMPERNICKEL are used for sandwiches. See also CORNELL BREAD, SOURDOUGH, BOSTON BROWN BREAD, MONKEY BREAD, ANADAMA BREAD.

"Bread and skip" is an archaic New England colloquialism meaning a scanty meal, while "bread and with it" refers to a meal of bread and some other foods.

bread line. A term first used in 1825 to describe the lines of poor, hungry people who received loaves of bread and other food from charitable institutions. Bread lines became a common sight in American cities during the Great Depression of the 1930s.

breakfast. The first meal of the day. The word means "to break one's fast" and dates back at least to 1425. "Brekkie" is a modern colloquialism for "breakfast."

The Native American breakfast consisted of cornmeal mush and perhaps corn bread, both items the first European settlers adapted for their own breakfasts. The settlers also breakfasted on a quickly pre-pared porridge called "hasty pudding," made with cornmeal and molasses. Later bread or toast and coffee or tea were the usual breakfast, while in the nineteenth century affluence brought more variety to the diet and larger portions of meats, fish, cheese, bread, jams, and, often, a tot of rum or cider. Scotsman John Melish visited America in 1811 and reported in his *Travels in the United States of America* on "A Backwoods Breakfast," at which his humble hostess sought to wring the necks of two chickens.

> I told her to stop, and she gave me a look of astonish-ment. "Have you any eggs?" said I. "Yes, plenty," replied she, still keeping in a stooping posture, with the chicken in her hand. "Well," said I, "just boil an egg, and let me have it, with a little bread and tea, and that will save you and I a great deal of trouble." She seemed quite embarrassed, and said she never could set down a breakfast to me like that. . . . She detained me about half an hour, and at last placed upon the table a profu-sion of ham, eggs, fritters, bread, butter and some excellent tea. . . . I mention the circumstance to show the kind of hospitality of the landlady, and the good living enjoyed by the backwoods people.

Also popular were PANCAKES, especially buckwheat pancakes, which were consumed in stacks with butter and molasses or maple syrup. Of these the English author of *Mrs. Beeton's Every-Day Cookery* (1909 ed.) wrote, "Hot cakes at breakfast are quite a national institution [in America]. These are made with soda and baking-powder, and must be regarded as some-what beyond the capacities of average digestive organs."

In different parts of the United States different food items are served for breakfast, although a meal of eggs, bacon, toast, and coffee seems ubiquitous, with the addition in the South of GRITS, HAM, or BISCUITS, in the West with CHILE peppers, in the Northeast with sausages and hash-brown potatoes, and in urban restaurants with preparations of EGGS BENEDICT, finnan haddie, melon, FRENCH TOAST, CAVIAR, WAFFLES, DANISH PASTRY, fruit, ENGLISH MUFFINS, and many other items. In Jewish communities breakfast may consist of BAGELS and cream cheese.

The popularity of breakfast CEREALS began in the middle of the nineteenth century and has continued since then, especially as a children's breakfast item. Americans have to a large extent curbed their hearty breakfasts in recent years because of dietary concerns (although the midmorning "coffee break" often serves

to bolster an early light breakfast with a roll or muffin), and increasing numbers of women in the work force, saving the tradition of a big breakfast for weekends or Sunday BRUNCH. "Business breakfasts" held at hotel dining rooms are also popular, for, as James Villas contends in *American Taste* (1982), "Show me the fool who finds something sensible and digni-fied about offering plastic cups of instant coffee and a puny piece of bread as an excuse for a business break-fast, and I can only hope that he collapses from lack of adrenaline before the meeting is finished."

The American food industry has marketed scores of breakfast foods designed to save time in the kitchen, including frozen waffles, packaged pancake batter, heat-and-serve eggs, powdered eggs, imitation CREAM, already cooked sausage, fake bacon, canned fruit, and tarts shaped to fit conveniently into the toaster. FAST-FOOD restaurants also offer' standard fare, such as scrambled eggs, sausage, pancakes, and coffee, and many restaurants, diners, and luncheonettes advertise the fact that "breakfast is served 24 hours a day." One out of four Americans eats breakfast in the car on the way to work, but only 42 percent of Americans eat breakfast every day of the week

breakfast cream. A New Orleans term for light cream.

breakfast club. A business or social organization that holds regular meetings over breakfast, often with a featured speaker. Most clubs are either all male or all female and have between twenty and thirty members. The concept dates back at least to the 1940s.

breakfast dance. A term used to describe all-night parties held in nightclubs in Harlem, New York, dating in print to 1934.

brick cheese. A smooth, cow's-milk cheese created in 1877 by John Jossi of Wisconsin. It is formed into bricks about five pounds in weight, has small holes, and is aged about three months.

bridge mix. Also, "bridge assortment." A mixture of snacks or candies customarily served at a social gath-ering like a bridge game. Many snacks or candies are packaged under this term, which dates back to the 1950s.

bret. Winemakers' term for wine that has been con-taminated with the genus of the wild yeast *Brettanomyces.*

brew. As a slang term, a beer (1907). Also, "brewski" (1978) among students.

broccoflower. A registered trademark (1990) of the Tanimura and Antle company of Spreckels, California, for a vegetable that is a genetic cross between BROCCOLI and CAULIFLOWER. Originally grown in Holland, the vegetable was brought to the United States by Rick Antle in 1987 and is now grown exclusively at the company's farms in the Salinas Valley and elsewhere. In 1991 the harvest averaged 25,000–30,000 cartons per week.

broccoli (*Brassica oleracea botrytis*). A plant in the mustard family having a flowery green head and related to CABBAGE and CAULIFLOWER. The word is from the Italian *broccolo,* "cabbage sprout," and was first recorded in English in 1699 as a plant from Naples. The plant arrived in England about 1720, and John Randolph of Williamsburg wrote of it in *A Treatise on Gardening by a Citizen of Virginia* (1775) that "the stems will eat like Asparagus and the heads like Cauliflower." Nevertheless, broccoli virtually disappeared from American soil until its reintroduction in the twentieth century. According to film producer Albert Broccoli in an interview in *USA Today* (July 28, 1987), his uncle reintroduced the seeds in Long Island, New York, in the 1920s. The Italian variety of broccoli began to grow slowly in favor with the creation of a popular dish containing broccoli called CHICKEN DIVAN in the 1930s. In the United States the green sprouting varieties are most often grown.

"Broccoli rabe" (*B. rapa parachinensis*), also called by a variety of names and pronunciations like "broccoli di rabe," "broccoli rape," "broccoli di rape," "broccoli raab," and "rapini," is a winter vegetable with slightly indented leaves with small sprouts and a bitter taste (it is sometimes called "bitter broccoli"). The word "rabe" or "raab" denotes its relation to the turnip family (Latin *rapa*). It is a widely grown and beloved vegetable of Italian Americans and Chinese, and is now cultivated in the United States in California, Arizona, Florida, and New Jersey.

Broccoli is usually boiled or steamed and served with butter sauce. Americans ate 1.9 pounds per person in 1982.

broken victuals. Leftovers, a colloquialism dating to 1861 in print.

Bronx cocktail. A cocktail made of gin, sweet and dry vermouths, and orange juice, concocted by bartender Johnnie Solon at the Waldorf-Astoria Hotel in New York City sometime between 1899 (when he joined the establishment) and 1906 (when the word first appeared in print). As Solon related the story (to Albert Stevens Crockett, author of *Old Waldorf Bar Days* [1931]), Solon was challenged by a customer to come up with a new cocktail. The bartender thereupon mixed two jiggers of Gordon's gin with one jigger of orange juice, then a dash each of French and Italian vermouths. The success of the cocktail caused the Waldorf to use a case of oranges per day. According to Solon, he chose the name on the spur of the moment because he had recently been to the Bronx Zoo and was reminded that some of his customers saw strange animals when they drank too much. The addition of an egg yolk to the following recipe makes the drink a "silver Bronx," while the juice of a blood orange makes it a "Bloody Bronx."

BRONX COCKTAIL

Shake over ice cubes 1½ oz. gin, ½ oz. dry vermouth, ½ oz. sweet vermouth, and ½ oz. orange juice. Strain into cocktail glass and serve over ice cubes.

Brooklyn cake. A nineteenth-century light cake whose name probably has nothing to do with the borough of New York City, but rather with Brooklyn, Connecticut, or, perhaps, a misreading of Brookline, Massachusetts.

BROOKLYN CAKE

The recipe given in The Pentucket Housewife *(1882) calls for a batter of 1½ c. sugar, 6 egg whites beaten with 1 t. cream of tartar folded into ½ c. creamed butter, ½ t. baking soda, ½ c. cornstarch, 1½ cups flour, and lemon juice.*

Brother Jonathan's hat. A suet pudding of nineteenth-century New England. The name derives from a derisive term used by the British and the Loyalists during the Revolutionary War for American rebels. Later the name was applied to any American citizen, and the *Dictionary of Americanisms* disputes the claim that it originally referred to Governor Jonathan Trumbull (1710–85) of Connecticut. As a dish it seems to be synonymous with DEACON PORTER'S HAT, but may predate the latter.

brown bag. A term used to describe a meal packed in a brown paper bag, usually for lunch consumed at work. Brown paper bags were first made in Pennsylvania in 1852, though not patented (by Luther C. Crowell of West Dennis, Massachusetts) until 1872, two years after Francis Wolle had patented a machine that fabricated the paper into a flat-bottomed, easily folded bag that became the standard of the food-service industry.

Today there are about 60 million Americans who eat lunch out of a brown bag, and the phrase "to brown bag it," meaning to eat one's lunch in this manner, goes back at least to the 1950s, according to David Lyon, head of the Brown Bag Institute in Connecticut.

In 1979 cheaper plastic grocery bags began to replace paper bags in grocery stores and now account for half the bags used.

brown goods. Liquor industry term for spirits that are usually brown in color, like scotch, BOURBON, and BLENDED WHISKEY. "White goods" are spirits usually colorless, like GIN and VODKA.

brownie. A rich chocolate cake cut into squares and eaten as a dessert or snack. The name comes from the deep brown color of the confection, and it has been an American favorite since the nineteenth century, first appearing in print in 1906 in *The Boston Cooking-School Cook Book.* (Earlier references to "brownies" include the Sears, Roebuck Catalog for 1897, although the reference is to mail order chocolate candies named after cartoon elves created by author Palmer Cox in a series that began with *The Brownies: Their Book* [1887], and the 1896 edition of the *Boston Cooking-School Cook Book* for a browned molasses confection containing no chocolate.) Some brownies are quite moist at the center, while others are more cookielike. In the South, a brownielike cake made without chocolate, baked in two layers, and topped with butterscotch meringue is called "mud hen," "mud hen cake," or "butterscotch brownies."

BROWNIE

Combine 2 c. sugar, ½ c. flour, and ½ c. cocoa. Add 4 beaten eggs, ½ lb. melted cooled butter, 2 t. vanilla, and 1 c. chopped pecans or walnuts. Pour into buttered pan and place in a larger pan half-full of hot water. Bake for 45 min. at 300°.

brownstone front cake. A rich chocolate cake, with a vanilla or caramel icing. According to culinary historian Meryl Evans, recipes for the cake date back at least to 1903, but the origin of the name is unknown, but would seem to refer to the reddish-brown color of brownstone buildings' facades

bruiss. A dish of boiled bread and milk. The origin of the name is unknown, but the dish is mentioned in *The Pentucket Housewife* (1882) with the instructions to add milk to crusts of bread, boil slowly, and add salt and butter.

brunch. A portmanteau word combining "breakfast" with "lunch" for a meal taken late in the morning or just around noon. According to the English magazine *Punch* (August 1, 1896), brunch was "introduced . . . last year by Mr. Guy Beringer, in the now defunct *Hunter's Weekly,* and indicating a combined breakfast and lunch," probably one taken just after arriving home from hunting.

The practice of having brunch did not really take hold in the United States until the 1930s, but today it is part of many hotel and restaurant menus on weekends, as well as a popular form of social entertaining for weekend hosts. "There may be some perfectly nice people who use the word 'brunch,' " commented humorist Heywood Broun, "but I prefer not to know about them."

Brunswick stew. A stew made originally with squirrel, now made with chicken or other meats. There have been many claims as to the dish's origins, especially from the citizens of Brunswick County, North Carolina, but the most creditable claim comes from Brunswick County, Virginia, where in 1828 Dr. Creed Haskins of the Virginia state legislature requested a special squirrel stew from "Uncle Jimmy" Matthews to feed those attending a political rally. This original Brunswick stew was said to have contained no vegetables except onions, but it soon went through several transformations before the squirrel itself dropped from most recipes after the turn of the century. The first mention in print of the dish was in 1856.

brush roast. A North Carolina term for a dish of oysters cooked on a wire netting over a wood fire and served with butter, chow-chow, and corn bread (1939).

Brussels sprout (*Brassica oleracea gemmifera*). A small cabbage of the mustard family originally developed from primitive cabbage in fourteenth-century

Brussels, Belgium. It is first mentioned in English print in 1796, but did not enter England until the midnineteenth century. In the United States Brussels sprouts are grown predominantly in California and New York, with the most popular variety being the "Improved Long Island."

buck. Originally a Prohibition-era drink made with gin (and called a "gin buck"), ginger ale, and the juice of a lemon whose shell was then added to the drink. It contains no sugar. Later bucks were made with other carbonated drinks and spirits. "Buck" is also a term used for fermented mash used to make MOONSHINE (1933).

BUCK

Over ice cubes pour 1½ oz. gin, squeeze the juice of half a lemon into the glass, add the lemon shell, and top with ginger ale.

---

buck and breck. A cold pickle condiment like CHOW-CHOW. The origin of the name is unknown.

BUCK AND BRECK

To 1 gal. of vinegar add 1 lb. brown sugar, 1 c. salt, 2 oz. black pepper, 2 oz. ginger, 2 oz. white mustard seed, 2 oz. dry mustard, 2 oz. cloves, 2 oz. celery seed, 1 oz. turmeric, 1 c. grated horseradish, 2 oz. cloves, 2 chopped onions, 1 head of chopped cabbage, 2 lb. chopped, peeled tomatoes, 2 each of red and green peppers, mix, pour into bottles, seal, and, according to old advice, "let stand until Thanksgiving."

---

bucket candy. According to the *Dictionary of American Regional English*, "The type of small candies packed and sold from a bucket," such as gumdrops, lozenges, and various bonbons. The term dates in print to 1950, and is associated with South Carolinians.

bucket of blood. A western term for a very tough saloon or bar. Originally the term referred to the Bucket of Blood saloon owned by Shorty Young in Havre, Montana, the fame of which became the basis for describing any similar establishment by the same name by about 1880. One may also find such places referred to as "bucket shops." See also BLOODY MARY.

buckeye. A peanut-butter-and-chocolate candy made in little balls resembling buckeye nuts. The term is dated in print by the *Dictionary of American Regional English to 1970*, which describes it as "Cheap candy that used to be sold years ago." But according to Marcia Adams in *Heartland* (1991), "If Ohio were to declare a state candy, this recipe would be it. . . . Some cooks like to leave a bit of peanut butter ball exposed when dipping in the chocolate so it more closely resembles a real buckeye."

BUCKEYE

Mix together in a bowl 4 c. peanut butter, 1 c. softened butter, 6 c. confectioners' sugar, and 2 T. vanilla. Cover bowl, chill until firm, then pinch off pieces about an in. in diameter, place in waxed paper-covered pans, and chill again until firm. In a double boiler melt 12 oz. semisweet chocolate morsels and ½ c. shaved paraffin. Using a toothpick, dip the peanut balls into the chocolate, drain, then refrigerate until firm. Makes about 36 buckeyes.

---

buckle. A kind of cake made with berries, most commonly blueberries. The use of the term is probably quite old, but its first record in print is only in 1959 in Elsie Masterton's *Blueberry Bill Cookbook*. Blueberries are tossed with flour and added to a cake batter that is sprinkled with more batter or a topping.

buckwheat. Any plant of the genus *Fagopyrum*, whose seeds are coarsely ground to make flour. The name is from the Middle Dutch *boecweite*, "beech wheat," so called because the seeds resemble the nuts of the beech tree. The word was first recorded in English in 1548. The plant is a native of Central Asia, but it was propagated in the New World for fodder and cereal, as is known through a reference by Adam Smith in 1776. "Buckwheat cakes," pancakes made with buckwheat flour and dating in print to 1772, were popular everywhere in the country in the nineteenth century. "It is hard for the American to rise from his winter breakfast without his buckwheat cakes," wrote English traveler George Makepeace Towle in *American Society* (1870). It was American painter James Abbott McNeill Whistler (1834–1903) who introduced buckwheat cakes to London society. "Slip go down" is a slang term for buckwheat pudding.

There are two basic forms of buckwheat—unroasted and roasted—the latter known by the Russian word, "kasha," which is also the word used for a cooked porridge made from the roasted buckwheat.

buffalo. An erroneous name for the American bison (*Bison bison*), a shaggy-maned, short-horned, hoofed mammal of the cattle family with a large, low-slung head and massive hump, reaching a height of five feet, a length of nine feet, and a weight of twenty-five hundred pounds. The word "buffalo" correctly applies to various species of Asian or African oxen, but Americans have called their native bison by this name ever since explorer Hernando de Soto spotted the animal in the New World in 1544 and called it by the Portuguese, *bufalo*.

Once the buffalo population in this country spread on both sides of the Mississippi River in thick waves, numbering more than 60 million at the beginning of the nineteenth century. The Native Americans' respect for the buffalo was borne out of their total dependence on its meat and hide for sustenance, clothing, tepee coverings, and rope, while other parts of the beast went into making utensils, medicines, even children's toys. The buffalo was deified by the Great Plains Indians for good reason.

By slicing the meat from the carcass and drying it in the sun or smoking it in their tepees, the Native Americans produced a jerky they called PEMMICAN, which they pounded and perserved in buffalo-skin pouches and often enriched with fat and wild berries.

Despite their respect for the buffalo, the Native Americans engaged in wanton killing of the herds, sometimes driving them off a cliff into a ravine. But this was as nothing compared with the deliberate and wholesale slaughter of the herds brought on by the easterners who killed the buffalo for its hide, for sport, and for its importance to the Native American tribes. Buffalo hunters sent back tens of thousands of pelts to be made into coats. The Kansas Pacific Railroad, desiring an efficient way to remove the herds from their westward path, arranged special hunting tours on which well-dressed easterners with long rifles shot from the moving train windows and cut down the animals, only to have them rot where they fell. But the main reason for the deliberate destruction of the herds was to eliminate the life-sustaining animal as a resource for the Native Americans, who were the real object of the slaughter.

By the mid-nineteenth century the buffalo was extinct east of the Mississippi, and by the end of the century less than a thousand remained on the whole continent. Only the interdiction of President Theodore Roosevelt, who in 1905 established in Kansas and Montana two protected reservations for the beast, saved the buffalo. Today herds have been restocked and expanded, most in private hands, so that the buffalo now numbers about 250,000 head, some of which are raised for sale as meat. The state of Kansas named the buffalo its state animal, and for a time this most American of cattle appeared on the nickel coin.

The buffalo has never been of much gastronomic interest to Americans, although today there is a certain exotic curiosity about the meat, which is occasionally found on menus. The early pioneers were forced to eat buffalo meat and Indian pemmican on the long trek westward, but later on the cattle breeders preferred the more passive longhorn steer to the ornery bison. A few attempts have been made to breed the buffalo with other cattle. One such crossbreed, by Charles Goodnight, between a bison and a Polled Angus steer, produced the "cattalo," and since 1973 there has been some interest in a hybrid called the "beefalo," a cross between the buffalo and a Hereford or Charolais. There is even an American Beefalo Association, with 950 members worldwide. The beefalo is said to be easier and faster to bring to full weight, and its meat leaner. Still, the beefalo has never fulfilled its early promise as the "meat of the future."

Buffalo meat itself tastes a good deal like beef and has no pronounced gamy flavor. Young bulls make for the best meat, especially if marinated.

"Buffalo cider" is a euphemism for the liquid in a buffalo's stomach that a Great Plains hunter would drink if he was far from water.

Buffalo chicken wings. Deep-fried chicken wings served with a HOT SAUCE and a blue-cheese dressing. The dish originated at the Anchor Bar in Buffalo, New York, on October 30, 1964, when owner Teressa Bellissimo, having just received an oversupply of chicken wings, was asked by her son Dominic and his friends for something to nibble on. According to Dominic in an interview for *Nation's Restaurant News* in 1991, "She cut off the doohickeys, fried them, drained them and swished them around in margarine. Then she improvised on the hot sauce and put blue cheese dressing—our house dressing—on the side." Being Catholics, the Bellissimos did not eat meat on Fridays, so they waited until midnight to serve the first wings.

The dish became an immediate sensation at the restaurant (which today sells seventy thousand pounds of chicken per month), and soon Buffalo chicken wings (sometimes called "Western New York chicken wings") were being served all over the city. In 1977 the city of Buffalo declared July 29 "Chicken Wing Day."

Today the dish is a staple in restaurants and bars across the United States.

BUFFALO CHICKEN WINGS

Separate the wing bone at the joints of 20 chicken wings, then cut off the tip of each wing. Deep-fry in peanut oil for about 10 min., until golden brown and cooked through.

Melt 4 T. butter in a saucepan and add 4 T. bottled red-hot pepper sauce. Add salt and pepper to taste, and a dash of cayenne pepper. For the dressing, blend 1 c. mayonnaise with 2 T. chopped onion, 1 t. minced garlic, ½ c. sour cream, 1 T. white vinegar, and ¼ c. blue cheese. Serve chicken wings with the sauce and the dressing. Serves 4.

buffet. A form of food service whereby diners move along the length of tables set with various cold and hot foods. The word, from the French and dating in print to 1718, also applies to the sideboard or cabinet on which the food is placed. In euphemistic slang, "buffet" is also applied to a tavern or SPEAKEASY.

bug juice. Also, "bugjuice." Cowboy slang for whiskey, in print since 1863. The *New Dictionary Of American Slang* (1986) suggests it derives from the drink's "resemblance to the *juice* secreted by grasshoppers," but among schoolchildren the term has come to mean (at least since its first appearance in 1889) any very sweet, usually noncarbonated soft drink, and, commonly, to the product Kool-Aid, in which case the tendency of the drink to draw bugs may better explain its usage.

bull and bear. A sandwich created at the Caucus Club restaurant in Detroit, Michigan, made with corned beef, chopped liver, lettuce, tomato, COLESLAW, and RUSSIAN or THOUSAND ISLAND DRESSING. The name has nothing to do with the ingredients, but instead with the traditional symbols of buyer and seller on the stock exchange, which provides much of the Caucus Club's clientele.

A "bull and bear" cocktail, also created at the Caucus Club.

BULL AND BEAR

Mix 1½ oz. vodka, ½ oz. clam juice, ½ oz. beef bouillon, a slice of lemon, and a dash each of celery salt, A.1 sauce, and Tabasco sauce.

bull cheese. A Western term of the nineteenth cen-

tury for dried strips of buffalo meat. The Spanish words *carne seca* were also used for the same item.

bullshot. An alcoholic drink made with vodka, beef bouillon, and seasonings. The drink originated at the Caucus Club restaurant in Detroit, Michigan, in the early 1960s when then-owner Lester Gruber and a representative of a national soup company created the cocktail together. The name, a play on the expletive "bullshit," derives from the blend of beef bouillon and shot of vodka. A "Danish bowl" cocktail, also invented at the Caucus Club, substitutes aquavit for vodka in the recipe.

BULLSHOT

Mix 1½ oz. vodka with 3 oz. beef bouillon. Add dashes of Worcestershire sauce, A.1 sauce, Tabasco, and angostura bitters. Stir, pour over ice, and garnish with slice of lemon and a sprinkling of celery salt.

bumper to bumper. A New England cooking term for foods set in a pan so that their sides are touching. As cited by food writer Christopher Idone in *The New York Times* (January 5, 1991), "bumper scallops [are] a dish of scallops moistened with a little clarified butter, lightly dusted with paprika and broiled in a pan into which they fit snugly side by side, or bumper to bumper, as Nantucket natives put it."

Bundt cake. Any of a variety of cakes baked in a round, tubular Bundt pan, developed by H. David Dalquist of Nordic Products in Minneapolis, Minnesota, in 1950 upon being asked by members of the local Hadassah to make an aluminum version of the European cast iron kugelhopf pan. The pan (now a registered trademark of Northland Aluminum Products, Inc. of Minnesota) became very popular after it was featured in a pound cake recipe published in the *Good Housekeeping Cookbook* (1960). According to culinary historian Jean Anderson in *The American Century Cookbook* (1997) the Bundt pan became ubiquitous in American kitchens after a "Tunnel of Fudge Cake" recipe was printed from the Pillsbury Bake-Off for 1966, followed by a Bundt Streusel Spice Cake in the same contest for 1972.

buñuelo. A round pastry deep-fried and sprinkled with sugar, very popular in the Southwest. Buñuelos were brought from Mexico, where hot chocolate and buñuelos are part of the Christmas Eve meal.

burbot (*Lota lota*). Also, "maria." A freshwater cod found on both coasts and throughout the Great Lakes. The burbot has a slightly oilier flesh than the saltwater varieties. The name is from Middle English *borbot,* and Old French *bourbeter* "to burrow in mud."

burgoo. A southern stew of various meats and vegetables. Burgoo is often associated with Kentucky and is frequently seen at political rallies in the South. One authority believes the word may derive from a mispronunciation of "barbecue," but the word was known to British sailors at least as early as 1700 as a kind of oatmeal porridge, making some etymologists suspect that it may derive from the Turkish wheat pilaf called *burgbul* (or *bulgur),* meaning "bruised grain."

No one knows how this word might have been applied to an American stew. As of 1700 in print the word referred to a sailor's oatmeal gruel. But an 1853 reference in a book entitled *Western Characters* identifies a "burgou pot" used for an "impromptu barbecue," and by 1885 the *Magazine of American History* cites "burgoo" as a Southern and Southwestern barbecue dish made of hunter's contributions to a "vast stew."

There is a highly suspect story about a Civil War soldier with a speech impediment who cooked up some blackbirds in a five-hundred-gallon copper kettle used for making gunpowder. When he called his fellow soldiers to dinner, the word came out, not "bird stew," but "burgoo." Another story, dating to 1941, contends the dish was first introduced to Kentucky by a Frenchman in the American cavalry during the days of deprivation under Reconstruction, following the Civil War. "Burgoo" also came to be applied to the outdoor social gathering itself by 1889.

Whatever its origins, it was a very popular stew. In 1895 Gus Jaubert cooked up a batch for the Grand Army of the Republic that came to six thousand gallons, and the so-called Kentucky burgoo king, James T. Looney, was used to serving crowds of people numbering up to ten thousand. A recipe for a mere five thousand people was printed in the *Louisville Courier-Journal* not long ago that called for 800 lb. of beef, 200 lb. fowl, 168 gal. tomatoes, 350 lb. cabbage, 6 bu. onions, 85 gal. tomato puree, 24 gal. carrots, 36 gal. corn, 1,800 lb. potatoes, 2 lb. red pepper, ½ lb. black pepper, 20 lb. salt, 8 oz. angostura bitters, I pint Worcestershire sauce, ½ lb. curry powder, 3 qt. tomato ketchup, and 2 qt. sherry.

A somewhat less gargantuan portion printed in the same journal goes as follows:

BURGOO

Place in a large kettle 2 lb. pork shank, 2 lb. veal shank, 2 lb. beef shank, 2 lb. breast of lamb, one 4-lb. hen, and 8 qt. water. Bring slowly to a boil and then simmer until meat falls from bones. Pare and dice 1½ lb. Irish potatoes and 1½ lb. onions. Remove and chop up the meat, discard the bones. Return to stock with potatoes and onions, together with 1 bunch scraped, chopped carrots; 2 seeded, chopped green peppers; 2 c. chopped cabbage; 1 qt. tomato puree, 1 c. whole corn; 1 pod red pepper; 2 c. diced okra; 2 c. lima beans; 1 c. diced celery. Add salt, cayenne pepper, Tabasco, A.1 sauce, Worcestershire sauce to taste. Cook about 10 hr. or until thick but still soupy. Stir frequently. Add chopped parsley.

burrito. A TORTILLA rolled and cooked on a griddle, then filled with a variety of condiments. Burritos are a Mexican-American staple. The word, from Spanish for "little donkey," first saw print in America in 1934. If fried, the burrito becomes a CHIMICHANGA.

busboy. A restaurant worker who helps the waiter by clearing ("busing") and setting a table and by keeping water glasses filled. The term was first in print in 1913. A "busgirl" would be a female helper.

business lunch. A lunch at a restaurant where business is discussed. The term has been in currency at least since the 1950s. A "businessman's lunch" is a restaurant term for a fixed-price lunch designed to attract businessmen, especially those on a short lunch hour. See also POWER LUNCH.

butter. An emulsion of fat made from churned milk, usually whitish yellow to yellow in color and used as a cooking fat or as a spread on bread and other preparations. The word is from the Greek *bouturon,* for cow's cheese, becoming, in Middle English, *buter.*

Butter has been widely used for centuries as a cooking fat, at first by herdsmen, and it is mentioned several times in the Bible. It was not until the Middle Ages, however, that Europeans began to use butter extensively, but because of its tendency to turn rancid quickly, it was not a preferred food until well into the eighteenth century. Even today other oils are preferred for cooking in warm Mediterranean countries.

There is no evidence that Native Americans made butter, but the early European settlers made their own with whirling wooden blades inside a butter churn. The surplus was sold to neighbors and local stores, for there was no commercial creamery in the United States until the mid-nineteenth century; possibly the first was opened in 1856 in Orange County, New York, by R. S. Woodhull. Today very little butter is made at home, and, in fact, Americans now buy far more butter substitutes, such as MARGARINE, than real butter. In 1997 U.S. per capita consumption of butter was 4.2 pounds, and total U.S. production of butter was 1.5 billion pounds.

All American butter is made from cow's milk and is pasteurized, that is, heated to 163 degrees for thirty minutes or to 182 degrees for ten minutes (called "high temperature short-time pasteurization"). It is then cooked and churned. FDA gradings of AA, A, B, and C are then assigned.

Only after 1900 was creamery butter widely available, first made into quarter-pound bars by a cooperative of creameries (later called Land O'Lakes) in Meeker County, Minnesota, in 1922. New processes in the 1930s that allowed continuous production boosted sales.

Today the United States and the Soviet Union are the world's leading producers. The leading butter-producing states are Minnesota, Wisconsin, and Iowa, with the butter industry as a whole using up 20 percent of all milk produced.

"Sweet butter," or "unsalted butter," contains no salt. "Sweet cream butter" has some salt added. "Whipped butter" is combined with air to give a more spreadable texture when cold. "Clarified butter" is made in the kitchen by melting butter and letting the casein and other nonfat ingredients drop out, thereby creating a clear liquid with a higher burning point but less flavor.

"Buttermilk" is the liquid left after butter granules have reached the breaking point on the milk's surface during the production process (see also MILK).

butterfish (*Peprilus triacantbus*). A fatty fish ranging from Nova Scotia to Cape Hatteras that grows up to twelve inches and one-and-a-half pounds. Butterfish are usually found fresh in summer in New York and Boston markets. The name dates back at least to 1674 and is often applied to various other fish, such as the POMPANO.

buttermilk pie. A pie made from buttermilk, eggs, sugar, and vanilla, it is particularly popular in the South. For a description of buttermilk, see BUTTER and MILK.

BUTTERMILK PIE

Beat together 4 eggs and 1½ c. sugar until well blended, then mix in 1 T. flour, ¾ c. buttermilk, ½ t. vanilla, a dash of salt, and ½ c. melted, cooled butter. Mix until a smooth batter is formed. Pour into pie shell and bake in a 300° oven until set. Serve warm.

butternut. Also, "white walnut" and "oil nut." A native tree of eastern America in the walnut family (1741).

butterscotch. A confection made from butter, brown sugar, and lemon juice. The association with Scotland has never been satisfactorily explained. Butterscotch sauce, or butterscotch topping, is an American dessert sauce with the flavor of butterscotch candy and is served over ice cream (for a "butterscotch sundae"), on POUND CAKE, and on other sweets. The word was first printed in 1855, earlier as "butterscot."

BUTTERSCOTCH

Combine ½ c. butter with 1 lb. brown sugar, heat to 290° (use a candy thermometer), and flavor with 1 T. lemon juice. Beat to make creamy in texture, then pour out on a marble slab and let cool.

BUTTERSCOTCH SAUCE

In a double boiler combine 2 c. brown sugar, ½ c. butter, ¼ pt. heavy cream, and 1 T. lemon juice. Cook for about 1 hr., stirring to thicken.

buttery. A larder or pantry where provisions are stored, dating in print to 1654.

buyback. Bartenders' term for a complimentary drink given a customer who has already paid for three or four others.

BX. Also, "Body Shop." Abbreviation for "body exchange," a slang term from the 1960s to describe a bar where people go primarily to meet partners of the opposite sex.

BYOB. Slang abbreviation for "Bring your own booze," meaning a guest should bring his own liquor or beer to a party. As "BYOL" ("bring your own liquor") the phrase dates in print to 1928.

cabbage (*Brassica oleracea capitata*). A plant whose large head of tightly wrapped leaves is eaten in a variety of ways—boiled, stuffed, or raw, as in COLESLAW. The word is from Vulgar Latin *bottia,* "bump," which in Middle English became *caboche.*

The term cabbage includes BROCCOLI, BRUSSELS SPROUTS, CAULIFLOWER, KALE, and collard greens, but it usually refers more specifically to the white and red cabbages, as well as the purple and green varieties, with their characteristic large heads and firmly packed leaves.

The "savoy cabbage" (not related to SALAD SAVOY), mostly grown in Europe, is considered among the finest, while "Chinese cabbage" (*B. pekinensis),* also called "celery cabbage" and "petsai," is an Oriental cabbage of a different species.

Cabbages were brought to the New World by the European settlers, and the plant grew well in temperate climates, particularly in the Middle Atlantic colonies. German immigrants especially valued the cabbage, which was a major vegetable in their diet, and the Dutch made coleslaw from it. After the Civil War, with the proliferation of railroads, cabbage became widely available to all Americans, and it remains a very popular garden plant.

Cabernet Sauvignon. A variety of vinifera grape that makes a rich, tannic red wine with a distinctive varietal character. The word was first printed in 1941. Cabernet Sauvignon (also called just "Cabernet" or "Cab," for short, though distinguished from another varietal called "Cabernet Franc") is the predominant grape in the wines of Bordeaux and has, since the 1960s, become one of the premium varietals of California, where many examples may contain 100 percent Cabernet Sauvignon. In 1989 wine writer James Laube assessed more than twelve hundred examples from nearly one hundred wineries in his book *California's Great Cabernets,* and as of 1991 about 5 percent of the total tonnage of wine grapes grown in California were Cabernet. Out of thirty-two thousand acres planted with grapes in the Napa Valley (consid-ered the prime area for growing good Cabernet) about eight thousand acres are Cabernet Sauvignon. Cabernet also flourishes in the Northwest, and some wine from this varietal is also made in Ohio, Texas, New Jersey, New York, Arkansas, and Virginia.

cabinet. A Rhode Island name for a soda-fountain confection of milk, syrup, and ice cream blended in a mixer. The *Dictionary of American Regional English* cites 1957 as the first evidence in print, and another from 1968 by a resident of Fall River, Massachusetts, named Dorothy Cahill that the drink's name was originated by a pharmacist in that town who kept the ice cream in a cabinet at the soda fountain. Elsewhere such a drink is called a MILK SHAKE.

cab joint. Also, "steer joint." An illicit bar and bordello of New York City's Prohibition era. As described by Charles G. Shaw in *Nightlife: Vanity Fair's Guide to New York After Dark* (1931), " 'Cab' or 'steer' joints operate as 'clubs' and depend largely on taxi-drivers to corral their victims. The formula, nine times out of ten, is identical. 'Like to meet some pretty girls?' asks the affable cabbie. 'I'll show you a place with real hot mammas, good booze, and all you want.' A knowing wink, a sidelong leer, and fate arranges the rest. Either the joy-hunter falls for the bait (and enters) or wisely turns elsewhere." See SPEAKEASY.

cactus. Any of a variety of plants in the family *Cactaceae* whose branches have either spines or scales (1767). Cactuses grow mainly in desert areas, where the branches are sometimes used in cooking, especially in the Southwest, where the edible parts are called NOPALS.

Caesar salad. A salad of romaine lettuce, garlic, olive oil, croutons, Parmesan cheese, Worcestershire sauce, and, often, anchovies. It was created by Caesar Cardini, an Italian immigrant who opened a series of restaurants in Tijuana, Mexico, just across the border from San Diego. On Fourth of July weekend in 1924 at Caesar's Palace, Cardini concocted the salad as a main course, arranging the lettuce leaves on a plate with the intention that they would be eaten with the fingers. Later Cardini shredded the leaves into bite-sized pieces. The salad became particularly popular with Hollywood movie people who visited Tijuana, and it became a featured dish at Chasen's and Romanoff's in Los Angeles. Cardini was adamant in insisting that the salad be subtly flavored and argued against the inclusion of anchovies, whose faint flavor in his creation he believed may have come from the Worcestershire sauce. He also decreed that only Italian olive oil and imported Parmesan cheese be used. In 1948 he established a patent on the dressing, which is still packaged and sold as "Cardini's Original Caesar dressing mix," distributed by Caesar Cardini Foods, Culver City, California. Cardini himself died in 1956, and the business is now carried on by his daughter, Rosa Cardini.

The Caesar salad was once voted by the International Society of Epicures in Paris as the "greatest recipe to originate from the Americas in fifty years."

The following recipe is the original and does not include anchovies.

CAESAR SALAD

Cut up white bread into ½-in. pieces to make about 2 c. Mash 2 cloves garlic in some olive oil. Dry out the croutons in the oven, basting them with the garlic and oil. Strip the leaves from 2 medium heads of romaine lettuce to provide 6 to 8 leaves per person. Wash gently, shake dry, and refrigerate in a plastic bag until ready to serve. Puree 2 cloves mashed garlic with ¼ t. salt and 3 T. olive oil, strain, and place in frying pan. Add croutons, heat briefly, and toss, then turn into serving bowl. Boil 2 eggs exactly 1 min. Grate ¼ c. Parmesan cheese. In a very large bowl pour 4 T. olive oil over the lettuce leaves and scoop in large motions to coat. Sprinkle lettuce with ¼ t. salt, 8 grinds of fresh black pepper, and 2 more t. oil, toss again, add juice of 1 lemon, 6 drops Worcestershire sauce, and break in eggs. Toss and add cheese. Toss and top with croutons. Serve on a chilled plate.

café. A coffeehouse or other inexpensive, usually small, restaurant. The term, first in English print in 1802, is from the French for coffee.

café au lait. Creole term for hot, strong coffee served with an equal amount of hot milk. The term (first in print in English in 1763) comes from the French, "coffee with milk," and was first advocated in the late seventeenth century by Dr. Monin of Grenoble, France, as a healthful alternative to powdered coffees that were often adulterated with other substances like toasted bread, fava beans, and peas.

café brûlot. A dark coffee mixed with the flavors of citrus rind and brandy. The name of this traditional New Orleans coffee is a compound of the French *café*, coffee, and *brûlot*, "burnt brandy." Although it is not mentioned in *The Picayune's Creole Cook Book* (1901), it is apparently an old recipe, since flame-proof "brûlot bowls" made especially for the coffee were known before 1900.

CAFÉ BRÛLOT

In a fireproof brûlot bowl or saucepan place 2 sticks of cinnamon, 6 cloves, 1½ T. sugar, the rind of 1 lemon, and 3 oz. brandy. Heat to below boiling point, ignite with a match, and mix. Pour strong, hot coffee into bowl, then pour into small coffee cups.

cafeteria. A restaurant at which people move along a line and select the food and drinks they want, then carry them on trays to a table to eat their meals. The word is an American rendering of a Spanish word for coffee shop, a meaning it had in print as of 1839.

The first self-service restaurant was the Exchange Buffet in New York City, opened September 4, 1885, which catered to an exclusively male clientele. Food was purchased at a counter, and patrons ate standing up. The word "cafeteria" was first used by John Kruger, who ran a self-service eatery at the 1893 World's Columbian Exposition in Chicago, although he also nicknamed them "conscience joints" because customers tallied their own bills.

The Childs brothers of New York City introduced the tray about 1898, and New Yorkers called such establishments "grab joints." In 1900 in New York Bernarr Adolphus Macfadden opened the first "penny restaurant," where every item cost a penny. The AUTOMAT, in which people chose their food from a wall of boxes covered with glass doors, was begun in Philadelphia in 1902 by Joseph Horn and Frank Hardart.

The first cafeteria in the West was opened in 1905 by Helen Mosher in Los Angeles, and easterners called such western examples "California-style restaurants." The first cafeteria in the South—where the industry proliferated most and thrives today—was in 1918 at Britling's Department Store in Birmingham,

Alabama. Many current cafeteria chains also came out of the South—S&W Cafeteria in Ashville, North Carolina, the Morrison chain in Mobile, Alabama, the Piccadilly chain in Baton Rouge, Louisiana, Furr's in Lubbock, Texas, Wyatt's in Dallas, and Luby's in San Antonio.

Cafeterias are the most common form of eating room at American schools, so that "cafeteria" has become synonymous with such dining halls.

The suffix "-eria" has led to all manner of words meaning a kind of shop—"pizzeria," "chocolateria," "fruiteria," "meateria," "caviarteria," and others.

Cajun. A descendant of the French Acadians who settled in Louisiana after the British deported them from Acadia in Nova Scotia and the Maritime Provinces of Canada in 1755 for refusing to pledge allegiance to England. In Louisiana these people were soon called " 'Cadians," and, by 1842, "Cagians." The spelling "Cajuns" first saw print in 1927.

Cajun cuisine, with its French, Spanish, African, and Indian influences, is distinctive, but Louisiana authorities and gastronomes have argued for decades about just what is and is not Cajun cookery. Few would refuse to list the following dishes in the Cajun canon: JAMBALAYA, ÉTOUFÉE COUSH-COUSH, BOUDIN, ANDOUILLES, CHAUDIN, GUMBO and all manner of crab dishes and dishes requiring heavy doses of HOT SAUCE.

Cajun festivals often revolve around food, including the Breaux Bridge Crawfish Festival, a yam festival, and "boucheries" (large-scale butchering parties), where Cajuns consume prodigious amounts of food and drink and everyone works hard to live by the Cajun motto, *"Laissez le bon temps rouler"*—"Let the good times roll." In *American Cooking: Creole and Acadian* (1971), Peter S. Feibleman wrestled with the problem of defining Cajun cookery and finally realized there was no final word on the matter:

What, then, is the difference between the terms Creole and Acadian as applied to food? Most authorities will start with a simple answer: they will tell you that it is the difference between city French cooking and country French cooking. But then the reservations and qualifications begin. Both Creole and Acadian cooking are Louisiana French in style, of course—which (authorities will add) isn't French at all. Is that clear? No? Well, Acadian cooking is a little spicier than Creole—sometimes, not always. Acadians like a lot of rice—well, of course, the Creoles like a lot of rice, too. Acadian cooks are likely to put all the ingredients for a course into one big pot, while Creoles like these in-

gredients separate. Yes, that's true—at least, most Creoles like them separate. "Look [the authorities will finally say], maybe you'd better just taste it. . . ."

Louisiana cooking authority Tom Fitzmorris, in *The New Orleans Eat Book* (1991), noted, "Unalloyed Cajun food is almost never found in restaurants, not even in Cajun country. I suspect the reason for this is that Cajun cooking, for all its glorious flavor, looks ugly (unless, of course, you grew up with it). Much of it is pot food from very big pots. Getting the polished look restaurant patrons require screws up the flavor." And, as Louisiana culinary authority JoAnn Clevenger has said, "Cajun food can only be corrupted, but Creole food must evolve."

Interest in a particular form of Cajun food was fueled by Cajun chef Paul Prudhomme, who began serving his own highly seasoned version of his family's recipes at his New Orleans restaurant, K-Paul's Louisiana Kitchen, which opened in 1979 and where he popularized nontraditional dishes like BLACKENED REDFISH and "Cajun popcorn" (fried CRAYFISH tails).

cake. A baked confection usually containing flour, butter, eggs, and sweetener, although some cakes do not contain flour. The word derives from Old Norse *kaka*, which in Middle English became *cake*.

Until the last quarter of the nineteenth century cakes were usually baked in pans shaped to resemble bread loaves and were often studded with fruit. With the availability of the more modern bake ovens after 1870, it became possible to make much lighter cakes with the new baking sodas and powders. The "layer cake," composed of two or more layers of cake between various fillings, started to become popular by the 1870s, especially as celebratory wedding and birthday cakes. After the turn of the century layer cakes were among the favorite of American confections, especially after The General Foods Company and the Pillsbury Company brought out boxed cake mixes between 1947 and 1948, so that by the end of the 1950s more than half the cakes Americans baked were from such mixes. The "ice cream cake" was a layer cake or cake roll filled with ice cream.

"Cake flour" is regular white soft-wheat flour often containing a proportion of baking powder and salt.

A "cake social" is a social gathering at which cake is either served or sold to raise money for a charitable purpose. A "cakewalk" (dating in print to 1879) is a term used mainly by African-Americans to describe a social entertainment wherein the participants dance or strut fancifully in order to win the prize of a cake.

cala. A New Orleans Sunday-morning breakfast confection made of rice that is mixed with flour, spices, and sugar, and then deep-fried. Sometimes it is made with ground black-eyed peas. The word, first printed in 1880, derives from one or more African languages such as Nupe *kàrà*, "fried cake."

Calas (the term is used almost exclusively in the plural) were sold by African-American street vendors in the city's French Quarter, and one would hear the cry, "*Belles calas tout chauds!*"

"Cala" is also a term for a shoulder cut of HAM, usually referred to as "shoulder bacon," "picnic ham," or "California ham."

CALAS

Mix 3 cups cooked rice, 3 beaten eggs, ¼ t. vanilla, ¼ t. nutmeg, ¼ t. cinnamon, and ¼ t. lemon rind. Sift ½ c. flour with ½ c. sugar, 3½ t. baking powder, and ½ t. salt. Stir into rice. Drop by spoon into deep, hot fat and fry for about 2 min. Sprinkle with confectioners' sugar. Makes about 2 dozen.

---

callabasate. A candied pumpkin, usually made at home. In print the word (from the Spanish *calabazate*) dates to 1967.

calabash. Also, "calipash," "capapash," and other forms. This word refers to two plants, one an Old World vine, *Lagenaria siceraria*, the other a tropical American tree, *Crescentia cujete*, also called the "bottle gourd" for its large, round shape, dating in print to 1590. The word is from the Spanish *calabaza*, "gourd."

In South Carolina "calabash" is also the name for a dish of turtle cooked in its shell, now served rarely.

In North Carolina "calabash style" refers to fish that is breaded or coated with a batter and fried, the name deriving from the seacoast town of Calabash, where many restaurants specialize in this style of cooking.

calcium (or sodium) propionate. A preservative used to prevent the growth of mold in bread products.

calcium (or sodium) stearyl lactylate. An additive mixed with dough to strengthen its texture. It is also used in artificial whipped cream, cake fillings, and processed egg whites.

calibougas. Also, "calibogus" and other spellings. A beverage of rum, spruce beer, and molasses known

since the middle of the eighteenth century, but a word of unknown origins.

California roll. Also, "carifonia roll." A form of sushi made with avocados, crabmeat, cucumbers, and other ingredients wrapped in vinegared rice. It was supposedly created at a Japanese restaurant in Los Angeles named Tokyo Kaikan about 1973 for the American palate but has also gained popularity in Japan, where it is called *kashu-maki*, a literal translation of "California roll."

call liquor. Bartenders' term for a brand-name liquor specified by a customer.

calzone. An Italian-American pastry made from PIZZA dough that is stuffed with a variety of fillings like cheese, sausage, or ground meat and folded into a half-moon shape that resembles trousers, which in Italian is *calzoni*. The word entered English print in the 1950s. "Calzone" is also applied to a sweet sugar cookie of Mexican origins.

cambric tea. Also called "hot-water tea," and "kelly tea," cambric tea is merely hot water, milk, sugar, and perhaps a dash of tea, given to children to make them feel part of a social gathering. The term comes from cambric fabric, which is white and thin, like cambric tea; it is American slang, used at least since 1888.

camper. Bartender slang for a customer who "camps out" in a bar for the entire evening, as cited in *Newsweek* magazine (July 22, 1991).

canaigre (*Rumex hymenosepalus*). Also, "wild rhubarb," "pie dock," "wild pie-plant," and "tanner's dock." Canaigre is a species of buckwheat found from Wyoming to Utah, Western Texas, New Mexico, Arizona, and California (1879). It has long green leaves and a reddish stem. The Indians of the Southwest, including the Maricopa, Pima, Navaho, and Hopi, prepared it in various ways, and the plant was used for soothing sore throats and for tanning leather. The Maricopa used the seeds in a flat bread; the Navaho blended them into a mush.

canapé. A slice of thin toast or cracker spread with any of a variety of meats, vegetables, cheeses, or fish, usually served on trays before the first course. The word is from the French for "couch."

According to the *World Famous Chefs' Cook Book* (1941), compiled by Ford Naylor, "It is correct to offer [canapés] to guests in the living room, just before dinner; or as a first course at luncheon or dinner; or at receptions and teas. When canapés or tidbits are served with relishes, the combination is known as an hors d'oeuvre."

The term first appears in English print in 1895 as a reference to a tidbit served with anchovies, still a popular canapé. Other canapés might include hard-boiled, minced eggs, sliced olives with pimiento, cheese puffs, ham, liver, or fish pâté, smoked salmon, pickles, small frankfurters wrapped in pastry (called "pigs-in-a-blanket"), and oysters wrapped in bacon (an English canapé known as "angels on horseback"). "Devils on horseback" are an American canapé made with chicken livers wrapped in bacon.

"Canapés" are often synonymous in America with hors d'oeuvres.

candy. Any of a wide variety of sweet morsels, bars, lozenges, figures, or other confections eaten on their own, as a snack or treat beyond the usual mealtime foods. Candy may take the form of fluffy marshmallow, chocolate-covered nuts, citrus rinds, spun sugar, bars with cream centers, tiny hard drops, gums, and many other shapes and types. Many are based on crystallized sugar, whose once-high price made such sweet confections a delicacy indulged only by the wealthy.

The ancient Egyptians preserved nuts and fruits with honey, and by the Middle Ages physicians had learned how to mask the bad taste of their medicines with sweetness, a practice still widespread. Boiled "sugar plums" were known in seventeenth-century England and soon were to appear in the American colonies where maple-syrup candy was popular in the North and benne-seed confections were just as tempting in the South. In New Amsterdam one could enjoy "marchpane," or "marzipan," which is very old decorative candy made from almonds ground into a sweet paste.

While the British called such confections, "sweet-meats," Americans came to call "candy," from the Arabic *gandi*, "made of sugar," although one finds "candy" in English as early as the fifteenth century. Originally Americans used the word to mean a "toffee" (a hard candy made from sugar and butter), but by the nineteenth century "candy" was a general term for all kinds of sweet confections.

CARAMELS were known in the early eighteenth century, and LOLLIPOPS by the 1780s, as were PRALINES— named after French diplomat César du Plessis-Praslin, later duc de Choiseul—a candy that became particularly well known in Louisiana.

"Hard candies" made from lemon or peppermint flavors were popular in the early nineteenth century, and Eliza Leslie, in her *Directions for Cookery* (1837), speaks of chocolate-covered nuts and "bonbons" (from the French, for "good-good") wrapped in papers on which were printed lines of verse. "Peppermint sticks" were enjoyed by midcentury, as was HOARHOUND CANDY and other lozenges used as sore-throat remedies. Soft, chewy TAFFY was made at taffy pulls during this period, and people also delighted in peanut brittle and a candy so hard it was called a "jawbreaker." "Vinegar candy" was boosted by being continuously mentioned throughout the popular series of *Dotty Dimple Stories* of 1867–1869 by Rebecca Sophia Clarke, whose pen name was Sophie May. By the 1860s there were "gumdrops."

A significant moment in candy history occurred at the 1851 Great Exhibition in London, where "French-style" candies with rich cream centers were first displayed. These caught on immediately in America, and within a few years there were more than 380 candy factories in the United States, many turning out candy that cost one cent (called "penny candy"), a price that extended well into the twentieth century. Most of these candies were sold in batches or by the pound and displayed behind glass cases. Hard, clear candies, traditional at Christmas, were made at home in patterned molds, most of which were made by Thomas Mills and Brothers, a Philadelphia company established in 1864.

Flavored gums from tree resins had been known throughout the nineteenth century, but chewing gum did not come along until the 1870s. Bubble gum appeared by the end of the century. FUDGE originated at women's colleges in the late nineteenth century, sourballs appeared by the turn of the last decade, and "Cracker Jack" was the hit of Chicago's Columbian Exposition of 1893. "Jelly beans" came along in 1905.

But it was the discovery of milk chocolate in Switzerland in 1875 that made the American CANDY BAR such a phenomenon of the late nineteenth century. The first such chocolate bar was produced in 1894 by Milton Snavely Hershey, and there soon followed an endless array of candy products containing peanuts, cream centers, fruit fillings, nougat, coconut, and many other sweet fillers with names like "Milky Way," "Snickers," "3 Musketeers," "Mary Jane," "Goo Goo Cluster," and hundreds of others.

In 1912 Americans began buying "Life Savers," made by Clarence A. Crane of Cleveland, Ohio. These were round white peppermints with distinctive holes in the middle (thus, their resemblance to a life preserver on a boat); later five more flavors were added. Crane sold his formula for $2,900 to New Yorkers Ed Noble and Roy Allen, who solved a problem of keeping the Life Savers fresh by "shrink-wrapping" them in aluminum foil—a first in the industry.

Nineteen twelve was also the year "NECCO Wafers" (an acronym for the New England Confectionary Company, which opened in 1847) appeared. These were previously called "Peerless Wafers" and had been carried to the Arctic and South Pole by Donald MacMillian and Richard Byrd (Byrd allegedly brought two and a half tons of them with him). In 1920 the newest candy on the market was JU-JUBES, tiny morsels of colored candy, and "Juicyfruits," shaped into fruit forms.

Americans went to the "candy shop" specifically to buy various kinds of candies, usually sold by the pound or produced in bars by the shop itself. "Candy stores" were small shops selling mostly commercially produced, packaged candies, as well as everything from newspapers and magazines to ice cream sodas and cigars, and, in fact, were more or less synonymous with "soda fountains" and "cigar stores" by the twentieth century. At such stores a child could purchase penny candy, which sometimes was merely icing in a little tin plate, or malted-milk balls, or strings of licorice, or sweet liquids inside small wax bottles. One favorite was hard pellets of candy stuck to long strips of paper.

COTTON CANDY, made by spinning colored sugar in a centrifuge, causing it to puff into cottonlike strands, came along in 1900 and was usually sold at carnivals, circuses, and state fairs, rarely at candy stores.

Today Americans consume about 24.9 pounds of candy per person each year, not including chewing gum, for an industry sale of $22.7 billion. The American candy industry turns out more than two thousand different items.

candy apple. Also, "candied apple." A confection made by immersing an apple in a red sugar syrup that forms a hard, candylike crust on the fruit. Candy apples are usually eaten on a stick and are a specialty of carnivals and county fairs.

candy bar. A bar of candy, usually coated with or containing chocolate, that may include nuts, jellies, peanut butter, fruit, nougat, caramel, coconut, cookie wafers, and other-fillings.

The first candy bars were made by François Louis Cailler in Switzerland in 1819, and by 1842 Birmingham's Cadbury Limited offered eating choco-

late for sale through its catalog. But the candy bar as we know it was the idea of Milton Snavely Hershey, who manufactured the first American chocolate bars, the Hershey Almond Bar and the Hershey Milk Chocolate Bar, in 1894 after seeing some German chocolate-making machines at the 1893 World's Columbian Exposition in Chicago. Hershey had before then made caramels at his Lancaster (Pennsylvania) Caramel Plant, which he sold in 1900. After a trip to Europe Hershey built a plant in Derry Church, Pennsylvania, and opened the Hershey Company in 1904.

Before long the Bunte Brothers were making chocolate-coated bars, and by 1912 Howard H. Cambell of the Standard Candy Company of Nashville, Tennessee, produced the first combination bar, called the "Goo Goo Cluster" (supposedly named after the sounds made by his infant son), which contained caramel, marshmallow, peanuts, and milk chocolate. The Goo Goo has long been advertised as "the South's Favorite Candy."

After World War I the candy-bar craze swept the country, giving impetus to dozens of candy manufacturers, including the Curtiss Candy Company, the Fox-Cross Candy Company, Peter Paul Candies, the Clark Company, Mars Candies, the Charles N. Miller Company, and many others. During the war candy bars were given to servicemen for nourishment, to provide quick energy, and to build morale.

The first candy bars sold for ten cents, which at the time was too much for a public not hooked on such confections, especially when a pound of loose candy cost the same price. After World War I a drop in the prices of sugar and chocolate helped lower the price of candy bars to five cents, and a nickel was the prevailing price of most candy bars until the 1960s. By 1968 the average candy bar cost ten cents again, and by 1980 thirty-five cents was the usual tab for a bar that changed shape, size, and weight through competition and as the result of failing or rising sugar prices.

Although there have been a few attempts to make "health bars," containing honey instead of sugar, carob instead of chocolate, and vitamins instead of caramel, the American candy bar remains a persistent reminder of the American sweet tooth. Americans today consume about 20.8 pounds of candy per person annually, with chocolate being the most popular type by far (3.1 billion pounds). Some of the most famous and popular candy bars over the years include:

Baby Ruth (1920). A chocolate-covered bar with a caramel-and-peanut center (originally called "Kandy Kake" produced by the Curtiss Candy Company of Chicago. The item was not named after New York Yankees baseball player George Herman "Babe" Ruth (1895–1948), but instead honored the daughter of former president Grover Cleveland, whose name was Ruth and who as a child had won the hearts of the nation.

Bit-o-Honey (1924). A bar made of almond bits and honey-flavored taffy, produced by the Schutter-Johnson Company of Chicago, now produced by the Chunky Corporation of New York City.

Charleston Chew (1922). A chocolate-covered bar with a vanilla-nougat center, manufactured by the Fox-Cross Candy Company of Emeryville, California. The current producer is Nabisco Confections, Inc.

Chuckles (1921). A jellied candy coated with sugar crystals, created by Fred W. Amend of Chicago and now produced by Nabisco Confections, Inc.

Chunky (mid-1930s). A square chunk of chocolate containing Brazil nuts, cashews, and raisins, created by New York confectioner Philip Silverstein, who named the candy after his "chunky" little daughter. It is now manufactured by the Ward-Johnston Division of the Terson Company.

Clark (1917). Usually referred to as the "Clark bar," it was made by the D. L. Clark Company and contained roasted peanuts and a milk-chocolate covering. The company is now merged with the M. J. Holloway Company, a division of the Beatrice Foods Company.

5th Avenue (1936). A peanut-butter-and-almond bar covered with milk chocolate, first produced by William H. Luden of Reading, Pennsylvania.

HeatH Bar (1932). Introduced as "HeatH's English Toffee" in 1928 by L. S. Heath, this chocolate-covered toffee bar was considered a premium item because it was smaller than most other candy bars. People often referred to it as the "H and H Bar," because the two H's in the word "HeatH" were capitalized around lowercase letters.

Junior Mints (1949). These small morsels with a creamy mint center covered with chocolate were produced by the James O. Welch Company (now part of Nabisco Confections, Inc.). Welch himself named the candy after seeing a performance of a Broadway play entitled *Junior Miss,* based on *The New Yorker Magazine* short stories by Sally Benson.

Hershey's Kisses (1907). Small chocolate droplets wrapped in foil and with identifying paper plumes. Kisses were made by the Hershey Company, although the Wilbur Chocolate Company of Lititz, Pennsylvania, had been making similar candies called "Wilbur Buds" since 1894.

M & M's Plain Chocolate Candies (1941). Usually called "M & M's," these chocolate morsels coated with variously colored sugar shells were produced by M & M Limited of Newark, New Jersey. In 1954 "M & M's Peanut Chocolate Candies" appeared, and both are known by the slogan "The Milk Chocolate Melts in Your Mouth—Not in Your Hand."

Mary Jane (1914). A molasses-and-peanut butter candy bar made by the Charles M. Milter Company.

Milk Duds (1926). Caramel-and-chocolate morsels, first made by the Holloway Company of Chicago, now by Beatrice Food Company.

Milky Way (1923). Introduced by Frank C. Mars, this bar of chocolate nougat, caramel, and chocolate covering has been one of the most popular of all candy bars.

Mr. Goodbar (1925). A chocolate-and-peanut bar produced by the Hershey Company.

Mounds (1922). A double bar of dark chocolate covering and coconut center, manufactured by Peter Paul Halajia of Naugatuck, Connecticut. In 1948 a similar bar using milk chocolate and almonds became another success for the company, which called the new candy Almond Joy.

Oh Henry! (1921). Made by the Williamson Candy Company of Chicago, this milk chocolate-and-peanut bar was not named after short-story writer William Sydney Porter, whose pen name was O. Henry. According to Ray Broekel in *The Great American Candy Bar Book* (1982):

Mr. Williamson was operating a combination retail and wholesale candy store, and every day about the same time, a young fellow named Henry would come into the store and kid around with the girls who were making candy. Before long, the girls got into the habit of asking Henry to do little odd jobs and favors for them . . . [and] you'd hear, "Oh, Henry, will you get me this?" Or, "Oh, Henry, will you get me that?"

Later in the year, when it came time to find a name for the nut roll that was being manufactured, Mr. Williamson's salesmen said, "All we hear around here is 'Oh, Henry,' so why not call the candy bar Oh Henry!"

Reese's Peanut Butter Cups (1923). Produced by H. B. Reese in Hershey, Pennsylvania, these chocolate-and-peanut-butter candies came in waxed-paper containers. The candy is now made by the Hershey Company.

Sky Bar (1937). A combination bar of chocolate segments containing centers of caramel, vanilla, peanut, or fudge, made by the NECCO Company of Cambridge, Massachusetts.

Snickers (1930). A bar of peanut-butter nougat, peanuts in caramel, and a milk-chocolate coating. Snickers was produced by Frank C. Mars of Chicago and is the largest-selling candy bar in the United States.

3 Musketeers (1932). Originally three bars of chocolate coating on fluffy chocolate nougat, these were named after the 1844 novel by Alexandre Dumas, *The Three Musketeers*, and were created by the Mars Company. Today the item is all one bar.

Tootsie Roll (1896). Leo Hirschfield of New York City named these chocolate, chewy morsels after his daughter, Clara, whose nickname was Tootsie. In the 1930s he came up with Tootsie Roll Pops, which were lollipops filled with the original product's chocolate.

candy stew. Also, "candy boiling." A party where candy is made by everyone. It dates in print to 1837.

cane beer. A kind of beer fermented from the skimmings of boiling sugarcane syrup. It is said to have a sweet-sour taste, and dates in print to 1938.

cane corn. Slang term for corn whiskey made from corn and cane sugar.

canoe race. A campus phrase for drinking beer in relay teams.

cantaloupe (*Cucumis melo reticulatus*). A musk melon, elsewhere called the "netted" or "nutmeg" melon, that is round or oval, weighs about two to four pounds, has orange flesh, and is known for its sweetness. The word is from the name of a papal villa near Rome, Cantalupo, where the fruit was supposedly first grown, but in Europe the cantaloupe is specifically *C. melo cantalupensis*. The melon is first mentioned in print in 1739. It may have been first brought to America by Columbus before March 29, 1494, when the first European melons were planted. The crops are now primarily raised in California, Arizona, and Texas.

Americans often eat cantaloupe for breakfast, sometimes with cottage cheese.

cantina. A saloon in the Southwest; also, "canteen," which has the additional meaning of a metal flask used to carry water. The word "cantina" is from the Italian (for "wine cellar") and the Spanish (for "wine cellar" or "storage room"); by extension it came to mean a place where one could buy a drink of wine or spirits. The word was first printed in 1844.

canvasback duck (*Aythya valisineria*). A wild North American duck found throughout the United States whose name derives from the light color of its neck and back. Thomas Jefferson first mentioned the bird by this name in 1782, and it has long been considered one of the tastiest of all American fowl, its flavor the result of its wild-celery diet. The most preferred canvasbacks came from the Chesapeake Bay, Long Island Sound, and along the Delaware and Susquehanna rivers; for these gastronomes paid a high price and Europeans had the ducks imported. In the Chesapeake Bay region the canvasback almost became extinct after Army Ordnance appropriated some of the fowl's feeding grounds in 1917.

Cape Cod turkey. Also, "Cape Ann turkey." A slang euphemism for baked codfish at least since 1805. The term may have derived from the gratefulness of Cape Codders for nature's bounty of cod, their major industry in the eighteenth and nineteenth centuries. So, perhaps in the spirit of the Thanksgiving turkey, the people called the fish by this name. Others believe it may derive from Boston Catholics' attempt to make more palatable the thought of eating fish every Friday, when no meat was allowed for religious reasons.

CAPE COD TURKEY

Season a 3-lb. cod with salt and pepper, then fill its cavity with 3 c. bread crumbs, 1 chopped onion, 2 T. parsley, ⅓ c. dill pickle, salt, pepper, 3 beaten eggs, and 4 T. melted butter. Close cavity and bake for 45 min. at 350°. Serves 6.

caper (*Capparis Spinosa*). Any of 150 species of shrub bearing a flowered bud pickled for use as a condiment. Capers may have originated in Asia Minor; the word is from the Greek *kápparis*. Capers are grown in the United States in Florida and California.

cappuccino. A dark coffee served with a foamy head of milk or cream. A traditional beverage of Italy, cappuccino is made by forcing steam through milk or cream to form a creamy topping for the coffee, though in America it may be served simply with whipped cream on top. The drink is supposedly named after a Capuchin monk in whose garden coffee was grown in Brazil in 1774. Others say the name derives from the drink's resemblance to the tonsured heads of Capuchin monks. The word is first found in American print in 1948.

carambola (*Averrhoa carambola*). Also "star fruit," five-angled fruit, and "Chinese star fruit." An elongated, lantern-shaped yellow fruit that when cut in slices resembles a star shape. It is sweet, resembling a plum, and is of Asian origins, but the name "carambola" is of Indian origins via the Portuguese, and dates in print to 1598. The carambola is grown in Hawaii, especially the "Arkin" and "Golden Star."

caramel. A confection made from sugar, cream, butter, and flavorings, or merely melted sugar used as a flavoring, topping, or coloring in soups, desserts, and spirits.

The term came into English from the French, via Old Spanish, and, ultimately, the Greek *kalamos*. It first appears in English print in 1725, referring to the melted-sugar variety. The candy caramel was first mentioned in 1884 by the *Philadelphia Times*. To "caramelize" sugar is to heat it to the melting stage, just before it begins to burn. Some recommend the addition of a small bit of water during the cooking of caramel.

carbo-load. A slang term, particularly popular among athletes in the 1980s, to describe eating large portions of foods rich in carbohydrates, such as potatoes, rice, and pasta, before strenuous activity or athletic competition.

caribou (*Rangifer tarandus*). Also, "cariboo," "carraboo," and other spellings. A large wild deer of the arctic and subarctic regions of North America, taxonomically the same as the reindeer but never domesticated. The domesticated reindeer, on the other hand, was introduced into Alaska from Siberia only in the 1890s and became an essential part of the Alaskan Eskimo's way of life.

The caribou has shaggy hair, grows to about eight feet in length and four feet in height at the shoulder, migrates in herds, and is highly prized by hunters. The name comes from French Canadian, in turn from Micmac *khalibu* or other Native American words meaning "pawing the snow," and has been traced to 1610. By 1972 it had other Indian names, such as *maccarib* and *Pohano*.

Usually caribou meat would be marinated and stewed. *Nipku* is a Canadian Eskimo trail food made by partially thawing chunks of the meat, slicing them very thin, and drying the slices on bushes.

carob. A chocolate substitute made from the pods of the carob tree (*Ceratonia siliqua*). The word is derived from Middle French *carobe,* and dates in English print to 1548.

carp (*Cyprinus carpio*). A warm-water fish native to Asia and introduced to the United States from Germany in 1876, by the United States Fish Commission. The fish proliferated so fast that 260,000 carp were distributed throughout 298 congressional districts in an effort to make fishermen out of the constituencies. It propagated so successfully that it invaded the habitats of trout and other fish, and efforts were made to eradicate the oversupply of carp. Despite its widespread distribution in muddy waters throughout the United States, the carp has never been favored by Americans as an eating fish, although it has been a principal ingredient used by Jewish Americans to make GEFILTE FISH.

The name of the fish is of unknown origins and is first mentioned in English in 1440.

carpetbag steak. A grilled steak of beef into which is cut a pocket enclosing a stuffing of oysters. The name derives from a handbag for travelers that was popular from about 1840 to 1870. The dish resembles the sacklike bag with its top closure. There does not seem to be any specific association with an American slang term, "carpetbagger," for a hated post-Civil War opportunist who took advantage of both white and black southerners politically and economically. In fact, the carpetbag steak is much more popular in Australia and is only mentioned for the first time in American print in 1941 in Louis Diat's *Cooking à la Ritz*. Although there is no proof the dish originated at Chasen's restaurant in Los Angeles, which opened in 1936, it did become one of the restaurant's signature dishes.

carrageenan. A thickening and stabilizing agent obtained from Irish moss seaweed, often added to ice cream, chocolate milk, and infant formula (1889).

carrot (*Daucus carota*). A long orange root vegetable having fine leaves called "carrot tops." The carrot originated in the Middle East but is now propagated worldwide. The word is from the Greek *karōton,* and first appears in English print in 1533.

The carrot was not much appreciated in Europe until the sixteenth century, but the roots were brought to America by the early English settlers, and, with improved types developed in France around 1830, the vegetable took on commercial interest. Today carrots are grown in half the states in the Union, especially in Texas, California, Michigan, and Wisconsin.

Americans nibble on carrots raw, often cut into "carrot sticks" served as appetizers at parties. They are also boiled and buttered, sometimes made into puddings, and often baked into a cake, especially popular since the 1960s, topped with a cream cheese frosting.

casaba. A variety of winter melon (*Cucumis melo*) with a yellow skin and sweet white flesh (1885). The name comes from the Turkish town of Kasaba (now Turgutlu). The melon may have been brought to California by Turkish or Armenian immigrants, although, notes Waverley Root in *Food* (1980), "The first officially recorded import . . . seems to have been the Netted Gem variety, imported from France in 1881. This started commercial melon cultivation in the United States, though not until 1895 did they develop reliable quality in this country, starting in Colorado."

The "Crenshaw" (also, "Cranshaw") melon is similar to the casaba.

cassabanana (*Sicana odorifera*). An orange-crimson colored squashlike fruit with a pronounced aromatic flavor. The term dates to 1911 in print. The cassabanana is grown to some extent in the Gulf and is often cooked like a sweet potato.

casserole. A dish or pot made from a material such as glass, cast iron, aluminum, or earthenware in which food is baked and, often, served. The word, which may also refer to the food itself, as, for example, a "tuna casserole," is from the French and was first printed in English in 1708.

Cooking in such dishes has always been part of most nations' gastronomy, but the idea of casserole cooking as a "one-dish meal" became popular in America in the twentieth century, especially in the 1950s when new forms of lightweight metal and glassware appeared on the market. The virtues of easy-to-prepare meals were increasingly promoted in the women's magazines of the era, thereby supposedly freeing the housewife from the lengthy drudgery of the kitchen. Casserole cooking also coincided with the popularity during this same era of buffets, brunches, patio parties, and other casual social meals at which guests could help themselves from a common dish. By the 1970s "casserole cookery" took on a less-than-sophisticated image, even though many such dishes were still served at formal dinners and casual meals without characterizing them by the name.

TUNA-NOODLE CASSEROLE

Combine 2½ c. canned tomatoes, 1 chopped onion, 1 minced clove garlic, salt and pepper, and ¼ c. chopped parsley. In a buttered baking dish place 2 oz. cooked noodles, half of the tomato mixture, ½ c. chunk-style tuna, and ¼ lb. Cheddar cheese slices. Add another 2 oz. cooked noodles, the rest of the tomato mixture, ½ c. tuna, and ¼ lb. Cheddar cheese slices. Bake, uncovered, for 40 min. at 350°.

Catawba. An American labrusca grape originally found growing along the banks of the Catawba River in North Carolina in 1823 and popularized by John Adlum of Washington, D.C. It became a popular wine grape of Ohio in 1842, when Nicholas Longworth made the first American CHAMPAGNE from it. Catawba is still widely used in the East to make sweet red, white, and rosé wines, often blended with the DELAWARE grape.

cat beer. Army slang for milk (1941).

catfish (Family Ictaluridae). Any of a wide range of spiny, scaleless fish with eight barbels (or "whiskers") on the snout, jaw, and chin. Catfish have bristlelike teeth, and some species contain a poison gland at the base of the pectoral spines. There are two thousand species of catfish, whose name, derived from its whiskered appearance, was first mentioned in print in 1612.

North America has twenty-eight species of catfish, about a dozen of which are eaten and three of which make up the most important edible species: the "channel catfish" (*Ictalurus punctatus*), also called the "black warrior," "blue catfish," "canal boater," and many other names; the "white catfish" (*I. catus*); and the "blue catfish" (*I. furcatus*), also called the "Mississippi catfish." Smaller catfish, called "mad toms" (genus *Noturus*), are used mainly for bait.

Catfish are greatly enjoyed in the South, where they are usually dredged in cornmeal and fried. These are usually served with hush puppies and coleslaw on the side. "Catfish Friday" is a common term in the South for Good Friday, when tradition dictates that Christians consume fish. A "catfish row" is a slang term for a neighborhood where African-Americans live, so called because of their supposed affinity for catfish.

In the southern states catfish are produced on fish farms (90 percent in Mississippi) and sold fresh or frozen. U.S. commercial landings of catfish (and bullheads) totaled 15.2 million pounds in 1997.

cauliflower (*Brassica oleracea botrytis*). A plant with a large head of crowded white flowers, related to the CABBAGE and BROCCOLI. The word is probably from the Italian *cavolfiore*, "flowered cabbage," and is first recorded in English in 1597. Cauliflower originated in Asia Minor and did not reach America until the seventeenth century, when it was first grown on Long Island, New York, where it has been cultivated ever since. The most popular United States variety is the "snowball."

caviar. Specifically, the eggs or roe of the STURGEON, but generally referring to the eggs of other fish as well, such as tuna, lumpfish, and salmon (1560). The word "caviar" originates in the Turkish *havyār*, and for most of man's history the eggs of the sturgeon were consumed as a matter of course throughout the Middle East and Eastern Europe.

It was hardly considered a delicacy in nineteenth-century America, when caviar was given away in saloons as part of the FREE LUNCH designed to build a thirst for beer. At the end of the nineteenth century America was the largest supplier of caviar in the world. American caviar was obtained from "Atlantic sturgeon" (or "sea sturgeon"), which Henry Hudson had noted in abundance in 1609 but which were not much prized as a food fish among the white settlers, though a mainstay of the Indians' diet.

In 1873 German immigrant Henry Schacht set up a caviar business near Chester, Pennsylvania, catching his sturgeons in the Delaware River and shipping his product to European markets for a dollar per pound. Seven years later another plant opened in Bay Side, New Jersey, and business boomed for the next quarter-century. So successful was the sturgeon industry in those years that it soon depleted its own product, so that by 1900 such fisheries found themselves without a source of supply. Sturgeon fisheries were also established along the Columbia River in the Northwest in 1888, and by 1892 6 million pounds of the fish were caught. By 1900 these, too, were depleted almost to the point of extinction, although the state of Pennsylvania that year reported that 90 percent of so-called Russian caviar sold in Europe and the United States was coming out of the Delaware River.

During those boom years America shipped much of its caviar supply to Europe and then imported it back again under the label "Russian caviar," for ever since the word "caviar" was first printed in English in 1591, the best examples were thought to come from Russian rivers. With the end of the American sturgeon industry, caviar prices jumped wildly, and true Russian and Iranian caviar needed to be imported.

Americans not willing to pay such prices were forced to switch to domestic fish roe. In the 1960s the Romanoff Caviar Company (which began when German immigrant Ferdinand Hansen came to Penns Grove, New Jersey, in 1859 to supervise caviar production and which is now owned by Iroquois Foods) began marketing more affordable varieties made from the roe of salmon (called "red salmon caviar"), lumpfish, and, in 1982, whitefish (called "golden whitefish caviar").

FDA regulations forbid the use of the word "caviar" alone on a label unless it is truly from sturgeon roe; if other fish roe is used, the name of the fish must precede "caviar." During the 1970s there was increased interest in the production of domestic sturgeon caviar because of an encouraging rise in the number of the fish in Arkansas, Oklahoma, and Oregon rivers. California also has sturgeons, but it is illegal to catch them for commercial purposes. The two main wild species are the "white" and "green" sturgeons, the former now farm-raised. The largest sturgeon farm in the world is Sierra Aqua Farms, begun in 1980 in Elverta, California, which produces about 100,000 pounds of white sturgeon per month.

Other companies market the roe of the Mississippi paddlefish (*Polyodon spathula*) as "American sturgeon caviar," because the paddlefish is similar to the sturgeon. In Louisiana the roe of the local fish called "choupique" (see BOWFIN) is used as caviar.

Caviar is traditionally made by pushing the roe through a sieve in order to remove fatty tissue and membranes. It is then salted and packed in tins or jars.

cayenne pepper. Also, "cayenne." A seasoning of pulverized chile peppers and salt (1756). The word comes from the seasoning's association with the peppers of Cayenne Island, French Guiana, but the powdered peppers were made elsewhere. Today the term "cayenne" connotes no particular type of ground chile or degree of heat, according to the American Spice Trade Association, which believes the term should be phased out of the market.

Eliza Leslie, in her *Directions for Cookery* (1837), gives the following instructions for mixing cayenne, advising one to "wear glasses to save your eyes from being incommoded by [the peppers]. Dry ripe chilis before a fire the day before. Trim the stalks, pound the pods in a mortar until powdered, add one-sixth their weight in salt".

celery (*Apium graveolens dulce*). A plant of the CARROT family, related to the PARSNIP and PARSLEY, used as a flavoring or vegetable in soup, salads, and sauces or eaten raw as an appetizer. The word derives from the Greek *sélinon*, and first appears in English print in 1664, thirty-two years after its first cultivation in France as a soup ingredient. Celery grows wild in Europe and Asia, and some wild varieties, which are believed to have escaped from cultivated varieties, are found in California. Florida and California grow most of the United States celery crop, and most of that is of the Pascal variety.

"Celery salt" was first advertised in the Sears, Roebuck Catalog for 1897 and is still used as a milder flavoring.

cellar kitchen. A kitchen located in the basement. The term dates back in print to 1830 and usually referred to inferior housing conditions, especially in the northeastern cities, but in the twentieth century many immigrant families, especially Italians who were able to move up to a certain affluence and buy homes, would very often put in a cellar kitchen as a second kitchen where much of the everyday cooking took place.

cereal. Generally, any edible grain, such as wheat, oats, barley, or corn. In America, however, the word (from the Latin *cereālis*, "of grain") has since the end of the nineteenth century meant a breakfast food prepared from such grains. Such dishes are often called "breakfast cereals," such as oatmeal and cornflakes.

The first examples of American cooked cereals were the corn-mush porridges adapted from Native American cookery. "Quaker Oats," made by a process of hulled oats developed by Asmus J. Ehrrichsen, appeared in 1877. "Cream of Wheat" was created by flour miller Tom Avidon of Grand Rapids, Michigan, in 1894. But the interest in nutrition in the mid-nineteenth century as promoted by Reverend Sylvester Graham, creator of "graham flour," led to pronouncements on the value of grain in the diet. One of Graham's followers, Dr. James Caleb Jackson of New York, created the first packaged breakfast cereal, which was called "Granula."

In the 1890s another nutritionist, Dr. John Harvey Kellogg (1852–1943), head of the Battle Creek Sanatorium in Battle Creek, Michigan, doled out portions of "Battle Creek health foods" to his patients, who consumed great quantities of bran and zwieback. Kellogg developed packaged cereals at this time—the first named "Granola," quickly changed to "Granose" to avoid conflict with Jackson's Granula. Later Kellogg's brother, Will Keith Kellogg, created one of the most popular and enduring of all American breakfast cereals, "Kellogg's Toasted Corn Flakes," introduced in 1907.

One of Kellogg's patients, Charles William Post, founded the Postum Cereal Company in 1896, marketing a coffee substitute made from cereal and called "Postum Cereal Food Coffee," and, in 1898, a wheat-and-malted barley cereal called "Grape-Nuts" (which contained neither grapes nor nuts; Post claimed grape sugar was formed in the baking process). Post's other contribution of that era was a cornflake cereal he originally called "Elijah's Manna" in 1904, but, after being criticized for his use of a biblical name, changed it to "Post Toasties" two years later.

In 1892 a Denver lawyer named Henry Perky traveled to Watertown, New York, to work with an air-brake designer named William Ford on a corn cereal, but discovered instead a process for pressing wheat into shreds that could be formed into biscuits. These he called "Shredded Wheat" and returned to Denver to open a bakery and restaurant and to sell the item door to door by wagon. He set up the Shredded Wheat Company in Niagara Falls, New York, which was bought in 1928 by the National Biscuit Company (today called Nabisco Brands, Inc.).

"Maltex," a toasted-wheat-and-barley cereal, made by the Standard Milling Company of Kansas City, Missouri, appeared in 1899. "Wheaties," a wheat-flake cereal, was accidentally created in 1921 when a Minneapolis health theorist named Mennenberg (or perhaps Minniberg) spilled some gruel on a hot stove, making a crisp wheat flake. The Washburn Crosby Company (changed in 1928 to General Mills, Inc., of Minneapolis, Minnesota) bought the rights to this cereal and introduced it in 1924. The same company's corn-puff cereal, "Kix," was marketed in 1937, and their ring-shaped oat cereal, "Cheerioats," appeared in 1941 (the name was changed to "Cheerios" in 1945 and marketed as "the first ready-to-eat oat cereal").

In 1935 the Ralston Purina Company of St. Louis, Missouri, came out with "Shredded Ralston," a cereal of small wheat squares in a waffle pattern. Later the name was changed to "Wheat Chex," and "Rice Chex" (1950) and "Corn Chex" (1958) followed.

Because of criticism of breakfast cereals in the 1960s as being of little nutritional value on their own, many cereal manufacturers have since added vitamins and minerals to their products and cut down on the sugar content, which had become very high in cereals aimed at the children's market. Many of these were named after cartoon or movie characters like Dracula ("Count Chocula," chocolate-flavored), Frankenstein ("Frankenberry," fruit-flavored), and others.

Also in the 1960s there was a surge of interest in "natural grain" cereals that were supposedly unadulterated by sugar and additives, although many of these contained high amounts of honey, brown sugar, or raisins, as well as dried fruits. The most successful was "Granola," a mixture of various cereal grains. Wheat germ was also promoted as an additive giving a nutritional boost to packaged cereals.

Hot cereals made from grains include cream of wheat, farina, and oatmeal, which are all variations of basic porridge.

challa. Also, "challeh" or "challah." A shaped loaf of white, slightly sweetened egg bread coated with an egg-white glaze. Challa is a traditional Jewish bread served on the Sabbath and assumes different shapes at

different holiday feasts: for Shabbat it is braided; for Rosh Hashanah and Yom Kippur it is rounded and might be topped with a dove-wing or ladder pattern made from the dough. By tradition, when the bread is baked, a small morsel is thrown into the oven as a sacrifice to commemorate the Hebrew term *challa*, "the priest's share," mentioned in the Bible, Num. 15:20 and Ezek. 44:30. It first appeared in English print in 1927.

CHALLA

Dissolve 2 pkgs. yeast in ½ c. warm water. Add a pinch of saffron that has steeped in some hot water to 2 c. boiling water, 3 T. vegetable oil, I T. salt, and I T. sugar. Cool to lukewarm and add yeast. Add 2 beaten eggs and mix with 3 c. flour. Set aside for 10 min., add enough flour to make a dough, and knead. Shape into a ball, grease the surface, and cover to let rise until doubled. Knead again, then cut dough into two loaves. Cut each half into three long pieces, fasten the ends together, and braid. Place on greased sheet, let rise until doubled, brush with egg white in I T. water, bake at 400° for 15 min., reduce to 350°, and bake for 45 min.

---

chalupa. A tortilla formed in the shape of a "little boat" (from the Mexican) and filled with various ingredients, such as shredded pork, beef, poultry, fish, tomatoes, onion, or cheese. The term dates in American print to 1895. Chalupas are often served as an appetizer and are a staple of Mexican-American menus.

champagne. Also, "bubbly." A sparkling wine. True champagne comes from the Champagne region of France, northeast of Paris, which is centered around the cities of Reims and Epernay. Sparkling wine (as opposed to the still wines produced in the same region) were produced in the seventeenth century in the Champagne area, but much credit has been given to a Benedictine monk named Dom Pérignon, cellarmaster at the Abbey of Hautvillers; until his death in 1715, for his work in stopping the bottles from exploding because of the excessive effervescence by using better corks and thicker bottles. Dom Pérignon is also credited for important work in the blending of champagnes.

Champagne became extremely popular at the French court, and soon afterward it came to be considered a wine for special occasions and lavish dinners; it is still so used to celebrate weddings, anniversaries, births, holidays, and other feasts in America and the rest of the world,

Champagne is made by any of three methods: The first, called the "champagne process" (*méthode champenoise* in French), involves pressing the grapes and fermenting them for about three weeks. The wine is then chilled either by fresh winter air or refrigerated tanks, and a small amount of sugar dissolved in old wine is added to initiate a second fermentation in the bottle. The yeasts and sugar create additional carbon dioxide and alcohol. Sediment in the bottle is positioned in the neck by a process called "riddling," or turning the bottles periodically to force the sediment down the neck. This process, traditionally done by hand, is now occasionally done by machine. The sediment is then disgorged from the bottle by freezing the neck and removing the cork with the sediment behind it. The wine lost in disgorging is replaced with more wine and with a concentration of sugar dissolved in mature wine. This last addition gives the wine its final degree of sweetness, which ranges from "brut" (very dry), to "extra dry" or "extra sec" (dry), to "dry" or "sec" (somewhat sweeter), to "demi-sec" (quite sweet), to "doux" (very sweet). The bottle is then recorked. About forty U.S. wineries use the *méthode champenoise*.

The second method is called the "Charmat" or "bulk process," invented by French enologist Eugène Charmat in 1907. Fermentation takes place in large tanks, and bottling is done under pressure all in a continuous process. About 70 percent of American sparkling wines is made by the Charmat method.

The third method is a "transfer process," developed in Germany, in which a second fermentation does take place in the bottle but in which the bottles are not riddled. Instead the cork is removed after being chilled, the sediment is twice filtered out under pressure, and the wine is put into clean bottles.

The first American champagnes were made in 1842 by Nicholas Longworth from Catawba grapes grown on twelve hundred acres of vineyards near Cincinnati, Ohio, and these wines enjoyed great success and acclaim even in England, where a writer for the *Illustrated London News* reported that Longworth's sparkling wine "transcends the Champagne of France." There were other attempts after Longworth's, including those of Agoston Haraszthy de Mokcsa in California's Sonoma Valley in the 1860s, based on methods learned at France's Moët et Chandon cellars, but his efforts failed. In 1884 Frenchborn Paul Masson brought champagne-making equipment to his employer Charles Lefranc in Santa Clara, California, and began making sparkling wine there after the phyl-

loxera blight destroyed the French vineyards. In 1892 Masson founded his own Paul Masson Champagne Company, and his wines won awards both in America and abroad, including honorable mention at the Paris Exposition of 1900. Masson prospered and became known for his lavish parties, at one of which singer Anna Held took a notorious bath in Masson champagne in 1917. During Prohibition Masson continued to make some champagne for "medicinal purposes," but federal agents raided his winery in 1929 and severely crippled the operations there.

Another name in California champagne making of that era is that of the Korbel brothers, whose winery dates to 1886 but whose first sparkling wines were not made until 1896 by winemaker Franz Hazek from Prague. Both the Paul Masson Vineyards and Korbel Champagne Cellars thrive today.

New York State also produced champagne in the nineteenth century. In 1860 Charles Davenport Champlin opened the Pleasant Valley Winery in Hammondsport in the Finger Lakes district. By 1865 Champlin had made the first New York champagne from Catawba grapes, and he won an honorable mention at the 1867 Paris Exposition. In 1870 the winery blended Catawba with Delaware grapes; on tasting it, horticulturist Colonel Marshall Wilder said, "Truly, this will be the great champagne of the West!" (meaning west of Europe), and soon afterward the wine was called Great Western, which took a gold medal at the 1873 Vienna Exposition. Great Western was an enormous success, and the company even built a railroad in 1872 to haul its product. It was called the Bath & Hammondsport Railroad, but was nicknamed "the Champagne Trail."

Although the French rage at the practice of American wines being labeled "champagne," there is nothing in United States law to prevent it. (It is interesting to note that when the French champagne producer Moët-Hennessey built a winery in California's Napa Valley in 1973, the company labeled its product "sparkling wine," refusing to call it "champagne.") Americans have also referred to their sparkling wines as "the bubbly" since the 1890s, and, more colloquially, "gigglewater" by the 1920s. There are also other American wines labeled "Sparkling Burgundy" or "Sparkling Moscato" that may or may not possess any of the characteristics associated with the true wines of Burgundy or Italy.

American champagnes have traditionally been fermented somewhat sweeter than their European counterparts, although this has changed in the last decade, as drier wines have become more popular.

The grapes used in the production of California champagne include the traditional PINOT NOIR and CHARDONNAY used in France, along with FRENCH COLOMBARD, CHENIN BLANC, Sémillon, Folle Blanche, and others. New York State champagnes are principally made from CATAWBA and Delaware varieties. In 1998, Americans produced 8.4 million cases of champagne and sparkling wine, about a quarter of which was produced in the United States, mostly in California.

chardonel. A white hybrid grape made from a cross between CHARDONNAY and SEYVAL BLANC grapes. It was cultivated in the Finger Lakes region of New York by Cornell University. The grape was first developed in 1953, with vine propagation begun in 1960. The technical name was "Geneva White 9" ("GW9"), and "Chardonel" became the official name in September 1991.

Chardonnay. A white vinifera grape that produces a well-balanced, fruity wine. It is the grape used in the finest whites of Burgundy and within the last twenty years has become the premium white grape of California and the Northwest. Some plantings are also found in the East. The label on American Chardonnays may read "Pinot Chardonnay," but the grape is not now believed to be related to the Pinot family. The word was first printed circa 1941.

In 1991 California alone had 56,600 acres of Chardonnay planted.

Charlie Taylor. A mixture of sorghum or syrup and bacon grease, used by westerners as a substitute for butter (1933).

charlotte russe. A French dessert (supposedly created by Marie-Antonin Carème) made in mold with ladyfingers and Bavarian cream. The term is from the French for "Russian charlotte." (See also APPLE CHARLOTTE.)

While this confection is known and made in the United States, a simple version consisting of a square of sponge cake topped with whipped cream (sometimes with chocolate sprinkles) and a maraschino cherry was also called a "charlotte russe," a variation of which appeared in Lafcadio Hearn's *La Cuisine Créole* (1885). This was a standard item in eastern cities, particularly among urban Jewish Americans (some of whom pronounced the item "charley roose" or "charlotte roosh"), who made it at home or bought it at a pastry shop, where it was set on a frilled cardboard holder whose center could be pushed up so as to reveal more cake as the whipped cream was consumed.

chaser. A drink imbibed immediately after swallowing a first, different drink; for instance, a "beer chaser" would be a glass of BEER drunk after one has had a jigger of spirits. The term has been in print since 1897.

chaudin. A stuffed pig's stomach that is browned and then cooked in a kettle. It is a traditional Cajun dish, and the word is derived from the French, *chaud,* "hot." The pig's stomach itself is called a "ponce" (from the French *panse,* "belly").

chaurice. Also, "hot sausage." A Creole and Cajun hot pork sausage made with a good deal of chile powder and fresh vegetables. The name probably derives from the spicy, dry Spanish sausage called *chorizo.* It is most often pan-fried and served with beans.

chayote (*Sechium edule*). Also, "vegetable pear" and, in Louisiana, "mirliton" (because it resembles a small hornpipe like a kazoo). A squashlike, pear-shaped fruit with a taste similar to cucumber, often served as a vegetable (1885). The name derives from the Spanish, via Nahuatl, *chayotli.* Chayote is pale green to dark green in color and shaped like a pear. It is raised throughout the Caribbean and Latin America, as well as in small gardens of Louisiana, where stuffed mirlitons are served as a main dish.

Cheddar. A cow's-milk cheese produced in many states, ranging from mild to quite sharp in taste and from white to pumpkin orange in color (the deeper hues come from the American annato-bean vegetable dye). Americans consume about 9.6 pounds of Cheddar annually, most in the form of processed cheese. The name was first used in print in 1661.

The name and the cheese derive from the village of Cheddar, a district of Somerset, England, where it has been made at least since the sixteenth century. American Cheddars are usually made in blocks, with a firm, not crumbly, texture, or they may be dipped in paraffin. The main varieties are:

coon. Very sharp, aged for more than a year and cured at high temperatures. Coon has a more crumbly texture than other Cheddars.

goat's milk Cheddar. Made in Iowa, this variety

is not commonly found in the rest of the states. It is rich and has a slightly sweet flavor.

New York Cheddar. Some varieties are white and sharp, like Herkimer Cheddar; mild and yellow, like Cooper Cheddar; or smoked.

pineapple Cheddar. Made in Litchfield County, Connecticut, pineapple Cheddar is now uncommon. Its name derives from its hanging shape in the netting during the curing process.

Tillamook. A highly esteemed yellow Oregon Cheddar that may be well aged, but may also range from mild to sharp.

Vermont Cheddar. A sharp cheese, light yellow in color and distinctive in taste—especially the Crowley variety, which may have a tangy taste after aging. Vermont sage Cheddar is flavored with sage.

Wisconsin Cheddar. Wisconsin produces the most Cheddar cheeses in the country, ranging from Colby (after the town in Wisconsin where it was created), to Longhorn, which is somewhat mild. In the 1964 World's Fair in New York a six-ton Cheddar, made from Wisconsin and Canadian cheese, was exhibited; it was later served in a London restaurant. "Cheddar cheese soup" is said to have been created, or at least popularized, at Emily Shaw's Restaurant in Pound Ridge, New York.

Cheddar cheese is often served in New England with a slice of apple pie and coffee.

cheese. A food made from the pressed curd of milk. The word is from the Latin *cāseus*, and became *cese* in English about the year 1000. Medieval monks raised cheesemaking to a sophisticated and diverse craft.

Americans developed their own cheesemaking talents mainly from English traditions, although German methods had a distinct effect on the production of nineteenth-century cheeses, and Scandinavians who settled in the Midwest brought their own talents to bear. American colonists in the North loved cheese and enjoyed it frequently; the Dutch of the Middle Atlantic colonies ate it twice a day, and it was certainly a staple of the Germans' diet in New Jersey and Pennsylvania. Most of the cheese eaten by English colonists was imported from the mother country, and after the Revolution high duties were placed on imported Cheshires and CHEDDARs.

In the South, where fresh milk quickly soured in the heat, cheese was brought in from the North. As in other countries, cheese was a delectable way to preserve milk all over the United States. The basic technique for cheesemaking begins with mixing milk with rennet, the stomach lining of a slaughtered calf. The rennet curdles the milk, leaving the whey on top to be drawn off. The curds are then pressed into a mold and eaten fresh or aged for flavor and texture, Cheese was used with other foods of the Colonial period as barter for goods.

Good cheeses were considered something of a luxury, however, and served as part of celebrations. On New Year's Day, 1802, President Thomas Jefferson was presented at the White House with a 1,235-pound Cheshire cheese from Cheshire, Massachusetts. A fourteen-hundred-pound cheese was delivered to President Andrew Jackson's last reception in 1837—the ten thousand citizens who attended left the cheese and the White House in shambles. It is said the smell of the cheese lingered in the carpets and furniture for a month afterward.

The most popular cheese of the nineteenth century was Cheddar. American varieties of this English cheese were sold in every New England grocery as "store cheese," largely as a result of improved techniques developed by Englishman Joseph Harding. Vermont and New York became famous for their Cheddars. In the years following the California Gold Rush of 1849 in Monterey farmer David Jacks created a cheese called "Monterey Jack" that was similar to cheeses made by the Spanish friars. A Wisconsin farmer named Adam Blumer, recently arrived in the United States from Switzerland, began making imitation "Swiss cheese," complete with the identifying holes, about 1850. Brick cheese was made first in Wisconsin, about 1877; Liederkranz was the creation of Swiss-born Emil Frey of Monroe, New York, in 1892. Creditable Limburgers, first made in Belgium, were produced by the German immigrants in upstate New York and became a standard item at beerhalls, where the drinks were accompanied by large slabs of cheese and pumpernickel bread.

The best-known United States cheese is termed, simply, "American cheese" or "American Cheddar," so called after the Revolutionary War when proud dairy workers scorned English items. This factory-made cheese was popularized further when a Chicago grocery clerk named J. H. Kraft had the idea of wrapping individual portions of cheese for his customers to buy and, as of 1903, of selling his cheese door-to-door by horse and wagon. In 1918 Wisconsin cheesemaker

Hubert Fassbender created a cheese spreadable at room temperature and sealed it in a small ceramic pot he called a "cheese crock."

Today the United States is the largest producer of cheese in the world. New York State alone produces about twenty-six pounds of cheese for every American. The total United States cheese production for 1998 was 6.3 billion pounds, much of which was bought by the federal government as part of a dairy-support price system. Cheese is made in thirty-seven states. Wisconsin, California, Minnesota, and New York are the country's largest cheese producers, making all sorts of traditional cheeses, as well as process-cheese spread, pasteurized process-cheese food, and other dairy products. In 1997 Americans ate 28 pounds of cheese per person, with 15.7 pounds being domestic.

Several small commercial cheese producers, led by Laura Chenel of Santa Rosa, California, in the early 1980s, now make goat cheese, and in recent years there has been a growth in the amount of mozzarella cheese (primarily used on pizza), low-fat cottage cheese (used in diets), and cream cheese, while imported cheeses sold at cheese stores have become readily available year-round.

The following list of American-made cheeses includes the main varieties.

American. A form of CHEDDAR (1795).

Amish Baby Swiss. Produced by Ohio Amish farmers; sometimes smoked.

baker's. Made from skim milk for commercial use.

Bandon. An Oregon-produced Cheddar.

Bel Paese. An Italian cheese (the name means "beautiful country," the title of a children's book by Father Antonio Stoppani) created by Egidio Calbani of Lombardy in 1929, also produced in America.

bierkäse. In Germany this cheese is called Weisslacker käse, but it is made in Wisconsin. Bierkäse means "beer cheese" and is associated with the strong-tasting cheeses, like Limburger, usually consumed with beer.

blue. A blue-veined cheese under various names. Originally made from goat's milk by the United States Department of Agriculture and California Experiment Station in 1918 by using *Penicillium roqueforti,* American blue cheeses were later made with cow's milk after further successful experiments in universities in Washington and the Midwest.

brick cheese. See main entry.

Brie. A French cheese now made in small amounts by small dairies in the United States. Brie, whose name derives from the region of Brie in Northeast France, is creamy inside and has a white rind.

Camembert. A soft-centered cheese originally made in France's Normandy (wherein lies the village of Camembert), but for some years made in the United States. The best known is Borden Camembert, made by the Borden Company in Van Wert, Ohio.

Cheddar. See main entry.

cheese food. Cheese that has been processed with cream, milk, skim milk, cheese whey, or whey albumin. Under FDA regulations, at least 51 percent of the product must be pure cheese.

Colby. A granular cheese first made at the end of the nineteenth century by the Steinwand family in Colby, Wisconsin. Colby is now made outside the United States as well (1940). FDA standards require that it contain not less than 50 percent milk fat.

coon. A sharp American Cheddar, usually aged a year or more.

Cornhusker. Developed by the Agricultural Experiment Station at the University of Nebraska (nicknamed the "Cornhusker State") about 1940, this cheese is similar to Colby.

cottage cheese. See main entry.

Cougar Gold. A form of Cheddar first made at the State University of Washington at Pullman.

cream cheese. See main entry.

Creole. A very rich and moist New Orleans cheese made from clabber and heavy cream.

Cup. A cheese made in Pennsylvania-Dutch country whose name derives from the white china cups in which it was carried to market. According to Evan Jones in *The World of Cheese* (1979), "Berks Cup Cheese is the result of baking curds in the oven, with new curds added each day for a week. The baked curds are poured into a heated pan and simmered slowly to a boil, without stirring; salt, cream, butter, and baking soda are added, and the mixture is boiled 15 minutes, during which time eggs are mixed into the curds. The cheese is cooled in cups."

coldpack. A cheese made from one or more varieties of Cheddar. Flavorings, such as wine, are sometimes added to this unheated, tangy cheese, which may also be called *club cheese*.

Edam. Originally a cheese of Holland, Edam is formed into a ball and usually coated with a red covering of paraffin or other substances. It must contain not less than 40 percent milk fat.

farmer. Also "farmer's." A general term applied to fresh cottage cheese, although there are regional farmer cheeses of firmer, dryer textures (1945).

feta. A crumbly white cheese made in the style of Greek goat's milk cheese, although American varieties are more often made from cow's milk (1935). After curds are formed, the cheese is pickled in a brine solution. The word "feta" is from the Greek.

goat. Also "goat's." Called *chèvre* in France, this is a fresh, sourish cheese made from goat milk by about 100 producers around the United States, including California, Iowa, New Jersey, and Pennsylvania.

Gold'N'Rich. A semisoft loaf developed from Port Salut cheese at Elgin, Illinois.

Gorgonzola. A crumbly, blue-veined cheese of Italian origin (named after a town in Piedmont where the cheese was first produced), Gorgonzola is injected with *Penicillium glaucum*. The American version must contain at least 50 percent milk fat.

Gouda. Named after a Dutch town, this is a firm cheese formed into a compressed sphere. It is similar to Edam and must contain not less than 46 percent fat solids.

Herkimer. An American Cheddar made in New York's Herkimer County.

Liederkranz. See main entry.

Limburger. A strong cheese of Belgian origins (the town of Limburg), it was made popular by German cheesemakers of the nineteenth century and served at beerhalls with pumpernickel bread, onions, and draughts of beer (1810).

Longhorn. An American Cheddar.

Maytag Blue. See main entry.

Minnesota Slim. An orange, loose-textured cheese good for melting developed by the University of Minnesota. It was named at the Lund Market in Minneapolis, Minnesota.

Monterey Jack. A mild cheese that originated in Monterey, California, it resembles the cheeses made by early Spanish friars in that territory and is named after David Jacks, who first made the cheese just after California's Gold Rush years (1845). It is widely used as a topping for Mexican-American dishes.

Mossholder's. First developed by Otto Mossholder in 1925 in Appleton, Wisconsin, this cow's milk cheese has a pronounced flavor and semisoft, creamy texture.

mozzarella. Of Italian origins, this fresh white cow's milk cheese comes in two forms: a mild unsalted fresh cheese kept in water (commonly made in Italian-American groceries), and a firmer, salted cheese primarily made for pizza toppings. Both must contain at least 45 percent milk fat.

Muenster. Of Alsatian origins, this cheese was developed in monasteries by medieval monks (the word "Muenster" derives from the Latin *monasterium*. In the United States (where it is sometimes spelled "Munster") the cheese must contain not less than 50 percent milk fat.

Nuworld. A white-mold cheese developed by the universities of Wisconsin and Minnesota after World War II. It must contain at least 50 percent milk fat.

Parmesan. This hard, well-aged cheese takes its name from the Italian city of Parma. In Italy there are strict regulations as to region, quality, and aging of the cheese (which they call *parmigiano*), whereas in the United States domestic Parmesan is used primarily for grating and must contain no less than 32 percent milk fat.

pecorino. Although in Italy this cheese is made from sheep's milk (the name is from the Italian *pecora,* for sheep), U.S. versions are made from cow's milk and are used primarily as grating cheeses that have a very sharp tangy flavor.

pineapple. An extra-rich Cheddar cheese made in a wooden mold so as to resemble the shape of a pineapple, this cheese originated in New York, with its first mention in print in 1830, though similar cheeses had been produced in England earlier. In 1808 Lewis M. Norton of Goshen, Connecticut, received a patent for the cheese, and it was produced there until 1904. A relative named Eugene Norton bought rights to the company, however, and built a factory in Attica, New York, which closed in 1918 when the Kraft Company bought the patent. Another version of pineapple cheese was produced by O.A. Weatherly in Milford, New York, until 1945, when his company was sold to Dairylea, which produced the cheese for another decade, although the equipment was moved to Wisconsin where a form of the cheese continued to be made.

processed. A product made from melting various kinds of cheeses with emulsifiers, acids, flavorings, and colorings to produce a smooth consistency (1915). A "processed cheese food" contains less real cheese than "processed cheese spread," whereas the latter has more moisture and less butterfat than cheese.

ricotta. A fresh, moist white cheese originating in Italy, where its name means "recooked." Ricotta is similar to cottage cheese and most often used in Italian-American cookery.

romano. A hard grating cheese whose name derives from the Italian capital. American versions tend to be quite salty and are used mostly on pasta dishes (1905).

Swiss. A generic term for all imitations of the original Swiss Emmenthaler (1815). The words "imported Swiss" on a label mean only that the cheese is of this type and not necessarily made in Switzerland. American Swiss cheese is aged about four months, has holes, and originated in the work of Wisconsin's Adam Blumer about 1850.

Teleme Jack. A melting cheese said to have originated around 1922 by makers of Monterey Jack who had emigrated from Greece. The cheese was named after a Romanian brine-cured cheese.

Tillamook. An American Cheddar made in Oregon's Tillamook County.

Trappist. A generic term for cheeses made by the monks of the Trappist order. A form of this cheese is made by Trappists near Gethsemane, Kentucky.

cheesecake. A dessert cake or pie made with cream cheese, cottage cheese, or ricotta. Various forms of cheesecake have been popular for centuries. The first mention in print of such a dessert dates to 1440, and recipes for such a dish can be found throughout the eighteenth and nineteenth centuries.

American cheesecakes are primarily of two varieties. "Jewish cheesecake," has a smooth, cream cheese filling, commonly set on a graham-cracker crust. Because of their association with New York restaurants and bakeries, such items are commonly called "New York cheesecake," especially outside of New York. Particularly light examples are sometimes called a "French cheesecake." Such examples are sometimes topped with fruit, which itself may be glazed with jelly. Jewish cheesecakes have become a staple of American steakhouses. One of the most famous cheesecakes of this type is that associated with Lindy's restaurant in New York City, now a trademark name of Lindy's Food Products of New York. The supposed recipe for the original Lindy's cheesecake is given below.

The second basic variety is the "Italian cheesecake," usually made from ricotta cheese and set on a pastry crust and commonly containing bits of candied fruit.

LINDY'S CHEESECAKE

Combine 1 c. flour, ¼ c. sugar, 1 t. grated lemon rind, and 1 t. vanilla in a large bowl. Make a well in the center, add 1 egg yolk and ¼ lb. softened butter, adding water if necessary to make a pliable dough. Wrap in waxed paper and chill 1 hr. Meanwhile, with an electric mixer, combine 2½ lb. cream cheese, 1¾ c. sugar, 3 T. flour, and ½ t. each of grated orange and lemon rind. Add 5 whole eggs, 2 egg yolks, ¼ c. vanilla, and beat well. Add ¼ c. heavy cream and blend thoroughly. Butter the sides and bottom of a 9-in. springform pan. Roll out one third of the dough to ⅛-in. thickness and mold into the pan's bottom. Bake at 400° for 15 min. until lightly browned, then cool. Place the top of the pan over the base, roll the remaining dough to a ⅛-in. thickness, cut into strips, and press into the pan to line the sides completely. Pour in the cheese mixture, bake for 10 min. at 550° reduce heat to 200° and continue to bake for 1 hr.

ITALIAN CHEESECAKE

Combine 2 c. flour sifted with ½ t. salt, cut in 1 c. butter to make a coarse meal. Make a well in the center and add 2 beaten egg yolks and 1–2 T. cold water to make a soft, pliable dough. Roll to a thickness of ¼ in., place in a buttered pan, trim edges, and set aside. Beat 4 eggs until light in color, gradually adding 1 c. sugar. Combine 3 c. ricotta cheese, ¼ c. flour, 2 t. candied fruit, 2 T. each of grated lemon and orange rind, 1 T. vanilla, and ⅛ t. salt. Beat in egg mixture till smooth, pour into pastry, bake for 1 hr. at 350°. Cool before serving. If desired, dust with confectioners' sugar.

Chenin Blanc. A white vinifera grape that makes a slightly spicy wine that is sometimes slightly sweet. It is an important grape in France's Loire Valley and has been used by high-volume California wineries. Before Prohibition, California winemakers referred to the grape as "White Zinfandel," then later as "White Pinot." Then, in 1955, the Charles Krug winery began making the varietal under the name "Chenin Blanc," which has since been adapted as standard in the industry.

cherimoya (*Annona cherimola*). A South American fruit with scalelike skin and soft fruit. The word is from American Spanish and dates in print to 1736. It is also called the "custard apple," although properly that fruit is *A. reticulata*. It is now being grown in California and eaten cold or made into a custard.

cherries jubilee. A dessert made with black cherries flambéed with kirsch or brandy, then spooned over vanilla ice cream. The dish is a standard CONTINENTAL menu item, especially fashionable from the

1930s through the 1960s in deluxe restaurants, and also a popular dinner-party dish of the same period. The origins of the dish are unknown. *Larousse Gastronomique* (American edition, 1988) lists a dish of cherries called *cérises jubilées* cooked with a sugar syrup, then arranged in small ramekins and flamed with kirsch.

CHERRIES JUBILEE

Combine 1 c. sugar and 2 c. water in a saucepan and bring to a boil. Poach 1½ lb. pitted black cherries in the sugar syrup until tender. Drain the cherries and reserve 1 c. of the syrup. Add 1 T. cornstarch to the syrup, warm until somewhat thickened, add cherries. Warm ½ c. kirsch or brandy slightly in a saucepan, pour over cherries, and carefully ignite with a match. Serve over vanilla ice cream.

cherry. Any of a variety of trees in the genus *Prunus*, but especially *P. avium*, the "sweet cherry," bearing small red berries that are eaten raw, baked in pies, made in relishes, ice creams, cordials, brandies, and used as flavorings. The word "cherry" is from the Greek *kerásos*, which in Middle English became *chery*.

The cherry originated in Asia but was widely dispersed throughout Europe and North America in prehistoric times. European colonists found wild cherries in America and cultivated them, also crossbreeding them with European varieties.

Today the United States is the leading producer of cherries, with 85 percent of the country's crop grown in Michigan, California, Oregon, and Washington. The total crop is sold as follows: 44 percent canned, 35 percent fresh, 20 percent dried, 1 percent frozen. The leading variety is the "Bing" cherry, developed in 1875 by Seth Luelling in Milwaukie, Oregon, and named, according to Janie Hibler in *Dungeness Crabs and Blackberry Cobblers* (1991), after Luelling's Manchurian foreman. Other principal varieties include the sweet cherry "Lambert" and the tart cherries "Early Richmond," "English Morello," and "Montmorency." See also MARASCHINO.

cherrybarb. A drink of brandy and sugar.

cherry soup. A Midwestern soup of Scandinavian and Eastern European origins, where wine is commonly used instead of lemon juice. It is traditionally served cold in the summer, but may be served hot or cold in the winter.

chervil (*Anthriscus cerefolium*). An aromatic plant used in soups and salads. It originated in Russia, though the name is from the Greek *khaiéphullon*, and the herb is raised mostly in the northeastern United States.

chess pie. Also, "chess-cake pie" and "chess tart." A simple egg, butter, and sugar pie (commonly made with buttermilk) long associated with the South. Meringue is sometimes added as a topping. The origin of the name has escaped a definitive answer. Some believe it may be a derivation of "cheese pie," although traditional chess pies do not contain cheese of any kind. According to Sarah Belk in *Around the Southern Table* (1991), old cookbooks often referred to cheesecakes and pies that do not actually contain cheese, using the term more to describe the curdlike texture of the confection, citing a selection of cheeseless "cheese" pastries in *Housekeeping in Old Virginia* (1979) made with eggs, sugar, butter, milk, and lemon juice—ingredients often used in a chess pie. Belk also cited Elizabeth Hedgecock Sparks, author of *North Carolina and Old Salem Cookery*, who said chess pie was "an old, old tart which may have obtained its name from the town of Chester, England." A recipe for "Old Virginia Chess Cakes," which are actually filled pies, is printed in *World Famous Chefs' Cook Book* (1939) by Ford Naylor.

In *Southern Food* (1987) John Egerton offered two stories as to why the confection is called "chess pie." The first involves a mutation of "chest pie," that is, a pie kept in a piece of furniture called a "pie chest" (or "pie safe") that was a cupboard with perforated tin panels to allow air flow. The other, more folkloric, story involves an unknown southern housewife who, when asked what kind of pie it was, answered, "It's jes' pie." The earliest printed reference to the pie was in a cookbook published by the Fort Worth Women's Club in 1928.

Belk noted that chess pies made with white sugar were called "sugar pies," those with brown sugar "brown-sugar pies," and those with raisins "Osgood" pies (an elision of "Oh-so-good").

CHESS PIE

🅐 *Beat 3 eggs for 1 min., gradually add 1½ c. sugar, 3 T. cooled melted butter, ⅓ c. buttermilk, ½ t. salt, and ½ t. vanilla extract. Mix well and pour into a 9-in. pie shell. Bake in 375° oven for 15 min., reduce heat to 250°, and bake 20 min. until set. Top with meringue and brown if desired.*

---

chestnut. Any of a variety of trees in the genus *Castanea* that bear a sweet bud eaten roasted, boiled, in a stuffing, or as a flavoring. The name is from the Greek *kastenea*.

The first American colonist found the land covered with tall American chestnut trees (*C. dentata*) whose nuts were eaten by the Indians, but the Europeans also brought their own varieties with them. Far East varieties were planted in 1904 on Long Island, New York, which carried a blight (*Endothia parasitica*) that virtually wiped out the native chestnut trees over the next three decades, so that most chestnuts today are still imported from Europe, especially the "Spanish chestnut" (*C. sativa*) and the "Chinese chestnut" (*C. mollissima*), this last now grown in the United States. Efforts are currently being made in New York State to create a new fungus-resistant hybrid that is 99 percent American chestnut and one percent Chinese chestnut.

chewing gum. A sweet, flavored chewable substance made from "chicle" (from the Nahautl *chictli*), a gummy juice of the tropical evergreen enjoyed as an idle snack. The word "gum" is from Middle English *gumme*.

Americans had long chewed gum resins from trees, as they had seen the Indians do. Spruce gum was particularly popular in the early eighteenth century and is mentioned in Mark Twain's 1876 novel *Tom Sawyer*, wherein Tom and Becky pass a single piece of "chewing gum" (a term that saw print as of 1755) back and forth. The first commercial gum was made by John Curtis around 1755, who called it "Maine Pure Spruce Gum." In the 1870s a chewing gum was created from chicle by a Staten Island New York inventor named Thomas Adams, who had observed the exiled Mexican general Antonio Lopez de Santa Ana chewing the substance (which the general had hoped could be made into a rubber substitute). Adams called his invention "Adams' New York No. 1," which he persuaded a Hoboken, New Jersey, druggist to sell for a penny per piece. Adams's son, Thomas, Jr., sold the product as far as the Mississippi as "Adams' New York Gum—Snapping and Stretching," and introduced the first flavored gums—sassafras and licorice (which he called "Black Jack").

In the 1880s William White produced the first corn syrup-based, peppermint-flavored, flat sticks of gum, called "Yucatan," and by the turn of the century New Yorkers could buy chewing gum from the new VENDING MACHINES at railroad platforms and in "gumball machines." A candy-coated gum named Chiclet was the creation of Henry Fleer, whose brother Frank made the first "bubble gum" in 1906 that could be blown into a bubble, but not until 1928 did an accountant named Walter Diemer come up with a formula, which he sold to Fleer, that wouldn't stick to the blower's face. The new gum was at first called "Blibber Blubber," then "Dubble Bubble." The Topps Chewing Gum Company produced another bubble gum in 1947 called "Bazooka," so named because its tubular length resembled the World War II weapon.

The man who would become the world's largest maker of chewing gum was William Wrigley, whose brands such as "Spearmint" (introduced in 1892), "Juicy Fruit," and "Doublemint" made him the largest gum producer in the world.

A "low-sugar gum" called "Dentyne" (a contraction of the words "dental hygiene") was invented in 1899 by drugstore manager Franklin V. Canning, and sugarless gum was first sold as of 1969.

One of the most popular pastimes of American children was collecting bubble-gum trading cards, which were packed inside the gum packages and which featured pictures of popular sports figures and movie and television heroes. Trading cards were first packed with cigarettes in 1879, but by the 1880s Old Judge Tobacco was printing up "baseball cards" with pictures of baseball players on them. In 1951 the Topps Chewing Gum Company came out with a line of Bazooka Gum packaged with a card series called "Freedom's War," depicting scenes from the Korean War; that same year they also began issuing packages with baseball cards in them, which now sell more than 500 million each year. Baseball cards have since become a much sought-out collector's item that may sell for thousands of dollars apiece at auction.

American' per capita consumption of chewing gum is 1.8 pounds, with industry sales of $2.2 billion.

Chicago. A slang term for pineapple or, as in "Chicago sundae," a sundae made with pineapple, so called because of the tendency of Chicago gangsters during Prohibition to use hand grenades called "pineapples." A jelly-filled doughnut is often called a "Chicago" in the Midwest.

chicken (*Gallicus domesticus*). A common name for the domestic fowl raised throughout the world as a food and cooked in every conceivable way, except as a dessert. The word is from the Old English *cīcen*.

The domesticated chicken first appeared about 2000 B.C. in India, and was brought to America by Columbus in 1493. In Hawaii, European travelers found a domesticated fowl called the *moa*, a descendant of a wild jungle fowl probably brought from Malaysia. In 1826, however, the ship *Wellington* docked in Hawaii, dumping its old water into the harbor. This water contained a mosquito larva carrying a bird pox or "bumblefoot" that immediately infected the island's birds and devastated the chicken population.

Early on in American history, chickens were not everyday foods, although in the nineteenth century poultry breeding resulted in some excellent stocks that increased the yield. The "Plymouth Rock" breed was noted in 1849, and the "Wyandotte" received its name from a Mr. Houdette of Worcester, Massachusetts, in 1883. The state bird of Rhode Island, the "Rhode Island red," was developed by William Tripp of Little Compton, Rhode Island, in 1902 by crossing a "Brown Leghorn" with a "Malay Hen," while the "Rhode Island White" was developed in 1926. The "Cornish game hen" was developed from a Plymouth Rock and a "Cornish game cock," and weighs between one and two pounds. A "squab chicken" is not a true SQUAB, but is instead a very small chicken weighing between three-quarters and one-and-a-half pounds. "Chickalona" is a kind of chicken BOLOGNA developed from chicken necks and backs by Cornell University's poultry department.

Federal law regulates the following standards for chickens: A "broiler," also known as a "fryer," is a bird two and a half to four pounds. A "roaster" weighs between five and seven pounds. A "capon" ranges up to ten pounds. A "hen," "stewing hen," or "boiling fowl" is above ten pounds and is a year and a half old. "Deedie" is a southern colloquialism for a young chicken.

The Department of Agriculture grades chickens "A" (the best and most readily found in markets), "B," and "C." They are sold "fresh-killed," which may actually mean they have been shipped at about the standard 35-degree refrigerator temperature or in shaved ice, or "deep chilled" at 30 degrees, as well as frozen, canned, and freeze-dried. Americans eat about 74.4 pounds per capita of chicken a year (and about 245 eggs), preparing the fowl in many ways, including such standard dishes as SOUTHERN FRIED CHICKEN, CHICKEN À LA KING, CHICKEN TETRAZZINI, CHICKEN CACCIATORE, COUNTRY CAPTAIN, BARBECUE CHICKEN, and many others.

chicken à la king. A dish of chicken with a cream sauce garnished with pimientos. Several theories as to the dish's origins date from the late nineteenth century. One credits New York's Brighton Beach Hotel, where chef George Greenwald supposedly made it for the proprietors, Mr. and Mrs. E. Clark King III. Chef Charles Ranhofer of Delmonico's Restaurant in New York City suggested that Foxhall P. Keene, son of Wall Street broker and sportsman James R. Keene, came up with the idea at Delmonico's in the 1880s. A third story credits James R. Keene himself as the namesake and the place and time of origin as Claridge's Restaurant in London after Keene's horse won the 1881 Grand Prix. However the dish got its name, first mentioned in print in 1912, it became a standard luncheon item in the decades that followed, often served from a chafing dish and with rice or on a pastry shell.

CHICKEN À LA KING

In a saucepan blend 4 T. flour with 4 T. butter and cook for about 2 min. Add 2 c. chicken broth and 2 c. light cream, thicken, and remove from heat. In a skillet sauté 1 T. minced onion, ¼ lb. sliced mushrooms, and 1 sweet green pepper cut in strips. Add ½ c. chopped pimiento and 3 c. diced cooked chicken. Season with salt and pepper. Spoon a little sauce into 2 beaten egg yolks, then stir eggs and the rest of the sauce into chicken mixture, and cook over low heat for 1 min. Remove from heat and stir in ½ c. sherry and ½ c. blanched toasted almonds. Serve on toast, rice, or pastry shells. Serves 6.

chicken bog. North Carolina slang for a chicken PILAU made with rice and sausage. The name may derive from the fact that a bog is a section of wet, soggy ground, and the chicken in this dish would be mixed with wet, soggy rice. Loris, South Carolina, holds a Great Loris Bog-Off cooking competition each year.

chickenburger. A patty of ground chicken broiled, grilled, or fried to resemble a beef HAMBURGER. The chickenburger followed the latter sometime in the first quarter of this century.

chicken cacciatore. Also, "chicken alla cacciatore." A dish of chicken cooked with mushrooms and, often, tomato sauce. It is an Italian-American specialty whose name means chicken "hunter's style," but there is no traditional dish by this name in Italy. Chicken cacciatore appears on Italian-American menus at least since the 1930s.

CHICKEN CACCIATORE

Cut a chicken in several pieces, dredge in flour, and sauté in 3 T. olive oil. Add 1 lb. sliced mushrooms and cook together. Add 1 sliced onion, then 1½ c. seasoned tomato sauce, and salt and pepper. Cook, covered, until chicken is tender.

chicken Divan. A dish of sliced chicken breast poached in chicken broth and served on broccoli with a sherry-laced cream-and-cheese sauce. The chicken is placed in a casserole, layered with the broccoli spears, topped with the sauce, and set briefly under a broiler until browned. It was created in the 1930s at the Divan Parisien restaurant in New York (also credited with introducing BROCCOLI to the United States).

chicken fixings. Also, "chicken-fixins." A Western colloquialism for a fancy chicken dinner, and, by extension, any fancy food. The term dates in print to 1838.

chicken francese. An Italian-American dish of sautéed chicken cutlets with a lemon-butter sauce. The word *francese* is Italian for "French style," although there is no specific dish by this name in either Italian or French cookery.

CHICKEN FRANCESE

In a shallow bowl beat together 2 eggs with ½ c. milk and 3 T. minced parsley. Dredge 2 lb. pounded, flattened chicken cutlets in flour, then dip into egg mixture. Sauté in hot oil until golden brown, turn and sauté the other side the same way. Remove from pan and drain on paper. In another pan melt ⅓ c. butter, add ½ c. chicken broth, squeeze in 3 T. lemon juice, add salt and pepper to taste. Add the chicken cutlets and cook until thoroughly heated through.

chicken-fried steak. Also, "chicken-fry steak." A beefsteak that has been tenderized by pounding, coated with flour or batter, and fried crisp. Usually a lesser cut of beef is used. The name refers to the style of cooking, which is much the same as for SOUTHERN FRIED CHICKEN. Chicken-fried steak has been a staple dish of the South, Southwest, and Midwest for decades, although it dates in print only to 1952.

CHICKEN-FRIED STEAK

Pound until thin and tender 4 slices of round steak. Dip in a mixture of 1 beaten egg and 1 c. milk, dredge in flour seasoned with salt and pepper, and fry in shortening, or other oil until crisp and well done. Pour off the oil. Sprinkle 1 T. flour into skillet and cook with pan drippings until browned. Add 1 c. milk and bring to boil, then lower to simmer and cook until thickened. Pour gravy over steaks.

chicken-in-the-shell. A dish of chicken in a creamed mushroom sauce served in a cockleshell; well known in San Francisco at the turn of the present century, it was first served at the Iron House on Montgomery Street.

Chicken Raphael Weill. A dish of chicken parts sautéed in butter, then simmered in chicken broth and white wine and finished with a sauce of heavy cream, sherry, and egg yolks. The dish dates to the turn of the century in San Francisco and is named after its creator, Raphael Weill, owner of that city's White House Department Store.

chicken tetrazzini. A dish of chicken (though turkey is often substituted) in a cream sauce, served over spaghetti and browned in the oven with bread crumbs and Parmesan cheese. It is named after the Italian coloratura soprano opera singer Luisa Tetrazzini (1871–1940), who was extremely popular in the United States after 1908. It is not known when or where the dish was created, though some say it was in San Francisco (the dish was first mentioned in print in 1931), and Tetrazzini herself does not mention the dish in her autobiography, *My Life of Song* (1921). The rather stout singer did write of her eating habits, however: "I eat the plainest food always, and naturally, being Italian, I prefer the foods of my native land. . . . I allow the tempting pastry, the rich and over-spiced patty, to pass by untouched, consoling myself with fruit and fresh vegetables."

CHICKEN TETRAZZINI

In a saucepan make a roux of 4 T. flour and 4 T. butter, add 2 c. heavy cream and 1 c. chicken broth, stir, and cook until thickened. Remove from heat, blend in 3 c. cooked chicken meat cut into small pieces. In a buttered dish place ¾ lb. cooked buttered spaghetti, pour chicken mixture on top, spread with bread crumbs and Parmesan cheese, and brown in oven or under broiler. Serves 6.

chicken Vesuvio. An Italian-American dish of chicken sautéed with garlic, olive oil, oregano, lemon, and wine, piled with potato wedges. According to an article in *Nation's Restaurant News* (April 27, 1987), the dish was "created in Chicago by a Neapolitan cook shortly after World War II." It has become a staple item in Italian-American restaurants in that city. Although it is obviously named after the volcano Mount Vesuvius near Naples, Italy, there are several stories as to the reasons why. It has been speculated that the name derives either from the amount of smoke produced in the cooking process when the wine is added to the hot pan. But, according to *The Italian Cookbook,* published by the Culinary Arts Institute of Chicago in 1954, "the rim of this casserole is topped with deep-fried potatoes and seems to be erupting flavorful fried chicken."

CHICKEN VESUVIO

In a large skillet brown a 2–3 lb. chicken cut up into pieces in ½ c. olive oil. Remove the chicken pieces from skillet and place in a single layer in a large casserole dish. Drain all but 2 T. olive oil from skillet, sauté 2 cloves of sliced garlic, stir in ½ c. Marsala wine, the juice of half a lemon, 1 t. oregano and 1 t. chopped parsley. Reduce for 1 min. Pour over chicken and bake at 325° for 45 min., turning the chicken pieces once. When chicken is done, place fried potatoes around the rim of the baking dish to form the look of a volcano.

chick-pea (*Cicer arietinum*). A hard seed of a plant indigenous to the Mediterranean and central Asia. The chick-pea is not actually a pea, though both are of the same subfamily, *Papilionoideae*. The name for the seed comes from the Latin, *cicer,* but in the United States, where it was introduced by Hispanics, it is called a "garbanzo" (a word that worked its way from Latin, *ervum,* "bitter vetch," through Old Spanish, *arvanço,* to Spanish, *garbanzo*). The word was first printed in 1548 and in American print in 1844. Chick-peas are usually soaked for several hours, roasted, and eaten as a snack or put into stews and salads.

chicory. American nomenclature is very confusing for this salad green called *Cichorium intybus,* with its curly leaves and bright blue flowers (it is sometimes called "blue sailors"). Chicory is quite bitter and is often mixed with other salad greens.

The same plant's roots are dried and ground into a granular powder, often referred to as "succory," that resembles coffee and is used as an additive to or substitute for real coffee in Creole and Cajun cooking, a legacy of the French influence on these cuisines.

The confusion begins with what Americans call "endive," which is a form of *C. intybus* cultivated to produce silky white leaves for salad and which is often referred to as "Belgian endive" or "witloof." The Belgians, however, call that *chicon.*

True endive is another variety, called *C. endivia,* with curly, succulent leaves, more commonly known in America as "escarole" (from the Italian *scarola),* first in print in 1822.

chicory coffee. Also, "chicken coffee." Adding chicory to coffee began in New Orleans during the food-scarce Civil War. Chicory adds a bitterness to coffee, which may be moderated with milk to make CAFÉ AU LAIT, although morning coffee tends to be black, café noir. In New Orleans the coffee and chicory can be bought already blended into light or dark mixtures, and it is meant to be made by a drip method. Most of this chicory is imported from Spain. There is an old saying among Catholic Creoles in New Orleans to the effect that "good coffee and the Protestant religion can seldom if ever be found together." And the same people are fond of the description of chicory coffee as being "Black as the devil,/Strong as death,/Sweet as love,/Hot as Hell!"

chief cook and bottle washer. A slang phrase, dating back to 1840 in print, for a handyman or someone who can do many menial jobs well.

chiffon. A very light, sweet, fluffy filling for a pie, cake, or pudding. The word is from the French, meaning "rag," and ultimately the Middle English word "chip," as chiffon also refers to pieces of sheer, delicate ribbon or fabric for women's clothing.

Chiffon pie is first mentioned in American print in 1929 as a "chiffon pumpkin pie" in the *Beverly Hills Women's Club's Fashions in Foods.* The 1931 edition of Irma S. Rombauer's *Joy of Cooking* gave a recipe for lemon chiffon, and the *Better Homes and Gardens Heritage Cook Book* (1975) said that "chiffon cake was invented by a professional baker and introduced in May 1948. Made with cooking oil instead of solid shortening and beaten—not creamed—this light cake was the first new cake to have been developed in one hundred years of baking." Other authorities, however, credit an amateur baker with creating the confection in 1927. In the 1953 cookbook *250 Superb Pastries,* edited by Ruth Berolzheimer of the Culinary Arts Institute, forty chiffon recipes are given.

chile (*Capsicum annuum*). Also, "chili," "chilli," "chile pepper," and "chili pepper." Although the American Spice Trade Association continues to use the spelling "chili" for such peppers, most authorities, including *Chile Pepper* magazine, generally prefer the spelling "chile" for the pepper and "chili" for the dish CHILI CON CARNE.

Chile pepper is a very hot red, green, or yellow fruit of a New World plant, or the powder made from this fruit. There are more than three hundred varieties, originating in South America. The word is from the Nahuatl *chilli,* and came into English in the mid-seventeenth century via the Spanish.

Christopher Columbus found that the Indians of the New World had cultivated the plant and used the fruit as a principal seasoning for their food. In fact, the Indians of Central and South America had done so from at least as early as 3300 B.C., and chiles were among their most beloved and revered foods, used as everything from a seasoning to a medicine and aphrodisiac. It was reported in 1529 by a Spanish missionary that the Aztecs put chile peppers in everything they ate, including chocolate.

The chile was brought back to Spain as early as 1514, but a German botanist named Leonhard Fuchs, believing Columbus had landed in India, called the chiles "Calcutta peppers," despite the fact that chiles were not true peppers (nor did they reach India until 1611). Nevertheless the English and Americans have continued to refer to the plant as the "chile pepper." Chiles may first have been brought into what is now the United States by General Juan de Oñate, who founded Santa Fe around 1609, although it is possible they were brought north much earlier by missionaries. By the early 1800s commercial seeds were for sale in North America; by 1888 the Burpee Seed Company offered twenty varieties, and by the beginning of the next century, 114 varieties (more than half of the bell variety) were counted by the U.S.D.A. In 1991 the Chile Institute was founded at New Mexico State University to study chile peppers.

Chiles are used both fresh and dried, some roasted over open fires or in ovens, others left to dry in braided strands called "ristras."

"Chile powder" was first made commercially by café owner William Gebhardt of New Braunfels, Texas, in 1894. In Texas chile powder is commonly the basis of CHILI CON CARNE and is a prime ingredient in TEX-MEX and Mexican-American cuisine, including stuffed chiles called CHILES RELLENOS.

Chiles' heat is measured by "Scoville Units," originally developed in 1912 by pharmacologist Wilbur

Scoville, based on human tasters' reaction to solutions of chile peppers in alcohol and sugar water. Today "High Pressure Liquid Chromatography" has replaced the Scoville test, but chiles are still rated according to Scoville Units, ranging from 0 for "sweet banana" chiles up to 300,000 for "habanero." The major United States growing regions for chiles are New Mexico, California, Texas, and Arizona, where several hybrids have been created. Today there are about 125,000 acres of commercially cultivated peppers, of which about 40 percent are of the hot varieties. India, however, grows the largest acerage (2,230,000 acres), with the U.S. seventh in production among the world's chile growers. In 1997 the total production of chile peppers in the U.S. was 125 million pounds.

The main varieties of chiles used in the United States include:

Anaheim. A generic name for several long green chiles, they are a fairly mild chile. Originally these chiles were New Mexican in origin and later grown in California, around Anaheim, although they are no longer a significant crop in that region. The preferred name, "New Mexico," is now used instead of "Anaheim." When dried, they are sometimes called "chile colorado."

ancho. Also "pasilla" and "mulato." A dark reddish brown, slightly hot, dried "poblano." Measures 1,000–1,500 Scoville Units. The name in Spanish means "wide chile."

banana pepper. Also, "sweet banana." Very mild, yellow, often pickled. Measures 0 Scoville Units.

cayenne. See main entry. Measures 30,000–50,000 Scoville Units.

chilaca. Mildly hot to hot, this is often used in soups and sauces. When dried, it is called "pasilla" or "chile negro." Measures 1,000–1,500 Scoville Units.

chipotle. A dried jalapeño (see below), this is a very hot brown chile. Also called "chile ahumado" or "chile meco." Measures 2,500–5,000 Scoville Units.

de arbol. Extremely hot, measuring 15,000–30,000 Scoville Units. The name in Spanish means "treelike." The de arbol pepper is usually ground into a powder or used to season oils, soups, and sauces.

Fresno. A mild chile, cone-shaped, mainly cultivated in the United States. It goes under the more general name "New Mexico." It is often used in salsas.

Guajillo. Very hot, grown in Mexico but imported. When dried it is called *mirasol*, or, erroneously, "dried Anaheim." Measures 2,500–5,000 Scoville Units.

habanero. Extremely hot yellow-orange pepper. The name is Spanish for "Havana-like," possibly referring to the chile's origins in Havana, Cuba. In Jamaica it is known as "Scotch bonnet" or "Scot's Bonnet" and "Bahamian" or "Bahamian Mama" in the Bahamas. It belongs to the *C. chinese* species. It is commonly used in sauces and barbecue recipes. Measures 200,000–300,000 Scoville Units.

jalapeño. Green, about two inches long, hot. The most widely consumed chile in the United States. Dried jalapeños are called "chipotle." Texas is the largest producer of jalapeños. Commercially, jalapeños cut into slices are sometimes called "NACHO slices" or "nacho rings," for use on nachos. Measures 2,500–5,000 Scoville Units.

New Mexico. Both green and red, dried and roasted chiles, formerly called "Anaheim," but now descriptive of various strains originally grown in New Mexico. The main varieties include "NuMex Big Jim," "New Mexico No. 6–4," and "Española Improved." New Mexico chiles make up 50 percent of all chiles grown in the United States. 100-1,000 Scoville Units.

pasilla. A wrinkled, dark brown chilaca chile, whose Spanish name means "little raisin." It is fairly mild, measuring 1,000–1,500 Scoville Units, and is mainly used as a powder to flavor mole dishes. In California it is often (erroneously) called the "Anaheim."

pequin. Also, "piquin," "chiltepin," "bird pepper," "chile mesquito," and "chile bravo." Very hot dried pepper, usually canned. This small pepper probably takes its Spanish name from *pequeño*, "small." It is usually crushed and put into soups or sauces. Measures 50,000–100,000 Scoville Units.

pimiento. Also, "pimento." A sweet, quite mild pepper like the bell pepper.

poblano. Fairly hot, large dark green pepper. It is the fresh ancho. Measures 1,000–1,500 Scoville units.

serrano. Long, slim, very hot chile, sold green. The name is from the Spanish for "from the mountains," referring to their origins in the Mexican mountains of northern Puebla and Hidalgo. The main varieties include the "Balin," the "Tipico," and the "Largo." The "Hidalgo," bred in 1985 by the Texas Agricultural Experiment Station, has become very popular in the United States. The serrano is most often used in fresh salsas. Measures 10,000–23,000 Scoville Units.

Chilean sea bass. Also, "Patagonian toothfish." A deepwater fish (*Dissostichus eleginoides*) found along the length of Chile that grows to about 20 pounds. Its high oil content had made it an extremely popular fish in American restaurants as of the mid 1990s, so much so that it is now considered close to being an endangered species.

chiles rellenos. Also, "chilies relienos." A Mexican dish of fried stuffed chile peppers (the term means "stuffed chiles"), served throughout the Southwest and in Mexican-American restaurants (1890).

CHILES RELLENOS

Peel 12 charred chiles, leaving on the stems, and slit them open to remove seeds. Stuff the pockets with 8 oz. of Monterey Jack cheese cut in thin strips. Sift together 1 c. flour, 1 t. baking powder, ½ t. salt, ¼ c. cornmeal, and add 1 c. milk blended with 2 beaten eggs. Dip the chiles in the batter and cook in hot oil until golden. Drain and serve with guacamole, onions, and other Mexican condiments. Serves 4.

---

chili con carne. Also, "chile con carne," or simply "chili." A dish of well-seasoned and well-cooked beef with chile peppers. Chili con carne is one of the most famous dishes of Texas, although wide variations are known throughout the United States. In New Mexico, for instance, chili is commonly made without meat at all and is more a stew of chile peppers and vegetables, and is called "chili verde" (green chili, from the green peppers used), first mentioned in print by author

Stephen Crane in his description of the food stands in San Antonio, Texas.

According to Dave DeWitt and Nancy Gerlach in *The Whole Chile Pepper Book* (1990), a dish that sounded identical to what came to be called chili was described by J. C. Clopper, who visited San Antonio in 1828, and commented on how poor people would cut the little meat they could afford "into a kind of hash with nearly as many peppers as there are pieces of meat—this is all stewed together." The first mention of the word "chile" was in a book by S. Compton Smith entitled *Chile Con Carne, or The Camp and the Field* (1857), and there was a "San Antonio Chili Stand" at the 1893 Chicago World's Fair. As Waverley Root and Richard de Rochemont point out in *Eating in America* (1976), "One Mexican dictionary [Francisco J. Santamaria's *Diccionario de Mejicanismos* (1959)] even goes so far as to define chili con carne as 'a detestable food with a false Mexican title which is sold in the United States from Texas to New York.' "

Ironically, derogatory slang terms like "chili chaser" and "chili eater" are used by Americans to refer to low-class Mexicans, and when writer Stephen Crane visited San Antonio, Texas, in 1895, he wrote, "Upon one of the plazas, Mexican vendors with open-air stands sell food that tastes exactly like pounded fire-brick from hades—chili con carne, tamales, enchiladas, chili verde, frijoles." A "chili joint" referred to a cheap restaurant, more often than not serving inferior quality food.

Although chili most probably originated in Texas and has become a staple of TEX-MEX cooking, chili con carne (the preferred spelling among chile purists) is found throughout the United States in diverse forms. Chili was introduced in the Northern states in 1893 at the Chicago World's Fair, which had a San Antonio Chilley Stand. In 1902 a German immigrant in New Braunfels, Texas, created a "chili powder" that helped popularize the dish throughout the state and Southwest. In Texas cubed or shredded meat is preferred, while in other parts of the country ground beef is more common. In New Mexico one may find lamb or mutton used instead of beef. In the Old West cowboys would often throw bull's eyeballs into their chili.

In chili's native state of Texas there are several quasi-organizations devoted to the glories of the dish, and every year there are several chili contests held. The most famous is the Annual World Championship Chili Cookoff in Terlingua, Texas, sponsored by the Chili Appreciation Society International and begun in

1967 as a promotional aid for restaurateur Frank X. Tolbert's book, *A Bowl of Red: The Natural History of Chili with Recipes* (1953). ("Bowl of red" is a common term for chili in Texas.) The championship is held on the first Saturday of November, with participants from all over the world. Although the hotness of the chili is a virtue, it is the blend of flavors that ultimately decides a champion recipe.

Texas chili purists consider the addition of red kidney beans to their favorite dish (except perhaps as a side dish) as tantamount to a criminal act. Yet chili both in and outside of Texas is commonly cooked or served with beans. Chili is traditionally served with rice and beer.

In many parts of the country chili is served on top of a hamburger and called, for unknown reasons, "chili size."

"Cincinnati chili" was the creation of Macedonian immigrant Athanas Kiradjieff, who settled in Cincinnati and opened a hot-dog stand called the Empress (named after the Empress Burlesque Theater in the same building), where in 1922 he concocted a layered chili (seasoned with Middle Eastern spices) that could be served in various "ways." "Five-way" chili was the most elaborate—a mound of spaghetti topped with chili, then chopped onions, then red kidney beans, then shredded yellow cheese, and served traditionally with oyster crackers and a side order of two hot dogs topped with shredded cheese. Kiradjieff later changed the name of his chain of eateries to Empress Chili, although the popularity of another restaurant chain's Cincinnati chili—Skyline Chili (opened in 1949 by Nicholas Lambrinides)—has for some made the term "Skyline Chili" synonymous with "Cincinnati chili."

Chili con carne has even become a partisan issue in the United States Senate. In 1974 Arizona senator Barry Goldwater challenged Texas senator John Tower on the floor of the Senate to a cooking contest with the words, "A Texan does not know chili from the leavings in a corral." The following spring a panel of five "experts" judged chilis made by the two legislators, and Goldwater's came out the best of the lot.

Today chili con carne is sold in restaurants called "chili parlors" or "chili joints." Chili is also widely available in cans. The Department of Agriculture stipulates that products labeled "chili con carne" must contain at least 40 percent meat; "chili con carne with beans" at least 25 percent meat; "chili hot dog with meat" 40 percent meat; "chili mac" (with macaroni and beans) at least 16 percent; and "chili sauce with meat" at least 6 percent.

CHILI CON CARNE

Cut up 4 lb. beef chuck into cubes and brown in hot oil, then remove and drain off excess grease. Brown in oil 1½ c. chopped onions with 6 green or red chile peppers, then add to meat and mix well. Add 3 T. cumin, 2 T. oregano, 1–2 bay leaves, ¾ c. hot paprika, 1½ T. chili powder, 3 T. chopped coriander (cilantro), 5 Cloves chopped garlic, ¼ t. ground pepper, 1 t. salt, and 1 c. water. Simmer until meat is tender, add a little water if necessary, adjust salt, pepper, and hot seasonings to taste. Serves 10.

CINCINNATI FIVE-WAY CHILI

Brown 1 lb. ground beef with 2 chopped onions and 3 cloves minced garlic in a skillet with 3 T. vegetable oil. Add 1 c. tomato sauce, 1 c. water, 1 T. red-wine vinegar, ¼ c. ketchup, 1 t. black pepper, salt to taste, 1–2 T. chili powder, ½ t. ground cumin, ½ t. marjoram, ½ t. turmeric, ½ t. nutmeg, ¾ t. cinnamon, ½ t. allspice, ¼ t. ground cloves, ¼ t. mace, ¼ t. cardamom, 1 crumbled bay leaf, and ½ t. unsweetened cocoa powder. Bring to a boil, lower heat to a simmer, and cook, covered, for about one hour.

Boil ¾ lb. thick spaghetti until soft, drain and divide into 4–6 portions on plates. Spoon some of the chili onto the spaghetti. Spoon some warmed red kidney beans onto chili. Spoon chopped onions on top of the beans. Grate yellow Cheddar cheese on top of the dish. Serve with oyster crackers and cheese-topped hot dogs on the side. Serves 4–6.

chili con queso. An appetizer dip made of chile peppers and cheese (the Spanish term means "chile pepper with cheese"), it is a staple of Tex-Mex and Mexican-American menus.

CHILI CON QUESO

Melt 1 c. Monterey Jack cheese with ¾ c. sharp Cheddar in a double boiler. Add ¼ c. heavy cream and blend with 1 chopped tomato, 1 chopped onion, 1 chopped charred chile pepper, and 1 clove minced garlic. Serve with corn chips.

chili queen. A Texas slang term for a Mexican in the downtown section of San Antonio who sold tamales from quickly set-up stands, which started appearing in the municipal market in Military Plaza in the 1880s.

These stands were prohibited for sanitary reasons by Mayor Charles Kennon Quin in 1937. According to Green Peyton in his book, *San Antonio: City in the Sun* (1946), "The singers still gather around your car and serenade you. But without the chili queens to exchange the anatomical insults with them in sonorous Spanish, they seem a bit lackadaisical and depressed."

chili sauce. Any of a variety of well-seasoned, chile pepper-based condiments, most often used with Mexican-American dishes (1880).

chimichanga. A deep-fried wheat tortilla stuffed with minced beef, potatoes, and seasonings. The term was long considered a nonsense word—a Mexican version of "whatchamacallit" or "thingamajig"—reputedly coined in the 1950s in Tucson, Arizona, although Diana Kennedy, in her *Cuisines of Mexico* (1972), reports that fried burritos in Mexico are called by the similar name *chivichangas*. But in *The Food Lover's Handbook to the Southwest* (1992), Dave DeWitt and Mary Jane Wilan noted that Tucson writer Janet Mitchell found that *changa* means a female monkey in Spanish and *chimenea* a chimney or hearth. When put together this becomes, according to Jim Griffith of the Arizona Southwest Folklore Center, a polite version of an "unmentionable Mexican expletive that mentions a monkey." According to DeWitt and Wilan,

> *Investigator Mitchell heard tales about the first* chimichanga *being created when a burro was accidentally knocked into a deep-fat fryer, and the cook exclaimed, "Chimichanga!" She had also heard that a baked burro cooked in a bar in Nogales [Arizona] in the 1940s bad been called a toasted monkey.*
>
> *The logical conclusion, then, was that the idiom* chimichanga *means toasted monkey and is an allusion to the golden-brown color of the deep-fried burro.*

CHIMICHANGA

Coarsely chop 2 lb. chuck steak, add 2 diced potatoes, 6 green or red chiles that have been charred, peeled, and deseeded, 1 onion, 3 cloves garlic, 1 t. oregano, salt, pepper, and enough water to cover. Boil, then lower heat and simmer for 1 hr., till meat is tender and texture is stew-like. Place the mixture in 12 wheat tortillas and fold into a packet, then fry in hot oil until golden brown. Drain, serve with shredded lettuce, sour cream, guacamole, and chili sauce. Serves 6.

Chinese cabbage (*Brassica rapa pekinensis*). Also, "celery cabbage," "Chinese white cabbage," "Chinese mustard cabbage," and "white celery mustard." A long-stemmed, leafy cabbage used in salads and Oriental cooking.

The term has been used in print since the 1830s. "Bok choy" (*Brassica rapa chinensis*) also goes by the name "Chinese cabbage," and is a similar plant.

chinese grits. A slang term for rice. See GRITS.

chipped beef. Dried beef. The term derives from early English usage of the word "chip," "to strip or pare away a crust." The dish has been known at least since 1819 in print.

Dried beef was a staple of the early American diet, and even much later, when more desirable forms of beef were readily available, chipped beef in a flour-based gravy continued to be a popular luncheon or buffet item called, in slang, SHIT ON A SHINGLE.

"Chipped ham" is a similar form of dried meat, especially popular in Pittsburgh, Pennsylvania.

CREAMED CHIPPED BEEF

Shred ½ lb. dried beef into strips. Melt ½ c. butter in pan and brown meat. Add salt and pepper and sprinkle with 6 T. flour. Add 2 pt. milk gradually, stirring constantly until blended, and cook until it boils. Lower heat and simmer until thickened. Serves 12.

---

chitterlings. Also, "chitlins." A hog's innards, which are either fried or boiled, most popular in the South and as soul food in the northern cities. The term dates in print to 1250.

Chitterlings were rarely found in American cookbooks until recently, and sometimes disguised under the name "Kentucky oysters." Most African-Americans pronounce the word "chitlins," but the origins of the word are in Middle English *chiterling*, "body organs." Chitterlings may also be called, euphemistically, "wrinkled steak."

Salley, South Carolina, calls itself the "Chitlin Capital of the World," and has held a post-Thanksgiving "Chitlin Strut" each year since 1966.

CHITTERLINGS

Chitterlings should be well washed so as to remove any residue. For 5 lb. of chitterlings, add 1 large chopped onion, 1 t. salt, ¼ c. vinegar, and about ½ c. water, simmer for 2 hr., stirring occasionally, then cut into smaller pieces and continue cooking for two more hours. Correct seasoning and add water as necessary.

To fry chitterlings, repeat steps above, but do not cut up into small pieces. Make a batter from ⅔ c. milk, 1 beaten egg, ⅔ c. flour, ½ t. baking powder, ¼ t. salt, and stir until smooth. Dip chitterlings in batter and fry in hot fat.

choc. An inferior beer originally made by the Choctaw Indians, dating in print to 1929. The term came to mean any such low-grade beer.

chocoholic. A slang term for a person with a very strong appetite for chocolate. The term, a play on "alcoholic," gained currency in the 1980s.

chocolate. Both chocolate and cocoa come from the tropical bean known as *Theobroma cacao*. The use of chocolate in everything from hot and cold drinks to candymaking to pastries and other confections makes it one of the world's most versatile flavorings. The word "chocolate" comes via the Spanish from the Aztec Indian word *xocolatl,* meaning "bitter water." The Aztecs drank the pounded beans with spices but no sugar and believed that the bean was brought from the heavens by the gods (indeed, *Theobroma* means "food of the gods"). So valuable were these beans that a hundred of them were worth the price of a slave in Mexico, where they were used as currency. Recent scientific studies have indicated that the cacao bean cultivated today is more closely related to wild South American plants rather than to domesticated Mayan trees.

Some authorities say Columbus brought cocoa beans to Spain, but they were of little interest until Hernando Cortés returned with the beans and some Aztec hints on how to process them. Cortés first tasted chocolate at a ceremony with the Aztec king Montezuma, who reputedly believed in the drink's aphrodisiac powers and consumed up to fifty large cups a day. The Aztecs also enjoyed chocolate with red peppers and chilled with snow. The Spanish found their bitterness off-putting, but, with the addition of sugar, a chocolate drink was prepared that became immediately popular throughout Europe. The term "chocolate" appears in print in England as of 1604, and by 1657 a Frenchman had opened a "cocoa house" in London that sold prepared chocolate at the very high price of ten to fifteen shillings per pound.

Chocolate became the fashionable drink in Europe in the eighteenth century, and was first manufactured in America in 1765 at Milton Lower Mills, near Dorchester, Massachusetts, with beans from the West Indies. By 1780 John Hannan had opened the first chocolate factory under the financing of Dr. James Baker, and the products sold from there were called "Baker's Chocolate." (There is still a product called "Baker's Chocolate" made by General Foods, Inc.) Baker's also produced a sweet chocolate named "Baker's German Sweet Chocolate," after an English confectioner at the factory whose name was Samuel German, which forms the basis of GERMAN'S SWEET CHOCOLATE CAKE. Cocoa powder was first produced in 1828.

But hard chocolate, of the consistency of candy, was still unknown at the beginning of the nineteenth century, while the liquid form was promoted mainly as a restorative. (Thomas Jefferson believed chocolate superior to tea or coffee in this regard.)

On the basis of a Mexican Indian's process of using sifted wood ashes to refine the raw cocoa into a more digestible form, Holland's C. J. Van Houten found a way to alkalize chocolate and make it darker through a process, which also released cocoa butter, that came to be called "dutching." When combined with sugar and chocolate, the butter enabled processors to make a hardened candy bar, and by 1842 the Cadbury Company of England was selling such confections; Americans were eating "chocolate creams" (candies with sugar-cream centers) by the 1860s.

In 1875 a Swiss chocolate manufacturer named Daniel Peter combined his product with sweetened condensed milk, recently discovered by Henri Nestlé, a Swiss chemist, thereby creating the first milk chocolate, which became extremely popular in Europe and the United States. The Nestlé Food Company opened facilities in New York in 1905 to act as a sales agency for its products. But America's first mass-produced milk-chocolate candy was the Hershey Bar, manufactured in 1894 by Milton Snavely Hershey of Lancaster, Pennsylvania.

In the present century chocolate took powerful hold of the candy and confections market, and "cocoa" or "hot chocolate"—a mixture of cocoa powder, sugar, and milk or water—became a popular wintertime beverage. Hershey's first manufactured such a cocoa in 1894. This was in time packaged with dried milk which needed only water to turn it into a beverage.

After World War II powdered and sugared chocolate were processed so that they would dissolve in cold milk, and "chocolate milk" became a household word. Chocolate is also made into syrups, sodas, milk shakes, fudge, cookies, cakes, and every imaginable kind of dessert. Its association with Valentine's Day (February

14)—represented by giving chocolate hearts or boxes of gift-wrapped chocolate candies filled with sweet sugar creams, fruits, liqueurs, or nuts—was well promoted by the 1890s. Chocolate Easter bunnies and Easter eggs have made that feast a rather sweet one, and one may well throw in chocolate Santas for Christmas. Commercial "chocolate kisses" (a large droplet of milk or other chocolate shaped something like an acorn cap), made by the Hershey Company since 1907, were called "Wilbur Buds" when first introduced in 1893 by a manufacturer of that name (although there are recipes for kisses before then). "Chocolate babies" (once called "nigger babies" in less enlightened times), tiny figures of babies molded in chocolate, have been known since the 1890s.

Within the last decade the world consumption of cacao beans has averaged six hundred thousand tons annually, most of it coming from Africa. The "chocolate belt" of countries producing the bean extends around the middle of the tropical regions of the earth, from places like Guatemala, Nicaragua, Panama, Costa Rica, Nigeria, Trinidad, and the Ivory Coast. The largest producer is Ghana, where the "Forastero" bean constitutes the staple of the world's consumption. The "Maracaibo" bean, from Venezuela, and the "Puerto Cabello," also South American, are highly prized and are blended in the more expensive chocolates.

The production of chocolate begins with the picking of the pods with a "cacao hook." Each pod on the tree contains between twenty and forty beans, which are removed from the pods by hand and then left in the open air before fermenting in "sweating boxes," boxes with perforated slats that allow the beans to drip their juices. The beans are then dried, washed, and put in sacks for shipping. At the chocolate plants the beans are roasted in various ways to produce several different flavors that will be blended. The shells are removed by a machine, called a "cracker and fanner," that separates the nibs and shells and blows away the debris.

The beans are approximately 50 percent fat, called "cocoa butter," and 50 percent liquid, called "chocolate liquor." The former is expressed as a gold liquid, while the latter becomes a thick paste that, unsweetened, is turned into baking or cooking chocolate. "Cocoa powder" is made by melting the chocolate liquor and pressing out more of the cocoa butter. The remaining hard mass is then ground into a fine powder and sold, either as a flavoring or for making cocoa and hot chocolate.

To make "sweet" chocolate for candy and other confections, sugar and a little vanilla are mixed with the chocolate liquor. It is then processed to a smooth texture in the form of a paste, to which is added cocoa butter before being hardened by cooling. "Milk chocolate" is mixed from this sweetened chocolate and more cocoa butter, sugar, and milk, and then processed to remove moisture and to give smoothness. "Semisweet chocolate" has a lower quantity of sugar than sweet chocolate.

In 1997 Americans consumed 3.1 billion pounds of chocolate (11.7 lbs. per person) for an industry sales total of $12.5 billion, 96.7 percent of which was made in the United States. Most American chocolate is made with large amounts of cocoa powder and some lecithin emulsifier to reduce the required amount of cocoa butter.

chocolate velvet cake. A very rich, densely textured chocolate cake that originated at The Four Seasons restaurant in New York. It was the creation of pastry chef Albert Kumin in 1959. Since then chocolate velvet cake has become synonymous with very rich, thick cake with a fudgelike consistency.

chop house. In its most basic form, a restaurant that specializes in serving beef, lamb, veal, and pork chops. In the nineteenth century the term, which dates in print to 1690, usually referred to an inexpensive, very rudimentary eating establishment. But according to Charles G. Shaw in *Nightlife: Vanity Fair's Intimate Guide to New York After Dark* (1931), chophouses became far more elaborate establishments after the turn of the century and grew out of the older "dining saloons" or "oyster rooms" of the nineteenth century and were originally based on English models:

The New York chophouse of to-day, wrote Shaw, has acquired a true Yankee tang and in many cases has gone so far as to outstrip its London counterpart. Native, and even local dishes, will frequently be featured; elaborate dressings introduced; while in some instances a "ladies section" has been actually installed. On the whole, you will find the chophouse plain and I fear rather noisy. You may feel a certain primness in the dearth of brilliant color. For its aspect is seldom a gay one. . . . On the other hand, the chophouse has a real solidity, a thorough, wholesome quality in everything from the furnishings to the cooking.

Everyone talks at the top of his voice (to be heard above the din of jingling cutlery, rushing waiters, and orders from the kitchen), and if, perchance, the man at the table next to you bellows in your ear, do not be alarmed. It is all in the game, and the tenderness of the sirloin is the first consideration. For these are halls of honest worth and simple fare, where show and chi-chi are unknown and the vigor of grills and roasts triumph supreme.

chop suey. A Chinese-American dish of widely varying ingredients, but usually containing bamboo shoots, water chestnuts, bean sprouts, celery, soy sauce, and either pork or chicken. Although there is no such dish by this name in China, there is a story that when the first Chinese statesman to visit the United States, Viceroy Li Hung-chang, arrived in 1896, he was asked by American newspapermen what kind of food he ate. "Chop suey" was supposedly their transcription of the Mandarin words *"tsa tsui,"* which means "a little of this and that." Yet "chop suey" appears in American print at least as early as 1888.

Chop suey is probably derived from the mixture of vegetables and meat concocted by the Chinese cooks who fed the workers on the Pacific railroad lines in the middle of the last century. When Chinese began opening restaurants in Chinatowns in New York, San Francisco, and other cities in the late nineteenth century, they became known as "chop suey parlors."

Americanized Chinese dishes such as this and chow mein were served in Chinese restaurants to American customers, but rarely would a Chinese indulge in such a food. In his book *Bohemian San Francisco* (1914), Clarence E. Edwards noted that after the earthquake of 1906 "a number of places [in Chinatown] have been opened to cater to Americans, and on every hand one sees 'chop suey' signs and 'Chinese noodles.' It goes without saying that one seldom sees a Chinaman eating in the restaurants that are most attractive to Americans." And in the 1944 motion picture *Destination Tokyo*, a flight officer warns a B-24 bomber crew, "If you land in China, don't order chop suey. That's strictly an American dish."

"American chop suey" is a New England dish of ground beef, noodles, and tomato sauce.

CHOP SUEY

Slice 2 chicken breasts into thin strips, then sauté in 2 T. oil until lightly cooked. Add 1 c. sliced button mushrooms, 1 chopped green pepper, ½ c. sliced water chestnuts, 1 can Chinese vegetables, 1 chopped stalk of celery, 3 T. soy sauce, and ½ c. chicken broth. Bring to a boil, then simmer for 3 min. Blend 1 T. cornstarch into 4 T. cold water, mix, then add to simmering chicken. When thickened, remove from heat and serve over hot white rice.

chorizo. A spicy pork sausage found in Hispanic cooking from Spain to California. Called "chaurice" in Louisiana, chorizo is used in egg dishes and tortillas, as appetizers, or as part of a main dish. The word was first printed in 1846.

chow. A slang term (dating in print to 1856), especially popular with American servicemen, for food served to them by the cook. It also referred to mealtime, although "chow time" was also heard. A "chowhound" was someone who was first in a "chow line" for food. These were well-known army terms by World War I, but the word "chow" goes back to the era when Chinese laborers worked on the Pacific railroads during the 1850s. The word may have been picked up by sailors from Pidgin English, which in turn got it from the Mandarin Chinese *ch'ao,* "to fry" or "cook."

chow-chow. A relish of pickles or other vegetables. The word may be from the Mandarin Chinese *cha,* "mixed," and dates in print to 1785, when Chinese laborers worked on the railroads of the American West.

CHOW-CHOW

Mix together 1 qt. small cucumbers, 1 qt. large cucumbers, 1 qt. sliced green tomatoes, 1 qt. sliced onions, 1 qt. small onions, 1 qt. chopped cauliflower, and 4 chopped peppers. Cover with 1 c. salt in 4 qt. water. Let stand for 24 hr., then heat until scalded. Drain. Mix 1 c. flour, 1½ c. sugar, 6 T. mustard, and 1 t. turmeric with 1 pt. vinegar. Pour into 2 pt. vinegar and heat in double boiler until thickened. Add to vegetables and pack into clean jars and seal.

chowder. A seafood soup associated with New England, the most popular of which is clam chowder. The term may also describe a buttery, hearty soup made with corn, chicken, or other chunks or bits of food still evident in the blend.

The origins of the word "chowder" are somewhat obscure, but most authorities, including the *Dictionary of American Regional English,* believe it derives from the French word for a large cauldron, *chaudière,* in which Breton sailors threw their catch to make a communal stew, a custom carried to Newfoundland, Nova Scotia, and down to New England in the seventeenth and eighteenth centuries. But in *Down East Chowder* (1982), John Thorne contends that evidence for such a derivation is very tenuous, noting that "the phrase *'faire la chaudière'* seems no longer to exist in Brittany, while *chaudrée,* another touted source of origin, resembles chowder no more and no less than any fish soup resembles another. (The French word for cauldron, by the way, is *chaudron,* not *chaudière*—that latter word has more the meaning of a steam boiler.)"

Although the *Oxford English Dictionary* suggests *chaudière* as the etymological link, it also lists "chowdee" as a dialectical variation of an old Cornwall or Devonshire word, "jowter," for a fish peddler. Certainly fish stews existed in almost every sea-bound country in the world, and the distinction between these and the earliest chowders of New England are a matter of interpretation. New England chowders have been known at least since the 1730s, and were first mentioned in print by a New England diarist in 1732, by which time salt pork seemed to have already attained the status of a prerequisite ingredient. The first printed recipe for chowder was a piece of doggerel published in the *Boston Evening Post* for September 23, 1751, that called for fish, onions, salt pork, sweet marjoram, savory, thyme, and biscuit, to which was added a bottle of red wine. This and other early chowders were undoubtedly more like a pudding or thick stew than a soup, a perfect consistency for onboard consumption, especially since, as Thorne notes, "it uses a minimum of one of the most precious of shipboard supplies: water."

The first American cookbook to give a chowder recipe was the second edition of Amelia Simmons's *American Cookery* (1800). It called for bass, salt pork, crackers, and a side dish of potatoes. Ketchup and flour were suggested to thicken the dish in early-nineteenth-century recipes, by which time New England chowders had become more like a soup. Although by 1836 "clam chowder" was known in Boston, where its associations are still strong, throughout the century chowder was less commonly a dish of clams than of fish, usually cod or haddock, and by the 1840s potatoes had become a traditional ingredient.

Chowder was a staple dish of New Englanders, and for sailors merely another way to make a constant diet of fish palatable. In *Moby Dick* (1851) Herman Melville wrote of the Try Pots, a chowder house in Nantucket, where one might have a choice of either cod or clam chowder. Melville's hero, Ishmael, ordered the latter: "Oh! sweet friends, hearken to me. It was made of small juicy clams, scarcely bigger than hazel nuts, mixed with pounded ship biscuits, and salted port cut up into little flakes! the whole enriched with butter, and plentifully seasoned with pepper and salt." Melville went on to describe the menu at the Try Pots—"Chowder for breakfast, and chowder for dinner, and chowder for supper, till you began to look for fish-bones coming through your clothes."

By the end of the century certain New England regions became known for their various interpretations of chowder—one might find cream in one spot, lobsters in others, no potatoes elsewhere—but most were by then a creamy white soup brimming with chopped fish or clams, crackers, and butter. By the 1830s in Rhode Island, however, cooks often added tomatoes to their chowder, a practice that brought down unremitting scorn from chowder fanciers in Massachusetts and Maine, who associated such a concoction with New York because the dish came to be called, for no discernible reason, "Manhattan clam chowder" sometime in the 1930s. By 1940 Eleanor Early in her *New England Sampler* decried this "terrible pink mixture (with tomatoes in it, and herbs) called Manhattan Clam Chowder, that is only a vegetable soup, and not to be confused with New England Clam Chowder, nor spoken of in the same breath. Tomatoes and clams have no more affinity than ice cream and horseradish." In her 1954 *New England Cookbook* she goes on to note that Rhode Islanders and Connecticut cooks believe Cape Cod milk chowder is fit "only for babies and sick people," to which Early replies, "Nonsense! Cape Cod is full of happy octogenarians." She nevertheless includes a recipe for tomato-laden Rhode Island clam chowder.

Just why tomato-based chowder is called "Manhattan" has never been satisfactorily explained. A note in *The New York Times* for January 24, 1990, cites a letter dated December 25, 1978, from Austin Phelps Winters to the effect that his father, William H. Winters, and his uncle James ran a fish store at New York's Fulton Fish Market where the two brothers made a chowder with tomatoes instead of milk because milk "was too expensive" and called it "Manhattan clam chowder." There is no other corroboration of this report, however.

The issue of whether one should add tomato to chowder is merely a regional preference, for tomatoes fill the fish stews of many countries' kitchens, and neither Manhattanites nor Rhode Islanders are original or adamant on the matter.

Today chowders made with clams predominate, but fish chowders are also popular. Noting that in Oregon a "first-rate chowder is made with corn and fresh salmon," Thorne recommends cod, haddock, whiting, flounder, cusk, hake, and halibut. The best clams for a chowder are traditionally the large quahogs.

CLAM CHOWDER

Shell 3 doz. clams, remove tips and chop up coarsely. Peel and dice 5 potatoes. Fry ¼ lb. salt pork with 2 diced onions until soft. Add potatoes to 1 qt. boiling water, then add pork and onions. Cook until tender. Scald and strain 1½ c. clam liquid, then add to kettle. Add clams, bring to a boil, add 1 qt. milk, pepper to taste, and several common crackers. Serve when warm.

FISH CHOWDER

Cook 3 diced onions in 2 T. salt pork until soft. In 2 c. water boil 4 diced potatoes until tender, add onions, 2 lb. cut-up fish, ½ lb. butter, salt, pepper, ¼ t. savory, 1 can evaporated milk, and 3 c. milk. Heat but do not boil. Serves 6.

MANHATTAN CLAM CHOWDER

Brown 2 oz. salt pork in a skillet, then remove and drain. In a large kettle place the salt pork, 1 pt. opened clams chopped fine, 1½ c. clam liquid, 2 peeled and diced potatoes, ½ c. water, 1 chopped onion, 1 stalk celery, 1 chopped carrot, 6 peeled, seeded, chopped tomatoes, 1 chopped green pepper, ⅓ c. tomato paste, 1 bay leaf, ½ t. thyme, salt, and pepper. Bring to a boil, reduce heat, and simmer for 2 hr.

chow mein. A Chinese-American dish made of stewed vegetables and meat with fried noodles. The term comes from Mandarin Chinese *ch'ao mien,* "fried noodles," and probably was brought to the United States by Chinese cooks serving the workers on the western railroads in the 1850s. The word first appears in print in 1900. Although most chow mein bears scant resemblance to true Mandarin cooking, it has become a staple in Chinese-American restaurants. H. L. Mencken noted that at least one Chinese authority vouched for the Chinese origins of the dish, though in America it is "a bit flavored up for Western palates."

Owing to its inexpensive ingredients, chow mein has long been a lunch dish in American school cafeterias.

CHOW MEIN

Heat 3 T. oil in a saucepan over high heat, and sauté 1 c. sliced beef or chicken until brown. Add 1 c. sliced celery, 1 c. diced onion, and 1 c. water. Stir and cook until tender, covered. Add 1 can of Chinese vegetables, 3 T. flour mixed with ½ c. water, 2 T. soy sauce, 1 t. salt, ½ t. paprika, and ¼ t. celery salt. Serve on rice and top with 1 can Chinese fried noodles.

Christy Girl. A cocktail that originated at the Howard Chandler Christy Room of New York's Sherry Netherland Hotel. Christy (1873–1952) was a prominent illustrator of the early part of this century and later a sought-after portrait painter. His illustrations of the American girl as a perky outdoorswoman of considerable daring for the era inspired the cocktail, though it is rarely ordered today.

CHRISTY GIRL

Shake together ½ jigger peach brandy, ½ jigger dry gin, a dash of grenadine, and the white of 1 egg with ice cubes. Strain into a cocktail glass and decorate with a maraschino cherry.

chuck. A western term for food of any kind, dating back to 1840 in print; also used as a verb, "to eat." A "chuck habit" is a fear of or obsession for a certain kind of food.

"Chuck" is also a butcher's term for a cut of BEEF extending from the neck to the ribs, including the shoulder blade. This cut is often used to make hamburgers and a rib roast (or "blade roast"). One oval-shaped part of the chuck may be sliced into slabs to make "chicken steaks," which are quickly grilled or pan-fried.

chuck wagon. A converted farm wagon that served as a mobile kitchen and center of social activity in the West. The chuck wagon was manned by a cook who had to store utensils and food enough to feed the range cowboys three hot meals a day. Early Texans called it the "commissary," and other terms were "mess wagon" and "growler." A "chuck box" of shelves and storage space, attached to the rear of the wagon, swung down on hinges as a worktable. Underneath was a dishpan called a "wreck pan," and under that a "cooney," a piece of dried cowhide slung to carry firewood and buffalo or cow chips. A good chuck wagon was one that could carry at least a month's provisions. The word was first printed in 1860; by the 1940s "chuck wagon" was also used for a roadside or neighborhood lunch counter. "Chuck-wagon chicken" was a cowboy term for fried bacon.

chug-a-lug. Also, "chug." A campus term, dating in print to the 1930s, that describes the sound of someone drinking a long draught of beer or spirits. Usually to chug-a-lug a drink means to swallow it down without pausing between gulps.

church key. Slang term for a bottle or can opener (1951).

cider. Pressed apple juice that is used to make both vinegar and an unfermented drink called "sweet cider" or a slightly fermented drink called "hard cider." The word derives from the Hebrew *shēkār,* which in Middle English became *cidre.* In America, "to cider," that is, to make cider, is known in the Appalachians.

Cider was by far the most popular drink of Colonial America. Everyone, including children, drank it, and it was bought very cheaply by the barrel, if not made at home. "Ciderkin" was a diluted form of cider made from a second pressing of the apple pulp residue and more water. "Cider royal" was a more pungent form that might be mixed with brandy or boiled down for strength. If mixed with rum it became a drink called "stonewall." "Cider wine" is a mixture of cider and cider brandy.

There was not only variety but a great range of quality in ciders, and the French gastronome Anthelme Brillat-Savarin (1755–1826), who spent three years in America, pronounced the native product "so excellent that I could have gone on drinking it forever." President John Adams (1735–1826), who lived to be ninety-one, prided himself on drinking a pitcher of cider every morning.

The popularity of cider waned in the nineteenth century as beer predominated with the adult population, but cider is still extremely popular with Americans, especially in autumn, when the pressings take place. "Hard cider" ranges from 3-7 percent alcohol, while "sweet cider's" alcohol content must fall below 3 percent. Above 7 percent alcohol the drink becomes wine or APPLEJACK. "Cider vinegar" is cider that has decayed beyond the vinous stage and become vinegar, widely used in cooking and salads. "Cider molasses" or "cider sauce" is cider cooked to a syrup and used as a sweetener.

In the eighteenth century the word "cider" was

occasionally applied to drinks made from the pressings of other fruits, like peaches and pears.

cilantro (*Coriandrum sativum*). Also "coriander," "Mexican parsley," and "Chinese parsley." A leafy herb of the parsley family whose dried seeds, more commonly called "coriander," are also used as a flavoring. Coriander (from the Middle English *coriandre*) has been enjoyed as a flavoring agent for millennia, though it was never much in favor in Europe, with the exception of Portugal (where it is called *coentros*), whose people may have brought it to America. The word "cilantro," which entered English print in 1903, comes from the Spanish (who have never much cared for the herb), and Americans more commonly refer to it by this name because of its prevalence in Mexican food. Indeed, cilantro has only achieved real popularity in the past decade because of the increased interest in Mexican and Oriental food. Cilantro is now grown in California's Central Coast and the Coachella Valley, with 3,500 acres under cultivation as of 1996.

cinci. Midwestern slang for a short glass of beer. The term, dating in print to 1981, refers in some way to Cincinnati, Ohio, and is often applied to a small glass.

Cincinnati oyster. A slang term for pickled pig's feet, because Cincinnati was so associated with pork products (1877).

cinderella. A muffin flavored with wine or sherry and nutmeg. The name comes from the heroine of the old fairy tale and may have something to do with the muffin's fancy appearance, just as Cinderella emerged as a grand, fancily dressed girl for the prince's ball. The recipe is from *Directions for Cookery* (1837) by Eliza Leslie, who notes that these muffins are also sometimes called "German puffs."

CINDERELLA

Beat 8 eggs until light in color, mix in 8 T. flour, 1 qt. milk, ½ lb. cooled melted butter, ¼ t. powdered nutmeg, and 1 t. cinnamon. Make a smooth batter. Fill in buttered muffin tins, bake for 15 min. at 375°. Turn muffins out on rack and sprinkle sugar over them. Serve hot with whipped cream flavored with sherry and nutmeg.

cioppino. A fish stew cooked with tomatoes, wine, and spices, and associated at least since the 1930s with San Francisco, where it is still a specialty in many restaurants (1935). The word is Italian, from a Genoese dialect, *ciuppin*, for a fish stew, and the dish seems to have originated with the Italian immigrants of San Francisco, who often used the crabmeat available in the city's markets.

CIOPPINO

In a large kettle with 4 T. olive oil sauté 4 chopped onions, 8 chopped garlic cloves, 1 diced carrot, 1 diced leek, 1 diced celery stalk, until limp. Add 1 c. tomato purée and ⅓ t. crumbled saffron. Add the meat from 2 or more crabs, 10 shrimp that have been peeled and deveined, 2 doz. clams, 2 doz. mussels, ½ lb. bay scallops, 8 oz. each of two or more fish (such as snapper or sea bass), and stir to coat with oil and other ingredients. Add 2 c. white wine, 3 c. fish stock, 2 bay leaves, ½ t. oregano, ½ t. thyme, salt, pepper, and 4 peeled and seeded chopped tomatoes. Cover, bring to a boil, then simmer for 15 min. Remove fish and reduce stock for 15 min. Return fish to stock, bring to a boil, then serve. Serves 8.

---

citric acid. Abundant in citrus fruits, this is used as an additive (as an antioxidant and flavoring agent), imparting a tart flavor to processed food.

clabber. Sour, curdled milk, rarely seen now in the United States because most milk is pasteurized and will not naturally turn to curd before it goes bad. In the South clabber was often eaten with sugar, or even with black pepper and cream. *New York Times* food writer Craig Claiborne recalled that "it was a common dish of my Southern childhood. My father raised and milked cows. The milk was allowed to stand in churns and more often than not became clabber, a semifirm, very white liquid on the bottom and a semifirm layer of yellow cream on top. The clabber was a pure product, the result of a natural bacterial action. Clabber tends to 'break apart' when dipped into. It is quite sour but of a different texture and flavor than yogurt. When you 'churned' the clabber, you wound up with butter (from the top cream layer) and buttermilk." The word comes from the Irish *bainne clabair* ("thick milk") and dates in print to 1625.

A "clabber biscuit" is a BISCUIT made with clabber. "Clabber cheese" is a synonym for COTTAGE CHEESE.

clam (class *Pelecypoda*). Any of a variety of bivalve mollusks that burrow in sand in both salt and fresh water. The word derives from Old English *clamm*, "bond" or "fetter," for its clamped shell. The mollusk has had this name in English at least since the end of the fourteenth century, although a Scot may mean a scallop when he says "clam."

Clams, of which there are more than two thousand species, exist in most regions of the world and have been consumed since prehistoric times. The earliest white settlers of North America found clams to their liking, and the Native Americans used the clamshell as money, or wampum. They also showed the New England colonists how to hold "clambakes"—social gatherings, often held at the beach after a fresh catch, which have endured to this day in that region.

The two main varieties of clams eaten on the East Coast are the "soft-shell" (*Mya arenaria*) and the "hard-shell" (*Mercenaria mercenaria*), better known as the "quahog" (from the Narraganset word *poquaûhock*), and as the "round clam." "Quahog" in English dates at least to 1753.

The soft-shell clam, also called the "long-necked clam," "piss clam" and, via Algonquin dialect, "maninose," found from the Arctic Ocean to Cape Hatteras and introduced to Pacific waters north of San Francisco, is generally used for making clam CHOWDER and frying, though it is most commonly steamed. Soft-shell clams are often called "steamers" or "clam bellies."

The hard-shell clam is preferred raw and in chowders, its size often determining its use. The smallest quahogs, less than 2¼ inches, are called "littlenecks" (after Littleneck Bay on Long Island, New York; but William and Mary Morris in their *Morris Dictionary of Word and Phrase Origins* [1971] give "Little Neck" as a clamming region of Ipswich, Massachusetts); the next size, up to three inches, is "cherrystone" (after Cherrystone Creek, Virginia); still larger quahogs are called "chowder clams" and used for that purpose. Sometimes clams less than two inches are called "Philadelphia Nicks," while those larger than two inches are called "New York Nicks."

The "razor clam" or "jacknife clam" of the East (*Ensis directus*), so called because of its sharp shell, is not as popular because it is difficult to catch. The "bar clam" (*Spisula solidissima*), also called the "beach clam," "Atlantic surf clam," "hen clam," "sea clam," and "skimmer clam," is used for chowders or deep-fried as "clam strips."

There are several clams of culinary interest on the West Coast: The "razor clam" (*Siliqua patula* and other species) is not related to the eastern variety named above; the "Pacific littleneck" (*Protothaca staminea* and others) is not related to the eastern variety either, nor is the "Philippine littleneck" (*Tapes philippinarum*); the "California bean clam" (*Donax californicus*) is eaten in soups; the "geoduck" (*Panopea generosa*)—pronounced "gooey-duck"—is very large, up to eight inches in length and five pounds in weight (it is also called "giant clam"), and has a tough texture. Its name, first appearing in English in 1883, is most probably from the Nisqualli Indian for "digging deep." This last species is dug out of beds twenty to seventy feet deep, and most of the supply is shipped to Japan, where it is considered a great delicacy. Americans may find the clam on Pacific beaches during very low tides. The process of catching one is described by Lila Gault in *The Northwest Cookbook* (1978):

The digger must first find the neck of the geoduck, which is directly below the "mark," and then center a stovepipe over it. The stovepipe is then driven into the sand as deeply as possible and the fun truly begins. The neck is held with one hand and the other scoops sand away from it, making a large hole in the process. Unlike razor clams, geoduck do not move their bodies when disturbed. Once the neck is grabbed, if the diggers are persistent, they will always get their clam! When the body of the clam is reached, often two and sometimes as much as four feet below the surface, the geoduck can be lifted out of the hole. This chase and capture actually works better with two or three people at work—a single digger must be extremely agile and tenacious to get even one of these clams.

The "Manila clam" (*Venerupis japonica* or *T. japonica*) was imported from the Orient after 1900 and became a dominant species harvested in the Northwest.

Clam farming was pioneered at the National Marine Fisheries at Milford, Connecticut, around 1930, with the first commercial hatcheries established on the East Coast in the 1960s. U.S. commercial landings of clams totaled 129.7 million pounds in 1997.

CLAMBAKE

Build a fire in a deep pit, place a layer of large, flat rocks on top of the burning wood, and repeat procedure with more wood and rocks twice more. Let burn until very hot. Rake the fire, retaining embers, and lay on top wet seaweed to a depth of about 6 in. Then place clams, mussels, lobsters, potatoes, corn, and onions on top. Cover with layers of wet canvas, cook about 1½ hr. Serve with butter.

clam fritter. A deep-fried clam in batter, supposedly first made by Lawrence Woodman at Woodman's Restaurant in Essex, Massachusetts, on July 3, 1916. Clam fritters are also called "fannie daddies" on Cape Cod and "boat steerers" in other parts of New England.

CLAM FRITTER

Beat 2 egg yolks, add ½ c. milk, 1 T. butter, 1 c. flour, salt, pepper, and 1 T. lemon juice. Beat in 2 stiffly beaten egg whites, mix in 1 pt. clams, and chill for several hours. Fry small amounts in hot oil till golden brown.

clams casino. A dish of clams mixed with butter, paprika, and shallots, then baked with small strips or pieces of bacon on top. The recipe originated at the Casino at Narragansett Pier in New York City around 1917. In his autobiography, *Inns and Outs* (1939), restaurateur Julius Keller described how society woman Mrs. Paran Stevens asked Keller, then maître d' at the Casino, to create a new dish for a luncheon she was holding for friends. Keller came up with a recipe for clams baked with bacon. When Stevens inquired as to the dish's name, Keller replied, "it has no name, Mrs. Stevens; but we shall call it clams casino in honor of this restaurant."

CLAMS CASINO

In a bowl combine 8 T. softened butter, ⅓ c. minced shallots, 1 minced pimiento, ⅓ c. minced green pepper, 3 T. minced parsley, salt and pepper to taste, ½ t. Worcestershire sauce, a dash of cayenne, and 2 T. lemon juice. Mix well, then spoon over 2 doz. opened clams on the half shell. Top each clam with half a slice of uncooked bacon. Place on a bed of rock salt on a baking sheet, cook in a 450° oven for 6–8 min. until bacon is crisp.

clams posillipo. An Italian-American dish of clams cooked with garlic, red peppers, tomatoes, and seasonings. The dish is named after the cape of Posillipo near Naples, Italy, but there is no specific, traditional dish by this name in Italy. Neither is there a "classic" Italian-American recipe, but the following recipe is typical.

CLAMS POSILLIPO

Wash and drain 4 doz. clams (littlenecks or cherrystones). In ½ c. olive oil sauté 1½ T. minced garlic and

2 seeded dried red peppers for about 1 min. Add ½ c. dry white wine, reduce by half, add 3 c. canned tomatoes and 1 T. tomato paste. Add salt and pepper, 1 T. oregano, and ¼ c. chopped parsley. Cover, bring to a boil, then simmer for 15 min. Add clams, cover, and cook until clams open, about 8–10 min. Serves 4–5.

club. A term for a bill or check for one's meal. It was first mentioned in print in 1793 but is now obsolete.

club sandwich. A sandwich usually made with three slices of toast enclosing fillings of lettuce, mayonnaise, cooked chicken breast, tomato slices, cooked bacon strips, and a garnish. James Beard, in *American Cookery* (1972), insists, however, that the original club sandwiches were made with only two slices of toast (sometimes called a "Junior club") and called the three-slice rendition "a horror." He and others have also cited the alternate name of "clubhouse sandwich," which suggests its origins were in the kitchens that prepared food for men's private social clubs.

The first appearance of the club sandwich in print was in Ray L. McCardell's *Conversations of a Chorus Girl* in 1903, and recipes were printed in Fannie Farmer's *Boston Cooking-School Cookbook* in 1906, indicating the item had been popular for some time. A letter to *The New York Times* (March 9, 1983) cited an explanation of the sandwich's origins in a book entitled *New York, a Guide to the Empire State* (1962): "In 1894 Richard Canfield (1865–1914), the debonair patron of art, purchased the Saratoga Club [in Saratoga, New York] to make it a casino. Canfield Solitaire was originated in the casino's gambling rooms and the club sandwich in its kitchens."

cobbler. A cold drink made from wine, sherry, liquor, or other alcohol with citrus juice and sugar. The word's origins are obscure; one conjecture has it associated with a shortened form of "cobbler's punch," meaning that it had the effect of "patching up" the imbiber. Washington Irving's reference to a "sherry-cobbler" in his *History of New York . . . by Diedrich Knickerbocker* (1809) is the first appearance of the word, used to describe a drink, in print.

Another kind of cobbler is a western deep-dish pie with a thick crust and a fruit filling. This dish is called BIRD'S NEST PUDDING or "crow's-nest pudding" in New England; it is served with a custard but no topping in Connecticut, with maple sugar in Massachusetts, and with a sour sauce in Vermont.

Cobb salad. A chopped salad made with avocado, lettuce, celery, tomato, bacon, chicken, chives, hard-boiled egg, watercress, and Roquefort cheese. The dish was created at the Brown Derby in Los Angeles in 1926 by owner Bob Cobb, who invented it as a way to utilize leftovers in the refrigerator. According to food writer Merrill Shindler, "The name Cobb has become generic for every sort of chopped salad, even concoctions that are more shredded or julienned than chopped." The original recipe, from the *Brown Derby Cook Book,* is given below.

COBB SALAD

Cut ½ head lettuce, ½ bunch watercress, one small bunch chicory, and ½ head romaine into fine pieces and arrange in salad bowl. Cut 2 medium, peeled tomatoes in half, remove seeds, dice finely, and arrange in strips across the salad. Dice 2 boiled chicken breasts and arrange over the greens and tomatoes. Chop finely 6 strips crisp bacon and sprinkle on salad. Cut 1 avocado in small pieces and arrange around the edge of the salad. Decorate by sprinkling the top with 3 chopped hard-boiled eggs, 2 T. chopped chives, and ½ c. grated Roquefort cheese. Just before serving, mix the salad with French dressing. Serves 4–6.

cobia. Also, "Seargeantfish," "lemon fish," "black salmon," "crabeater" and other names. A warm-water fish (*Rachycentron canadum*) of the Mid-Atlantic coast, up to five feet long, with wide stripes and a spindle shape. The origin of the word is unknown, appearing first in 1879.

cocktail. A beverage combining liquors with juices, sodas, or other ingredients. Examples would include MARTINIS, MANHATTANS, SAZERACS, SCREWDRIVERS, and many others. The term does not usually refer to punches or any hot drinks and is usually associated with apéritifs.

The word "cocktail" has been a subject of some controversy among etymologists and historians. H. L. Mencken, in his first supplement to *The American Language* (1945), notes seven sources of origin for the term, including references to the British "cock ale," a seventeenth-century concoction of chicken broth and ale. The word has been traced in print to 1800, but it appears to be somewhat older than that. Stuart Berg Flexner, in *Listening to America* (1982), strongly supports the contention that the word derives from the French *coquetier,* for "egg cup," the container in which

French apothecary Antoine Peychaud served his concoction of bitters and Sazerac-du-Forge brandy after his arrival in New Orleans about 1795. Other authorities have problems with this assertion, including Professor Arthur Schlesinger, Jr., who wondered how the word could have so quickly found its way into a Hudson, New York, newspaper (the *Balance*) by 1806 if it had only recently been coined from the French word for egg cup.

A "cocktail dress" would be a fancy dress worn by a woman to a "cocktail party," a social gathering that became popular in the 1920s, during Prohibition when alcoholic drinks were hard to find outside the home, except illegally. A "cocktail table" is a low table, usually set between sofa and chairs, around which guests sit and enjoy cocktails. A "cocktail pianist" is an entertainer who plays while people sip cocktails. A "shrimp cocktail" is a variation on the "oyster cocktail," created about 1860 by a San Francisco miner who dipped his oysters in ketchup. A "cocktail finger" is a finger-shaped piece of crabmeat similarly served as an hors d'oeuvre.

"Cocktail lounges," where one would go to enjoy cocktails, have been so called since the 1930s.

By the nineteenth century any mixture of various whiskeys was called a cocktail. Since the 1870s a mixture using champagne or a sparkling wine was called a "champagne cocktail." A "cocktail shaker," in which to mix cocktails with ice, was created as of the 1860s.

The "cocktail hour" is a period in the late afternoon or early evening when people enjoy a cocktail before dinner. The term is said to have originated in New York during Prohibition when speakeasies had a tacit understanding with police officials not to open until 6:00 P.M. An establishment named Tony's restaurant at 42 East Fifty-third Street defied this agreement by opening at 4:00 P.M., and a press agent took to calling this period between 4:00 P.M. and 6:00 P.M. "the cocktail hour."

coconut. Also, "cocoanut." The large pod fruit of the coconut palm (*Cocos nucifera*). The interior white meat of the fruit and its milky liquid are eaten fresh or dried as desserts, as a garnish, or as an oil for cooking. The word is a combination of a Portuguese children's term, *coco*, for the "goblin" shell of the fruit, and the English word "nut." The fruit was first mentioned in English print in 1555, and the first American reference was in 1834.

The origins of the coconut have never been fully understood, but some believe it is native to tropical America and was dispersed to Pacific islands by the drift of the pods through the ocean. Coconuts were known in Egypt by the sixth century A.D., and Marco Polo noted them in India and elsewhere in the Far East. Certainly coconuts were encountered on the Pacific shores of South America and Hawaii, but coconut is not a major crop of the latter. Most of the coconut enjoyed by Americans is imported from Indonesia, the Philippines, and other Pacific countries. Half the coconuts used in the food industry actually come from noncultivated trees.

The dried meat of coconut, called "copra" (probably from the Hindi *khopra*, for "coconut") is shredded or flaked, often sweetened, or processed to make coconut oil. Americans eat coconut fresh, but most often use it in its dried form in desserts such as coconut cake, known at least since 1830. By 1909 coconut ices were enjoyed. Coconut cream, a viscous, sweet, homogenized liquid made with coconut, sugar, and various thickeners, was created in 1948 by Don Ramón Lopez-Irizarry of Puerto Rico, who sold the item under the name "Coco Lopez." It is principally used to make cocktails like the PIÑA COLADA.

cod (family Gadidae). Also, "codfish." Any of a variety of marine fishes in this family. Cod is one of the most important food fishes in the world, both fresh and, especially, salted and dried. The word is possibly related to the Middle English word "cod," meaning a "bag," the shape of which resembles the hefty codfish. The first printed mention of the word as a fish was in 1460.

Cod is a fish inextricably linked to the history and fortunes of America; the fish's abundance in eastern waters was excitedly noted by Venetian navigator Giovanni Caboto (who sailed for England as "John Cabot") on his exploration of Newfoundland in 1497. An English adventurer, Bartholomew Gosnold, found so many of the fish when he sailed south of Nova Scotia in 1602 that he named the arm of land in those waters "Cape Cod," later a center of the New England fishing industry. In 1630 Francis Higginson wrote, "The abundance of Sea-Fish are almost beyond beleeving, and sure I whould scarce have baleeved it except I had seene it with mine owne eyes." Ten years later Massachusetts, whose fishing industry had begun in Gloucester in 1623, sent three hundred thousand dried codfish to market. By 1640 the Massachusetts Bay Colony was shipping 300,000 cod to the world market.

The cod trade developed rapidly. American shipbuilders in 1713 created the New England schooner for fishing in the worst of weather, and the newly rich fishing families of the region were slightly referred to as the "codfish aristocracy." So important was the cod to the livelihood of Massachusetts that the state's House of Representatives voted in 1784 to hang a white-pine carving of the "Sacred Cod" in their meeting room, where it is still displayed today.

Cod also had a role in maintaining the lucrative triangular trade between England, the North American and West Indian colonies, and Africa. Dried cod would be shipped to Europe, the boats would then pick up slaves in Africa, stop in the Caribbean to load on molasses and sugar, and sell the latter goods to New England-run distilleries, a continual journey of economic barbarism that lasted for more than eighty years.

The American Revolution's peace treaty included provisions for American boats to fish in English waters, thanks to Massachusetts's John Adams.

Young cod is called SCROD, which is also the name of a dish of young cod baked with white wine and milk. Dried cod is sometimes called "dunfish" in New England.

Per capita U.S. consumption of cod is 1.12 lbs. annually, with about 28.6 million pounds of Atlantic cod and 661 million pounds of Pacific cod brought to market in 1997.

The principal types of cod found in American waters include:

Atlantic cod (*Gadus morbua*). This enormous cod dominates the industry, with nearly 7 billion pounds caught annually around the world. It ranges the North Atlantic, rarely going as far south as Virginia. It is sometimes called "rock cod."

haddock (*Melanogrammus aeglefinus*). Ranging throughout the North Atlantic as far south as New Jersey, the haddock usually weighs between two and five pounds and is preferred fresh rather than salted (1275). "Finnan haddie" (from a Scottish port, Findhorn, and the Scottish word for haddock) is a smoked haddock popularized by John Ross, Jr., in the nineteenth century.

The haddock population has been severely reduced in recent years but has started to make a comeback, with 3.3 million pounds landed by U.S. commercial fishing in 1997.

lingcod. Also, "blue cod." A large Pacific coastline fish (*Ophiodon elongatus*) with a greenish hue to its skin (1929). The BURBOT (*Lota maculosa*) also goes by this name (first in print as of 1946), as well as by "buffalo," "cultus cod," and "green." U.S. commercial landings of lingcod totaled 4.1 million pounds in 1997.

coddes. Also, "coddies" and "codfish ball." Salt-cod cakes mixed with mashed potatoes, coated with bread crumbs, deep-fried, and served at room temperature with mustard between two Saltine crackers, either as a snack or a lunch item. They are a specialty of Baltimore, Maryland, where they were commonly sold at drugstore soda fountains.

coddle. To cook in a liquid just below the boiling point, as with eggs. Coddled apples are made by cooking apple slices in a syrup of water and sugar in the ratio of 2 to 1. The term goes back at least to the sixteenth century.

coffee. Roasted, ground beans from the coffee plant (genus *Coffea*), or a beverage made from these beans. The main species, *C. arabica*, indigenous to Ethiopia, is now grown throughout the so-called coffee belt that rings the world between latitudes of 25 degrees North and 30 degrees South. Arabica beans now constitute about 75 percent of the world's coffee-bean production. "Congo coffee" (*C. robusta*), with a more robust taste, makes up most of the rest of the world's production.

Coffee plants originated in Ethiopia, and the word's etymology derives either from its shipping point, Kaffa, in that country, or from the Arabic *guhiya*, or Turkish *kahveh*, which referred to a wine tonic that restored the appetite.

There are several legends as to who first brewed coffee: One involves a goatherd of Kaffa named Kaldi whose goats were particularly sprightly after consuming the caffeine-rich coffee beans—an activity noticed by a local monk named Mullah, who brewed a beverage from the beans and spread word of its restorative virtues throughout the region. An Arab legend of the fifteenth century contends that the ninth-century mufti of Aden was the first to make the drink, after which it became a favorite of the Middle Eastern courts. The first mention of coffee in English is in 1590.

Coffee beans were brought to Italy by 1615, and by 1644 to France, where, thanks to the efforts of Turkish ambassador Suleiman Aga, it became a fashionable beverage in 1669 at the court of Louis XIV, who introduced a single coffee seedling to the Caribbean island of Martinique and began a spread of the plant throughout Central and South America that eventually made Brazil the world's largest coffee producer. (The Dutch introduced the plant to Indonesia and Java, and "Java" became an American slang term for all coffee as of the mid-nineteenth century.)

The first coffeehouse in London was opened in 1688 by Edward Lloyd (who later built the insurance company Lloyd's of London), and more sprouted quickly, as they did in America, where the Dutch had introduced coffee by 1670. The Merchants Coffee House in New York had by the middle of the eighteenth century become known for entertaining several of the leading revolutionary dissenters of the day. In protest against the high taxes imposed by the British on tea, Americans turned to coffee, causing coffee sales to increase during the Revolutionary War by 600 percent. But coffee's own high price prevented it from becoming a truly popular drink for decades afterward, and mock coffee made from rye (called "Boston coffee," although in the twentieth century this refers to a cup of half coffee and half cream), peas ("Canadian coffee"), and burnt bread ("crumb coffee") was often substituted.

In the 1860s tea importers George Huntington Hartford and George Gilman organized the American Coffee Corporation to buy beans directly from Brazil and Colombia; thereby making coffee less expensive for the American consumer—twenty-five cents per pound, as compared with the two dollars per pound Americans had paid before—and helping it to become America's favorite beverage.

Americans got the coffee percolator from the English, but "drip pot" was an American term by the end of the century. The "Neapolitan flip" (so called because it is of Southern Italian origins) is a method of pouring boiling water over ground coffee placed in a paper filter inside a funnel inside a pouring pot.

"Iced coffee" was first served at the Philadelphia Centennial Exposition in 1876.

In 1878 James Sanborn and Caleb Chase produced the first ground coffee sealed in tin cans. The American taste in coffee was largely due to a blend developed by Joel Cheek of Nashville, Tennessee, and served in the 1880s at the Maxwell House hotel in that city. It became extremely popular, especially after President Theodore Roosevelt in 1907 pronounced the coffee "good to the last drop," which is the motto of the brand Maxwell House, to this day.

In New Orleans, the people were drinking CHICORY coffee, a more bitter brew than most American blends. In 1903 a caffeine-free coffee called "Sanka" (from French *sans caféine*, "without caffeine") was developed by Dr. Ludwig Roselius of Bremen, Germany, but was not successful until it was promoted in the 1930s by the General Foods company. Decaffeinated coffee is made by various methods utilizing either water processing or chemical solvents like ethyl acetate. Today decaffeinated coffee makes up nearly 22 percent of the American market.

Powdered coffees had been known as of the eighteenth century, but it was not until 1901 that "instant coffee" from powder first appeared, introduced by Satori Kato at the Buffalo Pan American Exposition (later marketed as Nescafé in 1939). Credit for instant coffee also goes to G. Washington, an Englishman living in Guatemala, who discovered in 1906 a practical process of condensing coffee so that it could be reconstituted merely by adding boiling water in a cup, calling his "soluble" product "G. Washington's Red E Coffee."

Today there are two basic methods for producing instant coffee: "Spray-dried" (or "regular") instant is sprayed through hot air after being brewed, thereby removing the water. "Freeze-dried" instant is made from brewed coffee frozen into slabs, then ground and passed through a vacuum and heat in order to remove the water. "Aglomerization" is a process by which spray-dried coffee powder is made into more appealing little nuggets.

Coffee is almost always a blend of beans from various sources. Brazil provides the beans for one third of the world's consumption, Colombia is the second-largest producer, and there are large plantations in Costa Rica, Mexico, Cuba, India, Java, and various African countries. Some of the best beans come from Jamaica, and Hawaii produces a coffee, known as "Kona," that is highly esteemed.

Americans have generally preferred a lighter, less robust coffee than the rest of the world, and instant coffee makes up a great share of the domestic market. The term "American coffee" has become useful to restaurants within the last decade to describe a blend that is percolated, as opposed to ESPRESSO, "café filtré," or Hispanic coffees, which are very hearty and rich and brewed by a drip method. An "American roast," also called a "regular roast," is somewhat heavier than a "light roast." A "heavy roast" (sometimes called "Dark French") is extremely dark, while "Italian roast" (preferred for espresso) is glossy and dark brown. "Viennese roast" is a blend of one third heavy and two thirds regular, while "European roast" transposes the ratio. "Mocha" is either a coffee from Ethiopia (whose name is derived from the city of Mocha there) or a Yemeni coffee having a taste of chocolate. "Mocha" may also refer to a beverage made with coffee and cocoa mixed together with water or milk or to any flavor derived from these two beans. "Jamoke" (also, "Jamoca") is an early-twentieth-century term for coffee in general, a combination of "Java" and "mocha."

The popularity of darker coffees like espresso was fueled by a new interest in coffee shops with stylish decor, baked goods and new, expensive varitions on Italian and European coffees. This trend was started in 1983 by Howard Schultz, who opened Starbucks Coffee in Seattle, Washington, that year and built 2,000 locations, with 170 abroad, by 1999. The number of coffeehouses has grown from about 500 in 1991 to about 7,000 in 1999.

Americans consume half the world's coffee supply, and 52 percent of Americans (over the age of ten) drink coffee—down from the high of 74.7 percent in 1962—consuming about 100 billion cups each year, which translates to 23.5 gallons per person. The U.S. only produces about 9 million pounds of coffee annually, with the rest imported. Thirty-nine percent of Americans drink their coffee black. Americans drink coffee with breakfast, in the middle of the morning at a "coffee break" (so called since the mid-1940s), at lunch, with snacks (especially doughnuts), and with or after dinner. In many restaurants the coffee cup and saucer will be placed on the table at the start of the meal. Coffee mugs are popular at inexpensive restaurants, diners, and lunch counters, and take-out eateries offer plastic or cardboard coffee cups. Americans take their coffee either "black" (with no sugar, milk, or cream), "light" (with a lot of milk or cream), or "regular" (which usually refers to coffee with some sugar and milk or cream, although regional differences may eliminate one or the other in usage).

coffee and. A colloquial abbreviation for "coffee and (doughnuts, pastries, cake, etc.)" served at a social function. The phrase is most commonly used to describe the snacks served after a business meeting (1869).

coffee filter. Cooks' slang for the tall, white paper hat they traditionally wear (formally called a "toque"), because it resembles a paper filter through which coffee is dripped (1999).

coffee klatch. An informal get-together over coffee. The term, which comes from a similar German term *kaffee-klatsch* ("coffee gossip"), first in English print in 1890, was especially popular during the 1950s and 1960s.

coffee milk. A blend of a little coffee in a glass of sweetened milk. It is a specialty of Rhode Island, where the tradition dates back to 1905, when Daniel Ablesen began selling coffee milk in Pawtucket. In 1914 Eclipse Food Products began bottling a coffee syrup, using the slogan "You'll smack your lips when it's Eclipse." Today the drink may also be purchased in containers, already mixed. "Coffee milk" also refers to simple coffee with hot milk.

coffin. A pastry crust, a deep-dish pie, or the pan it is baked in, with reference to a coffin in which a body is laid.

cola cake. A cake made with marshmallows and Coca-Cola soda.

COLA CAKE

In a bowl sift 2 c. sugar with 2 c. flour. Add 1½ c. small marshmallows. In a saucepan mix 1 stick butter, ½ c. vegetable oil, 3 T. cocoa, and 1 c. Coca-Cola. Bring to a boil, pour into dry ingredients, blend well, add ½ c. buttermilk, 1 t. baking soda, 2 eggs, and 1 t. vanilla extract. Mix well, pour into a greased 9 x 13-inch pan, bake in 350° oven for 45 min. Remove and frost with a frosting made by combining 1 stick butter, 3 T. cocoa, and 6 T. Coca-Cola in a saucepan. Bring to a boil. In a bowl put 16 oz. confectioners' sugar. Pour frosting liquid over sugar, blend, add 1 t. vanilla extract and 1 c. chopped pecans.

---

cola roast. A southern dish made by basting a roast beef with cola soda as it roasts.

colcannon. A dish of boiled cabbage and potatoes. The term dates in print to 1843 and comes from the Irish Gaelic *cál ceannan*.

cold cut. Usually meant to refer to a thin slice of meat served cold for lunch, either on a SANDWICH or with various salads, mayonnaise, vegetables, mustard, and snacks. The most common meats are bologna, liverwurst, beef, turkey breast, chicken, tongue, pastrami, and various salamis. The first printed reference to the term appeared in 1940.

Cold Duck. A mixture of American sparkling red and white wines (1965), it is a semisweet, low-alcohol beverage that achieved widespread popularity in the 1970s and then faded by the beginning of the 1980s.

There are several versions of how Cold Duck got its name, though most authorities agree that it is a mistaken transformation of the German words *Kalte Ende,* "cold ending." Some assert the drink originated in Bavaria, where hunters would begin the day with a glass of sparkling wine. The unused wine was then mixed together with other leftover wines and drunk cold at the end of the day.

Another story credits the court of German emperor and king of Prussia Wilhelm I (1797–1888) with the drink's origins, when General Von Pape, attending a dinner at the emperor's, remarked that he preferred a "cold ending" rather than coffee at the end of a meal and proceeded to mix *Sekt* and a Moselle wine with lemon juice. Enjoying a *Kalte Ende* became popular after that.

Somehow *Kalte Ende* was erroneously transformed, perhaps in dialect, into *Kalte Ente,* meaning "cold duck."

The drink came to America by way of a German immigrant named Harold Borgman, original owner of the Pontchartrain Wine Cellar in Detroit, Michigan, where, he contended, he first made the drink with champagne and still Burgundy wine in 1935. It remained a local favorite until, in 1963, the general manager of an importing firm sampled the drink and talked one of his suppliers into bottling the concoction. A year later the first commercially sold Cold Duck was produced, followed by examples from California and Michigan. American Sparkling Burgundy replaced the still Burgundy originally used, and American champagne was used instead of *Sekt* or true French champagne. (Germany has bottled a lemon-flavored version of *Kalte Ente* since 1948 and a red variation called *Turkenblut.*) After 1971 Cold Duck was a semisweet apéritif with enormous sales in America, but the American palate soon grew tired of the soda-poplike quality of the beverage, and sales had dropped precipitously by the end of the decade.

coleslaw. Also, "cabbage salad." Shredded cabbage, mayonnaise, and seasonings, usually served cold as a side dish. The words are from Dutch *koolsla,* a combination of *kool,* "cabbage," and *sla,* "salad," a dish that was known in America in print by 1785. Because it is usually served cold, some call the dish "cold slaw" in contrast to "hot slaw," but there is no relation to the temperature in the etymology.

COLESLAW

In a large bowl stir together 1 c. mayonnaise, 1 T. lemon juice, 4 c. shredded cabbage, and 1½ c. shredded carrots. Add ½ c. raisins if desired. Makes about 5 c.

---

collard greens. Also "collards." A variety of kale (*Brassica oleracea acephala*) with a rosette of green leaves. The word comes from "colewort" and dates in American print to 1745. This nutritious green vegetable is one of the staples of southern cooking, particularly among African-Americans, who often refer to collards simply as "greens." They are usually boiled and seasoned with ham hocks, and they form the basis for POTLIKKER.

collation. A light meal or refreshment served to one's guests.

combination platter. Also, "combo platter." Restaurant term for a dish composed of several items on the menu. It is especially associated with barbecue, Chinese, and Mexican restaurants.

comfort food. Any food that a person considers to put him at ease, often as part of nostalgia for a favored childhood food. Often it is of a soft consistency, like mashed potatoes. In her book *Comfort Food* (1986), Sue Kreitzman wrote of her subject:

> [Comfort foods] don't take us back to the womb but to the period shortly thereafter when we were safely cradled and gently fed. Fragrant, gutsy stews, thick chunky soups, and bubbling gratins make us feel safe, warm, and well protected from the raging elements. Old-fashioned desserts that contain plenty of texture and temperature contrasts help us surrender to sensual pleasure and so forget the stresses of a sometimes cruel world.

common cracker. Very crisp, hard, thick wheat-flour cracker that may be split and grilled with butter or Cheddar cheese, ground into bread crumbs, or eaten in chowders; similar to BOSTON CRACKER. The term first appears in print in 1939. One manufacturer claims common crackers were first baked by Charles Cross about 1830 in his Montpelier, Vermont, bakery, and were called "Cross crackers" or "Montpelier crackers." But in *New England Cookbook* (1954), Eleanor Early credits the cracker's invention to Artemus Kennedy of Menotomy, Massachusetts, almost two hundred years ago. Early wrote that "Artemus had a large family and it was said that the children learned to retrieve the crackers [that Artemus tossed on the floor of a big Dutch oven] . . . before they could walk. Baking was done three times a week, and Artemus rode about the countryside on his horse, selling them from his saddlebags."

Whatever their origins, common crackers are no longer easily found, and the news that a Rockingham, Vermont, citizen named Vrest Orton had bought the original Charles Cross machinery and begun to sell common crackers again in 1981 was greeted with considerable interest by those who remember the taste of dry, crisp morsels split opened and eaten with good Vermont cheddar. See also TRENTON CRACKER.

COMMON CRACKER

A recipe from Louise Andrews Kent's Mrs. Appleyard's Kitchen (1942) gave the following recipe for "Puffed Montpelier Crackers": "Split each cracker in half.... Put ice cubes into a large bowl of cold water. When the water is very cold, put in the split cracker halves.... At the end of three minutes—or sooner, if they seem to be getting too soft—remove the crackers from the ice water....When they have drained about five minutes, put them into iron dripping pans and dot them thickly with soft butter. Dust them with paprika, if you wish. Heat the oven to 450° and bake them until they are puffed, crisp, and golden brown. They should be done in 25 to 35 minutes.

common doings. A frontier term dating in print to 1838 for any plain food.

commons. A college or university dining hall, where the students are served a "common" meal. It may also refer to the food itself, a meaning dating to the sixteenth century in England.

conch (genus *Strombus*). A brightly colored gastropod mollusk eaten in the Caribbean and Florida. The word (which is pronounced "conk") is from the Latin *concha,* and as slang has been applied at least since 1852 to the inhabitants of Key West, Florida, especially to those with a Bahamian ancestry of mixed cockney and African-American blood, probably because of their fondness for the marine food. (Low-class white North Carolinians have also been called "conchs" for the same reason.)

Because of its popularity, conch was almost fished out in Florida waters, and commercial fishing of the mollusk has been banned for more than a decade. Most conch comes from Bahamian and other waters.

Conch meat is tough and must be pounded or finely chopped. It is often served in salads, as fritters, or in a chowder.

Concord. A labrusca hybrid grape used to make wine and jelly, jam, and preserves. Introduced in 1849, this dark red grape was propagated from a seedling grown in Concord, Massachusetts, by Ephraim Wales Bull, whose discovery enriched others but not himself: His gravestone reads, HE SOWED, BUT OTHERS REAPED.

Concord was especially successful in New York State, both as a wine grape and as an eating grape. Oversupply in the 1890s led to a bust, which in turn prompted two dentists named Welch to set up the world's first large grape-juice plant at Westfield, New York. The Welch Grape Juice Company prospered under Prohibition by selling unfermented wine and the juice to make jellies, jams, and preserves. Jacob Merrill ("Jack") Kaplan bought the company in 1945 and began making a very sweet kosher wine from Concord grapes. He neglected to put the word "kosher" on the label, however, and thereby lost out to other kosher-wine producers like Manischewitz and Mogen David.

Today more than 80 percent of New York's vineyards are planted with Concord grapes, the majority going to make jams, jellies, and preserves as well as grape juice and concentrates.

Coney Island. Also, "coney." Principally this refers to a HOT DOG whose popularity was associated with Brooklyn, New York's Coney Island amusement-park vendors, but it may also refer to a hamburger, HERO sandwich, or, prior to World War I, fried clams. In Syracuse, New York, a "coney" refers specifically to a white pork sausage much like a German *Weisswurst* served in a bun.

convenience store. Also, "C-store." A small market carrying an array of basic packaged foods, coffee, some fast food and other nonfood goods intended for customers stopping quickly along the road to pick up a few items. The term dates in print to 1960, but credit for the idea has gone to Joe C. Thompson of Dallas, Texas, who in 1927 began selling bread, milk, and eggs at his ICE HOUSE, out of which grew the largest chain of convenience stores—the "7-Eleven" stores, owned by the Southland Corporation. Indeed, according to an article about a murder at a convenience store in Port Arthur, Texas, in *Newsweek* (October 17, 1983), "*all* convenience stores were called 7-Elevens in the language of the street."

Many convenience stores are located within gas stations, and most stay open for long hours or twenty-four hours a day.

conversation heart. Also, "candy hearts." A small, heart-shaped candy made from sugar paste, corn syrup, and dextrose and imprinted with a Valentine's Day message such as I LOVE YOU and KISS ME. They were created in 1902 by the New England Confectionary Company, better known as NECCO (which also produces NECCO wafer candies from the same ingredients) of Cambridge, Massachusetts. They were originally called "Tiny Conversation Hearts." NECCO makes about 8 billion pieces each year, although the candy is also produced by other companies.

cookbook. A term for a book of recipes (1800). Before 1809 such volumes were referred to as "cookerie books," "recipe books," "receipt books," or "culinary reviews." The first American cookbooks were family collections of favorite recipes handed down from one generation to the next, as well as American editions of English volumes like *The Compleat Housewife* (1742) by Eliza Smith. But in June of 1796 Amelia Simmons, who called herself "An American Orphan," published the forty-seven-page *American Cookery, or, the art of dressing viands, fish, poultry and vegetables, and the best modes of making pastes, puffs, pies, tarts, puddings, custards and preserves, and all kinds of cakes, from the imperial plumb to plain cake. Adapted to this country, and all grades of life.* It was the first published volume to include recipes for specifically American dishes such as cranberry sauce and pumpkin pie.

Cookbooks began appearing rapidly after Simmons's successful venture. Lydia Child's *The American Frugal Housewife* (1832), Mary Randolph's *Virginia Housewife* (1824), Eliza Leslie's *Directions for Cookery* (1837), Sallie Rutledge's *Carolina Housewife* (1847), Elizabeth H. Putnam's *Mrs. Putnam's Receipt Book* (1850), and others were very popular. Catharine Esther Beecher's *Treatise on Domestic Economy for the Use of Young Ladies at Home and at School* (1841), and *Miss Beecher's Domestic Receipt Book* (1846) were significant for their tips on food storage and the use of ovens and kitchen utensils.

In 1896 Fannie Merritt Farmer published *The Boston Cooking-School Cook Book,* which for the first time applied scientific terms and precise measurements to recipes. In it appeared the first American instructions to use a "level teaspoon," rather than the usual "dash" or "pinch" other writers decreed. Farmer's cookbook, originally published in a three-thousand-copy edition at her own expense, was an immediate and tremendous best-seller, and she was to become one of the most important women in America for changing the way women of the period cooked and managed their households.

In the twentieth century cookbooks were often issued by food companies to promote their product, cooking institutes to promote their schools, and newspapers to promote their sales. The *Boston Post Cook Book,* for instance, which originated in *The Great Breakfast Table Paper of New England,* listed favorite dishes of famous American women, including Mrs. Calvin Coolidge, and pages of "household hints" ranging from the use of a corn popper to methods for removing tea stains. Various food-industry organizations—for apple growers or meatpackers, for example—offered cookbooks to the public, and there is a long tradition of church groups, Junior Leagues, and women's clubs that publish their own, usually based on members' own recipes. Some of these grew into best-selling books, such as *Joy of Cooking,* by Irma S. Rombauer and Marion Rombauer Becker, published in numerous editions since 1931 (the first commercial edition was published in 1936 by the Bobbs-Merrill Company). Other popular cookbooks issued forth from the editorial department of the "ladies' magazines," such as *Better Homes and Gardens, McCall's, Good Housekeeping.* The *Betty Crocker Cookbook,* first issued in 1950, has since sold more than 22 million copies.

Ethnic foods formed but a small section of most of these books, and only after World War II did ethnic cookbooks begin to interest the American public, although the authors almost always "adapted" foreign recipes to an American palate that supposedly did not care for highly seasoned or spicy foods or for dishes that took much time to prepare and cook. Such modifications led to a mistaken notion among many Americans about the true nature of ethnic foods, and foreign restaurateurs followed by catering to the same conventions about adaptions or transformations of dishes on their menus.

In the 1950s and 1960s there appeared a number of very popular cookbooks that were sold on gimmickry, from an attempt to sympathize with the housewife who really did not much enjoy cooking (with titles such as Peg Bracken's *I Hate to Cook Book*) to small volumes, often enhanced by strong graphic design, that catered to a specific approach to cookery, such as patio, fondue, backyard, or hibachi cookbooks in which every recipe was adapted to the book's idea.

Also in the 1960s, however, came the first series of serious, specialized, and challenging cookbooks that demonstrated some of the more sophisticated and authentic techniques of preparing French, Italian, Chinese, and other ethnic cuisines, beginning with Julia Child's *Mastering the Art of French Cooking,* first published in 1961 and keyed to a very well-received public-television show. Mrs. Child abated the fears of some American cooks who regarded French classic cuisine as intimidating, and there quickly followed volumes by other authors on regional Italian cookery, authentic Cantonese and Szechuan cookery, and true Mexican cookery. Later came Vietnamese, Indian, and Thai cookbooks of great authority, as well as translations of the cookbooks of the French practitioners of LA NOUVELLE CUISINE.

In the late 1960s and 1970s there appeared a series of beautifully designed and thoroughly researched volumes by Time-Life Books, under the general editorship of Richard L. Williams, entitled *Foods of the World.* These books surveyed the cuisines of Japan, Russia, Italy, and other countries along with several volumes on American cooking, from the South to the Northwest, including a volume gathering up the various ethnic influences in American food entitled *The Melting Pot.*

There was increased interest in American food in the 1980s, resulting in large numbers of regional cookbooks that more often than not provided a good deal of information on the region's food culture and history. One of the most important was *Chef Paul Prudhomme's Louisiana Kitchen* (1984), which sparked a national interest in Cajun cooking. "Celebrity chefs" who had cooking shows on television, like Jeff Smith (The Frugal Gourmet) or ran celebrated restaurants, like Wolfgang Puck of Spago in Los Angeles and Jasper White of Jasper's in Boston, wrote cookbooks that expressed their own sense of style and personality as much as they did good taste. Two of the best selling cookbooks of the 1980s were "lifestyle" books in which the settings in which food was photographed were every bit as important to set a mood as the food itself. These were Martha Stewart's *Entertaining* (1982) and *Lee Bailey's Country Weekends* (1983), and their imitators grew numerous in the decade to follow. In the late 1980s the genre turned more towards culinary memoirs and authoritative ethnic works on regional cookery of various parts of the world, expecially Italy and France, such as *A Taste of Alsace* by Sue Style (1990), *The Cooking of the Eastern Mediterranean* by Paula Wolfert (1994), *The Foods of Vietnam* by Nicole Routheir (1989), *The Food and Wine of Greece* by Diane Kochilas (1990),

Memoirs of a Cuban Kitchen by Mary Urrutia Randelman and Joan Schwartz (1992), *Catalan Cuisine* by Colman Andrews (1988), and *Naples at Table* by Arthur Schwartz (1998), as well as a number of general cookbooks such as Julia Child's *The Way to Cook* (1989) and Mark Bittman's *How to Cook Everything* (1998) that attempted to show how recipies go wrong and how dishes can best made in the home.

Today there are hundreds of cookbooks published each year, though only a handful reach a large public.

cookie. A small, flat, sweet cake eaten as a snack or with other desserts. The word is from the Dutch *koekje,* "little cake," and first appears in print in 1695. The term is little used in England, where "cake" is still preferred, as it was in America until the late twentieth century; in Scotland "cookie" refers to a small bun. In America the cookie has long been a favorite snack food since the Dutch made cookies popular in their early settlements. A "filled cookie" is a form of cookie sandwich stuffed with a fruit filling, usually date or raisin, as in a FIG NEWTON.

One finds dozens of cookie recipes in eighteenth- and nineteenth-century cookbooks, but the most popular cookie in America today—the chocolate-chip or TOLL HOUSE cookie, created by Mrs. Ruth Wakefield, who owned the Toll House Inn in Whitman, Massachusetts—did not appear until after 1930. The next popular cookies are oatmeal raisin, peanut butter and oatmeal.

See also, MOON PIE, GIRL SCOUT COOKIES, WHOOPIE PIES, and OREO.

cooking wine. Any wine primarily intended to be added to cooked foods for flavor. The alcohol in cooking wine is burned off, leaving a faint taste of the wine. Although gourmets recommend using a good wine for cooking, most wines used for this purpose are inexpensive and lack distinction. During Prohibition many of these wines were salted so as to make them undrinkable.

cooter. A southern dialect word for a box TURTLE. From either a West African word, *kuta,* or a Kongo word, *nkuda,* it was first printed in English in 1832, though probably used for a long while before that on southern plantations. Cooter stew is still part of southern cookery.

coquina soup. A Florida soup of periwinkle clams. "Coquina" derives from the Spanish, "small clam," and since the 1800s has referred to a buildup of marine shells bound by calcareous cement and used as a building material.

cordial. A sweet, syrupy spirit, synonymous with "liqueur," which is the preferred term in England and France, though it is often heard in America. "Cordial" derives from the Medieval Latin *cordialis* from the Latin *cor*, "heart."

Cordials once had medicinal uses, and the oldest-known example dates back to Hippocrates, who concocted one of cinnamon and wine-sweetened honey about 420 B.C. The tradition was carried on by European monks, and many cordials now made commercially were first created by such men of the cloth.

Cordials are made by three processes: infusion (or maceration), in which the flavorings steep in alcohol; percolation, in which the alcohol percolates above the flavorings; and distillation, in which ingredients are distilled directly from their extracted flavors in copper stills, a method that results in clear, colorless liquids of varying proofs. A fruit-flavored brandy is a cordial made with a brandy base, but other spirits are used for other kinds of cordials.

Most American cordials are quite sweet, with up to 35 percent sugar, and are made from various fruits, beans, and herbs, ranging from cherry to chocolate to mint. Some are milk-based, with low alcohol. A "dry" cordial must have less than 10 percent sugar, but no cordial may have less than 2.5 percent sugar by weight.

corn. Any of a variety of a cultivated cereal plant, *Zea mays*, yielding a sweet kernel that is made into oil, eaten fresh, or cooked in a wide variety of dishes. In Great Britain the word generally refers to any major cereal crop and was applied to this new cereal they found in North America in 1608. But the word "maize" (from the West Taino Indian *mahiz*) was more common in the New World. Because the cereal was so associated with the Native Americans, it was soon being called "Indian corn" by the white settlers, to distinguish it from their own cereals such as barley and wheat.

Corn was not only a staple crop of the Native Americans, it was the staff of life for many tribes ranging from Canada to South America long before Columbus arrived in the West Indies. It was grown in Mexico in prehistoric times and reached the territory that is now the United States more than two millennia ago, where it became part of Native American rituals and religion. Many legends and deities were devoted to the cycle of raising corn. The Native Americans called the cereal "Sacred Mother" and "Giver of Life," and the Zunis dusted their doorways with cornmeal in the belief its miraculous powers would prevent the marauding conquistadores from entering. According to Alfred Whiting in *Ethnobotany of the Hopi* (1966), the Hopi of the Southwest had at least twenty different varieties of cultivated corn in a rainbow of colors, each of which was symbolic in some way.

Native Americans roasted their corn and ground it into meal to make cakes, breads, and porridges. Tortillas were made with cornmeal before the Spanish introduced wheat, and succotash was a Native American vegetable stew that provided a great range of nutrients. When the Spanish landed in Cuba on November 5, 1492, they were treated to *mahiz* in at least two forms, baked and in flour.

When Captain John Smith explored the Virginia territory in 1607, he commented on "great heapes of corn" stored away by the Native Americans, and the colonists from the ship *Susan Constant* were met at Chesapeake Bay in April 1607 by friendly Native Americans led by Powhatan, who gave them a feast of corn bread, venison, and berries. When Miles Standish alighted from the *Mayflower* at Plymouth in 1620, he immediately came upon an Indian cache of corn and collected it for the winter ahead. By the following spring the Pilgrims were planting corn in the Native American method, by poking a hole in the ground and putting in the corn kernels with a dead fish that served to fertilize them. By the fall twenty acres of corn were harvested—the European grains of barley and wheat having failed—and served at the first THANKSGIVING. The Native Americans even brought a remarkable delicacy to the feast—POPCORN. The new cereal was precious and helped the early settlers to survive those first harsh years. There is a record of a public whipping in the Plymouth Colony in 1622 of settlers who dared eat the new corn before it was fully ripe (although immature corn, called "green corn" or "roasting corn," was long a staple of southern cooking until the 1920s).

Before long uniquely American dishes were being developed on the basis of this new grain, including an Indian bread called "pone" or "corn pone" (from the Algonquian word *apan*, "baked") made of cornmeal, salt, and water. This was later called "corn bread" and has been a staple of American cooking to this day.

HOMINY was, as of 1629, a term for a cornmeal porridge, though it referred specifically to dried, hulled corn kernels. Once the crops took hold throughout the colonies, cornmeal foods were everyday fare, and slaves on the southern plantations lived on a diet of corn bread and water, as did the poorest white settlers. "Dodger" (or "corn dodger") was a fried corn cake (first mentioned in print in 1831), the meaning of which is obscure but may derive from a Scots word, *dadge*, for a BANNOCK.

Mature "sweet corn" (also called "sugar corn") fit to be boiled and buttered was first found along the banks of the Susquehanna River in an Indian village in 1779, but it was not until the 1820s that it garnered much attention among farmers and not until the 1840s that it became a ubiquitous item on American dinner tables. In fact, the term "corn on the cob" only entered the language as of 1876.

Throughout the nineteenth century the corn crop increased as the settlers moved into the western territories, utilized both for food and fodder. In the mid-1800s a new hybrid called Reid's Yellow Dent (after the farmer who discovered it, Robert Reid of Tazewell County, Illinois), created by chance cross-pollination, began to be widely cultivated in the Midwest, and by 1882 people were referring to the great corn-producing states of the Midwest as the "Corn Belt." "Corncrackers," mills for grinding corn, were known by 1844, and "corn poppers" were marketed in the 1870s. A breakfast CEREAL called "cornflakes," developed by Dr. John Harvey Kellogg and his brother Will Keith Kellogg of Battle Creek, Michigan, made its appearance in the market in 1907. "Corn roasts" were popular social events by 1899, and CORN SYRUP was known by 1903.

From 1877 through 1920 American horticulturists developed many new hybrids that became standard on the country's farms, including "Golden Chaff," "shoepeg," "Country Gentleman," and "Bantam." In 1924 Henry A. Wallace of Iowa (later vice president under Franklin D. Roosevelt) showcased a hearty hybrid called "Copper-cross" that survived the great windstorm of 1836 and was thereafter widely planted. In 1950 Dr. J. R. Laughnam of the University of Illinois discovered very sweet strains of corn, which, because their dried kernels looked shriveled, were called "shrunken two" or "SH2," called in the market "supersweet," "ultrasweet," or" extrasweet." Even sweeter corn was produced in the 1960s by Dr. A. M. Rhodes, also at the University of Illinois, and called "sugar-enhanced" or, in seed catalogs, "Everlasting Heritage."

The major varieties of corn include "dent" (*Z. m. indenta*), so called because the kernel becomes dented in shrinking, but also called "field corn"; a very hearty strain called "flint" or "Indian" (*Z. m. indurata*) "flour" (preferred by the Indians), of which "blue corn" is a variety; "waxy" (introduced from China as a tapioca substitute in 1907); and "popcorn" (*Z. m. everta*), also called "rice" or "pearl corn."

Today the United States corn crop is equal to the combined crop of wheat, oats, barley, rice, rye, and sorghum, although most is used for feed. The principal corn-producing states are Ohio, Indiana, Illinois, Nebraska, South Dakota, and, the largest, Iowa.

Depending on the region of the country they live in, Americans often stand firmly on the merits of either white or yellow cornmeal in their recipes, white generally being preferred in the South and Midwest.

Americans enjoy corn in a wide variety of ways, especially in late summer when the fresh corn on the cob is boiled and buttered. Corn on the cob is also available frozen, and shucked corn kernels are widely bought in cans. Creamed corn, sold canned, consists of whole or partially whole cut kernels packed in a creamy liquid from the kernels or other ingredients (including monosodium glutamate, starch, butter or margarine, and often pieces of green or red pepper). In the South fried corn is common, and fried "corn fritters" (also called "corn oysters") made with an egg batter are popular throughout the United States.

Aside from those recipes given below, many corn items and dishes will be found under main entries, including HUSH PUPPIES, CRACKLING bread, SPOON BREAD, INDIAN PUDDING, SUCCOTASH, TORTILLAS, MAQUECHOU, and others.

CORN BREAD

Pour 2 T. butter or bacon fat into a skillet and place in 450° oven to heat up. Combine 2 c. cornmeal, 4 t. baking powder, and 1½ t. salt. Beat 1 egg in 1½ c. milk, combine with dry ingredients, pour into skillet, and bake for 20–25 min.

CORN CHOWDER

Brown ¼ lb. salt pork and add 1 chopped onion. Put in 4 c. peeled potatoes, 2 c. water, salt, and pepper, and simmer until potatoes are tender. Stir in 4 c. scalded milk and 2 c. kernel corn. Correct seasonings, serve with pat of butter. Serves 6.

corn chip. A snack food made from ground corn-meal that is flattened by machine and cut into chips of various sizes. It is often flavored or seasoned and is a staple of Mexican restaurants, usually served with a SALSA. It is also the basis for FRITO PIE.

Mexicans have long made corn chips at home, but it was not until the invention in 1932 of a special rolling machine by I. J. Filler of San Antonio, Texas, and its subsequent adoption by Elmer Doolin for producing the item in large bulk, that the corn chip became a commercial product. Doolin called his product "Fritos Corn Chips."

corn dog. A hot dog covered with a cornmeal batter, deep-fried, and eaten on a stick. The item was perfected in 1942 by vaudevillians Neil and Carl Fletcher of Dallas, Texas, who originally called it "Fletcher's Original State Fair Corny Dog" because they sold it from a stand at the State Fair of Texas. "We have heard some fellow had used a mold to put cornbread around a wiener, but that was too slow," Neil Fletcher told a *New York Times* reporter in 1983. "So we started experimenting in the kitchen and finally came up with a batter that would stay on. It tasted like hell. When we got one that tasted O.K. it wouldn't stay on the weenie. We must have tried about 60 times until we got one that was right."

CORN DOG

Fry ½ lb. mashed spicy sausage with 1 chopped onion, 1 t. cayenne, and 2 T. beef stock. Grease corn-stick pans and heat in 375° oven. Mix together 1 c. cornmeal, 1 c. flour, 2 T. melted butter, 3 t. baking powder, ¼ t. salt, 2 beaten eggs, and ¾ c. milk. Fill corn-stick pans, cover each stick with some of the sausage mixture, cover with more corn mixture, and bake at 375° for 25 min.

---

corned beef. Beef that has been cured in salt. Corned beef is served either as a main dish or as a sandwich in America. The term has nothing to do with American corn, but rather with an English term, "corn," for any small particle, such as a grain of salt. Beef brisket is the usual cut, although rump, eye round, bottom round, and tongue may also be used.

Saltpeter (sodium nitrate or potassium nitrate) is added to most of the corned beef sold in the United States.

Cornell bread. A bread made with soya flour, wheat germ, and nonfat dry milk. It was developed as a high-protein bread in the 1930s by Clive M. McKay, professor of animal nutrition at Cornell University in Ithaca, New York. Originally created with the help of the Dry Milk Institute as a way of improving the diet of patients in mental hospitals, Cornell bread became popular during World War II at a time when meat was rationed or increasingly expensive, and a high-protein alternative was needed.

The formula called for adding to the bottom of each cup of white flour in a bread recipe one tablespoon soya flour, one tablespoon dry-milk solids, and one teaspoon wheat germ. The rest of the cup would then be filled with sifted unbleached white flour.

corn syrup. A sweet, thick liquid derived from corn-starch treated with acids or enzymes and used to sweeten and thicken candy, syrups, and snack foods. By far the most popular and best-known corn syrup is Karo, introduced in 1902 by Corn Products Company of Edgewater, New Jersey. The name "Karo" may have been in honor of the inventor's wife, Caroline, or, some say, derivative of an earlier trademark for table syrup, "Kairomel." So common is the use of Karo in making pecan pie that the confection is often called "Karo pie" in the South. See also SUGAR.

corn whiskey. Also, "corn." Whiskey made from corn (1835). BOURBON is the primary example of American spirits made from corn. By the time of Prohibition it came to connote cheap moonshine whiskey.

cottage cheese. A moist, soft white cheese made from skimmed milk (1840). Cottage cheese may be eaten on its own, in a salad, or with melon, and is sometimes used as a substitute for ricotta in American lasagnas. It is consumed fresh, not aged. Cottage cheese sales in the U.S. in 1997 totaled 707 million pounds, with per capita consumption at 2.7 pounds.

After milk has soured, it solidifies into a wet mass called "clabbered milk," which leaves behind the curds as the liquid ("whey") drops away. Sometimes this process is hastened by the addition of rennet. Cottage cheese is the product of one of the first stages of the process.

In the early part of the nineteenth century the name for such cheese was "pot cheese" (which today is almost synonymous with" cottage cheese," though sometimes the term suggested a cheese that has drained for a longer period and acquired a slightly sour taste) or "card cheese" (a variation of "curd cheese"). Finely textured cottage cheese is sometimes called in the Southwest "cream cheese" (but see main entry for CREAM CHEESE). By the 1820s "smear case" (from German, *Schmierkäse*, a spreading cheese) was also heard, particularly in Pennsylvania-Dutch communities, and by mid-century the name "cottage cheese" entered the language. Cottage cheese to which thick cream has been added was called "cheese butter."

Today cottage cheese may be bought in various forms. "Sweet-curd cottage cheese" is mild because it has been washed to remove acid; "creamed cottage cheese" contains 4–8 percent cream; and "California-style" or "small-curd cottage cheese" has smaller curds than regular cottage cheese. "Medium-curd" and "large-curd" cottage cheese, also sometimes called "popcorn cheese," are also available.

cottage-fried potatoes. Also, "cottage fries" and "country fries." Potatoes that are sliced into thin disks and deep-fried. The term dates in print to 1965 and is predominantly used in the North.

cottage pudding. A plain cake that is smeared with a sweet sauce. It was listed in the original *Fannie Farmer Cooking-School Cookbook* in 1896 and mentioned by O. Henry in 1909.

cotton candy. A confection made by spinning sugar at high speed in a large tub so as to create what appears to be candy cotton set on a cardboard stick. The item originated in 1900 at the Ringling Bros. and Barnum & Bailey circus when snack vendor Thomas Patton began experimenting with the long-common process of boiling sugar to a caramelized state, then forming long threads of it with a fork waved in the air. Patton heated the sugar on a gas-fired hot plate that spun, creating a kind of cottony sugar floss. Patton sold his patent on the machine, which was refined by the Electric Candy Machine Company of New York and Nashville, selling the new confection—called "Fairy Floss Candy"—at the 1904 St. Louis World's Fair.

Cotton candy (which dates in print to the 1920s) continues to be a popular item at circuses, amusement parks, and fairs, with most cotton-candy machines now made by the Gold Medal Products company. Cotton candy is now flavored and colored.

country captain. A curried-chicken dish often attributed to Georgian origins. Eliza Leslie, in her mid-nineteenth-century cookbooks, contended that the dish got its name from a British army officer who brought the recipe back from his station in India. Others believe the dish originated in Savannah, Georgia, a major shipping port for the spice trade.

COUNTRY CAPTAIN

Fry 4 bacon strips until crisp. Remove from pan, then sauté in 2 T. bacon fat, 1 chopped green pepper, 1 chopped onion, 2 minced garlic cloves, and ½ c. celery for about 5 min. Add 6 chopped tomatoes and 1 c. orange juice, sprinkle in 2 T. curry powder and ½ t. thyme. Bring to a boil, then simmer for 5 min. Add 8 slices chicken breast and cook 30 min. Garnish with chutney or sprinkle with dried currants, roasted almonds, and minced parsley.

country pie. A southern term for a liver pie.

court-bouillon. In classical French cuisine, a poaching liquid composed of various vegetables, vinegar or white wine, herbs, salt, and pepper. The word, first printed in English in 1715, is from the French for "short broth." In Creole and Cajun cuisine, however, the term usually refers to a dish of redfish cooked with a seasoned tomato sauce, as mentioned in *Mme. Bequé and Her Recipes: Old Creole Cookery* (1900), from which the following recipe is adapted.

COURT-BOUILLON

Roll six slices of redfish in seasoned flour and brown in hot oil, but do not cook through. Set aside. In a skillet sauté 1 large onion, chopped, with 1 t. flour in 2 T. oil. When brown, stir in ½ cup red wine, 2 T. chopped garlic, 3 bay leaves, a little fresh thyme and parsley, a piece of chile pepper, and salt and pepper to taste. When slightly reduced, add fish and cook over low heat for about 45 min. Serve with toast.

cowboy slang. The lingo of cowboys is a colorful language of the West and includes a great number of slang terms for various foods, cooks, and utensils used for cooking. Many of the following were first noted by Ramon F. Adams in his *Western Words: A Dictionary of the American West* (1968).

Arbuckle's. A brand name for coffee in the Old West. Arbuckle's coffee was so ubiquitous that recipes for coffee would read, "Take a pound of Arbuckle's . . ."

baldface dishes. Used since 1840 to describe real china plates and dishes, in contrast to the tin or granite dishes usually used on the trail.

bar dog. A bartender.

Basque barbecue. A barbecue made from lamb, so called because many nineteenth-century sheepmen were of Basque ancestry.

bean eater. A Mexican or Chicano, because beans were a predominant ingredient in Hispanic cooking.

bear sign. A doughnut, probably because of its resemblance to a bear's excrement (1903).

belly-wash. Weak coffee, whiskey, or soup (1889).

big antelope. An animal belonging to someone else and killed for food. Ramon F. Adams, in *Western Words* (1968), notes, "It was the custom in the old days for a ranchman never to kill his own cattle for food, and many an oldtimer was accused of never knowing how his own beef tasted."

biscuit roller. The cook on a ranch, used since the 1870s. Also called a "biscuit shooter," which was sometimes applied to a restaurant waitress as well.

canned cow. Canned or condensed milk (1925).

cíbola. A southwestern cowboy term, from the Spanish for buffalo. A "cíbolero" is a buffalo hunter.

coffin varnish. Cheap, inferior whiskey. The term first appears in print in 1935.

cookhouse. A ranch building where food is prepared and served (1785). Cookhouses were also called "feed bags" or "feed troughs" (referring to the bags and troughs from which horses fed on grain).

cookie. A nineteenth-century term used by ranchers or cowboys for a cook or by sailors for a cook's helper (1852). The ranch cook was responsible for three hot meals a day, and he had to possess a good deal of imagination to please his men with dishes that often had to be prepared from meager sources on the open range.

A "cook's louse" was a cook's helper, and a cowboy's cook might also be called a "coosie" (from the Spanish *cocinero*), as well as "bean master," "belly cheater," "belly robber," "biscuit roller," "boarding-house man," "boiler," "dinero," "dough-belly," "doughboxer," "dough-puncher," "dough roller," "dough wrangler," "flunky," "grease ball," "grease burner," "grease belly," "grub-spoiler," "grub worm," "gut burglar," "gut robber," "hash-burner," "hash slinger," "kitchen mechanic," "lizard," "scorcher," "mess moll," MULLIGAN mixer," "old woman," "pothook," "pot rustler," "Sallie," "sizzler," "sop and 'taters," SOURDOUGH," "star chief," "stew builder," "stomach robber," "swamper," and, doubtless, scores of other appellations.

cookie pusher. A restaurant waitress (1936).

cowboy cocktail. Straight whiskey.

cowboy coffee. Black coffee without sugar, a term dating back to 1943 in print. Cowboys themselves called their coffee "Arbuckle's," "belly-wash," "black-jack," "black water," "brown coffee," "jamoka" (from the words *java* and *mocha*), "six-shooter coffee" (strong enough to float a six-shooter pistol), and "Indian coffee" (a weakened, reboiled coffee made from used grounds that was considered not fit for cowboys but good enough for Indian visitors).

cowboy toast. Biscuits baked with butter, sugar, and spices. According to *Western Kitchen Cook Book of Original Chuckwagon and Mexican Foods* (1937) by C. C. and Dudley Yaws, "This dish has been enjoyed in ranch homes and cow camps in the west for many years."

COWBOY TOAST

Break 6 cold biscuits in half, place in bread pan, and brown in hot oven. Sprinkle with sugar and replace in oven until sugar is browned. Cover with ½ c. milk, sprinkle with a dash of allspice, pour melted 1 T. butter over the dish, replace in oven, and let simmer for 10 min.

eatin' iron. A knife, fork, or spoon.

gun-wadding bread. A light bread eaten by cowboys (1919).

gut-eaters. Native Americans, because of some tribes' taste for the entrails of animals.

hot rock. A biscuit.

immigrant butter. Grease, flour, and water.

John Chinaman. Boiled rice, so called because the Chinese in nineteenth-century America subsisted on the grain. It has been a slang term for Chinese immigrants since the 1820s.

Kansas City fish. Fried salt pork.

know your cans. A cowboy game in which players had to recite from memory the exact ingredients listed on the labels of canned foodstuffs, with every punctuation mark in the right place.

larrup. MOLASSES, which was also called "long sweetenin'." The origin of the name (1938) is unknown, though the same word in dialectical English means a "beating."

man at the pot! An expression directed at a colleague who went to refill his cup with coffee. On hearing this call, he was duty-bound to fill his companions' cups too.

Mexican strawberries. Dried beans, which were often red.

Mormon dip. Gravy made from milk. The name refers to the Mormons, members of the Church of Jesus Christ of Latter-Day Saints, who founded Salt Lake City, Utah, in 1841.

niggers-in-a-blanket. A dessert whose name derived from the dark raisins in the dough. A similar pastry made with blackberries goes by the same derogatory name in Louisiana.

pair of overalls. An order of two drinks served at once.

pig's vest with buttons. Salt pork or sow belly.

piloncillo. From the Spanish *pilón*, for a small loaf of unrefined sugar, often given as something for good measure. The term has been in print since 1844.

pooch. A dish made from tomatoes, sugar, and bread.

poor doe. Tough venison.

prairie beeves. A buffalo.

prairie bitters. A popular Old West beverage, also considered medicinal, made from the gall of the buffalo and water.

salt hoss. Corned beef.

sea plum. An oyster.

skunk egg. An onion.

snake-head whiskey. A cheap whiskey known among cowboys. The name came from the assumption that the drink's potency was due to the addition of snake heads in the distilling barrel.

sourdough bullet. Disparaging term for a poorly made biscuit.

spotted pup. Dish made from cooked rice and raisins.

swamper. A cook's helper.

swamp seed. Rice.

wasp nest. A light bread.

whistle berries. Beans, perhaps because of the flatulence they often cause.

woosher. A hog.

cowcumbers. An early variant of "cucumber" dating at least to the seventeenth century, but also cowboy slang for pickles.

cow grease. Also, "cow salve." Slang for butter.

cowpea (*Vigna unquiculata*). Also, "black-eyed pea" (so called because of a black rim on the inner curve of the coat seam), "black-eyed bean," "black-eyed Susan," "blue-eyed bean," "bung belly," "'chain gang pea" (presumably because it was such a staple of the Southern prison diet), "China bean," "cream pea," "Jerusalem pea," "field pea," "whippoorwill pea," "marble pea," "Tonkin pea," "crowder pea," and "zipper." George Washington Carver listed varieties called the "Extra Early Black-Eye," "New Era Lady Cuban Blackeye,"

"Iron," "Speckled," "Groot," "Clay," "Red Ripper," "Brabham," and "White Crowder." The cowpea has been known by that name at least since 1776, but "black-eyed pea" is probably in wider usage, especially in the South, where the term dates in print to 1728.

The cowpea is a native Asian vine-bearing pod, also used in Africa as food and fodder and probably brought to the West Indies in 1674 during the slave trade. It is said that James Oglethorpe brought the cowpea to Georgia in 1734, after which it became an important crop in the South and one of the staples of the Negro diet. Today it is still a cherished ingredient of African-American SOUL FOOD. Cowpeas are a main ingredient in HOPPING JOHN, and, with green peppers, green onions, vinegar, and red peppers, in a dish called "Texas caviar."

cowpuncher's sandwich. According to food writer Craig Claiborne, "A cowpuncher's sandwich is quite simple to make. Slice red onions about one-quarter-inch thick. Put them in a bowl with a generous sprinkling of crumbled oregano. Add equal amounts of ice water and vinegar to cover and let stand overnight. Drain the onions, sprinkle with salt and pepper and use as a filling for two slices of buttered bread."

crab (order Decapoda). Any of a large variety of crustaceans, mostly inhabiting salt water, with a hard shell and five pairs of legs, the front ones having pincers. The word is Middle English in origin. There are more than forty-four hundred species, all edible, ranging from tiny pea crabs to giant, thirty pound Tasmanians. After shrimp, crab is the most popular crustacean on American dining tables. Scores of preparations have been created region by region for the shellfish, and there are more varieties in North America than anywhere in the world. Crabs from Maryland's Chesapeake Bay are particularly savored in the East, while the Pacific's "Dungeness" and "king" crabs are highly popular in the West. Southerners pride themselves on their many different crab recipes, from CRAB CAKES to GUMBOS.

The most important crabs in American cookery are:

blue crab (*Callinectes sapidus*). With its bluegreen shell and romantic Latin name, which means "beautiful swimmer," the blue crab is the most important species on the East Coast. The female carrying eggs is called by various names—"sponge," "ballie," "punk," "sook," and others. A mature male is called a "jimmy." A crab that is getting fat and get-

ting ready to shed its shell is called a "comer." The shedding crab, called a "buster" or "peeler" (a "rankpeeler" is a crab one to three days before it sheds its shell) is particularly valued for its culinary interest. These "soft-shell crabs" are harvested alive, just as the crab has molted his hard shell and is in the process of growing a new one that is at first soft. If the shell begins to harden too much and turn brittle, it is first called a "buck" or "buckram," then a "papershell," and, finally, a "buckler." They are shipped to market and sold alive or flash-frozen. The soft-shell crab industry was begun in the nineteenth century in Crisfield, Maryland.

Blue crabs are sold according to size, ranging from the smallest, called "mediums" (which run 3½–4 inches across the back), "hotels" (4–4½ inches), "prime" (4½–5 inches), "jumbo" (5–5½ inches), and "whale" (5½ or more inches).

Dungeness crab. See main entry.

king crab (*Paralithodes camtschaticus*). A large Pacific crab, also called "Alaska King crab," "Alaskan king crab," "Japanese crab," and "Russian crab," which derives its name from its regal size, which can reach 25 pounds. The term "king crab" has been in print since the end of the seventeenth century.

Only about 25 percent of the crustacean is actually edible, and most Americans buy its claws frozen. Only the male crab is harvested; it is thereupon cooked and frozen before sale. The meat of the claws and legs is marketed, usually in five-pound units, and it is particularly popular in salads.

land crab (*Cardisoma quanhumi*). Also, "mulatto" or "white crab." Land crabs are found throughout the Gulf of Mexico and the Caribbean. A. J. McClane, in his *Encyclopedia of Fish Cookery* (1977), notes that "this species was so abundant in south Florida until the 1950s that our streets were often overrun at night with migrating crabs. Evidently their place has been usurped in a changing ecology."

rock crab (*Cancer irroratus*). An East Coast crab that lives among rocks and in deep water. The similar "Jonah crab" (*C. borealis*) and "spider crab" (*Libinia emarginata*) also go by this name and others, including "sand crab" and "white legger."

With its spindly legs that make it resemble a spider, this crab is given market names that would make a consumer less squeamish, such as "snow" (more specifically *Chionoecetes opilio*), "tanner," and "queen crab." Another so-called "spider crab" (*Stenocionops furcata*) of the Southeast also goes by the name "decorator crab" because it "decorates" itself with algae, grass, and other items. In Maine the crab is locally called "peekytoe," a name seafood wholesaler Rod Mitchell of the Browne Trading Company in Portland, Maine, began using to sell the product to chefs in New York in the mid-1990s, and the crab took on a new popularity by that name in upscale restaurants.

stone crab. See main entry.

Much American crab is marketed as "crabmeat," either frozen or vacuum-packed, which constitutes the overwhelming majority of crab used in restaurants. Crabmeat may be labeled "lump" meat, "flake" (small pieces), or "flake and lump," mostly from blue crabs. "Back fin" meat is from the breast of the blue crab. The mature female crab with eggs is colloquially called a "bally," "lemon-belly," or "punk." U.S. commercial landings of crabs totaled 430 million pounds in 1997.

crab butter. The white-yellow fat inside the back shell of a large crab. Crab butter is much prized as a delicacy and is often added to a dressing or sauce.

crab cake. A sautéed or fried patty of crabmeat. The term dates in print to 1939 in Crosby Gaige's *New York World's Fair Cook Book,* where they are called "Baltimore crab cakes," suggesting they have long been known in the South. A "crabburger" is a crab cake eaten on a hamburger bun.

CRAB CAKE

In a bowl combine 1 lb. crabmeat, 1½ t. salt, 1 t. dry mustard, 2 t. Worcestershire sauce, 1 egg yolk, and 2 t. mayonnaise. Pat lightly into small cakes, dip in flour, then into beaten egg and fry in butter or hot oil.

crab house. A place where crabs are cooked, processed, and packed for distribution. Also, a restaurant that specializes in crab dishes.

crab lantern. A fried apple pastry. According to the *Dictionary of American Regional English,* the name may derive from "crab apple" and "lantern," "from the ventilating slashes that expose the fruit filling." The term dates in print to about 1770.

crab Louis. Also, "crab Louie." A crabmeat salad made with hard-boiled eggs. The dish has been credited to chefs at Solari's restaurant (where it was served at least as early as 1914) or the dining room of the St. Francis Hotel, both in San Francisco, while others say it was the creation of the chef at the Olympic Club in Seattle, Washington, at the turn of the last century. In their book *Northwest Bounty* (1988) Schuyler Ingle and Sharon Kramis described "Dungeness Crab Louie" as a "classic Northwest Salad." There are many versions of the dish.

CRAB LOUIS

On a salad plate place a bed of shredded lettuce, add a mound of lump crabmeat, top with claw meat. Chop 6 hard-boiled eggs and sprinkle on crabmeat, then decorate with chopped chives. Dress with a mixture of 1 c. mayonnaise, ¼ c. French dressing, ½ t. tarragon, ½ c. chili sauce, 2 T. chopped green olives, 1 t. horseradish, 1 t. Worcestershire sauce, salt and pepper to taste. Serves 6.

crabmeat à la Dewey. A crabmeat dish made with green pepper, mushrooms, and cream sauce. There are two stories as to the dish's origin: One claims it was created at the Gage & Tollner restaurant in Brooklyn, New York, and named after proprietor Seth Bradford Dewey. But, according to Ned and Pam Bradford in *Boston's Locke-Ober Café* (1978), the dish was created by the chef at the Maryland Yacht Club in honor of Commodore George Dewey's victory over the Spanish fleet in Manila Bay on May 1, 1898.

crabmeat Remick. A dish made from crabmeat, chili sauce, mayonnaise, and other seasonings. It was created in 1920 at the Plaza Hotel in New York City by chef Albert Leopold Lattard in honor of William H. Remick, president of the New York Stock Exchange from 1919 to 1921.

CRABMEAT REMICK

Combine 1 c. chili sauce, 1 cup mayonnaise, ½ oz. dry mustard, 1 t. paprika, 1 t. celery salt, ½ t. Tabasco sauce, and ½ t. Worcestershire sauce. Blend half of this mixture with 1 lb. crabmeat. Spoon the crabmeat mixture into 2 doz. empty clam shells, pour the rest of the sauce mixture on top of shells, sprinkle with Parmesan cheese, and set in 350° oven until sauce bubbles.

crab Norfolk. A dish of crabmeat baked and seasoned with vinegar, Tabasco, and Worcestershire sauce. The name supposedly derives from the city of Norfolk, Virginia, where the dish was made in what was called a "Norfolk aluminum pan," a small oval cooking pan in which the crabmeat was placed. According to Craig Claiborne, the dish was created by W. O. Snowden at the Snowden and Mason Restaurant in Norfolk, which opened in 1924.

CRAB NORFOLK

Combine 1 lb. crabmeat with 2 T. vinegar, ½ t. Tabasco sauce, ½ t. Worcestershire sauce, salt, and pepper. Place portions in small pans each containing 1 T. melted butter. Bake in 350° oven until well heated.

cracker. A thin, unsweetened wheat-flour wafer made from unleavened dough and usually eaten as a snack, as a canapé, with soups, and with dips. The word comes from the "cracking" sound it makes when broken. Since the eighteenth century Americans have spoken of these wafers by this term, first appearing in print in 1739, but it is still a word rarely used in England, where "biscuit" is preferred. (To Americans, a biscuit is a small yeast-dough form of bread.) In the 1830s Americans called the wafers "soda crackers," and COMMON CRACKERS or "oyster crackers" (see TRENTON CRACKERS) were placed in New England chowders or split and buttered. Graham crackers are sweet and made with GRAHAM FLOUR, while Saltines is a trademark of the National Biscuit Company for a very popular cracker made with salt on top.

In the nineteenth century crackers were sold at grocery stores from cracker barrels or packaged in cracker boxes or Boston tins. "Cracker pudding" is a New England dish made from crackers, milk, eggs, and raisins.

"Animal Crackers" are actually a COOKIE, first produced as Christmas tree ornaments in 1902 by the National Biscuit Company (now Nabsico). They are formed in the shapes of various circus animals and packed in a box decorated like a circus train. Nabisco currently produces about 7 million Animal Cracker cookies per day.

cracker barrel. A large barrel, found in turn-of-the-century groceries and general stores, for holding crackers that were to be sold in quantity. The term first appeared in print in 1875.

crackling. Also, "cracklins." A crispy morsel left over after most of the fat has been rendered by cooking pork, a meaning the word has had since the beginning of the eighteenth century and first seen in print in 1834. Cracklings may be added to a variety of dishes—bean's and other vegetables, for instance—and a particular favorite in the South is "crackling bread," which appears in print in 1842, and may also be called "scrap johnnycake" or "goody-bread." In Cajun Louisiana cracklings are called "grattons" or "gratons," from the French cretons. In Mexican-American regions cracklings are called *chicharrons*.

CRACKLING BREAD

To 1 qt. cornmeal, add enough boiling water to make a stiff dough. Add 1 c. cracklings, mix and form into oblong cakes. Bake at 400° until inserted knife comes out clean and top is golden-brown. (Modern-day recipes usually include eggs and butter.)

crackseed. A snack in Hawaii available in scores of varieties and eaten like candy. The term first appeared in print about 1970. Crackseeds are made by smashing the seed of a fruit and preserving the pulp with salt; they have a salty-sweet pungency with a faint taste of licorice. Some of the varieties sold in small packages include sweet *li hing mui* (plum), rocksalt plum, salted mango, wet lemon peel, and wet *li hing mui*.

cranberry (*Vaccinium macrocarpon*). Also, "bearberry." A very tart red berry grown in bogs from low, trailing vines. Cranberries are used in sauces, jellies, and beverages and as a traditional accompaniment at Thanksgiving dinners (1640). There are several species of wild cranberry in the world, but the American or large cranberry is the only one in wide cultivation. This variety makes up a major crop of Massachusetts, New Jersey, Wisconsin, and Oregon. Cranberry bogs are sandy and often flooded, and some continue to be productive after a century. In New England the bogs are picked between Labor Day (when the "Early Blacks" ripen) and the end of October (when the "Late Howes" are brought in).

The Native Americans of New England, who called them *sassamanesh* or *ibimi,* long enjoyed cranberries, both raw or sweetened with maple sugar, and they often added them to their PEMMICAN.

The first European settlers found the fruit similar to their lingonberry, but somewhat too tart unless sweetened or made into a condiment.

There is no hard evidence that the Pilgrims ate cranberries at the First Thanksgiving, held in October of 1621, but it is a fair assumption that the Native Americans might have brought them to the feast at a time when the cranberries were at their ripest in that region. The name "cranberry" was not English, however; the settlers probably called the berries "fenberries," after a fruit they knew at home. Years later the Dutch introduced the word *kranbeere* (from the Low German *kraanbere,* "crane berry," because its stamen resembled a beak). Others referred to them as "bounce berries," because of their bouncy quality. There is a story that a New Jersey grower named John I. Webb ("Peg-Leg John") initiated the development of the first cranberry separator after he transferred the berries from his loft to the ground by allowing them to tumble down the stairs—the ripest, firmest berries bounced to the ground, the bruised fruit remained on the steps. Commercial cranberry cultivation began after another accidental discovery, this time on Cape Cod about 1816. Henry Hall noticed that bogs that had had sand blown over them produced a sturdy crop of cranberries, so he spread some sand on his own property and duplicated the results. There is a cherished legend on Cape Cod about how the cranberry bogs began there. It seems that a Native American medicine man cast a spell over the Reverend Richard Bourne and then mired him in quicksand. For the next fifteen days the two men waged a battle of wits, during which the motionless Reverend Bourne was sustained only by a white dove who fed him cranberries. The Native American fell exhausted from the strain, and the spell was lifted from the minister. The story goes on to tell how one of the berries fell to the ground and became rooted forever in the Cape Cod soil, which is acknowledged to produce some of America's best cranberries.

The commercial production of cranberries grew so rapidly that supply far outpaced demand by the turn of the century. In 1912 Marcus L. Urann of the Cape Cod Cranberry Company began canning "cranberry sauce" for sale throughout the year, calling his product "Ocean Spray Cape Cod Cranberry Sauce." Urann merged in 1930 with several other growers to form the "Ocean Spray growers' cooperative," which today has 900 members representing 70 percent of all American cranberry growers. In 1946 the growers began selling fresh bagged berries, and in 1930 developed a cranberry juice "cocktail."

In 1996, 200 billion cranberries were harvested. Americans consume 400 million pounds of cranberries annually, with about 80 million eaten over Thanksgiving week.

crayfish. Also, "crawfish," "crawdad," "crawdaddy," and "Florida lobster." Any of various freshwater crustaceans of the genera *Cambarus* and *Astacus.*

Although considerably smaller, the crayfish resembles the LOBSTER, and there are 250 species and subspecies found in North America alone. The name is from Middle English *crevise,* and, ultimately, from the Frankish *krabītja.*

Crayfish formed a significant part of the diet of the Native American of the South and still hold their highest status among the Cajuns of Louisiana. Louisianans have an enormous passion and appetite for what they call "crawfish" (a name used by Captain John Smith as early as 1615), "mudbugs," "creekcrabs," "freshwater lobsters," "yabbies," "cheval du diable" (Creole French for "devil's horse"), and other names. The crayfish figures in Louisiana folklore, and the natives hold "crawfish boils" whenever the crustacean is in season. Breaux Bridge, Louisiana, calls itself the "Crawfish Capital of the World" and holds a yearly festival of eating and drinking to prove it, cooking up crayfish in pies, gumbos, stews, and every other way imaginable. Yet one would not easily find crawfish on restaurant menus in Louisiana much before 1960 because they were considered a common food to be eaten at home.

Crayfish are commercially harvested in waters of the Mississippi basin, most of them of the Red Swamp and White River varieties, with the season running approximately from Thanksgiving Day to the Fourth of July. In 1997 about 23 million pounds were farmed, with Louisiana producing 90 percent of the crop. These are eaten with the fingers, picking the white meat out of the body (mostly out of Vermillion and Acadia parishes). "Squeezing the tip" refers to squeezing the meat from the tail. It is also considered a delicacy to "suck the head" to extract the fat in the animal's thorax.

"Cajun popcorn" is a dish of battered, deep-fried crayfish popularized by Cajun chef Paul Prudhomme in the 1980s.

CRAWFISH ÉTOUFFÉE

Sauté 1 chopped onion, ½ c. chopped green pepper, 2 chopped shallots or scallions, and 2 chopped cloves of garlic in 6 T. butter for about 15 min. Add 3 lb. crayfish and continue cooking for another 15 min. Add salt and pepper to taste, ¼ t. cayenne, and enough water to moisten bottom of pan. Bring to boil, simmer for 5 min., basting crayfish. Serve over boiled rice.

cream. The fat-rich, unhomogenized part of the milk that rises to the surface. FDA Standards of Identity mandate that a product cannot be called "cream" unless it contains at least 18 percent butterfat.

half-and-half. A mixture of half cream and half whole milk.

heavy cream. Must contain not less than 36 percent butterfat; may contain emulsifiers, stabilizers, nutritive sweeteners, and flavoring ingredients.

light cream. Also called "coffee cream." Light cream must contain less than 30 percent, but not less than 18 percent, butterfat and may contain emulsifiers, stabilizers, nutritive sweeteners, and flavoring agents.

light whipping cream. Must contain not less than 30 percent but less than 36 percent butterfat and may contain emulsifiers, stabilizers, nutritive sweeteners, and flavoring ingredients.

pouring cream. A nineteenth-century term for cream poured out of a pitcher.

sour cream. Cream that has been treated with lactic acid producing bacteria and containing not less than 18 percent butterfat (1815). Sour cream may contain optional ingredients such as rennet, salt, sodium citrate, and flavoring ingredients.

cream cheese. A cow's-milk cheese with a very smooth consistency and a mild, slightly tangy flavor (1575). Under FDA regulations cream cheese must contain not less than 33 percent milkfat and not more than 55 percent moisture. The cheese is not aged, but gum arabic may be added to increase firmness and shelf life. Diluted cream cheese may be called "imitation cream cheese" (although this may also refer to a nondairy product).

Cream cheese became available to everyone after Isaac and Joseph Breakstone of the Breakstone Company produced "Breakstone's Downsville Cream Cheese" (named after the New York community where it was made) in 1920. It became immediately popular among Jewish communities in New York City as a spread for BAGELS.

In 1872 a dairyman named Lawrence in New York State began mixing cream and milk to make a particularly savory form of cream cheese that was soon being manufactured by various dairies. A cheese distributor named Reynolds enlisted Lawrence and the nearby Empire Cheese Company of South Edmeston, New York, to produce the cheese under the name "Philadelphia Brand," which in 1928 became a trademark of Kraft food company of Glenview, Illinois.

cream toast. A dish of toast with a cream sauce on it.

credit card. A card that identifies a person who seeks to purchase an item on credit. The term has been in use since 1885, and "charge accounts" have been part of American business since 1807, established at Cowperthwaite & Sons in New York. The first popular card for charging was made by Western Union about 1914, and "charge plates," usually in the form of thin metal cards called "metal money," came in around the same time at hotels. But the most important innovation for food service came in 1950 after businessman Francis X. McNamara (who himself worked for a credit company in Manhattan) found himself unable to pay for a restaurant meal in New York because he'd forgotten his money. This gave him the idea to create the "Diners Club" with the help of attorney Ralph Schneider. For a fee of three dollars per year, cardholders could charge their meals at any of twenty-seven participating restaurants in New York. By the end of 1951 more than $1 million had been charged on the new cards, and McNamara sold out his share to Schneider in 1953 for $200,000. Diners Club later became a subsidiary of Citicorp.

crème brûlée. Also, "burnt cream." A dessert custard topped with a burnt-sugar crust. *The Random House Dictionary of the English Language* traces the first appearance in print of crème brûlée to 1885, from the French, meaning "burnt cream," which it is often called in England. But the dish is probably not of French origins. Escoffier does not mention such a dish; *Larousse Gastronomique* refers to a similar dish under the name *crème anglaise au miroir* ("mirrorlike English cream"). As "burnt cream," the dish originated in England, where, according to English food authority Jane Grigson, recipes for the dish appeared in seventeenth-century cookbooks. By the turn of the twentieth century it had become a favorite dessert at Trinity College, Cambridge, and, according to Jane Garmey in *Great British Cooking* (1981), it is often referred to as "Trinity cream."

Recipes for "burnt cream" have been included in

Creole cookbooks since the nineteenth century, though *The Picayune Creole Cook Book* (1901) indicates that the confection is made merely by adding caramel to a custard base that is then reduced, strained, garnished with fruits, and served cool. In *The New Orleans Eat Book* (1991), Tom Fitzmorris says, "*Crème brûlée* is a variation on caramel custard in which the custard part is much richer, yet semi-liquid in texture. The caramel part is baked into a hard shell over the top." The classic American cookbook *Joy of Cooking* calls it "A rich French custard—famous for its hard, caramelized sugar glaze." There are recipes for a burnt glaze custard under the name "creme brulee" in *The Cordon Bleu Cook Book* (1947) by Dione Lucas and *The White House Cookbook* (1964) edited by Jane Halliday Ervin.

But the popularity of the dish in the United States soared after it was made fashionable when chef Alain Sailhac brought the idea back from a trip to Spain (where the dish is known as an old Catalan dessert called *crema quemada a la catalana*) in 1982 and began making it at the restaurant Le Cirque in New York City. After that it became a standard dish in American fine-dining restaurants, as well, ironically, as in France.

Creole mustard. A hot, spicy mustard made from seeds marinated in vinegar. It is a specialty of Louisiana's German Creoles, who brought the mustard seeds from Austria and Holland.

Crisco. The trademark of a shortening made from vegetable oils, principally soybean. By a process called "hydrogenation" the oils are suspended in fat solids so as to form a white, soft mass that is packed in airtight tin cans.

The product is manufactured by the Procter & Gamble Company, which began marketing the new shortening in 1911. Its virtues over lard, butter, and other vegetable oils at that time were that it did not pick up odors or flavors from foods fried in it, did not smoke when heated, and could be kept for long periods without going rancid. (In the early 1960s the product was altered to double the amount of polyunsaturates, considered by some scientists to be important to health.)

The name "Crisco" was the result of a contest held among Procter & Gamble employees. The two leading choices were "Krispo" and "Cryst," meant to suggest the hissing sound of the shortening in the pan, and these were combined into "Crisco."

From the beginning the product was marketed with recipes attached, and the name became fairly synonymous with "shortening," especially "white shortening," and was used as an alternative to heavier fats such as lard. It has been particularly favored in the South, where, according to James Villas in *American Taste* (1982), it is the essential ingredient in making good SOUTHERN FRIED CHICKEN.

Artificially flavored "Butter Flavor Crisco" was introduced nationally in 1983.

crockery cooker. A large, lidded kettle containing its own heat unit for cooking. The first example was the "Crockpot," brought on the market by the Rival Manufacturing Company of Kansas City, Missouri, in 1971. Foods are placed in the Crockpot, the pot is turned on, and the food is slowly cooked through.

crumb bun. A pastry topped with crumbs made of flour, fat, and powdered sugar, usually eaten as a breakfast item or snack.

crummin. A Texas dish of crumbled-up corn bread and sweet milk.

crust coffee. A coffee substitute made at home in New England. It was made by toasting bread until almost burned, pouring boiling water on it, straining the liquid, and drinking it with sugar and cream. The term dates in print to 1863.

Cruvinet. Trademark name for a system developed in France to preserve wines from oxidation in bottles that have been opened. The system, which puts nitrogen into the opened bottle, is most often used in restaurants that offer several wines by the glass. The first restaurant in the United States to use the Cruvinet was Lavin's in New York City on November 15, 1982, to celebrate the arrival of the Beaujolais Nouveau wine from France.

Cuba libre. A cocktail made from rum, cola, and lime juice. The name in Spanish means "free Cuba," but its origins are obscure, probably dating from the Spanish-American War (1898), when Cuba was liberated from Spanish rule.

According to a deposition by Fausto Rodriguez on October 24, 1965, this blend of ingredients was made in August of 1900 by a "Mr. X," who worked in the office of the United States Signal Corps in Cuba. (Mr. Rodriguez was a messenger for the Corps.) The drink became immediately popular among the American soldiers.

Cuban-Chinese food. A mixture of Cuban and Chinese food items sold at restaurants opened by Cuban-Chinese who fled Cuba in the 1960s after Fidel Castro seized power. Many settled in New York City's Hispanic neighborhoods, where they opened such restaurants primarily to serve the Latino community.

cucumber (*Cucumis sativus*). A long green vegetable in the gourd family that is generally eaten raw, as in a salad.

The word is from the Latin *cucumis,* which in Middle English became "cucumber."

Though the cucumber was long believed to have originated in India, there is now evidence that it came from Thailand and was cultivated there ten thousand years before Christ. By the fourteenth century A.D. it was being cultivated in England. Spaniards brought the cucumber to America, and it was then readily cultivated by the Pueblo Indians. In 1998 the U.S. produced 615 million tons of cucumbers for processing, mostly for pickles.

cuitlacoche (*Ustilago maydis*). Also, "huittacoche." A gray-black fungus that grows on the ears of corn, used in cooking as one would wild mushrooms. The word is from the Nahuatl *cuitlatl* ("excrement") and *cochi* ("black") and is pronounced "hweet-la-KO-chay." In *The Cuisines of Mexico* (1972; revised 1986), Diana Kennedy spelled the word *huitlacoche,* citing *cuitla-coche* as an alternative in her *Recipes from the Regional Cooks of Mexico* (1978), then gave the latter spelling in her 1989 book *The Art of Mexican Cooking.*

The fungus does grow wild on American corn, but most farmers burn it as a crop nuisance called "smut." Though a regional specialty of Mexico City cookery, cuitlacoche began to be treated as a delicacy among American chefs, particularly in the Southwest, only in the 1980s. Almost all cuitlacoche used in cooking is imported from Mexico canned, although it may grow wild in some American gardens and farms and has been cultivated in very small quantities in California and Georgia. Cuitlacoche is usually sautéed with garlic and oil.

cull. Fishermen's term for a lobster with only one claw, usually the result of a battle with another creature.

currant. Any of a variety of prickly shrubs of the genus *Ribes* that bear small dark berries that are often dried and used as a flavoring. The word is from Old French *Corinthe,* referring to the city of Corinth, because the berries were called in Middle English "raysons of coraunte"—that is, "raisins of Corinth."

Currants first began to appear in England in the seventeenth century and were brought to America soon afterward, even though there were already native varieties in the New World, specifically the "American black currant" (*R. americanum*). Until the present century currants were cultivated in the United States, but their growth has now been discouraged because currants carry the parasite *Cronartium ribicola,* which does not harm the plant itself but attacks precious white pines in its vicinity. Most currants on the American market are therefore dried and imported.

cush. A cornmeal pancake made in the South. The name (first recorded about 1770) arrived in America with the African slaves brought to the Caribbean and the South; it derives from the Arab, *kuskus,* "to grind small," and the grain dish of Morocco called "cous-cous." In Louisiana "coush-coush caille" is a dish of corn bread and clabber.

cushaw (*Cucurbita moschata*). An American crook-necked SQUASH popular among the Cajun people of Louisiana. The name comes from the Indian, probably the Algonquian of North Carolina and Virginia, *coscushaw,* and first appears in English in 1580.

cut straw and molasses. Western slang term for inferior food, dating in print to 1857.

cyclone candy. A sweet confection mentioned by Marjorie Mosser in her *Foods of Old New England* (1957). The reasons for its name are unknown.

czarnina. Also "czarina." A Polish-American soup made from duck's blood, from the Polish *czernina.* It is usually served on feast days.

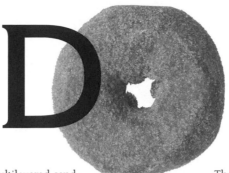

Dagwood sandwich. A multilayered sandwich made with slices of bread enclosing various kinds of meats, lettuce, vegetables, and other condiments. The name derives from the comic-strip character Dagwood Bumstead, created and drawn by Murat Bernard "Chic" Young for "Blondie"—which began on September 6, 1930, as part of the King Features Syndicate.

The sandwich first appeared in the comic strip on April 16, 1936, and, according to Dean Young, son of Chic Young and now co-author of the strip with Bill Yates, it was not at first as colossal a sandwich as it eventually became through the years. The character and the sandwich became immediately linked, and Americans began referring to such overstuffed items as "Dagwoods." The sandwich was also a regular feature in the series of twenty-eight *Blondie* motion pictures made from 1938 to 1950 and in two television series, in 1954 and 1968, of the same name.

daiquiri. Sometimes "Daiquiri." A cocktail made from rum, lime juice, and sugar. It is named after the town of Daiquiri, near Santiago, in Cuba, where, after the Spanish-American War (1898), Americans came to work the mines, retiring on weekends to the Venus Hotel to drink such a cocktail. Chief engineer Jennings S. Cox has been credited with naming the drink in 1900 after the mines. Some say he himself invented the cocktail. The drink was supposedly brought to the United States by Lucius W. Johnson, a medical officer on the U.S.S. *Minnesota,* who enjoyed the drink in Cuba in 1909 and introduced it to Washington's Army and Navy Club. The cocktail was first cited in print in F. Scott Fitzgerald's 1920 novel *This Side of Paradise.*

DAIQUIRI

Combine 2 t. lime juice, ½ t. superfine sugar, and 2 oz. light rum over ice, shake, and strain into a chilled cocktail glass. Sometimes the rim of the glass is sugared.

A frozen daiquiri, often made with banana, strawberries, or other fruit, is made by adding about 4 ice cubes to the mixture and pulverizing it in an electric blender.

A pink daiquiri is made by adding 1 t. each of maraschino or grenadine.

The "frozen daiquiri," for which crushed ice is added before blending, was supposedly created at the La Florida Bar (known to customers in Ernest Hemingway's day as the "Floridita") in Havana, Cuba.

daisy. A cocktail made from citrus-fruit juice, a cordial or fruit syrup, and liquor. Daisies are generally synonymous with "fixes," which were originally based on pineapple syrup, while daisies were based on raspberry or grenadine, but these distinctions have blurred since the mid-nineteenth century, when both drinks were especially popular. The name probably derives from a slang term meaning "something excellent," rather than directly from the flower.

dandelion (*Taraxacum officinale*). A native Eurasian plant that has become naturalized as a weed in North America. The word is from the Medieval Latin *dens leonis,* "lion's tooth," via Old French. Its leaves are sometimes added to salads, and its flowers are used to produce a HONEY, especially in Colorado. It is also used to make "dandelion wine." See DUTCH SALAD.

Danish pastry. Also, "Danish." A term encompassing a variety of yeast-dough pastries rolled and filled with cheese, prune, almond paste, fruit preserves, nuts, or other condiments. These pastries are a staple breakfast item, especially on the East Coast, where one orders a "Danish" prefixed by the filling desired. Although the pastries may have Danish origins, these flaky buns and rolls are more often associated with New York Jewish delicatessens and bakeries. With this meaning the word first appeared in print in 1928. In California Danish pastries are sometimes called "snails," because of their snaillike appearance.

date. The fruit of the date palm (*Phoenix dactylifera*), a tropical tree. The sweet fruit is especially popular in Asia and the Middle East. The name is from the Greek *daktulos,* finger, after the shape of the fruit. The date began to be cultivated in California about 1902, principally from the variety Deglet Noor (meaning "Date of the Light"). Dates are classified as "soft," "semi-dry," and "dry." More than 99 percent of the dates marketed in the United States are grown in California, where "date milk shakes," blended with ice cream and milk, are a popular local confection.

date fish. Name of either of two mollusks, the "piddock" (*Zirfaea crispata*) or the "chubby mya" (*Platyodon cancellatus*). The term was first mentioned in print in 1838, but Goode's *Fisheries U.S.* (1884) notes that both mollusks "are esteemed delicacies on the coast of California under the name of 'Date fish.' "

Deacon Porter's hat. A suet pudding steamed in a long, cylindrical mold. It is fairly similar to the pudding called BROTHER JONATHAN'S HAT. According to Eleanor Early in her *New England Cookbook* (1954), "When this pudding . . . made its first appearance at dinner one noon in 1837, a student [at] Mount Holyoke Female Seminary, cried, 'Oh, see the Deacon's hat!' " referring to Deacon Andrew W. Porter, a member of the school's first board of trustees, who wore a stovepipe hat every day. Early also notes that "there is said to have been a light-colored pudding, made in a similar mold, called the Deacon's Summer Hat, but that is only a legend."

dead soldier. Also, "dead marine." An empty beer bottle (1899).

Delaware. An American red labrusca grape that makes wines that rarely need the sugaring that other eastern varieties require. It was introduced in the 1840s and is today used as a table grape as well as a champagne grape.

delicatessen. A grocery store that usually sells cooked meats, prepared foods, and delicacies. The word is from the German *Delikatesse,* "delicacy." In the 1880s it referred to preserved foods. During the period of post-Civil War emigration to America, many Jews set up butcher shops called *schlact* stores, but as more foods were added to the shelves, the term "delicatessen shop," "delicatessen store," and "delicatessen" became common, though some preferred the non-German term "appetizing store." Later on "delicatessen" was shortened to "deli" or "delly," which sometimes also refers to the foods sold in such an establishment.

New York City is still the hub for deli culture and sets the standards for those elsewhere. Delicatessens specialize in serving pastrami, potato salad, pickles, rye bread, liverwurst, and many other items enjoyed by the Jews of the eastern cities. To call such a store a "Jewish delicatessen" is, therefore, something of a redundancy, and many delicatessens maintain KOSHER regulations. But today many other ethnic groups run their own delis, as in "Italian deli" or "Latin-American deli."

Delmonico potatoes. Potato balls boiled and buttered and sprinkled with lemon juice, parsley, pepper, and salt. The dish was featured at New York's Delmonico's Restaurant in the nineteenth century.

Democrat. A sweet, baked buttermilk confection of the nineteenth century. The nature of the connection is obscure, but the dish somehow refers to the Democratic party.

DEMOCRAT

Combine 1 pt. buttermilk with 1 c. confectioners' sugar, 3 beaten egg yolks, ½ c. butter, 3 t. baking powder, and 1 qt. flour. Fold in 3 stiffly beaten egg whites. Bake in muffin tins, 1 T. of batter to a tin, for about 20 min. at 375°.

---

depth charge. A bar drink made by dropping a shot glass of whiskey into a glass of beer (1956). The imbiber is supposed to drain the glass and end up with the shot glass between his teeth. The name derives from the depth-charge explosives dropped in the water from a ship in an effort to destroy a submerged submarine. In an article about Johnstown, Pennsylvania, in *Esquire* (April 1984), Adam Smith observed, "If you get three steelworkers at a bar, [drinking depth charges] can become a competitive sport."

Derby pie. Trademark name of the Kerns Bakery in Louisville, Kentucky, for a very thick, rich chocolate-chip pecan pie. Its name derives from the tradition of serving it on Kentucky Derby Day, the first Saturday in May.

designated driver. A person who volunteers or is appointed not to consume alcoholic beverages while at a party or restaurant so that he may drive his friends home safely without fear of accident or of being arrested by police for "driving while under the influence" of alcohol ("DWI"). The term gained currency in the 1980s.

deviled. Also, "devilled." Any of a variety of dishes prepared with hot seasonings, such as cayenne or mustard. The word derives from its association with the demon who dwells in hell. In a culinary context the word first appears in print in 1786; by 1820 Washington Irving had used the word in his *Sketchbook* to describe a highly seasoned dish similar to a curry.

Deviled dishes were very popular throughout the nineteenth and into the twentieth centuries, especially for seafood preparations and some appetizers. The first U.S. food product to be granted a trademark (number 82) by the U.S. Patent Office (1870), to William Underwood & Company of Boston, was for "deviled entremets," introduced in 1867.

devil's food. A cake, muffin, or cookie made with dark chocolate, so called because it is supposedly so rich and delicious that it must be somewhat sinful, although the association is clearly made with humor. Its dark color contrasted with the snowy white of ANGEL-FOOD CAKE, an earlier confection. The first devil's-food recipe appeared in 1900, after which recipes and references became frequent in cookbooks. The "red devil's food cake," given a reddish-brown color by the mixture of coca and baking soda, is a post-World War II version of the standard devil's food cake.

dewberry (genus *Rubus*). Any of a variety of trailing forms of the BLACKBERRY (1570), including the "nagoonberry" (*Rubus acaulis*) of Alaska (1914). In his *Soul Food Cookbook* (1969), Bob Jeffries refers to dewberries baked in pastry as "dubies." The word first appeared in print in 1578.

dextrose. A sugar (also called "glucose" or "grape sugar") derived from the sap and juice of grapes and other plants (1865). Dextrose provides the major source of energy in animals and is used to thicken and sweeten caramel, soda pop, baked goods, and candy.

Dick Smith. Also, "Dick Smither." Colloquialism for a man who drinks liquor by himself or one who never buys drinks for anyone else at the bar. The term, which may also be used as a verb, dates in print to 1876.

dill (*Anethum graveolens*). An herb, native to the Old World, used as a seasoning in sauces, soups, and salads. Its name derives from the West Germanic, *dilja*. Pickles are often flavored with dill, which in the United States is grown primarily in Ohio and the Midwest. In *Food* (1980), Waverley Root noted that "the Romans mixed aneth oil in their gladiators' food in the belief

that it was a tonic, and it may have been for the same reason that dill seeds were given to American children a century or two back to chew in church, perhaps to keep them awake during long sermons, for which reason they were called 'meetin' seeds.'"

dime-a-dip dinner. Also, "ten-cents-a-dip." A meal held to benefit a charity or raise funds at which all food items cost ten cents or some other specific amount of money. The term dates in print to 1976 and seems closely associated with Mormon communities.

diner. An inexpensive RESTAURANT originally made to look like a railroad dining car. *Roadside,* a journal for diner aficionados, defined a diner as "a prefabricated structure with counter service, hauled out to its site" in its Fall 1990 issue. Diners grew out of the concept of the lunch wagon, at first a pushcart wheeled into city streets where workers could get a quick bite to eat. In 1872 in Providence, Rhode Island, Walter Scott improved on the idea with his "Pioneer Lunch," a horse-drawn lunch wagon that was quickly copied in New England and led to elaborately decorated versions with complete working kitchens and stained-glass windows, led by Thomas H. Buckley's New England Lunch Wagon Company, which also was the first to try out the idea of a stationary lunch stand, in Worcester, Massachusetts, which was not a success.

But the proliferation of lunch wagons (sometimes called "dog wagons") in New England and their unsavory reputations as blue-collar hangouts caused many towns to force the owners to close down by 10:00 P.M. As a result, many lunch-wagon owners removed their horses and set down their wagons as immobile units, which were allowed to stay open day and night. By renovating dilapidated electric trolley cars, these same entrepreneurs upgraded the image of their eateries, and, led by men like Patrick J. "Pop" Tierney of New Rochelle, New York, the roadside eateries grew in number, popularity, and design, usually copying the look, finish, and details of the railroad dining cars of the era. By the 1930s streamlining made such restaurants—by then called "diners"—gleaming beacons by the road, known for their fast, efficient service and crisp, clean lines.

The industry grew rapidly and came to be dominated by Greek immigrants, whose families might own several diners, many of which were designed around traditional Greek motifs and given Greek names like "Apollo" and "Pegasus."

By the late 1940s at least thirteen manufacturers were involved in building diners at a rate of 250 a year, but, owing to the changing eating habits of Americans and the intrusion of FAST FOOD chain restaurants in every American town, the diner went into a slow decline after 1960, although there has been a revival of nostalgic interest in diners since the mid-1980s, and several new ones have been built around the United States to evoke the design elements, atmosphere, and food of the 1930s, 1940s, and 1950s. Currently there are about 2,000 diners in the United States.

dinner. The main meal of the day. Until the 1820s this was commonly the midday meal, supper being a lighter meal at the end of the workday. Today, dinner is usually the evening meal.

The word "dinner," dating to the thirteenth century in England, derives from the French *dîner.* "Supper" is also found in English as of the thirteenth century, from the French *so(u)per,* itself possibly related to "soup," which was often the simple repast of the evening meal. In American usage, "dinner" dates in print to 1622.

In America the tradition of eating the heaviest meal at midday was superseded in the 1820s by the demands of workers whose mealtime was often not paid for by their employers, thereby necessitating a quick, light meal before getting back to work. This became known as LUNCH, and the main meal of the day, "dinner," was consumed after work ended. The tradition of eating the main meal in the afternoon was carried on as the "Sunday dinner," since Sunday was for most people the only day of the week off from work. Even after the five-day workweek became the norm, the Sunday dinner, held anywhere from noon onward, continued to be an American family gathering.

Today southerners still speak of "supper" as the evening meal, though it may be eaten somewhat earlier than in the rest of the country. In the North the term "supper" may refer to a light meal served after an evening's entertainment, as in "after-theater supper." "Pre-theater dinner" is served before the eight o'clock curtain. "Din din" is a childish expression for dinner.

dinnerhouse. Restaurant industry term for a moderately priced, fairly casual, family-oriented restaurant, often connected with a chain or franchise.

dip. A condiment, often made with mayonnaise or sour cream, into which one dips any of a variety of vegetables or snacks. Dips are usually served with party food. In the mid-nineteenth century "dip" referred to a sauce of pork fat served on fish. By the

next century "dip" was a sauce for puddings, and "dipping" or "dippy" referred to both a gravy or sauce to dip meats into or a sweet sauce for desserts. In the 1950s "party dips" were sauces in which guests dipped snack foods like potato chips. The most popular party dips were cream-cheese dip, onion dip, clam dip, and other creamy sauces. "Salsa" is a term used for a dipping sauce for tortilla chips.

In 1952 the Lipton food company developed a dehydrated onion-soup mix that became even more popular as the base for an onion dip (two envelopes of soup mix plus 1 c. sour cream), which Lipton thereafter printed as a recipe called "California Dip" on the back of the package.

dirt. Known anthropologically as "geophagy," the eating of dirt is common to nearly every culture on earth, especially during famine, as a way of absorbing minerals. In the United States it is specific to African Americans and poor rural whites (called "clay eaters" or "sand-lappers," which term dates in print to 1841) in the South. The custom apparently was carried to the New World by African slaves, whose masters sometimes masked slaves' mouths to prevent the practice. Native Americans of the Southwest are also known to consume clay with acorns and tubers.

In this century the eating of dirt is still indulged by some southerners, who tend to favor particular patches, especially "hill dirt" from slopes. In 1975 a study done by anthropologist Dennis A. Frate revealed that of fifty-six African-American women in rural Mississippi, thirty-two admitted to eating dirt, especially during pregnancy. Others consumed cornstarch or baking soda, a possible cause of anemia.

dirty rice. A Louisiana Cajun dish of rice cooked with chicken gizzards and livers, so called because the meat gives the rice a "dirty" appearance. The term dates in print to 1967.

DIRTY RICE

Boil 10 each of chicken gizzards, necks, livers, and hearts in 2 qt. water until tender. Remove and retain liquid. Fry 4 lb. hot sausage and retain fat. Sauté 2 minced onions, 1 minced bell pepper, and 4 stalks minced celery in 3 T. of the retained fat, then add 5 chopped scallions and cook for about 10 min. Add 1 c. chopped ham and chicken mixture, 8 T. melted butter, and 2 T. chopped parsley. Add water from kettle, salt, and pepper, and let simmer for 15 min. Blend in 3 lb. cooked rice.

dish night. A night when movie theaters gave away free dishware as a promotional gimmick. The practice began in the late 1920s and continued through the 1950s. Moviegoers would go to the theater on dish night (usually a weeknight) and receive a different dish—a cup, saucer, plate, gravy boat, or other item—thereby encouraging the moviegoer to return week after week to get a complete set.

dishwater. Slang for very weak or badly made coffee.

Dixie Cup. Trademark name for one of the first paper cups. It was produced by the International Drink Cup Company of New York in 1908.

Dixie wine. Slang term, used mostly by Mormons, for fermented grape juice with a pronounced, rough taste. The term dates in print to 1873.

dog (*Canis familiaris*). A domesticated carnivorous mammal of many breeds. In America the dog has never been a food animal except among Native Americans and Hawaiians, although the first settlers from England who landed in Virginia in 1607 staved off starvation by boiling and eating their mastiffs.

In precolonial Hawaii dogs, which were brought from Polynesia, were called *'ilio* and raised in large herds for food; they were actually preferred to pig in those days, and in 1830 the Reverend William Ellis reported that dogs were "mostly fed on vegetables; and we have sometimes seen them kept in yards, with small houses to sleep in. A part of the rent of every tenant who occupies land, is paid in dogs for his landlord's table." Ellis claimed to have seen two hundred dogs baked at one time for a feast and to have heard that when King Taumuarii of Tauai visited the governor of Hawaii, Kuakini, four hundred dogs were baked for the dinner.

dogfish. Any of several species of small sharks, especially *Mustelus canis*, called "smooth dogfish," "smooth dog," and "grayfish," and *Squalus acanthias*, called "spiny dogfish," "spur dog," "piked dogfish," and "grayfish." The name probably refers to the small size and shape of the species, which resemble dogs or puppies. In print the term dates back to 1425.

dog-in-a-blanket. A steamed pudding containing fruit preserves (1887).

doggie bag. Also, "doggy bag." A bag in which a customer may carry home the edible remains of a restaurant meal to be eaten the next day, though its name suggests—in a rather too-cute manner—that the contents will be fed to one's pet. Although leftovers have long been packed up for customers, the term "doggie bag" dates in print to 1963. Two claims have been made for the idea under that name, Lawry's Prime Rib, a Los Angeles restaurant that dates its usage back to the 1930s, and the Old Homestead Steak House in New York City, whose owner, Harry Sherry, also began to use the term in the 1930s.

Dolly Varden (*Salvelinus malma*). Also, "bull trout" and "Oregon char." This char or trout, which grows up to three feet in length, is a multicolored, spotted fish found from Alaska to northern California in both salt and fresh water. Its beautiful markings have caused some Alaskans to call the fish "golden trout" or "golden-finned trout," but the more common name, "Dolly Varden," comes from a character in Charles Dickens's novel *Barnaby Rudge* (1841) who wore a tight-fitting dress with a flowered skirt over a brightly colored petticoat. The *Yreka Union* (California) of June 3, 1876, insisted the fish were "first caught in McCloud River by white men—Messrs. Josiah Edson of Shasta Valley and Geo. Campbell of Soda Springs, and were given the name of Dolly Varden by Elda McCloud, a niece of Mr. Campbell." But Goode's *Fisheries* (1884) contends that "in the Sacramento the name 'Dolly Varden' was given to [the fish] by the landlady at the hotel, and this name it still retains in that region." "Dolly Varden" is also the name of a New England cake, mentioned in *The Pentucket Housewife* (1882).

DOLLY VARDEN CAKE

Beat 4 egg yolks separately from 4 egg whites. Fold the two together, add 1 c. creamed butter, 2½ c. sugar, 1 c. milk, 4 c. flour, ½ t. baking soda, and 1 t. cream of tartar. Divide the mixture in two. To each half of the mixture add 1 T. molasses, 1 t. spices, and some raisins and currants. Pour each mixture into separate loaf pans and bake in medium-hot oven.

---

dolphin. Either of two varieties of marine fish, *Coryphaena hippurus* or *C. equisetis*, ranging in size from two pounds to fifty pounds or more and inhabiting both oceans of North America. The reference to the former was first noted in 1862. These food-fish dolphins (also called "dorado") are not in any way related to the mammals of the same name.

The word comes from Greek *delphis*.

These varieties are better known in Hawaii as MAHIMAHI (1926), and there are considered a delicacy. They are also sought in Florida, where the roe is eaten. U.S. commercial landings of dolphin totaled nearly 2 million pounds in 1997.

dope. Slang term in the South for cola drinks, because the caffeine in some soda pop acts as a slight stimulant. Originally it applied to true narcotics, especially heated opium, which became a gloppy substance like the Dutch sauce called *doop*, from which the word derives.

"Dope" is also a slang term for GRAVY (1807) and for dessert topping or molasses (1904).

doughnut. A deep-fried yeast pastry that has a hole in the middle. Doughnuts are a favorite snack and confection throughout the United States and are known in other forms throughout Europe.

The first American doughnuts did not have holes at all; they were quite literally little "nuts" of dough. The Pilgrims, who had spent the years 1607–20 in Holland, learned to make doughnuts there and brought them to New England; the most direct antecedent of the pastry seems to be of German origin, and these doughnuts came in all shapes and sizes. The first mention of the term in print was in Washington Irving's *History of New York . . . by Diedrich Knickerbocker* (1809), in which he describes the Dutch settlers of New Amsterdam in the seventeenth century: "[The table] was always sure to boast an enormous dish of balls of sweetened dough, fried in hog's fat, and called doughnuts or olykoeks [oil cakes]—a delicious kind of cake, at present scarce known in the city, excepting in genuine Dutch families."

Eliza Leslie's *New Cookery Book* (1857) refers to the German origins of the doughnut, which by then had become quite popular. The Pennsylvania Dutch traditionally served doughnuts called *fossnocks* or *fastnachts* on Shrove Tuesday (Fastnacht) as the last sweet before Lent; at other times of the year they were called "Fett Kucke" or "fat cake." On Fastnacht Day these doughnuts are served at breakfast (the last person to arrive at the table is labeled a lazy "fastnacht" and served the last of the dough).

The Pennsylvania Dutch were probably the first to make doughnuts with holes in their centers, a perfect shape for "dunking" (Pennsylvania Dutch *tunke*; German *dunke*) in coffee, which has become a standard method of eating doughnuts for Americans. There seems little real evidence to support the story of a Rockport, Maine, sea captain named Hanson Crockett Gregory, who claimed to have poked out the soggy centers of his wife's doughnuts in 1847 so that he might slip them over the spokes of his ship's wheel, thereby being able to nibble while keeping an even keel. Nevertheless, in 1947 a centenary plaque commemorating Gregory's alleged culinary creation was placed on the house where he had lived.

By the middle of the nineteenth century the hole must have been widely accepted, and a housewares catalog of 1870 shows a doughnut cutter including a corer, as does the 1897 Sears, Roebuck Catalog, which priced the gadget at four cents. "Crullers" (Dutch *krullen*) were an early egg-dough pastry shaped by the New Amsterdam Dutch into "love knots" or "matrimony knots" or the elongated shape that became familiar throughout the country. Sometimes crullers were called "wonders," and, among the Creoles, *croque-cignole*.

By the twentieth century doughnuts, dusted with powdered sugar or cinnamon, iced, or stuffed with jelly (sometimes called a CHICAGO) or cream (sometimes called a "cream doughnut" or "cream stick") had become a great American favorite.

It is improbable that the reason American soldiers in France during World War I were called "doughboys" was because of their affection for the confection, or, as Evan Jones asserts in *American Food* (1981), that the name "doughboy" appeared after a Salvation Army worker in France made a batch for the soldiers away from home, although the term "doughboy" as meaning a flour or cornmeal dumpling goes back at least to 1753 in print, as meaning a doughnut, to 1887. Elizabeth Custer (widow of General George Custer) believed the name to derive from the similarity of doughnuts' shape to the infantry's globular brass buttons. Other associations have been made: a pipe clay, called "dough," with which the infantry cleaned their white belts, and a slang term of southwestern Hispanics for American soldiers quartered in adobe structures. The term is found even in a British soldier's reference in 1809 to Lord Wellington's retreat after the battle of Talavera in Spain. Wellington's soldiers made bread by grinding wheat flour with their hands and stones—"from which wretched practice we christened the place Dough Boy Hill." "Doughboy" is also a Rhode Island term for deep-fried and sugared dough. "Doughgod" is a variant term, used in the Northeast and West, for the same confection. People in the North and Northwest commonly call an oblong doughnut "long-john" or "BISMARCK," a term also used by northeasterners for a "jelly doughnut," though the origin of "bismarck" is not known. A "cake doughnut" is a doughnut made with baking powder or soda rather than yeast.

Doughnuts, often spelled "donuts," are as popular as ever, and shops specializing in selling them have been around for decades, sometimes called "doughnuteries." Although the majority of homemade doughnuts are still deep-fried in oil, there are on the market electric appliances for making doughnuts without having to deep-fry the dough. "Sinker," once a term applied to a pancake or roll, became by the 1920s a term for a very heavy doughnut.

"Doughnut holes," the dough ball supposedly from the center of the doughnut, have been sold separately at least since the 1960s.

REGULAR DOUGHNUTS

Sift 2 c. flour, ½ c. sugar, 1 t. salt, and 3 t. baking powder. Beat 1 egg with ½ c. milk and 2 T. cooled melted butter. Mix with flour and knead the dough lightly. Roll on a board to ¼-in thickness and cut with doughnut cutter. Deep fry in a light oil heated to 360–375° and of a depth that allows doughnuts to float to surface. Brown on one side, turn over, and brown other side. Drain on brown paper or crisp in warm oven.

RAISED DOUGHNUTS

Cream 1 c. butter with ½ c. sugar, then add 3 eggs, 1 t. salt, 1 cake yeast dissolved in lukewarm milk, and the grated rind of one lemon. Blend in 3 c. flour and knead into an elastic dough. Cover and let rise overnight in a warm place until doubled. Roll into ¼-in. sheet, cut into rings, let stand again until doubled, then fry in deep oil. Drain and roll in powdered sugar.

---

downhome. A colloquialism used to describe anything, including food, that has a simple, folksy, often rural quality to it. It is most commonly used to refer to foods in the South, like fried CATFISH, HUSH PUPPIES, SOUTHERN FRIED CHICKEN, GRITS and many other items. The term has been in usage at least since the early nineteenth century.

Dr. Brown's Cel-Ray Soda. Trademark name for a celery-flavored carbonated beverage first bottled in 1869 and now bottled by Canada Dry Bottling Company of New York in Queens, New York. Its unique flavor, from celery seeds, was supposedly developed by a Brooklyn doctor named Brown, though this had never been verified. The trademark was long owned by the American Beverage Company.

Long popular with New York City's Jewish community, the beverage was originally called "Dr. Brown's Cel-Ray Tonic," and its label proudly proclaimed it "contains vitamins G B D." But the federal government forced the makers to change the name to "Soda" because the original name implied the drink had medical or health benefits.

Today, Dr. Brown's Cel-Ray Soda sells in excess of a million cases a year.

Dresden dressing. A cold sauce, made with hard-boiled eggs, onion, mustard, and other seasonings, to accompany meats. The name derives from the German city of Dresden, and the sauce itself may be of German origin, though it first appears under the name "Dresden dressing" in American cookery of the nineteenth century.

dressing. A general term, dating in print to 1504, referring to gravies, salad sauces, dessert sauces, cake frostings, and STUFFINGS. Most common usage would denote a "salad dressing," e.g., vinegar and oil, FRENCH DRESSING, GREEN GODDESS DRESSING, THOUSAND ISLAND DRESSING, RANCH, and ITALIAN DRESSING. "Boiled dressing" is particularly associated with the Midwest and South, although the ingredients are not necessarily boiled.

BOILED DRESSING

Combine ½ c. water and ⅔ c. vinegar in a saucepan and bring to a boil. Mix together 2 T. flour, 2 T sugar, 1 t. salt, ⅛ t. pepper, and ¼ t. dry mustard. Stir in the liquid and then one beaten egg, stirring rapidly. Return to heat to thicken. Cool before using.

---

dried apple. A staple of early American tables and travelers' provisions. Apples left to dry over the winter were often made into pies on the trail westward, causing one passenger on the overland stagecoaches to remark that it was "apple pie from Genesis to Revelation along the Platte." A bit of doggerel from the same period goes: "Spit in my ears/And tell me lies, but give me no dried apple pies." See also MCGINTY.

drink box. A commercially made waxed or plasticized paper carton for beverages.

drinking straw. A paper or plastic straw used for sipping beverages. Before 1888, Americans sipped drinks through stalks of rye or other hollow stalks, but in that year Marvin Chester Stone of Washington, D.C., took out a patent for drinking straws made from paraffin-coated manila paper. Today drinking straws are made of various materials, some constructed to bend according to the level of the glass.

dropped egg. New Englander's term for a poached egg, dating in print to 1884.

drown the miller. Slang phrase meaning to dilute liquor with too much water or to add excessive water to a dough. The phrase first saw print in 1899.

drum (family Sciaenidae). Any of a variety of fish that inhabit temperate and tropical marine waters, with species ranging from those weighing less than eight ounces to giant "totuava" that may reach 225 pounds or more. The name comes from a "drumming muscle" that makes a drumlike sound when expanded against the gas bladder. The fish was so-called at least as early as 1676. Many species are called "croakers," because the sound resembles croaking. Some of the more important drums for culinary purposes include the "Atlantic croaker" (*Micropogon undulatus*); "banded croaker" (*Larimus fasciatus*); "black drum" (*Pogonias cromis*); "freshwater drum" (*Aplodinotus grunniens*), also called "sheepshead," "crocus," "gaspergu," "jewelhead," and other names; "spot drum" (*Leiostomus xanthurus*), also called "Lafayette," after a visit to New York City by General Lafayette at a time when the fish was particularly numerous in the harbor; "white sea bass" (*Cynoscion nobilis*); and "yellowfin croaker" (*Umbrina roncador*). The "red drum" (*Sciaenops ocellata*), also called "channel bass" and "redfish," took on amazing popularity in the 1980s after Cajun chef Paul Prudhomme popularized his recipe for BLACKENED REDFISH—so much so that the federal government banned commercial fishing of the species in the Gulf of Mexico in 1987.

drunk. Intoxicated with liquor. This word is only the most easily identifiable among hundreds of others to indicate intoxication. As Stuart Berg Flexner writes in his appendix to the *Dictionary of American Slang* (second supplemented edition, 1975):

The concept having the most slang synonyms is drunk. *This vast number of* drunk *words does not necessarily mean that Americans are obsessed with drinking,*

though we seem obsessed with talking about it. Many of these words are quite old. . . . Later immigrant groups brought their own words for drink and drunkenness, and it seems that some, during their first period of adjustment had a fair number of members who turned to whiskey as a compensation for the rejection they suffered as newcomers in a strange land. Most of the words for drunk, however, originated or became popular during Prohibition.

Flexner's list included 353 terms ("and I didn't exhaust the subject," he wrote later). The American penchant for "drunk" slang was first noted by Benjamin Franklin in the *Pennsylvania Gazette* in 1737, when "have a glass eye," "loose in the hilt," "nimtopsical," "moon-eyed," "top heavy," "been to Barbados" were all used to describe drunkenness. Franklin listed 228 terms, 90 of which (as pointed out by Edward D. Seeber in *American Speech* [February 1940]) were not listed in either the *Oxford English Dictionary* or the *English Dialect Dictionary*.

The following list gives only a small sampling of the more familiar terms for "drunk," with the dates of their first appearance in print in parentheses): "soused" (sixteenth century), "blind" (seventeenth century), "oiled" (1737), "stewed" (1737), "bent" (1833), "stinking" (1837), "lushed" (1840), "tight" (1843), "pixillated" (1850s), "swizzled" (1850s), "D and D"—that is, an abbreviation for the legal phrase "drunk and disorderly" (1870), "paralyzed" (1888), "looped" (1890), "pickled" (1890s), "woozy" (1897), "tanked" (1905), "plastered" (1912), "hooted" (1915), "potted" (1922), "dead to the world" (1926), "bombed" (1940s), "shit-faced" (1940s), "feeling no pain" (1940s), "sloshed" (1950s), and "zonked" (1950s).

duck. Any of a variety of webbed-footed birds of the family Anatidae that may be either wild or domesticated and that inhabit open water, marshes, ponds, lakes, and rivers. The word is from Old English *dūce*.

Ducks have been esteemed for their culinary value by most cultures of the world, and it is possible that the Indians in Central America domesticated the bird even before the Chinese did. The first European explorers were amazed at the numbers of ducks in American skies and soon commented on the delicious and distinctive flavor of the native CANVASBACK, whose name figures in every cookbook of the nineteenth century to the extent that no banquet would be considered successful without serving the fowl.

On March 13, 1873, however, the arrival in New York of a Yankee clipper ship with a tiny flock of white

Peking ducks—one drake and three females—signaled the beginning of a domestic industry of immense proportions. The birds were introduced to Connecticut and then to eastern Long Island, where they propagated at an encouraging rate. Domestic ducks were bought mostly by newly arrived immigrants, who bought them plucked, cooled, and packed in a barrel (called "New York Dressed"). Only in this century did the fowl, by now called the "Long Island duckling," attain gastronomic respect; Long Island now produces half the ducks sold in America and exports some as well.

In the nineteenth century wild ducks were usually eaten rare, but today domestic ducks are generally preferred cooked with a very crisp skin and served either roasted with applesauce or in the classic French manner, with orange sauce. "Peking duck" now refers to a Chinese dish of specially prepared duck skin and meat detached and served in thin pancakes or buns with scallions and a sweet sauce.

The wild ducks of culinary importance to Americans include the canvasback (*Aythya valsineria*), also called the "bullneck," the "redhead" (*A. americana*), the "mallard" (*Anas platyrhynchos*), the "black duck" (*Anas rubripes*), the "ring-necked duck" (*Aythya collaris*), and the "scoters" (*Melanitta fusca, M. perspicillata,* and *M. nigra*), also called "coots." The "mergansers" (any of, a variety in the genus *Mergus,* which derives its name from the Latin *mergus,* "diver," and *anser,* "goose") are not preferred and are often referred to by hunters as "trash ducks."

The "Muscovy duck" (*Cairina moschata*) was originally called the "musk duck" for its distinct, musky smell. Its first printed mention, in 1774, notes that the name "Muscovy duck" had already been erroneously applied to the bird, which was native to South and Central America. Because of the bird's strong flavor it has been domesticated and crossed with other breeds. It is sometimes called the "Barbary duck," because it was assumed to be an African bird. The Muscovy duck is available at American markets in the fall and winter. It is usually roasted.

The United States Department of Agriculture grades ducks as it does chickens, "grade A" being the highest, "grade B" next, and "grade C" the lowest.

duck. African-American slang for an alcoholic beverage.

duff. A steamed pudding containing fruit, as an "apple duff" or "plum duff." It was usually boiled in a bag. The word, which first appeared in print in 1816, is a nineteenth-century Scots or Northern England rendering of "dough," pronounced like "rough." In his novel *Two Years Before the Mast* (1840), Richard Henry Dana, Jr., notes that on the sabbath seamen would be "allowed on that day a pudding, or, as it is called, a 'duff.' "

du jour. A French term meaning "of the day" that in America is usually attached to "soup," "fish," "dish," or other items. The term refers to a special item on the menu for that particular day.

dulse (*Rhodymenia palmata*). A coarse red seaweed that grows in profusion on the rocky coasts of the North Atlantic. The word derives from a Scottish dialect word and dates in print to 1540. It is dried and packaged, eaten raw, fried, and toasted, and is a local specialty of New Brunswick.

dump cake. A cake made by "dumping" the ingredients directly into the baking pan, mixing them, and baking the batter.

Dungeness crab (*Cancer magister*). A Pacific crab that is found from Alaska to Baja (1920). It is one of the rock crabs, colored pinkish green and yellow and weighing between one-and-three-quarters and four pounds. It is named for a small town on the Olympic Peninsula in Washington, where it was first commercially harvested. Only males at least six and a quarter inches long may be harvested, mainly during the winter months. Today the Dungeness is a major industry of the Northwest, and each season in San Francisco Bay a Roman Catholic priest blesses the fishing fleet that will bring in the crabs. It is a very popular seaside delicacy sold by vendors who get "cracked crabs" fresh from the boat, scoop out the yellow-white fat called CRAB BUTTER, and serve them with mayonnaise.

In the Northwest "crab feeds" are social gatherings (similar to New England clambakes or southern crab boils) where Dungeness crabs are featured.

dusty miller. An ice-cream sundae made with powdered malted-milk topping. The term derives from a noctuid moth of the same name whose speckled wings resemble the dusty topping on the sundae. The moth's name is first mentioned in print in 1909; the sundae probably dates from the 1920s.

Dutch courage. A slang term (dating back at least to 1809) for false courage induced by alcohol. Also, an English term for gin imported from Holland.

Dutch grocery. A slang term for a dirty grocery store. It was in use in the last quarter of the nineteenth century.

Dutch lunch. A slang phrase usually referring to a buffet lunch consisting of cold meats, cheese, and beer, dating in print to 1904.

Dutch oven. Also, "Dutch bake oven." Usually a large, covered cast-iron kettle used for slow cooking. It may indeed have been of Pennsylvania-Dutch heritage, though the word itself first appears in print in 1760. In Colonial America such kettles were often hung from a hook in the open fireplace, while at other times set on legs over the fire. In the West the term referred to a thick, three-footed skillet used as an all-purpose cooking utensil that was placed over hot coals, with more coals placed on the lid in order to brown baked items like biscuits. In this century a wall oven may also be called a "Dutch oven."

Dutch salad. According to the *Dictionary of American Regional English*, a Pennsylvania colloquialism for a dandelion salad.

dyspepsia coffee. A supposed aid for indigestion made by mixing half coffee and half cornmeal moistened with molasses. This is browned in the oven and used as one would ground coffee. The term dates in print to 1940.

early-bird special. A restaurant dinner meal served earlier and at a cheaper price than is usual at the regular dinner hours of 5:00 P.M. or later. It is popular with those on a budget, senior citizens, and especially in resort areas like Florida.

eau sucrée. This French-Creole term, which means "sugar water," refers to a glass of water in which has been dissolved one tablespoon sugar. Eau sucrée is drunk after a heavy meal, supposedly to ease digestion, and, notes *The Picayune's Creole Cook Book* (1900), it "is used by all Creole mothers as a sedative for their little ones. Just before kissing her babes 'Good-night,' the Creole mother will give them a small glass of 'eau sucrée.' It is claimed that it insures easy digestion and perfect sleep."

Eau sucrée parties were frequent in old New Orleans, often held as a substitute for the more lavish parties of wealthier Creoles but no less enjoyed for their simple pleasures.

EDTA (Ethylenediaminetetraacetate). An additive, used in mayonnaise and other processed foods, for preventing trace metals from mechanical rollers, blenders, and containers from causing rancidity.

eel (*Anguilla rostrata*). A long, snakelike fish of the order Anguilliformes, found in eastern waters. The word is from Old English *ael*.

Long considered a delicacy by Europeans and Asians, eels have not been of much gastronomic interest to most Americans, but in Colonial New England "eel time" in autumn was anticipated with the same enthusiasm that attended the run of the shad or the apple harvest. Later, Mediterranean immigrants— the Italians, Greeks, Portuguese, and others—kept their traditions of eating eel on certain holidays, especially Christmas, and the eel industry in America is still seasonal. Eels are prepared in diverse ways, boiled, steamed, stewed, grilled, or fried. U.S. commercial landings of eel totaled 1.07 million pounds in 1997.

egg. A shelled ovum of a bird, especially from domesticated fowl. The word is from Old Norse. Eggs are a staple food of the world's people, and although the eggs of wild fowl, turkeys, geese, doves, and other birds are eaten, it is the egg of the chicken that is most widely cultivated. Americans consume about 245 eggs per capita each year.

The Native Americans did not have chickens until the Europeans brought them to America, but wild fowls' eggs—quail, geese, turkey, and pigeon—were part of the Native Americans' diet, as were turtle and crocodile eggs in the territories near the Gulf of Mexico. Columbus brought chickens to the West Indies in 1493, and the Puritans and English settlers of Jamestown brought them to North America. Since chickens—and, therefore, eggs—were common but not abundant enough to provide everyday meals in the Colonial era, they remained expensive items well into the nineteenth century, especially in the West, where domesticated fowl were rare. In fact, the dish called HANGTOWN FRY was made in the California Gold Rush days from the two most expensive ingredients of the kitchen—eggs and oysters.

The egg industry was revolutionized in 1934 when John Kimber realized it was more efficient to breed chickens specifically for egg-laying. Today egg production is a finely mechanized science, overseen by both federal and state inspectors. The U.S. currently produces 63 billion eggs per year. Eggs are sized by weight, averaged by the dozen. "Jumbo" eggs must weigh thirty ounces or more, "extra large" between twenty-seven and thirty, "large" between twenty-four and twenty-seven, "medium" between twenty-one and twenty-four, "small" between eighteen and twenty-one, and "peewee" between fifteen and eighteen.

Eggs are also graded on the basis of physical condition, with the more viscous yolks scoring highest, from "grade AA" ("Fancy Fresh") to "A," "B," and "C." About 10 percent of the country's eggs go into egg products, such as frozen and dried eggs. "Egg substitutes," produced for those concerned about cholesterol in their diet, are made from egg whites alone with added food coloring, although a process developed by Michael Foods of Minneapolis, Minnesota, in 1992 cut cholesterol in real eggs by using centrifugal force to drive out the substance.

Indeed, concern over the supposed high cholesterol content of eggs (about 215 milligrams per egg) cut into Americans' egg consumption throughout the 1980s and 1990s, but recent studies, including a 1999 study by the Harvard School of Public Health published in *The Journal of the American Medical Association*, found that healthy people eating up to seven eggs a week did not increase their risk of heart attack or stroke.

Americans eat their eggs poached (in New England called "dropped eggs"), boiled (or hard-boiled), as an omelet (or "omelette"), or, since 1864, scrambled, that is, sautéed in butter by mixing the eggs around in a skillet. Americans also created the term "shirred eggs" as of 1883, for eggs cooked unshelled in molds. A well-known egg sandwich or omelet is the WESTERN, made with green pepper, chopped ham, and eggs on toast. A "Spanish omelet" is made with onions, peppers, tomatoes, and other seasonings. See also main entries for EGG FOO YUNG, EGGS BENEDICT, EGGS SARDOU, and EGGNOG.

egg bread. A corn bread without leavening, known since the middle of the nineteenth century. It was first mentioned as an American bread in 1854.

egg butter. A sweet spreading butter made with molasses. *The Buckeye Cookbook* (1883) gives the following recipe:

EGG BUTTER

Boil 1 pt. molasses slowly for 15-20 min., stirring frequently. Add 3 beaten eggs, stirred in quickly so as not to curdle. Boil a few minutes longer, partially cool, and add lemon juice to taste.

---

egg coffee. Coffee to which an egg has been added, dating in print to 1896.

egg cook. Restaurant workers' slang term for the breakfast cook.

egg cream. A New York City soda-fountain confection made from chocolate syrup, milk, and seltzer. The simplicity of the egg cream is deceptive, for its flavor and texture depend entirely on the correct preparation. There is no egg in an egg cream, but if the ingredients are mixed properly, a foamy, egg-white-like head tops off the drink.

Nevertheless, as David Shulman pointed out in *American Speech* (1987), there was a confection called an "egg cream" syrup listed in W. A. Bonham's *Modern Guide for Soda Dispensers* (1896) that was made with both eggs and cream, but no chocolate. This was probably not the egg cream that gained legendary fame in eastern cities. Also, Lettice Bryan in *The Kentucky Housewife* (1839) gives a recipe for an orange-flavored custard dessert called "egg cream."

There seems no basis to believe the legend that Yiddish actor Boris Thomashefsky brought the idea for the egg cream back from Paris after having tasted a drink called *chocolat et créme*. Indeed, the unchallenged claim for the invention of the egg cream is that of Louis Auster, a Jewish immigrant who came to the United States about 1890 and opened a candy store at Stanton and Cannon streets, then another at Third Street and Avenue D. According to Auster's grandson, Stanley, the egg cream was a matter of happenstance: "[My grandfather] was fooling around, and he started mixing water and cocoa and sugar and so on, and somehow or other, eureka, he hit on something which seemed to be just perfect for him."

Auster's egg creams became famous (he'd sell three thousand on a hot day) and were based on a secret formula that has never been revealed, although the Schrafft's ice-cream company supposedly offered him twenty thousand dollars for it. The chocolate syrup used was made in the rear of the store, and windows were blacked out for privacy. "The name of the egg cream was really a misnomer," recalled Stanley Auster. "People thought there was cream in it, and they would like to think there was egg in it because egg meant something that was really good and expensive. There never was any egg, and there never was any cream." Auster also insisted a glass, not a paper cup, and ice-cold milk were basic to the success of a good egg cream.

After Louis Auster died in 1955, the candy store closed, and the recipe passed to his family, with the last batch of the secret syrup made up by Stanley and his uncle Mendy around 1974. The first printed reference to the egg cream was in 1950.

Without access to Auster's syrup, other soda fountains and candy stores make the drink with "Fox's u-bet Chocolate Flavor Syrup," created by Herman Fox some time before 1920 in Brooklyn, now considered the most widely accepted ingredient in the mix.

EGG CREAM

In a tall soda fountain glass, pour 1½ oz. chocolate syrup, add 1½ oz. ice-cold milk, stir to blend, then, while stirring, fill to the top with a fast jet of seltzer deflected off a spoon in order to create a foamy white head.

egg foo yung. A dish of scrambled eggs and Chinese vegetables. Egg foo yung is a Chinese-American menu item not found in authentic Chinese cooking. The name may derive from a Guangdong word meaning "egg white."

EGG FOO YUNG

Beat 4 eggs lightly and combine with 1 c. bean sprouts, 1 T. chopped scallions, 1 T. bamboo shoots, 1 T. water chestnuts, and salt to taste. Add ¾ c. chopped seafood or cooked meat. Mix well. In a skillet or wok with 3 T. oil, drop ⅓ c. egg and vegetable mixture in small cakes and cook until browned. Pile cakes together and pour over them sauce made from 1 c. chicken broth, ¼ t. sugar, salt, 2 T. soy sauce, 2 T. monosodium glutamate, and 1 T. cold water in which 1 t. cornstarch has been dissolved.

eggnog. Also, "egg nog" and "egg pop." A rich beverage made with eggs and spirits traditionally served in America at Christmastime. The word "nog" is an Old English term for ale, a meaning known since the late seventeenth century. In England the drink was often made with red Spanish wine, but in America, where the first printing of the word was in 1765, rum and later other spirits were substituted.

According to FDA standards, commercially produced eggnog must contain at least one percent by weight egg-yolk solids and must be pasteurized; it may also be homogenized.

EGG NOG

Separate 6 eggs and beat the yolks with ½ c. sugar until light yellow. Add ½ c. bourbon or blended whiskey and ½ c. brandy and blend well. Chill in refrigerator for several hours. Beat egg whites until soft peaks are formed. Whip 1½ pt. heavy cream until slightly thickened, then fold into yolk mixture. Fold in egg whites, chill again. Serve with a sprinkling of grated nutmeg.

eggplant (*Solanum melongena*). The plump deep purple fruit of a plant in the potato family native to India. The name, derived simply from the egglike shape of the fruit, was first mentioned in English print in 1767. Thomas Jefferson has been credited with introducing the eggplant to America, though it has never achieved great popularity with most of the population. It is usually sautéed or baked, often as "eggplant parmigiana," an Italian-American dish of breaded, sautéed eggplant baked with tomato sauce. Because of its association with Italian-Americans, eggplant is sometimes called, in derogatory slang, "guinea squash."

"Eggplant caviar" is a snack dip made from roasted eggplant pureed with garlic, oil and other seasonings.

eggs Benedict. ENGLISH MUFFINS topped with a slice of ham or Canadian bacon, poached eggs, and a hollandaise sauce. It is a very popular BRUNCH and breakfast item. The word first appeared in print in 1893.

The *Dictionary of Americanisms* and the *Morris Dictionary of Word and Phrase Origins* agree on the story of how the dish got its name, with Morris reporting: "The legendary Delmonico's Restaurant in New York City has been the birthplace of eggs Benedict. According to a well-founded report, two of the regular customers were Mr. and Mrs. LeGrand Benedict. One Saturday at lunch Mrs. Benedict complained that there was nothing new on the menu, so the maître d'hôtel asked what she might suggest. Out of their colloquy came the now internationally famous recipe." Another story attributes the dish's inspiration to Wall Street broker Lemuel Benedict, and food writer George Lang contends that the famous maître d'hôtel of the Waldorf-Astoria Restaurant and Hotel in New York City, Oscar Tschirky, changed the recipe by adding truffles and a *glace de viande,* but *The Waldorf-Astoria Cookbook* (1981) follows the traditional form of earlier years.

EGGS BENEDICT

Split two English muffins and toast lightly. Spread with butter. Sauté in butter 4 slices baked ham or Canadian bacon and place one slice on each muffin half. Keep warm in slow oven. Boil water and add 1 T. vinegar and 1 t. salt. Lower heat to a simmer and poach 4 eggs for about 5 min. Remove and drain, then place over muffins. Pour over them a freshly made hollandaise sauce.

eggs Sardou. A dish of poached eggs with artichoke hearts, anchovies, chopped ham, truffle, and hollandaise sauce. Eggs Sardou is a specialty of New Orleans, and, specifically, of Antoine's Restaurant, where it was created by owner Antoine Alciatore (1824–77) on the occasion of a dinner he hosted for French playwright Victorien Sardou (1831–1908), author of a satire on America entitled *L'Oncle Sam* (1873).

EGGS SARDOU

Place 2 cooked artichoke hearts on a serving dish, set 4 anchovy fillets and 2 poached eggs on top, and pour 1/3 c. hollandaise sauce over them. Sprinkle with 1 T. chopped ham and garnish with a slice of truffle. Serves 1. (Some recipes call for creamed spinach to be set under the artichoke hearts.)

election cake. A raised fruitcake of New England, first mentioned by Amelia Simmons in her *American Cookery* as early as 1796, although, as the name indicates, records show that such cakes have been baked to celebrate Election Days at least as early as 1771 in Connecticut. Although this practice spread throughout the Midwest and West in the nineteenth century, the cake is usually associated with Hartford, Connecticut, and, by the 1830s, was often called "Hartford election cake." There were also "election buns," which were doled out along similar party lines. Cookies, usually of gingerbread, served at such functions were often called "training cakes," because another name for Election Day was "Training Day."

ELECTION CAKE

Heat 1/2 c. dry sherry in a saucepan, add 1/2. c. raisins, and remove from heat. Let stand several hours until raisins soften and absorb sherry. Heat 1 1/2 c. milk to lukewarm and remove from heat. Combine 1 1/2 c. flour, 1/3 c. sugar, 1 pkg. yeast, and 1/2 t. salt. Add milk, blend, cover, and let rise until doubled. Punch dough down. Mix together 3/4 c. butter, 1/2 c. brown sugar, 2 beaten eggs, and 3 1/2 c. flour. Add 1 t. ground cinnamon, 1/2 t. ground nutmeg, 1/4 t. ground cloves, 1 c. chopped pecans or walnuts, and 1/2 c. candied citron. Drain the raisins, but reserve the sherry. Add sherry to yeast flour, then into egg flour, blend well together, add raisins, and place batter in greased and floured 10-in. tube pan. Let rise again, bake at 350° for 1 hr., covered with aluminum foil for the last

15 min. Invert on rack and cool. Combine 2 c. confectioners' sugar, 1 t. vanilla, and 2 T. sweet sherry to make an icing. Frost cake, garnish with nuts and flower shapes of citron.

elevener. Southern slang for a person who waits until midmorning before having his first drink of spirits.

el presidente. A cocktail whose name is Spanish for "the president," supposedly named after (and perhaps concocted by) General Marco Garcia Menocal y Deop, President of Cuba from 1913 to 1921. A recipe was printed in Ford Naylor's *World Famous Chefs' Cook Book* (1939).

EL PRESIDENTE

Shake with ice 1 1/2 oz. gold rum, 1/2 oz. dry vermouth, 1 t. dark rum, 1 t. curaçao, 1/4 t. grenadine, 2 t. lime juice. Serve in a chilled cocktail glass.

Emmaline sauce. A nineteenth-century flavoring sauce included by Sarah Tyson Rorer in *McIlhenny's Tabasco Sauce Recipes* (1913). The origin of the name is not known.

EMMALINE SAUCE

Pare and grate raw pumpkin, squash, or pawpaw to make 1 pt. Add 1 chopped Spanish onion, 4 mashed garlic cloves, 1 t. celery seed, 2 red peppers, 2 green peppers, 1 t. turmeric, and 1 bottle Tabasco. Add 1 pt. vinegar, stir, then bring to boil and simmer for several minutes. Bottle and seal. Use as a flavoring for soups or stews.

empanada. A fried turnover pastry of Mexican origins and now a staple of Mexican-American restaurants. The word was first printed in 1920. *Empanar* in Spanish means "to bake in pastry."

EMPANADA

Dissolve 1 pkg. yeast in 1/2 c. lukewarm water. Cut 4 T. lard or butter into 4 c. flour, add 1 t. salt and 1 T. sugar. Pour in yeast and make a dough. Roll into thin sheet and cut into rounds. Fill with mincemeat or fruit preserves, moisten edges of dough, and seal one round to another. Deep-fry in hot oil to a golden brown, drain, and dust with powdered sugar or cinnamon.

enchilada. A TORTILLA stuffed with various fillings of meat, cheese, chili sauce, chorizo sausage, and other ingredients. It is a Spanish-American term meaning "filled with chili" and was first printed in America in 1885. An article in *American Speech* in 1949 asserted that an enchilada was "a Mexican dish prepared more for *turista* than for local consumption." The dish has become a staple of Mexican-American restaurants.

ENCHILADA

In a blender puree one 16-oz. can tomatoes, 2 red chile peppers, ½ t. salt, and ¼ t. pepper. Add 1 c. sour cream. Mix 2 c. chopped cooked chicken with ½ c. shredded Monterey Jack or Cheddar cheese. Sauté briefly a dozen tortillas in 1 T. oil until golden on both sides. Drain and spread chicken on each tortilla, roll up, and place in greased baking dish. Pour tomato and chile mixture over them, cover with aluminum foil, and bake at 350° for 30 min. Remove foil, sprinkle with more cheese, place under broiler until top melts and browns. Serves 6.

English monkey. A cheese dish similar to Welsh rabbit made with bread crumbs, milk, butter, and cheese poured over crackers but with the addition of tomatoes. The term dates in print to 1896.

English muffin. A round, flat muffin made from white flour, yeast, malted barley, vinegar, and farina. English muffins are usually split and toasted, buttered, and spread with jam or preserves. Although tea muffins that were once popular in England resembled the American "English muffin," there is no single muffin in Britain by this specific name. Nor do Americans often make English muffins at home, preferring to buy those sold at a grocery. Most of these store-bought varieties derive from those made by the S. B. Thomas Company of New York, whose founder, Samuel Bath Thomas, emigrated from England in 1875 with his mother's recipe and began making muffins at his Ninth Avenue bakery in 1880. The name was first printed in 1925.

Recipes for English muffins generally do not contain many of the ingredients in the Thomas formula.

For muffin rings, *Joy of Cooking* (1964) by Irma S. Rombauer and Marion Rombauer Becker recommends using "small unlacquered fish cans and deviled meat cans [with the] tops and bottoms removed and the rims . . . thoroughly scrubbed."

"English muffin pizza" gained popularity in the early 1970s.

entrée. The main course of a meal, or, occasionally, a dish served between two chief courses. The word is French for "entry," and in France the word formally has the second meaning, as it does in England, where it might also be called a "made dish." In America menus usually list the entrée as the main course, although this has been its principal usage only over the last forty years. Noted Ford Naylor in 1941 in his *World Famous Chefs' Cook Book,* "It is only in the less expensive restaurants and lunchrooms, where the word 'entrée' has come to describe any main dish, including roasts." Often in America the word is spelled without the accent mark, and first appeared in 1761.

Eskimo ice cream. An Eskimo confection originally made as a mixture of salmon berries, seal oil, and snow. Today it is more commonly made with salmon berries, CRISCO, sugar, and mashed potatoes. The term dates in print to 1913.

espresso. A very dark, bitter Italian coffee, often, incorrectly, spelled "expresso." The name has nothing to do with the idea of a "quick cup" of coffee, but everything to do with the Italian meaning "pressed out," for in the preparation of this coffee the essence of freshly ground beans (almost always the Arabica variety) is pushed out of a special espresso machine by steam and water, creating a very concentrated half-cup of brew.

The word "espresso" first appears in English print in 1940, but in Italy it has been known at least since the turn of the century. Its invention has been traced to the Italian railway station in Milan where those about to board a train wanted a quickly made cup of coffee, and some espresso makers contend the term *espresso* may be associated with the "express trains" of those stations. The first espresso machine manufacturer was a company named Bezzera in 1902.

In America espresso often comes out as a full cup of less-strong Italian coffee. Espresso may also be prepared in a drip pot. Often in America espresso will be garnished with a sliver of lemon peel, and a generous restaurateur may offer a complimentary shot of anisette liqueur to be added to the cup, but this, too, is rarely seen in Italy.

estomacs mulâtres. Louisiana gingerbread made with flour and cane syrup. The name is from the French, "mulatto stomachs," and refers to the light brown color of the puffy little confections.

étouffée. A cooking term, dating in print to the 1930s, connoting a kind of stewed dish served over white rice. The term is derived from French cuisine, meaning a braised dish. According to Cajun chef Paul Prudhomme in *Chef Paul Prudhomme's Louisiana Kitchen* (1984), "in Louisiana cooking [étouffée] signifies covered with a liquid." For a recipe of "crawfish étouffée," see CRAYFISH

F

fajita. A Tex-Mex dish made from marinated, grilled skirt steak (the diaphragm from the rib cage of cattle) served in a wheat tortilla. The word derives from the Spanish *faja,* for "girdle" or "strip" and describes the cut of meat itself. There has been much conjecture as to the fajita's origins, though none has been documented. Grilling skirt steak over mesquite coals would be characteristic of Texas cooking since the days when beef became a dominant meat in the American diet. But the word "fajita" did not appear in print until 1975.

In 1984 Homero Recio, a lecturer on animal science at Texas A&M University, obtained a fellowship to study the origins of the item, coming to the conclusion two years later that, ironically, it was his grandfather, a butcher in Premont, Texas, who may have been the first to use the term "fajita" to describe the pieces of skirt steak cooked directly on mesquite coals for family dinners as far back as the 1930s. Recio also hypothesized that the first restaurant to serve fajitas—though under the name "botanzas" (appetizers)—was the Roundup in McAllen, Texas. But Sonny "Fajita King" Falcon claimed to have opened the first "fajita stand" in Kyle, Texas, and in 1978 a "Fajita King" stand in Austin (though he does not claim to have created the fajita itself). The popularity of the dish certainly grew after Ninfa Laurenza introduced it on her menu at Ninfa's Restaurant in Houston, Texas, on July 13, 1973, but that was under the name "tacos al carbon," and increased still further as a "fajita" after the item was featured at the Austin Hyatt Regency Hotel, which by 1982 was selling thirteen thousand orders per month. Since then the term "fajita" has been corrupted to mean any kind of meat or seafood served in a flour tortilla, as in "lobster fajita" or "chicken fajita." Usually these items are marinated and grilled.

FAJITA

Marinate a skirt steak in ½ c. lime juice, 1 T. crushed garlic or 1 t. garlic powder, ¼ c. vegetable oil, and ¼ c. vinegar. Grill meat over hot coals. Cut into smaller pieces and serve in a wheat tortilla.

---

family restaurant. A food service establishment that specializes in offering menus and atmosphere particularly suited to families. Amenities usually include separate, limited-choice "children's menus," high chairs or booster seats, booths, counters, bright, colorful decor, and inexpensive food. Many are part of national restaurant chains like Denny's and Roy Rogers.

farkleberry. A native American shrub (*Vaccinium arboreum*) of the South with black, many-seeded berries (1755). The origin of the name is unknown.

fast food. A casual, inexpensive restaurant or eatery that dispenses food quickly. The term took on currency in the 1960s after expansion of multi-unit chains like McDonald's, Pizza Hut, and Kentucky Fried Chicken (now KFC), but the term was used by writer George G. Foster in his *New York in Slices* (1848) to describe the frenetically paced "fast food" establishments in New York's business district.

Most of the fast-food restaurants are drive-ins, places where one buys one's meal either in the restaurant or from one's car. Fast-food restaurants proliferated in the 1960s, when a variety of chain restaurants (usually franchised) expanded, including McDonald's, Burger King, Pizza Hut, Wendy's, Kentucky Fried Chicken, Arby's, Roy Rogers, and many others. The average cost for a hamburger, French fries, and soft drink in the U.S. in 1999 was about $4.49.

Today the term "fast food" is often synonymous with JUNK FOOD, which would also include store-bought items such as potato chips, candy, brownies, cakes, and cookies, considered to have little nutritional value or to contain "empty calories."

FDA. See Food and Drug Administration.

fennel. A plant in the parsley family (*Foeniculum vulgare*) with small yellow flowers and feathery leaves, used either as a flavoring or eaten as a vegetable in a salad or cooked as a side dish. The word is from Middle English, *fenol,* and the plant was first grown in

America from European seeds acquired by Thomas Jefferson at Monticello in 1824. Because of its anise-like flavor, it is sometimes confused with the latter, which is actually another member of the parsley family (*Pimpinella anisum*), whose seeds are used as a flavoring.

fern bar. A bar or restaurant with a bar whose stereotypical decor includes an abundance of hanging plants, especially ferns. Varnished oak, brass railings, and Tiffany-style glass are also common to such establishments, which tend to attract young adults interested in meeting people of the opposite sex. The term appeared in print in an article by Eric Pace in *The New York Times* for February 20, 1984, in which he cited it as "Young adult slang, heard as far away as New Haven." See also SINGLES' BAR.

fettuccine Alfredo. Also, "fettuccine all'Alfredo." A dish of fettuccine egg noodles mixed with butter, Parmesan cheese, and cream. The dish has been a staple of Italian-American restaurants since the mid-1960s. It was created in 1914 by Alfredo Di Lelio, who opened a restaurant in Rome, Italy, under his first name on the Via della Scrofa in 1910. The dish supposedly helped restore the appetite of his wife after she gave birth to their son. The original dish was made with a very rich triple butter Di Lelio made himself, three kinds of flour, and only the heart of the best *parmigiano*.

Fettuccine all'Alfredo became famous after Hollywood movie actors Douglas Fairbanks and Mary Pickford ate the dish at Alfredo's restaurant while on their honeymoon in 1927. They dined at Alfredo's daily and at the end of their stay presented the owner with a gold-plated spoon and fork with which to mix the pasta and inscribed "To Alfredo the King of the noodles July 1927." The international press picked up on this item and spread the fame of Alfredo's noodle dish around the world. Within a year a recipe had appeared in the United States, printed in *The Rector Cook Book* by George Rector (who in 1939 reported Di Lelio had given the golden utensils to be melted down for Mussolini's war efforts).

After World War II Di Lelio moved to the Piazza Augusto Imperatore, and in the 1950s his restaurant became a mecca for visiting Americans, most of whom came to sample fettuccine Alfredo. (The trademark to the name "Alfredo's the Original of Rome" was bought by Guido Bellanca to open a series of restaurants under that name in the United States, with branches in New York, Miami Beach, and Lake Buena Vista, Florida.)

Because most American cooks could not reproduce the richness of the original butter, today the dish almost always contains heavy cream. (In Italy this would be called *fettuccine alla panna* or *fettuccine alla crema*.)

FETTUCCINE ALFREDO

Boil in salted water 1 lb. fresh fettuccine until tender but firm. In a saucepan melt 7 T. butter with 7 T. Parmesan cheese and 1 c. heavy cream. Drain fettuccine, add to sauce and toss. Serve with more grated Parmesan. Serves 4–6.

fiambre. A Southwestern salad made with avocados, oranges, and beets. It is of South American origins and traditionally served on All Saints' Day.

FIAMBRE

Mix together in a blender or food processor 1 clove crushed garlic, 3–4 sprigs parsley, 3 T. tarragon vinegar, ½ c. orange juice, 1½ t. salt, ¼ t. chile powder, and ⅔ c. vegetable oil. Slice in julienne strips 3 c. chicken and slice 4 hard-boiled eggs and 3 cooked beets. Slice 2 avocados into strips. Place several leaves of romaine lettuce on a plate, arrange chicken, eggs, and beets on top. Garnish with avocado and orange slices and pour on dressing. Garnish with diced scallions. Serves 6-8.

fiddlehead fern (*Matteucia struthiopteris, Amsinckia intermedia*, and *Phacelia tanacetifolia*). Also, "fiddleneck." Several ferns having tips shaped like a violin's scroll fall under this name, though the "cinnamon," "brake," and, especially, the "ostrich fern" are the varieties most commonly referred to. Ostrich ferns from Maine are highly valued and are sometimes found canned or frozen. Because of their delicacy, fiddleheads should be eaten immediately after picking, boiled in saltwater, and served with butter or in a salad. The earliest citation of a fern by this, with reference to the cinnamon variety, was in 1882.

fig (*Ficus carica*). A sweet multiseeded fruit of the fig tree or shrub, usually eaten dried. It originated in northern Asia Minor. The word is from the Latin *ficus*.

Figs were introduced into America on the island of Hispaniola in 1520 by the Spaniards, and the Mission fig owes its name to the Spanish missions set up in California, in the 1700s, where 100 percent of the fig crop is cultivated, predominantly around Madera, Fresno, and Merced counties.

Today the most important varieties of figs cultivated are the "Mission," "Calimyrna," "San Pedro," "Kadota," "Adriatic," and "Brown Turkey."

Most of the fig crop goes into making a sweet filling for "Fig Newtons," cookies baked by Nabisco Brands, Inc., of East Hanover, New Jersey. The cookie was first produced after Philadelphian James Henry Mitchell developed a machine in 1892 to combine a hollow cookie crust with a jam filling. This machine he brought to the Kennedy Biscuit Works, which tried it out in Cambridgeport, Massachusetts, and the resulting cookie was christened "Newton's cakes," after the nearby Boston suburb of Newton. In 1898 the company combined with others to form the National Biscuit Company (now Nabisco Brands). The most frequently used jam in the cookie was fig, and soon the name became "Fig Newton."

filet mignon. A very tender center cut of beef, usually about one to one and a half inches thick. The term, first used in American print on a menu for New York's Architectural League for February 9, 1899, as "Filet Mignon Sauté à la Péigueux," the word is from the French *filet,* "thick slice," and *mignon,* "dainty."

Filet mignon is considered a very tender cut and is usually simply broiled or grilled, often served with a sauce of black pepper or cream and brandy. It may also be part of a shish kebab.

filling. A Pennsylvania-Dutch side dish made of potatoes that are mashed, mixed with eggs, and baked.

"Filling" is also a synonym for a poultry stuffing in the East and for ICING in the South and West.

finger food. Any food item that is picked up and eaten with the fingers, like snacks and canapés. The term has been in print at least since 1928.

fire. Used as a verb by restaurant workers, meaning to "begin cooking a dish."

fire cake. A very simple cake made with flour and water and cooked before an open fire. The term dates in print to 1777.

fish boil. A social gathering at which various kinds of fish are boiled in a large kettle and served with many side dishes like potatoes, coleslaw, and bread. They are especially popular in the lake country of the upper Midwest, from which the fresh fish are taken and boiled in large outdoor kettles set over fires. The vegetables are often added to the boiling water, along with copious amounts of salt. In Wisconsin in the 1960s restaurants began featuring fish boils for their customers.

fish camp. Originally the term referred to a camp where people went to fish, but in the Carolinas restaurants set on the grounds of such camps and specializing in fried-fish dinners were called fish camps. By extension the term has also come to mean any roadside restaurant serving fish dishes. The original meaning dates in print to 1897.

Fish House punch. A PUNCH made of lemon juice, brandy, and peach brandy. It was first created about 1732 at Philadelphia's Colony of the State in Schuylkill (reorganized in the Revolutionary War as the State in Schuylkill) Fishing Club, which was limited to thirty members, all of whom were expected to be good cooks. Each meeting is opened with a toast and a glass of Fish House punch and closed with a glass of Madeira and a toast to the memory of George Washington, who, legend has it, once dined at the club and for days afterward left blank pages in his diary. There are many variations of Fish House punch, some made with brandy, some made with rum or other whiskeys, though the "official" version given below was adopted in 1873.

FISH HOUSE PUNCH

Dissolve 5 lb. sugar in 1 qt. lemon juice, 1 qt. brandy, 2 qt. rum, and 4½ qt. water and ice.

fish muddle. A North Carolina term for a fish stew. "Muddle" refers to a jumble or something mixed up together. "Pine bark stew" is a fish muddle cooked in an iron pot over a pine-bark fire.

FISH MUDDLE

In a large pot sauté ⅓ c. diced salt pork in 1 T. oil for about 5 min. Add 1 chopped red or green pepper, 1 chopped onion, 1 chopped stalk of celery, 1 chopped carrot, and sauté for about 15 min. on a low heat. Add 1 lb. peeled, quartered white potatoes, sauté briefly, then add 2½ c. fish stock, bring to a boil, lower to a simmer, cover and cook for 15 min. Add 1 lb. or more of various seafood like cod, haddock, scallops, and clams and cook

> for about 5 min., until seafood is done. Add salt, pepper, and a pinch of mace. Add 1 t. or more hot sauce, stir, then add ¼ c. heavy or light cream. Blend well, cook for 1 min. Serves 6.

fish stick. A fillet of fish that has been sliced into sticks about one inch wide, battered or rolled in bread crumbs, and fried or baked. Frozen fish sticks were an outgrowth of frozen CRABCAKES made and sold to grocers by Edward Piszek of Philadelphia in 1946. In 1952 Piszek introduced frozen fish sticks under the brand "Mrs. Paul's Kitchens" (named for one of his business partners), which became the leader in the field. *Time* magazine reported in 1953 the sale of frozen fish sticks made by the Birds Eye Company.

flanken. A cut of beef similar to short ribs of flank steak particularly popular in Jewish-American communities. The term itself is Yiddish for "beef flanks" and dates in print to 1945.

flanker. Food-industry term for products made in "healthier" versions by removing some or all of the sugar and salt content, as in soft drinks.

flatbread. An unleavened, very thin bread, usually applied to Scandinavian breads and derived from the Norwegian *flatbrod*. The term dates in print to 1875.

flat car. African-American and hobo slang for pork chops (1936) or PANCAKES (1927). The term first saw print in 1936.

flauta. A tortilla that is rolled with various fillings and then fried. Flautas, whose resemblance to a flute gives them their Mexican name, are made by heating a masa tortilla on a sheet-metal grill called a *comal,* then rolling a filling of meat or poultry in the center, and frying the roll in hot oil. They are then drained and garnished with shredded lettuce and chili sauce.

fletcherism. A fad of the early twentieth century based on *The ABC of Nutrition* (1903) by Horace Fletcher (1849–1919), in which the author mandated that each mouthful of food be chewed exactly thirty-two times—once for each tooth in the mouth. "To fletcherize" meant to chew one's food thoroughly. The theory had the support of many prominent Americans, including John D. Rockefeller, William James, and Thomas Edison. After Fletcher's death in 1919 his theories quickly lost their bite.

flip. A drink made with beer, sugar, molasses, dried pumpkin, and rum, all heated with a hot iron. A fireplace poker was called an "iron flip dog," hence the drink's name. A "yard of flannel" was flip with a beaten egg added, which gave it a flannellike appearance on top. Flip is first mentioned in 1695 in England, and Herman Melville's hero Ishmael in *Moby-Dick* (1851) expounded on the drink:

> *Flip? Did I say we had flip? Yes, and we flipped it at the rate of ten gallons the hour; and when the squall came (for its squally off there by Patagonia), and all hands— visitors and all—were called to reef topsails, we were so top heavy that we had to swing each other aloft in bowlines; and we ignorantly furled the skirts of our jackets into the sails, so that we hung there, reefed fast in the howling gale, a warning example to all drunken tars. However, the masts did not go overboard; and by and by we scrambled down, so sober, that we had to pass the flip again, though the savage salt spray bursting down the forecastle scuttle, rather too much diluted and pickled it for my taste.*

"Flip" is also a southern slang term for a pancake.

floating island. A dessert made with fluffs of meringue set in a custard sauce (1630). The dish originated in France but became known in America by the late eighteenth century. The term is a translation of the French *île flottante,* and *Larousse Gastronomique* describes another version of the dessert made with sponge cake spread with jam, whipped cream, and nuts and set in a bowl of custard. Benjamin Franklin mentions eating a "custard with floating masses of whipped cream or white of eggs" in his *Letters* (1771), and Thomas Jefferson called the dessert "snow eggs," a translation of the French *oeufs à la neige.* By the nineteenth century the dish was well known and served at lavish dinners.

flounder. Any of a variety of flatfishes in the families Bothidae and Pleuronectidae, sometimes erroneously sold as SOLE. The name comes from Norman French, *floundre.* The main American species of fish that fall under the name include: American plaice (*Hippoglossoides platessoides*), also called the "dab" or "sand dab" (*plaice* is from the Latin *platessa,* "flatfish"); "Atlantic HALIBUT" (*H. hippoglossus*); "California halibut" (*Paralichthys californicus*); "Pacific halibut" (*H. stenolepsis*); "Pacific sand dab" (*Citharichthys sordidus*); "Southern flounder" (*P. lethostigma*); "starry flounder" (*Platichthys stellatus*); "fluke" (*P. dentatus*), also called "summer flounder"; "winter flounder" (*Pseudopleuronectes americanus*), also called "blueback flounder," "blackback flounder," and "lemon sole"; "yellowtail flounder" (*Limanda ferruginea*), also called "rusty flounder."

flour. A powdery substance made by grinding and sifting grains such as wheat, corn, rye, and others. The word is from the Middle English.

Native Americans used corn flour almost exclusively for their breads, porridges, and other staple foods, and corn was the flour most readily available to the first settlers who came from Europe, their own grains, like wheat and barley, having failed in several instances. Cornmeal flour continued to be the most important variety until well into the nineteenth century, when wheat became a major crop in America. The production of wheat flour picked up after the invention in 1834 of the Swiss steel roller that ground the meal very finely, a process vastly improved in 1865 by French-American Edmund LeCroix, by separating bran from granual middlings with a middling purifier and fan-driven air currents to clean the wheat as it moved through the mill. The first all-roller flour mill was displayed in the United States at the 1876 Philadelphia Centennial Exposition.

After 1900 American wheat flour was processed to appear white by bleaching and removal of the wheat germ and other flecks of grain, thereby lessening its nutritive value. Today there has been a trend favoring unbleached and whole-wheat flours. Americans' per capita consumption of wheat flour in 1996 was 148 pounds. The main types of flour available in the American market include:

all-purpose flour. A blend of hard- and softwheat flours suitable for general use in all baked goods. Now enriched with thiamine, niacin, iron, and riboflavin and available bleached or unbleached, this is the flour usually meant when no other is specified.

arrowroot flour. A flour made from the arrowroot plant, used mainly as a starch for thickening sauces and gravies.

barley meal. A coarse whole-kernel flour made from barley.

cake flour. A flour made from soft wheats, although the term may also refer to a self-rising flour that contains baking powder and salt.

cornstarch. Also called "corn flour." A flour made from corn and used as a thickener in gravies and

sauces. The process was invented in 1842 by Thomas Kingsford, who eventually merged with the Argo Manufacturing Company of Nebraska and others to form the United Starch Company.

farina. A flour made from hard, but not durum, wheat.

gluten flour. A starch-free flour made by washing the starch from a high-protein wheat flour.

hard-wheat flour. Milled from winter or spring wheat grown mainly in North and South Dakota, Montana, and Kansas. Hardwheat flour has a higher gluten level than other flours and is excellent for bread making.

oat flour. A flour milled from oats, rarely used. But oatmeal, with a much coarser texture, is used for a porridge and in breads and cookies. Flaky rolled oats are used the same way.

pastry flour. A finely milled, soft, low-gluten flour found in the South, where it is used to make pastries.

potato flour. A flour made from potatoes, used primarily as a thickener in gravies and sauces or in sponge cakes.

rice flour. A flour made from milled rice, often combined with all-purpose flour in recipes.

rye flour. A coarse whole-kernel flour milled from rye.

semolina. A granular durum-wheat flour used to make macaroni, spaghetti, and other pastas. It is high in gluten.

soft-wheat flour. Milled from winter wheat and grown mostly in Illinois and Indiana. Softwheat flour is used for biscuits and pastries.

stone-ground flour. A coarse flour milled with stone rather than steel rollers.

tapioca flour. A flour made from the cassava root, used primarily as a thickener in sauces and gravies.

whole-wheat flour. Also called GRAHAM FLOUR. Whole-wheat flour is made from the entire wheat kernel, and for baking is usually combined with a white all-purpose flour.

Fluffernutter. A sandwich made with peanut butter and Marshmallow Fluff, a spreadable marshmallow product. The sandwich was named by Marshmallow Fluff's advertising agency, Durkee-Mower, in 1961.

flummery. Also, "furmenty." A very old term for a custard or fruit pudding or a gruel made from oats. The word dates at least to the early seventeenth century and derives from the Welsch *llymru*. In America it often connoted a pudding with fruit, and the name dates in print to 1615.

foie gras. Fowl liver that has been fattened through a process of overfeeding the animal. The term is from the French for "fattened liver" and is specifically applied to goose liver and considered a great delicacy, but American laws prohibit the importation of most fresh meat. French foie gras must be cooked before it is allowed into the United States. Only within the last decade or so have American companies (currently three) produced foie gras, which is from the liver of a moulard duck (a crossbreed between a female Muscovy and male Pekin). The first California producer of foie gras (from Muscovy ducks) was Marc Leinwand, but the largest producer is Hudson Valley Foie Gras and Duck Products in Ferndale, New York, started by Michael A. Ginor and Izzy Yanay in 1990 and now producing 80 percent of U.S. foie gras.

In 1999, however, the ban was lifted by the F.D.A. after several European countries guaranteed that a poultry virus named Newcastle disease had been eradicated, allowing fresh goose foie gras to be exported to the U.S.

The birds are fed increasing amounts of corn for several weeks, then fed through a tube (a process called "gavage"), although at least one American producer insists the birds are not force-fed but are induced to eat large amounts of corn naturally.

American foie gras is usually graded "A," "B," or "C," depending on the size ("A" liver is about 16 to 22 ounces, "B" 12 to 16 ounces, and "C" under 12 ounces), condition of the skin with regard to bruises or blood, shape, and color.

fonda. A hotel or restaurant in the West. The term dates back at least to 1844 and derives from the Spanish.

fondant. A sugar paste eaten as candy or as icing. The word is from the French, from the past participle of *fondre*, "to melt." The word first appeared in English in 1877. Candies made from fondant were called "ice cream candy" in print as of 1873.

fondue. A method of fast cooking by which bite-size pieces of meat, fruit, or bread are impaled on skewers and dipped into a bubbling liquid either to be quickly cooked or coated. Individual eaters insert their own skewers into the pot, and, because of the communal nature of the activity, fondue cooking has been very much part of social gatherings and parties (1875).

Fondue originated in Switzerland, where it was part of peasant families' one-pot cooking methods and a means of using hardened cheese. The word comes from the French verb *fondre*, "to melt." The classic fondue, called *fondue neuchâteloise*, is made with Emmenthaler or Gruyère cheeses and a Swiss white wine intended to provide acidity. This mixture is placed in a flame-heated earthenware pot called a *caquelon* and melted; a cherry brandy such as Kirsch is added, and skewered crusts of bread are dipped into the blend.

Although the French gastronome Brillat-Savarin referred to fondue in the nineteenth century, the dish actually remained a peasant meal of little interest until it was introduced in the United States in the 1950s. In 1952 chef-owner Konrad Egli of New York's Chalet Swiss restaurant made a *fondue bourguignonne*, made with beef cubes cooked in hot oil, that became an overnight sensation that spread rapidly to other restaurants. In the early 1960s Egli, who noticed that many of his diet-conscious customers avoided his rich chocolate desserts, consulted with his public-relations agent, Beverly Allen, and came up with a chocolate fondue (introduced on July 4, 1964) into which one dipped pieces of cake, fruit, or cream-puff pastry—a variation completely unknown in Switzerland but one that became popular even there within the last few years.

These various fondues were enormously popular as party food with Americans, particularly during winter and especially on skiing holidays. Fondue pots and skewers were a standard entertaining item in American homes throughout the 1960s, but the popularity of the dish has faded considerably since then.

CHOCOLATE FONDUE

Break 8–9 oz. of good Swiss chocolate (preferably Toblerone brand with honey and crushed almonds) into fondue pot, add ½ c. heavy cream and 2 T. Kirsch or other brandy. Skewer morsels of any or all of the following—cake, fruit, cream-puff pastry—and dip in bubbling chocolate.

Food and Drug Administration (FDA). An agency of the Public Health Service division of the United States Department of Health, Education and Welfare whose purpose is to protect public health by monitoring standards of the food and drug industries.

The Food and Drug Act of 1906 was the first instance of such monitoring, and in 1931 the FDA was formed. The Food, Drug and Cosmetic Act of 1938 (amended in 1958 and 1962) increased the powers of the agency.

The FDA controls bureaus of food, product safety, drugs, and veterinary medicine, and its role in drawing up "Standards of Identity" has helped enormously in defining what American food products may or may not be or contain by law. For example, a product labeled "fruit jam" must contain forty-five parts fruit and fifty-five parts sugar or other sweetener, while "raisin bread" must have raisins equaling 50 percent of the weight of the flour. Skim milk is required to have two thousand International Units of Vitamin A in each quart. "Standards of quality" set minimum specifications for such factors as tenderness, color, and freedom from defects in canned fruits and vegetables, limiting, for example, excessive peel in tomatoes, hardness in peas, or pits in pitted canned cherries. (These standards are not to be confused with the Department of Agriculture's USDA voluntary "grades of meat." See BEEF.)

The FDA also monitors "fill-of-container standards," setting requirements as to the volume of food product that must be packaged in a container, sometimes specifying minimum weights of solid food that must remain after the drainable liquid has been poured off (referred to as "minimum drained weight"). Other items must have a minimum fill in terms of the total food as a percentage of the container.

In 1990 Congress passed the Nutrition and Labelling Act, which gave the FDA until May 8, 1993, to standardize food labels at a time when twelve thousand new food items were appearing in the market annually, many with dubious health claims or questionable use of terms like LIGHT, "cholesterol free " and "fat free." Regulations include definitions for serving sizes for some foods, nutritional information on calories, calories from total fat, total fat in grams, saturated fat in grams, cholesterol in milligrams, total carbohydrates in grams, complex carbohydrates in grams, sugars in grams, dietary fiber in grams, protein in grams, sodium in milligrams, vitamins A and C, calcium, and iron. Restaurants, roadside markets, grocers, and prepared foods made on the premises are currently exempt from these regulations. See also main entry for LIGHT foods.

The FDA may take the following actions against those who violate these standards: seizure of the product itself; prosecution of the packer or distributor with possible fines or jail sentence; and court injunction to prohibit shipment of illegal goods.

food court. A space within a building, usually in a shopping mall, featuring a range of fast food eateries and a sit-down area (1980).

foodie. A slang term coined in an article in *Harpers & Queen* magazine (August 1982) entitled "Cuisine Poseur" to describe people who are intensely fascinated by food and talk about food. "A Foodie is a person who is very very interested in food," wrote Paul Levy (who edited the original article) and Ann Barr in their book *The Official Foodie Handbook* (1984). "Foodies are the ones talking about food in any gathering—salivating over restaurants, recipes, radicchio. They don't think they are being trivial—Foodies consider food to be an art, on a level with painting or drama."

food stamp. A federally funded program designed to provide nutritional assistance to the poor in America by giving them coupons that may be exchanged at grocery stores for food products. During the Depression the federal government alleviated both hunger and surplus farm products by allowing families to exchange money for stamps of equal value and additional stamps with which to buy food. Reduced surpluses during World War II canceled such federal programs, but in 1961 President John F. Kennedy directed the Agriculture Department to establish an experimental program, which in 1964 became a full-fledged program under the Food Stamp Act. By 1971 Congress had established uniform standards of eligibility. Since then various changes in the regulations and funds available for food stamps have occurred under different administrations. As of 1994, 71 percent of eligible people living in the U.S. received food stamps.

food wine. A phrase used by American wine producers to describe a wine that goes particularly well with different kinds of food, as opposed to a wine that may be drunk on its own. The phrase gained currency in the mid-1980s, used in an article in the December 16–31, 1983, number of *The Wine Spectator.* "No one admits to coining the term," wrote Harvey Steiman in a later article, entitled "What Is a 'Food Wine' Anyway?" for *Wine Spectator* (April 1–15, 1984), "but several winemakers suggested that it developed to counter an oftern-heard [sic] criticism of California wines—that they are too big and flavorful to make pleasant companions to food. Another possibility is that the term is a reaction to wines that are simply high in alcohol. Such wines stand out in tastings, but may not be the best choices with dinner."

foo-foo. An African-American term for dough made from boiled and pounded plantain. The word derives from West African and dates in print to 1889.

fool. A dessert of cooked, pureed fruit served with cream. The word dates to 1590 in print, though the derivation of its usage is unknown.

fortune cookie. A Chinese-American cookie into which has been folded a printed message predicting one's fortune.

Fortune cookies are not known in Chinese food culture, but they have long been part of the hospitality of Chinese-American restaurants, which traditionally serve them free of charge with tea after the meal. *The Random House Dictionary*, 2nd ed., dates the item in print only to 1960, though they have certainly been served for much longer than that. An article by food historian Meryle Evans in *Diversion* magazine (October 1987) provides several stories as to the possible origins of the fortune cookie. One story concerns Japanese landscape architect Makoto Hagiwara, who emigrated to San Francisco at the turn of the twentieth century and designed a teahouse where, sometime before World War I, he and his daughter Sada Yamamoto began serving fortune cookies to the patrons. Another suggests that just after World War I a Los Angeles baker named David Jung handed out such cookies containing words of encouragement to the poor and homeless people on the streets. He later started the Hong Kong Noodle Company and did produce cookies with fortunes inside.

By the 1930s there were fortune-cookie factories, one of the first being William T. Leong's Key Key Fortune Cookie Company in New York City.

Until the late 1960s fortune cookies were always folded by hand. Then, Edward Louie, owner of the Lotus Fortune Cookie Company in San Francisco, invented a machine to do the job. Louie also pioneered giant fortune cookies up to six inches wide and was the first to insert bawdy fortunes into the confections.

In 1992 Donald H. Lau of Wonton Food Company in Long Island City, New York, planned to produce fortune cookies in Guangzhou, China.

Franconia potatoes. Boiled potatoes baked with butter. The name refers to the Franconia range of the White Mountains in New Hampshire. The recipe below is from a 1944 cookbook.

FRANCONIA POTATOES

Boil potatoes in salted water, place on a buttered pan, pour melted butter over them, season with salt and pepper, and bake until browned at 400°.

free lunch. A midday meal offered free of charge to saloon customers in order to entice them to drink more beer or spirits. The word dates in print to 1835. In her book *The New Orleans Restaurant Cookbook* (1967), Deirdre Stanforth contends that the practice began in the New Orleans French Quarter at the St. Louis Hotel and was created for the business clientele who could not get home for lunch. So successful was the free lunch that the management sought to stop it, but by then it had become firmly entrenched and before long was practiced in other restaurants across the country, and especially in beerhalls. In those days the free lunch might consist of large platters of beef, ham, soup, potatoes, caviar, and oysters, all set on the bar, but as time went on, sliced meats, cheese, and bread became more the norm. By the middle of the twentieth century the free lunch had deteriorated into a complimentary snack of pretzels, potato chips, or other cocktail nibbles, though one occasionally will still find a crock of Cheddar cheese and crackers set out on a bar.

free-range. A restaurant industry and butchers' term for animals, most commonly referring to chickens, that are allowed to forage on their own and are not penned in (1910). The term gained currency in the 1980s among chefs doing the so-called NEW AMERICAN COOKING.

French Colombard. A white vinifera grape used both in blending wines and as a varietal. In France the grape is known as the "Colombard" and by other names, but in California it has been called "West's White Pacific" in the nineteenth century (when West & Sons of Stockton, California, brought it back from France) and "Winkler" (after viticulturist Dr. Albert J.

Winkler) after the repeal of Prohibition. Later it was identified by enologist Harold P. Olmo of the University of California as French Colombard. The first varietal from this grape appeared in 1964 under the Parducci Wine Cellars label.

French cruller. A fried DOUGHNUT-like cake that is crimped on the top and topped with frosting. The term dates in print to 1965.

French dip sandwich. A sandwich made of sliced beef, lamb or pork and hot mustard set on a sliced French loaf that has been dipped into the pan juices. It was created at Philippe's the Original, a restaurant that opened in Los Angeles in 1908.

French dressing. A salad dressing made by mixing three parts oil to one part vinegar, though some other seasonings like mustard or bleu cheese may be added (1880).

french fry. A method of cooking potatoes or other vegetables cut into narrow strips or rounds. "French fries" (also a "side of fries" or just "fries") are easily the most popular form of potato preparation in America and are a staple of FAST-FOOD restaurants. In France they are called *pommes frites* and were not mentioned in French print until 1858, and in 1868 as a low-class food item. In England they are known as "chips," first mentioned in a letter by Oscar Wilde dated March 1876, wherein he writes, "My dear Bouncer, I am very glad to hear from Mark that you have come back safe out of the clutches of those barbarous Irish. I was afraid that the 'potato-chips' that we live on over there would have been too much for you."

The term "french fry" has nothing to do with the country of origin, but instead refers to a method, called "frenching," of cutting the potatoes into narrow strips. The *Oxford English Dictionary,* which traces "French-fried potatoes" back to 1894, suggests the usage is American in origin. "French frieds" dates to 1915; "french fries" to the 1930s. "French fried onion rings" appears in print in 1939. "Shoestring potatoes," which are cut in very thin strips, dates in print to 1898.

Most of the commercial french-fried potatoes are precut, partially cooked, and frozen for delivery to groceries and restaurants. In fact, it is now infrequent to find freshly made french fries outside the home. At home the potatoes may be fried in pure lard, but vegetable oil is the more common medium today. "Steak fries" and "Texas fries" are usually cut thicker than reg-ular french-fried potatoes. Thickly cut potatoes cooked in a small amount of fat or oil are called "American fried potatoes," while thinly sliced potatoes done the same way are called "American raw fry." "Onion rings" are onion slices usually battered in flour, milk, and cornmeal before frying.

French 75. A cocktail made from gin, Cointreau, lemon juice, and champagne, though ingredients vary with different recipes. The drink is named after a French 75-millimeter gun, considered the finest field-piece of World War I.

"Count" León Bertrand Arnaud Casenave, owner of Arnaud's restaurant in New Orleans, which opened in 1918, claimed to have created the drink, but *Harry's ABC of Mixing Cocktails* (1919, revised 1939) refers to a " '75 Cocktail" made from 1 t. absinthe plus two parts Calvados and one part gin as "the original 1915 recipe of the French '75 Cocktail," and gives another recipe for a French '75 calling for 2 oz. gin, the juice of a lemon, sugar, ice, and champagne as having originated at Harry's New York Bar in Paris in 1925. David A. Embury, in his *Fine Art Of Mixing Drinks* (1958), notes unpersuasively that "gin is sometimes used in place of cognac in [a French 75], but then, of course, it no longer should be called French." Embury's version calls for the juice of 1 lime or half a lemon, 2 t. sugar syrup, and 2 oz. cognac.

Arnaud's recipe for a French 75, given in Deirdre Stanforth's *New Orleans Restaurant Cookbook* (1967), is as follows:

> ## FRENCH 75
>
> *Shake with ice the juice of 1 lemon with 1 oz. gin and ½ oz. Cointreau, strain into a champagne glass, and top with champagne and a lemon twist.*

French toast. A breakfast dish made from white bread dipped in an egg-and-milk mixture, then fried in butter and served with either syrup or powdered sugar. It is a very popular item both at home and in restaurants, and it is often accompanied by bacon, ham, or sausage.

The dish does have its origins in France, where it is known as *ameritte* or *pain perdu* ("lost bread"), a term that has persisted, in Creole and Cajun cookery; in Spain it is called *torriga* and in England "Poor Knights of Windsor," which is the same name for the dish in Denmark, *arme riddere,* and Germany, *arme Ritter.* At one time or another in America it has been referred to as "Spanish," "German," or "nun's toast," and its first appearance in print as "French toast" was in 1871. In her 1893 cookbook Mary Lincoln calls it "egg toast," as does *The Picayune's Creole Cook Book* (1900).

FRENCH TOAST

Dip a slice of white bread into a batter made from 1 beaten egg and ¼ c. milk or cream. Sauté in butter until brown on both sides. Serve immediately with maple syrup, cinnamon, powdered sugar, or honey.

---

fress. To eat greedily. The word is from German, *fressen,* "to devour," and is used primarily in Pennsylvania-Dutch communities and among Jewish Americans. The word dates in print to 1916.

fried chicken. A cowboy term for bacon that is rolled in flour and then fried. See also SOUTHERN FRIED CHICKEN.

Frito pie. Also, "chili pie" and "corn chip chili pie." A Texas snack made with Fritos Corn Chips (a company trademark), CHILI, grated cheese, and onion. According to Texas food writer Alison Cook, "purists" demand that the chili, cheese, and onion be poured directly into a torn-open bag of Fritos, called "walk around corn chip chili pie." "THIS DISH MUST," wrote Cook, "REPEAT, MUST BE EATEN OUT OF THE SACK WITH A PLASTIC FORK OR SPOON, lest the whole effect be lost." The more "traditional" form of the pie is made in a baking dish.

The Frito-Lay company, based in Dallas, has claimed that Daisy Dean Doolin, mother of the company's founder, Elmer Doolin, may have invented the dish in the 1930s as a way of using leftovers. (Fritos Corn Chips themselves were first sold in San Antonio by Doolin as of 1932.) Cook, however, noted that a recipe for the dish appeared in 1946 in the *Fredericksburg Home Kitchen* as "Chili-Frito Loaf," submitted by Viola Mae Schmidt. Another claim has been made for the wife of a Travis County, Texas, deputy sheriff's wife, who cooked up the pie for prisoners in the local jail.

FRITO PIE

In a 9" x 12" baking dish spread 2 c. Fritos Corn Chips evenly. Distribute 1 c. chopped onion and ½ c. grated Cheddar cheese on top. Pour on enough chile to cover. Top with another cup of Fritos and ½ c. Cheddar cheese. Bake in pre-heated 350° oven until bubbling, about 10–20 min. Serves 4–6.

Frogmore stew. A southern dish of boiled shrimp, crab, sausage, onions, and corn on the cob, traditionally served outdoors, similar to a New England clambake or Maryland crab boil. The name probably derives from a town on St. Helena Island (the town is now called St. Helena). A similar dish is elsewhere called "Buford stew," possibly after Buford, Georgia.

FROGMORE STEW

Bring to a boil 3 qts. of water and add 2 T. seafood boil seasonings. Add 1 lb. cooked hot smoked sausage, 1 whole onion, 1 t. hot red pepper flakes, and a wedge of lemon. Lower heat and simmer for 5 min. Add 6 ears of corn and cook for 2 min. Add 2 lb. unshelled shrimp and cook for 3–5 min. Serve with red beans and rice.

---

frogs' legs. Any of various preparations using the legs of three United States species of frog, the "green frog" (*Rana clamitans*), the "American bullfrog" (*R. catesbeiana*), or the "northern leopard frog" (*R. pipiens*). The majority of these are caught in Florida and Louisiana, where they are a delicacy, either deep-fried or made with a spicy sauce

---

DEEP-FRIED FROGS' LEGS

In a bowl with 1 c. vinegar, 1 sliced onion, and 3 chopped cloves of garlic marinate 2 doz. frogs' legs for about 3 hr. Make a batter of 1 beaten egg, 1 c. flour, ½ c. milk, ¼ t. cayenne pepper, and 1 t. salt. Drain frogs' legs, dip in batter, fry in deep fat at 375° until golden brown.

---

from the well. Bartender slang for the inexpensive house brands of liquor used for drinks when a customer does not specify a brand.

frosted. A half-frozen citrus-juice drink, made by freezing a fruit juice until almost firm, then whirling it through a blender. Frosteds may also be made by putting ice cubes made from one fruit juice, such as grapefruit, into a glass containing another fruit juice, like lemonade. Sometimes MILK SHAKE is used as a synonym for a frosted.

fruit cocktail. A cup of various fruits served as an appetizer, usually containing pineapple slices, grapefruit slices, and, if canned, a sweetened liquid. (For the origins of COCKTAIL, see main entry.) In the 1850s recipe books called the item a "fruit salad." The term "fruit cocktail" was first used in print in the *New York Hotel Review* for 1922; "fruit cup" followed in print in 1931.

fruit soup. A Scandinavian-American soup made with dried fruits and thickened with tapioca or sago. The term dates in print to 1950.

fry bread. A bread of the Southwest Native Americans, particularly the Navaho and Hopi, that is deep-fried and sometimes served with honey and powdered sugar. Wheat flour was brought to the Americas by the Spanish, and this is one of the few Native-American breads not based on corn flour. Fry breads are often featured at county fairs and Native-American festivals throughout the Southwest, and a fry-bread contest, overseen by a Navaho woman named Hazel Yazza since 1946, is held annually at the Navaho Nation Fair and Rodeo in September.

FRY BREAD

Mix 2 c. flour with 2 T. baking powder and 1 t. salt. Add ½ c. warm water, or more, to achieve an elastic dough. Divide into 2-in. balls, roll out to a ¼-in. thickness, and fry in hot oil. Drain and serve with honey, cinnamon, or confectioners' sugar. (If Navaho bread is desired, punch a hole in the center of each flattened piece before frying, since the Navaho lowered their bread into the oil with a stick, leaving a hole in the bread.)

frying-pan bread. Cowboy bread made in a skillet from flour, water, and baking powder made into a thin batter that was spread on a skillet placed over hot coals.

fudge. A semisoft candy made from butter, sugar, and various flavorings, the most usual being chocolate, vanilla, and maple. The candy was first made in New England women's colleges. The origins of the term are obscure. The *Oxford English Dictionary* suggests it may be a variant of an older word, "fadge," meaning "to fit pieces together." "Fudge" had been used to mean a hoax or cheat since about 1833, and by midcentury "Oh, fudge!" was a fairly innocuous expletive.

It has long been speculated that American college women, using candymaking as an excuse to stay up late at night, applied the then-current meaning to the new candy, which was undoubtedly responsible for helping many students gain their "freshman fifteen," that is, fifteen pounds gained during the first year at college. In *Oh, Fudge!* (1990) Lee Edwards Benning cited a 1921 letter in the Vassar College archives written by alumna Emelyn B. Hartridge, who contended that "fudge, as I knew it, was first made in Baltimore by a cousin of a schoolmate of mine . . . [and] sold in 1886 in a grocery store [at 279 Williams Street] for 40 cents a pound. . . . From my schoolmate, Nannie Hagner . . . I secured the recipe and in my first year at Vassar, I made it there—and in 1888 I made 30 pounds for the Senior Auction, its real introduction to the college, I think."

The word "fudge" as a candy first showed up in print in 1896, and by 1908 was commonly associated with women's colleges, as in "Wellesley Fudge," "Smith College Fudge," and "Vassar Fudge." "Divinity fudge" (known at least since 1913), a light confection made with egg whites and, often, candied cherries, came along about 1910 and was especially popular during the holidays. The name probably referred to its "divine" flavor. "Fudge frosting" was being applied to cakes at the Wellesley College Tea Room by 1898.

Most fudge is made from chocolate, though vanilla and maple are very popular, as is fudge riddled with walnuts or pecans. "Fudge brownies" are more cake-like than fudge, but have a similar semisoft, moist texture.

CHOCOLATE FUDGE

Combine 2 c. sugar, 2 T. corn syrup, ⅔ c. evaporated milk, 2 oz. unsweetened chocolate, and 3 T. butter in saucepan, bring to boil, and cook to 236° on a candy thermometer. Pour mixture onto marble slab and turn edges in with spatula until glossy sheen is gone. Add 1 t. vanilla and, if desired, chopped nuts.

fumaric acid. An additive used to give a tartness to the flavor of processed foods like pie fillings, gelatin, and powdered drinks.

funeral pie. Also, "raisin pie." A PennsylvaniaDutch pie traditionally baked before the imminent death of a family member for the purpose of easing the grief of the mourners at the funeral. The pie is also sometimes called a "rosina" or "rosine" pie, because *Rosine* in

German means "raisin." The term dates in print to 1949 but is certainly much older.

FUNERAL PIE

Soak 1 c. raisins in 2 c. warm water for 2 hr. In a double boiler combine 1½ c. sugar, 4 T. flour, 1 beaten egg, the juice of 1 lemon and the lemon rind, ¼ t. salt, then raisins and water. Cook for 15 min., pour into unbaked pie shell, top with a lattice of dough, and bake at 375° for 45 min.

---

funnel cake. A deep-fried pastry made from batter dripped through a funnel. This Pennsylvania-Dutch breakfast dish (which dates in print to 1950 but is certainly much older) is swirled in a spiral in hot fat and then served with sugar or maple syrup.

FUNNEL CAKE

Combine 1 c. flour, ¾ c. milk, 1 t. baking powder, ⅛ t. salt, and 1 egg to make a batter. Let stand for 10 min. Drip the batter through a funnel, swirling to form a spiral design, in very hot fat or oil. Turn when browned and brown the other side. Drain and serve with powdered sugar or maple syrup.

---

funny cake. As defined in its first printed reference (1965) in the *Woman's Day Encyclopedia of Cookery*, this is a single-crust pie made with sugar, shortening, egg, milk, flour, baking powder, and vanilla poured into a pan lined with a mixture of cocoa, vanilla, water, and sugar.

fusion cuisine. A term that gained currency in the late 1980s to describe a cuisine that draws on elements of many regional cookeries, especially by matching European and Asian ingredients and techniques.

fuzzy navel. A cocktail made with peach schnapps and orange juice. The "fuzzy" refers to the effect of inebriation on the imbiber as well as to peach fuzz; the "navel" refers to the navel orange. A drink made with peach schnapps, and grapefruit juice is called a "fuzzy pucker," because of the tartness of the grapefruit juice. Both became popular in the 1980s.

galley queen. Airline workers' slang for a lazy flight attendant who spends too much time loafing in the galley, first mentioned in print in 1990.

gap 'n' swallow. Cornmeal mush. The term dates in print to 1939. Described by Josephine H. Pierce in *Coast to Coast Cookery* (1951) as "an emergency pudding made of cornmeal, much like Hasty Pudding. Also a plum pudding served with maple syrup." It is an old New England dish, whose name is a fanciful description of opening one's mouth and swallowing the dish either with relish or mere endurance.

gar. Also, "needlefish" and "alligator gar." Any of a variety of predatory fish in the species *Lepisosteidae,* of which five species occur in United States waters, principally in the southern and central states. The word "gar" is an American shortening of the English "garfish," which derives from the Middle English "geren". Gars were a basic food fish of the Florida Seminoles. The fish is often smoked.

Garbo. Also, "garbo." An uncommon term for a toasted English muffin, perhaps named after movie actress Greta Garbo.

garden vegetables. The American gardening tradition is basically derived from English roots. But the availability of fruits and vegetables at American markets has made a food-producing garden on one's own property more of a hobby than a necessity. On southern plantations before the Civil War, slaves were often encouraged to keep their own gardens to add to their own diet; if there was a surplus, the food would be sold.

During World War I Americans were urged to plant "liberty gardens" in vacant lots or their own backyards in order to release other foodstuffs for shipment overseas to troops. This same practice came about again in 1942, when such plantings were called "victory gardens."

During the 1960s gardening took on a revival owing to studies that showed many commercially grown fruits and vegetables were treated with pesticides and chemicals that rendered some items dangerous to consume. Many books appeared that encouraged Americans to raise some of their own food on their own land, while at the same time food raised without any chemical additives was pronounced natural or ORGANIC. Today more than half of all American households grow some or all of their own food. The Midwest has the most home gardeners, the South the least. The tomato, grown by 94 percent of home gardeners, is easily the most popular vegetable among such planters.

garlic (*Allium sativum*). An onionlike plant having a bulb that is highly aromatic and distinctly flavored. The word is from Old English *garleac,* "spear leek." The plant is native to Central Asia and has long been enjoyed as a seasoning in Asia, Africa, and Europe, especially around the Mediterranean.

In America there grew a wild garlic (*A. canadense*) eaten by pre-Columbian Indians, but the familiar market varieties (American, Creole, Mexican, Italian, and Tahitian) came via Europe and were only appreciated as a seasoning in those regions bordering the Gulf of Mexico, where the French, Spanish, African, and Caribbean influences were the strongest. In the rest of the country garlic's usage was confined to ethnic neighborhoods in large cities until the middle of the present century. "Garlic has been the vehicle in the United States of a self-reversing snobbery," wrote Waverley Root in *Food* (1980). "Before I left America to live in Europe in 1927, you were looked down upon if you ate garlic, a food fit only for ditchdiggers; when I returned in 1940, you were looked down upon if you *didn't* eat it. It had become the hallmark of gastronomic sophistication, and I was overwhelmed by the meals offered by thoughtful friends, who catered to my supposedly acquired dashing Gallic tastes by including garlic in every dish except ice cream." It was hardly surprising, therefore, that lunch-counter slang terms of the 1920s and 1930s for garlic included "Bronx vanilla," "halitosis," and "Italian perfume."

Ninety percent of America's garlic is grown in California, which grows predominantly "Early" and "Late California" varieties. "Green garlic" is young garlic picked in late winter or spring. "Elephant garlic," so called for its three-to-four-inch diameter size, is technically not a garlic but more related to a leek. Two thirds of the domestic garlic crop is dehydrated and processed into flakes or garlic salt, a milder-flavored seasoning that appeared in the 1930s; in the late 1940s "garlic bread" was being served in Italian-American restaurants as a standard item. In 1970 the per capita U.S. consumption of garlic was less than a half a pound; in 1997 it had grown to 1.7 pounds.

Gatorade. Trademark name for a sweet soft drink developed by Dr. Robert Cade at the University of Florida in Gainesville, Florida, in 1965 to help athletes replenish fluids and minerals. It was so called because the university's football team was nicknamed the "Gators." The beverage later became a very popular soft drink nationally, especially after it was adopted by the National Football League in 1967 as an official drink.

gazpacho. Also, "gaspacho." A cold tomato-and-vegetable soup popular as summer fare and a staple of American restaurant menus, especially in the West. Another dish of the same name is "gazpacho salad," a layering of greens, sliced tomatoes, cucumbers, onions, bread crumbs, and French dressing. As such it was characterized by Mrs. Mary Randolph in *The Virginia Housewife* (1824). As a soup, "gazpacho" has been in print since 1835.

Although antecedents of the soup are mentioned in the Bible and Greek and Roman literature (the word comes from the Arabic for "soaked bread"), gazpacho is more specifically an Andalusian dish, itself open to numerous interpretations—some thick, some hot, some cold—and often served with several garnishes, such as chopped eggs, bread cubes, peppers, onions, and scallions. In fact, *Cassell's Spanish Dictionary* defines gazpacho as an "Andalusian dish made of bread, oil, vinegar, onions and garlic; crumbs of bread in a pan" and makes no mention of the strained tomatoes that most identify gazpacho for Americans. Maite Manjón, in *The Gastronomy of Spain and Portugal* (1990), contended that the original dish was a garlic soup called *ajo blanco* and was of Moorish origins. Tomatoes and peppers were added after the Spanish explorers brought those ingredients back from the Americas, and today there are many regional "gazpachos" throughout Andalusia, including hot versions.

Although long known in this country, gazpacho's popularity was for a great while confined to the South. Later, in the West, it took on a vogue that has made it one of the most often found contemporary soups on a menu.

GAZPACHO

Peel and seed 2 tomatoes and chop together with 1 seeded sweet red pepper, 2 cloves garlic, and 2 T. seasonings, such as basil, tarragon, parsley, scallion, onions, and chives. Add ½ c. olive oil, 3 T. lime juice, and about 3 c. chicken broth. Puree in a food blender or food mill, add salt, pepper, and chopped cucumber, and chill for several hours. Serve with bread crumbs or bread cubes and white onions.

gefilte fish. Also, "gefulte fish." A small fish dumpling or quenelle seasoned with chopped eggs, onion, and pepper, which according to tradition should be made from several varieties of freshwater fish. The dish is frequently served at Jewish-American homes on Friday night and at holiday dinners. The term is from the German for "stuffed fish" and first appeared in print in 1890.

GEFILTE FISH

Fillet 3 lb. whole fish of two or three varieties, such as whitefish, carp, or pickerel. Lightly salt the fillets and chill for several hours, then grind finely, adding 2 eggs, ½ c. water, 3 T. matzo meal, 2 t. salt, and ⅛ t. pepper. Chill for 10 min., shape into loaves. Salt and chill the bones, skin, and head of the fish, rinse, and place in large pot with 2 chopped onions and 3 chopped carrots in a layer. Season with salt and pepper, cover with water, and bring to a boil. Cook for 5 min., then add fish mixture to broth and place sliced carrots on top. Cover, bring to boil, simmer gently for 1 hr. Cool slightly before serving, garnish with carrots, broth, horseradish, and dill pickles. Serves 6.

gelatin. A thickening agent used in powdered desserts, yogurt, puddings, ice cream, cheese spreads, and other foods. Gelatin is a protein derived from animal bones, hooves, and other parts.

gem. A muffin baked in a rectangular, sectioned pan with a round bottom. It is known mostly in the North and first saw print in 1875.

German's Sweet Chocolate cake. A cake made with Baker's German's Sweet Chocolate and topped with a coconut-pecan frosting. The original recipe, when first submitted to a Dallas newspaper in 1957 by a reader, caused the sale of Baker's German's Sweet Chocolate (a trademark name of the General Foods Company) to soar in Texas. A General Foods district manager brought the recipe to the attention of the company, and the recipe was perfected and promoted throughout the United States.

The recipe has become so widespread over so many decades that it is often called "German chocolate cake," and many believe the cake is of German origins and, because of the inclusion of pecans and buttermilk, a specialty of Texas bakers. But in fact the name of the chocolate derives from Dr. James Baker, who in 1780 financed the first chocolate factory in America. His descendant, Walter Baker, hired an employee named Samuel German, who developed a "sweet chocolate," which was added to the Baker's line under German's name.

A similar cake, apparently newer and adapted from German's Sweet Chocolate cake, is called a "Texas sheet cake" (also "Texas cake"), because it is baked in a large baking pan and not set in layers.

GERMAN'S SWEET CHOCOLATE CAKE

Melt 1 4-oz. package of Baker's German's Sweet Chocolate in ½ c. boiling water, then remove from heat to cool. In a bowl mix 2¼ c. cake flour, 1 t. baking soda, and ½ t. salt. In another bowl cream 1 c. butter or margarine, and beat in 4 egg yolks, one at a time. Blend in 1 t. vanilla extract and melted chocolate. Add flour mixture, alternating with 1 c. buttermilk. Beat until smooth. Beat 4 eggs whites until stiff and fold into batter. Pour batter into three 9-in. cake pans lined with waxed paper, and bake 30 min. at 350° until set. Remove from oven and remove cakes from pans. Let cool on a rack.

Make a frosting by combining 1½ c. evaporated milk, 1½ c. sugar, 4 beaten egg yolks, ¾ c. melted butter, and 1½ t. vanilla extract. Cook over medium heat, stirring until it turns a light brown color. Remove from heat, add 2 c. Baker's Angel Flake coconut and 1½ c. chopped pecans. Beat until cool and spreadable. Spread on each layer of the cakes, including the top.

gibraltar. A hard candy associated with Salem, Massachusetts, and described in the book *Old Salem* (1886) as "a white and delicate candy, flavored with lemon or peppermint, soft as ice cream at one stage of its existence, but capable of hardening into a consistency so stony and so unutterably flinty-hearted that it is almost a libel on the rock whose name it bears. The Gibraltar is the aristocrat of Salem confectionery."

Gibson. A MARTINI cocktail garnished with a small white onion (1925). The drink was apparently named after the American illustrator Charles Dana Gibson (1867–1944), famous for his drawings of the turn-of-the-century "Gibson Girl." The story goes that Gibson ordered a martini—usually served with an olive—from bartender Charley Connolly of the Players in New York City. Connolly found himself out of olives and instead served the drink with two tiny white onions. The drink caught on, took the name of the more famous of the two men, and ever since has caused confirmed martini drinkers to shudder at the thought of drinking their favorite cocktail with such a garnish. The recipe, however, differs not at all from that of a dry martini.

gimlet. A drink of gin and lime juice. The word derives from a term for a boring tool (from Middle English and, ultimately, Middle Dutch *wimmelkijn*), which supposedly was used to puncture the kegs of lime juice shipped after 1795 to the British colonies as a preventive for scurvy. As a cocktail, the word first appears in print in 1923.

Bartenders disagree as to the proportions for a gimlet, some adding carbonated water as with a gin RICKEY, others not. In America carbonated water is not usual. In his novel *The Long Goodbye* (1953), Raymond Chandler insists "a real gimlet is half gin and half Rose's Lime Juice and nothing else."

GIMLET

Stir with ice 2 oz. gin and ½ oz. Rose's lime juice. Strain into sour glass.

gin. A distilled spirit made from grain and flavored with juniper and other aromatics. Gin was first made as a medicine in Holland by Franz de le Boë (1614–1672), also known as Doctor Sylvius, professor of medicine at the University of Leiden. Sylvius redistilled a pure alcohol with the oil of the juniper berry (*Juniperus communis*), the result of which he called "Genièvre (French, from the Dutch *jenever*, "juniper berries"). He believed the new spirit would have therapeutic effect, a claim that made its creator famous and created an immediate market for the then-inexpensive spirit, which was sometimes called "Hollands" or "Schiedam" (after a gin-distillery center near Rotterdam).

The English imported gin, which they called "Dutch courage," but during Queen Anne's reign (1702–14) the spirit was produced locally and became the favorite—and least expensive—alcoholic drink sold throughout England, especially after the monarch raised excise taxes on foreign spirits and lowered them on domestic. "London Dry Gin" used to mean a gin produced in or near that city, and such spirits differed in taste from the heavier Dutch gins. These lighter London-style gins became just as popular in the English colonies and have remained the preferred American variety ever since.

English gins run 80 to 97 proof, slightly lower than most American gins, and their taste has a bit more character than ours. (The English also make a rarely seen sweetened gin called "Old Tom," which purists insist is the correct spirit for a Tom Collins cocktail.)

During Prohibition those who opposed enforced temperance would often make liquor illegally at home, and so-called "bathtub gin"—that is, liquor mixed in one's bathtub—was the easiest spirit to produce. By obtaining a doctor's prescription for pure alcohol on some pretext of illness, one merely had to flavor the liquid with juniper berries, or their extract, and other botanicals such as coriander, lemon peel, or angelica. Glycerin was often added to soften the home brew's rawness.

Commercially produced gin in America may be either distilled or made by combining distilled spirits with botanical oils, a process called "compounding." By law all gins must have the flavor of juniper, though "sloe gin," which is really a cordial and not a gin, is allowed to carry the name by tradition. Minimum proof by federal law is 60 (30 percent alcohol by volume).

Gin is almost never aged, although there are some "golden gins" produced whose color comes from brief aging.

Gin is principally mixed with other spirits or citrus juices to make cocktails such as the MARTINI, the GIBSON, the GIMLET, the RAMOS GIN FIZZ, and others. The United States is the biggest producer of gin, with 8.7 million 9-liter cases produced by the U.S. in 1997. The U.S. imports more British gin than any other country.

ginger (*Zingiber officinale*). This native plant of tropical and subtropical regions of Asia, especially Indomalaysia, is no longer extant in its wild form, but its cultivated root is valued for its pungent, aromatic spiciness and is a seasoning used throughout the world in everything from curries to desserts.

The name derives from the Sanskrit *Srngaveram* ("horn root"), Greek *ziggiberis,* Latin *zinziberi,* and on to Middle English "gingivere." Ginger was well known to the ancient Romans, but it nearly disappeared in Europe after the fall of the Roman Empire. Marco Polo brought ginger back from the Orient, and afterward the European appetite for spices made it once again a treasured and expensive condiment. Legend has it that Queen Elizabeth I of England invented the "gingerbread man," a cookie in the shape of a man, especially popular during Christmastime.

There was no ginger in the New World except a wild variety called "Indian ginger" (*Asarum canadense*) used in colonial times, but the English brought it to the American Colonies early on, and ginger cookies were handed out to the Virginia voters to persuade them to elect certain candidates for the House of Burgesses. Ginger became a popular spice in Caribbean and Creole cookery, but in the rest of the country it was more often used in cakes, breads, and cookies. Virginian William Byrd in 1711 remarked that he "ate gingerbread all day long," and Amelia Simmons's *American Cookery* (1796) gives a recipe for molasses gingerbread. Eliza Leslie's 1828 volume, *Seventy-five Receipts,* listed both a common gingerbread and an enriched LAFAYETTE GINGER BREAD with lemon juice and brown sugar. Fannie Merritt Farmer, in her 1896 *Boston Cooking School Cook Book,* speaks of three available grades of ginger—"Jamaica, best and strongest; Cochin [Indian], and African."

Today fresh gingerroot is available in American markets, but Americans usually depend on dry, powdered ginger for use in cakes and cookies. Crystallized ginger is often found in specialty shops, and candied ginger was long served in the North as an after-dinner digestive. Ginger ice cream was a flavor popular in New England, though now rarely seen.

Booker T. Washington, founder of the Tuskegee Institute in Alabama, recalled the childhood he spent as a slave and how he envied the white people's enjoyment of ginger cakes: "I remember that at one time I saw two of my young mistresses and some lady visitors eating ginger-cakes, in the yard. At that time those cakes seemed to me to be absolutely the most tempting and desirable things that I had ever seen; and I then and there resolved that, if I ever got free, the height of my ambition would be reached if I could get to the point where I could secure and eat ginger-cakes in the way I saw those ladies doing" (*Up From Slavery* [1901]).

GINGERBREAD

Sift together 1 t. powdered ginger and 1 c. flour. Cream ½ c. butter with ½ c. brown sugar. Add flour mixture and blend well. Beat in ½ c. molasses and 1 well-beaten egg. Dissolve 1 t. baking soda in ½ c. boiling water and add to batter. Mix well, then bake in well-greased shallow pan at 350° for about 20 min. or until inserted knife comes out clean.

ginger beer. A nonalcoholic beverage flavored with fermented ginger (1800). Ginger beer was popular in England at the beginning of the nineteenth century and later in America as a substitute for real beer. A MOSCOW MULE is a cocktail made with ginger beer and vodka.

GINGER BEER

In a large earthenware vessel put 2 oz. pounded gingerroot, ¼ pt. lemon juice, 1 lb. sugar, and 1 gal. boiling water. Cool to 110°, then add 1 oz. yeast dissolved in a little water. Let ferment for 1 wk. When fermentation ends, pour through strainer into bottles. Makes 1 gal.

ginger champagne. A substitute cocktail without alcohol made with ginger flavoring. The drink has been known by this name since at least 1842.

gingersnap. A cookie made from ginger and molasses. "Snap" probably derives from an informal meaning for something easy, from German, or Middle Dutch, *snappen,* "to seize quickly." The word was first printed in 1795.

"Gingerbread men" are cookies cut in the form of human shapes and usually decorated with icing for eyes, mouth, and buttons.

gin mill. Slang term for a bar or saloon, known in print since 1865.

Girl Scout Cookies. A trademark name for a series of cookies sold by the 2.5 million Girl Scouts of America to raise money for their organization. When the idea was created in the 1920s, the cookies were actually made by local Girl Scout units and peddled door-to-cloor each spring. Today the cookies are baked by two companies, Interbake Foods, Inc., of Richmond, Virginia (since 1938) and Little Brownie Bakers of Louisville, Kentucky (since 1975) and still sold door-to-door by the Girl Scouts. In 1997, 183 million boxes were sold, gener-

ating $500 million in business. The most popular cookie of fourteen varieties is called "Thin Mints."

glycerin. Also, "glycerol." An additive, derived from fat and oil molecules, for retaining the moisture of foods to which it is added, such as marshmallow, candy, and baked goods.

goat. Any of a variety of horned ruminants in the genus *Capra,* including the American mountain goat. Goat's meat is not of much interest to most Americans, though it finds favor among some westerners and among certain immigrant groups like the Italians, Greeks, and Spanish. In Mexican or Latin communities and in the Southwest, a suckling kid is often called by its Spanish name, *cabrito.* Slang terms for goat are "Adirondack steak" and "mountain lamb."

goatfish. Any of a variety of fish in the family Mullidae, usually golden or red (circa 1639). In America the name refers to several fish, especially the "red goatfish" (*Mullus auratus*), known as the Hawaiian "kumu" (1926) and "moano," which means "white" in Hawaiian and refers to either the species *Parupeneus bifasciatus* or *P. multifasciatus.*

goetta. A specialty dish of Cincinnati made from ground meat and oatmeal boiled together, then molded, sliced, and fried, most commonly as a breakfast meat. It is similar to SCRAPPLE. The word is pronounced "get-ta" or "gheu-tuh," and must in some sense derive from German origins, although the exact reason for the name is not known. The *Dictionary of American Regional English* notes in a cookbook entitled *Cincinnati Recipe Treasury* (1983), "Martha Finke Oehler of Covington, Kentucky, claims that her ancestors 'invented' goetta (pronounced get-ta) back around the turn of the century. . . . The goetta became popular, and packages were transported across the Ohio River to Cincinnati markets, where the meat purveyors began selling their homemade versions in a German atmosphere."

GOETTA

In a large pot boil 2 lb. pork cut into cubes and 1 onion cut in two for about 30 min. Remove from the liquid, grind into a fine mince. Into the liquid stir 2½ c. oatmeal and the pork and season with salt and pepper. Cook until liquid is absorbed, about 45 min., remove from pan and cool. Pack into a loaf pan and chill well. Serve cut into slabs and fried in butter.

gohan. Cooked rice with vinegar and sugar, often used to wrap sushi. This is a term used in Japanese-American communities and comes from the Japanese word for cooked rice, although *shari* is more commonly used when referring to the vinegared rice used to make sushi. "Gohan" dates in American print to 1958.

golden Cadillac. A cocktail made from Galliano liqueur, white crème de cacao, and heavy cream. The name derives from the golden color of the drink and its richness, a characteristic associated with the American luxury car, the Cadillac. In 1956 Columbia Pictures produced a motion picture entitled *The Solid Gold Cadillac,* and the cocktail may date from that period.

GOLDEN CADILLAC

In an electric blender mix with crushed ice 1 oz. Galliano, 2 oz. crème de cacao, and 2 oz. heavy cream. Pour into cocktail glass.

Gooey Butter Cake. A yeast-raised coffee cake whose butter-rich center gives it its "gooey" name. It is a specialty of St. Louis, Missouri, but its creator is unknown. In an article in *The New York Times* (April 4, 1989) Ann Barry suggested it probably came out of South St. Louis, where many German bakers lived in the 1930s, and may have been an accident whereby the baker added too much butter or other ingredients but, rather than waste expensive ingredients, served the cake anyway, much to customers' delight.

GOOEY BUTTER CAKE

In a bowl cream 1 c. sugar, ⅓ c. vegetable shortening, 3 T. butter, 1 T. dried milk powder, 1 large egg, a few drops yellow food coloring, and a pinch of salt. Add ¼ c. bread flour, ¼ c. cake flour, ¼ t. vanilla extract, 1 T. light corn syrup, and 2 T. water. Mix briefly just enough to blend ingredients. Take a 10-oz. Danish coffee cake and cut to fit an 8-by-8-in. buttered pan, leaving a rim around the edge of the pan. Pour the butter mixture over the cake. Bake for 30 min. in a 375° oven. Sprinkle with confectioners' sugar. Makes 8–10 servings.

goose. Any of a variety of wild or domesticated large birds of the family Anatidae, especially of the genera *Anser* and *Branta.* The word is from Old English *gōs.*

Geese were plentiful in the New World, but they have never been successfully mass-marketed and must be raised on small farms or taken in the wild, where the following species are found: "Canada goose" (*Branta canadensis*); "brant" (*B. bernicla*), a western subspecies of which is the "black brant"; "emperor goose" (*Philacte canagica*); "white-fronted goose" (*Anser albifrons*); "snow goose" (*Chen caerulescens*); and "Ross's goose" (*Chen rossii*).

Geese are almost always roasted but have never achieved much popularity with Americans.

goozlum. Also "googlum." Slang term for a gravy, sauce, or other viscous food. The etymology is unknown but possibly refers to the "oozing" quality of such a food. The term dates in print to 1911.

gordos. Also, "gordas." A trapper's term for wheat pancakes. But Blanche and Edna V. McNeil in *First Foods of America* (c. 1936) indicate that gordos were made from chiles, meat, frijoles, avocados, and masa, while "gorditas" ("little fat ones" in Spanish) are masa cakes made with cheese, chili, and avocados.

gorp. As a verb, to eat noisly or greedily, a meaning found in print since 1913. As a noun, "gorp" refers to a mixture of dried fruit, seeds, nuts, and chocolate chips used as high-energy food for athletes, particularly hikers and mountain climbers, a meaning known in print since 1968. "Glop" and "goop" are similar terms used to describe such foods.

goulash. Also "Hungarian goulash." A Hungarian-American stew of meat and vegetables seasoned with paprika. The Hungarian word is *gulyás,* which originally meant "shepherd," then was synonymous with the kind of stew. Its first printed reference in English was in 1865, as "Hungarian goulash" to 1950. It may be made with beef, veal, lamb, or chicken. The FDA requires canned or packaged goulash to contain at least 25 percent meat.

GOULASH

Brown 2 lb. beef in ¼ c. butter or lard. Add 2 chopped onions and sauté until golden. Add 1 c. beef stock, 1 t. salt, 1 t. paprika, and, if desired, 1 chopped green pepper. Cover and cook for about 1 hr., then add 6 small peeled potatoes. Continue cooking until meat and potatoes are tender. Serve with buttered egg noodles.

go south. Restaurant cook's slang for food that is beginning to spoil.

graham flour. An unsifted whole-wheat flour containing the bran of the wheat kernel (1825). It is named after Reverend Sylvester Graham (1794–1851), a tenacious advocate of temperance, healthy nutrition, and the virtues of home baking with this kind of flour. So influential was Graham's theory that he and his followers' appearance in Boston drew a protesting group of local bakers who were routed only after Graham's people had pelted the demonstrators with lime.

Graham set up "Graham hotels" serving strictly controlled meals quite in line with the belief of the temperance movement that food should not contain any stimulants or seasonings that might enflame the blood. Graham began his crusade in 1830, and within four years people were talking of "Graham bread." By 1882 a flat, slightly sweet cookie called a "graham cracker" was well known, and the cookbooks of the nineteenth century always included recipes for such foods made with graham flour.

Graham's legacy survives today mostly in the form of the cookies named after him and graham-cracker crust, a pastry crust that is used often in lemon-meringue pies, Key lime pies, cheesecakes, and other confections. Graham crackers made by Nabisco Brands, Inc., of East Hanover, New Jersey, have long been one of America's most popular cookies.

grape. Any of a large number of species of fruit berries from vines in the genus *Vitis*, 90 percent of which are vinifera grapes, a species encompassing at least five thousand varieties. The word is from the Germanic.

The earliest colonists found America abundant with wild grapes. In fact, it has been estimated that North America has 50 percent of the world's wildgrape species, including *V. labrusca*, with its characteristic "foxy" taste and aroma, and *V. rotundi folia*, the MUSCADINE grape.

The settlers on the eastern coast immediately set to make WINE from the native grapes, but found that their own European vinifera vines fared poorly. On the western coast, however, the Spanish missionaries successfully introduced vinifera varieties and made a great deal of wine from the 1780s onward. In the nineteenth century many new varieties were imported to California, and these thrived until the blight of *Phylloxera vastatrix* hit in the 1870s and devastated many vineyards, as it had in Europe before the vines were grafted onto resistant American roots.

In those same years a grape industry had been building in New York and the West, providing table grapes, jellies, jams, preserves, juices; and raisins. The most popular table-grape varieties include "Almeria," "Calmeria," "Cardinal," "Emperor," "Italia," "Muscat of Alexandria," "Ribler," "Thompson Seedless," and "Tokay." Most grape juice, jelly, jams, and preserves are made with "Concord" grapes, a labrusca hybrid. Most raisins are made from either Thompson Seedless or Muscat of Alexandria.

Garden-variety grapes include: the "mustang" or "winter" grape (*V. candicans*), the "post-oak" or "turkey grape" (*V. lincecumi*), the "little mountain" (*V. berlandieri*), the "sweet mountain" (*V. monticola*), the "frost" or "sour" grape (*V. cordifolia*), the "sweet winter" or "ashy" grape (*V. cinerea*), the "adobeland" or "dog ridge" grape (*V. champini*), the "Texas Panhandle" large grape (*V. doaniana*), the "solonis," "bush," or "gulch" grape (*V. longii*), the "sand bush," "sugar," or "rock" grape (*V. rupestris*), and the "riverside" or "riverbank" grape (*V. riparia*).

In 1869 a Methodist prohibitionist named Dr. Thomas B. Welch of Vineland, New Jersey, developed a method of pasteurizing and bottling grape juice that would not ferment. For a long while he sold this beverage locally to church groups as "Dr. Welch's Unfermented Wine" as a curative for all sorts of maladies. Then, after the onset of Prohibition, his son Charles promoted what he called "Welch's Grape Juice" with great success, and by 1923 his company was making grape jelly, which itself became an American best-selling product and the common basis for a peanut-butter-and-jelly sandwich. Today the Welch's company is owned by a cooperative of New York State grape growers and is headquartered in Concord, Massachusetts.

Americans consumed per capita 8 pounds of fresh grapes and nearly 12 pounds of processed grapes in 1997.

grapefruit (*Citrus paradisi*). Also called "pomelo." A tropical tree bearing a yellow, globular fruit that grows in grapelike clusters that give it its name, first mentioned in print in 1805 in *Hortus Jamaicensis* by John Lunan, who also noted that the fruit had the flavor of a grape. The fruit was originally confused with the true pomelo (or pummelo), known taxonomically as *C. grandis*, which was also called the "shaddock" after an English captain named Shaddock brought seeds from Indonesia to Barbados in 1696. But the grapefruit that Lunan described was not the pomelo, although it may have been a mutant of it.

The grapefruit was introduced to Tampa, Florida, in 1823 by a French count named Odette Philippe, but it achieved no gastronomic notice until well into the nineteenth century, when the first shipments of the fruit were made to northern markets. The first commercial plantings in Florida were in 1885, and by 1900 the grapefruit had taken on some interest as an alternative to oranges, and, with the introduction of the "Marsh Seedless" variety, it became all the more attractive as a breakfast fruit. In 1924 the pink-fleshed "Thompson Seedless" was marketed, followed five years later by a red variety named "Red Blush." The "Ruby Red," originally discovered as a bud mutation on a Thompson pink tree, is one of the most popular of the pink-fleshed grapefruits and is the primary variety grown in Texas.

Today the United States produces between 75 percent and 90 percent of the world's crop, mostly in Florida (3.6 billion pounds), the rest in California, Arkansas, and Texas. More than half of the crop is canned or made into fruit juice or frozen concentrate. Grapefruit is eaten fresh and, occasionally, broiled with sugar.

grape pie. A pie made from eastern grapes of the labrusca variety and its hybrids. This pie in some form was originally made by the Indians living along the vine-rich regions of Canandaigua Lake in New York, and it is rarely made anywhere else in the United States.

grasshopper pie. A dessert pie made with green crème de menthe cordial, gelatin, and whipped cream. It derives its name from the green color of the cordial. The pie is popular in the South, where it is customarily served with a cookie crust, and probably dates from the 1950s.

GRASSHOPPER PIE

Crumble 1 ½ c. chocolate cookies very fine, combine with ¼ c. melted butter and ⅛ t. cinnamon. Press into buttered pie pan to create a thin crust. Sprinkle 1½ t. unflavored gelatin over ⅓ c. milk and mix. Stand bowl in double boiler and dissolve gelatin. Beat 4 egg yolks until thickened, beat in ¼ c. sugar, ¼ c. green crème de cacao, and blend completely. Stir in gelatin, chill mixture until quite thick, fold in 1 c. whipped cream, pour into pie crust, and chill overnight. Serve with a sprinkling of chocolate curls.

---

graveyard stew. Slang for any soft, easily digestible food, like milk toast, fed to sick people. The connotation is that such food is served to those near death. The term dates in print to 1911.

gravy. A sauce, usually flour-based, served with meat, poultry, and other foods. The word is from Middle English, "gravey," from Old French *grave,* which, according to the *American Heritage Dictionary,* is a misreading of *grane,* perhaps "(dish) seasoned with grains," from *grain,* "spice." In America "gravy" is a more common term than "sauce" or "sop" (which may indicate a basting sauce) and has been in print since the middle of the nineteenth century. By 1900 the word had metaphoric connotations of money obtained with little or no effort, so that to be on the "gravy train" was to acquire money gratuitously, often through political graft.

The FDA requires processed gravy to contain at least 25 percent meat stock or broth or at least 6 percent meat.

grayling (*Thymallus arcticus*). Also, "Arctic grayling." A cold-water fish found throughout the Arctic and northern United States, where it has been widely introduced. The name of the fish, first used in the fifteenth century, comes from its color. Although graylings are no longer marketed commercially, they were from 1860 to 1880 the mainstay of the diet of the lumberjacks in Michigan, when, according to A. J. McClane in *The Encyclopedia of Fish Cookery* (1977), "enterprising merchants hauled them away by the wagonload to feed lumber camps, or down the Au Sable and Lake Huron in the live wells of houseboats to supply restaurants of Detroit and Chicago." Ecological and climatic changes have decreased the fish's population considerably, so that today the grayling is mainly a sport fish.

grazing. An early 1980s synonym for snacking or for eating small portions of many foods, usually at a restaurant, some of which were called "grazing restaurants." The activity may take place at various times throughout the day instead of at regular mealtimes. Grazing is also sometimes called "modular eating."

greasy spoon. A cheap restaurant serving low-quality food. The connotation is that such a place has poor sanitation and uses a good deal of grease in the kitchen. The term dates in print to 1918.

Green Goddess. A salad or salad dressing made

from anchovies, mayonnaise, tarragon vinegar, and other seasonings. The salad was created at San Francisco's Palace Hotel (now the Sheraton-Palace) in the mid-1920s at the request of actor George Arliss (1868–1946), who was appearing in town in William Archer's play *The Green Goddess* (which had opened in New York in 1921 and was twice made into a motion picture [1923 and 1930] starring Arliss).

The following recipe is from the Sheraton-Palace:

GREEN GODDESS

Mince 8–10 anchovy fillets with 1 green onion. Add ¼ c. minced parsley, 2 T. minced tarragon, 3 c. mayonnaise, ¼ c. tarragon vinegar, and ½ c. cut chives. Chop romaine, escarole, and chicory and mix together dressing and greens in a bowl that has been rubbed with garlic. The salad may be topped with chicken, crab, or shrimp.

greenings. Also "greens." The tops of leafy vegetables or the vegetables themselves, in print since 1940.

green lamb. Rancher term for a newborn lamb.

greenling (family Hexagrammidae). Also, "sea trout." A fish of the Pacific that ranges from Baja California to the Aleutians, the two dominant species being the "kelp greenling" (*Hexagrammos decagrammus*) and the "painted greenling" (*Oxylebius pictus*). Greenlings are often made into steaks and broiled or grilled.

green meat. Rancher term for meat that has not been aged.

grenadine. A sweet syrup with a deep red color and the flavor of pomegranates, from which it takes its name (French *grenadier*). Grenadine may be bought with a small amount of alcohol (about 5 proof) or with no alcohol, and it is used both as a sweetener and coloring for cocktails. The first printed English reference was in 1700.

grillade. A dish of veal or beef round braised with seasonings and served with grits. It is, in fact, usually referred to in Louisiana as "grillades and grits" and is a specialty of that region, especially for Sunday brunch. *Grillade* is a French term meaning "broiled meat," usually ham, but veal or beef are more usual in America. The term first appeared in print in 1650.

GRILLADE

Pound 2 lb. veal or beef that has been cut into pieces about 2–3 sq. in. and brown in 2 T. oil, then remove. Brown 1⅓ T. flour in the same amount of hot oil to make a roux, add 1 T. oil, brown 1 chopped onion, ½ chopped green pepper, 1 chopped celery stalk, 2 cloves minced garlic, a pinch of thyme, 2 t. chopped parsley, and ⅛ t. cayenne pepper. Add 1 coarsely chopped tomato that has been peeled and seeded, stir in 1 ½ c. water, salt, and pepper, bring to a boil, then simmer for about 10 min. Add meat, cover, and simmer until meat is cooked through and tender. Serve with grits.

grits. Finely ground dried, hulled corn kernels that are prepared in a variety of ways as a side dish, pudding, soufflé, and breakfast food. Grits are a form of HOMINY and, especially when cooked, are often called "hominy grits." The word is from Old English "grytt," for "bran," but the Old English word "greot" also meant something ground. Americans have used the word "grits" at least since the end of the eighteenth century.

Grits have been called an "institution" in the South, but they are rarely encountered in the North. Satisfying and filling, grits are a traditional southern breakfast food, but they are just as often served as a side dish. GRILLADES and grits is a Louisiana specialty of braised meat and buttered grits. "Shrimp and grits" is a Carolina dish.

BOILED GRITS

Soak ½ c. grits in 1 c. cold water overnight. Add ½ t. salt, ½ c. cold water, heat and stir until boiling, then lower heat to simmer and stir. Cover and let thicken, adding some more hot water to keep consistency from getting too thick. Serve with butter.

GRITS SOUFFLÉ

Heat 1½ c. water with 1 c. milk, add ½ c. grits, add 4 beaten egg yolks, and stir until thickened. Cool, then add ¼ c. Parmesan cheese, Tabasco sauce, and salt and pepper to taste. Fold in 4 stiffly beaten egg whites, pour into buttered soufflé dish, and bake at 425° for about 30 min.

grog. A mixture of hot water and rum, often with the

addition of spices and citrus fruit (1770). The name supposedly derives from a British admiral named Edward Vernon (1684–1757), whose nickname was "Old Grog" and who tried to prevent scurvy among his crew by giving them a rum-and-water mixture, a concoction that did nothing for scurvy but warmed the seamen's souls and gave the world "Old Grog's drink."

The United States Navy, following the British Navy's lead, included in the sailors' rations "one half pint of distilled spirits per day," and this was usually served from a "grog tub," kept locked away until seven bells, when the master's mate pumped the spirits and water into it.

On land grog became a very popular stimulant among workers in the iron mills of the Northeast and was an ordinary drink for others. Americans usually sweetened the grog with molasses, which gave it the name "blackstripe," a variation on "blackstrap," which was a cold mixture of molasses and rum in New England.

"Grog blossoms" are a slang term, dating in print to 1791, for the broken blood vessels in the nose caused by too much alcohol.

GROG

In a heated mug combine 1 oz. rum, 1 t. molasses, and top with boiling water.

---

grouper (family Serranidae). A common name for a carnivorous member of the sea BASS family having over four hundred species. Only two genera of true groupers, *Epinephelus* and *Mycteroperca,* including about one hundred species, are of culinary interest. The name is from the Portuguese *garoupa,* its first printed mention in English being in 1671. In California the "rockfish" (*Sebastichthys*) is also called a grouper.

The groupers of culinary importance in North America include the "black grouper" (*Mycteroperca bonaci*); JEWFISH (*Epinephelus itajara*); "Nassau grouper" (*E. striatus*); "red grouper" (*E. morio*); "spotted cabrilla" (*E. analogus*); and "yellowmouth grouper" (*M. interstitialis*), the most common market species of the South and especially popular in the Carolinas and Florida. In Hawaii the deepwater hapu'upu'u (*E. quemus*) may be called a SEA BASS. U.S. commercial landings of grouper totaled 10.3 million pounds in 1997.

growler. A bucket or pitcher used to carry beer from

a tavern to one's home. The term appeared in the last quarter of the nineteenth century. The vessels, suggests Flexner in *I Hear America Talking* (1976), were so called "perhaps because they made a growling, grating sound when they slid across the bar."

grub. A colloquial expression for any kind of food, often heard in the West among cowboys, ranchers, miners, and loggers. The term is quite old, however, deriving from Middle and Old English words meaning "to dig" and suggesting a person who had to dig for roots to eat. As a slang term for food "grub" dates in print to 1659.

grunt. A very old Colonial dessert made with berries and a dough steamed in a kettle. In New England, the term (which dates in print to 1896) is often synonymous with the more widely used term SLUMP.

GRUNT

Cook 1 c. blackberries or blueberries in 1 c. water and ½ c. sugar for about 5 min. until soft, then place in a buttered mold. Sift 3 T. baking powder with 1½ c. flour and ¼ t. salt. Cut in 1 T. butter to make a coarse meal, then stir in ½ c. milk to form a dough. Place dough over berries, cover, and set in a kettle of boiling water to steam for about 1 hr. Serve with a hard or foamy sauce. Serves 6.

A grunt is also an American fish of the family Pomadasyidae, genus *Haemulon* and allied species, deriving its name from the grunting sound it makes. (It is not the same fish as the Dutch grunt [*Cyprinus gobio*].) The "pigfish" (*Orthopristis chrysopterus*) is a species of eastern American grunt, so called because of its piglike mouth. So, too, is the "sargo" (*Anisotremus davidsonii*), abundant in Pacific waters, a species of grunt. The "margate fish" (*H. album*) probably named after Margate, England, is found in Florida waters, although other species also take this name. The first mention of the grunt was in 1713 as the "Gray Grunt" in *Synopsis Piscium.*

"Grunt" is also a slang expression from the Old West meaning pork or ham, sometimes bacon. "Cluck and grunt" would be eggs and bacon, imitating the sounds made by the animals who provide them. Finally, "grunt" is a slang term from the late 1940s meaning a check or bill for a restaurant meal.

guacamole. A dip made from avocados and chile pepper. Guacamole is a staple of Tex-Mex and

Mexican-American menus (the word is from Mexican Spanish via Nahuatl *ahuacamolli,* "avocado sauce") and became especially popular in the 1960s and 1970s as an appetizer at parties and buffets. The first printed reference to the word in English was in 1915.

GUACAMOLE

Remove the pits from 2 avocados and mash the flesh with 2 t. lime juice, ½ t. salt, 2 chopped scallions, ½ chopped and seeded tomato, 1 minced garlic clove, a minced green chile or pickled jalapeño, and ½ t. coriander. Serve with corn chips or over lettuce leaves as a salad.

---

gum. A variety of thickening agents and stabilizers, such as guar, locust bean, arabic, ghatti, karaya, tragacanth, and others, used in ice cream, beverages, puddings, salad dressings, candy, and other foods. See also CHEWING GUM.

gumbo. A Louisiana soup or stew usually containing okra and any of a variety of meats, seafood, and vegetables. The dish reflects the influence of an amalgam of cultures, including those of the Indians of the region, the French and Spanish settlers, and the African slaves who gave it its name (from the Bantu *gombo,* akin to Umbundu *ochinggombo,* okra). The word "gumbo" first appears in American print in 1795, and throughout the nineteenth century the dish is mentioned with affection and relish. "Gumbo" sometimes referred to okra itself (a usage cited in 1859) and by 1823 people also spoke of "gumbo filé" (or "filé gumbo"), which was a gumbo thickened with filé powder (ground sassafras leaves) as used by the Choctaw Indians.

There are several forms of gumbo, incorporating meats and vegetables, vegetables alone, shrimp and crawfish, and, usually, okra pods. There is no such thing as an "authentic" gumbo, except that the tastes of such dishes seem to share a common heritage of heartiness. Even "gumbo z'herbes" (a corruption of the French, *aux herbes,* "with herbs"), traditionally served on the meatless Maundy Thursday, is usually described as containing only vegetables, but the "Gumbo aux Herbes" recipe given in the esteemed

volume, *The Picayune's Creole Cook Book* (1900), contains veal brisket and ham. Gumbo z'herbes also traditionally contains seven greens for good luck.

Gumbo Ya-Ya (dating in print to 1941) is a Creole expression meaning a group of women who are all talking at once or something that is all mixed up, a meaning that lends itself to various gumbo recipes.

SEAFOOD GUMBO

(From the Gumbo Shop restaurant in New Orleans): Peel and devein 3 lb. shrimp and chill. Boil shrimp shells and 1 ham bone in 2 qt. water to make a stock. In a skillet sauté 1 qt. okra cut into small pieces in 1 T. oil for about 3 min. In a large kettle make a roux with ⅔ c. oil and ½ c. flour, add 2 chopped onions, 1 chopped bell pepper, 2 chopped celery stalks, 2 chopped garlic cloves, and ¼ c. chopped parsley, and sauté until tender. Add one 16-oz. can stewed tomatoes, cook 15 min., then add sautéed okra, the ham-and-shrimp stock, 2 small boiled crabs broken in quarters, salt and pepper, 2 bay leaves, 2 T. Worcestershire sauce, and ½ t. cayenne pepper. Bring to a boil, then simmer for 2 hr., stirring occasionally. Add shrimp and continue cooking until done. Serve over steamed rice.

---

gundinga. According to the *Dictionary of American Regional English,* this is a Northeast Florida term for a pudding made with sausages and innards, dating in print to 1949.

gyro. A Greek-American sandwich made from rotisserie-roasted, seasoned lamb that is sliced and served with onions in a pocket of pita bread. The word (which first appears in print in 1970) is from the Greek *gyros,* meaning a "turn," and is pronounced "JEER-o." The dish is better known in America than in Greece and possibly created in New York, where gyros are sold at Greek lunch counters and by street vendors, although some say it originated in the Pláka neighborhood of Athens. It is not a dish found in classic Greek cookery or listed in Greek cookbooks. It also seems possible that the name "gyro" may have some association with the Italian-American sandwich called the HERO.

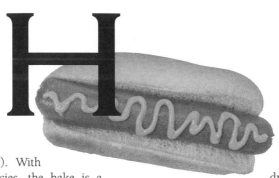

H

hake (Genus *Urophycis*). With more than a dozen species, the hake is a member of the cod family and is found in both eastern and western waters. The name is from Middle English. The two main species in the Atlantic are the "white hake" (*U. tenuis*), the "Silver hake" (*M. bilinearis*), also called "whiting" and "New England hake," and the "red hake" (*U. chuss*), also called "ling" and "squirrel hake," which when washed ashore in winter are picked up by people who live along the shore, who call them "frostfish." The Pacific hake (*Merluccius productus*) is abundant on the coast from Alaska to Baja California. U.S. commercial landings of Pacific hake totaled nearly 500 million pounds in 1997, with red, silver and white hake totaling 42 million pounds together.

halibut. A term used for two large flounders, *Hippoglossus hippoglossus*, a North Atlantic fish, and *H. stenolepis*, a North Pacific fish, as well as other flatfish. The Atlantic halibut is very large, reaching seven hundred pounds in weight, and is caught from Virginia to Greenland. It has firm white meat usually cut into fillets or steaks, and is sometimes smoked. The cheeks of the fish are particularly prized. The Pacific species swims in waters from central California to the Bering Seas, with most caught in Alaskan waters. The "California halibut" (*Paralichthys californicus*) is much smaller (up to sixty pounds) and generally cut into fillets. U.S. commercial landings of halibut in 1997 totaled 69.9 million pounds

halvah. Also, "halavah." A confection of mashed sesame seeds and honey. Halvah is of Turkish origin and was first sold in America at the turn of the century by Turkish, Syrian, and Armenian street vendors. (The word is from the Turkish *helve*.) The candy soon became a favorite of the Jewish immigrants in New York, and today halvah is still associated with Jewish delicatessens, even though one of the most popular commercial brands still depicts a turbaned Turk on its wrapper. The word was first printed in 1840.

Halvah is often sold in oblong bars from which slabs may be sliced according to one's request or in cellophane-wrapped smaller bars.

ham. The smoked or cured dried thigh of the hind leg of the hog. The word is from Old English.

Hams in America are cured in a variety of ways. Dry curing involves salting the meat heavily and allowing it to absorb the salt over a period of time. Sweet-pickle curing involves immersing the meat in a sweet brine. Injection curing, which is today the most common practice, involves a sweet-pickle cure coupled with injections of brine into the meat's interior in order to speed the process. After curing, the hams are then smoked (though not all hams are so treated), the degree of smoking differing from region to region and ranging from a few hours to many weeks. The woods used for smoking are usually hickory or maple, though some large companies use sawdust or liquid-smoke flavorings. Most hams are then cooked, either partially or fully, and carry labels such as "fully cooked," "heat-and-serve," and "ready-to-eat," meaning they require no further cooking and may be eaten straight from the can or wrapper. "Sugar-cured ham" is a term that entered the language in the 1830s.

The most popular hams are sold "boneless. "Bone-in hams" are sold whole, as shanks and rumps and center slices. "Half sections" are called "butt halves" or "shank halves," while "portions" are halves with center slices removed. "Semiboneless hams" have the shank and aitch bones removed but leave the round leg bone in.

Most hams are prepared "urban style"—that is, made on a large scale—resulting in meat that is less expensive, because the processing is shorter and less complicated, and, usually, blander in taste. The first canned hams in the United States were made in 1926 by George A. Hormel & Company. "Country hams" (first recorded in 1949) are salt-cured; in Kentucky they are called "old ham." "Country-style" hams or "country-cured" hams (first recorded in 1944) go through more complex curings and smokings in rural sections of Virginia, Georgia, Tennessee, Kentucky, Vermont, and other states, though the term denotes a ham merely made in the "style" of a true country ham.

The famous "Smithfield ham" is coated with salt, sodium nitrate, and sugar, refrigerated for five days, salted again, refrigerated again for one day per pound of meat, washed, refrigerated for another two weeks, smoked for ten days, and then aged six to twelve months. In order to carry a Smithfield label, a ham must be prepared in this manner in the town of Smithfield, Virginia, though the hogs may come from the surrounding area. This ham is sometimes called the "Virginia ham," but that name is more generally applied to a specific method of roasting a smoked ham, as given below. In the South ham steaks or ham slices are often served with REDEYE GRAVY made from the drippings.

"Scotch hams" once referred to hams produced in Scotland but now refer to uncooked, boneless, mildly cured hams sold in casings. PROSCIUTTO is a dry-cured ham of Italian origin. FDA regulations for ham labeling are as follows:

Ham—contains no added water and at least 20.5 percent protein after removal of fat.

Ham with natural juices—contains at least 18.5 percent protein.

Ham, water added—contains up to 10 percent added water, but at least 17 percent protein.

Ham and water product—contains any amount of water (amount must be listed).

hamburger. Also, "burger" and "beefburger." A grilled, fried, or broiled patty of ground beef, usually served on a "hamburger bun" and topped with ketchup, onions, or other condiments. Hamburgers, along with HOT DOGS, are considered the most identifiably American of food items, despite the German-sounding name. Certainly ground meat, served either raw or cooked, is not indigenous to America or Germany, but the name obviously derives from the German city of Hamburg, where some sort of pounded beefsteak was popular by the middle of the nineteenth century. *The Dictionary of American English* traces "Hamburg steak" to 1884 in an article in the *Boston Evening Journal*, but the term hamburger appeared on a menu from Delmonico's restaurant in New York believed to be printed in 1834. Residents of Hamburg, New York, have long claimed that the item was created in the summer of 1885 at the Erie County Fair when vendors Charles and Frank Menches ran out of pork with which to make sandwiches (the brothers supposedly first wanted to name the new item after Erie County).

By the 1890s "Hamburg" (or "Hamburgh") steak specifically referred not to a ground-meat patty but to

a piece of beef that had been pounded so as to tenderize the meat by breaking up the fibers. Both Oscar Tschirky in *The Cook Book by "Oscar of the Waldorf"* (1896) and D. A. Mary Johnson (Bailey) Lincoln in her *Boston Cook Book* (1896) refer to such a treatment, with fried onions enfolded by the edges of the meat, which was then broiled.

In one of the most widely used cookbooks of the day, *Mrs. [Sarah Tyson] Rorer's New Cook Book* (1902), however, Hamburg steak is described as beef put twice through a meat grinder and mixed with onion and pepper, which is close to the present concept of what a hamburger should be.

The first appearance in print of "hamburg" alone was in 1903, and, according to James Villas in *American Taste* (1982), a "hamburger steak" was featured at the 1904 Louisiana Purchase Exposition in St. Louis, Missouri. By 1912 ground-meat patties we now call "hamburgers" were being served in a soft yeast bun having the approximate shape of the patty itself, and soon the suffix "-burger" was attached to all sorts of other foods, such as "lamb," "chicken," "clam," and, the most famous and colloquially successful, "cheese" (known since at least 1938), which is a hamburger topped with a slice of American cheese that melts in the cooking process. *The Dictionary of American Slang* notes that the suffix came to mean "any hot sandwich served on a bun, often toasted, with many condiments. . . . Occasionally a 'burger' is associated with a famous person, event, or historic spot [such as the] Ike-burger[,] somewhat pop[ular] during [the] first presidential campaign of Dwight D. Eisenhower [1952]." Still, the word "-steak" was used with "hamburger" well into the 1920s. In his novel *A Farewell to Arms* (1929), Ernest Hemingway makes such a reference to World War I versions of the dish.

"Hamburger stands" came along with the opening of a chain of roadside restaurants called White Castles (the first in Wichita, Kansas, in 1921) and the popularity of the hamburger grew rapidly with the increase in the number of Americans traveling the roads in automobiles. White Castle hamburgers (and their imitators) steam-cooked their hamburgers, which were quite a bit smaller than other versions and were advertised with the slogan "Buy 'em by the Sack." Among White Castle's most devoted patrons these hamburgers became known affectionately as "sliders," "belly bombs," and "gut grenades."

By the 1930s the hamburger—now loaded down with "the works," that is, onion, pickles, ketchup, and other condiments—was a standard item in inexpensive restaurants, and without its roll took on haughty pretensions at high-class restaurants, where it was called "chopped steak." Some Americans were calling hamburgers "Wimpy burgers"—inspired by an insatiable hamburger addict named J. Wellington Wimpy from the Popeye comic strip drawn by Elzie Segar since 1919 and featured in movie cartoons after 1929. Even today "Wimpie" is a synonym for a hamburger in England, and there is a chain of Wimpy restaurants there and in the United States.

By the 1940s the hamburger was firmly entrenched as a quintessential American dish—beefy (though sometimes made with filler and usually with fat or gristle), easy to eat while on the move, and found almost everywhere in the country. In his annotations to H. L. Mencken's *The American Language* (1963), Raven I. McDavid, Jr., notes that "the ultimate horror, *Trumanburger* [after President Harry Truman (1945–53)], coined during the dying days of the meat rationing in 1946, consisted of mashed baked beans."

A fresh leap of popularity came in the 1950s with the opening of the McDonald's chain of hamburger stands in Des Plaines, Illinois. The first McDonald's however, was opened in San Bernardino, California, just before World War II. Modern, spanking clean, with an assembly-line efficiency and youthful atmosphere, these restaurants, immediately identifiable by their golden arches set outside the front-door parking lot, ushered in a new era of drive-in eating, featuring prepackaged hamburgers with the condiments already added. McDonald's spawned competitors like Burger King and Wendy's throughout the United States, and although such places sold other items, a "burger and fries" (with french-fried potatoes) is still the most common order.

Today hamburgers are just as likely to be made at home from beef patties or ground meat purchased at a market and broiled, fried, or barbecued and served year-round.

A "veggie burger" or "vegeburger" is a patty made from ground vegetables, then cooked like a hamburger and, usually, served on a bun. It dates to the 1970s and was particularly popular among vegetarians and HEALTH FOOD adherents.

Americans eat three hamburgers per week per person—about 38 billion annually—or 59 percent of all sandwiches consumed.

Hangtown Fry. A dish of oysters, eggs, and bacon supposedly concocted during the California Gold Rush of 1849 when a recently lucky miner brought a sack of gold to the Cary House Restaurant in Hangtown and ordered the most expensive meal in the place. When the chef suggested oysters and eggs—

which were very high-priced items at the time—the miner asked that bacon be added for good measure, and the dish gained local celebrity as the Hangtown Fry. (Hangtown, now called Placerville, got its name from the notoriety of several public hangings held during the Gold Rush days.)

HANGTOWN FRY

Dredge a dozen oysters in seasoned flour, then in a beaten egg, then in bread crumbs. Fry in butter, then add 8 beaten eggs, and cook until firm. Season with salt and pepper. Turn and cook on the other side. Serve with bacon. Serves 4.

---

happy hour. The period of one or two hours before dinner when people enjoy a cocktail or other beverage. It is very common that bars advertising a happy hour offer discounts on drinks in order to attract an after-work clientele. In April 1984 the army chief of staff, General John A. Wickham, Jr., ordered the end of happy hours at U.S. military base clubs and service-sponsored social events, citing such promotion of liquor as "not consistent with Army policies and programs to eliminate alcohol-related problems." Several states in the 1980s also banned the idea of happy hours.

The term "happy hour," which first saw print in 1961, refers back to the connotation (used as early as the 1920s) of "happy" as meaning slightly intoxicated.

hard sauce. A dessert topping made with butter, confectioners' sugar, eggs, and vanilla, dating in print to 1880.

HARD SAUCE

Cream ¼ lb. butter with 1 lb. confectioners' sugar. Blend in 2 beaten eggs, then add 1 t. vanilla, and, if desired, rum or brandy to taste. To make a "foamy sauce," cream the butter with ½ lb. confectioners' sugar and slowly add 1 beaten egg and ¼ c. hot water. Flavor with vanilla and, if desired, rum or brandy, and heat over hot water until thickened. Serve warm.

---

hardtack. Also, "sea biscuit," "sea bread," "ship biscuit," and "pilot bread." A hard biscuit made with flour and water but no shortening or yeast. The word is a combination of "hard," for the firm consistency of the biscuit, and "tack," an English word meaning "food." The first mention of hardtack in print was in

1830, but in 1833 there was mention of "soft tack," referring to loaves of bread.

Hardtack was long part of the staple diet of English and American sailors, because of its ability to keep for lengthy periods of time at sea.

Other, more recent slang terms for hardtack include "hard Tommy," "artillery," "dog biscuits," "jawbreakers," and "pantile," the last being the name of a roofing tile. Hardtack and molasses is called "dandy funk."

hartshorn. A source of ammonia used in baking cookies or, as "salt of hartshorn," as smelling salts. Once the word meant literally the ground horn of a hart's (male deer's) antler, but ammonium carbonate was later used as a substitute, which also went by the name of "salt of hartshorn." This is still available in American pharmacies and used occasionally in making cookies. "Hartshorn jelly" is a nutritive jelly once made from hartshorn and later from calves' bones.

Harvard beets. A dish of beets cooked in vinegar, sugar, and cornstarch. The name probably comes from the deep crimson color of the cooked beets, similar to the color of the Harvard football team's jerseys. The dish is more than fifty years old, but its origins are still unknown. A letter to *The New York Times* on the subject (January 13, 1982) insisted that the dish was conceived at a seventeenth-century English tavern called Harwood's, whose customers included a Russian emigré who, in 1846, opened up a restaurant in Boston under the same name. But the emigré kept pronouncing his establishment's name more like "Harvard," so the dish he brought from England became known as "Harvard beets."

HARVARD BEETS

Gently wash a dozen beets and simmer until tender, about 40 min. Drain and chop up or dice. Mix together ½ c. sugar, 2 t. cornstarch, and ½ c. vinegar, and bring to a boil, then simmer for 5 min. Pour over the beets and reheat, then toss with 2 T. butter.

"Yale beets," of even more obscure origins, are boiled beets prepared exactly as above except for the substitution of 1/2 c. orange juice and 1 T. lemon juice for the vinegar.

Harvard cocktail. A drink whose name derived from Harvard University in Cambridge, Massachusetts, probably in the 1930s after Prohibition ended.

HARVARD COCKTAIL

Shake together with ice ¾ oz. brandy, ¾ oz. sweet vermouth, a dash sugar syrup, and 2 dashes orange bitters. Strain into chilled cocktail glass.

Harvey restaurants. Originally, eating houses opened at the Atchison, Topeka & Santa Fe Railway stations throughout the Southwest by Englishman Frederick Henry Harvey, who came to the United States in 1850 at the age of fifteen to work on the railroads. Appalled at the conditions under which the workers and travelers had to eat, he opened a clean dining room with good food and varied menus above the Topeka, Kansas, station in 1876, and convinced the railway to open a restaurant at each of their depot towns along the route. By 1887 there was a "Harvey House" every hundred miles along the twelve-thousand-mile line. The establishment of a Harvey House restaurant in a depot had a civilizing effect on these rudimentary towns, and the importation of well-groomed, well-mannered waitresses called "Harvey Girls" had the further effect of bringing tens of thousands of prospective brides and mothers to the West, and the Harvey Girls became part of American folkore, as exhibited in the 1946 Metro-Goldwyn- Mayer musical motion picture *The Harvey Girls*.

"Where the name Fred Harvey appears," wrote bohemian philosopher Elbert Hubbard in 1901, "the traveling public expects much. It may be on the desert of Arizona, a hundred miles from water, but if it is a Fred Harvey place, you get filtered spring water, ice, fresh fruit and every other good thing you can find at the same season in the best places in New York City or Chicago. How the miracle occurs, you do not know— it is a Fred Harvey concern—that is enough."

By the time of his death in 1901 Harvey ran fifteen hotels, forty-seven lunch and dining rooms, and thirty dining cars. By 1928 there were "Harvey diners" and, by 1941, "Harvey House restaurants." By 1930 the company was serving 15 million meals each year. But with the decline of the railroads after World War II, the Harvey restaurants declined, too, although their partnership with the Sante Fe Railroad lasted until 1968.

Harvey Wallbanger. A cocktail that supposedly originated at Pancho's Bar in Manhattan Beach, California, and was named after a late-1960s surfboard enthusiast named Harvey, who consoled himself after the loss of a tournament with several of these cocktails, which thereupon caused him to bang into the wall on his exit.

The name and drink are now a trademark of "21" Brands, Inc., which is the importer of Galliano liqueur, which introduced the cocktail in 1970.

HARVEY WALLBANGER

Shake together with ice 2 oz. vodka, ½ T. Galliano, 4 oz. orange juice, and ½ t. sugar, pouring the mixture over ice cubes in a glass and floating some Galliano on top. Some prefer to omit the sugar.

hash. A dish of chopped pork or beef combined with various chopped-up vegetables and seasonings. Hash is generally considered an odds-and-ends kind of dish and was thought of as such when the word first came into English in the mid-seventeenth century, from the Old French word *hacher,* "to chop," after which it was soon found in America to describe a form of shepherd's pie or other mélange of meat and vegetables. A recipe for "chicken hash" was printed in *Rector's Oyster House* in 1897.

By the middle of the nineteenth century hash became associated with cheap restaurants called "hash houses" or "hasheries" (an 1850 menu from the Eldorado Hotel in Hangtown, California, lists "Low Grade Hash" for seventy-five cents and "18 Carets Hash" for a dollar) and the workers in such places were called "hash slingers." By the turn of the century "corned beef hash" was being ordered, sometimes called "cornbeef Willie." By the 1930s the curious jargon of lunch counters and diners was referred to as "hash house Greek" owing to the large numbers of Greeks who owned such establishments.

haupia. A Hawaiian dessert pudding made with coconut and sugar, dating in print to 1955. The name is from the Hawaiian.

HAUPIA

In a saucepan combine 3 c. frozen coconut milk that has been thawed out (or 2 c. fresh coconut milk mixed with 1 c. water) and ½ c. sugar. Gradually add ½ c. cornstarch, blending carefully, then add 1 t. vanilla and a pinch of salt. Cook over medium heat, stirring constantly, until thickened. Pour into buttered cake pan and refrigerate overnight. Cut into squares and serve.

Hawaiian food. The food of Hawaii is a diverse blend of all the island and mainland cuisines, especially those of Polynesia, Japan, China, and Korea, wed to Portuguese and American tastes. Hawaii was settled by Polynesians who themselves derived from the Indomalayan region. Except for the bat (*'ope'ape'a*), which was inedible, Hawaii had no indigenous animals, and all present animals on the islands were at one time or another brought to Hawaii. These included the DOG (*'ilio*), which was bred for food, the pig (*pua'a*), domesticated fowl (*moa*), and other animals.

Fish, which is a mainstay of the Hawaiian diet, was plentiful in the island waters, and every species was eaten, for no poisonous fish existed in the region. TURTLE (*honu*), porpoise (*nai'a, nu'ao, pahu*), sperm whale (*palaoa*), octopus (*he'e*), squid (*muhe'e*) CRAYFISH (*ula*), CRABS (*papa'*), SHRIMP (*'opae*), yellowfin TUNA (*'ahi*), wahoo (*ono*), red MULLET (*moana*), and pink SNAPPER (OPAKA-PAKA) were relished by the natives.

Wild plant foods were numerous and included the "tree fern" (*hapu'u*), the "wild raspberry" (*'akal*), "lambs'-quarters" (*'aweoweo*), and seaweed (LIMU), while other plants were introduced into the region, such as COCONUT (*niu*), breadfruit (*'ulu*), BANANA (*mai'a*), TARO (*kalo*), SWEET POTATO (*'uala, uwal*), YAM (*uhi*), Polynesian arrowroot (*pia*), and sugarcane (*ko*).

Taro was easily the most important staple of the Hawaiian natives, and today it is still pounded into a thick, fermented paste called POI.

Hawaiian agriculture has made fruit and nuts one of the state's most important industries, with pineapple, papayas, and macadamia nuts the major exports.

The "luau" is a Hawaiian feast of some dimensions, and the featured dishes are often poi, LOMILOMI SALMON, and KALUA PIG cooked in a covered, smoky pit.

Hawaiian snacks are varied among CRACKSEEDS of dried fruit, MALASADOS (a Portuguese-inspired doughnut), and MANAPUA (a stuffed yeast-dough bun). A traditional dessert of the state is HAUPIA, a kind of gelatinous square pudding made from fresh coconut milk and cornstarch.

Hawaiians drink the same beverages as do the mainlanders, with the addition of indigenous beverages that include an abundance of fruit juices, drinks made with coconut milk, and Kona coffee, made from plantation beans on the island of Hawaii. There is some wine produced in Hawaii, both from grapes and from pineapple.

Hawaiian haystacks. A dish made of successive layers of rice, gravy, chow-mein noodles, shredded cheese, tomatoes, onions, celery, coconut, Mandarin oranges, and maraschino cherries, all of which resembles a haystack; the coconut lends a Hawaiian association to the name. It is especially popular with young people.

"Haystack" is also a term for several multilayered dishes, desserts, and cookies, especially those made with coconut.

hazelnut. The nut of any of a variety of shrubs or trees of the genus *Corylus*, especially the "American hazelnut" (*C. americana*), the "beaked hazelnut" (*C. cornuta*), and the "California hazelnut" (*C. californica*). The name is from the Old English *hoesel*.

The hazelnut is sometimes called the "filbert," because it supposedly ripens on Saint Philbert's Day, August 22.

Up until about 1940 most hazelnuts were imported to the United States from Sicily and Naples, but a native industry has since developed in Oregon, where the first trees were planted in Scottsburg in 1858 and whose 1000 growers produce 99 percent of the U.S. crop of between 20,000 and 39,000 tons annually from more than 3.6 million trees. The nuts are often ground or roasted to be used in pastries and desserts.

headcheese. A sausage made from a calf's or pig's head and molded in its own jelly and seasoned. Headcheese is usually served as an appetizer or, according to C. Major's *Dictionary of Afro-American Slang* (1971), as a lunch meat in African-American communities.

In England headcheese is called "brawn," from a Germanic word referring to flesh or muscle. In French, however, the item goes by the name *fromage de tête de porc*, "cheese of the pig's head." Both the French and American usages refer to the crumbly, cheeselike texture of the meat, and its first appearance in American print was in 1841.

health food. A vague term first used in 1882 to describe food that is supposedly healthier than most of the processed, packaged, or prepared food sold in the market. Sometimes "health food" is a synonym for "organic" or "natural foods," somewhat less vague terms that suggest foods grown or raised without any ADDITIVES, pesticides, or special treatment whatsoever, but the term covers a wide range of food items, from fresh vegetables and fruits to herb teas and vit-

amin supplements. In fact, the average "health food store," a trend of the 1960s, 1970s, and 1980s, holds shelves full of vitamin and mineral supplements, literature on various diets, and expensive grain cereals. Organic foods were popularized after 1948 by J. I. Rodale, publisher of *Organic Gardening and Farming* magazine.

The Federal Trade Commission has taken no position on the term "health food" (although it does monitor false claims for "healthfulness") but has proposed that such a phrase be prohibited in advertising food products, because that claim may cost the consumer more than twice what a food item without the "health food" label would.

heavenly hash. A dessert made of vanilla wafers and whipped cream popular in the Midwest.

HEAVENLY HASH

Beat 2 eggs with 1 c. confectioners' sugar and ½ c. butter, and mix with ½ pt. whipped cream and ¾ c. walnuts. Place a layer of vanilla wafer cookies in a pan, add the whipped cream mixture, then another layer of wafers. Chill until firm and serve with more whipped cream.

Herman. A Midwest colloquialism for a bread starter made with sugar or honey, often kept by families over decades. It is used to make sweet breads and coffee cakes. In *Real American Food* (1986) Jane and Michael Stern wrote, "Where did Herman come from and how did he get named? We have seen explanations that trace the first Herman starter back to Jesus and a certain Mount Herman in Israel; to Hermann, Missouri; and to a little girl in Richmond, Virginia, who simply wanted to give a silly name to her mommy's bubbly sourdough starter."

According to Harlene H. Watland and Dawn W. Johanson, editors of *The Herman Sourdough Herald* newsletter published in Cambridge, Minnesota, from 1980 to 1983, the origins of Herman are obscure, but many of their subscribers told them Herman starters had been in their families for generations.

HERMAN

In ½ c. tepid water dissolve 1 pkg. dry yeast. When foamy, blend in 2 t. honey or sugar, 2½ c. flour, and 2 c. water. Store in a large jar, cover with a damp cloth, and clasp with a rubber band. Let stand for 48 hr. Stir down

> *bubbles, refrigerate, and stir each day for 5 days. Mix together 1 c. flour, 1 c. milk and ½ c. sugar and add to the yeast mixture. On the tenth day remove 2 c. of starter for baking, add another flour-milk-sugar mixture, and keep going this way.*

hermit. A cookie containing raisins, cloves, and nutmeg. They are made with either sugar or molasses. The first printed reference dates to 1896, and the name may refer to the brown lumpy appearance of the cookie, like that of a hermit's robe. The cookies are sometimes called "Harwich hermits," suggesting they originated in Harwich, Massachusetts.

HERMIT

Cream ⅓ c. butter with ⅔ c. sugar. Add 1 beaten egg, then 2 T. milk. Add ⅓ c. chopped raisins. Sift together 2 c. flour, 2 t. baking powder, ½ t. cinnamon, ¼ t. powdered cloves, ¼ t. mace, and ¼ t. nutmeg. Add to raisin mixture and blend. Mold into a ball, cover with waxed paper, and chill for 2 hr. Roll out to about ¼ in. thickness. Cut into cookie rounds and bake for 15 min. in a 325° oven.

hero. Also, "hero sandwich," "hero boy " and "Italian hero sandwich," but see below for other variations. A loaf of Italian or French bread sliced lengthwise and filled with a variety of meats and cheeses, spices, lettuce, peppers, and other items. A meatball hero would contain meatballs and tomato sauce; a veal parmigiana hero would contain a breaded, fried veal cutlet, mozzarella cheese, and tomato sauce.

In the 1930s food writer Clementine Paddleford noted that the name derived from the hyperbole that one must be a hero to eat such a sandwich. In other parts of the country, however, the same item is known by other names. "Bombee" is heard in upper New York State. "Grinder" (first printed appearance in 1954), "Italian grinder," and "guinea grinder" ("guinea" is ethnic slur for an Italian) are used widely in New England and derives from the amount of chewing needed to "grind through." New Englanders also use "Italian sandwich" and, in Boston, "spuky." Also common in New England is "submarine," a term coined by grocer Benedetto Capaldo for the sandwich he made during World War II in Groton, Connecticut, which has long been a submarine base for the U.S. Navy.

"Wedge" (for the shape of the sandwich, usually cut at an angle) is another common alternative for hero, as is a "hoagie," most often associated with Philadelphia and New Jersey. There are several versions of the hoagie's origins. One holds that they were named after the Hog Island shipyard in Delaware County during World War I when many Italian immigrants worked there and ate such a sandwich at lunch. Another story credits Antoinette Iannelli, owner of Emil's restaurant in South Philadelphia, who said she created the first hoagie in 1936 for a policeman who'd had a fight with his wife and left the house without lunch. Before long she was making the sandwiches for policemen and shipyard workers at Hog Island. According to culinary historian William Woys Weaver, "hoagie" probably derives from "hokey-pokey," which referred both to a cheap form of ice cream sold by street vendors and to the vendors themselves, "hokey-pokey men." ("Hokey-pokey" may be a an American corruption of the Italian *O che poco*—"Oh, how little"—or a variant of hocus-pocus.) "Hoagie" dates in print to 1955.

In Chicago an "Italian beef sandwich" is made with thinly sliced beef and warm garlicky gravy served on Italian bread with sweet or hot peppers and, commonly, onions, carrots, and olives. In the South—especially in New Orleans—such an item is called a PO' BOY (since it is a relatively inexpensive item for a great deal of food) and made with thin slices of well-cooked meat such as shoulder roast in a rich gravy placed on a small, sliced French loaf with mayonnaise, tomatoes, and shredded lettuce. The most famous variant in that city is called the "peacemaker" or "la médiatrice," because in the nineteenth century husbands coming home late from the saloons would bring their wives a sandwich made with fried oysters and seasonings such as tartar sauce or cayenne.

A "Cuban sandwich" is a popular Cuban-American version made with pork, smoked ham, Swiss cheese, mustard, mayonnaise, pickles, and other condiments, while a "medianoche" (Spanish for "midnight") is served on an egg roll there. A Cuban sandwich made with turkey breast, creamed cheese, and strawberry preserves is called an "Elena Ruiz," named after a Cuban socialite.

Still another New Orleans version is the MUFFULETTA, made on a round loaf of bread specially baked in the local bakeries, and contains salami, provolone cheese, ham, minced garlic, and a mixture called "olive salad," made from chopped green olives, pimientos, chopped Greek olives, oregano, and parsley.

herring. Any of various fishes of the Clupeidae family, but especially *Clupea harengus*. The name "herring" is from Old English *haering*.

The herring is an important figure in European history; wars have been fought for control of its grounds, and there was even a Battle of the Herrings in 1429 at Rouvray, France, between the British and the French. The Hanseatic League dwindled in power with the decline of the herring in the Baltic, and by 1665 the Dutch raided St. John's, Newfoundland, to halt the English herring industry that had developed there. In America fishermen sought the fish both in the Atlantic and Pacific, and in 1877 United States fleets paid England $5.5 million for the rights to fish the waters of the Gulf of St. Lawrence and Newfoundland. The agreement was not supported by Newfoundland sailors, who proceeded to cut the herring nets of the Americans, which precipitated the Fortune Bay Riot.

Herrings come in all sizes, but the two main species for American consumption are the "Atlantic herring" (*C. harengus*), also called "sea herring," and "Pacific herring" (*C. pallasi*), both ocean fish. The "alewife" or "spring herring" (*Alosa pseudoharengus*) of the Atlantic coast spawns in freshwater streams and is of some commercial interest when smoked or pickled. A Hawaiian species called the "makiawa" (*Etrumeus micropus*), is about ten inches long (1926). U.S. commercial landings of herring in 1997 was 347.9 million pounds.

The following terminology for herring preparations are used in the United States:

Bismarck herring. Cured with its skin on in strong vinegar, this herring made from "schmaltz" fishes (see below) derives its name from a German process of the nineteenth century.

bloater. A golden, hot-smoked, dry-salted herring whose name derives from its swollen appearance.

hard-salted or hard-cured herring. A lean herring cured in salt alone.

kipper. A brined, air-dried, cold-smoked fat herring; the name probably comes from its copperlike color, which in Old English is *coper*.

pickled herring. In the United States this term refers to a herring in vinegar and spices, but elsewhere it refers to a dry-salted herring cured in brine or blood pickle.

rollmops. See main entry.

schmaltz herring. A herring containing at least 18 percent fat, but usually more, and filleted and traditionally served with sliced onions, boiled potatoes, and black bread. The word is from the German for "melted fat."

hibachi. A Japanese brazier using charcoal as its burning medium. The name is Japanese for "fire bowl." The hibachi became a faddish implement for cooking meats and fish in America in the 1960s. Ingredients are marinated in soy sauce and other seasonings and grilled over the open fire. The word "hibachi" dates in English to 1860.

hickory. Any of a variety of trees of the genus *Carya*, with seventeen species, thirteen of them native to North America. Of culinary importance is the native PECAN (*C. illinoiensis*), but the word "hickory" derives from a Virginia Indian name for a food made from crushed hickory nuts, *pawcohiccora*.

higdom. A pickling brine made with green tomatoes, onions, cabbage, peppers, and other condiments and spices. According to William Woys Weaver in *America Eats* (1989), "Higdom is one of those recipes, like Bordeaux pickle, that appears with great regularity in Victorian charitable cookbooks . . . [and] was once a popular feature of church suppers and picnics." The origins of the term are unknown.

highball. A cocktail served in a tall glass, usually containing a carbonated beverage. The term's origin is obscure, though some have suggested it derives from the railroad semaphore signal having a large ball on top that means "Go ahead," which dates back at least to 1880. The W.P.A. guide *Missouri* (1941) attributes its creation to The Planter's Hotel in St. Louis. By 1932 Americans were familiar with "highball glasses," and the Sears, Roebuck Catalog for 1944 sold them by that name.

hip flask. A slender container, usually made of metal, for holding liquor. Its shape made it easy to insert in one's hip pocket and keep out of sight during the days of Prohibition. The term first appeared in print in 1923.

historical flask. A molded glass flask, used to hold liquor, decorated with American emblems, symbols, and nationally known figures, such as presidents of the United States. Historical flasks first appeared in the early nineteenth century and came in the colors light green, aquamarine, amber, and, occasionally, olive amber.

hoarhound candy. Also, "horehound" and "slug." A candy, shaped as balls, drops, or squares made from hoarhound, an aromatic plant (*Marrubium Vulgare*), and often used as a lozenge for sore throats.

HOARHOUND CANDY

To 3 c. hot water add 3 oz. hoarhound and simmer for 20 min. Strain, then add 3½ lb. brown sugar and cook until the syrup reaches the hard-ball stage (265° on a candy thermometer). Pour into a buttered pan and cool, then cut into small balls or squares. Makes about 5 doz.

---

hobo egg. Slang term for an egg dish made on camping trips by cutting a hole in a piece of toast, setting it on a griddle, and frying an egg inside the hole. The term dates in print to 1980.

Hoboken special. Pineapple soda with a scoop of chocolate ice cream. The term refers to Hoboken, New Jersey, presumably for no other reason than that this 1920s drink was popular in that section of the country.

hockey puck. A slang term used to describe compact meats like hamburgers or filet mignons that have an overcooked, tough texture.

hogfish (*Lachnolaimus maximus*). Also, "hog snapper" and "Irish pompano." A fish of the wrasse family with a hoglike snout, found from Brazil to North Carolina and particularly popular in Florida (1590). North Carolinians also refer to the "pigfish" (*Orthopristis chrysopterus*), so called because of its grunting sound, as "hogfish."

holiskes. Used in the plural. A Jewish-American dish of stuffed cabbage leaves. The term, which dates in print to 1949, is from Yiddish.

home meal replacement. A food industry term for higher quality take-home foods, usually prepared on the premises of a supermarket or gourmet food store as opposed to frozen prepared meals.

hominy. Dried, hulled corn kernels cooked in a variety of ways in breads, puddings, and other preparations. It was one of the first foods European settlers readily accepted from the Native Americans, and the word, from one or another Algonquian words, such as *rockahominie* ("parched corn") or *tackhummin* ("hulled corn"), was used as early as 1620. Different terms describe hominy that has been treated or ground in different ways. "Great hominy," also called "whole hominy," "pearl hominy" (from its pearly appearance), and "samp" (from the Narraganset *nasàump*, "corn mush"), is coarsery ground and prepared by scalding shelled corn in water and wood ash to separate the hulls, called the "eyes." The corn is dried and then boiled until soft and porridgelike. Sometimes lye is used instead of wood ash, and this is often called "lye hominy." If the corn is ground more finely, or ground twice, the result is called "hominy grits" or, as is usual in the South, just GRITS.

Further grinding results in cornmeal. (Since grits are a major food item in the South, they are treated in more detail under the main entry.)

"Hogs and hominy" is an old southern dish of hominy and fried pork.

honey. A sweet liquid produced by bees from flower nectar. Honey, whose name comes from Old English *hunig,* was the first and most widespread sweetener used by man. About 80 percent of honey is sugar (mainly fructose and glucose). Worldwide about 1 million tons of honey are produced each year, most of it gathered from various flowers rather than a single variety.

America has always had many species of honey-producing bees, and Waverley Root in *Food* (1980) noted that the Spaniards found the Aztecs and Mayas consuming honey made by the species *Melipona beecheii.* But it was not until 1638 that honey was available to New England settlers, who had introduced the bee species *Apis mellifica* (possibly Italian or Dutch varieties), which the Indians called "English" or "white man's flies."

In *Food and Drink in America* (1981), Richard J. Hooker cited a chronicler's description of New York in 1670: "You shall scarce see a house, but the South side is begirt with Hives and Bees." By 1812 the honeybees had moved as far as Texas, where in 1821 Stephen F. Austin found a bee tree that provided his party with a gallon and a half of honey. In 1852 the Reverend L. Langstroth had invented the "movable frame hive," which made the collection of honey far easier than it had been, and, after the A. I. Root Company of Medina, Ohio, developed a roller press to make consistently thin wax foundation plates for the bees' hives, wide-scale honey production became feasible.

Today there are several hundred kinds of honey sold in the United States (one of the world's largest producers) in three basic forms: "comb," which comes straight from the hives; "chunk," which is bottled with bits of the honeycomb; and "extracted," which is usually pasteurized to prevent crystallization. Honey's flavor comes from the type of nectar used, and these may include, as James Trager lists in *The Enriched, Fortified, Concentrated, Country-Fresh, Lip Smacking, Finger-Licking, International, Unexpurgated Foodbook* (1970), "orange-blossom honey from Florida, raspberry honey and strong buckwheat honey from New Jersey, chewy dandelion honey from Colorado, tupelo honey from the swamps of Florida and Georgia, firewood honey (pale-gold and molasses-thick) from Oregon and Washington, river-willow honey from the banks of the Mississippi, . . . manzanita honey from California, sage-blossom honey from Arizona, gallberry honey from Georgia, hearts-ease honey from Illinois, tulip-tree honey from Maryland, linden honey from New York, anise-hyssop honey from Iowa, spearmint honey from Indiana, milky-white guajillo honey from Texas, and alergoba honey from Hawaii."

Americans consume about 1.1 pounds of honey per person annually. The United States is one of the world's largest producers of honey, with 212,000 beekeepers tending nearly 4 million hives. In 1998 the United States produced 221 million pounds of honey.

honeydew. A variety of muskmelon, *Cucumis melo,* having a pale, yellowish skin and light green flesh. Its name comes from the fragrant, sticky sweetness of its flesh. The word dates in print to 1570. The honeydew is a winter melon, first brought to America about 1900 and originally called the "French White Antibes."

hooch. Also, "hootch." A cheap whiskey. The term, which became widespread during Prohibition, has been cited back to 1895. It was derived from the name of a Chinook Indian tribe, the Hoochinoo, that made a form of distilled spirits bought by United States soldiers who had recently occupied the new Alaskan territory and who had been forbidden liquor by their government. By 1877 the soldiers were using the term "hoochinoo," which, in the Gold Rush era after 1896, was shortened to "hooch."

Hoosier cake. Also "Hoosier bait." A kind of rough-textured gingerbread. The association with Indiana (the "Hoosier state") was explained in *Bartlett's Americanisms* (1859): *"Hoosier Cake.* A Western name for a sort of coarse gingerbread, which, say the

Kentuckians, is the best bait to catch a hoosier with, the biped being fond of it."

hopping john. Also, "hoppin' John" and "happy John." A southern dish made of COWPEAS and rice, served traditionally on New Year's Day to ensure good luck for the year. The origin of the name is obscure, but several stories abide. One ascribes the name to the custom of inviting guests to eat with the request to, "Hop in, John." Another suggests it derives from an old ritual on New Year's Day in which the children in the house hopped once around the table before eating the dish. The first mention of the dish by name was in 1830.

In *Rice & Beans: The Itinerary of a Recipe* (1981), John Thorne suggests that the name is a corruption of *"pois à pigeon,"* a French term for "pigeon peas," which flourished in the Caribbean but not in the American South, resulting in an etymological dissolve into "hopping john." Whatever the origins of the name, the dish quite definitely was a staple of the African slaves who populated southern plantations, especially those of the Gulla country of South Carolina, and one will find similar dishes throughout the Caribbean. In Puerto Rico, for instance, such dishes are called *gandules,* while RED BEANS AND RICE is a staple of Louisiana cookery, just as black beans and rice (called *moros y christianos,* "Moors and Christians") is a famous Cuban dish. See also LIMPIN' SUZAN.

HOPPING JOHN

Rinse 1 c. dry cowpeas in 8 c. water and boil for 2 min. Remove from heat and let stand for 1 hr., then drain, reserving 6 c. of the cooking water. In a skillet sauté 6 pieces of bacon, 1 chopped onion, and 1 chopped clove of garlic, then stir in cowpea mixture. Season with salt and pepper and add cooking water. Stir in 1 c. rice, bring to a boil, then simmer for 1 hr., stirring occasionally. Serves 8.

---

horse (*Equus caballus*). A hoofed mammal up to five-and-one-half feet at the shoulder and weighing up to eleven hundred pounds. Horses were brought to America by the Spanish, and wild horses, called "mustangs" in the West, are all descendants of these domesticated herds. Because of the horse's utility for both the white and the red man from the beginning of American history, it was never used for food, except in times of starvation, and Americans continue to respect the horse for its beauty, strength, and herding abilities.

Horsemeat, then, is a rarity in the United States, though common in Europe and the Middle East, where American slaughterhouses send most of their available horsemeat. In fact, most of the sixteen American firms that sell horsemeat are owned by Europeans. Until recently it was illegal in many states to sell horsemeat.

horseradish (*Armoracia lapathifolia* and *A. rusticana*). A perennial plant of the mustard family cultivated for its roots, which produce a very pungent flavor and aroma when cut, shredded, or made into a paste. The word first appears in print as of about 1590, and probably derives from its connotation of being strong as a horse.

Just when the root was brought to America is not known, although it was once called "German mustard." The three principal horseradish-raising regions in the U.S. are around Silver Lake, Wisconsin, St. Louis, Missouri, and Tule Lake, California.

horse's neck. A strip of lemon or orange peel cut from the fruit in a continuous spiral and usually served as a garnish in a cocktail (1900). The term is also a euphemism for "horse's ass," but it had not been established when a drink by the name "horse's neck" first appeared. A nonalcoholic variety was made with just ginger ale and the lemon peel, but there are recipes that add bourbon, blended whiskey, or gin.

hot ball. Also "red hot," "fireball," and "hot dollar." A cherry- or cinnamon-spiced candy with a strong, hot flavor. It is a common candy in the Mid-Atlantic states and dates in print to the 1960s.

hot bird and a cold bottle. A double entendre used to describe those late-night pleasures sought out by young men-about-town in New York City during the period just before World War I. The "hot bird" referred both to a warm dish and to a woman of easy virtue; the "cold bottle" would usually be champagne.

hot bricks. A drink of whiskey, boiling water, and a ball of butter. Also called "stirrups," it was a drink of Louisville, Kentucky, now obsolete. "Hot bricks" was also a nineteenth-century term for something very dangerous.

hot brown. A sandwich of chicken, bacon, or ham with a cheese sauce, created at Louisville's Brown Hotel in the late 1920s.

hot dog. Also, "frankfurter," "frank," "wiener," "weenie," "wienie," "dog," and "red hot." "Tube steak" is a servicemen's term for a hot dog, which is a pork or beef sausage, sometimes skinless, served on a soft yeast roll.

The hot dog is, with the hamburger, considered one of the quintessential American food items—inexpensive, easy and fast to cook, readily purchased all over the country, and ideal for eating while standing up. Most Americans eat hot dogs with combinations of mustard, pickle relish, and sauerkraut. Sometimes the hot dog is eaten without the roll but with beans, a dish called "franks and beans."

The hot dog is either boiled, grilled, or fried, and in Baltimore some make split, deep-fried versions called "frizzled hot dogs." Today frankfurters are almost never made from scratch at home, though they are eaten in 95 percent of American homes, usually sold ready-to-eat but generally heated through by boiling or grilling in butter. Grilling hot dogs outside on a BARBECUE is a very popular method of cooking them, and American children enjoy inserting a stick through them and cooking them over an open fire. "Corn dogs" are fried with a cornmeal batter. A "Kansas dog" is served with mustard and melted cheese, while a "Chicago-style dog" comes in a poppyseed bun with several relishes. In delicatessens hot dogs are named for their sizes: "Regulars" are about six inches in length. Small frankfurters wrapped in puff pastry are called "pigs-in-a-blanket" and are served at cocktail parties or catered parties. "Lillies," short for "Lilliputians" (after the fictional city of Lilliput in Jonathan Swift's *Gulliver's Travels* [1726]) are about half the size of one's thumb. An "Irish frank" is made from corned beef.

A great deal of etymological research has gone into the term "hot dog" (1895), but there is still no certainty as to just who first used the words to describe the sausage, which in various forms had been a favorite of German Americans since the middle of the nineteenth century, when it was known as *Wienerwurst* from the German for "Vienna sausage." German immigrants in New York sometimes called smoked sausages *bundewurst* ("dog sausage") by 1845 in print. By 1904 hot dogs were also called "wieners," and by the 1920s people were attending "wienie roasts," parties at which the attendees roasted their own hot dogs over an open fire. The "frankfurter" (from the German city of Frankfurt) is reputed to have been introduced in St. Louis in the 1880s by a German immigrant named Antoine Feuchtwanger, who did popularize the roll the sausage came to be served in, but a crucial moment in the promotion of the item came in 1901 at New York City's Polo Grounds, where director of catering Harry Magely Stevens is reputed to have heated the roll, added the condiments, and exhorted his vendors to cry out, "Red hots! Get your red hots!" (Credit for the introduction of the heated roll in 1889 has also gone to Charles Feltman, owner of Feltman's Gardens in Brooklyn's Coney Island amusement park.) Stevens himself said the term "hot dog" was coined by Hearst sports cartoonist T. A. "Tad" Dorgan, who often caricatured German figures as dachshund dogs and who, by 1906, was drawing talking sausages in his newspaper's pages, playing off the suggestion that the cheap sausages sold at Coney Island and elsewhere contained dogmeat. So accepted was this myth of the sausages' contents that the Coney Island Chamber of Commerce in 1913 banned the use of the term "hot dog" from all signs there.

The greatest promotion of the item was at Nathan Handwerker's frankfurter stand at Coney Island called Nathan's Famous (today a franchise operation with many branches in the Northeast). The sausage became so associated with his concession that people began calling the item a "Coney Island" (a term reserved thirty years before for fried clams). By the 1920s "hot dog stands" were well known throughout the United States, and the hot dog had become one of American's favorite foods, particularly at sporting events, county fairs, and carnivals. Americans eat 14 billion hot dogs per year or 37 million a day, and the average person consumes eighty hot dogs per year. Most are consumed at home, about 15 percent purchased from street vendors, and 9 percent at ballparks. Nearly 90 percent are eaten with mustard.

July has been "National Hot Dog Month" in the United States since 1957.

hot fudge. A thick topping for ice-cream sundaes containing chocolate, butter, and sugar kept hot so as to have a slight melting effect on the ice cream. John Schumacher, owner of an ice-cream parlor in Los Angeles called C. C. Brown's, contends that hot fudge was invented by the original proprietor soon after opening the place in 1906. In the East credit for one of the region's first hot-fudge recipes has been claimed for Sarah Dow, who bought Bailey's ice-cream parlor in Boston in 1900 and started making the confection soon afterward.

HOT FUDGE

In a double boiler heat ½ c. milk, ¼ c. butter, and a dash of salt. Add 2 c. bittersweet chocolate and stir until smooth. Remove from heat, add 1 t. vanilla extract, and stir. Keep warm for serving.

---

hot sauce. Any of a number of commercially bottled seasoning sauces made with chile peppers, salt, and perhaps vinegar. Bottled cayenne-based sauces were known in Massachusetts by 1807, and by 1849 Lea and Perrins Worcestershire Sauce from England was being imported into New York. The most famous hot sauce is TABASCO Pepper Sauce, made by the McIlhenny Company as of 1859. One of the first was named after Maunsel White, a planter who brought slave-made hot sauce with him to the Gem Restaurant in New Orleans before the Civil War. Today hot sauces can have extravagant names, often based on the high degree of hotness or their origins, such as "Hawaiian Passion," "Texas Gunpowder," "Cajun Power," "Sweet Fire," "Inner Beauty," and "Jamaican Hellfire."

hot scotch. An alcoholic drink made with a little scotch whiskey and hot water, so called at least since 1882.

hot water. A Colonial-era term for distilled liquors.

house pie. A pie of cooked crushed apples, including the peel and core. It dates back to the mid-eighteenth century.

houska. A sweet yeast bread shaped into a braid. It is of Bohemian origins, and the word derives from the Czech, dating in print to 1952.

Hubbard squash (*Cucurbita maximus ohioensis*). Also, "Ohio squash." A winter SQUASH with a very thick, bumpy, green-to-orange skin and yellow-orange flesh, it was supposedly brought to America from the West Indies. The origin of the name was explained by James J. H. Gregory in a letter published in the December 1857 issue of the *Magazine of Horticulture*:

Upwards of twenty years ago, a single specimen was brought into [Marblebead, Massachusetts], the seed from which was planted in the garden of a lady, now deceased; a specimen from this yield was given to Captain Knott Martin, of this town, who raised it for family use for a few years, when it was brought to our notice in the year 1842 or '43. We were first informed of its good qualities by Mrs. Elizabeth Hubbard, a very worthy lady, through whom we obtained seeds from Captain Martin. As the squash up to this time had no speciflc name to designate it from other varieties, my father termed it the "Hubbard Squash."

huckleberry. Also, "dangleberry." Any of a variety of deep blue native American berries of a tree in the genus *Gaylussacia*, often confused with the blueberry (1660). The name may be a variation of "whortleberry."

Henry David Thoreau praised the huckleberry as among the finest fruits of the wild and cautioned interested eaters:

> *If you would know the flavor of huckleberries, ask the cow-boy or the partridge. It is a vulgar error to suppose that you have tasted huckleberries who have never plucked them. A huckleberry never reaches Boston; they have not been known there since they grew on her three hills. The ambrosial and essential part of the fruit is lost with the bloom which is rubbed off in the market cart, and they become mere provender.*

Those unfamiliar with the huckleberry and blueberry may have difficulty telling them apart, the latter having a softer texture and many tiny seeds. On the West Coast what is referred to as the "mountain huckleberry" is actually the "evergreen blueberry" (*Vaccinium ovatum*).

The "common huckleberry" (*G. resinosa*) is itself called the "black huckleberry," while the "bush huckleberry" (*G. dumosa*) is also called the "gopherberry." Like the blueberry, the huckleberry is most often eaten raw, in muffins, in breads, or in pies, this last called in slang "fly pie."

huevos rancheros. A Mexican dish of fried eggs set on tortillas and covered with a tomato-and-chile-pepper sauce. The dish has become a staple of Mexican-American menus, especially as a brunch or luncheon item. The name is from the Spanish for "ranch eggs" and, as "eggs ranchera," dates in print to 1932 in Sheilah Hibben's *National Cookbook*.

HUEVOS RANCHEROS

Briefly sauté 2 tortillas on both sides, drain, and keep warm. Fry two eggs, place on the tortillas, and cover with a sauce of 1 tomato, 1 chopped clove of garlic, 1 chopped red or green chile pepper, 1 chopped onion, salt, and pepper blended together and cooked with 1 T. oil for about 5 min. Often shredded Monterey Jack or Cheddar cheese is sprinkled on top.

hukilau. A Hawaiian word for a beach party. Originally the term was used as a verb meaning to fish with a seine net or to "pull rope." But it came to mean the party held on the beach when the fish nets were gathered in.

humble pie. A pie made from the innards of deer (1640). There is a double pun in the name, for "umble" is a very old English word for the heart, liver, and gizzard of a deer, the kind of food eaten by servants and hunters while the lord of the house ate venison. And since certain British dialects delete the *h* in the word "humble" when speaking, "humble pie" would be pronounced "umble pie," or connote a dish for those of few pretensions.

The English brought the dish to America, and in Susannah Carter's *The Frugal Housewife,* published in Boston in the eighteenth century from an English cookbook, a recipe for humble pie includes the entrails of the deer together with beef suet, apples, ½ pound sugar, salt, mace, cloves, nutmeg, and more than a pound of currants.

It is no longer a dish to be found in America, except as a curiosity or as a version of the English steak and kidney pie.

Humboldt dressing. A dressing of crab butter, mayonnaise, and seasonings to be mixed with a dish of crabs. Supposedly created in the 1940s by a Eureka, California, woman named Humboldt who sold crabs from a stand, although it might also have originated in the town of Humboldt, California.

HUMBOLDT DRESSING

Mash crab butter from 2 crabs, stir in ½ c. mayonnaise, 1 t. Worcestershire sauce, 4 dashes hot pepper sauce, 1 c. diced celery, ½ c. chopped parsley, and 2 T. chopped scallion. Cover and chill for 30 min.

humbug. A term used to describe a variety of very simple, plain foods of a kind often advocated by members of very strict religions. A printed reference dating to 1838 calls a peppermint-flavored molasses taffy by this name, and "humbug" is also used to describe fried-dough fritters sprinkled with cinnamon. A nineteenth-century pie made with a short crust, molasses, sugar, raisins, and bread or cracker crumbs is also called "humbug," because the simple ingredients of the pie were determined by Methodist prohibitions against luxury ingredients, especially festive Christmas puddings that were often doused with spirits. The original meaning of "humbug" means to deceive or delude (the origins of the word are uncertain, but it dates in this form in print to the 1730s), so that such confections were made to "deceive" the palate of the person eating them.

HUMBUG PIE

In a bowl mix 1 c. molasses, 1 c. chopped raisins, 1 c. cracker crumbs, ½ c. vinegar, 1 c. cold water, 2 T. melted butter, 1¼ t. mace, 1 t. allspice, 1 t. cinnamon, and 1 t. salt. Pour mixture into 10-in. pie shell, brush with cold water, and sprinkle with sugar. Bake for 10 min. at 400°, reduce heat to 350° and bake for 35–40 min. more until center is set.

hummer. A drink created at Detroit's Bay View Yacht Club from Kahlúa, light rum, and heavy cream. It was so called because after drinking two or three hummers, imbibers would start humming happily. Bartender Farouk El-haje of Detroit's London Chop House, which made the drink its specialty, replaced the cream with vanilla ice cream.

HUMMER

In a blender mix 1 oz. Kahlúa, 1 oz. light rum, and 1 oz. heavy cream or vanilla ice cream. Serve in a stemmed old-fashioned glass.

hurricane. A cocktail made with passion-fruit flavoring, dark rum, and citrus juices. The drink was created as a promotional cocktail that was featured at Pat O'Brien's French Quarter Bar in New Orleans, Louisiana. There is even a tall "hurricane glass" in which the cocktail is served. O'Brien's has since given birth to similarly named cocktails like the "cyclone," the "squall," and the "breeze."

HURRICANE

Fill a hurricane glass with crushed ice, add 2 oz. Jero's Red Passion Fruit cocktail mix, 2 oz. lemon juice, 4 oz. dark rum, 1 orange slice, and a maraschino cherry.

hush puppy. A dumpling of cornmeal that is deep-fried, especially popular in the South. The term appears in print for the first time about 1915. Although unconfirmed, the common assumption regarding the hush puppy's origin is that it dates from the period of scarcity following the Civil War, when cooks would toss scraps of corn batter to hungry dogs with the words "Hush, puppies!" But the *Morris Dictionary of Word and Phrase Origins* cites a southern reader's account that in the South the aquatic reptile called the salamander was often known as a "water dog" or "water puppy" (also "dwarf waterdog" *[Necturus punctatus]* and "mud-puppy" *[N. maculosus)*, because of its squat, stout legs. These were deep-fried with cornmeal dough and formed into sticks, and, so the account goes, they were called "hush puppies" because eating such lowly food was not something a southern wife would want known to her neighbors.

Hush puppies are the traditional accompaniment to fried catfish.

HUSH PUPPY

Sift together 1½ c. cornmeal with ½ c. flour, 2 t. baking powder, and ½ t. salt. Beat 1 egg in ¾ c. milk and add 1 grated onion. Mix with cornmeal and flour until well blended, then drop from a T. into hot fat. Fry until golden brown, drain, and serve hot.

hydraulic sandwich. Sailor's term for a liquid lunch like beer. It was first cited as a buzzword of 1991 in *Newsweek* magazine.

hydrolyzed vegetable protein (HVP). A flavor enhancer used in processed foods like soup, frankfurters, and stews. It is vegetable protein (such as from the soybean) that has been chemically broken down to the amino acids.

ice. Water that has been frozen solid. Ice has been long used as a preservative, as a substance with which to cool food and drinks, and as a solidifier for ice cream and sherbets.

Pits for ice storage have been found in the colonial ruins of Jamestown, Virginia, which were common in Europe and date back to the days of the ancient Romans.

Since the nineteenth century Americans have always enjoyed abundant, available ice in various forms, first used in ice houses or ice cellars, where food was kept right through spring and summer through storage in structures filled with ice blocks cut in winter and well insulated with straw and sawdust. From 1806 until the 1850s the ice-cutting industry was dominated by the "Ice King," Frederic Tudor of Boston, who eventually shipped ice as far away as China. Tudor's business was increased considerably when Nathaniel Wyeth invented an ice cutter with parallel sawtooth runners, dragged through frozen ponds and lakes by horses. In 1802 Maryland farmer Thomas Moore designed an insulated "icebox" that was commonly used in homes by the 1830s. These insulated chests were supplied by "ice men," who brought hundred-pound blocks of ice on horse-drawn "ice wagons" (which first appeared on the streets of New York about 1827), became common household fixtures. The delivery of ice was part of a standard of life enjoyed by most Americans well into the twentieth century, when electric refrigerators with freezers became affordable to everyone. The relative purity and accessibility of American waters caused visitor Charles Dickens in New York to remark on "gaining refreshment from the heat in the sight of the great blocks of clean ice which are carried into shops and bar rooms." In 1833 a Boston ship sailed four months carrying 180 tons of ice to Calcutta, and as of 1830 American ice was bound for England for use on British fishing trawlers.

The first refrigeration unit to produce ice was made by Englishman Jacob Perkins in 1834. The first United States patent for an ice-making machine went to Dr.

John Gorrie of the College of Physicians and Surgeons at Columbia University in 1844, who used it as an air conditioner for fevered patients. Gorrie later moved to Apalachicola, Florida, where, in 1850, he saved the reputation of the local French consul by using the machine's ice blocks to cool down champagne for a Bastille Day celebration.

Artificial ice was soon being made by refrigeration in ice plants, the first of which was built in 1865 in New Orleans, and by 1875 restaurants had their own ice-making machines. Much later, about 1925, "dry ice" (carbon dioxide) became available for purchase in bulk, though it is almost never used at home.

Ice takes various forms in the preparation of food and drink. "Shaved" ice or "chipped" ice was once standard in bars and restaurants, where a bartender might actually chip his own from a large block. Ice crushers are mechanical or hand-cranked tools for making "crushed" ice, often used for blending or shaking cocktails. After the Second World War ice cubes predominated in bars, as they have in home iceboxes.

"Aged ice" is commercially made ice that has been frozen very hard in order to retain the coldness. This form of ice is available in groceries or vending machines, and, through a process called "zone fractionalization" of water continually run over a cold surface, driving impurities to the center, resulting in a much clearer ice cube.

Many Europeans consider Americans' passion for ice a national characteristic. It is true that Americans drink few beverages aside from coffee and tea that are not served ice-cold, whereas in Europe room temperature drinks are more usual.

The "ice bucket," known since at least 1919, is a bucket of ice in which one places wine bottles to chill.

icebox pie. A crusted, creamy pie that is frozen or chilled firm. It became a popular item by the 1920s, when Americans began buying refrigerators that made such confections easy to make. "Icebox cookies" were also popular.

ICEBOX PIE

Scald 2 c. milk with 1½ squares baking chocolate. Mix in ⅔ c. sugar, 3 T. cornstarch, ½ t. salt, and then stir in milk and cook in double boiler for 10 min. until thickened. Stir a small amount of the liquid into 3 beaten egg yolks, being careful not to curdle them, then add the rest of the liquid. Stir and cook for 2 min. Add 2 T. butter and 1 t. vanilla, then cool. Beat well and pour into pastry shell, top with whipped cream, and chill until quite firm.

ice cream. A confection made from cream, sugar, and flavorings chilled to a semisolid consistency and consumed as a dessert or snack food. The specific phrase "ice cream" dates in print to 1735, in a description by Virginian Thomas Black, who sampled some at Governor Thomas Bladen's mansion in Annapolis, Maryland.

Ice cream, in various forms, goes back at least as far as the ancient Greeks and Romans, who cooled their wine with mountain snow and ice. Marco Polo brought back from the Orient a recipe for a frozen dessert based on milk, and there is evidence that some form of ice cream was brought by Catherine de Médicis from Italy to France.

About 1700 a pamphlet of ice-cream and sherbet recipes was published entitled *L'Art de Faire des Glaces,* and by then the major capitals of Europe were well familiar with the dish. The first known advertisement for ice cream in America appeared on May 12, 1777, in the New York *Gazette,* placed by confectioner Philip Lenzi, who said he offered ice cream "almost every day." And a 1786 advertisement in the New York *Post Boy* noted that the City Tavern served the confection every day.

Most ice cream of that period was made through an arduous method of beating cream in a pewter pot that was concurrently being shaken in a larger pot of salt and ice. But rudimentary ice-cream machines were for sale by the 1780s; George Washington, who spent £51.6s.2d. (about two hundred dollars) for ice cream in the summer of 1790 alone, owned a "Cream Machine for Making Ice," and Thomas Jefferson, who wrote extensive notes on making the confection, has been credited with bringing "French-style" ice cream, made with egg yolks, to America. He also had an ice-cream-making machine he called a "sorbetière" at Monticello, where he followed a recipe that called for a stick of vanilla (which Jefferson brought back from Europe), two bottles of cream, and an egg-custard mixture, boiled, stirred, reheated, strained, and put in an "ice pail."

President James Madison's wife, Dolley, is said to have popularized ice cream by making it a frequent dessert at the White House between 1809 and 1817 (and she had also helped the bachelor Jefferson with his White House parties after 1801). But the dish had been making considerable headway on its own, both in recipe books of the eighteenth century and in confectioners' shops, very often run by Italians. Consequently ice creams were often called "Italian ice creams" or "Neapolitan ice creams" throughout the nineteenth century, and the purveying of such confections became associated with Italian immigrants.

Philadelphia became renowned for its ice cream, and the phrase "Philadelphia ice cream," used since the early nineteenth century, came to mean a specifically American style of rich ice cream. One proud Philadelphia confectioner of the nineteenth century, James W. Parkinson, who also opened the grand Parkinson's Broadway Saloon selling ice cream in New York City, wrote of the prejudicial distinctions made between American and French frozen desserts (as well as other foods): "The admission is well nigh universal that the French 'Made Us,' and that we are 'The Sheep' of French 'pastures.' . . . So deeply rooted in this sentiment in the public mind . . . that when an American confectioner or caterer makes any invention in his craft, he feels that to secure its sales, and to establish its popularity, he must give it a French name." Parkinson had little reason to fear French competition, for he was enormously successful and claimed proudly to have created the first pistachio ice cream. He nevertheless played it safe occasionally by listing "biscuit glacé" among his confections.

The availability of ICE in America made ice creams and sherbets equally available to everyone, whereas they had continued to be expensive items in Europe. Even in hot climates, ice cream was offered on a year-round basis; by 1808 ice cream was available every day in New Orleans, where it was first sold at the Exchange Coffee-House. In 1835 English traveler Harriet Martineau reported "towers of ice cream" available daily in Kentucky. Two years later Englishman Frederick Marryat marveled at seeing "common laborers" lapping up ice cream on their midday break.

A breakthrough in ice-cream production came in 1846 when a small, compact ice-cream freezer was invented by a New Jersey woman named Nancy Johnson, about whom little is known. The freezer was cranked by hand and made ice-cream making a pastime (though still a chore) of American homelife. For some reason Johnson did not patent her invention, but in 1848 William G. Young did, calling it the "Johnson Patent Ice-Cream Freezer" (later known as the "Johnson-Young" ice-cream maker).

By midcentury ice cream was no longer a novelty, and the editor of *Godey's Lady's Book* for 1850 noted that "a party without ice cream would be like breakfast without bread or a dinner without a roast." The confection had become relatively cheap to buy at the market, thanks to the efforts of Baltimore ice-cream manufacturer Jacob Fussell, who began by using an oversupply of cream to make the confection and to undercut the confectioners' prices by more than half in 1851. He opened ice-cream plants in several eastern cities, while his associate Perry Brazelton moved the industry into the Midwest. By the end of the century Americans were eating 5 million gallons of ice cream a year, prompted by technological improvements in mechanical ice-cream makers.

By the 1870s Americans were going to "ice-cream parlors" and stopping at "ice-cream stands." They sat at "ice-cream parlor chairs" made from bent wood or wire, mass-produced after 1870, and ate from "ice cream dishes" made from tinned steel. Many parlors were set in pharmacies, which had separate "ice-cream fountains," which grew more and more ornate as the nineteenth century wore on. With marble counters and silver spigots, these ice-cream saloons were among the most extravagant creations of the Victorian era in the United States. The marble fountain at James Tuft's concession at the Philadelphia Centennial Exposition of 1876 was two stories tall. Elaborately decorated, molded ice cream became the fashion, and women who specialized in making such confections were called "fancy ladies."

Two claims have been made for the invention of the "ice cream soda:" In 1868 Herr Harnisch, owner of the Harnisch & Baer Ice Cream Parlor in San Antonio, Texas, introduced soda water to the city and, thereafter, placed a scoop of ice cream into the soda itself. Also, in 1874 an "ice cream soda," made with milk, a flavored syrup, and a scoop of ice cream, was first featured by Robert M. Green at the Franklin Institute in Philadelphia. By 1893 *The Critic Magazine* could proclaim, "The ice cream soda is our national beverage." Americans also loved "milk sherbets" (from the Turkish *sherbet,* and Arabic *sharbah,* "drink"), which if made without milk were called "ices" or "Italian ices" (these last were scooped into pleated paper cups and licked).

MILK SHAKES, "malteds," and "frappes" came along toward the end of the nineteenth century, too, as did the "sundae" and the "ice-cream cone." The origins of both items have been argued over the years. A 1913 reference to "sundae" noted that in New England the word was "now in established usage for college ices," a term that may have preceded "sundae" and hints at its origins at college soda fountains. But Paul Dickson, in his *Great American Ice Cream Book* (1972), cites two main contenders for the honor of creating the sundae, although he refers to several others with less credibility. The first claim concerns the Evanston, Illinois, civic moralists of the 1890s who inveighed against drinking soda water on the Sabbath, prompting confectioners to create a dish that would not corrupt public morals—scoops of ice cream with flavored syrups or toppings—called "Sundays." The other claim dates to the same period, when a man named George Hallauer of Two Rivers, Wisconsin, ordered such a dish at Ed Berner's soda fountain. The ice-cream-and-syrup confection became so popular that other parlor owners had to serve it, and George Giffy, a fountain owner in Manitowoc, Wisconsin, began serving it only on Sundays as a loss leader. Although the original name was spelled with a *y* (the dish early on was called the "Soda-less Soda"), the *ae* ending, contends Dickson, "came about when those who orated from the pulpit on the sinful soda went to work on the sacrilegious use of the name of the Sabbath for its stand-in." In any case, by 1900 soda-fountain suppliers were selling tulip-shaped sundae dishes.

The ice-cream cone is equally as confusing as to its origins. It seems clear that the cone (a wafer rolled to hold a scoop of ice cream) became popular at the 1904 St. Louis World's Fair, but there are several claims as to just who started hawking it there. Some authorities credit a Syrian immigrant named Ernest A. Hamwi with the invention, which was actually a Persian pastry, *zalabia,* that Hamwi rolled to hold ice cream when another concessionaire ran out of ice-cream dishes. Another claim was made by David Avayou, a Turkish ice-cream parlor owner from New Jersey, who got the idea from seeing ice cream eaten in paper cones in France and who then purveyed the wafer cones at the St. Louis Fair. Still another contender at that same exposition, Abe Doumar, claimed to have created the cone from waffles at a stand in the "Old City of Jerusalem" section of the fair; he called them "Cornucopias." (A 1905 version of Doumar's cone-making machine from Coney Island is still exhibited at Doumar's Cones and Barbecue Since 1904 restaurant in Norfolk, Virginia.) There are other stories, too, but Dickson believes the most creditable claim is that of Italo Marchiony, an Italian immigrant who once offered documentary evidence that he took out a patent on an ice-cream cone as of December 13, 1903, but had made them since 1896. It would appear, writes Dickson, "that the Marchiony patent wins for him the credit as American inventor of the ice cream cone, but since he never achieved any success or popularity with his invention the distinction of introducing it to a waiting America goes to a group of men—which one is not sure—at the St. Louis Fair of 1904," where there were at least fifty ice-cream booths selling five thousand gallons a day. In 1910 Frederick A. Bruckmann of Portland, Oregon, invented an ice cream cone machine that could produce 3,000 cones each hour.

Today cones are made in a variety of shapes. The "sugar cone" has a cookielike texture, while the "waffle cone" is lighter and more airy. Sometimes the latter is colored with food dyes.

A good deal of American ice cream was sold by street vendors in large cities. The slang term for their product as of the 1880s was "hokey-pokey," which may derive from the Italian "*O che poco!*" ("Oh, here's a little!") or *occi-pocci* (mixed colors or flavors) because the "hokey-pokey man" who sold this cheap ice cream was often of Italian descent.

An advance in technique came when William A. Breyer of Philadelphia began using brine instead of salt and ice to freeze his ice cream.

During World War I ice cream was declared an "essential foodstuff," so that its ingredients were not rationed. By 1919 Americans were eating 230 million gallons of ice cream, and it became known as an "American typical food," like hamburgers and hot dogs. By 1940 the figure was up to 318 million gallons.

Americans would go to a soda fountain and order "hand-packed" ice cream (ice cream that was scooped from large containers behind the counter and packed in a cardboard container); otherwise the ice cream was packed at a factory and shipped, often with a considerable lag of time between its manufacture and its sale. "Ice-cream cakes" were layer cakes filled with ice cream rather than icing, custard, or cream. "Banana splits," a dish of sliced bananas topped with scoops of ice cream, different syrups, ground nuts, and MARASCHINO cherries, became popular after 1892, when the United Fruit Company began bringing in large quantities of bananas to the United States. The banana split was mentioned in the 1915 edition of *The Dispenser's Formulary or Soda Water Guide* as the first "fancy fountain dessert [meaning a sundae with fruit] to win favor—and it still maintains its popularity."

The first chocolate-covered ice-cream bar was invented by Christian K. Nelson in Onawa, Iowa, in 1920. Nelson, a Danish immigrant who became a schoolteacher and part-time candy-store owner, dubbed his confection the I-Scream Bar" ("I scream, ice cream!" was recorded as a street vendor's in the New York *National Advertiser* as early as 1828), and in 1921 became partners with an Omaha, Nebraska, ice-cream company superintendent named Russell Stover, who changed the item's name to "Eskimo Pie," in a reference to the Alaskan Eskimos' frigid climate. The promotion (and success) of Eskimo Pie was largely based on its claims of purity at a time when problems of sanitation in the industry were of real public concern. Eskimo Pie was wrapped in aluminum foil and advertised as "automatically frozen in silver-lined vessels, enrobed in chocolate, wrapped by machinery in a spotless, sun-lit factory and protected by zero temperature until served to you." By 1922 the company was selling 2 million ice-cream bars a day. After a period of trouble defending their patent from imitators, Nelson and Stover sold their company to become a subsidiary of U.S. Foil, whose product was used to wrap the confection.

The sanitation problem was also met with the creation of the "ice-cream sandwich" (slabs of ice cream sandwiched between cakelike cookies), which began appearing in the late 1890s on New York street vendors' carts. In San Francisco the IT'S IT ice-cream bar was a similar item made with oatmeal cookie layers, and in the 1980s a considerable success was made with an ice-cream sandwich using chocolate-chip cookies called the "Chipwich."

Credit for the first person to put ice cream on a stick goes to a Youngstown, Ohio, parlor owner named Harry Burt, who called his creation—a chocolate-covered ice-cream bar set on a wooden stick—the "Good Humor Ice Cream Sucker," which was sold by vendors driving clean white trucks. After Burt's death in 1926, several Cleveland businessmen bought the company and began selling national franchises, which proliferated and made the "Good Humor man" a summertime fixture in American communities.

In 1905 an eleven-year-old boy named Frank Epperson, of Oakland, California, accidentally left a mixing stick in a glass of juice on a windowsill while visiting friends in New Jersey. The juice froze with the stick in it, enabling the ice to be held in the hand and licked.

In 1922 Epperson introduced this new "ice lollipop" at a fireman's ball in Oakland, California, and called it an "Epsicle," then later "Popsicle." (Frozen "juice bars" had been known in the nineteenth century, including one called the "Hokey Pokey," but none was marketed well until the Popsicle in 1923.) In 1934 a Greek immigrant named Thomas Andreas Carvel of Yonkers, New York, started selling a new form of soft ice cream he called "frozen custard," which was extruded from a machine he had invented. Carvel ice-cream stores proliferated in the Northeast, while in the Midwest Sherwood (Sherb) Noble opened similar soft ice-cream stands under the name Dairy Queen, beginning with a store in Joliet, Illinois, in 1940.

Ice-cream sales suffered during the Depression of the 1930s, but the small-town soda fountain survived even as many of the large and opulent pharmacy fountains lost ground. Promoted as healthful and wholesome by the industry, ice cream took on a positively sanitary image in the 1940s, and Hollywood movies pictured ice-cream soda fountains as oases of innocent Americana. In World War II newspapers printed photos and stories of GIs and sailors who missed few things back home so much as ice cream. By 1946 Americans annually were consuming more than twenty quarts of ice cream per capita.

In the 1950s Americans began buying more ice cream in groceries and in the new supermarkets than in soda fountains and drugstores, and the flavor and texture of American ice creams began to change as large companies cut costs by adding stabilizers, more air, and artificial ingredients. Supermarkets and large food corporations marketed their own brands nationally, at the same time that a number of smaller companies began in the 1960s to sell "premium ice creams"—many resembling the kinds made before the 1950s—with rich flavors of chocolate, vanilla, and other old favorites. Companies like Howard Johnson's, a restaurant chain begun in Wollaston, Massachusetts, in 1925, advertised "28 Flavors," and Baskin-Robbins, begun in Los Angeles in 1946, thirty-one. These premium, and very high priced, ice creams and sherbets begat a new generation of small shops selling "homemade ice creams" that purported to be more "natural" and certainly more delicious than the supermarket varieties. In 1973 Steve Herrell, owner of Steve's ice-cream parlor in Somerville, Massachusetts, began blending his customers' choice of cookie and/or candy morsels into his ice cream and called the item a "Mix-in," a copyrighted trademark he sold with the store in 1977. This idea, under other names (including "Smoosh-in," the new term used at Herrell's next shop, in Northampton, Massachusetts), became very popular in the 1980s in the new ice cream shops opening in towns and suburban shopping malls.

In 1997 America produced 1.56 billion gallons of frozen desserts (which includes frozen YOGURT), with about 8.8 percent of milk production going toward such confection. Americans consumed 5.4 gallons of frozen desserts per capita in 1997, which makes Americans the largest ice cream consumers in the world, followed by Australia and Sweden. The four most popular flavors of ice cream are vanilla, chocolate, strawberry, and butter pecan. The top five toppings for ice cream are HOT FUDGE, chocolate fudge, BUTTERSCOTCH, CARAMEL, and STRAWBERRY.

ice house. While the term "ice house" refers simply to a place where ice is made, stored or sold (1830), it is also a Southern term for a local beer bar (1988) or convenience store (1967). As Rebecca Trounson has written in the *Houston Chronicle* for March 3, 1986, "Distinguished by their garage doors, their dank, dark interiors and their ice-cooled beer, *icehouses* are places men. . . can head straight from their jobs and not feel embarrassed to be in their uniforms or other work clothes." Icehouses usually have a few chairs out front for their regular customers. According to Texas historian Joe Frantz, icehouses first appeared along the Gulf Coast in the mid-1800s when ice was first shipped in boats with straw insulation to Texas from New England. The ice was then stored in insulated buildings that before long began stocking beer and, later, a few other dry goods. Others, including historian Tom Denyer, contend the icehouse as it came to be known in Texas started in San Antonio in the 1920s, and that by 1970 there were 287 in the city, though by 1999 the number had dwindled to 60.

icing. A term often interchangeable with "frosting" and preferred in America to describe the sugar-and-water mixture used to decorate and cover cakes. Icing may also contain other ingredients and flavorings such as marshmallow, chocolate, nuts, and fruit.

"Frosting" actually precedes "icing" in print, the former appearing around 1610, the latter in 1760, with icing considered a somewhat lighter, decorative glaze than frosting. But in America it became normal to use "icing" (and the verb "to ice") to describe either form of the confection.

I.D. Bartender slang meaning to check a person's identification, such as a driver's license, to determine if he is of legal drinking age. To "card" someone is to ask for similar identification. "Fake I.D." is falsified identification used to gain access to drinking establishments.

imitation. Under FDA regulations, this term must be used on the labels of all products that are not as nutritious as the product that it resembles and for which it is a substitute.

imperial crab. Also, "crab imperial." Either of two preparations of molded, baked crabmeat, one a variation of deviled crab made as a gratin bound with cream or a cream sauce, the other bound with mayonnaise and topped with bread crumbs, first mentioned in print in 1932. In an article in *The Washingtonian* (March 1990), Robert Shoffner traced the origins of the dish to Thompson's Sea Girt House in Baltimore in the late nineteenth century (a second Thompson's, opened in 1940, contends it still serves the original recipe), where it was probably a mounded gratin containing mayonnaise, sautéed onions, bell peppers, pimientos, and egg yolks. Shoffner traces the second, later, form of the dish to the Crisfield Restaurant in Silver Spring, Maryland, where it was created by Lillian Landis in 1944. This version is traditionally served in a real or ceramic crab shell.

IMPERIAL CRAB

Combine 1 T. chopped onion with 2 T. chopped green pepper, 1 T. chopped pimiento, and 1 T. chopped celery. In 1 T. butter sauté vegetables until lightly browned. In a bowl blend together 1 beaten egg, ½ t. dry mustard, and 1 lb. lump crabmeat. Add vegetables and blend. Divide the mixture into four mounds or place in crab shells or shell-shaped ramekins. Dot the top of each portion with 1 T. mayonnaise, sprinkle with paprika, and bake for 15 min. at 350°. If preferred, the tops may also be sprinkled with bread crumbs.

Imp 'n' Ahrn. A drink associated with Pittsburgh made from Imperial whiskey and Iron City beer.

imu. A hole dug in the ground, in which heated lava stones are placed, then foods to be cooked, covered with earth or banana leaves. It is a Hawaiian cooking technique, very popular at outdoor parties called "luaus." Often a KALUA PIG is roasted this way.

inamona. Hawaiian dish made from mashed roasted candlenuts and salt, used as a relish (1930).

Indian. Since colonial times the word "Indian" has been applied to a wide variety of fruits, vegetables, grasses, foods and drinks, most often to those foods containing corn or cornmeal, as in INDIAN BREAD and INDIAN PUDDING, but also as a slur indicating something of inferior quality, as INDIAN WHISKY.

Indian bread. As described by Adams in *Western Words*, "A tasty strip of fatty matter extending from the shoulder blade backward along the backbone of a buffalo. When seared in hot grease and then smoked, it became a tidbit the buffalo hunter used for bread. When eaten with lean or dried meat, it made an excellent sandwich." The term also referred to cornmeal bread.

Indian lemonade. Fragrant sumac (*Rhus canadensis*), first in print in 1898, as well as a beverage made from the berries.

Indian pudding. A cornmeal-pudding dessert made with milk and molasses. The name comes from the fact that corn was called "Indian corn" by the early English settlers, and anything containing corn or cornmeal might have the adjective "Indian" so applied. This dish was called *sagamite* by the Native Americans, and, in the late seventeenth century, "hasty pudding" by the colonists.

"Indian pudding" was first printed in 1722 in the *New England Courant*, where the dessert's color was described "to the great surprise of the whole family" as "Blood-red."

INDIAN PUDDING

Scald 4 c. milk in a double boiler, stir in ⅓ c. cornmeal, and cook, stirring, over boiling water for 15 min. Stir in ¼ c. dark molasses, cook for 5 min., and remove from heat. Stir in ¼ c. butter, ¾ t. salt, a pinch of ginger or cinnamon, if desired, and 1 beaten egg. Pour into buttered baking dish and bake at 350° for about 2 hr. until set. Serve with whipped cream or vanilla ice cream.

Indian whisky. A very low-grade alcoholic spirit that white men sold to the Native Americans during the days of the Missouri River trade of the nineteenth century. One recipe (from E. C. Abbott and Helena Huntington Smith's *We Pointed North* [1939]) suggests the horrifying nature of this brew:

Take one barrel of Missouri River water, and two gallons of alcohol. Then you add two ounces of strychnine to make them crazy—because strychnine is the greatest stimulant in the world—three bars of tobacco to make them sick—because an Indian wouldn't figure it was whisky unless it made him sick—five bars of soap to give it a head, and half-pound of red pepper, and then you put some sage brush and boil it until it's brown. Strain this into a barrel and you've got your Indian whisky.

ingredients statement. A listing on a food product's label, mandated by the Federal Trade Commission, that must include the ingredients in order of predominance—that is, the most abundant ingredient must be listed first.

in the weeds. Restaurant workers' lingo for having too much work to do that night.

invert sugar. A sweetening additive blended from dextrose and fructose and used in candy, soft drinks, and other foods.

Irish coffee. A blend of hot coffee, Irish whisky, and whipped cream. According to a plaque outside the Buena Vista Bar in San Francisco, "America's first Irish coffee was made here in 1952. It was inspirationally invented at Shannon Airport [Ireland] by [chef] Joe Sheridan. It was fortuitously introduced by [newspaper writer] Stan Delaplane. It was nurtured to a national institution by [the bar's owner] Jack Koeppler." Sheridan actually created the drink in 1942 at Foynes Dock, where flying boats docked in World War II. It was promoted as of 1947 at Shannon Airport as an official welcoming beverage.

IRISH COFFEE

Rinse out an 8-oz. goblet with hot water, place 2 t. sugar in goblet, and pour in 1½ oz. Irish whisky and 5 oz. strong hot coffee. Stir, then top with whipped cream.

Irish moss. Also, "carrageen moss" and "sea moss."

An edible moss (*Chondrus crispus*) of the North Atlantic coast (1853) that is used as a stabllizer in milk-based puddings and to smoothe out ice cream.

isinglass. A transparent gelatin made from the air bladder of fishes, such as the STURGEON. Isinglass was used until the present century to make jellies and clarify liquors. The name is from the obsolete Dutch *huizenblas,* and ultimately from German *hūsōn,* "sturgeon," plus *-blase,* "bladder." Its first mention in English was in 1535.

isleta bread. A Pueblo Indian bread shaped like a bear's claw, hence the alternate names "bear claw" or "paw bread."

Italian beef stand. An inexpensive restaurant or streetside stand selling sliced beef in a spicy gravy. Italian beef is a specialty of the Midwest, especially Chicago. The name merely refers to some vague idea of how Italians would serve their beef—highly, seasoned—but there is no such dish in Italy.

It's It. An ice-cream sandwich made from vanilla ice cream between two oatmeal cookies, covered with chocolate and frozen hard. This confection originated in 1928 at the Playland-at-the-Beach amusement park in San Francisco, and credit for its creation is given to park owner George Whitney. San Franciscans still remember a "trip to the It stand," and today the confection is available in food stores and supermarkets under its original name, made by the It's-It Ice Cream Company in that city.

izer cookie. A cookie baked on a long wafer iron that is impressed with figures of designs that then appear on the cookie. The term derives from the Dutch word *izer* (or *yser),* meaning "iron," and the cookies were made by the Dutch immigrants in New York and elsewhere in the Colonies.

jack (genus *Caranx*). Any of a variety of ocean fish that includes the POMPANO, most of which are not significant food fishes in the United States. The origin of the name is obscure, the first mention being in 1587. The principal eating fishes of this type include the "amberjack" (*Seriola dumerili*); the "bar jack" (*C. ruber*); the "blue runner" (*C. crysos*); the "crevalle" (*C. hippos*), also called "jack crevalle" or "crevalle jack"; the "jack mackerel" (*Trachurus symmetricus*), also called the "horse mackerel," though it is not a true mackerel; the "rainbow runner" (*Elagatis bipinnulatus*); the "yellow jack" (*C. bartholomaei*); and the yellowtail (*S. dorsalis*).

Jack Rose. A cocktail made from apple brandy, lime or lemon juice, and grenadine. The name seems to be based on the drink's color, which resembles that of a rose named after French general Jean-François Jacqueminot (1787–1865), though it may refer to a pre-World War I gangster named Jack Rose. The drink is first mentioned in print in Ernest Hemingway's novel *The Sun Also Rises* (1926).

JACK ROSE

Shake together with ice 8 parts apple brandy, 2 parts lemon or lime juice, and 1 part grenadine. Strain into cocktail glass and add lemon twist.

---

jake. An alcoholic beverage made from Jamaican ginger during the Prohibition era.

jambalaya. A main dish of rice, pork, ham, sausage, shrimp, crayfish, and seasonings—or any combination of the above. Jambalaya is one of the most famous Cajun-Creole creations, with as many versions and incorporating as wide a variety of ingredients as any dish in American gastronomy. Most etymologists believe the name came from the Spanish word for ham, *jamón*, a prime ingredient in the first jambalayas of the eighteenth century, but others prefer the beloved story of a gentleman who stopped by a New Orleans inn late one night to find nothing left for him

to dine upon. The owner thereupon told the cook, whose name was Jean, to "mix some things together"—*balayez*, in the dialect of Louisiana—so the grateful guest pronounced the dish of odds-and-ends wonderful and named it "Jean Balayez."

The word itself first appeared in print only in 1872, and *The Picayune's Creole Cook Book* (1900) calls it a "Spanish-Creole dish." Missouri Creoles call it "jambolail." But today it is a great favorite and synonymous with Louisiana cuisine.

Jambalaya may be made with beef, pork, chicken, shrimp, oysters, crayfish, or any number of other ingredients, and none is more authentic than the next. Most will use the local sausage called "chaurice" (or CHORIZO), and green pepper and chile or cayenne pepper are fairly standard. Louisianans are passionate about jambalaya and even hold an annual jambalaya cook-off in the old Cajun town of Gonzales, the self-proclaimed Jambalaya Capital of the World.

JAMBALAYA

Sauté ½ lb. sliced smoked sausage and ½ lb. cubed ham in ¼ c. hot oil until browned. Remove from saucepan and then sauté 1 c. chopped onions, 1 c. chopped bell pepper, 1 c. chopped celery, 1 c. chopped scallion, and 2 cloves minced garlic in meat drippings until soft. Add one 16-oz. can drained tomatoes, 1 t. thyme, 1 t. black pepper, ¼ t. cayenne, 1 t. salt, and cook for 5 min. Stir in 1 c. converted rice. Mix together liquid from tomatoes, 1½ c. chicken stock or water, and 1½ T. Worcestershire sauce to equal 2½ c. Bring to boil, reduce to simmer, add 2 lb. raw, peeled shrimp, ham, and sausage, and cook uncovered for about 30 min.

Jansson's Temptation. A dish made from potatoes, onions, anchovies, and cream baked in a pan. Although the dish is associated with Sweden, where it is called *Jansson's frestelse,* and Norway, it is widely believed to be of American origins. In the September 1989 number of *Food & Wine* magazine, Sharon Kapnick wrote of the dish:

In 1846, Erik Jansson, a Swedish religious reformer fleeing persecution, came to America with his followers. They settled in northwestern Illinois, where Jansson founded the village of Bishop Hill, named after his hometown of Biskopskulla. Jansson advocated strict asceticism, calling for a meager diet barely sufficient for survival. As the legend goes, an ardent follower discovered Jansson surreptitiously devouring a steaming casserole of potatoes and anchovies enriched with milk, onions, and butter. He was gorging so passionately that his reputation was forever ruined, and the dish was thereafter called Jansson's Temptation.

JANSSON'S TEMPTATION

Cut up 2 lb. of peeled potatoes into ¼-in. strips and place half of them in a buttered baking dish. Layer on top 2 c. sliced onions and enough canned anchovies to cover. Cover with another layer of potatoes, add salt and pepper to taste, then pour on 1½ c. of light cream. Dot with butter and bake at 375° for about 45–50 min.

Japanese steakhouse. A Japanese-American restaurant at which foods are cooked directly in front of the customer on a flat griddle called a *teppanyaki* by a chef who displays remarkable showmanship in cutting and flipping the food. The concept was begun in 1964 by Rocky Aioki, who opened his first Benihana of Tokyo restaurants in New York City and later built them into a worldwide chain (in Japan a similar restaurant opened by Aioki's father was called Benihana of New York).

Teppanyaki-style restaurants are a tradition in Japan, although the traditional country ranch decor has taken on elements used by the Benihana restaurants with a full-scale Western-style bar. The chef wears a puffy toque and wields a sharp knife called a *hocho* while he cooks a variety of dishes on a griddle surrounded by counters where the customers sit. The usual menu at such restaurants includes soup and salad, followed by steak, shrimp, chicken, and seafood, accompanied by bean sprouts, zucchini, onions, and mushrooms.

jawbreaker. Also, "jawbone breaker." Very hard, round candies in various colors, so called because they are very difficult to bite into.

Jeff Davis. A Northern slur first used during the Civil War for the kinds of inferior and substitute foods Southerners were forced to consume because of the deprivations caused by the conflict. The name derives from American statesman Jefferson Davis, who, as president of the Confederacy during the war, was an object of Northern scorn. Thus, "Jeff Davis coffee" was a substitute made from wheat grain rather than coffee beans, and to call someone a "Jeff Davis" was to label him a Southern ignoramus. The term is not found in Southern cookbooks of the nineteenth century, but "Jeff Davis pie" and "Jeff Davis pudding" have since lost all condescending connotations.

In an article in *Food & Wine* (September 1989) Sharon Kapnick asserted that "Jefferson Davis pie" was actually created by a former slave named Mary Ann, cook for a Missouri merchant named George B. Warren, for Sunday dinners during the Civil War and so-named because of Warren's admiration for the Confederacy's president.

The following recipe, from a Washington, D.C., woman named Florence Berryman, printed in the *D.A.R. Cookbook* (1949), is said to have gone back three generations in her family, suggesting that Jeff Davis pie was well known during Davis's own lifetime (1808–1889). A similar pie or tart in the South, based on English recipes known also in New England, was called CHESS PIE.

JEFF DAVIS

Cream 1 c. butter with 2 c. sugar. Mix 3 beaten egg yolks with ½ c. milk, 2 T. flour, and the juice of 1 lemon. Add to creamed butter. Pour into pie plate with bottom crust and bake at 300° until set. Make a meringue and cover the pie, then brown in oven.

Other recipes call for more spices and raisins and nuts to be added to the batter. A very similar confection was called "Osgood pie."

Jell-O. A trademark name for a gelatin dessert made from sugar, gelatin, adipic acid, disodium phosphate, fumaric acid, artificial color, natural flavor with BHA, and artificial flavor. A patent for a "gelatin dessert" was taken out in 1865 by Peter Cooper, and Charles B. Knox packaged unflavored instant powdered gelatin for making aspic in the 1890s. In 1897 Pearl Bixby Wait of LeRoy, New York, came up with a flavored gelatin his wife, May Davis Wait, called "Jell-O," whose rights were sold for $450 to Orator Francis Woodward of the Genesee Pure Food Company, which he renamed the "Jell-O Company." The rights for the product were purchased in 1925 by the Postum Cereal Company, but today the product is made by Kraft Foods, which sells more than 400 million packages each year.

Some slang terms for gelatin desserts of this type include "shivering Liz," "shimmy," and "nervous pudding." The numerous gelatin desserts to be found in so many Junior League Cookbooks of the South and Midwest is somewhat explained by the fact that refrigerators and iceboxes required to make the dessert were owned only by families who could afford their high prices.

A "Jell-O shot," supposedly created in New Orleans in the 1980s, is a small paper cup of Jell-O mixed with vodka, schnapps, or other spirits.

jelly. A sweet, semisolid translucent condiment made by boiling fruit juice and sugar with pectin or gelatin. Jelly is used as a spread on toast or as a dessert filling. Sometimes it is added to sauces or gravies, and mint jelly is customarily served with roast lamb or lamb chops.

The word "jelly" derives from Middle English, geli, and ultimately from the Latin *gelare,* "to freeze."

FDA standards require that commercial jelly must contain not less than forty-five parts by weight fruit ingredients to fifty-five parts sweetening.

"Jam" differs from jelly in being made with fresh or dried fruit rather than juice and has a thicker texture. The word may derive from the sense of the verb "jam," to force something to congeal together.

"Preserves" differ from jams and jellies by containing pieces of the fruit, although jams and preserves are treated under the same heading in the FDA's *Code of Federal Regulations, Title 21* (revised April 1, 1982).

Commercial jellies, jams, and preserves are usually made by adding pectins rather than relying on the natural pectins of the fruit. Grape jelly, made with Concord grapes, is the most popular of commercial jellies.

jelly bean. An egg-shaped candy with a chewy texture made by boiling sugar with a flavoring like fruit juice and setting it with gelatin or pectin. Jelly beans were first advertised in the July 5, 1905, edition of the *Chicago Daily News* at nine cents a pound.

jelly roll. A dessert of sponge cake rolled around a jelly filling, with currant or raspberry traditionally used in the preparation. "Jelly cakes" were known at least since the 1860s, but jelly rolls were not cited in print until 1895.

jerky. Beef that has been cut thin and dried in the sun. The word comes from the Spanish *chargui,* which itself came from a Peruvian word, *quechua.* It first appears in English in 1700 as a verb, *jerk,* then as a noun in the nineteenth century.

Jerky, in the form of PEMMICAN, was a staple food among the native Americans on the plains. It is very rich in protein and may be cooked in a soup or smoked, but more commonly it is sold as a "meat snack" in the form of a thin stick sold at convenience stores and bars.

In Hawaii, jerky is referred to as *pipikaula.*

Jerusalem artichoke (*Helianthus tuberosus*). Also "ground artichoke." A tuber with lumpy branches, reddish-brown skin, and a slightly sweet-ish flavor. The tuber is not a true ARTICHOKE and has nothing to do with Jerusalem, for it is a native American sunflower, which in Italian is *girasole,* the name given the plant when it was introduced to the garden of Cardinal Farnese in Rome about 1617. In 1620 the Italian word had been transformed into the English "Artichocks of Jerusalem," and, thereafter, "Jerusalem artichokes."

The plant had been noted by Samuel de Champlain in 1605 as a garden vegetable of the Indians on Cape Cod, but the settlers who came after him developed little interest in the tuber. Very few Americans are familiar with the food at all, though some commercial growers have tried to market it under the less foreign-sounding name of "sunchokes."

Jerusalem artichokes are usually chopped up raw and used in salads, or they may be boiled or steamed and served with butter.

jewfish (*Epinephelus itajara*). Also, "giant sea BASS." A large, grayish-brown GROUPER that may weigh up to seven hundred pounds, found near Florida and in the Gulf of Mexico. The first mention of the name in print was in 1697, when William Dampier, in his *Voyages and Descriptions, A Voyage to New Holland,* wrote, "The Jew-Fish is a very good Fish, and I judge so called by the English, because it hath Scales and Fins, therefore a clean Fish, according to the Levitical Law." (See main entry for KOSHER, for Jewish dietary rules.)

Jewish penicillin. A slang term for chicken soup, because of its supposed curative powers. In 1987 a mock court called the Court of Historical Review and Appeals in San Francisco awarded chicken soup the "official" title of "Jewish penicillin."

jicama (*Pachyrhizus erosus*). Pronounced "Hee-ka-mah," this tropical American tuber is a legume eaten as a vegetable. The name is from the Nahuatl *xicama*, appearing first in English print circa 1909. The tuber gained popularity, first in the West and South, in the 1980s, although most jicama is imported from Mexico.

Jim Hill mustard. A northwestern term for a wild mustard (*Sisymbrium altissimum*) discovered in the 1890s and first in print in 1923, when James Jerome Hill (1838–1916) built the Great Northern Railroad to Seattle, Washington.

jimmies. Very small pellets or rods of colored candy or chocolate used as a topping for ice cream. The word is first in print in 1963 but goes back much further.

Joe Frogger. A thick New England cookie spiced with ginger, nutmeg, cloves, and other spices. The origins of the name are unknown, though the most often cited story concerns an old man named "Uncle Joe" who lived near a frog pond in Marblehead, Massachusetts. He loved rum and always put it into his cookies, which resembled the frogs in the pond. The cookies are a traditional Sunday-night snack in New England.

JOE FROGGER

In a bowl combine ¼ c. molasses, 4 T. melted butter, ½ c. honey, 2 T. hot water, 3 T. rum, ½ t. baking soda, 2 c. flour, ½ t. ground ginger ¼ t. ground cloves, ¼ t. nutmeg, and ⅛ t. allspice. Blend well to form a dough. Chill for 1 hr. Pinch off a ball of dough about the size of a walnut, flatten to about ¼-in. thickness, place on buttered cookie sheet, and bake for 10 min. at 375°. Cool on rack. Makes 10 cookies.

Johannisberg Riesling. A white vinifera grape, properly called the "White Riesling," that goes into some of Germany's finest white wines. It has been increasingly planted as a wine grape in the United States, especially in California, where it is vinified either as a dry, spicy wine or as a LATE HARVEST sweet dessert wine.

johnnycake. Also "jonnycake" and "jonny cake." A form of PANCAKE traditionally made with Rhode Island ground flint ("Indian"). The name has been in print at least as early as 1739, but its derivation is very much clouded in speculation. Some authorities believe it may derive from an Indian word for flat cornmeal cakes, *joniken*. Others think it a derivative of "Shawnee cake," after the tribe of the Tennessee Valley. It is also possible that *johnnycake* is a form of the Dutch *pannekoeken*, for a *j* could be easily interchanged for the *p*, and the word is often spelled "johnnycake," without the *h*.

Most Rhode Island aficionados of the johnnycake—especially those who belong to the Society for the Propagation of the Jonnycake Tradition—insist that the word is from "journey cake" (1754), because it might be carried on a long trip, and the word "journey" is commonly pronounced as "jonny" in that part of New England. The traditional thinness and brittleness of johnnycakes seem hardly substantial or durable enough, however, to pack in saddlebags for a long trek through the New England wilderness.

The society also states that a true johnnycake must be made with an obsolete strain of Indian corn called "whitecap flint corn," which is cultivated in very small quantities because of its low yield (twelve tons to an acre, as opposed to twenty tons for dent corn). In 1940 the Rhode Island legislature again considered the johnnycake question by deciding that only those made with flint corn could be labeled "Rhode Island johnnycakes." (Johnnycake mixes are sold in packages.) Flint cornmeal is still made by Gray's Grist Mill in Adamsville, Carpenter's Gristmill in Perryville, and Kenyon's Gristmill in Usquepaugh, Rhode Island.

In Newport County, Rhode Island, johnnycakes are made commonly with cornmeal, salt, and cold milk; in South County they are made with cornmeal, salt, and boiling water, resulting in smaller, thicker johnnycakes than those in the north.

The johnnycake became part of New England folklore with the publication of a series of articles from 1879–1880 in *The Providence Journal* entitled *The Jonny-Cake Papers of "Shepherd Tom"* by Thomas Robinson Hazard. As might be expected, Rhode Island holds a Johnnycake Festival annually in the last week of October and the item is common to "May Breakfasts."

JOHNNYCAKES, NEWPORT COUNTY STYLE

Mix 1 c. stone-ground white cornmeal, ½ t. salt, 1½ c. cold milk, and 2 T. melted butter. Mixture will be thin. Spoon onto buttered griddle in 5-in. rounds and fry until golden.

Johnny Marzetti. Also "Johnny Mazetti." A baked dish of ground meat, tomato, and macaroni. It was created at the Marzetti Restaurant in Columbus, Ohio, in the 1920s, and named after the owner's brother, Johnny.

JOHNNY MARZETTI

Brown 1½ lb. ground beef with 1 chopped onion, add 1 can tomatoes, 1 can mushrooms, 1 can tomato paste, and ¼ lb. Cheddar or mozzarella cheese. Cook until tender and well blended, place on top of 8 oz. boiled noodles, sprinkle with cheese and bread crumbs, and bake at 300° for about 40 min. Serves 8.

jojoba. A shrub (*Simmondsia chinensis*) and its nut, which is considered better used in a beverage than in other forms of food (1920).

jolly boy. A nineteenth-century New England fried cake. Jolly boys were sometimes split in half, buttered, and served with maple syrup.

JOLLY BOY

Stir ½ t. baking soda into 1 c. sour milk, then add 1 beaten egg and ½ c. molasses. Mix in 2½ c. cornmeal or rye meal to form a biscuit dough. Drop balls of dough into hot oil and fry until golden brown. Makes about 25.

jook. A rice gruel sold in inexpensive Chinese-American "jook house" restaurants (see JUKE below) in San Francisco's Chinatown. Such places became popular just after World War II. See also JUKE.

jujube (*Ziziphus jujuba*). Also, "Chinese date." The fruit of an Old World tree having dark red skin and yellowish flowers. The term, which comes from the Middle English *iuiube*, also applies to several varieties of candies that are fruit-flavored and chewy, though not necessarily similar in taste to the jujube fruit.

A commercially produced candy called "Jujubes" (which probably took its name from the ju-ju gum that gave the tiny morsels their chewy texture) came on the American market sometime before 1920 and was followed by "Jujyfruits," which were shaped like candy berries, in 1920. Both candies are produced by the Heide company of New Jersey.

juke. Also, "jook" or "juke house." A roadside saloon, usually of a very low grade and long associated with prostitution in the South, where most jukes were operated. The word, which found its way into print only in 1934, derives from the African Wolof *dzug*, "to lead a disorderly life," and many of the jukes were frequented by African Americans.

By the 1940s "to juke" meant to go around to various bars and taverns, often in search of prostitutes. The word survives today in "jukebox," an automatic record player operated by dropping a coin in a slot and pushing buttons that indicate a listed song.

The food in such places usually included barbecued ribs and sandwiches, aside from liquor and beer, and jukes became known for their bold and intimidating signs, such as the one printed outside a Florida juke—YOU CAN DRINK IN HERE, BUT YOU GO OUTSIDE TO GET DRUNK—or this one printed on the ceiling of an Alabama juke—WHAT THE HELL ARE YOU LOOKING UP HERE FOR?

julekake. Also, "julekage" and "julicokki." A Christmas cake of dried fruits and nuts, served traditionally in Scandinavian-American homes. The term, which means "Yule cake," dates in print to 1940.

jumble. Also, "jumbal." A simple spiced butter cookie, usually with nuts "jumbled" up in the dough (1827). Jumbles, among the first American cookies, came in various shapes, sometimes dropped on a baking sheet, sometimes cut with a cookie cutter. The first printed recipe appeared in Lettice Bryan's *The Kentucky Housewife* (1839), where they are called "common jumbles" made into rings; they do not contain nuts.

JUMBLE

Blend ¼ c. butter with 2 c. flour. Blend in 2 beaten eggs, ½ c. grated coconut, ½ t. rosewater, and ¾ c. walnuts. Make a stiff dough. Drop by teaspoon onto a buttered baking sheet and bake for 10 min. at 450°.

junk food. Inexpensive food with little nutritional value, often eaten as snacks or bought at fast-food establishments. Junk food might include potato chips, pretzels, tortilla chips, sodas, french-fried potatoes, sugared cereals, candy, and ice cream. The first appearance of the term in print was in an article by food writer Gael Greene called "Confessions of a Sensualist" in *New York* magazine for May 17, 1971, in which she wrote, "My respect for the glories of French cuisine are unsurpassed, but I am a fool for junk food."

K

kaiser roll. Also, "Vienna roll" and "hard roll." A crisp, puffy, light roll used to make sandwiches in delicatessens or eaten as a breakfast roll. The name is from the German *kaiser,* "emperor," and refers to the crownlike appearance of the roll.

The kaiser roll originated in Vienna. Some say it was named after Franz Josef (1830–1916), emperor of Austria from 1848 to 1916, and was brought to America by German and Jewish immigrants. Today the confection is usually called simply a "hard roll" and is often topped with poppyseeds.

kalua pig. A Hawaiian form of barbecue in which a whole pig is baked in a pit dug in the ground called an *imu.* The pit is lined with wood, rocks are added, and a fire lighted. Once the fire is burning well, the wood is removed, and the pit is lined with ti or banana leaves. The pig is also wrapped in leaves and placed in the pit, which is then covered with more leaves. The pig is usually seasoned beforehand. It is commonly accompanied by servings of roasted bananas, sweet potatoes, or taro.

kamikaze. A cocktail made with citrus juices, Cointreau, and vodka. The name derives from the Japanese term, meaning "divine wind," for the Japanese pilots of the last years of World War II who would commit suicide by crashing their planes into American ships; metaphorically, drinking such a cocktail would be a suicidal act.

The drink may have once had less dramatic associations. Bartender Tony Lauriano claimed he created the drink at Les Pyrénées Restaurant in New York City in 1972 to honor the Broadway show *Jesus Christ Superstar,* after which the cocktail was originally named. Later the same ingredients came to be mixed into what was called the "kamikaze," but the person who coined that name is unknown.

KAMIKAZE

Shake with ice the juice of 1 lemon and 1 lime, 1½ oz. Cointreau, and 1½ oz. vodka. Garnish with sprig of mint.

kaukau. Hawaiian word for food or, as a verb, to eat or drink (1820), derived from pidgin Chinese *chowchow.*

kedgeree. An East Indian dish brought to America by seamen that was originally composed of rice, lentils, eggs, and spices (1916). New Englanders had added cod or other fish by the eighteenth century. The word comes from the Hindi *khichrī* from the Sanskrit *khiccā.*

KEDGEREE

In a double boiler combine 2 c. cooked rice, 2 c. cooked cod, 4 chopped hard-boiled eggs, 2 T. minced parsley, ½ c. heavy cream, 1 t. salt, and ⅛ t. pepper. Heat thoroughly. Serves 6.

keech cake. Also, "keeling." A Pennsylvania-German small cake made with cornmeal but without yeast and fried in fat. The name derives from the German *Küchlein.*

Kentucky breakfast. A colloquial slur defined as "three cocktails and a chaw of terbacker" (1882).

ketchup. Also, "catsup" and "catchup." A variety of condiments, the most common of which contains pickle and tomato. The word derives from Chinese *ket-tsiap,* "pickled fish sauce," which was picked up by English sailors in the seventeenth century and first mentioned in print circa 1690. Since in America most ketchups were made with tomato (bottled tomato ketchups were sold as of 1876 by the F. & J. Heinz Company of Pennsylvania), "tomato ketchup" as a description was little used after the end of the nineteenth century. Few Americans make their own ketchup any longer, though the bottled variety has come to be thought of as a necessary condiment with hamburgers, and much facile criticism of American food is aimed at the frequency with which Americans pour ketchup on their food, even though it is a traditional item both here and in England. "Tomato soy" is a nineteenth-century form of ketchup.

The following recipe is from Jacqueline Harrison Smith's *Famous Old Receipts* (1908):

KETCHUP

Peel 4 qt. tomatoes and place in a kettle with 2 qt. vinegar, 6 chopped red peppers, 4 T. salt, black pepper, 2 T. dry mustard, and 3 T. allspice. Boil for 4 hr. until thickened. Bottle, seal, and serve as a condiment for meat and fish.

---

kettle meat. Offal and meat from the head of an animal (1968).

Kickapoo Indian Medicine. A trademark name for a beverage produced by John Healy and Charles Bigelow of New Haven, Connecticut. It was promoted as a tonic for neuralgia and "impure blood" and derived its name from a band of Native Americans from various tribes whom the two hucksters called "full-blooded Kickapoo Indians" (an actual branch of the Algonquian tribe originally from the Midwest) and featured as of 1881 in a series of traveling Wild West-type shows throughout New England. The name of the drink was later adapted by cartoonist Al Capp as "Kickapoo Joy Juice" in his hillbilly comic strip "L'il Abner."

kidney bean (*Phaseolus vulgaris*). A species of kidney-shaped bean, the most familiar being reddish brown in color. The word was first printed in 1540.

kielbasa. Also, "kolbasy" and other spellings, or "Polish sausage." A pork sausage (sometimes containing beef or veal) seasoned with garlic. Kielbasa is sold in long links and is usually smoked and pre-cooked, then eaten in smaller chunks. The word is from the Polish for the same sausage. *Kolbasa* is a Russian alternative. The term was first printed in the 1920s. The word was also mentioned in American print in Saul Bellows's 1953 novel *The Adventures of Augie March:* "Just catch the picture of this lousy classroom, and all these poor punks full of sauerkraut and bread with pig's-feet, with immigrant blood and washday smells and kielbasa and homebrew beer."

killer bar. A bar whose liberal policy toward customers' alcohol limit results in many accidents traced to inebriation. According to an article in *The New York Times* (March 29, 1987), the state of Massachusetts began in 1982 to ask intoxicated offenders where they'd had their last drink in an effort to find bars that were habitually serving customers already intoxicated. In local parlance these establishments were called "multiple offender bars" or "killer bars."

King cake. A brioche-style cake made during the Louisiana carnival season, beginning in January and ending at Mardi Gras, during which time bakeries produce about 250,000 such cakes and many "King cake parties" are held (1889). By tradition the cake contains a red bean (sometimes covered in gold or silver leaf) or a figurine of the baby Jesus. It is sold widely throughout Louisiana during the weeks prior to Mardi Gras, and the person who finds the bean or figurine is promised good luck.

There are various stories as to the origins of the cake, though most in some way derive from the legend of the Three Kings visiting the infant Jesus in Bethlehem, as described in the New Testament. In the first half of the sixteenth century France commemorated Kings' Day—the twelfth day after Christmas—with a "Twelfth Night cake." A century later King Louis XIV took part in such a feast at which a *gâteau des Rois* ("Kings' cake") contained a hidden bean or ceramic figure, as it does to this day.

Before the Civil War American King cakes often contained gold, diamonds, or valuables instead of beans; after the war, with the end of gala Creole balls in Louisiana, peas, beans, pecans, and coins were used, and in 1871 the tradition of choosing the queen of the Mardi Gras was determined by who drew the prize in the cake. Then, in 1952, Donald and Gerald Entringer, owner of a New Orleans bakery called McKenzie's, began baking china dolls (late plastic) into the cake, which is the predominant tradition today.

The colors of purple (for justice), green (for faith), and gold (for power) that traditionally tint the cake's icing first appeared in 1872 after the Rex Krewe, a Mardi Gras parade organization, chose those colors to celebrate that year's festival.

KING CAKE

Proof 2 envelopes yeast with a little sugar in 1 c. warm water. In a saucepan melt 1 stick butter, 1 c. evaporated milk, ½ c. sugar, and 2 t. salt. In another bowl beat 4 eggs until light, then into the yeast mixture. Add milk mixture and blend well. Gradually add 5 c. flour and knead for about 8–10 min. Place in a greased bowl, turn to grease all sides, cover the bowl with a cloth, and let the dough double in bulk, about 2 hr. Punch dough down and roll out to about 18 in. by 36 in. Brush with melted butter.

> *Sprinkle with a mixture of 1 c. sugar, ½ c. brown sugar, and 2 T. ground cinnamon. Cut dough into three strips, roll each one up, braid, insert a bean or figurine somewhere in the dough, then cover with damp cloth and let rise again until double.*
>
> *Bake at 350° for 20–30 min. Glaze with icings colored green, yellow, and purple.*

kingfish. Also, "black mullet," "hogfish," "whiting," "sea mink" and other names. Either of two saltwater fish, *Menticirrhus americanus* or *M. saxitilis* (1743), although the name is also applied to the Spanish MACKEREL (*Scomberomorus cavalla* or *S. regalis*).

King Ranch chicken. Also, "King Ranch casserole." A layered casserole dish made with cut-up poached chicken, cream of mushroom soup, chilies, chicken soup, grated cheese, corn tortillas, and tomatoes (most often Ro-Tel brand). The dish is very commonly served at Texas clubwomen's buffets. For unknown reasons, the name, which dates in cookbooks at least to the 1950s, refers to the King Ranch in Kingsville, Texas, but there is no evidence that the dish was created there.

kishka. A Jewish-American baked sausage made with beef, flour, and spices. The word, from the Russian for "intestines," was first printed circa 1935.

kiwifruit (*Actinida chinensis*). Formally known as the "Chinese gooseberry," this round green fruit with black seeds originated in the Chang Kiang Valley of China, where it was called *yang tao*. Plants were brought to the United States in 1904 and seeds to New Zealand in 1906. But agricultural testing of the berries did not begin until 1935 in the United States, and the first commercial cultivation in America, by John Heinke, was in 1960, with nine vines, in Paradise, California. The first New Zealand-raised fruit was served a year later at Trader Vic's restaurant in San Francisco.

In 1962 a request for the fruit by a customer in a Los Angeles Safeway supermarket led the manager to contact Frieda Caplan of Produce Specialties, Inc. (now called Frieda's, Inc.) of Los Angeles who began importing the fruit from New Zealand. A year later, customs broker Norman Sondag of Ziel Growers suggested to Caplan that the name might be more appealing to Americans if changed to "kiwifruit" (because of its association with New Zealand and its resemblance to the fuzzy little kiwi bird), which the New Zealand growers thereupon did.

Caplan went on to buy the entire harvest of Heinke and other American growers in the late 1960s, and the kiwifruit gained enormous popularity as part of the NOUVELLE CUISINE movement of the 1970s and 1980s, when it was used in everything from desserts to sauces and garnishes.

Today 95 percent of the U.S. crop is grown in California on about 9,300 acres by 650 growers, primarily in the San Joaquin Valley. The overwhelmingly predominant variety is the "Hayward," developed by New Zealand horticulturist Hayward Wright.

klatch. Also, "coffee klatch" or "kaffeeklatch." An informal get-together, usually with the service of coffee and sweet confections (1888). From the German *Klatsch*, "gossip."

knish. A Jewish-American pastry stuffed with mashed potato, cheese, buckwheat groats, or chopped liver. Usually knishes are baked, though sometimes they are fried.

Knish is a Yiddish word (first in print in 1916) that comes from the Russian *knys*, or Polish *knyz*. The ubiquity of the knish in New York's Jewish community led to the lower section of Second Avenue being nicknamed "Knish Alley." A. Gross's *Kibitzer's Dictionary* (1930) humorously defines knishes as "dyspepsia."

KNISH

> Mix 1 c. mashed potatoes with 1 beaten egg, 1 T. chicken fat, ½ t. salt, a pinch of pepper, 1 T. minced onion, and enough flour to make a dough that is stiff enough to be shaped into oval patties about 4½-in. long. Make a depression in the center of each patty, fill with cooked chopped chicken liver, mashed potato, cheese, or buckwheat groats, and enclose filling with folds of dough. Brush the dough with egg yolk, bake on a greased sheet at 350° for about 20 min. Makes about 6.

knockwurst. The common American spelling (first in print in 1929) for the German word for smoked beef and/or pork sausage *knackwurst* (also used in American English), whose name refers to the crackling sound the skin of the sausage makes when bitten into. The sausage also goes by the name *Regensburger* in Germany. Knockwurst may be boiled, grilled, or steamed, and is often eaten with sauerkraut. A "special" is a New York term for a beef knockwurst eaten like a HOT DOG and sold at DELICATESSENS.

kolache. Also, "kolach" and "kolacky." A sweet pastry bun filled with cheese, poppyseeds, sausage, or, more commonly, jam or fruits like cherry, apricot, peach, pineapple, or prune, first mentioned in print in Willa Cather's novel *My Ántonia* (1919). It is of Czechoslovak origins (the Czech word is *koláce)* and, as "kolacky," entered print about 1915.

Kolaches are most popular in West Texas, where Czech immigrants settled in 1852.

kosher. A Yiddish term for food prepared according to strict Jewish dietary laws. The word is from the Hebrew kāshēr, "proper," and has taken on colloquial meanings in America to mean "correct" or "honest" or "acceptable."

According to kosher laws, meat and milk may not be eaten together, a prohibition that even necessitates separate cooking utensils and dishes both in the home and at food-processing plants. There are also "clean" and "unclean" animals that are listed in Leviticus and Deuteronomy, kosher animals being those that have a cloven hoof and chew their cud. A nonkosher (*trayf*) animal chews its cud but is not cloven-hoofed. Fish with scales and fins are kosher; birds of prey are not.

Slaughter of animals must be done according to a ritual by a *schochet*, who slashes the throat, and the meat must then be stamped by a supervisor, the *mashgiach*.

These laws are biblical in origin, and, as Leo Rosten notes in *The Joys of Yiddish* (1968):

> *Eating and drinking, to the ancient Jews, involved grave religious obligations, and strongly reinforced the idea of the Jews as a people "set apart," chosen by the Lord as "Mine . . ." "holy unto Me" (Leviticus). The strict observance of dietary rules was believed to strengthen the dedication of a Jew to his role as one of God's instruments for the redemption of mankind.*

There are 97 kosher-certifying organizations in the United States, with 23,590 U.S. food products certified kosher as of 1993.

Some American Jews have modified adherence to kosher rules over the years, especially in food stores or restaurants catering to a non-Jewish clientele. When the first New York City nonkosher DELICATESSENS opened at the turn of century, store owners often used the term *wurshtgesheft* ("sausage shop") in their window rather than the Hebrew letters for "kosher," but a group of rabbis forced the city to ban its usage in favor of "kosher-style."

Kossuth cake. A sponge cake filled with whipped cream or ice cream, covered with icing, and set in individual paper cups. According to tradition, the cake was created in 1851 by an East Baltimore confectioner to honor the arrival in that city of Lajos Kossuth (1802–94), a Hungarian revolutionary leader who sought funds from the Marylanders. (Legend has it that he collected only twenty-five dollars.)

kreplach. A dumpling containing chopped meat or cheese, often served in soup. The word derives from the German *kreppel*. Kreplachs are by tradition served on Purim, Rosh Hashanah, and the day before Yom Kippur. In its use as a Jewish dish, the word was first mentioned in print circa 1890.

KREPLACH

Mix together 1 beaten egg, 1 c. flour, and ¼ t. salt, and knead into an elastic dough. Roll out very thin and cut into 3-in. squares. Mix together 1 c. chopped cooked beef, 2 T. minced onion, 2 T. chicken fat, and ½ t. salt, place some in each half of the squares, then fold them to form triangles. Secure edges with a fork and boil in salted water for 20 min. Serve in soup or fry in hot fat. Makes 24.

kringle. A lemon-flavored Christmas cookie (1950). The name derives from the German *Christkindlein*, "gifts of the Christ Child," which in American became "Kris Kringle" (also an early name for Saint Nicholas or Santa Claus).

"Kringle" is also the name for a multilayered pastry with a variety of fruit or nut fillings. It is a specialty of the Wisconsin city of Racine, whose nickname is Kringleville because of its large Danish immigrant population, who called cookies and tea cakes made with butter "kringle." According to Jane and Michael Stern in *A Taste of America* (1988), Racine's kringle refers to a "broad cake wider than a dinner plate . . . less than an inch high, a lightweight sheaf of several dozen near-microscopic layers of dough and butter—like an enormous croissant but flakier—glazed with brown sugar and cinnamon, then filled with pecan, apple, date, prune, or cheese, and finally iced with a clear sugar frosting. One kringle serves about a dozen people."

KRINGLE COOKIES

Cream 8 T. unsalted butter with ½ c. sugar. Beat 6 egg yolks and 2 whole eggs until creamy and add to *butter and sugar mixture. Add grated zest of I lemon and I t. lemon extract. Sift 3½ c. flour into the batter to make a soft dough. Roll out to ¼-in. thickness, cut into ring shapes, and set on greased cookie sheets. Bake at 375° for I0 min. Cool on racks.*

kugel. A noodle or potato pudding served on the Jewish Sabbath. The word is from the Yiddish for a "ball." If made with noodles, the more frequently prepared of the two varieties, the dish is called *lukshen kugel*. Raisins are sometimes added to sweeten the dish. It is also commonly served with apple sauce. "Kugel" first appears in English print in 1840.

KUGEL

Cook ½ lb. noodles in boiling water and drain. Beat 3 egg yolks with 2 T. chicken fat, 2 T. sugar, and ½ t. salt, then fold into noodles. Beat 3 egg whites until stiff, fold into noodle mixture. Pour into greased pan, bake in 350° oven for about 30 min., then brown under flame. Serves 6.

kulolo. Hawaiian word for a steamed pudding made with taro and coconut (1938).

kumiss. Also, "koumyss," "koumiss," and other variants. A beverage of fermented milk, possibly originating with the Mongols, having an acrid flavor and a small bit of alcohol present. Kumiss was thought to have some digestive benefits. The word comes from the Russian and was first printed in English around 1600. "Laban" is a similar item.

KUMISS

Dissolve 4 oz. sugar in I gallon skimmed milk, pour into I-qt. bottles, add 2 oz. dry yeast to each bottle, and seal tightly. Set bottles in warm place to ferment, then in cool cellar, set on their sides. Fermentation takes about three days.

Kwanzaa. A Swahili term meaning "first fruits of the harvest," which in the United States has come to mean an African-American festival that runs from December 26 to New Year's Day. Kwanzaa was created by Maulana (Ron) Karenga of California State University in Long Beach, California, in 1966 as a way to encourage African-Americans to commemorate their African heritage, which is marked on the last day of the festival with a feast called *Kwanzaa Karamu*, featuring the foods—of Africa, South America, and the Caribbean. In 1991 Eric V. Copage published the first cookbook about the festival entitled *Kwanzaa: An African-American Celebration of Culture and Cooking.*

L

lactic acid. A spoilage inhibitor, added to cheese, desserts, carbonated drinks, and Spanish olives, that imparts a tart flavor to foods.

la cuite. Cooked sugar syrup in the last stage before it blackens and becomes bitter. The term is used among Louisiana Cajun cooks and derives from the French word for "cooking."

ladies' night. A bar promotion offering women lower prices on drinks on a certain night of the week. The idea is to attract more women and therefore more men to the bar. In 1972 the New York State Division of Human Rights prohibited ladies' night promotions at Yankee Stadium because they discriminated against men, and in 1986 the Connecticut Human Rights Commission ruled that ladies' nights be prohibited in all public bars for the same reason.

Lady Baltimore cake. A white cake filled with nuts and raisins and covered with a vanilla-and-egg-white frosting.

There are several stories of how the cake was named, but the most accepted version concerns a cake by this name baked by a Charleston, South Carolina, belle named Alicia Rhett Mayberry for novelist Owen Wister, who not only described the confection in his next book but named the novel itself *Lady Baltimore* (1906). In *American Food* (1974) Evan Jones noted that "it may also be true that the 'original' recipe became the property of the Misses Florence and Nina Ottolengui, who managed Charleston's Lady Baltimore Tea Room for a quarter of a century and annually baked and shipped to Owen Wister one of the very American cakes his novel had helped to make famous." Alicia Rhett Mayberry in *200 Years of Charleston Cooking* (ed. Lettie Gay, 1930) says the recipe came from the Woman's Exchange when Wister wrote his novel.

LADY BALTIMORE CAKE

Cream ½ c. butter and 1½ c. sugar, adding 1 c. water gradually, then 3 c. flour and 2 t. baking powder. Fold in 4 stiffly beaten egg whites and 1 t. vanilla. Bake in 3 buttered cake pans in a 375° oven.

Boil 1½ c. sugar and ½ c. water in a double boiler until syrup forms a thread. Beat well and pour slowly over 2 stiffly beaten egg whites. Beat until mixture may be spread on the cakes. Sprinkle on ½ c. raisins, 5 diced figs, ½ c. chopped pecans, and ⅓ c. candied cherries. Boil 2 c. sugar with ½ c. water in double boiler. Boil until syrup forms a thread, and beat well. Slowly pour over 2 stiffly beaten egg whites and 1 t. vanilla. Spread completely over layered cake.

ladyfinger. A light sponge-cake biscuit. The name comes from the usual shape of the confection, which is long and narrow, light and delicate. (OKRA is sometimes called "ladies' fingers" too.) The word often appears in the possessive, "Lady's finger," and the plural, "ladies' fingers," and was first mentioned by John Keats in his poem *The Cap and Bells* (1820). Ladyfingers have long been a popular confection in America, where some recipes call for the pastry to be pushed through a pastry tube.

LADYFINGER

Beat 1 egg white with a pinch of salt until foamy, add 1½ T. sugar and beat until stiff. Beat 1 egg yolk with ½ t. vanilla and 1½ T. sugar until light. Fold in whites and yolks together, then fold in ¼ c. flour. Spoon long, finger-shaped portions onto ungreased paper set on a cookie sheet and bake about 10 min. at 350° Cool, dust with confectioners' sugar. Makes 12.

lady lock. A spiral-shaped pastry filled with whipped cream or marshmallow cream and shaped to resemble a lock of hair (1920).

Lafayette gingerbread. Also called "Mary Ball Washington's ginger bread." A cakelike ginger-and-spice bread made by George Washington's mother when General Lafayette paid her a visit at her Fredericksburg, Virginia, home in 1784.

LAFAYETTE GINGERBREAD

Cream ½ c. butter, 1 c. brown sugar, and 1 c. molasses with ½ c. warm milk, 2 T. powdered ginger, 1½ t. cinnamon, 1½ t. mace, 1½ t. ground nutmeg, and ¼ c. brandy. Sift 3 c. flour with 1 t. cream of tartar and 3 beaten eggs, and add to butter mixture. Add the juice of 1 orange and its grated rind, 1 t. baking soda in 2 T. water, and 1 c. raisins. Blend thoroughly. Bake in a buttered 12-by-9-in. pan at 350° for about 45 min. Serves 15.

lagniappe. A Creole term for a small extra gift or bonus, such as a free roll given when one buys a dozen. It has been used in Louisiana at least since 1840 and is taken from the Spanish *la ñapa*, "the gift," by way of the Peruvian Quechuan word *yápa*, addition. In *Life on the Mississippi* (1883), Mark Twain wrote:

> We picked up one excellent word—a word worth traveling to New Orleans to get; a nice, limber, expressive, handy word—"Lagniappe." They pronounce it lan-nyyap. . . . It is the equivalent of the thirteenth roll in a "baker's dozen." It is something thrown in, gratis, for good measure. The custom originated in the Spanish quarter of the city. When a child or a servant buys something in a shop—or even the mayor or the governor, for aught I know—he finishes the operation by saying: "Give me something for lagniappe."
>
> The shopman always responds; gives the child a bit of licorice-root, gives the servant a cheap cigar or a spool of thread, gives the governor—I don't know what he gives the governor, support, likely.
>
> When you are invited to drink—and this does occur now and then in New Orleans—and you say, "What, again?—no I've had enough," the other party says, "But just this one more time—this is for lagniappe." . . . If the waiter in the restaurant stumbles and spills a gill of coffee down the back of your neck he says, "F'r lagniappe, sah," and gets you another cup without extra charge.

Lalla Rookh. A nineteenth-century dessert made with eggs, spirits, and whipped cream, although there are many variations. A 1910 cookbook by San Francisco chef Victor Hitzler of the Hotel St. Francis listed Lalla Rookh as nothing more than a crème de menthe cordial poured over ice in a sherbet glass to be served as a digestive between courses.

The name comes from a long poem about a beautiful princess of India, *Lalla Rookh* (1817), by Thomas Moore. The poem, praised for its "barbaric splendors" and exotic details, was a great success in both England and America, and this rich dessert was named after the poem's heroine.

LALLA ROOKH

In a saucepan beat 5 egg yolks with 1 c. sugar, stirring until thickened. Cool, then add ¾ c. brandy and ¼ c. rum. Fold in 1 qt. whipped cream and 5 stiffly beaten egg whites. Mix in a pinch of nutmeg, pack in ice and salt, and freeze.

lamb. A sheep (*Ovis aries*) less than a year old, usually slaughtered between four and twelve months for its meat. The word is from the Germanic *lambiz*. The meat of the lamb is considered one of the most desirable foods by many people, but it has never been among the more popular meats in the United States, where beef and pork are preferred. Americans have also tended to slaughter their lambs somewhat later than Europeans and Asians, so that the taste is not as delicate as it is in other countries. Also, the social divisiveness and bloodshed caused by the introduction of sheep herds into the steer country of the western territories in the nineteenth century gave lamb a bad reputation for most of the last century. In fact, Americans in 1998 ate only 1.3 pounds of lamb per person as compared to 68 pounds of beef and 53 pounds of pork. When lamb is eaten, it is usually in the form of a roast or in lamb chops, much of it shipped in frozen from New Zealand.

There are three categories of lamb recognized in the United States: "baby" or "hothouse lamb," which is milk-fed and usually slaughtered under six weeks of age; "spring lamb," milk-fed and slaughtered at under four months; and "lamb," weaned on grass and slaughtered under one year; after one year the animal's meat is termed "mutton, which is not very popular in America. Most United States lamb is sold as spring lamb, which federal regulations require be slaughtered between the beginning of March and the close of the week containing the first Monday in October. A very small amount of baby lamb comes from Pennsylvania and New Jersey.

Lamb is customarily served with mint jelly in the United States, and its greatest popularity is at the Easter meal.

lambs' quarters (*Chenopodium album*). Also, "lamb's quarters," and as a single word. A species of a wild plant, called "pigweed," "goosefoot," and "wild spinach," that originated in Europe and spread throughout the American West. The name, first in American print as of 1804, derives from "Lammas quarter," an ancient English festival at which a similar plant (*Atripex patula*) played a role. The Hopis packed the leaves around foods to be baked in order to keep in moisture, but others used them in stews or in salads. They may also be cooked like spinach, and the black seeds of the plant were used for breads. In the Southwest the plant is sometimes called by its Spanish-Mexican names *quelites* and *epazote*.

lamb's lettuce. Also, "Pawnee lettuce" and "fetticus." A salad green (*Valeriana locust*) that grows into the fall and is usually eaten fresh (1817).

Lane cake. A layer cake with a fluffy frosting and containing coconut, chopped fruits, and nuts in the filling. The cake was named after Emma Rylander Lane of Clayton, Alabama, who published the original recipe under the name "Prize Cake" in her cookbook *Some Good Things to Eat* (1898). But, according to Cecily Brownstone, author of the *Associated Press Cookbook* (1972) and friend of Mrs. Lane's granddaughter, the original recipe is very imprecise. In various forms it has become popular throughout the South.

According to Mrs. Lane, the cake "is much better . . . made a day or two before using."

LANE CAKE

Beat 2 c. sugar, 1¾ c. butter, and 2 t. vanilla until light. Combine 3½ c. flour, 4½ t. baking powder, and 1½ t. salt and add to butter mixture, alternating with 1½ c. milk until smooth. Fold in 8 stiffly beaten egg whites. Divide batter and pour into 3 buttered and floured cake pans. Bake for 20 min. at 375°, then cool. Melt ½ c. butter with 1 c. sugar, ⅓ c. bourbon, and ⅓ c. water, bring to boil, dissolve ingredients together, and stir half the mixture into 9 lightly beaten egg yolks. Return to saucepan and cook until thickened. Remove from heat, then stir in 1 c. chopped raisins, ¼ c. chopped pecans, ½ c. chopped maraschino cherries, ½ c. flaked coconut, and ¾ t. vanilla. Cool to room temperature, then spread over cake layers and on top. Combine 1 c. sugar, ⅓ c. water, ¼ t. cream of tartar, and a dash of salt in a saucepan and bring to boil, stirring until sugar is dissolved. Add 1 t. vanilla, then pour mixture very slowly into 2 beaten egg whites. Frost the cake with this icing.

lap lunch. A meal eaten on a plate set on one's lap at a casual party.

last call. Bartenders' announcement to customers just before closing time that last orders for drinks must be put in immediately.

Late Harvest. A term used by American winemakers to indicate a wine made from grapes picked late in the fall, after the grape has been attacked by the mold *Botrytis cinerea*. The mold allows moisture to escape and concentrates the sugars in the grapes, resulting in a very sweet, almost syrupy wine having high alcohol content. In California Late Harvest wines are often made from the JOHANNISBERG RIESLING grape.

lath-open bread. Appalachian biscuit-dough bread made into thin cakes so that when broken with the fingers breaks into flakes that resemble lath (1913).

latke. A Jewish pancake, usually made from potatoes, traditionally served at Chanukah (1927). The dish commemorates the biblical story of the Jewish Maccabees' defeat of the Syrians in 165 B.C. They found in the Temple of Jerusalem only enough oil to burn for one night, but the oil miraculously burned for eight nights. The oil used for frying the latkes symbolizes this miracle.

This tradition developed among the Ashkenazi Jews of Northern and Eastern Europe, many of whom came to America in the late nineteenth century and who carried the tradition with them. The potato latke has been made for over two hundred years, after the potato, brought from America in the sixteenth century, was accepted by Europeans as an edible food.

LATKE

Wash 6 potatoes and dice. Dry them, then grate, retaining some of the juice. Grate 1 small onion, add ½ t. salt and 1 egg. Blend well. Mix in 3 t. matzo meal with ½ t. baking powder, and blend into potatoes. Drop spoonfuls of the mixture into hot fat and cook until browned on all sides. Drain. Serve with applesauce or sour cream. Serves 4.

laulau. Hawaiian word for food cooked in ti leaves, usually steamed or baked in the IMU pit (1938).

leather. An early American confection made from dried-fruit "butters" or purees baked slowly and cut in long strips resembling strips of leather (1849).

LEATHER

🍴 Cook 1 lb. of fruit, such as peach or apricot, in simmering water until tender. Rub through a sieve or food mill, add 1 part brown sugar or honey to 4 parts fruit puree, then simmer for 5 min. Spread in thin sheets over a buttered baking pan and let dry out thoroughly in a slow, 250° oven for 2 hr. Cool, sprinkle with confectioners' sugar and, if desired, roll up. Serves 4.

leather or feather. Airline workers' slang for the choice between the beef or chicken entrées offered as part of in-flight service. The term was first in print in 1989.

lebkuchen. A Pennsylvania-Dutch spiced drop cake made especially at Christmastime (1906). The term is from German.

LEBKUCHEN

🍴 Boil 1 qt. honey in a pan, then mix ¾ lb. sugar with ¼ lb. citron, ½ lb. ground almonds, ¼ lb. orange peel, 1 oz. cinnamon, 1 pkg. yeast, 3 T. cherry brandy, some nutmeg, and 2¼ lb. flour. Knead for 15 min. Let stand overnight. Roll out and cut into 2-in. squares. Bake in a tin dish.

lecithin. An emulsifier and antioxidant found in animal and plant tissues and used in baked goods, chocolate, ice cream, and other foods. Lecithin also keeps oil and water from separating.

Lee cake. A white cake flavored with citrus rind and juice, supposedly based on recipes of cooks for General Robert E. Lee (1807–70), commander of the Confederate Army in the Civil War.

LEE CAKE

🍴 Beat 10 eggs until light in color and add 1 lb. sugar and 1 lb. flour, alternating the two ingredients. Grate in the rind of 1 lemon and add its juice, mix well, pour batter into cake pans, and bake at 350° until inserted knife comes out clean. Make icing of 1 lb. powdered sugar, 2 beaten egg whites, and the juice and rind of 1 orange. Coat layers of cake, sides, and top.

leek (*Allium porrum*). An onionlike plant of the lily family having green leaves and a white bulbous stalk. It is eaten as a vegetable, usually boiled, but has had little popularity in the United States until recently. Wild leek (*A. tricoccum*) is found in eastern North America. The word in Old English is *Lēac*.

lefse. Norwegian-American thin, flat bread made from potatoes (1902). From the Norwegian.

lemon (*Citrus limon*). A yellow-skinned, tangy citrus fruit native to Asia. Its juice, pulp, and rind are used in a wide variety of dishes, desserts, drinks, and COCKTAILS. The word is from the Persian *līmūn*, and first appears in print about 1400. "Lemonade" is sweetened juice and water.

Lemons have been cultivated around the eastern Mediterranean for at least twenty-five hundred years, and after the Crusades they became a desirable fruit in Europe, where they began to be grown in Sicily, Spain, and other Mediterranean countries. Legend has it that Columbus brought lemon seeds to Florida, and Spanish friars grew the fruit in California, where it flourished in the middle of the nineteenth century—especially the Eureka (possibly first cultivated in California or brought from Sicily) and the Lisbon (brought from Australia). In 1874 James W. Parkinson, writing of American dishes at the Philadelphia Centennial, noted that "citron" (*C. medica*), a lemon-like fruit, had "lately been transplanted in California, and promise[s] in the near future to equal the best."

In 1934 Irvin Swartzberg of Chicago began selling gallon bottles of fresh lemon juice to bars and restaurants, and, after perfecting a method of concentrating the juice with water, sold the product in the market under the name Puritan-ReaLemon.

"Lemon-meringue pie," made with lemon curd and topped with meringue, has been a favorite American dessert since the nineteenth century. "Shaker lemon pie," made from sliced onions, was beloved by the Shakers because lemons were one of the foods they themselves did not produce and were valued highly.

Today California produces most of the American lemon crop, with Florida and Texas also contributing. The common or "acid" lemon is the variety most used in the food industry and at home.

LEMON MERINGUE PIE

🍴 (A nineteenth-century dessert that has become one of the standards of the American kitchen.) Combine ⅓ c. cornstarch, ⅛ t. salt, and ⅔ c. sugar, stir in 1½ c. water, and cook over medium heat until mixture thickens and comes to a boil for 1 min. Remove from heat. Beat 4 egg yolks, stir in 2 T. of cornstarch mixture, then stir eggs into the rest of the cornstarch, being careful to stir out lumps. Add juice of 2 lemons and grated rind of 1 lemon. Cook in saucepan until thickened, but do not boil. Pour into pie crust and cool 10 min. Beat ½ c. sugar into 4 egg whites until stiff, mold on top of pie, bake in 400° oven until top is lightly browned. Cool.

lettuce. Any of a variety of plants in the genus *Lactuca,* especially *L. sativa,* cultivated for its leaves, which are used in salads. The word is from the Latin *lactuca,* which in Middle English became *letus.*

England had cultivated lettuce as of the fifteenth century, but Christopher Columbus may have been the first to bring it to America. Lettuce was grown only in home gardens until the twentieth century, when Americans' new appetite for salad made commercial production profitable. Today lettuce is raised in twenty of the states, cultivated in four main botanical varieties:

celtuce or asparagus lettuce (*L. s. asparagina*). Rarely seen in America.

head or cabbage lettuce (*L. s. capitata*). This variety includes the "butterhead," of which the "Bibb" (supposedly named after amateur breeder John B. Bibb of Frankfort, Kentucky, although the variety was introduced in 1890 as "Half Century") and the "Boston" are the principal horticultural varieties; and the "crisp head," which includes the "Imperial" and "iceberg" varieties, this last introduced by W. Atlee Burpee & Co. in 1894, which bacame the most popular lettice in America by the 1930s.

leaf lettuce (*L. s. crispa*). This variety includes the "oak leaf" and "salad bowl" lettuces.

romaine or Cos lettuce (*L. s. longifolia*). "Romaine" derives from Old French for the city of Rome, whereas "Cos" refers to the Greek island of Cos, or Kos, from which it may have originated.

liberty cabbage. A colloquialism created during World War I as a patriotic substitute for the German sauerkraut. The term was, as H. L. Mencken notes, "a complete failure."

Liederkranz. Trademark name for a strong-smelling cow's-milk cheese of distinctly American origins. Liederkranz began in 1889 when New York delicatessen owner Adolph Tode, who also owned the Monroe Cheese Company in Monroe, New York, asked his cheesemakers to try to duplicate the flavor of an imported German soft-ripened brick cheese known as *Bismarck Schlosskäse* ("Bismarck castle cheese") that was popular among German-Americans. Swiss immigrant cheesemaker Emil Frey took up the challenge and failed, although he managed to come up with a similar but distinctly different cheese that he sent to Tode, who ordered more. Unfortunately Frey was unable to duplicate the cheese until 1892, when Tode introduced it to a Popular singing group called the "Liederkranz Society" (whose members included Theodore Roosevelt) The word means "wreath of song" in German.

Liederkranz was an instant success, listed on a menu at the Liederkranz Halle in New York City for May 19, 1892, and its popularity caused the Monroe Cheese Company to expand production where there was more milk available, in Van Wert, Ohio. At first Tode could not reproduce the cheese, but did so after bringing in his old factory's equipment and allowing the bacteria to fill the air of his new plant.

In 1929 the Monroe Cheese Company was bought by the Borden Company, which in turn sold its natural cheese division to General Foods in 1982. This, in turn, was merged with Philip Morris's Kraft division in 1985, which has since stopped making the cheese altogether.

light. Also, "lite," "lighter" and "lower fat." A food industry term implying a fat content lower than other similar products. "Light beer" (which makes up 18 percent of the domestic market) may contain only one third the calories of regular beer.

But, according to the FDA Nutrition Labeling and Education Act of 1990, whose regulations were adopted in May 1993, a product labeled "light" may mean two things: First, that a nutritionally altered product contains one-third fewer calories or half the fat of the reference food. If the food derives 50 percent or more of its calories from fat, the reduction must be 50 percent of the fat. Second, that the sodium content of a low-calorie, low-fat food has been reduced by 50 percent. "Light in sodium" refers to a food in which sodium content has been reduced by at least 50 percent. The term "light" may continue to be used to describe properties such as texture and color if the label describes the intent, as in "light brown sugar" or "light and fluffy."

Meat, poultry, seafood and game products labeled "lean" must have less than 10 grams fat, less than 4 grams saturated fat, and less than 96 milligrams cholesterol per serving and per 100 grams. "Extra lean" products must contain less than 5 grams fat, less than 2 grams saturated fat, and less than 95 milligrams cholesterol.

"Reduced" means that a nutritionally altered product contains 25 percent less of a nutrient or of calories than the regular product (unless the regular product already meets the requirement). The rule for any food, altered or not, using the word less is the same.

"Low" (also "little, few," and "low source of") may be used on foods that could be eaten frequently without exceeding dietary guidelines for one or more of these components: fat, saturated fat, cholesterol, sodium, and calories. "Low fat" indicates 3 grams or less per serving; "low saturated fat," 1 gram or less; "low sodium," less than 140 milligrams per serving; "very low sodium," less than 35 milligrams; "low cholesterol," less than 20 milligrams per serving; "low calorie," 40 calories or less per serving.

"Free" means a product contains no amount of, or only physiologically inconsequential amounts of, one or more of the following: fat, saturated fat, cholesterol, sodium, sugars, and calories.

Under these regulations nutrition labeling is required on most foods (voluntary for many raw foods, many fresh fruits and vegetables, and raw fish).

lima bean (*Phaseolus limensis*). A green flat bean, called the "butter bean" in the South. The lima bean takes its name from the city of Lima, Peru, where it was cultivated very early. The bean was introduced to North America, where it was enjoyed by the Native Americans long before the arrival of the European settlers; it is the principal ingredient of SUCCOTASH.

The lima bean is first mentioned in print in 1756 and in William Cobbett's *American Gardener* (1819).

Lima beans are eaten fresh but are more often boiled and buttered. California produces most of the United States lima-bean crop.

lime (*Citrus aurantifolia*). A tangy green citrus fruit similar to the lemon. Its name derives from the Arabic *līmah*, and was first mentioned in English in 1615. Indigenous to Southeast Asia, the lime was introduced to Europe through Italy. In *Fading Feast* (1981), Raymond Sokolov writes, "Whether Columbus brought seeds of *C. aurantifolia* with him to Haiti in 1493 is a matter of conjecture, but it seems probable, since limes were flourishing on that island in 1520. Limes then spread gradually across the West Indies, westward to Mexico and northward to the Florida Keys." Lime trees

were established in the Keys by Dr. Henry Perrine in 1835, and these so-called "Key limes" (called "Mexican" in the Southwest) became a major commercial crop after 1906. But a hurricane in 1926 destroyed many of the groves. The groves were replanted with a more practical crossbreed called the "Tahiti" lime (particularly the "Persian," "Bearss," "Idemore," and "Pond" varieties), which had been grown in California since the 1850s and in Florida since 1883.

Today almost all limes grown in America are of the Tahiti variety, while true Key limes are a rarity grown only on private, noncommercial plots in the Florida Keys.

Americans use limes as a flavoring for desserts and cocktails and to enhance the flavor of fish and salads. The most famous confection made with limes is "Key lime pie," a tangy pie made with condensed milk and piled high with meringue or whipped cream. Because of the unavailability of true Key limes, except in the Florida Keys, Key lime pies are almost never made with anything but Tahiti limes.

Key lime pies were first made in the Keys in the 1850s. Jeanne A. Voltz, in *The Flavor of the South* (1977), explains that the recipe developed with the advent of sweetened condensed milk in 1856. Since there were few cows on the Keys, the new canned milk was welcomed by the residents and introduced into a pie made with lime juice.

The original pies were made with a pastry crust, but a crust made from graham crackers later became popular and today is a matter of preference, as is the choice between whipped cream and meringue toppings. There are three recipes for Key lime pie in *The Key West Cook Book* (1949), only one of which refers to a graham-cracker crust, and two of which do not require the pie to be baked. One has no topping, one whipped cream, and one meringue.

KEY LIME PIE

In a bowl combine ¼ c. graham-cracker crumbs, ⅓ c. sifted confectioners' sugar, and 6 T. unsalted butter, melted and cooled. Press the mixture into a pie plate to form a crust, bake in 350° oven for 10 min. until lightly browned, then cool on rack. Beat 4 egg yolks until light in color, stir in one 14-oz. can sweetened condensed milk, ¼ c. lime juice, ½ t. cream of tartar, then another ¼ c. lime juice. Spoon into shell and bake at 325° until it sets, about 10–15 min. Freeze for at least 3 hr. Beat 4 egg whites with ¼ c. sugar until stiff, spread over pie, and bake in 450° oven until meringue is golden.

limpa. Swedish-American rye bread made with molasses (1951). From the Swedish.

limpin' Suzan. A southern dish of red beans and rice (1952), a corollary to the more familiar HOPPING JOHN.

LIMPIN' SUZAN

Cover 1 lb. red beans with water and let soak for several hours. Drain, add 1 chopped onion, 1/4 lb. salt pork, and water to cover. Cook until tender, remove 1/2 c. of the beans and 2 T. of the liquid and mash into a puree. Add pepper and salt and 3–4 c. cooked rice. Cook through until heated, and top with the rest of the beans. Serves 6–8.

---

limu. Hawaiian word for edible seaweeds. In primitive Hawaiian culture women gathered and prepared seaweeds and made them a staple of their diet. Today Hawaiians eat about fifteen species, both fresh and salted but not usually dried. Some of the more popular "limu" include *wawae'iole*, *ogo*, and *manauea*. While many seaweeds are connected with legends and rituals, *limu kala* is specifically eaten at family gatherings called *ho'oponopono*, where grievances are aired and arguments settled peacefully. The word *kala* means "to forgive."

linguine. Also, "linguini." A flat pasta about one eighth of an inch wide. Linguine, a staple of Italian-American restaurants, is commonly served with a red or white clam sauce. The word, from the Italian ("little tongues"), was first printed in English in 1945.

liquor. A distilled spirit. The word, originally from the Latin, derives from Middle English *lic(o)ur*. Liquor is a general term for spirits that includes WHISKEY, BRANDY, RUM, VODKA, GIN, and CORDIALS. Malt liquor is brewed like BEER from malt, but has a higher alcohol content than beer, though it is usually nowhere close to the proof of most liquors.

American slang for liquor constitutes a freewheeling, sometimes hilarious, compendium of imaginative speech, with entries running into the hundreds for general terms and into the thousands for specific cocktails (most of which have not worn well or become part of the bartender's repertoire). For specific cocktail names look under main entries, for example, MARTINI, MANHATTAN, PIÑA COLADA, and others. The following list includes general terms for spirits, followed by dates indicating when they came into use or were first recorded in print: "Jersey lightning" (1780), "anti-fogmatic" (1789), "phlegm cutter" (1806), "firewater" (1817), "rotgut" (1819), "red eye" (1819), "coffin varnish" (1845), "tanglefoot" (1859), "tarantula juice" (1861), "sheep dip" (1865), "pick me up" (1867), "shot" (1906), "belt" (1921), and "panther sweat" (1929).

liquor sock. A knitted sock used in dry counties in the Midwest to carry liquor bottles to bring to restaurants forbidden to sell alcohol.

Little Joe's. A dish made of ground meat and spinach, with various seasonings according to taste. It would seem to be a variation on the kind of thrown together dish elsewhere called SLOPPY JOE or JOHNNY MARZETTI, but John Thorne in his *Simple Cooking* newsletter (1982) states, "Little Joe's is a popular San Francisco dish, named after the restaurant where, as legend has it, the meal was tossed together from leftovers in the kitchen late one night for a hungry customer."

LITTLE JOE'S

In 2 T. oil sauté 1 chopped onion until soft. Add 1 lb. ground beef and break up, cooking until gray. Add 1 c. cooked spinach, salt, and pepper, and cook until spinach is wilted. Beat 2 eggs with a dash of Tabasco sauce, add to beef and cook until eggs have set. Sprinkle with Parmesan cheese if desired, then spoon onto crisp rolls. Serves 4.

---

little roncador. Also, "roncador," "shiner," "tomcod," and other names. A fish (*Genyonemus lineatus*) of the California coastline (1882). The name derives from the Spanish *roncar*, "to grunt," bacause of the grunting sound the fish makes by inflating a bladder. A "ronco" (1880) is a GRUNT in the genus *Haemulon* found in West-Indian waters.

liverwurst. Also, "liver pudding." A sausage made with chopped liver that has a very smooth texture and is usually sliced in slabs. The word is derived from the German *Leberwurst*, "liver sausage," and was first printed in American English in 1869. Originally it was called "Braunschweiger," because it came from Germany's Brunswick Province (Braunschweig); it has long been associated with German immigrants.

Liverwurst is seasoned with onions, pistachios, and other spices, smoked, and packaged, usually to be spread on a sandwich or served as a canapé or cold cut. Occasionally it is sold fresh.

lobscouse. Also, "labskaus." A beef-and-potato stew described by Marjorie Mosser in her *Foods of Old New England* (1957) as "one of the most frequently used dishes in the galleys of New England sailing ships," first in American print in 1823. The dish seems to have originated in Hamburg, where it is still popular and called either *labskaus* or *lapskaus*.

LOBSCOUSE

Cut up 2 lb. bottom-round beef, 1 qt. potatoes, ½ lb. salt pork, 4 onions, cover with water and boil for 1 hr. Add 4 c. chopped corned beef, cook an additional ½ hr. Serves 6.

---

lobster. Any of a variety of crustaceans of the genus *Homarus* having five pairs of legs, including two large front claws. The name comes from the Old English *loppestre* and Latin *locusta*.

The American lobster (*Homarus americanus*) is today one of the more expensive food items in the market, owing to the difficulty of obtaining sufficient quantities to meet the demand. But when the first Europeans came to America, the lobster was one of the most commonly found crustaceans. They sometimes washed up on the beaches of Plymouth, Massachusetts, in piles two feet high. These settlers approached the creatures with less than gustatory enthusiasm, but the lobsters' abundance made them fit for the tables of the poor. (One observer remarked that "the very multitude of them cloys us.") In 1622 Governor William Bradford of the Plymouth Plantation apologized to a new arrival of settlers that the only dish he "could presente their friends with was a lobster . . . without bread or anything else but a cupp of fair water."

Lobsters in those days grew to tremendous size, sometimes forty or more pounds. (A record-holding forty-two-pounder was taken in Virginia in 1935 and now hangs in Boston's Museum of Science.) New Englanders might easily pick them off the beach for their tables, and ships carried them to other ports. When ships in New York Harbor were bombarded during the Revolution, the lobsters went to other waters, only to return at the cessation of hostilities.

The taste for lobster developed rapidly in the nineteenth century, and commercial fisheries specializing in the crustacean were begun in Maine in the 1840s, thereby giving rise to the fame of the "Maine lobster," which was being shipped around the world a decade later. In 1842 the first lobster shipments reached Chicago, and Americans enjoyed them both at home and in the cities' new "lobster palaces," the first of which was built in New York by the Shanley brothers. Here men made the consumption of several lobsters at one sitting a mark of one's affluence and joy in the good things of life.

Diamond Jim Brady thought nothing of downing a half-dozen, in addition to several other full courses. The March 1982 issue of *Yankee* magazine listed a professional wrestler named "André the Giant" as the all-time lobster-eating champion after he put away forty of the crustaceans at Custy's Restaurant in North Kingstown, Rhode Island. The news elicited a response from Tom Shovan of Woodlands, California, who claimed he had at the same restaurant once eaten sixty-one lobsters at a sitting. Shovan demanded from the magazine a "correction to this gross misstatement that would lead the naive to believe that a mere 40 lobsters are enough to satisfy a truly voracious appetite!"

By 1885 the American lobster industry was providing 130 million pounds of lobster per year. Soon afterward the population of the lobster beds decreased rapidly, and by 1918 only 33 million pounds were taken. Today, thanks to conservation efforts, the production is again above 83 million pounds, while millions of pounds of other lobsters come from South Africa, South America, Mexico, Australia, and elsewhere, usually in the form of "spiny lobsters," sometimes called "crawfish" but distinct from the true native freshwater CRAYFISH.

The so-called "Maine lobster" does not come only from Maine anymore either, but from beds in Canada as well. The average American lobster weighs between one and two pounds (in New England these are called "chicken lobsters," supposedly for their tenderness), although many eastern steak and lobster houses carry them at 'five or more pounds. Frozen lobster tails, 'usually broiled and served with clarified butter, are brought in in great quantities from South Africa and, now, from North Atlantic waters. Other preparations of lobster range from simple boiling or steaming to elaborate dishes, like LOBSTER NEWBURG and "lobster Thermidor," that require the removal of the meat from the tail and claws (Americans usually do not eat the innards) and combining it with cream, seasonings, sherry, and other ingredients.

Besides the American lobster, the following also

figure in culinary preparations in the United States, when available:

lobsterette (family Nephropidae). Lobsterettes are smaller members of the lobster family, ten species of which are found in the Atlantic and Caribbean, including the "Caribbean lobsterette" (*Metanephrops binghami*), the "Florida lobsterette" (*Nephrops aculeata*), and the "red lobsterette" (*Metanephrops rubellus*). In Europe these are called the *langoustine, scampo,* "Dublin Bay prawn," and other names.

Spanish lobster (*Scyllarides aequinoctialis*). Also, "shovel-nosed lobster," "sand lobster," "slipper lobster," "buccaneer crab," "gollipop," and other names. Rare in the United States, this lobster is usually brought in frozen from Southeast Asian waters.

spiny lobster (*Panulirus argus*). A favorite Floridian species, the spiny lobster ranges from the Carolinas to the Caribbean and is related to a Californian species, *P. interruptus*. At market, spiny lobsters are often called "rock lobsters."

lobster à l'américaine. A dish of lobster prepared with a sauce of tomatoes, brandy, white wine, cayenne pepper, and seasonings. It is certainly of French, not American, origins, and in France is called *homard à l'américaine*. Some gastronomes insist that it is actually a dish of Breton, or Armorican, origins, and that a *l'américaine* is an incorrect transcription of a *l'armoricaine*. Robert Courtine, however, in his book *The Hundred Glories of French Cooking* (1973), shows that the error was probably the other way around, pointing out that "no menu from any important restaurant, either in Paris or elsewhere, has ever been found with *armoricaine* antedating *américaine*. No, the latter has always preceded the former."

Courtine goes on to repeat the story told by Maurice-Edmond Sailland (called "Curnonsky") of how the dish was in fact created. Chef Pierre Fraisse had begun his cooking career in the United States, where he often prepared lobsters. Fraisse, known by the more American name "Peters," opened his own restaurant in Paris around 1860. One evening a group of Americans came in late, and Fraisse, having little left to work with, prepared a dish with lobsters that he called, in deference to his guests, "*homard a l'américaine*." *Sauce a l'américaine* is often used with other fish dishes.

LOBSTER À L'AMÉRICAINE

Cut the claws off a lobster and cut the tail into even rings. In 4 T. oil sauté the meat with salt and pepper until the shell has turned red. Remove from pan. To pan with oil add 1 finely chopped onion, 2 chopped shallots, and ¼ clove crushed garlic, and sauté until limp. Pour off the oil, add ½ c. white wine, ½ c. water, and 2 T. brandy, and burn off the alcohol. Add 2 peeled, seeded tomatoes, 3 sprigs of tarragon, and ⅛ t. cayenne. Place the lobster pieces on top, cover, and cook for 20 min. Remove lobster and place on serving platter. Remove tarragon. Over high heat reduce sauce in pan by half. Mash the lobster roe (called "coral") and green tomalley with 2 t. butter, a pinch of chervil, and a pinch of tarragon. Add to sauce in pan and stir to bind. Bring to boil, add 2 T. butter and 2 T. brandy, and pour over lobster. Garnish with chopped parsley and serve with rice.

---

lobster fra diavolo. An Italian-American dish whose name translates as "Lobster Brother Devil" made with lobster cooked in a spicy, peppery tomato sauce. It was a creation of Southern Italian immigrants, who did not have American lobsters in Italy (in Italy dishes termed "alla diavolo" indicate one made with a good deal of coarsely ground black pepper), and became a popular dish in Italian-American restaurants in New York by the 1940s.

lobster Newburg. Also "lobster à la Newburg" and "lobster Newberg." A rich dish of lobster meat, sherry, egg yolks, cream, and cayenne pepper. The dish was made famous at Delmonico's Restaurant in New York in 1876 when the recipe was brought to chef Charles Ranhofer by a West Indies sea captain named Ben Wenberg. It was an immediate hit, especially for after-theater suppers, and owner Charles Delmonico honored the captain by naming the dish "lobster à la Wenberg." But later Wenberg and Delmonico had a falling-out, and the restaurateur took the dish off the menu, restoring it only by popular demand by renaming it "lobster a la Newberg," reversing the first three letters of the captain's name. Chef Ranhofer also called it "lobster à la Delmonico," but the appellation "Newberg" (by 1897 it was better known under the spelling "Newburg") stuck, and the dish became a standard in hotel dining rooms in the United States. It is still quite popular and is found in French cookbooks, where it is sometimes referred to as "*Homard saute a la crème.*"

The sauce itself is used with other shellfish and such a preparation retains the name "à la Newburg." In some recipes the lobster is not sautéed in butter but only boiled. The first printed recipe appeared in 1895.

LOBSTER NEWBURG

Cook 2 lobsters in salted water until tender. Cool, then cut up meat into slices and saute with 6 T. butter. Salt to taste and add a dash of Tabasco or ¼ t. cayenne pepper. Pour in 1 c. heavy cream and 2 T. sherry and boil, reducing to half. Remove from heat and add 3 beaten egg yolks to thicken the sauce. Reheat, finishing it with a little more butter.

---

lobster roll. A sandwich made with lobster meat mixed with mayonnaise and seasonings on a hot-dog roll. About 1966–67 Fred Terry, owner of the Lobster Roll Restaurant (aka "Lunch") in Amagansett, New York, produced a recipe containing mayonnaise, celery, and seasonings; mixed with fresh lobster meat placed on a heated hot-dog roll that has come to be known as the "Long Island (New York) lobster roll," and is a version that has become very popular there and elsewhere, although a similar item was known in print in New England as of 1966. According to Carolyn Wyman in the *New Haven Register* (July 31 and August 7, 1996), lobster meat drenched in butter and served on a hamburger or hot dog roll has long been available at seaside eateries in Connecticut and may well have originated at a restaurant named Perry's in Milford, where owner Harry Perry concocted it for a regular customer named Ted Haley sometime in the 1920s. Furthermore, Perry's was said to have a sign from 1927 to 1977 reading "Home of the Famous Lobster Roll."

lobster shack. A roadside restaurant that specializes in selling freshly cooked lobsters. They are a fixture in New England and particularly in Maine.

loco moco. A Hawaiian dish made with a scoop of steamed white rice topped with a grilled hamburger patty, a fried egg, and meat gravy. It was created in 1949 as an after-school snack at the Lincoln Grill in Hilo, Hawaii.

logger slang. American loggers and lumberjacks have long had their own lingo for food and culinary terms, as indicated by the following:

bait can. A lunch pail used by loggers.

belly wash. A soft drink.

black Mike. Stew made from meat and vegetables.

boardinghouse man. The cook at camp.

boiler. A cook.

cackleberry. An egg. The cackle refers to the sound made by chickens, and in prison lingo eggs are referred to as "cacklers" (or "shells").

crib. A loggers' term for lunch, derived from the crib-shaped boxes in which lumber was sorted.

forbidden fruit. Pork.

forty-five-ninety. According to the *Dictionary of American Regional English*, loggers slang for a large sausage, so called after a large-caliber rifle cartridge.

lumberjack pie. A pie made with various vegetables and deer meat. The term is used by New England loggers.

mulligan car. A railroad car set in the woods from which the workers would take their lunch.

spud with the bark on. Logger slang for an unpeeled potato.

lollipop. A hard candy attached to a stick usually made of rolled paper (1785). It is a favorite children's snack and has been so since it was introduced in England in the 1780s. The name comes from an English dialect word, "lolly," "tongue," and the "pop" is probably associated with the sound made when the candy is withdrawn from the mouth.

The "Tootsie Roll Pop," a lollipop with a soft chocolate candy center, is a trademark of Tootsie Roll Industries, Inc., Chicago, Illinois.

lomi salmon. Also, "lomi-lomi salmon." A salted salmon dish of Hawaii often served at large feasts called "LUAUs." *Lomi* means "mashed with fingers" in Hawaiian. A recipe for the dish dates to the November 1828 issue of *Ladies' Home Journal*.

LOMI SALMON

Soak 1 lb. salted salmon in water and refrigerate overnight. Remove the skin, drain the fish, and cut up into *small pieces. Add 5 large chopped, peeled, seeded toma-toes, 1 finely chopped Maui onion, and 2 finely chopped scallions. Squeeze all these ingredients through fingers until well blended. Serve ice-cold. Serves 6.*

London broil. Flank steak that is broiled and cut into slices, though the term may also refer to another cut of beef appropriate for cooking in this manner. The name obviously derives from the English city of London, though the term is not used in England. It seems more specifically American in origin and dates in print at least to 1931, appearing in Charles G. Shaw's *Nightlife: Vanity Fair's Intimate Guide to New York After Dark* as a recommended dish at Keens Chophouse in New York City.

Long Island iced tea. A cocktail composed of various clear spirits including vodka, gin, and tequila with Coca-Cola and lemon. The drink is said to have been concocted by bartender Robert C. "Rosebud" Butt in 1976 at the Oak Beach Inn in Hampton Bays on Long Island, New York. "I was fooling around with some drinks," said Butt, "and I'm a tequila drinker, so I put together one shot each of tequila, light rum, vodka, gin, a dash of Triple Sec, a splash of sour mix, and topped it off with Coca-Cola and a slice of lemon, served it on the rocks in a Collins glass, and the thing tasted just like iced tea. I started serving them to the public about a year later."

longneck. A beer bottle or liquor bottle with a long neck, long known in the Southwest and particularly popular in Texas (1907). Beer drinkers carry the bottle around by the neck with considerable swagger and do not drink from a glass.

long sauce. Root vegetables with long roots, such as carrots, parsnips and beets (1809); also, a dish made from such vegetables. "Short sauce" refers to vegetables that grow above ground, such as peas, beans and tomatoes.

loose meat. Midwestern term for seasoned ground meat cooked loosely in a skillet and served with gravy or as a sandwich (1986). Common in the Midwest.

Louisburg pie. A pie made with chicken fricassée, potato balls, sliced mushrooms, and sausages. It may derive from the region around Louisburg, North Carolina.

love and tangle. Deep-fried doughnut that has been twisted and entwined.

love apple. A romantic colloquialism for tomatoes, so called because of a mistranslation of the Italian *pomo dei Moro*—"apple of the Moors"—(because tomatoes came to Italy from Morocco) into the French *pomme d'amour*, meaning "love apple." Certain aphrodisiacal attributes thereby accrued to tomatoes with no justification. The word was first printed in 1578.

low mull. A meat-and-vegetable stew whose ingredients vary according to the person preparing it. The origin of the word may derive from a colloquial verb, "to mull," "to make a muddle or mess" of something, used at least since 1821. Or the name may be a shortened form of MULLIGAN STEW.

lox. A Jewish-American version of smoked SALMON. The word is from the Yiddish *laks*, from Middle High German *labs*. According to Leo Rosten in *The Joys of Yiddish* (1968), "the luxurious practice of eating lox, thought to be so typical of East European Jews, actually began for them in New York. Lox was entirely unknown among European Jews and is rare to this day there—and in Israel." The word first appeared in English in 1940.

Lox is sliced very thin and usually served on a bagel with butter and cream cheese. The preferred variety is the Pacific salmon cured in saturated salt brine.

"Pickled lox" has been a specialty of the Concord Hotel in the Catskill Mountains of New York since 1939. The original recipe, given below, was refined by Frank Stubitz in 1949 and first printed in *The New York Times* (September 18, 1985):

PICKLED LOX

Place 3 lb. filleted, skinless brined salmon in a glass or stainless-steel dish, cover with cold water, cover with plastic wrap, and let stand in refrigerator for 48–60 hours, changing water frequently. Drain fish and trim away cartilage. In a saucepan combine 4 c. white vinegar. 1 c. water, 1½ T. pickling spices (without cinnamon) and 1 c. sugar and bring to a boil. Lower heat and simmer for 20 min. Allow to cool. Cut fish into ½ inch-thick slices and layer the slices with 2 sliced Bermuda onions in a glass dish. Strain the marinade liquid and pour over fish. Cover with plastic wrap and refrigerate for 23–36 hr. In a bowl whisk 4 c. sour cream, 1 t. sugar, and 1 T. fish marinade. Drain salmon and onions, then layer with the sour cream mixture. Serves 12.

luau. Hawaiian-style feast, usually held in the out-doors, often at the beach (1853) and featuring pig cooked in an IMU. The word, which in Hawaiian means "young taro tops," may also refer to the edible taro leaf or a dish made from taro leaves.

lunch. The midday meal. The word originally referred to a chunk or lump of something, including perhaps a slice of food, and in its first appearance in print (1591) it was related to the Spanish *lonja,* for "slice." By the seventeenth century it was often used to designate a piece of food or a light meal, but when the word "lunch" first appeared in print as an abbreviation of "luncheon" (1812), it was considered something of a fashionable colloquialism. Americans picked up the word quickly, however, and used it as a synonym for the midday meal taken quickly, as a worker might on the job. Before the 1820s the midday meal was called DINNER and the evening meal "supper." Today "luncheon" connotes a more formal lunch, usually given for friends or associates.

The midday meal at home was generally the heaviest meal of the day, but workers found neither the time nor the stomach for lengthy dinners while on the job, and so the custom of eating a sandwich or going to a lunchroom or CAFETERIA became common, although more affluent businesspeople of the nineteenth century would indulge in lavish midday dinners at city restaurants where six or more courses were not unusual.

For most Americans today lunch is a fairly light meal, with the largest meal of the day saved for the evening. The partially tax-deductible "business lunch" has become an American institution (see also POWER LUNCH), and opponents of lengthy, lavish restaurant lunches at taxpayers' expense have called such exemptions unfair to the average wage earner, who may not deduct the cost of his lunch.

Such business lunches have been characterized as "three-martini lunches" since the 1960s, sarcastically referring to the number of cocktails imbibed.

lunch box. Also "lunchbox" and "lunch pail." A portable container for one's lunch. Originally workers carried their lunches in "dinner pails" or "dinner buckets," first cited in print, respectively, in 1856 and 1901, which were designed to keep food warm. "Lunch boxes," cited in print in 1850, held cold food. Schoolchildren of the nineteenth century would often use their fathers' tobacco tins to carry their lunch in, but by the twentieth century manufacturers made lunch boxes especially for carrying to school.

The first licensed "character lunch box" appeared in 1935 with a picture of Mickey Mouse, from the Walt Disney cartoons, but the boom in lunch boxes began in 1950 when Aladdin Industries of Nashville, Tennessee, sold 500,000 lunch boxes with TV cowboy hero Hopalong Cassidy on it. Since then most lunch boxes have been made with pictures of children's favorite characters (the most popular ever was the "Disney School Bus," which sold more than 2 million units between 1961 and 1973). Today about 7 million lunch boxes are produced each year, all manufactured by two companies, Aladdin and the King-Seeley Thermos Company of Freeport, Illinois.

lunch counter. An inexpensive, casual restaurant serving simple food at a counter, although most lunch counters also have tables or booths. The term, first recorded in 1865, has many synonyms—"lunch stand," "hash house," "short-order restaurant," "snack bar," "lunchroom , and "lunch," superseded in the 1930s by "luncheonette." The term may also be used to refer to a DINER, which is a lunch counter originally made to look like a railroad dining car.

Lunch counters have provided etymologists and linguists with one of the richest stores of American slang, cant, and jargon, usually based on a form of verbal shorthand bandied back and forth between waiters and cooks. Some terms have entered the familiar language of most Americans—"BLT" (a bacon, lettuce, and tomato sandwich), "stack" (an order of pancakes), "mayo" (mayonnaise), and others—but most remain part of a bewildering and colorful language specific to the workers in such establishments. The following list is culled from various sources, including Supplement Two of *The American Language* (1948), by H. L. Mencken, who wrote, "The queer lingo used in transmitting orders from table to kitchen was noted by a writer in the *Detroit Free Press* so long ago as Jan. 7, 1852, *e.g., fried bedpost, mashed tambourine* and *roasted stirrups.* In 1876 J. G. Holland, then editor of *Scribner's,* discussed it in his *Everyday Topics,* p. 386. It was richly developed by the colored waiters who flourished in the 1870s and 80s, but is now pretty well confined to the waitresses and countermen who glorify third-rate eating-houses."

Many of these terms are shared by workers in soda fountains or ice-cream stores.

AC. A sandwich made with American cheese.

Adam and Eve on a raft. Two poached or fried eggs on toast (1909).

Adam's ale. Plain water.

alive. Raw (said of oysters).

all the way. A sandwich made with lettuce, mayonnaise, onion, and butter (1957); also, a chocolate cake with chocolate ice cream.

...and. Preceded by a food item, "and" indicates another food that invariably goes with the first, as in, "ham and" for "ham and eggs" or "burger and" for "hamburger and french fries."

Angel-food cake and wine. Also, "Lord's Supper." Bread and water (1942).

A-pie. Apple pie.

Arizona. Buttermilk, so called, according to Robert Shafer in "The Language of West Coast Culinary Workers," *American Speech* (April 1946), because "a waitress thinks any man drinking buttermilk ought to be in Arizona for his health."

axle grease. Also, "skid grease." Butter or margarine (1883).

baby. Also, "moo juice," "Sweet Alice," and "cow juice." Milk.

belch water. Seltzer or soda water.

birdseed. Cereal (1919).

black stick. A chocolate ice-cream cone.

blonde. Coffee with cream. "Blonde and sweet" is coffee with cream and sugar.

blue-bottle. Bromo-Seltzer, a trademark for a digestive aid of bicarbonated soda that comes in a blue bottle.

blue-plate special. A dish of meat, potato, and vegetable served on a plate (usually blue) sectioned in three parts.

Bossy in a bowl. Beef stew, so called because "Bossy" was a common name for a cow.

bottom. Ice cream added to a drink.

bowl of red. A bowl of chili con carne, so called for its deep red color (1900).

bowwow. A hot dog.

break it and shake it. Also, "make it cackle." Put a raw egg in a drink, especially a milk shake.

breath. An onion.

bridge. Also, "bridge party." Four of anything, so called from the card-game hand of bridge.

bucket of hail. A small glass of ice.

bullets. Also called "whistleberries" or "Saturday nights." Baked beans, so called because of the supposed flatulence they cause (1893).

bun pup. A hot dog.

burn it and let it swim. A float, made with chocolate syrup and ice cream floated on top.

burn one. Put a hamburger on the grill or add chocolate.

burn one all the way. A chocolate milk shake with chocolate ice cream.

burn the British. A toasted English muffin.

Canary Island special. Vanilla soda with chocolate ice cream.

carfare. Also, "subway." A worker's tip or percentage of the check as a gratuity. The meaning referred to the money to provide transportation home.

cat's eyes. TAPIOCA.

CB. A cheeseburger.

China. Rice pudding.

chopper. A table knife.

city juice. Water.

CJ. A cream-cheese-and-jelly sandwich.

clean up the kitchen. Hash or hamburger.

c.o. highball. Castor oil. See HIGHBALL.

coke pie. Coconut pie.

cold spot. A glass of iced tea.

Coney Island chicken. Also, "Coney Island." A hot dog, so called because hot dogs were popularly associated with the Coney Island stands at which they were sold.

cowboy. A western omelet or sandwich.

cow feed. A salad.

creep. Draft beer.

crowd. Three of anything (possibly from the old saying, "Two's company, three's a crowd").

deadeye. Poached egg.

dog and maggot. Cracker and cheese.

dog biscuit. Cracker (1908).

dog's body. A pudding of pea soup and flour or hardtack.

dough well done with cow to cover. Buttered toast.

draw one. Coffee (1896).

easy over. Eggs turned over and cooked briefly.

echo. Repeat the order.

eighty-one. A glass of water.

eighty-six. "Do not sell to that customer" (1943) or "The kitchen is out of the item ordered" (1936). Perhaps from the practice at Chumley's Restaurant (once a speakeasy) in New York City of throwing rowdy customers out the back door, which is No. 86 Bedford Street.

Eve with a lid on. Apple pie, referring to the biblical Eve's tempting apple and to the crust that covers it (1923).

fifty-five. A glass of root beer.

fifty-one. Hot chocolate.

filet. Served with ice cream.

first lady. Spareribs, a pun on Eve's being made from Adam's spare rib.

five. A large glass of milk.

fly cake. Also "roach cake." A raisin cake or huckleberry pie.

forty-one. Lemonade.

Frenchman's delight. Pea soup.

GAC. Grilled American cheese sandwich. This was also called "Jack" (from the pronunciation of "GAC"); a "Jack Benny" (after a radio comedian) was cheese with bacon.

gentleman will take a chance. Hash.

George Eddy. A customer who leaves no tip.

go for a walk. An order to be packed and taken out.

gravel train. Sugar bowl (1935).

graveyard stew. Milk toast (1911).

groundhog. Hot dog (1911).

hamlette. An omelet made with ham.

Harlem. Also, "Harlem soda." A soda made with chocolate, named after the section of New York City known for its predominantly black population. A "Harlem midget" was a small chocolate soda.

hemorrhage. Ketchup.

high and dry. A plain sandwich without butter, mayonnaise, or lettuce.

high, yellow, black and white. A chocolate soda with vanilla ice cream.

hold the hail. No ice.

hops. Malted-milk powder.

hot cha. Hot chocolate.

hot spot. Tea.

houseboat. A banana split, made with ice cream and sliced bananas.

ice the rice. Add ice cream to rice pudding.

in the alley. Serve as a side dish.

in the hay. A strawberry milkshake, punning on hay as straw.

Irish turkey. Corned beef and cabbage.

java. Coffee.

jerk. An ice-cream soda, referring to the jerking motion of a seltzer spigot.

joe. Coffee.

L.A. Serve an item with ice cream.

looseners. Prunes, so called because of their supposed laxative effect.

lumber. A toothpick.

maiden's delight. Cherries, so called because "cherry" is a slang term for the maidenhead.

make it virtue. Add cherry syrup to a cola soda.

mama. Marmalade.

M.D. Dr Pepper, a commercially produced soda.

Mike and Ike. Also, "the twins." Salt and pepper shakers.

monkey bowl. Plate used for a side dish.

Mud. Also, "Omurk." Black coffee or chocolate ice cream.

Murphy. Potatoes, so called because of their association with the Irish diet of potatoes, Murphy being a common Irish name.

natural. A commercially produced soda called

"7UP," from the combination of 5 and 2, called a "natural" in the dice game craps.

Noah's boy. A slice of ham, because Ham was Noah's second son.

no cow. Without milk.

O.J. Also, "Oh gee." Orange juice.

on the hoof. Meat done rare.

on wheels. An order to be packed and taken out.

pair of drawers. Two cups of coffee.

Pittsburgh. Toast or something burning, so called because of the smokestacks evident in Pittsburgh, a coal-producing and steel-mill city. In meat cookery, this refers to a piece of meat charred on the outside while still red within.

PT. A pot of tea.

put out the lights and cry. Liver and onions.

radio. A tuna-fish-salad sandwich on toast, punning on "tuna down," which sounds like "turn it down," as one would the radio knob.

sand. Sugar.

seaboard. Item wrapped for takeout, referring to "cardboard."

sea dust. Salt.

shoot it yellow. Add lemon syrup or slice of lemon to a cola soda.

shoot one from the south. Make an especially strong cola soda.

sinkers and suds. Doughnuts and coffee.

squeeze one. Orange juice.

stretch one. A cola soda.

through Georgia. Add chocolate syrup; because of Georgia's large black population, though possibly referring to General William Tecumseh

Sherman's infamous "scorched-earth policy" of the Civil War, when he marched his army through Georgia, burning everything in his wake.

to the left. Lemon syrup, customarily set to the left of the cola-syrup pump.

to the right. Cherry syrup, customarily set to the right of the cola-syrup pump.

twenty-one. Limeade.

Vermont. Maple syrup, because maple syrup comes primarily from Vermont.

warts. Olives.

wreath. Cabbage.

yum-yum. Sugar.

zeppelins in a fog. Sausages in mashed potatoes.

lutefisk. A Scandinavian dish made from dried cod preserved in lye and soda. The word is from Norwegian (also Swedish *lutfisk* "lye fish") first in print in English in 1924. It is traditionally served at Christmastime and is considered a delicacy among Scandinavian Americans, especially in the Midwest. Madison, Wisconsin, even calls itself the "Lutefisk capital of the U.S.A." Lutefisk is rarely made at home and is usually bought at specialty stores. It is softened by simmering in salted water for about ten minutes and served with a white sauce and potatoes on the side. It may also be made into a pudding.

macadamia nut. Also, "Queensland nut." The seed of two tropical trees, *Macadamia intergrigolia and M. tetraphylla,* originally native to Australia but now forming the third-largest crop of Hawaii. The tree is named after chemist John MacAdam (1827–65), who promoted the plant's cultivation in Australia. The name "macadamia" was first used in print in 1900. The alternate name, "Queensland nut," derives from Australia's second-largest state.

According to S. A. Clark in *All the Best in Hawaii* (1949), the nut was brought to Honolulu, Hawaii, from Tasmania about 1890 by E. W. Jordan.

Originally the tree was used merely as an ornamental shrub, but researchers at the Hawaiian Agricultural College forty years later discovered the nuts' culinary value, leading to widespread planting for commercial harvesting.

Today macadamia nuts are usually roasted and salted, eaten as snacks, or used in salads and fish and meat preparations.

macaroni. A form of dried pasta that is usually tubular or shaped in some way, in contrast to the long, thin shape of spaghetti. The word is of Italian origins (from *maccherone,* "mixture of elements," but the word serves as a name for the pasta too) and has been known in English at least since the sixteenth century. (The reference to "macaroni" in the famous eighteenth-century American song "Yankee Doodle Dandy"—"stuck a feather in his hat and called it macaroni"—refers not to the pasta but to a slang term of the period for a fop or dandy, after the London Macaroni Club.) Thomas Jefferson sent his emissary, William Short, to Naples for a macaroni machine (though Short returned with a spaghetti machine instead).

Macaroni is eaten in America in the traditional Italian manner—that is, with various sauces (most often tomato)—but a specifically American dish is macaroni and cheese, which is made by placing a layer of boiled macaroni in a buttered baking dish and grating over it American, Cheddar, or Swiss cheese, then baking it until the cheese has melted. This dish was first made in the nineteenth century but took on great popularity when the Kraft food company introduced the "Kraft Dinner" in 1937, a macaroni-and-cheese meal that today sells 300 million boxes per year.

Macaroni salad is a dish of cold macaroni to which is added mayonnaise and various vegetables and seasonings, like celery, onions, peppers, tomatoes, chives, and pimiento.

mackerel. Any of a wide variety of fishes in the family Scombridae. As a food fish the Atlantic mackerel *(Scomber scombrus),* also called "Boston mackerel," is the most important mackerel in the United States. It travels in large schools, ranging from Labrador to Cape Hatteras, and is known for its swiftness. The name mackerel derives from Old French *maquerel,* and has been found in print in English since the beginning of the fourteenth century.

Most American mackerel used to be salted. Much of the salting was done in Boston; hence, salted mackerel was called "Boston mackerel." It was not until ships stocked ice in their holds that the mackerel was sold fresh. In 1885 a fishery at Eastport, Maine, brought in 100 million pounds. As with other fish of this era, overworking the sea resulted in a decline in population, with the result that the mackerel has gone through cycles of scarcity and proliferation. The most important species for the table include the "cero" *(Scomberomorus regalis),* also called "painted mackerel"; "chub mackerel" *(S. japonicus),* also called "hardhead"; "king mackerel" *(S. cavalla),* also called "kingfish" and "cero"; "Spanish mackerel" *(S. maculatus);* and "wahoo" *(Acanthocybium solandri),* whose etymological roots are unknown and which in Hawaii is known as *ono* ("sweet"). U.S. commercial landings of Atlantic mackerel in 1997 totaled 33.9 million pounds, with 91 percent caught in Rhode Island and New Jersey waters. Chub mackerel landings totaled 40.6 million pounds.

Madeira nut. The English walnut *(Juglans regia),* now widely planted in California (1821). The name derives from the island of Madeira.

mademoiselle. Also, "layfayette," "corvian," maomao" (in Hawaii) and "croaker." A small fish

(*Bairdiella chrysura*) of the Gulf and Atlantic coasts (1882). They are usually pan fried.

maid of honor. A custard tart made with damson plums or other fruits. This popular early-American dish came from England, where the tarts were named after the maids of honor at the court of Elizabeth I (queen 1558–1603) and are associated with the palace at Richmond, Surrey.

MAID OF HONOR

Roll out pastry for a 2-crust pie and line 10 tart shells about 3½-in. in diameter. Beat 2 eggs with ½ c. sugar. Soften ½ c. almond paste with 2 T. dry sherry, 2 T. butter, and 1 T. lemon juice and add to egg batter. Mix in 2 T. flour. Drop 1 t. fruit jam or preserves into each shell, pour batter over each, and bake for 45 min. at 350°.

---

mai tai. A cocktail made from lime, curaçao, and rum, created in 1944 by Victor "Trader Vic" Bergeron, then owner of an Oakland, California, restaurant called Hinky Dinks and later owner of Trader Vic's. In his book *Trader Vic's Bartender's Guide* (revised, 1972), Bergeron told how the drink came about:

> I was at the service bar in my Oakland restaurant. I took down a bottle of seventeen-year-old rum. It was J. Wray Nephew from Jamaica—surprisingly golden in color, medium bodied, but with the rich pungent flavor particular to the Jamaican blends. The flavor of this great rum wasn't meant to be overpowered with heavy additions of fruit juices and flavorings. I took a fresh lime, added some orange curaçao from Holland, a dash of rock candy syrup, and a dollop of French orgeat for its subtle almond flavor. I added a generous amount of shaved ice and shook it vigorously by hand to produce the marriage I was after. Half the lime shell went into each drink for color, and I stuck in a branch of fresh mint. I gave the first two of them to Ham and Carrie Guild, friends from Tahiti who were there that night.
>
> Carrie took one sip and said, "Mai Tai—Roa Aé." In Tahitian this means "Out of this world—the best." Well, that was that. I named the drink "Mai Tai. . . ."
>
> Anybody who says I didn't create this drink is a dirty stinker.

There is, however, no evidence that the term does mean what Bergeron said it does in Tahitian.

MAI TAI

Squeeze juice of 1 lime into an old-fashioned glass, add ½ oz. orange curaçao, ¼ oz. rock-candy syrup, ¼ oz. orgeat syrup, 1 oz. dark Jamaican rum, and 1 oz. Martinique rum. Shake with shaved ice. Decorate with lime shell, fresh mint, and fruit stick.

---

maître d'hôtel butter. A classic preparation of butter mixed with pepper, salt, lemon juice, chopped parsley, and occasionally with chives. It is used as a garnish for grilled meats and fish, The term derives from the French for "master of the house," referring to a head waiter who usually takes reservations and assigns seating.

makoola. Home-brewed liquor. The word's earliest citation in print (1882) says the name comes from a "Russian brewer," while the *Dictionary of Alaskan English* (1991) suggests it may be derived from Russian *muka,* "flour."

malasado. Also, "malassada." A puffy pastry made from an egg batter that is deep-fried and rolled in sugar (1967). It is based on similar pastries brought by the Portuguese immigrants, and each year the Portuguese Society of Hawaii holds a contest to make the best version. The term is from two Portuguese words *mal,* "bad," and *assado,* "baked," and may have originated when scraps of Portuguese sweet-bread dough were hastily thrown into hot fat, thereby making a "badly baked" bread.

MALASADO

Dissolve 2 pkgs. dry yeast in 1 c. warm water with 1 T. sugar and 1 T. flour. Let stand until proofed. In a large bowl combine 5 lb. flour, 3 c. sugar, and 1 t. salt. Beat one doz. eggs, add 1 c. milk, add to flour mixture and blend. Add ½ lb. melted butter. Knead well, then let dough rise until doubled in size. Remove from bowl, pinch off pieces of dough the size of a walnut, deep-fry in oil, drain, and roll in sugar.

---

malted milk. Originally created in 1887 as an easily digestible infant's food made from an extract of wheat and malted barley combined with milk and made into a powder called "diastoid" by James and William Horlick of Racine, Wisconsin, this item, under the name "Horlick's Malted Milk," was featured by the

Walgreen drugstore chain as part of a chocolate milk shake, which itself became known as a "malted" and became one of the most popular soda-fountain drinks.

man-about-town. Term first used in 1903 by the New York *Herald Tribune* to describe a man who caroused in restaurants and saloons past 1:00 A.M.

manapua. A dough bun, filled with pork, bean paste, and other stuffings, that is steamed and usually sold from roadside stands in Hawaii (1938). The word derives from the Hawaiian *mea* (thing) + *ono* (delicious) + *pua'a* (pig), possibly once referring to various Chinese dishes.

mango (*Mangifera indica*). An oblong tropical fruit known for its sweetness. They are commonly used in salads, side dishes, and many desserts, as well as a puree added to cocktails. "Mango" entered English print in 1575, possibly via the Malayalam *mānna*.

Only about 15–20 percent of the mangoes in the American market are grown here—mostly in Florida—with the rest coming from Haiti, Mexico, Belize, and Brazil. Among the most popular varieties are the "Tommy Atkins" and "Keitt."

In the Midwest (especially the Ohio Valley) a sweet pepper is called a "mango."

Manhattan. Also, "Manhattan cocktail." An alcoholic drink of bourbon or blended whiskey with sweet vermouth and bitters.

The *Oxford English Dictionary* traces the drink back to 1890, but a writer in *The New Yorker* in 1948 referred to seeing a Supreme Court justice drinking such a cocktail in a Washington bar back in 1886, and the drink is certainly older than that. Spirits authority Emanuel Greenberg traces the origin of the drink to a banquet given by Winston Churchill's American mother, Jennie, at New York's Manhattan Club: "It was a bash celebrating Samuel Tilden's election as governor of the state [in 1874], and the bartender whomped up a new drink for the occasion, thoughtfully naming it for his place of employment."

Food writer James Villas disputed this in his book *Villas at Table* (1988) on the basis of an interview with colleague Carol Truax, who contended that her father, Supreme Court judge Charles Henry Truax, was responsible for the cocktail about 1890. Having been told by his doctor to stop drinking MARTINIS in order to lose weight, Truax went to his club, the Manhattan Club, and asked the bartender there to make him a new cocktail. The new drink was thereupon named after the club itself.

Modern versions of the Manhattan tend to be drier than those recipes from the early part of this century. Villas gives the following recipe as the original:

MANHATTAN

Combine 2 oz. rye, blended or bourbon whiskey, with 1 oz. sweet Italian vermouth and a dash of Angostura bitters in a pitcher. Add 2–3 ice cubes, stir quickly until well chilled, and strain into a cocktail glass. Garnish with a maraschino cherry.

A "Perfect Manhattan" uses ¼ oz. sweet vermouth and ¼ oz. dry vermouth with the whiskey, while a "Dry Manhattan" substitutes dry French vermouth entirely for the sweet vermouth. A "Sweet Manhattan" is synonymous with a regular Manhattan, except, perhaps, for the amount of sweet vermouth added. A "Scotch Manhattan," more often called a ROB ROY, is made with scotch instead of bourbon or blended whiskey.

manini. In Hawaiian waters a surgeonfish (*Acanthurus sandvicensis*), in print since 1926, as well as a kind of green-and-white striped banana, usually cooked (1948).

mannitol. A sweetener used in chewing gum and on low-calorie foods.

maple syrup. A sweet syrup or sugar made from the sugar-maple tree (*Acer saccharum*), also called the "hard maple" or "rock maple." The word is from Old English *mapel*. Although Europeans were familiar with various species of maple tree in their own countries, they were unaware of the American sugar maple's virtues as an agent for such a delicious sweetener as the Northeastern Native Americans obtained merely by slashing the bark and letting the sap drip out. This technique was learned by the early colonists, who found maple syrup and sugar a fine substitute for the expensive sugar imported from the West Indies. By the 1720s there was a good deal of "sugaring" of maple trees going on among settlers, who waited for the sudden thaw of the late New England winter when the sap would begin flowing through the trees. The colonists would gash the tree trunks, guide the sap into troughs, and boil it over fires.

Maple sweeteners became even more popular after the passage of the 1764 Sugar Act, which imposed high duties on imported sugar. After the Revolution, New England maple production boomed, providing products like maple candy, beer, wine, and molasses. Abolitionists urged their fellow citizens to eat more maple sugar than West Indian sugar in order to "reduce by that much the lashings the Negroes have to endure to grow cane sugar to satisfy our gluttony." In New Hampshire people called maple syrup "humbo," from an Indian word.

Maple products remained principal forms of sweetening well into the nineteenth century, especially after tin cans became available in which to pack the syrup. Before then, most maple was turned into sugar loaves. Today most of the maple sugar and syrup produced comes from Vermont, though a good deal of the syrup used on American foods like pancakes is no longer maple syrup at all. In 1887 P. J. Towle of St. Paul, Minnesota, produced a blend of maple and sugarcane syrup that was less expensive than pure maple syrup. He packed it in a tin can, shaped like a log cabin of the kind his childhood hero, Abraham Lincoln, grew up in, and called it "Log Cabin Syrup."

Since then many syrups have been produced from other sweeteners, and these by law must be labeled "pancake syrups."

The sugaring of maple trees has long been a New England social ritual. Both professional and amateur sugarers will head for a grove of maple trees, called a "sugar bush," to collect the sap, return to a "sugar house" to boil it down, and hope for a "sugar snow"—that is, a late snowfall that prolongs the running of the sap in the trees. It takes about thirty five gallons of boiling sap to produce one gallon of syrup. Often a late-season "sugar in the snow" party is held, during which maple syrup is poured on fresh snow and eaten like an ice.

Maple syrup is graded "Fancy" (the finest), "Grade A," "Grade B," and "Unclassified," a dark syrup used in commercially produced maple and blended syrups.

Maple sweeteners are used on breakfast dishes like pancakes, waffles, bacon, and sausage and in candies, cakes, ice cream, and many other confections. Vermont and New York produce more than two thirds of the country's maple syrup. In 1998 total U.S. production of maple syrup was 1,159,000 gallons.

MAPLE SUGAR

Boil 1 pt. maple syrup, then reduce heat to a simmer and stir for about 10 min., until candy thermometer registers 240°. Cool by stirring over a pot of cold water until it thickens to light taffy stage. Return to medium heat to liquefy again, pour into candy or other molds, cool for 15 min., and turn out.

maquechou. Also, "maque choux" and other variants. A Cajun dish made with corn, onions, peppers, and milk (1931). The meaning of the term, which is Cajun French, is not clear. According to the anonymous author of *New Orleans Cuisine*, published in the 1930s:

One of the most popular traditional dishes of south Louisiana is Mocquechou; also one of the most controversial as to origin. Some natives believe that this succulent stew was brought to Louisiana by the Spanish, and that the name originated with the Spanish name "machica" which was a dish of toasted corn meal sweetened with sugar and spices. Others think the name came from the word "maigrichou" which means "a thin child" as this dish was originally more soup than stew. The "Cajuns" of Louisiana have their own interpretation, making it a dish soaked with cabbage and calling it "moque-chou" or "mock cabbage."

The original dish was made of fresh scraped corn and tomatoes, simmered with water and butter.

Maquechou is often added to chicken or other meats.

MAQUECHOU

In a saucepan melt 2 T. butter, add 3 T. chopped onions and 2 T. chopped bell pepper. Cook on low heat for about 3 min. Cut off the kernels from 8 ears of corn and add to the saucepan. Cook for 3 more min., then add ½ c. milk, a pinch of cayenne, and salt and pepper to taste. Cook for about 15 min. Until creamy.

maraschino. A cordial made from the fermented juice of the Dalmatian marasca cherry or a maraschino-flavored preserved cherry. The cordial runs 60 to 78 proof. The cherry is used as a garnish in cocktails like the OLD-FASHIONED and the MANHATTAN, as well as a flavoring for some cakes and cookies.

The word comes from the Italian marasca, referring to the wild cherry tree from which the drink is made, and first saw English print in 1791. The drink was originally made along the Adriatic coast from cherries and honey allowed to ferment, then distilled into a liqueur. The, cherries themselves were often marinated in the liqueur and enjoyed on their own. The French flavored and colored their own local cherries bright red and called them maraschinos, a process used by American manufacturers around the turn of the last century in Ohio and Illinois and modified for use with any kind of cherry in the 1920s by food scientist E. H. Wiegand of Oregon State University. The cherries are put into a brining liquid of sodium metabisulfate, calcium chloride, and citric acid, then soaked in corn syrup and fructose solution, then artificially flavored and colored either red or green.

margarine. Also, "oleomargarine." A blend of animal and vegetable oils and fats mixed with milk and salt to form a semisolid often used as a substitute for BUTTER. Americans use far more margarine than butter. U.S. per capita consumption of margarine in 1997 was 8.6 pounds.

The word comes from the French *margarique*, referring to margaric acid, a fatty substance, and its pearly color (from Greek *margaron*, "pearl"). Oleo, too, derives from the French *oléo*, for "oil." Originally the product was called in French *oleomargarine*, first made by French chemist Hippolyte Mège-Mouries in the 1860s for a contest sponsored by Napoleon III to find a substitute for butter. By 1867 a French patent had been filed, by 1869 a British one, and by 1873 an American one. Dairymen in the United States fought the use of margarine as a substitute, but it was widely manufactured by the end of the century, first in 1881 by Community Manufacturing Company of New York. In 1886 Congress passed the Oleomargarine Act to regulate and tax the manufacture and sale of the product.

American margarine is usually made from corn, cottonseed, or soybean oil that is refined, deodorized, hydrogenated, homogenized, chilled, and reworked with salt, then often enriched with vitamins A and D. Although regular margarine is of about the same caloric count as butter, diet margarines are sold.

margarita. A cocktail made from tequila, Triple Sec or Cointreau, and lime juice. According to *The Tequila Book* (1976), by Marion Gorman and Felipe de Alba, there are several claims as to the creation of the drink. One story traces the margarita to the bar at the Caliente Race Track in Tijuana, Mexico, about 1930. Another credits Doña Bertha, owner of Bertita's Bar in Tasca, Mexico, as having made the drink about 1930. Former Los Angeles bartender Daniel Negrete claims to have originated the cocktail at the Garcí Crespo Hotel in Puebla, Mexico, in 1936 and named it after a girlfriend named Margarita. Still another story gives the credit to a San Antonio, Texas, woman, Margarita Sames, who made the drink for houseguests in 1948 while living in Acapulco. Yet another claim pinpoints the drink's birthplace as the Tale of the Cock Restaurant in Los Angeles about 1955 and says it was named after a Hollywood starlet.

An article in *GQ* magazine (October 1974) credited Pancho Morales, a bartender in Tommy's Place in Juárez, with the invention of the drink in 1942. Others say it was concocted at Dallas's El Charro Bar by Mariano Martinez, whose son, Mariano, Jr., supposedly made the first "frozen margarita" with crushed ice in 1971.

Whatever its origins, the margarita was the cocktail that increased American interest in tequila in the 1960s, particularly among college students in the West. The first appearance of the word in print was in 1963.

MARGARITA

Chill a stemmed cocktail glass and dip the rim in salt. In a metal shaker put a scoop of chopped ice, 1½ oz. tequila, ½ oz. Triple Sec or Cointreau, and 1 oz. lime juice. Shake gently a few times, strain into glass, and garnish with lime peel, if desired.

marinara. A spicy, quickly cooked tomato sauce of Italian origins but far more popular in American restaurants featuring southern Italian cuisines than in most of Italy. There is a 1905 printed reference to "eggs alla marinara" (*alla* in Italian means "in the style of") in an Italian recipe book, but the term was probably widely known by the 1920s, by which time Italian-American restaurants had proliferated. As a sauce for spaghetti "marinara" is mentioned in the film "Rain or Shine" (1930).

Often marinara sauce is called "red sauce," although that may also refer to a meat-and-tomato sauce.

The name means "mariner's style" and is perhaps associated with the custom of plopping the fresh catch of the day into steaming cauldrons of tomato, onion, and spices for the evening meal.

MARINARA

In a large skillet heat ½ c. olive oil. Add and brown 4 mashed cloves of garlic. Put through a sieve 3½ c. Italian canned tomatoes and add to skillet. Add 1¼ t. salt, 1 t. oregano, ¼ t. chopped parsley, and ⅛ t. pepper. Cook uncovered on medium heat for about 15–20 min., until tomatoes have broken down and thickened.

Marlborough pie. An apple-and-cream pie, sometimes called "Marlborough pudding" or "Marlborough tart," since there is no top crust (1869). The pie is a Massachusetts specialty, often served at Thanksgiving dinners, although the origin of the name is obscure. There is a town of Marlborough in Connecticut, while Massachusetts, New Jersey, New Hampshire, and New York all have towns called "Marlboro."

MARLBOROUGH PIE

Combine 1 c. applesauce with 3 T. lemon juice, 1 c. sugar, 4 beaten eggs, 2 T. butter, ½ t. nutmeg, 1 c. cream, and ¼ c. sweet sherry. Pour into a 9-in. pie crust and bake at 400° for about 10 min., then at 325° for about 45 min. more. Cool until the filling gels.

---

marlin. Any of a variety of fish in the genera *Makaira* and *Tetrapterus*, with a long, sword-like jaw (1915). The "striped marlin" (*T. audax*), in Hawaii called either "nairagi" or "a'u," is a great game fish that ranges from California to Chile. Also in Hawaii the shortbill spearfish (*T. angustirostris*) is called "hebi," usually used in stews and soups. The "blue marlin" (*M. nigricans*) swims in the north Atlantic, while the "white marlin" (*T. algidus*) can be found in warmer waters of the Atlantic.

marmalade. A form of thick jam that contains pieces of the fruit used. The name comes from the Portuguese *marmelada*, meaning "quince jam" and first appears in English print in 1515.

Early marmalades were in fact made with quince and served as dessert in the form of a bar, but by the eighteenth century Seville orange had become the preferred flavor and remains so today.

marshmallow. A pasty, sweet confection made from corn syrup, gelatin, and sugar. It was once made from the root of the marshmallow plant (*Althaea officinalis*), from which the word derives its name via Old English *merscmealwe*, "marsh" and "mallow." As a confection marshmallow dates back at least to the 1880s. In America marshmallows were once made by the "cast" method, like chocolates, in molds. In 1963 the Borden Company, which owned "Campfire Marshmallows," used a new "extruded" method of making marshmallows, cutting up a long rope of extruded marshmallow paste into small morsels. At the same time, Campfire also introduced "miniature marshmallows," which became popular as a salad ingredient. Marshmallow Fluff is a product (originally called "Toot Sweet") introduced in 1920 by H. Allen Burkee and Fred L.

Mower of Lynn, Massachusetts. Used as a topping for ice cream and desserts, it also became an ingredient in a peanut butter and Marshmallow Fluff sandwich on white bread called the "Fluffernutter." "Peeps" are variously colored marshmallow Easter candies in the shape of small chicks or bunnies, originally made by Rodda Candy in Lancaster, Pennsylvania.

Most marshmallows, however, are used as a topping and filling for cakes, candies, and desserts and as a traditional addition to hot chocolate or cocoa. Marshmallows are also a very popular children's treat when inserted on a stick and roasted over an open fire until crispy on the outside and melting within.

MARSHMALLOW

Soak 1 envelope gelatin in ½ c. cold water for 5 min. Bring ¾ c. water and 2 c. sugar to a boil until liquid forms a thread when dropped from spoon. Add gelatin and let stand away from heat until cooled. Add a dash of salt and 1 t. vanilla extract. Beat until white and thickened, pour into pans dusted with powdered sugar to a depth of about 1 in. Let cool, then turn onto greased marble, cut in cubes, and roll in powdered sugar.

---

martini. A cocktail made from gin and dry vermouth and served with a twist of lemon peel. The origins of the martini have never been satisfactorily explained, despite numerous claims for the drink's invention and the exhaustive research of Lowell Edmunds in *The Silver Bullet: The Martini in American Civilization* (1981), wherein he cites the first appearance of a drink called the "Martinez" in O. H. Byron's *The Modern Bartender* (1884), which contained curaçao, bitters, gin, and Italian vermouth. This is similar to a recipe for a "Gin Cocktail" in *The Bon-Vivant's Companion, or How to Mix Drinks* (1862) by "Professor" Jerry Thomas, a bartender at San Francisco's Occidental Hotel who has been credited with the invention of the drink in that year. Legend had it that the drink was named after a bone-chilled traveler on his way to Martinez, California, although others have claimed that the Martinez (and the weary traveler) first appeared at Julio's Bar in Martinez, California, concocted by bartender Julio Richelieu.

Thomas first gives the name for the cocktail as the "Martinez" in the 1887 edition of his book, while "Martine" appears in Harry Johnson's *New and Improved Bartender's Manual or How to Mix Drinks for the Present Style* (1888). As Edmunds pointed out, this confusing nomenclature seemed to describe pretty much the same drink, but the term "martini" came to be the preferred form by the turn of the century. Most probably the name is somehow connected to the Italian vermouth producer Martini, Sola & Company (later Martini & Rossi), which had been making vermouth since 1829 and is said to have exported it since 1843. (Little credence is given to the association of the name with a Swiss breechblock single-shot rifle, used by the British Army as of 1871, named after its inventor, Friedrich Von Martini; the drink was said to have the "kick of a Martini.")

Early forms of the martini had a definite sweetness to them. But by the 1920s sweet ingredients had pretty much been eliminated. "Dryness" came to be associated with the ratio of gin to vermouth. A pre-Prohibition recipe calls for two parts gin, one part dry vermouth, and a dash of orange bitters, and before World War I the gin had reached four parts to each part vermouth. After World War II the bitters vanished in the cocktail, and the vermouth was reduced to a literal shadow of its former self, with gin-to-vermouth ratios of 5, 6, or 7 to 1 becoming standard. There is one drink, called the "Montgomery," that has a ratio of 15 to 1, which is so called after England's World War II field marshal Bernard Law Montgomery's preference for having fifteen troops for every German troop in battle. Another, called the "naked martini," is no more than gin on the rocks with a lemon twist. This mania for dryness has led to joke recipes that direct the bartender to pour in some vermouth, swirl it around, toss it out, and pour in the gin, or the command for the bartender merely to look at the bottle of vermouth.

Martini fans will argue over the merits of their drink having a lemon twist or an olive as the perfect garnish, but there is general agreement that the addition of a white sour cocktail onion makes the drink a GIBSON. The "martini sandwich," devised by John Kepke, of Brooklyn, consists of a martini between two glasses of draft beer.

The vodka martini became very popular in the 1960s following the success of a series of books and movies based on the exploits of fictional British spy James Bond in novels and stories by Ian Fleming. Bond's first instance of ordering a vodka martini (made with "three measures of Gordon's [gin], one of vodka, half a measure of Kina Lillet" shaken, not stirred, and garnished with lemon peel) was in the book *Casino Royale* (1953).

Maryland stuffed ham. A dish of boiled ham with slits in the meat, into which is stuffed cabbage, onions,

mustard, hot pepper, and other seasonings. It is available only in southern Maryland, and, more specifically, will be found in St. Mary's County. Traditionally served at Easter, the dish may date from the time of Maryland's founder, George Calvert, Lord Baltimore (1580?–1632), who reportedly enjoyed stuffed ham as a boy in Yorkshire, England. In an article in *The New York Times* (December 5, 1982), Mary Z. Gray noted that "Stuffed Chine," calling for a ham cut to the bone to be slit and stuffed with herbs before being boiled, was a familiar recipe in Elizabethan England. She also records a story that Maryland stuffed ham may have originated in the early eighteenth century, "when a slave at St. Inigoe's Manor House dished it up as a special Easter treat for the Jesuit Fathers emerging from their Lenten fast."

Preparation of the dish is time-consuming, requiring that a whole corned ham be cut with ten or so deep slits into which a mixture of cabbage, kale, onions, mustard seed, celery seed, crushed hot pepper, and various other seasonings is stuffed by hand. More of the mixture is packed around the ham, which is then placed in a cloth bag, covered with water, and simmered for several hours. After the ham cools, the bag is cut away and the ham is refrigerated overnight, then served, usually cold, the next day.

masa. A finely ground, parched corn that has been treated with lime or a dough made from corn flour. The word "masa" comes from the Spanish for "dough." In 1953 the Quaker Oats Company registered the name "Masa Harina" for its cornmeal flour, which has since become a staple flour among Hispanic-Americans and is traditionally used in the making of southwestern breads, tortillas, and tamales.

mashu. Also, "masru." A sweet vetch (*Hedysarum alpinum*), sometimes referred to as the "Indian potato" or "Eskimo potato," because it tastes something like potato when cooked and is a staple of Eskimos. The word derives from the Inupiaq *masu*.

Mason jar. A glass jar with a removable threaded top and rubber gasket that keeps the contents airtight to prevent spoilage. The jar was invented in 1858 by John Landis Mason of Brooklyn, New York. A year later paraffin was used as a sealer. When Mason's patent ran out in 1878, the jar was further refined by the Ball brothers of Buffalo, New York, the Hero Fruit Jar Company, and the Consolidated Fruit Jar Company, although the Ball jar became the most popular with American consumers.

matzo. Also, "matzah" and other spellings. Unleavened bread made in thin sheets perforated for easy breaking apart. Matzo is the traditional bread of the Jewish Passover, a holiday commemorating the flight from Egypt of the Israelites, who had no time to wait for their bread to rise. The tradition has been passed on, as commanded in Exodus 12:15, "For seven days you shall eat unleavened bread." The word is from the Hebrew, first appearing in English print in 1846.

Today matzo is enjoyed year-round by Jews and non-Jews as a snack or cracker, with all commercially produced matzo made by just two companies, Streit's in New York City in 1914, and B. Manischewitz in Jersey City, New Jersey, whose combined production totals 20 million pounds annually.

"Matzo brei" is a breakfast dish made with broken, moistened pieces of matzo, eggs, and black pepper, which is sautéed in butter. It is often accompanied by cottage cheese.

mawmouth. Either of two freshwater fish of the American South—the warmouth (*Lupomus gulosus*), first in print in 1839, or a calico bass (*Pomoxys sparoides*), in print in 1890.

mayfish. A killfish of the Atlantic coast (*Fundulus majalis*), first in print in America in 1778.

mayhaw. Also "mayhull" and "May hawthorn." Either of two hawthorn trees or their fruit, *Crataegus aestivalis* (1868) or *C. opaca* (1960), native to the South and often made into jellies

mayonnaise. Also, "mayo." A mixture of egg yolks, oil, lemon juice or vinegar, and other seasonings. Mayonnaise is used as a salad dressing, in sandwiches, on canapés, in dips, and in some sauces and desserts. The name is French, but its origins are obscure. Antonïn Carême in his *Le Cuisinier Parisien* (1833–34) insisted the name should really be called "magnonaise," from the word *manier*, "to stir." *Larousse Gastronomique*, however, believes the word is a popular corruption of *moyeunaise*, itself derived from an old French word, *moyeu*, which means egg yolk. *The Oxford English Dictionary* lists the origins as "uncertain," while the *American Heritage Dictionary* mentions that the dressing is "possibly named in commemoration of the capture in 1756 of the city of Mahon, capital of Minorca, by the Duke of Richelieu." The first appearance of the word in English print was in 1841.

In France there are several classic mayonnaise dressings, but in the United States most people think of bottled mayonnaise, the first important example of which was marketed by New York City delicatessen owner Richard Hellmann in 1912 (although he actually created the formula in 1903). The Hellmann's name and facilities were later acquired by Best Foods, Inc., of California, and are now owned by CPC International, which produces a "real mayonnaise" sold east of the Rocky Mountains under the label "Hellmann's" and west of the Rockies as "Best Foods." The two brands account for about 43 percent of all the bottled mayonnaise sold in the United States. In 1937 Hellmann's developed a chocolate-cake recipe using mayonnaise that became an American favorite.

The FDA Standards of Identity require that mayonnaise have not less than 65 percent vegetable oil, whereas "mayonnaise-type salad dressings" (sometimes called "spoonable salad dressings") must contain not less than 30 percent vegetable oil.

MAYONNAISE

Beat 3 egg yolks until thickened and light yellow. Add 1½ t. dry mustard, a dash of cayenne, and ¾ t. salt. Beat in ¼ c. vinegar or lemon juice, then gradually add 1½ c. olive oil mixed with 1½ c. salad oil. Beat in another ¼ c. vinegar.

Maytag Blue. A blue-veined, tangy, smooth-textured cheese from Iowa made from the milk of holstein-friesian cows. The cheese was first made on October 11, 1941, by Robert and Frederick Maytag in cooperation with Iowa State University.

McGinty. A pie made in Oregon from dried apples. The recipe below is from Mrs. John James Burton and dates back to the 1870s. The name probably derives from a common name for Irish loggers and miners in the Northwest territory of those days.

MCGINTY

Wash, core, and skin 1 lb. dried apples, then soak overnight. Stew in water to cover, puree or push through a sieve, then add enough brown sugar to make a rich, thickened puree. Cool, add 1½ T. cinnamon. Line a pie pan with a pastry crust, place fruit mixture in crust, cover with top crust, make gashes in top crust, and press edges together. Cook in hot oven for over 15 min., then reduce heat. Serve hot with cream.

meadow tea. A Pennsylvania Dutch beverage made from meadow herbs like peppermint and spearmint steeped in hot water to make a form of TEA.

meat. According to the United States Department of Agriculture, "meat comes from the muscles of cattle, sheep, swine, and goats." Skeletal meat refers to the muscular cuts of tissue that had been attached to the animal's bone structure. A "meat food product" or "meat product" is "any food suitable for human consumption made from cattle, sheep, swine, or goats containing more than 3 percent meat." "Meat loaf" is a baked loaf of chopped meat and bread, first in print in 1899.

meat by-product. Also known as "variety meat." The edible and wholesome parts of cattle, swine, sheep, and goats, other than skeletal meat. The United States Department of Agriculture requires that meat by-products be listed on labels.

meeting seeds. A Puritan's term for fennel seeds, which were chewed at Sunday church meetings, probably to mask the smell of alcohol on one's breath.

melba toast. Also, "Melba toast." A very thin, crisp, dry toast first made in 1897 by chef Georges Auguste Escoffier of London's Savoy Hotel for Australian opera singer Nellie Melba (1859–1931), after whom Madame M. L. Ritz, wife of the hotel's owner, César Ritz, named the dish. The toast became a standard item served with salads or on a restaurant's bread dish. In the United States a flat version of melba toast was first mass-produced and packaged by Marjorie Weill, owner of the Devon Bakery in New York City in 1932, introducing round versions of the square toast in 1940, and gave her company a more English-sounding name—the Devonsheer Melba company.

Curiously Nellie Melba does not mention the famous toast in her autobiography, *Melodies and Memories* (1925), nor does Escoffier in his recipe book, *Le Guide Culinaire* (1921).

MELBA TOAST

Slice stale bread very thin, dry in a warming oven, then toast in a slow oven or under a grill.

menudo. Tripe soup or stew (1967), common in the Southwest. The word is derived from the Spanish for "entrails."

Meritage. Pronounced "MER-i-tage." A trademark name and symbol for an association of California wineries making wines from a blend of grapes traditionally used in Bordeaux winemaking. In 1988 a group of vintners formed "the Association in Search of a Name" for their organization, and the name "Meritage" was submitted by Neil Edgar of Newark, California, who combined the words "merit" and "heritage." The association sought to develop wines that had more complexity than traditional California varietals (which may contain 100 percent of a single grape variety), to be achieved by blending in classic Bordeaux varieties.

To obtain the right to use the Meritage trademark, a wine must meet the following criteria:

1. They must be a blend of the traditional Bordeaux grape varieties: Cabernet Sauvignon, Merlot, Cabernet Franc, Petit Verdot, Malbec, Gros Verdot, and Carminère for red; Sauvignon Blanc (Sauvignon Musque), Sémillon, and Muscadelle for white.

2. It must be the winery's best wine of its type.

3. It must be produced and bottled by a U.S. winery from grapes that carry a U.S. appellation of origin.

4. It must be limited in production to no more than twenty-five thousand cases from each vintage by a single winery.

Association members' blended wines may carry the word "Meritage" on their labels, although member wineries may instead carry only their own proprietary names. In 1993 The Meritage Association petitioned the BATF to recognize Meritage as a "designation of varietal significance."

meritfish. Also, "green smelt." A silversides fish (*Menidia menidia*) of the New England coast (1884).

mess. Although a mess of food may connote a sloppily presented meal of indiscriminate quality (1697), the term "mess" actually goes back to the Latin *missus,* a portion or course of food. Later, in England, mess referred to a group of people eating together, and in America a "mess house" (1865), "mess hall" or "mess tent" is a serviceman's dining room, for which a "mess sergeant" and "mess crew" prepare the food.

metate. A stone used by native Americans, Mexicans, and frontiersmen to grind cornmeal. The word is from the Mexican, first printed in English in 1834.

metzel soup. A Pennsylvania-Dutch sausage given as a gift by the person who slaughtered the animal (1872). The word is from the German *Metzelsuppe*, "sausage soup."

Mexican breakfast. Southern term, intending a regional slur, for a cigarette and a glass of water, usually prescribed for hangover victims (1954).

Miami grill. A dish of veal chops, orange slices, bananas, and tomatoes, all grilled or broiled together. It is associated with Miami, Florida, and probably dates from the 1930s.

MIAMI GRILL

On a greased rack place 4 veal chops, 4 lamb chops, 4 salted tomatoes, and 4 peeled and buttered bananas. Broil for 10–12 min., turning once.

mickey. A potato roasted over an open fire. Mickeys were sold by street vendors during the first half of this century, and the name derives from the potato's association with the Irish immigrants, who collectively had been referred to as "micks" since the nineteenth century. The word's usage in print, in reference to the potato, dates back only to the 1943 but is probably much older.

Mickey Finn. Also, "Mickey." A bartender's term for a secretly concocted beverage designed to induce diarrhea in an unwanted customer. It is also a term for "knockout drops," a drink that will induce unconsciousness (1925).

The origins of the drink are usually associated with San Francisco's Barbary Coast in the 1870s, when, according to Herb Caen in *Don't Call It Frisco* (1953), a discredited Scottish chemist-turned-bartender named Michael Finn helped shanghai sailors by serving them such potions. Sometimes these drinks contained Glauber's Salts, a horse laxative, or potassium tartrate, an emetic. There was even an infamous "Mickey Finn Case" involving the poisoning of an orchestra playing at a club on Fisherman's Wharf in San Francisco.

By the 1920s in some quarters Mickey Finn

referred to a "double," or two servings of liquor at once.

microwave oven. An electric oven that uses high-frequency electromagnetic waves to generate heat within foods by vibrating their molecules.

The microwave oven was developed by microwave researcher Percy Le Baron Spencer of the Raytheon Company in 1946 after noticing that a piece of chocolate in his pocket had melted as he stood next to a magnetron, which drives a radar set. By 1953 Raytheon had patented a very large, 750-pound "high frequency dielectric heating apparatus" they marketed to restaurants as a "Radar range." In 1964 Japan developed an improved electron tube that in 1967 was adapted for use in microwave ovens sold by Amana Refrigeration, Inc. (purchased by Raytheon two years before). In 1971 the federal government set safety standards for microwave ovens, and today a majority of American homes use them.

migas. A Mexican-American breakfast of scrambled eggs and corn tortillas. The word is from the Spanish for "crumbs" and refers to crumbled-up tortillas.

mile-high cake. Generally a tall cake of several layers, or cakes designed from recipes for baking at high altitudes. Mile-High Ice-Cream Pie was created at New Orleans's Pontchartrain Hotel.

milk. The white liquid produced by the mammary glands of cows, goats, sheep, and other animals, although in the United States almost all milk comes from cows. The word is from Old English *milc*.

Although milk has been drunk by most of the world's people, especially infants and children, it was not known to pre-Columbian Indians for the simple reason that they had no milk animals, which were brought to the New World by the Spaniards and English. In 1611 the first milk cows were brought to Jamestown, Virginia. At first the Europeans drank mostly goat's milk, but, notes Richard J. Hooker in *Food and Drink in America* (1981), "by 1634 all the 'better' plantations of Virginia were said to have plenty of milk, butter, and cheese, and throughout New England milk was drunk, made into cheese, or eaten with samp, suppawn, fruits, and baked pumpkins."

Until the nineteenth century, however, milk was still treated with caution, especially in the South, where the heat quickly spoiled fresh milk. Plantation slaves drank skim milk, while their masters drank the first milk of the morning. In the North, where it was cooler, Dutch and German settlers enjoyed their milk, especially when made into cheese. Still, milk was frequently contaminated, especially in the cities, where dairies were often run by breweries that fed the cows on fermented mash and adulterated the milk with water, chalk, and other ingredients, leading to *Leslie's Illustrated Newspaper's* pronouncement in 1858 that such actions constituted "milk murder." Indeed, even in the country people risked illness, even death, from a disease called "the milksick," "the milk evil," "milk poison," "the slows," and "the trembles" (from which Abraham Lincoln's mother died). Nevertheless, nutritionists and temperance leaders promoted the virtues of sanitary milk for their followers, and "milkmen" delivered their product from "milk ranches" (later "dairy farms") by "milk wagon," pouring it into customers' "milk cans."

A safer form of milk was developed by Gail Borden of Wolcottville, Connecticut, who had experimented with attar of meat and other concentrated foods but who made his fortune by creating condensed milk in 1853 after witnessing the deprivations of immigrant babies on a transatlantic crossing because the cows on board had milk sickness. Condensed milk was flavored with sugar and cooked under vacuum to remove 60 percent of the water, and it became standard issue among Civil War troops.

It was also during this period that French chemist Louis Pasteur (1822–95) developed a process for killing off harmful microbes in milk. This became known as "pasteurization" and was widely adopted in the United States by the 1890s, so that European visitors marveled at the amount of milk consumed here. State laws were soon instituted to regulate sanitary conditions in dairies—for example, inspections were mandatory in Newark, New Jersey, as of 1882. By 1908, 25 percent of New York's milk and 33 percent of Boston's was being pasteurized. The first known "milk bottle" dates at least to 1866, though the first patented bottle, called "Whiteman's milk jar," was not patented until 1884. The store-bought paperboard milk carton was created by Pure-Pak of Detroit, Michigan, in the 1930s.

Milk was wholesome, nutritious, and available to everyone; it was sold fresh or canned, condensed or, as of the 1920s, "evaporated," which was not sweetened like condensed milk. In 1927 Borden's marketed the first homogenized milk. "Powdered milk" or "dry milk" was pioneered by David Peebles in 1953 and first marketed by the Carnation Company the following year.

Before long the United States became the world's leading producer of milk and milk products, with Wisconsin and California leading the way. By 1950 Americans were drinking six hundred glasses of milk per person per year, but in the years that followed consumption decreased, owing to concerns over too much fat and cholesterol in the American diet. When low-fat milk containing between 0.5 percent and 2 percent milkfat (whole milk contains about 3.8 percent) came on the market in the 1960s, milk consumption rose again. Skim milk (or "skimmed milk") has nearly all the fat removed. In the South this is colloquially called "blue john." "Evaporated milk" is milk that has had 60 percent of its water removed, been heat sterilized, then canned (1870).

In 1997 Americans per capita consumed about 206 pounds of fluid milk items. Total fluid milk production was at nearly 157 billion pounds, with plain whole milk making up 18.5 billion pounds of sales. Lowfat milk sold nearly 24 billion pounds, skim milk 9 billion, flavored milk and drinks 2.8 billion, and buttermilk 695 million. Half-and-half sales were 889 million, light cream 120 million, heavy cream 509 million, sour cream and dips 803 million, eggnog 103 million, and yogurt 1.4 billion. Supermarkets make up the largest retail segment for milk (56 percent).

Most American milk is homogenized, and some is treated with a relatively new process called "ultra-pasteurization," by which the milk is heated for two seconds at 280°, which has the effect of killing some organisms but not affecting the taste. This process produces "long-life milk," able to be kept on a market shelf without souring for up to six months. "Dried milk," "powdered milk," or "dehydrated milk" is made from either whole or skim milk.

"Buttermilk" is made from the sour liquid containing some butterfat left after the making of butter. Markets also sell a cultured buttermilk made with a lactic-acid bacteria added to skim or partially skimmed milk. "Acidophilus milk" (or "LBA culture") is cultured with acidophilus bacteria and fortified with vitamins A and D. It is more easily digested by those people who cannot tolerate whole milk.

See also CREAM.

milk punch. Any low-proof drink made of liquor, sugar, and milk, usually served for brunches. Of rather recent origins, milk punches are an American streamlined version of EGGNOG and include drinks with names like the "Milky Way" (½ oz. brandy, ½ oz. rum,

½ oz. bourbon, 6 oz. milk, and a dash of vanilla shaken with ice).

milk shake. A drink made with milk, a flavored syrup, and ice cream blended to a thick consistency. It is a favorite soda-fountain item, only occasionally made at home.

When the term first appeared in print in 1885, milk shakes may have contained whiskey of some kind, but by the turn of the century they were considered wholesome drinks made with chocolate, strawberry, or vanilla syrups. In different parts of the country the item went by different names. One might order a "frappé" (from the French past participle of *frapper*, to "strike" or "chill"), which in the nineteenth century, and to some extent today, refers to a frozen sherbetlike mixture of fruit juice and ice. Frappé is today synonymous with milk shake and often pronounced "frapp." One may also hear "frosted," "thick shake," and, in Rhode Island, CABINET. A "malted" is made with MALTED MILK powder—invented in 1887 by William Horlick of Racine, Wisconsin, and made from dried milk, malted barley, and wheat flour—promoted at first as a drink for invalids and children. By the 1930s a "malt shop" was a soda fountain not attached to a pharmacy. "Date shakes" are popular in southern California.

mincemeat. Also, "mince." A mixture of chopped fruits, spices, suet, and, sometimes, meat that is usually baked in a pie crust. The word comes from "mince," "to chop finely," whose own origins are in the Latin *minuere*, "to diminish," and once "mincemeat" referred specifically to meat that had been minced up, a meaning it has had since the sixteenth century. By the nineteenth century, however, the word referred to a pie of fruit, spices, and suet, only occasionally containing any meat at all. In Colonial America these pies were made in the fall and sometimes frozen throughout the winter.

ming-mang. Ozarks colloquialism for a mixture of either butter and molasses or butter and gravy (1936), akin to the term "mishmash" for a mixture of things.

Minnehaha. A term for a variety of cakes, breads, or puddings that share little in common except the simplicity of ingredients and preparation. The name commemorates the Native American heroine of Henry Wadsworth Longfellow's epic poem *Hiawatha*, published in 1855, after which the Minnehaha foods appeared in recipe books. There is scant mention of Minnehaha's culinary talents in the poem, only a reference to the "Yellow cakes of the Mondamin" served at the wedding feast of Hiawatha and Minnehaha.

mint. Any of a variety of plants in the genus *Mentha* that bear aromatic leaves used for flavoring desserts, candy, gum, and other food. The name is from the Greek *minthe*.

The two most popular varieties of mint, "peppermint" (*M. piperita*) and "spearmint" (*M. spicata*), are not native to America but were brought over early by the European colonists, and the species proliferated without much need of cultivation.

"Mint jelly" is a customary accompaniment to lamb dishes in America, and peppermint sticks are a favorite hard candy, often crushed to make "peppermint-stick ice cream," served with hot fudge sauce.

mint julep. A COCKTAIL made from bourbon, sugar, and mint. It is a classic drink of Kentucky and is traditionally served at the running of the Kentucky Derby on the first Saturday of May. The word first appeared printed in John Davis's *Travels of Four Years and a Half in the United States of America* (1803), as a "dram of spiritous liquor that has mint in it, taken by Virginians in the morning."

The origin of the word "julep" is the Persian *gulāb* "rosewater," which is not an ingredient in the Kentucky cocktail but indicates a very sweet concoction known since the fifteenth century. Mint juleps were known in the United States by the end of the eighteenth century, long before bourbon became the ingredient most associated with the drink, and one will find mint juleps made with whiskeys other than bourbon, though this would be heresy in the state of Kentucky, where there is also great debate as to whether the mint leaves should be crushed in the traditional silver mug. Frances Parkinson Keyes once observed that "like a woman's heart, mint gives its sweetest aroma when bruised. I have heard it said that the last instructions which a Virginia gentleman murmurs on his deathbed are, 'Never insult a decent woman, never bring a horse in the house, and never crush the mint in a julep!' "

MINT JULEP

Chill a silver mug (made in the South especially for juleps). Dissolve 1½ t. confectioners' sugar in 1 T. water. Fill mug with crushed ice, pour in enough bourbon to cover, then stir in the sugar syrup. Garnish with sprigs of mint.

miracle. A nineteenth-century New England fried cookie.

MIRACLE

Beat 3 eggs with 3 T. melted butter, 2 c. flour, a dash of salt. Roll dough very thin, sprinkle with sugar, and cut into even, large squares. Fold in two, cut into long strips about 1 in. wide, and twist together to form a link. Fry in hot oil until golden brown.

Mission bell. A stevedore's term for a drinker of cheap wine, so called because of the widespread use of Mission grapes in such wines, especially in California.

Mississippi mud pie. A very dense chocolate pie that takes its name from the thick mud along the banks of the Mississippi River. According to Nathalie Dupree in *New Southern Cooking* (1986), the top of what she calls "Mississippi Mud Cake" should also be "cracked and dry-looking like Mississippi mud in the hot, dry summer." It does, however, seem to be of fairly recent origin; according to Mississippi-born food authority Craig Claiborne, writing in 1987, "I never heard of a Mississippi mud pie or Mississippi mud cake until I moved North."

MISSISSIPPI MUD PIE

In a saucepan melt 3 squares of bittersweet chocolate and 1 stick butter. In a bowl beat 3 eggs with 1¼ c. sugar, 2 T. corn syrup, and 1 t. vanilla extract, then pour slowly and blend into the chocolate mixture. Pour the batter into a pie crust (graham-cracker or chocolate-cookie crust is often used) and bake at 350° for about 35 minutes until set. The top should be fairly dry and crisp, the interior soft.

mixed grill. A dish composed of various grilled meats such as beef, pork, sausage, chicken, lamb, venison, and others. The term dates in print to about 1910. See MIAMI GRILL.

mock apple pie. A pie made with cheese-flavored Ritz crackers (introduced by the National Biscuit Company in 1933) and spices to resemble the taste of apple pie. The recipe first appeared during the Depression, when apples became a costly item.

mocktail. A colloquialism from the 1980s to describe a cocktail made without alcohol. See also SHIRLEY TEMPLE.

mock-turtle soup. A soup made from calves' brains to resemble true turtle soup. It is of English origins, made famous by the character of the mock turtle (with the shell of a turtle and the head of a calf) in Lewis Carroll's *Alice's Adventures in Wonderland* (1865). This recipe is from Mrs. James T. Halsey of Philadelphia, as published in *Famous Old Receipts* (1908):

MOCK-TURTLE SOUP

Boil the brains of a calf in 3 gal. water and reduce to 3 qt. Add a bunch of parsley, thyme, onions, 1 t. allspice, 1 t. cloves, 1 t. mace, 1 t. nutmeg, black and red peppers, and 1 t. salt. Cook for about 40 min. at a simmer. Remove meat, cool, then mince the meat. Return to pot with ½ pt. sherry, ½ c. walnuts, and ½ c. tomato ketchup. Make a roux of flour, 1 T. butter, and 1 T. vinegar and add to pot. Reheat, serve garnished with brain fritters, 6 hard-boiled eggs, parsley, and pepper.

moi. Hawaiian name for a threadfish (*Polydactylus sexfilis*) that is caught along the shoreline (1926). It is usually baked or steamed.

molasses. A sweetener made from refined sugar, including canesugar, sugar beets, and even sweet potatoes. The word is from the Portuguese *melaço,* derived from the Latin *mel,* for honey. The first use of the word was in Nicholas Lichefield's 1582 translation of Lopez de Castanheda's *First Booke of the Historie of the Discoverie and Conquest of the East Indias,* which described "Melasus" as "a certeine kinde of Sugar made of Palmes or Date trees."

Molasses became the most common American sweetener in the eighteenth century because it was much cheaper than sugar and was part of the triangular trade route that brought molasses to New England to be made into rum, which was then shipped to West Africa to be traded for slaves, who were in turn traded for molasses in the West Indies. When France forbade her West Indies colonies to export molasses to the mother country (where the French feared it would ruin the French brandy industry), the colonists began shipping molasses to America, and before long it was the principal sweetener of the British colonies. The Molasses Act of 1733 placed high duties on the substance, but widespread evasion of the tariff resulted in lowering tariffs in 1764. Nevertheless, John Adams said molasses was "an essential ingredient in American independence," because of England's attempts to tax the colonists in this manner.

Molasses remained Americans' most popular sweetener in the next century; it was used in drinks and confections and with meats, especially with pork, causing English traveler Frederick Marryat to write in his *Diary of America* (1839) that although the English "laugh at the notion of pork and molasses . . . it eats uncommonly well. . . . After all, why should we eat currant jelly with venison and not allow the Americans the humble imitation of pork and molasses?" A sweetener like molasses was especially needed with salt pork in order to temper the strong taste of the meat.

By the 1830s new brides measured their popularity by the number of layers of the molasses cake (or "stack cake") the guests brought, and molasses cookies and candy were very popular.

One of the stranger events in food history occurred on January 15, 1919, when an enormous vat of molasses exploded at the Purity Distilling Company in Boston, sending more than 2 million gallons into the streets and killing twenty-one people in what became known as the "Great Molasses Flood."

By the end of the century molasses vied with MAPLE syrup and sugar as the sweetener of choice, but when sugar prices dropped after World War I, both molasses and maple fell in popularity, so that today both are used as sweeteners in confections only when their specific taste is desirable, as in BOSTON BAKED BEANS.

In the production of molasses, the sugarcane is crushed and the juice concentrated by boiling; after crystallization the residue that remains is molasses, the residue of the first boiling being the best grade for table use. The top grades of molasses would include "fancy" or "all natural," and would include the first "strike" (also "centrifugal") made from the first extraction of sugar crystals. "Second strike" molasses is the residue from a second crystallization. Both first and second strikes are then bleached with sulfur-dioxide gas and termed "sulfured." The "third strike" is a very dark and thick molasses called BLACKSTRAP (also "mother liquor"), which may sometimes be found in health food stores but is generally distilled into animal feed or industrial alcohol. Molasses used to be called "long sweetening," while a darker, less-refined variety was called "short sweetening."

mom-and-pop. Most often used with "grocery,"

"store" or "restaurant," this refers to a small, homey grocery or eatery typically run by a family. The term has been in print since the 1950s.

mongole soup. A soup made from creamed split pea and tomato, usually from canned soups. It was especially popular during the 1930s, though its origins are uncertain. Food historian Jean Anderson has traced a recipe to 1935 under the name "puree mongole" for a soup using three bean purees, tomato, onion, and consomme in *Those Rich and Great Ones* by Henri Charpentier, whose restaurant in Lynnbrook, New York, featured the soup as a signature dish. The 1943 edition of *Joy of Cooking* contained a recipe for Mongole soup made with pea and tomato soups.

monkey bread. A sweet yeast bread, sometimes mixed with currants, formed from balls of dough, laid next to one another, which combine during baking. The origin of the name is unknown, though it has been suggested that the bread resembles the monkey puzzle tree (*Araucaria araucana*), whose .prickly branches make it difficult to climb. There is also a fruit called "monkey bread," from the baobab tree (*Adansonia digitata*) of Africa, but there is no evidence of any connection between it and the baked bread. It is probable that the name comes from the appearance of the baked bread itself, which resembles a pack of monkeys jumbled together.

Nancy Reagan made monkey bread a traditional dish of the White House Christmas celebration; she claims that the bread is so called "because when you make it, you have to monkey around with it." The following recipe is from the former First Lady:

> ### MONKEY BREAD
>
> Dissolve 1 pkg. dry yeast in ¼ c. milk. Add 2 eggs, beat, then mix in 3 T. sugar, 1 T. salt, 3½ c. flour, and 1 c. milk, and blend thoroughly. Cut in 6 oz. butter, knead well, and let rise to double. Knead again, let rise again for 40 min. Roll dough onto floured board, shape into a log, and cut into 28 pieces. Shape each piece of dough into ball and roll in ½ lb. melted butter. Butter and flour two 9-in. ring molds, place 7 balls of dough in each mold, place remaining balls of dough on top, and let rise again. Brush tops with 1 beaten egg, bake for 15 min. at 375°.

monkey food. Southern slang for snack food (1940).

monkey gland. A cocktail made with orange juice, grenadine, gin, and an anise cordial. It became popular in the 1920s, when Dr. Serge Voronoff (1866–1951), a Russian emigré to Paris and director of experimental surgery at the Laboratory of Physiology of the Collège de France, was promoting the benefits of transplanting the sex glands of monkeys into human beings in order to restore vitality and prolong life. His book, *Life,* appeared in 1920, but by the mid-1920s his theories had been generally discredited.

The cocktail, which facetiously promised similar restorative powers, may have been invented at Harry's New York Bar in Paris by owner Harry MacElhone.

MONKEY GLAND

Shake together with ice a dash of anise cordial, 2 dashes grenadine, and equal parts gin and orange juice. Strain into cocktail glass.

monkey rum. A spirit distilled from the syrup of sorghum. The first mention of this drink, which is produced in North Carolina, was in 1941.

monkfish (*Lophius americanus*). Also, "anglerfish," "goosefish," "fishing frog," and "allmouth." An Atlantic flatfish that usually dwells at the ocean bottom. Its European counterpart is *Lophius piscatorius.* The name "monkfish" has been used at least since the seventeenth century and refers to the species' remoteness of habitat in the same way a monk removes himself from the outside world.

Although long a favorite in European gastronomy, the fish was never a popular species in the United States because of its ugliness and its unappetizing name, "goosefish. It also mysteriously disappeared from American waters at the end of the nineteenth century. But the frequent use of the fish in French NOUVELLE CUISINE in the 1970s under the name "lotte," and the adoption by American chefs of the name "monkfish" or "anglerfish" led, in the 1980s, to an increased appetite for the species. The tail is the only part of the monkfish that is eaten and may be broiled, sautéed, poached, or baked. Its meat is white and quite firm, often cut into medallions. U.S. commercial landings of monkfish totaled 60.6 million pounds in 1997.

monoglycerides. An emulsifier that prevents spoilage in bread and baked goods and prevents the separation of oil in peanut butter.

monosodium glutamate (MSG). An amino-acid flavor enhancer used in seafood, cheese, sauces, and other foods both at home and in processing. The substance was first produced commercially in the United States in 1934. Monosodium glutamate is often found in Chinese food, giving rise to "Chinese restaurant syndrome," meaning the sensations of dizziness, tightness of the chest, and burning some people feel when they eat food with MSG in it.

Monte Cristo sandwich. A sandwich composed of ham, chicken, and Swiss cheese enclosed in bread that is dipped in beaten egg and fried until golden brown. The origin of the name is not known.

mooneye. Also, "gizzard shad," "toothed herring," "goldeye," and other names. A Midwestern fish of the genus *Hiodon* (1842), so called because the retina of the fish's eyes reflects light.

moonfish. Any of several American fish, including the spadefish (*Ephippus gigas*) that ranges from New England to the Gulf Coast (1842); a variety of fish in the genus *Selene*, including the "dollarfish," "horsehead," "humpbacked butterfish," and others (1878); the harvest fish (*Peprilus alepidotus*), first in print in 1911; and the Hawaiian fish "opah" (*Lampris luna* and *L. regius*), first noted in print in 1896.

Moon Pie. Trademark name for a cookie made by the Chattanooga Bakery in Chattanooga, Tennessee, consisting of two cookies with a marshmallow filling and chocolate icing. The Moon Pie is one of the most beloved confections in the American South. "It was the basis of the ten-cent lunch," southern cultural historian William Ferris told *The New York Times* (April 30, 1986). "A nickel for the Moon Pie and a nickel for an RC Cola."

The cookie supposedly originated in 1917 at the bakery when, around the turn of the century, a traveling salesman recommended creating just such a confection, whose size would be "as big as the moon." The Moon Pie was trademarked in 1919. In 1969 the bakery introduced a "Double Decker" version with three cookies and two layers of marshmallow. The company now produces 300,000 Moon Pies per day.

Moonshine. Illegally distilled WHISKEY, especially that made with corn. The term—which refers to the time of day when the cover of darkness hid the activities of the "moonshiners," those engaged in such illicit whiskey making—dates back at least to 1860 and was later sometimes shortened to "shine" or "moon." The number of moonshiners naturally increased during the Prohibition era. Moonshine is very potent, very raw, and often composed of dangerous elements, including battery acid, oil, and other ingredients used to speed up fermentation, thereby reducing the risk of being discovered. This unhealthy brew was called "scared whiskey." Moonshine filtered through charcoal was called "coal juice." Federal revenue agents were called "revenooers" by the hill people of Appalachia and the Ozarks, where most moonshine was produced, and a great deal of folklore grew up around the people and object of this cat-and-mouse game, depicted in comic strips like Al Capp's "Li'l Abner" and William de Beck's "Barney Google."

Southerners commonly call such spirits "white lightning"; white southerners sometimes use the term "black thunder."

moonshine. A dessert of egg whites and fruit preserves—a New England dish of the nineteenth century that has nothing to do with the illicit whiskey distilled in the South (circa 1885). It may be named after the silvery white flower called "everlasting" (*Anaphalis margaritacea*), which in the mid-nineteenth century was called "moonshine."

MOONSHINE

Beat 6 egg whites, add 6 T. confectioners' sugar, then fold in 1 c. peaches or 1 c. jelly or preserves. In a saucer pour cream flavored with vanilla and sugar and place egg-white mixture on top. Serves 6.

---

moose (*Alces alces* or *Alces americana*). A large, hairy, antlered, deerlike animal, standing up to seven and a half feet high at the shoulder and up to ten feet in length, that ranges from the coastal tundra of Alaska down to northwestern Colorado. Its name, according to the *American Heritage Dictionary*, is from the Natick *moos*, from Proto-Algonquian *mooswa*, while Flexner in *I Hear America Talking* cites Passamaquoddy *moosu*, "he trims smoothly," referring to the manner in which the animal strips bark from trees. In 1603 the first printed reference to the animal was made; by 1637, it was called "Mose," and by 1672 "Moose Deer."

Although the Native Americans hunted moose for their meat, early white settlers showed little interest in the animal as food. Even so, the moose's numbers dwindled in subsequent centuries, and the government finally had to step in to stave off extermination of the herds.

Today moose is rarely eaten, except as an exotic specialty in game restaurants. The meat is usually marinated and prepared as one would venison, or dredged in flour and pan-fried.

Moravian Christmas cookies. A traditional Moravian spice cookie served at Christmastime.

MORAVIAN CHRISTMAS COOKIES

Sift 2½ c. flour, ¼ t. ground cloves, ½ t. cinnamon ¼ t. nutmeg, and ¼ t. salt. Cream 1 c. butter and add 1½ c. sugar. Beat well, then add 2 beaten eggs and 1 T. brandy. Beat in the flour and chill for several hours. Roll out very thin and cut with cookie cutter. Place on buttered baking sheets and bake at 375° for about 8 min.

Moscow mule. A cocktail made from vodka and ginger beer. Its name refers to vodka's Russian heritage and ginger beer's zest, which combine to give the drink the kick of a mule.

The drink was created in 1947 by Jack Morgan, owner of a restaurant in West Hollywood, California, called the Cock 'n Bull, together with Jack Martin and Rudy Kunett of Heublein, a spirits distributor then trying to promote Smirnoff vodka. The drink helped spur the popularity of vodka drinks in the United States soon afterward. But during the Korean War the cocktail was used as an object of scorn when New York City bartenders marched with banners proclaiming WE CAN DO WITHOUT THE MOSCOW MULE, to which Smirnoff answered that their company had long ago disassociated themselves from the Communists and had long been making the vodka in New England—a perennial stronghold of American patriotism."

MOSCOW MULE

In a copper mug with ice cubes stir 3 oz. vodka, the juice of ½ lemon, a twist of lime peel, and a twist of cucumber peel. Fill with ginger beer. (Sometimes ginger ale is substituted.)

---

mountain dew. Illicit liquor, especially from the mountains of Kentucky and Tennessee, though the term originated in the whiskey-producing Highlands of Scotland. In America there is also a commercial soft drink, which is slightly lemony and carbonated, called "Mountain Dew."

The first American printed reference to the word was in 1850.

mountain oyster. The testicles of the bull, pig, or lamb (1890). Sometimes called "Rocky Mountain oysters" or "calf fries," they are usually breaded and fried in the West. The name derives from the general appearance of the final product and not a little euphemism. It is a term used both by cowboys and meat-packinghouse workers.

MOUNTAIN OYSTER

Wash 2 lb. lamb's testicles and place in large pot with 1 onion and 1 T. salt. Cover with water, bring to boil, lower to a simmer, and cook for 30 min. until tender, skimming top of water as necessary.

---

mountain tea. A wintergreen plant (*Gaultheria procumbens*) or a tea brewed from it (1785).

Moxie. Trademark for a fairly tart or bitter soft drink concocted by Dr. Augustus Thompson in Union, Maine, in 1884 and originally sold as a "Moxie Nerve Food" to help remedy "paralysis, softening of the brain, and mental imbecility."

The drink's name was speciously pronounced by Thompson to have been in honor of a "Lieutenant Moxie," who was said to have been a classmate of Thompson's at West Point and the discoverer of a mysterious plant food in South America that became the basis of the beverage. The problem was, Thompson was never enrolled at West Point, and the officer was said to have died in California shortly before Thompson secured the trademark for Moxie. It is possible that the name derived instead from a wintergreen vine (*Gaultheria hispidula*) that was called moxie (1894), itself possibly derived from the Algonquian base *maski-*, "medicine."

The beverage became a very popular soft drink, and "Moxie" itself came to have the additional meaning of courage, nerve, or shrewdness by 1930, when Damon Runyon wrote in *Collier's* magazine, "Personally, I always figure Louie a petty-larceny kind of guy, with no more moxie than a canary bird."

muckamuck. An Alaskan Chinook Indian word for food. When coupled to their word *hiu,* meaning "plenty," it means "plenty to eat." By extension, in American slang, a "high muckamuck" was not only someone who ate well, but also, at least since 1840, a very powerful politician. Today it also means any powerful person.

muddle. A fish stew or the gathering at which such a dish is made and served (1833).

muddler. A stick with a nubby end used to mash sugar or other ingredients at the bottom of a glass in making a cocktail or other drink. The word is from muddle, "to mix something up."

muffin. A small yeast cake usually sweetened with a bit of sugar. In England muffins were once called "tea-cakes," while in America muffins are served primarily for breakfast or as an accompaniment to dinner. Americans make plain muffins from flour, yeast, and sugar, but often add nuts and berries. Cornmeal muffins, blueberry muffins, and ENGLISH MUFFINS are particularly popular. Muffins are usually buttered.

The origins of the word are obscure, but possibly it is from Low German *muffe,* "cake." The term was first printed in English in 1703, and Hannah Glasse in her 1747 cookbook gives a recipe for making muffins. "Mush muffins" (called "slipperdowns" in New England) were a Colonial muffin made with hominy on a hanging griddle.

"Gems" were a popular muffin of the nineteenth century made with Gem commercial baking powder.

MUFFIN

Combine 1 beaten egg, 1 c. milk, and ¼ c. cooled, melted butter. In another bowl mix together 2 c. flour, 2 T. sugar, 1 pkg. yeast, and a pinch of salt. Add milk mixture and stir lightly. Add berries or nuts if desired. Bake for 25 min. at 400° until lightly browned. Makes 1 doz.

---

muffuletta. Also, "muffaletta." A HERO-type sandwich on a large, round Italian bread loaf stuffed with ham, Genoa and mortadella salami, cheeses, and pickled olives. It is a specialty of New Orleans, where it was created at the Central Grocery in 1906 by Salvatore Lupo based on a Sicilian sandwich. *Muffuletta* is a Sicilian dialect word for a round loaf of bread baked so that the center is hollow, so that it may be stuffed, usually with ricotta cheese.

The recipe below is purported to be the original Central Grocery muffuletta.

MUFFULETTA

Slice a 7-in. muffuletta bun or round Italian loaf with sesame seeds in half. Brush one half with olive oil. Layer fillings of 2 oz. sliced domestic ham, 2 oz. sliced Genoa salami, 2 oz. sliced Provolone or Swiss cheese, 2 oz. sliced mortadella, and add an olive vegetable condiment made with pimientoes, olive oil, garlic, vinegar, green and Greek olives, oregano, parsley, cauliflower, celery, and other vegetables on top. Cover with the other half of the bread, cut in half or into pie-shaped wedges.

mulacolong. A stewed chicken dish of obscure southern origins. In *200 Years of Charleston Cooking*, edited by Lettie Gay (1930), this dish is described thus: "The marching rhythm of this name is entrancing. Its origin is as mysterious as the flavor of the dish itself.

"A bird which has reached the age politely spoken of as 'uncertain' may serve as the pièce de résistance of any dinner and reflect glory on the hostess if it is prepared in this manner." The following recipe is from Gay's book.

MULACOLONG

Cut 1 fowl in pieces and fry until it is well browned. Then add 1 large chopped onion to the fat and allow this to brown also. Add 3 pt. veal stock, which should be very strong, and 1 t. turmeric mixed with 1 T. lemon juice. Season with salt and pepper and cook until the chicken is tender. The stock should cook down so that it forms a rich gravy, which should be served over the chicken.

mulberry. Any of a variety of trees in the genus *Morus*, especially the American red mulberry (*M. rubra*), which bears sweet berries used in making jellies, cordials, and pastries. The word is from Old English *mōrberie*, via the Latin *mōrum*.

Other varieties include the "Mexican" or "Texas mulberry" (*M. microphylla*) and the "black mulberry" (*M. nigra*).

mullet. Any of a variety of fish in the family Mugilidae, having more than a hundred species worldwide. The name is from Latin *mullus*, for the "red mullet" or "goatfish" (*Mullus surmuletus* and *M. barbatus*), known in Hawaii as *kumu*. In the United States two species are important: The "striped mullet" (*Muqil cephalus*), also called "black mullet" in Florida and "gray mullet" in other parts of the world; and the

"white mullet" (*M. curema*). Both are usually pan-fried or baked and in the South are often served as a breakfast fish. U.S. commercial landings of mullet totaled 19.6 million pounds in 1997

mulligan stew. Hobo slang for a stew made from any food he can find, but usually containing meat, potatoes, and vegetables. The term has been in use at least since 1904 and may be commemorative of some real or fictional cook of the hobo camps. It has been suggested, too, that it comes from "mulligatawny" (from the Indian Tamil word *milagutannir*, "pepper water"), an Indian curry soup still widely enjoyed. But the association with a typical Irish name like "Mulligan" seems true to an earlier meat-and-potatoes concoction of the nineteenth century called "Irish stew."

A "mulligan-mixer" is a cook in a hobo camp (or jungle). "Mulligan" was also a word for a bottle of hot pepper seeds and water once used in saloons to intensify the flavor of beer—a use of the term that may well refer back to the Indian Tamil word noted above.

munchies. A colloquial term for a craving for something to eat, especially snack foods like potato chips, pretzels, and popcorn. It may also refer to the snack food itself. "To get the munchies" was a phrase that was first heard in the 1960s, largely among marijuana smokers, whose appetites supposedly increased under the influence of the drug, a meaning first noted in print circa 1971, although the word itself has been around since at least 1917.

Muscadine (*Vitis rotundifolia*). A native American grapevine that proliferates in the Southeast (circa 1785). There are several species, including the SCUPPERNONG, sometimes called the "Bullace grape." The word is a variant of "Muscatel" or "Muscat grape," from Latin *muscus*, "musk."

Muscadine grapes were the first to be vinified in America, and as early as the 1560s the French Huguenots who settled in Florida were making wine from them. The grapes grow in bunches and are usually not picked but knocked to the ground with sticks.

Although Muscadine grapes and wines have always been made in the South and elsewhere, their greatest propagation in the nineteenth century was in North Carolina, where Colonel Paul Garrett built a very successful wine business selling Virginia Dare Scuppernong wine. During Prohibition the propagation of Muscadine fell, and only after 1965, with the help of the North Carolina state legislature and State

University at Raleigh, has the grape again been grown significantly. Many new varieties have been developed, including the "Mish," the "Hunt," the "Creek," the "Higgins," the "Tarheel," and others, most now marketed as wine under the general name of "Scuppernong."

mush. A porridge or cereal grain ground into a mushy consistency (1883).

mushroom. Any of a large variety of fungi of the class *Basidiomycetes*. The word is from the Gallo-Roman *mussiro*, which became *musseroun* in Middle English.

When the first European settlers arrived in America, they found the woods filled with wild mushrooms of thousands of varieties, but the fear of eating poisonous mushrooms has prevented Americans ever since from developing any interest in them whatsoever, relying only on the cultivated white or brown *Agaricus bisporus* for almost the entire crop offered at market. This variety was first cultivated in France at the beginning of the eighteenth century, probably by Louis XIV's agronomist, Olivier de Serres, near Paris. For this reason the mushroom was called *champignon de Paris*, or, outside France, the "Parisian mushroom." The English got hold of this fungus by the end of the nineteenth century and exported it to the United States, where some mushroom cultivation was undertaken after the Civil War. Before the 1940s the most available mushroom in the market was the "Italian brown" (*A. brunnescens*), also known as the "Crimini." The "Portobello" is merely a large Crimini, but because of its rich, meaty texture and woodsy taste, it has taken on enormous popularity in the 1990s, with 32.7 million pounds shipped to market in 1997. Then, in 1926, Lewis Downing of Downington, Pennsylvania, discovered pure white spores growing among his mushrooms. He propagated these new types and spawned an industry that has made Pennsylvania the leading producer of mushrooms in the country, especially in Butler and Armstrong counties. California is the second largest producer.

These were the only cultivated mushrooms in the United States until very recently, and considerable success has been achieved in the growing of the "shiitake" or "Black Forest" mushroom (*Lentinus edodesi*); "enoke" or "enoki" (*Flammulina velutipes*), originally imported from Japan); "oyster" (*Pleurotus ostraetus*); and "woodear" (*Auricularia polyticha*), also called "tree-ear," "cloud-ear," and "black tree fungus." There has even been some reported success with experiments in growing TRUFFLES in California, Texas, and Oregon, though American wild truffles do exist. Also found wild in the United States are "morels" (*Morchella esculenta* and *M. elata*), also called "dog pecker," "dry-land fish," "honeycomb," "moocher," "pine cone" and first cultivated in 1990 by Morel Mountain, Inc., of Mason, Michigan; "cèpes" (*Boletus edulis*), sometimes called "King Boletus," "red caps," and other names; "chanterelles" (*Cantharellus cibarius*), also called "egg mushroom"; "gyromitra" (*Gyromitra esculenta*) or "false morels"; "chicken mushrooms" (*Laetiporus sulphureus*), also called "chicken of the woods" or "hen of the woods" (though this name is also applied to *Grifola frondosa*); "man-on-a-horse" (*Trichloma flavovirens*), possibly so-called because of the elegant appearance of the mushrooms (1980); and "milk cap" (*Lactarius deliciosus*). The per capita U.S. consumption of commercially produced mushrooms in 1997 was 2 pounds. There is now an enormous amount of wild mushrooms being exported by the United States to Europe.

Americans eat mushrooms in salads, in sauces, and stuffed with a forcemeat of various ingredients and seasonings.

Music Hall Influence. A series of lavish restaurant/nightclubs begun the day after Prohibition took effect (January 16, 1920) by entrepreneur Billy Rose, whose Casino de Paris featured two orchestras, dancing, and a naked girl swimming in a fishbowl. The term was invented by press agent Bob Reud.

mussel. Any of a variety of both salt- and freshwater bivalve mollusks having a blue-black shell. The name derives from the Latin *musculus*, meaning "little mouse," and in Middle English the spelling is muscle.

Mussels have not been a major American food item except in communities with Mediterranean heritage. The most common mussel used in cooking is the "blue" or "edible mussel" (*Mytilus edulis*), which ranges from the Arctic Ocean to South Carolina and has been successfully introduced on the Pacific coast, where it joined the indigenous "California mussel" (*M. californianus*). U.S. commercial landings of mussels totaled 4.5 million pounds in 1997.

Mussels are usually eaten steamed or cooked in a stew. They are the main ingredient of the soup BILLI-BI.

mustard. A condiment in either paste or powdered form made from the seeds of any of a variety of plants in the genus *Brassica*, especially the "black mustard" (*B. Nigra*), the "white mustard" (*Sinapis alba*), and "brown mustard" (*B. juncea*), also called "Indian mustard."

The word in Middle English was *mustarde*, derived from the Latin *mustum*, meaning the "must" of new wine, which was usually blended with early forms of mustard paste.

"English mustards" have long been popular in America, the first of note having been blended with various spices by a Mrs. Clements of Durham, England, in 1729, and another prepared in the nineteenth century by Jeremiah Colman of Norwich, England. In 1904 George T. French of Rochester's R. T. French Company introduced a mild mustard called "French's Cream Salad Mustard," which became the world's best seller and became the standard for most American mustards, which fall into two categories: a brown paste having some pungency and a yellow paste flavored with sugar, vinegar, turmeric, and white wine.

"Yellow mustard" (also called "ballpark mustard" because of its prevalence in sports stadiums' food stands) is a fairly mild mustard that comes from the species *B. hirta* or *alba*, whose seeds were possibly brought to America by African slaves.

"Mustard greens" are the leaves of the mustard plants, and in America the brown mustard plant, sometimes called "leaf mustard," is used in cooking by southerners and in SOUL FOOD.

mystery meat. A schoolchild's term for cafeteria food that is unidentifiable because of poor preparation or cheap ingredients.

N

nab. Slang abbreviation for "no-alcohol beer," a BEER from which almost all the alcohol has been removed. The term has been in use since the 1980s, as has its corollary, "lab," meaning "low-alcohol beer." The beer trade itself lumps the two categories together as "nablabs."

nacho. A small TORTILLA chip topped with cheese and chile peppers or chili sauce. The word may be from the Spanish for "flat-nosed" or from the nickname for "Ignacio."

The origins of the nacho have been traced to Mexico in the 1940s, and may have been created by Ignacio "Nacho" Anaya, a chef at the Victory Club in Piedras Negras, Mexico, across the border from Eagle Pass, Texas. Having run low on certain food items one day, Anaya threw together the snack so that a group of Texas women having lunch at the club could have something to nibble on, calling the item "Nacho's Especial." This story seems confirmed by an advertisement for the Victory Club calling itself the birthplace of "Nacho Specials" that appeared in the *St. Anne's Cookbook,* published in 1954 by the Church of the Redeemer in Eagle Pass.

Another claim was made by Connie Alvarez King, who said she created the item in 1943 at her restaurant in Harlingen, Texas, naming the snack after her best worker, Ignacio, whose nickname was "Nacho."

The popularity of "ballpark nachos"—covered with chile peppers and a melted, liquid cheese and served at sports stadiums—has been credited to Sal Manriquez, who began serving such an item under the name "Margarita's State Fair Nachos," because that is what he called them when he first started serving them in 1964 at the State Fair of Dallas. Manriquez claims that he and his wife, Margarita, took broken, leftover pieces of tortillas, added beans and hot sauce, and began selling them, later substituting jalapeños and cheese. In 1975 Manriquez requested a permit to sell his nachos at Arlington Stadium but was turned down, and found that the stadium began selling its own nachos with cheese, which became known as "ballpark nachos."

'nana 'n' cookie pudding. According to Eric V. Copage in *Kwanzaa* (1991), this is an African-American dessert made from bananas, vanilla wafer cookies, and either meringue or whipped cream.

'NANA 'N' COOKIE PUDDING

In a double boiler combine 1⅓ c. sugar, ¼ c. flour, and 3 egg yolks. Blend with a whisk, then whisk in gradually 3 c. of hot milk. Continue to cook, stirring until the liquid thickens to a thin custard (180° on a kitchen thermometer). Remove from heat and stir in 1 t. vanilla. Spread one layer of a buttered 7" x 11" baking dish with about one third of a 12-oz. box of vanilla-wafer cookies. Pour half the custard over the wafers, then arrange 6 peeled bananas cut into rounds over the mixture. Top with the remaining wafers, top with more custard and bananas, and put on another layer of wafers. Top with meringue if desired, place on a baking sheet, and bake in a 350° oven for 5–10 mins. Cool and refrigerate before serving.

Naples biscuit. A light dessert or tea biscuit similar to a LADYFINGER. Its name comes from the Italian city of Naples, suggesting this was the sort of biscuit found there. Naples biscuits have been known in England since the seventeenth century and soon thereafter in America.

native beef. Moose or deer harvested out of season (1979), colloquially called "some of the governor's meat."

natural food. A term, which first appeared in 1917, that purports to describe unadulterated or unprocessed foods or foods that have been grown without the aid of pesticides or added enrichments. There is, however, no consensus as to just what a "natural food" is. The U.S. Department of Agriculture defines the term with reference to meat and poultry as meaning the product is minimally processed and contains no artificial colors or preservatives.

Because of the vagueness of the term, many manufacturers decide for themselves what they may or may not add. As a result, many "natural" foods may contain sugar, guar and carob gum, carrageenan, vitamin C, monosodium glutamate, artificial colors, and a long list of other substances.

To some people the term is synonymous with HEALTH FOOD.

Surveys have shown that Americans are willing to spend, on the average, 10 percent more money on foods they consider "natural."

navy bean. Also called "pea bean" or "beautiful bean." The navy bean is one of several varieties of KIDNEY BEAN (*Phaseolus vulgaris*). The name comes from the fact that it has been a standard food of the United States Navy since at least 1856, despite an old popular song that claims that "the Navy gets the gravy, but the Army gets the beans."

ned. A nineteenth-century slang term for pork. An 1833 account says the term was used in Tennessee for bacon, and by the 1840s, when the United States Cavalry entered the western Native American territories, soldiers were called "Neddies," because of the preponderance of pork in their diet.

needlefish. Also, "gar," "guardfish," "houndfish," "sea pike," "snipe" and other names. A fish of the family Belonidae, primarily in the genus *Strongylura* (1882). *S exilis* is a Pacific variety; *S. marina* lives in the Atlantic. The name comes from the fish's long body and long, sharp-toothed jaws. They are usually taken accidentally in nets designed to harvest other fish.

negative reservation. A restaurant term to describe a reservation taken for a table only when a regular customer calls to relinquish his usual reservation. The phrase has been in currency since the 1970s.

negimaki. A dish of thinly sliced beef wrapped around scallions and broiled with a soy-based sauce. The word is from the Japanese *negi* (onion) plus *maki* (wound around). The dish, which has become very popular in Japanese restaurants in the United States, was created at New York's Nippon Restaurant in 1963 by owner Nobuyoshi Kuaoka under the prompting of *New York Times* restaurant critic Craig Claiborne, who thought the restaurant should have more interesting beef dishes for the American customer. Kuaoka originally called the dish "negimayaki."

Negimaki is prepared by wrapping very thin slices of beef around several scallion stalks, cut like traditional Japanese *makisushi* (whose wrapper is made from *nori* seaweed). It is then broiled with a soy-based sauce and served with another, thicker soy-based sauce.

negro coffee. Also, "Mogdad coffee." The senna plant (either *Cassia occidentalis* or *C. Chamaecrista*) or a coffee-like beverage brewed from its roasted seeds (1889), so called because it was favored by Southern blacks.

negus. A sweet alcoholic beverage made from port and citrus flavors. It is said to have been named after Colonel Francis Negus (died 1732), and was so called in print by 1743. Legend has it that Negus averted a political free-for-all by diluting a dwindling bottle of wine that, in the words of the *Dictionary of National Biography,* was "passing rather more rapidly than good fellowship seemed to warrant over a political discussion" between Whigs and Tories.

NEGUS

Heat 1 qt. port and pour into warmed pitcher. Add 1 sliced lemon, 1½ oz. brandy, 1 T. sugar, a pinch of nutmeg, and 1 qt. boiling water.

---

nene (*Branta [Nesochen] sandvicensis*). A large Hawaiian goose eaten there in pre-Colonial times (1902).

New American cuisine. A phrase that developed in the early 1980s to describe foods made by American cooks with American ingredients but according to the principles of preparation, cooking, and presentation promulgated by the practitioners of France's NOUVELLE CUISINE, a trend of the late 1960s and 1970s by which lightness, expensive ingredients, untraditional marriages of foods, and less cooking time transformed classical French technique. In America many nouvelle-cuisine chefs opened establishments featuring similar methods in the 1970s and 1980s, while hard on their heels came young American cooks who adapted such techniques and philosophies to the American larder. Their development of menus based on regional American cooking and traditions led to the coinage of terms like "California Cuisine," "New New

England Cuisine," "New Southern Cooking," and "New Texas Cuisine."

The most influential of all these was California Cuisine, which itself was a development of two styles of cooking in the north and south of the state. In the north, especially around San Francisco and Berkeley, young chefs like Alice Waters of Chez Panisse searched out and supported local farmers and ingredients to create a kind of cooking based on the freshest, best ingredients from California's cornucopia and the Pacific Ocean. In the south, particularly in Los Angeles, this style of cooking became more eclectic, sometimes deliberately dazzling in presentation, other times extremely simple and low in calories. Grilling and smoking were the favored techniques, baby vegetables were hallmarks of the style, and salads were featured as main courses. Regional wines from the Napa and Sonoma valleys were also exhibited as being particularly suited to this kind of cuisine.

New Bedford pudding. A pudding made from cornmeal, flour, eggs, and molasses. The name commemorates the town of New Bedford, Massachusetts. The recipe below is from Elizabeth H. Putnam's *Mrs. Putnam's Receipt Book and Young Housekeeper's Assistant* (1850), published in Boston.

NEW BEDFORD PUDDING

Combine 4 T. flour, 4 T. cornmeal, 4 beaten eggs, 1 qt. boiling water, a pinch of salt, and 1 c. molasses. Bake for 3 hr. at a low temperature, about 300°.

New England boiled dinner. A very hearty dish of various meats and vegetables that was originally made with salt beef but that may also contain poultry. It was traditionally served at noontime, but begun early in the morning when the meat would be boiled with cabbage in a kettle over an open fire. Later the other vegetables would go in, and, notes Evan Jones in *American Food* (1974), "Some Yankees call for a sprinkling of cider vinegar, but the most common accents are homemade horseradish sauce or strong mustard."

Boiled meals have long been part of many countries' culinary heritage: In France such a meal is called *pot au feu,* in Italy *bollito misto,* and New England boiled dinners derive from English versions of the dish. The term "boiled dinner" was in print as of 1882, and "New England boiled dinner" as of 1896.

NEW ENGLAND BOILED DINNER

In a large kettle place a 4–5 lb. corned beef, 2 cloves garlic, ½ t. black peppercorns, and enough water to cover. Bring to boil, reduce to a simmer, and cook about 3 hr. Taste for desired degree of saltiness; if too strong, remove some of the simmering liquid and add fresh water. Add 1 chopped rutabaga, 10 red potatoes, 5 chopped carrots, and 1 chopped head of cabbage. Cook until vegetables are tender. Serves 8–10.

New England hardscrapple. A New England bread-pudding dish, dating in print to 1939. See SCRAPPLE.

New Jersey tea. Also, "redroot." A ceanothus tree, either *Ceanothus americanus,* also called "redhank," "spangles," and "wild pepper" or *C. herbaceus* (1785), whose leaves were brewed into an astringent beverage. It was a substitute for tea among Whigs during the Revolutionary War.

New York System. A term used in Rhode Island to describe an establishment that sells pork and veal HOT DOGS dressed with beef-based chili sauce, chopped onions, and celery salt. The New York System originated in 1927 when Gust Pappas opened a wiener stand on Smith Street, and today all the New York Systems are run by members of the Pappas family. According to Elaine Chaika of the University of Rhode Island:

> The wienies look as if they have been cut from a longer sausage at both ends. They are about four inches long, and are covered with a meat sauce. . . . At true New York systems the man at the grill—and it's always a man—wearing a white dirty apron, takes the order, then puts the required number of hot dog rolls (not "buns" here) on his arm, puts the wienies in the roll and then ladles on the sauce. . . . Those places that sell these things always have "New York System" in their names, such as "Olneyville New York System," "Mary's New York System," "Joe's New York System."

nic-nac. A form of simple shortbread cookie. The term is a variation of "nicknack" or "knickknack," meaning a simple trinket or toy. They were a favorite children's Christmas cookie in the nineteenth century.

nightcap. A drink, usually referring to one containing alcohol, taken just before bedtime or as the last drink of the night, dating in print to 1818.

nioi. A Hawaiian "chili water," made with chile peppers, water, and salt, that serves as a seasoning for various dishes.

nocake. Corn that is parched in ashes and ground into a meal that is afterwards mixed with water to make a paste (1634). The word is from the Narraganset *nokehick*.

noodle. Any of a variety of thin strips of paste made from flour, water, and sometimes egg. The word is from the German *Nudel,* and was first recorded in English in 1779. The word may refer to German or Pennsylvania-Dutch egg noodles or to Italian pasta as well as to Chinese and Japanese examples. *Spaghetti* (Italian for "little strings") did not enter the English language until the nineteenth century. American slang includes "apron string" for noodle.

EGG NOODLES

Combine 1 beaten egg, 2 T. milk, and ½ t. salt. Pour into a bowl of 1 c. flour in which a well has been made, mix to make a firm dough, and roll out very thin on floured board. Let rest for 30 min., then cut into strips about 1¼-in. wide.

---

nooning. A lunch break between New England church services. "Nooning sheds" were sheds, often where horses were held, where these meals were taken. The word "nooning" is, in fact, very old, dating back to Middle English in the fifteenth century.

nopall. Any of several cacti in the genus *Nopalea* that resemble the PRICKLY PEAR, although sometimes the prickly pear itself is called a "nopal," which entered print about 1720, from Nahuatl *nohpalli*. In Mexican communities, where they are called *nopales* or *nopalitos,* these cacti have become popular in the American Southwest in the past decade. The flavor is similar to a green pepper or okra, and they may be eaten raw or boiled or sautéed. They are often added to the fillings of tortillas or salads.

nosh. A Yiddish-American word meaning to munch on one's food. Used as a noun, the word refers to a snack of some kind. A "nosher" is a habitual snacker. The word is from the German *naschen,* "to nibble," and first appeared as a verb in English in 1956. A British reference to a "Nosh restaurant" appeared in 1917.

nougat. A confection made from sugar or honey with ground almonds (sometimes walnuts or pistachios). Nougat takes either of two forms: the first is white nougat, prepared from boiled sugar, egg whites, nuts, and sometimes dried cherries; the other is a caramel-based almond nougat molded into shapes. Either may be used in making candies.

The name originates in the Latin *nux,* for "nut." There is no truth to the old tale that a woman of the French town of Montélimar (known for its white nougat) created the confection in the eighteenth century to the approval of her friends, who complimented her with the words, *"Tu nous gâtes"* ("You spoil us"). The confection probably goes back to the Middle Ages, when it may have been introduced to Europe by the Arabs via Spain. The word does not appear in print in English until 1827, in a recipe book on Italian cookery.

In the United States nougat is principally used as a filling for commercially produced candies.

nouvelle cuisine, la. French for "new cooking." A style of cooking that developed in France in the 1960s and 1970s by which young chefs like Paul Bocuse, Roger Vergé, Jean and Pierre Troisgros, and Michel Guérard broke from the entrenched traditions of classic French cuisine in order to develop their own methods, techniques, and new dishes. The new style was formally christened "la nouvelle cuisine" by French food writers Henri Gault and Christian Millau in the October 1973 issue of their *Gault-Millau* magazine, wherein they pronounced what they called the ten commandments of this modern cookery to be:

1. Avoid unnecessary complications.

2. Shorten cooking times.

3. Shop regularly at the market.

4. Shorten the menu.

5. Don't hang or marinate game.

6. Avoid too rich sauces.

7. Return to regional cooking.

8. Investigate the latest techniques.

9. Consider diet and health.

10. Invent constantly.

Many believed that nouvelle cuisine was much lighter and less caloric than classical French cooking because of the attention given Guérard's diet menu, called "cuisine minceur," offered at his spa called les Près d'Eugénie at le Couvent des Herbes in Eugénie-les-Bains, France. In fact, much nouvelle cooking was based on white butter sauces (*beurre blanc*) and required extremely rich and expensive ingredients in its preparation, like foie gras, truffles, and smoked salmon.

The first nouvelle-cuisine restaurants in the United States were opened by young American chefs and entrepreneurs like Robert and Karen Pritsker of Dodin-Bouffant in Boston, Steven Spector and Peter Josten of Le Plaisir in New York, Jean Bertranou of L'Ermitage in Los Angeles, and Jean Banchet of Le Français in Wheeling, Illinois, all of which opened in the 1970s. The interest in such food and restaurants had a great effect on the development of what came to be called the NEW AMERICAN COOKING, by which young American chefs applied nouvelle principles to regional American menus.

As the nouvelle-cuisine movement evolved, exaggerated culinary effects, extravagant plate presentation, and exotic matches of ingredients became hallmarks of the style, so that by the mid-1980s to call something "nouvelle" connoted a dish that was overly stylized, preciously presented, and very expensive. As a result, many chefs avoided the term, preferring instead other terms like "cuisine moderne."

Nuevo Latino. "New Latin" (from the Spanish), referring to modern Latin-American cooking, a movement by young Latino chefs to incorporate traditional Central and South American ingredients and cooking techniques into a contemporary style and context. The term gained currency in the 1990s. See also, FUSION.

nutrition labeling. A listing of substances in a food product that is printed on the label. (Such a list is mandatory by Federal Trade Commission rules only on products for which specific nutritional claims are made, such as those said to be low in calories.)

The listing must include: serving size and servings per can; the amount of calories protein, carbohydrates, and fat per serving; and the percentage per serving of the Recommended Daily Allowances (RDAs) for protein, vitamins A and C, thiamine, riboflavin, niacin, and the minerals calcium and iron; although other nutrients may be listed, too, along with the cholesterol level per serving.

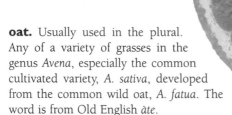

oat. Usually used in the plural. Any of a variety of grasses in the genus *Avena*, especially the common cultivated variety, *A. sativa*, developed from the common wild oat, *A. fatua*. The word is from Old English *àte*.

While 93 percent of the U.S. oat crop is used to feed animals, about 42 million bushels—out of a total U.S. crop of 176 million bushels in 1997—was made into breakfast cereals, especially the porridge called "oatmeal," made from rolled oats—that is, oats with the husks ground off which are then steamed and rolled flat to maintain their freshness longer. The largest and best-known oatmeal producer is the Quaker Oats Company, which was officially formed in 1901 but which had made the first trademarked American cereal—Quaker Oats—in 1877. The company also introduced a quick-cooking oatmeal in 1921.

The United States is the world's leading producer of oats, grown primarily in Iowa, Minnesota, Illinois, Wisconsin, and South Dakota.

octopus. Any of a variety of marine mollusks of the genus *Octopus*, having a sacklike head and eight tentacles with rows of suckers. The name is from the Greek *oktopous*, meaning "eight legs."

Except in Hawaii, where they are called *puloa* and *he'e*, octopuses are not consumed by Americans to any great extent, although Italian and Portuguese immigrants enjoy them, usually in a stew or salad. The "Atlantic octopus" (*Octopus vulgaris*) and the "common Pacific octopus" (*O. dolfleini*) are the two North American species. They are sometimes called "devilfish" because of their strange appearance.

O.D. gravy. A rural slang term of the South and Midwest that refers to brown gravy as "ox dung gravy" or "olive drab" gravy.

Ogeechee lime. Also, "Ogeechee tupelo" and "gopher plum." A Southern tupelo (*Nyssa ogeche*) used to prepare a summer beverage or preserves (1775). The name derives from the Ogeechee River in Georgia.

ohelo. Also, "Hawaiian huckleberry." A Hawaiian plant of the genus *Vaccinium*, especially *V. reticulatum* (1825), which are added to foods to give them a sour flavor. The word is from the Hawaiian for "berry."

ohelo-kai. A native Hawaiian red wolfberry (*Lyceum sandwicense*) with a salty pulp (1911). The Hawaiian word means "berry near the sea."

ohia. Also, "Malay apple." A native Hawaiian apple (*Eugenia malaccensis*) with a peach-like stone (1824). The Hawaiian word means "edible (fruit)."

Ohio pudding. A pudding of sweet potatoes, carrots, and brown sugar, popular in Ohio.

OHIO PUDDING

Combine 4 eggs with ¼ c. brown sugar, ½ c. cooked mashed sweet potatoes, ½ c. carrots, ½ c. squash, 1 t. salt, ¼ t. pepper, 1 c. bread crumbs, 1 qt. light cream, and 1 t. vanilla extract. Pour into buttered pan and bake 1¼ hr. at 350°. Serve with a sauce made from ¼ lb. butter beaten with 1½ c. confectioners' sugar, ½ c. heavy cream, and 1 T. lemon juice. Serves 6.

okolehao. Also, "oke." An 80-proof Hawaiian cordial made from cooked ti roots (*Cordyline australis*). The Hawaiian word means "iron buttocks," referring to an iron pot still and dates in print to 1924. Originally the liqueur was made by an Australian, William Stevenson, about 1790, but today it is produced commercially in column stills. Okolehao is not aged. It may be drunk straight, on the rocks, or in various Hawaiian-inspired cocktails.

okra (*Hibiscus esculentus*). Also, "lady's finger." A tropical or semitropical tree bearing finger-shaped green pods. The word, derived from the West African *nkruma*, was in use in America by the 1780s. Okra was brought to America by African slaves, who used it in stews or soups and cut it up as a vegetable. The most famous use for okra is in Louisiana GUMBO. Okra is particularly popular among African Americans in SOUL FOOD.

old-fashioned cocktail. A COCKTAIL made with WHISKEY, sugar, and BITTERS. According to an unsigned article in the *International Review of Food and Wine* (November 1978), the birth date of the old-fashioned cocktail

> could be no earlier than 1881 the year in which Louisville's aristocratic Pendennis Club first opened its doors to its members, one of whom was the then-reigning patriarch of fine Kentucky Bourbon, Colonel James E. Pepper. The Colonel's grandfather, Elijah, bad claimed twin birthdays for his distillery and the nation, and for generations his "Old 1776" brand of Bourbon would continue to be flogged under the proud slogan, "Born with the Republic." One might therefore surmise that the Old-Fashioned, created at the bar of the Pendennis and introduced in the East at the original Waldorf bar to honor Colonel Pepper some time in the 1890s, got its inspiration in part from Elijah's label. The term was first printed in 1901.

Most aficionados of the old-fashioned insist a sugar cube be placed at the bottom of the glass (which is squat and holds about six ounces), but others prefer to use sugar syrup.

OLD-FASHIONED COCKTAIL

In an old-fashioned glass place 1 sugar cube in 2 T. water, add a dash of bitters and 1½ oz. of whiskey (usually bourbon or rye). Add ice cubes and a slice of orange. Many prefer the drink topped off with club soda and a maraschino cherry, although some like the addition of a small amount of an orange cordial.

old maid. Southern and Midwestern colloquialism for a kernel of popcorn that failed to pop (1947).

Old Ned. Salt pork or home-cured bacon, especially in the South (1833). An article in the *Overland Monthly* in 1896 notes the name may be "an allusion to the famous Negro song, [and] was termed 'Old Ned' from its sable appearance."

olestra. A synthetic food oil that is not absorbed into the human body (1995). Used for weight control, the word derives from the Latin, *oleum* (oil) + polyester.

olive (*Olea europaea*). An Old World evergreen tree bearing a small fruit that is eaten on its own or pressed to make OLIVE OIL. The word is from the Latin *olīva*, first appearing in English about 1200. (The "American olive" or "devil wood" [*Olea americana*] and the "California olive" [*Oreodaphne californica*] are of no real culinary interest.)

The olive has long been cultivated throughout the Mediterranean, where it is a major food of the people's diet. It was first mentioned in records of seventeenth century B.C. Egypt. The Spaniards introduced three olive saplings to Lima, Peru, in 1560 that became the ancestors of all olives in America and introduced them to California's Mission San Diego de Alcalá circa 1769.

The English planted olives in 1670 in South Carolina, so that by the eighteenth century, Charleston's streets were lined with olive trees. In 1733 James Oglethorpe brought olive plantings to Georgia. Neither was ultimately successful. Thomas Jefferson planted olives in 1774 at Monticello, calling the vine "the worthiest plant to be introduced to America," but these efforts and subsequent plantings in South Carolina in 1791 came to naught, for the plants all died.

Nevertheless, olive trees flourished in California, where technology has bred a tree that matures in fifteen to twenty years rather than the usual thirty required in the Old World. By 1919 more than a million trees bore fruit, mainly used for olive oil. But because the product was cheaper to produce in Europe and had been so adulterated with cottonseed oil from the American South, the olive-oil industry languished in California.

In 1895 Mrs. Freda Ehmann of Marysville, California, produced a bumper crop of olives that she pickled (with the help of Dr. E. W. Hilgard of the University of California) and sold in groceries and restaurants to great success, earning her the title of "mother of the olive industry." Around the same time Professor Frederic T. Bioletti of the University of California invented a method of canning olives (called "green ripe") with an alkaline solution and brine so that they were available year-round.

Although Italy and Spain are the largest producers of olives in the world, California does produce a substantial crop (163,000 tons in 1993), mainly in the San Fernando and San Joaquin valleys. There, in contrast to European methods of leaving green olives to ripen to black on the vine, olives are picked in the fall at varying shades of green, given a lye cure, and, if marketed black (called "ripe"), are oxidized in a ferrous gluconate solution. California green olives thus treated with lye are called "Spanish-style olives." The predominant olives used in California are the large "Sevillano," the "Manzanilla," the "Mission" (used mostly for olive oil), the "Barondis," and the "Ascolanos." Olives are often sold stuffed with pimiento slices or already pitted.

Olives are sized, with some hyperbole, as "small" (3.2 to 3.3 grams), "medium," "large," "extra large," "jumbo," "colossal," and "supercolossal" (14.2 to 16.2 grams).

In 1998, 64.2 thousand tons of olives were canned, and 4.1 thousand tons were crushed for oil.

olive oil. An oil that is pressed from olives. It is a ubiquitous cooking ingredient around the Mediterranean, and much of it is imported by the United States from Italy, Spain, and other countries (in 1992 about 210 million pounds). Olive oil is monounsaturated and has a distinctive taste of the olive. In Europe the grades of quality range from "extra virgin" (the finest, with 1 percent acid) to "Fine" (1.5 percent), while others have more than 3.3 percent acid. "Pure olive oil" is extracted by solvent and refined, while "blended oils" may contain only 10 percent olive oil. None of this nomenclature is recognized by the FDA Standards of Identity.

In the late nineteenth century California had a thriving olive oil industry, but after World War II cheaper European olive oils nearly destroyed domestic production. Currently the U.S. produces about 325,000 gallons of olive oil out of a total world production of 460 million gallons.

onion. Any of a variety of pungent vegetables in the genus *Allium*, having a white, yellow, or red bulbous head. The word is from dialectial Latin *uniō*, which in Middle English became *unyon*.

Grown and eaten around the world, onions are a universal seasoning. Under the term "onion" fall GARLIC, LEEK, SCALLION, and SHALLOT, with about seventy species of onion native to North America. Hernando Cortés found onions in Mexico in the sixteenth century. Father Jacques Marquette, who explored the southern shore of Lake Michigan in 1624, survived for a time by eating a wild onion the Native Americans called "chicago," better known as the "tree onion" or "Egyptian onion" (*A. canadense*). Although the Native Americans and the pioneers certainly savored a wide variety of native onions, commercial production in the United States has largely been limited to one variety, the "common" or "seed" onion (*A. cepa*), brought from Europe in

Colonial times and now principally grown in California, Texas, and Oregon. Some of the other onion varieties in the American market include the "pearl" or "button onion," the "Red Italian" onion, the "Prizetaker" onion, the "Spanish onion," and the "Bermuda onion," though these last two names are often applied to a number of varieties. The "Vidalia onion" is a yellow hyrbrid Granex variety that has achieved popularity because of its sweetness, and the name "Vidalia" is protected under Georgia law, which specifies that, to be called by that name, the onion must be grown in any part of thirteen specified counties or in portions of six other specified counties in southeast Georgia.

Americans chop up onions for soups, stews, and sauces, boil them, roast them, sauté them, and use them in salads and as condiments. French-fried onion rings are very popular with meat dishes. "Tobacco onions" are deep-fried thin onion slices seasoned with chile power and so called because they resemble dried tobacco shreds. The per capita U.S. consumption of onions in 1997 was 16.8 pounds.

onion fish. Also, "rat fish." A grenadier fish, especially *Macrourus berglax* and *M. rupestris*, abundant along the Atlantic coast (1884), so called because its eyes resemble onions.

ono. A Hawaiian wahoo fish (*Acanthocybium solandri*), with a long, dark blue, purple-striped body (1926). Its Hawaiian name means "to have a sweet taste," and it is often used for sashimi.

on scholarship. Bartender slang for a bartender who spends too much time talking with the customers, thereby forcing his colleague to do most of the work. The term first saw print in 1991.

on the rocks. A term to describe a beverage being served with ice cubes. The phrase has become common usage in this century. Eric Partridge traces it in print to circa 1945.

oopu. Hawaiian freshwater fish (*Chonophorus genivittatus*), from the Hawaiian word *'o'opu* (1960).

opah. Also, "glance fish," "kingfish," "Jerusalem haddock," "moonfish" and "mariposa." A deepwater fish (*Lampris gutattus* and *L. regius*), first noted in print in 1750, whose name is native to Guinea.

opaka-paka. Hawaiian name for a saltwater [pink

SNAPPER] of the family Lutjanidae, especially *Pristipomoides microlepis* (1926).

opaleye. Also, "greenfish" and "bluefish" (though it is not the BLUEFISH species *Pomatus saltatrix*). A foot-long marine fish (*Girella nigricans*) that swims off the coast of California (1933).

opelu. A Hawaiian mackerel scad (*Decapterus pinnulatus* and *D. maruadsi*), which dates in print to 1926.

open dating. A system of dating products that outlines the various dates at which an item was packaged and should be discarded and past which it is no longer fit for consumption. The "pack date" tells when the food item was packaged; the "pull" or "sell date" indicates the last date on which the product should be sold, although some storage time in the home refrigerator is allowed for; the "expiration date" indicates the last date on which the food should be eaten or used; the "freshness date" is similar to the expiration date, but may allow for home storage. The "shelf life" of a product is the manufacturer's or grocer's indication of how long a product will last.

opihi. A Hawaiian limpet of the family Patellidae, especially of the genus *Cellana* (1915).

opossum. Also, "'possum." A nocturnal marsupial of the family Didelphidiae that is fifteen to twenty inches long, weighs six to eight pounds, has gray fur, and inhabits the woodlands of much of the United States. The only species in North America is the "Virginia opossum" (*Didelphus virginiana*), found mostly in the Southeast, California, the Northwest, and west of the Cascade-Sierra Mountains (where it was introduced in the 1920s). Its name is from the Algonquian for "white animal" and was used as early as 1610 by settlers. The opossum is no longer widely used as a food animal, though it is still occasionally eaten in the South either stewed or roasted.

orange. Any of a variety of trees in the genus *Citrus* bearing round, yellow-red fruit that is eaten fresh, made into juice, and used as a flavoring. The name is from the Sanskrit *nāranga*.

The orange is one of the most important fruits of the world and one of the oldest cultivated. Originating in the Orient, the fruit was cultivated in China as early as 2400 B.C. These were "bitter oranges" (*C. aurantium*), later brought to Spain, where they became known as the "Seville orange." The "sweet orange" (*C.*

sinensis) also originated in China and was also brought to Spain, possibly by the Moors in the eighth century.

Christopher Columbus brought Canary Islands orange seeds to Hispaniola in 1493, and plantings by the Spanish and Portuguese soon followed throughout the Caribbean, Mexico, and South America. Some believe that Ponce de Léon brought orange seeds to Florida, but the first recorded evidence of the fruit on North American soil credits Hernando de Soto with bringing the orange in 1539 to St. Augustine, Florida, where the trees flourished until Sir Francis Drake sacked the city in 1586 and destroyed them. These grew back quickly, but commercial plantings were of only minor importance for more than two centuries. In the West, meanwhile, Spanish missionaries brought oranges from Mexico into California and Arizona, but there, too, they were not developed into a commercial crop.

In Florida only one significant orange grower was to be found in the eighteenth century. His name was Jesse Fish, and in 1776 he shipped sixty-five thousand oranges and two casks of orange juice to England.

It was not until the United States acquired Florida in 1821 that orange growing became a profitable business for Americans. Before long the territory around St. Augustine and Jacksonville's Saint Johns River supported a thriving crop of orange trees, and by the 1830s the major eastern cities enjoyed relatively dependable shipments of the fruit, although much of the supply came from the Caribbean, especially from Cuba, until the 1880s. It became the custom in the period before the Civil War to give children a fresh orange in their Christmas stockings, and it remains a tradition to this day in some regions of the South.

The Florida groves increased in size until 1835, when a February freeze struck the orchards, wiping out all but one hardy variety—the "Indian River"— raised by Douglas Dummett, from whose orchard the entire Florida stock was begun again (and still again, in the winter of 1894–1895, when the Dummet grove was the sole survivor of another frost). The "Parson Brown" orange, developed by Reverend Nathan L. Brown of Webster, Florida, became extremely popular as an early-season variety.

By the 1880s orange production was growing rapidly, owing to the development of refrigerated ships that could carry the fruit from California and to the building of railroads into the heart of Florida. Also, a new orange, the "navel" (so called because of the bump on the skin of fruit, which prompted people to call it the "belly-button orange"), entered California in 1873 from Bahia, Brazil, by way of

Washington, D.C. (and is in fact called the "Washington Navel"). By the 1890s, the navel orange had become commercially important to the developing California orange industry—at a time when Florida was already shipping more than a billion oranges per year. By the 1920s nutritionists were promoting the benefits of orange juice, a juice especially high in vitamin C, and the drink became as ubiquitous as coffee on American breakfast tables, to such an extent that the industry's motto—"A day without orange juice is like a day without sunshine"—carried both figurative and literal truth. A concentrate of orange juice was formulated by John Fox of the National Research Corporation of Florida in 1946, under the "Minute Maid" label. After World War II orange juice became so popular that the sale of fresh oranges dropped 75 percent. Today most oranges grown are processed into juice, which more often than not reaches the consumer as a frozen concentrate that is sometimes reconstituted and sold in bottles or cartons. In 1993 orange juice made up 56 percent of all juices sold in the United States.

The "blood orange" (also called the "pigmented orange") was brought to the United States by Spanish and Italian immigrants and flourished in the 1930s, but did not become a productive commercial crop. Today the "Ruby Blood" and "Moro" varieties are raised in California and Florida.

Today the United States produces about 15.5 percent of the world's orange crop, with Florida contributing about three-quarters of American production (10.1 million tons in 1998, which was a severe reduction from the normal crop), with California, Arizona, Texas, and other states the rest. Ninety-three percent of the Florida crop goes into orange-juice concentrate. Before 1950 California produced most of the juice-orange crop, and Florida most of the eating oranges, but this has now been reversed.

Of all the oranges produced, the sweet orange is by far the most important; the bitter variety is used primarily in marmalade. The most common sweet oranges grown include the "Hamlin," the "Pineapple," the "Valencia," and the "navel," but hybrids such as the "King," "Temple," "Orlando," "Mineola," "Robinson," "Osceoloa," "Lee," "Nova," and "Page" are also well established.

The "mandarin orange" (*C. reticulata*), with its principal United States varieties such as the "Dancy," the "Clementine," the "Murcott," and the "Ponkan," is also called the "tangerine" (because it was first imported to Europe from Tangier, the earliest recorded shipment being in 1841). The "tangelo" (also called the "red tangelo" or "honeybell")—developed by the Department of Agriculture in Mineola, Florida, in 1931—is a cross between a "Dancy tangerine," a "Bowen" grapefruit, and an "Orchid Island" grapefruit.

The United States Department of Agriculture grades oranges "U.S. Fancy" and "U.S. No. 1," though these are not mandatory gradings and do not appear on most oranges.

The most popular culinary uses for oranges in the United States are in fruit salads, sherbets and ices, soda, and as a flavoring for many desserts, cakes, cookies, and candies. There are also several orange-flavored substitutes for the real thing, some in powdered form.

orange blossom. A drink made with orange juice and gin. The orange blossom was created during the Prohibition era to cut the taste of the gin and was sometimes called the "Adirondack Special" or "Florida," the first probably because illicit spirits could be had in the Adirondack Mountains and the latter because of Florida's great orange crop.

ORANGE BLOSSOM

 Combine 8 oz. gin, 4 oz. orange juice, and ½ oz. sugar syrup over ice.

Orange Julius. Trademark name for a drink made with orange juice, crushed ice, syrup, and a powder. The beverage was developed by real estate broker Willard Hamlin at the request of Julius Fried, who wanted to set up an orange-juice stand in Los Angeles. Since the citric acid of orange juice upset his and others' stomachs, Hamlin modified the raw juice to create a drink named after the entrepreneur. At the time of his death in 1987, there were more than 700 Orange Julius stands around the world.

orange roughy. A species of fish in the family Trachichthydiae that is harvested mainly around New Zealand, frozen, and sold at market. It became an important frozen fish in United States markets as of the 1980s.

oregano (*Origanum vulgare*). Also, "pot marjoram" and "wild marjoram." A strongly flavored herb common in Europe and North America that is used in Italy and the United States as a seasoning in tomato sauces, stews, and other preparations. It is similar to "sweet marjoram" (*Majorana hortensis*), which is milder and sometimes used as a substitute.

The word "oregano" is from the Italian *origano*, and Spanish, orégano. As a seasoning it was not popular in the United States until after World War II, when returning soldiers brought back a taste for the spicy food of southern Italy requiring oregano for reproduction.

Oregon tea. A brew made from boiling water and the shrub yerba buena (1891).

oreilles de cochon, les. Cajun confection of fried dough that is dusted with confectioners' sugar or syrup and chopped nuts. The term is French for "pig's ears" (which the item is sometimes called), because the flattened-out dough resembles the shape of a pig's ears. In the Midwest these are called "elephant ears," and in, the Low Country, similar pastries are called "marvels."

LES OREILLES DE COCHON

In a bowl beat together 2 eggs, 2 T. water, 2 T. melted butter, and a pinch of salt. Work in about 2 c. flour to make a smooth, slightly firm dough. Separate into pieces about the size of a walnut and roll each out into thin, flat circles about 4 in. in diameter. Place the tines of a fork on one end to grip the dough and give it a quarter-turn so that it resembles the crimp in a pig's ear. Drop the dough into hot oil and fry until brown and crisp. Drain on paper towels. In a saucepan heat 2 c. corn syrup and pour over the twists. Sprinkle with chopped pecans and confectioners' sugar.

OREO. A trademark name of the Nabisco Biscuit Company for a cookie composed of two thin chocolate cookies enclosing a white creme filling. The name (originally "OREO Biscuit") was apparently made up by the company. It has been suggested that the name may derive from the French word for "gold," *or*, because the original package had the product name in gold. Another guess is that the word is from the Greek for "mountain," the shape of which early test batches of OREOs resembled. The first OREOs were sold to a grocer named S. C. Thuesen on March 6, 1912; in 1921 the name was changed to "OREO Sandwich," then "OREO Creme Sandwich" in 1948 and "OREO Chocolate Sandwich" in 1974. OREOs were not, however, the first cookie of this type: "Hydrox Cookies" had been on the market since January 1, 1910, but OREOs have been far more successful. Since their inception, OREOs have sold more than 345 billion cookies, more than 7.5 billion each year, with nine out of ten American households purchasing them.

organic. With regard to food, this refers to any food grown without using chemical fertilizer, pesticides, or other unnatural substances. In this context the term gained currency in the 1970s and was allied to the HEALTH FOOD movement in the United States. Currently the FDA allows the use of the term "organic" on a processed-food label only if 95 percent of all the ingredients (excluding the salt and water content) were produced according to federal organic standards. In 1999 the USDA allowed farmers who raise meat and poultry without pesticide-treated feed, growth hormones or antibiotics to label their products "certified organic."

orgeat. An orange-and-almond flavoring used in cocktails and food. The word is from the French, originally from Latin *hordeum*. In the eighteenth century, when it became known in England, the syrup was made with barley, but later it was sweetened and used as a PUNCH. Orgeat may be bought commercially.

ORGEAT

Crush together 1 stick cinnamon with ¼ lb. almonds. Add 3 c. milk, 1 c. cream, and 1 T. rosewater. Sweeten to taste, bring to a boil, strain, and serve in punch cups.

ortolan. Also, "sora" and "rail." A small native American bird (*Porzana carolina*), which first appears in print in 1836, but not the true ortolan of Europe (*Emberiza hortulana*). It is a game bird caught in the fall and is considered a great delicacy to be roasted and eaten whole. The name is sometimes also applied to the bobolink (*Dolichoniz oryzivorous*), used more in stews (1859).

ostkaka. A type of Norwegian-American cheese pudding (1940) or milk and rennet custard (1967–68). The word is from the Norwegian *ostekake*.

Oswego tea. A horsemint (*Monardia didyma* or *M. fistulosa*) made into tea (1752).

OTW. An abbreviation for "on the way," used by restaurant maîtres d'hôtel to note that a party is late but has indicated it is in transit to the restaurant.

Oxford John. A simmered mutton dish named after Englishman John Farley, who compiled the *London Art of Cookery* in the eighteenth century. It became a very popular dish in Virginia during those years.

oyster (genera *Ostrea* and *Crassostrea*). Any of several edible mollusks found in brackish waters, marshes, inland waters, even on the roots of submerged trees and coral reefs. The name derives from the Greek *óstreon*.

Oysters have long been considered a delicacy and have been cultivated for at least two thousand years. The American Indians of the coastal regions enjoyed them as a staple part of their diet, and the earliest European explorers marveled at oysters that were up to a foot in length. Cultivation began soon afterward, and Virginia and Maryland have waged "oyster wars" over offshore beds since 1632. Although the oyster may have been an expensive delicacy in Europe, it was a common item on everyone's table in America. By the eighteenth century the urban poor were sustained by little more than bread and oysters. Colonial citizens dined regularly on chicken and oysters, and the mollusk was an economical ingredient for stuffing fowl and other meats. By the middle of the next century English traveler Charles Mackay could write in his book *Life and Liberty in America* (1859) that "the rich consume oysters and Champagne; the poorer classes consume oysters and lager bier, and that is one of the principal social differences between the two sections of the community."

Americans were oyster mad in the nineteenth century, and as people moved and settled westward, the demand for the bivalves in the interior regions grew accordingly. This demand was met by shipping oysters by stagecoach on the "Oyster Line" from Baltimore to Ohio, followed after the opening of the Erie Canal in 1825 by canal boats laden with oysters. Canned or pickled varieties were available as far west as St. Louis, Missouri, by 1856.

An American who sat down to a dish of oysters was not satisfied by a mere half-dozen. A man who could not put away a dozen or more was not considered much of an eater, and soup recipes of the nineteenth century call for quarts of oysters. Eliza Leslie's *Directions for Cookery* (1837) required two hundred of the mollusks for a stew, and there are records of prodigious feats of oyster consumption—not the least of which was the capacity of James "Diamond Jim" Brady (1856–1917), a wealthy financier who thought nothing of downing three or four dozen a day, in addition to soup, fowl, game, vegetables, desserts, chocolates, and gallons of his favorite drink, orange juice. (Lest anyone think the days of the great oyster

trenchermen are over, consider that in 1972 Bobby Melancon ate 188 oysters in one hour at the Louisiana State Oyster Festival in Galliano, Louisiana.)

Every coastal city had its oyster vendors on the streets, and "oyster saloons," "cellars," or "houses" were part of urban life. In New York City, where $6 million worth of oysters were sold in 1850, one looked for red-and-white-striped muslin balloons lighted by candles and set above basement restaurants where oysters were shucked day and night in quarters that might be remarkably ornate or rather sleazy. The city's "Canal Street Plan," named after a street in lower Manhattan, was an invitation to consume all the oysters a customer desired for the fixed price of six cents. By 1877 New York's Fulton Fish Market was selling fifty thousand oysters per day.

"The real Oyster House," wrote Charles E. Rector of Chicago's Rector's Oyster House, which opened in 1884, "is a specialized restaurant, the specialties of which are, in general, seafood, game, salads, certain delicatessen, and the choicest of wines, brandies and ales. In greater detail, it is a place where, in their season, the finest and freshest oysters of a dozen different varieties are to be found; where lobsters, and every variety of edible sea-food, from the hard-shell crab or the delicate soft-shell to the fragile, almost transparent shrimp are daily served."

Such places were frequented not only by men on the town but also by families, who ate to the rear, away from the bar. A few more refined spots, like Downing's on Broad Street, catered to a high-class clientele with dishes like oyster pie, scalloped oysters, and poached turkey with oysters.

On the West Coast oysters, including the indigenous Olympia variety, were just as popular. The dish called the HANGTOWN FRY was created at the Cary House in 1849 from what were then the two most expensive items of those Gold Rush days—eggs and oysters. A San Francisco miner accidentally created the "oyster cocktail" about 1860 (and by extension the "shrimp cocktail") by dipping the bivalve in ketchup.

Most oysters in those days were simply roasted, grilled, made into a stew, or eaten raw, with side dishes of lemon juice, mustard, and other condiments. The "oyster cracker" did not come along until about 1873.

Throughout the middle of the century oysters remained plentiful. Even when other foodstuffs were scarce in the Civil War, Union soldiers in Savannah sated their hunger with buckets full of oysters brought to them by the slaves they had liberated. In 1869 more than eighteen thousand pounds of oysters were sold during the racing season by one Saratoga, New York, hotel.

Nowhere was the oyster more appreciated than in New Orleans, where several classic oyster recipes, like OYSTERS BIENVILLE and OYSTERS ROCKEFELLER, were created. The *Picayune's Creole Cook Book* (1900) lists nearly forty recipes for the mollusk, including the famous city specialty, oyster loaf, or *"la Médiatrice"* (French for "Peacemaker"), so called because a husband who had stayed out too late would bring one home to his patient wife as an offering of peace.

The demand for oysters was so high that by the 1880s the eastern beds began to be depleted. Chesapeake Bay then produced 15 billion bushels of oysters a year, but by the end of the century many cultivators had gone out of business for lack of product, and new sources in the South were tapped to placate the American appetite. Also, the increase in water pollution in cities became so bad as to cause real concern that typhus might be spread by shellfish that had been soaked in local water after delivery and before serving. "The great century of the oyster was over," wrote Richard J. Hooker in *Food and Drink in America* (1981). "The joyous and uninhibited eating of oysters by rich and poor, Easterner and Westerner, Northerner and Southerner, had ended."

Americans harvested 39.7 million pounds of oysters in 1997. While many species of oyster are now brought in to the American market, five species are of widespread gastronomic interest. The Virginia oyster (*Crassostrea virginica*)—also known as "Apalachicola" (Apalachicola Bay, Florida), "Alabama Gulf," "Black Bay" (from Louisiana), "Blue Point" (originally from Blue Point, Long Island, New York, but now a widespread Atlantic oyster), "Bristol" (South Bristol, Maine), "Cape Cod" (Cape Cod, Massachusetts), "Chincoteague" (Chincoteague Bay, Maryland), "Cotuit" (Cotuit Harbor, Cape Cod), "Emerald Point" (Emerald Point Bay, Mississippi), "Florida Gulf" (Horseshoe Beach and Wakulla Bay, Florida), "Indian River" (Cape Canaveral, Florida), "James River" (James River, Virginia), "Kent Island" (Kent Island, Maryland), "Louisiana Gulf," "Lynnhaven" (Lynnhaven River, Virginia), "Malpeque" (Prince Edward Island, Canada), "Nelson Bay" (Nelson Bay, Alabama), "Rhode Island Select," "Texas Gulf" (Galveston Bay and Corpus Christi, Texas), "Wellfleet" (Cape Cod), and many others—ranges from the Gulf of St. Lawrence to the West Indies, is two to six inches long, has a gray, coarse shell, and is widely cultivated.

The "coon" or "raccoon" oyster (*Lopha frons*) ranges from Florida to Brazil, has an oval, ridged shell, and attaches itself to coral in shallow waters and also to trees—a phenomenon Sir Walter Raleigh described to Queen Elizabeth's court to the courtiers' disbelief. (The name, which dates in print to 1869, comes from their main predator, the raccoon.)

The "California oyster" (*O. lurida*), native to the West Coast, is purplish black or brown in color, has various shapes, and ranges from Alaska to Baja California. This species is more commonly called the "Olympia oyster" (from the Olympia Peninsula in the state of Washington) and is greatly valued for its flavor. Once very abundant, the species declined during this century owing to pollution, but efforts to clean up Puget Sound have resulted in higher yields.

The "Japanese oyster" (*C. gigas*), also known as the "Pacific oyster," "Golden Mantle" and "Portuguese" (Vancouver, British Columbia), "giant oyster," "Hog Island Sweetwater," "Tomales Bay" and "Preston Point" (Tomales Bay, California), "Kumamoto," (Kumamoto, Japan) "Quilcene" (Quilcene Bay, Washington), "Rock Point" (Dabob Bay, Washington), "Skokomish" (Hood River, Washington), "Westcott Bay" (Westcott Bay and Tiger Bay, Washington), "Willapa Bay" (Willapa Bay, Washington), and "Yaquina Bay" (Yaquina Bay, Oregon), is larger than the California variety and long in the shell, gray with purplish streaks. It ranges from British Columbia to Morro Bay, California, and was introduced from Japan in 1902.

The "belon" (*O. edulis*), which derives its name from the famous oysters of France's Brittany region, grows in the Northwest and Maine. It is also known as a "European oyster" or "European flat." They were first cultivated in Maine in 1975 by the York Harbor Export Company, whose first crop was available in 1978.

OYSTER STEW

Shuck 1 pt. oysters, retaining liquid. In large kettle simmer oysters in liquid for 3 min. Add 1 c. heavy cream and 3 c. milk. Heat until bubbles form at edge, add 1 t. salt, 1 T. Worcestershire sauce, and cayenne pepper to taste. Remove from heat, add 2 T. butter, and garnish with chopped parsley. Serves 4.

---

oysters Bienville. A New Orleans dish of oysters with a béchamel sauce of green pepper, onion, cheese, and bread crumbs. Named after the founder of the city, Jean Baptiste Le Moyne, Sieur de Bienville (1680–1767), the dish was created in the 1930s or early 1940s by Roy Alciatore, owner of Antoine's restaurant there, and chef Pete Michel. The following recipe, taken from Roy F. Guste, Jr.'s *Antoine's Restaurant Since 1840 Cookbook* (1979), differs considerably from other New Orleans versions that contain cayenne pepper, bacon, shrimp, and other ingredients.

OYSTERS BIENVILLE

Melt 4 T. butter in a skillet. Sauté 1½ c. minced bell pepper, 1 c. minced scallions, and 2 cloves minced garlic until limp. Add ½ c. dry white wine and bring to boil. Then add ½ c. chopped pimiento, 2 c. béchamel sauce, ⅔ c. ground American cheese, ½ c. bread crumbs, and salt and pepper to taste. Simmer for about 20 min. until very thick. Place 6 raw oysters on the half shell on each of six pie pans filled with rock salt. Cover oysters with sauce, bake in 400° oven for 10 min., until they begin to brown on top. Serve as an appetizer.

---

oyster shooter. A raw oyster placed in a shot glass or jigger and gulped down. It is commonly doused with vodka or another clear spirit and perhaps some cocktail sauce before being consumed.

oysters Kirkpatrick. A dish of baked oysters, green pepper, and bacon. The creation of this dish is credited to chef Ernest Arbogast of the Palm Court (later the Garden Court) of San Francisco's Palace Hotel. Named after Colonel John C. Kirkpatrick, who managed the hotel from 1894 to 1914, the dish was already well known by the end of his tenure, when Clarence E. Edwards wrote in *Bohemian San Francisco* (1914) that the dish was merely a variation on the "oyster salt roast" served at Mannings' Restaurant on the corner of Pine and Webb streets. The following recipe is supposedly the original:

OYSTERS KIRKPATRICK

Combine 1 c. ketchup, 1 c. chili sauce, 1 t. Worcestershire sauce, ½ t. A.1. sauce, 1 t. chopped parsley, and half a small chopped green pepper. Cut bacon slices into thirds, and cook halfway. Shuck oysters, dip them into sauce, and place them in shells. Place oysters on a bed of rock salt, cover with bacon, and sprinkle on Parmesan cheese. Bake at 400° until bacon is crisp.

---

oysters Rockefeller. A dish of oysters cooked with watercress, scallions, celery, anise, and other seasonings. It is a specialty created in 1899 by Jules Alciatore of Antoine's Restaurant in New Orleans. Roy F. Guste, Jr., great-grandson of Alciatore, writes in *Antoine's Restaurant Since 1840 Cookbook* (1979):

[In 1899] there was a shortage of snails coming in from Europe to the United States and Jules was looking for a replacement [he wanted] to be local in order to avoid any difficulty in procuring the product. He chose oysters. Jules was a pioneer in the art of cooked oysters, as they were rarely cooked before this time. He created a sauce with available green vegetable products, producing such a richness that be named it after one of the wealthiest men in the United States, John D. Rockefeller. Rockefeller (1839–1937) was indeed one of the country's richest men, having built a fortune in the oil, steel, railroad, and banking industries.

The original recipe for oysters Rockefeller has never been revealed, but although many renditions include chopped SPINACH in the dish, Guste insisted that spinach was not an ingredient of the original recipe. There does appear a recipe, however, in a 1941 compilation by Ford Naylor called the *World Famous Chefs' Cook Book,* in which the author contends, "Every recipe in this book, with few exceptions, is a secret recipe which has been jealously guarded. In many cases, its ingredients, proportions and blending have been concealed from the world for generations. Now, with as little change as possible in the directions of the chefs who produced them, these cherished recipes have been adapted for the use of the modern homemaker." The recipe for "Oysters à la Rockefeller" is given above the name "Antoine's Restaurant, New Orleans," and, allowing Naylor room for hyperbole and ambiguity of detail, it is possible that the following may be close to the original recipe, although Guste has denied that it is:

OYSTERS ROCKEFELLER

Select Louisiana oysters, open them and leave them on the half shell. Place the shells containing the oysters on a bed of rock salt in a pie pan.... Use the tail end tips of special onions [scallions], some celery, chervil, tarragon leaves, crumbs of stale bread, Tabasco sauce, and the best butter obtainable. Pound all these into a mixture in a mortar, so that all of the fragrant flavorings are blended. Add a few drops of absinthe [substitute an anise cordial] and a little white wine. Then force the mixture through a sieve. Place one spoonful on each oyster as it rests on its own shell, and in its own juice on the crushed rock salt, the purpose of which is to keep the oyster piping hot. Then place the oysters in an oven with overhead heat and cook until brown. Serve immediately.

P

pack. A liquor made from molasses. It is most familiar in the region around New Orleans, though rarely seen now. The name comes from English major general Sir Edward Michael Pakenham (1778–1815), who was killed at the Battle of New Orleans in January 1815, during the War of 1812.

package-goods store. Also, "package store." A store selling liquor in packages, as opposed to a bar dispensing liquor by the glass. The term came into use after the repeal of Prohibition in 1933, at a time when words like "saloon" and "barroom" still made some state legislators skittish. In many states such stores may also carry groceries and other items.

Palace Court salad. A salad of lettuce, tomato, and artichoke with a dressing of mayonnaise and crabmeat. The salad was created at the Palace Hotel (now the Sheraton-Palace) in San Francisco, though just when it first appeared on the menu is unclear. It may have been after 1909, when the restaurant there was named the Palm Court, or after 1942, when the name was changed to the Garden Court. The recipe below is used at the hotel.

PALACE COURT SALAD

Prepare a bed of shredded lettuce a half-inch deep. On the center place a thick slice of tomato and a marinated artichoke bottom. Mix 1 oz. chopped celery with 5 oz. crabmeat, and fold in just enough mayonnaise to hold the mixture together. Season with salt, pepper, and lemon juice. Form the salad into a tower-shaped mound and place an artichoke bottom on top. Garnish with a crab claw or pimiento strip. Border the lettuce with chopped egg and garnish the plate with an asparagus spear, black olive, and lemon wedge.

---

palm heart. Also called "swamp cabbage." The edible shoot of the cabbage palm (*Sabal palmetto*) sometimes called the "palmetto," which flourishes swampy land in Brazil and Florida. According to Howard Hillman in *The Cook's Book* (1981), "Palm hearts are quite bland, but extravagant; they are sometimes made into 'millionaire's salad,' so called not only because of the price but also because the fledgling tree has to be chopped down to get at its heart." The palm heart is protected by Florida state law and is usually available only canned. The palm heart is usually boiled and eaten as a vegetable mixed in a salad.

pancake. A flat cake cooked on a greased griddle and browned on both sides. Pancakes have long been a staple of the American breakfast table, and their history is as old as that of the Native Americans who shaped a soft batter in their hands and called it, in the Narraganset, *nokehick* ("it is soft"), transmuted by early white settlers into "no cake." Cornmeal pancakes were called "Indian cakes" as early as 1607. The Dutch in America made similar cakes from buckwheat, *pannekoeken,* which by 1740 were called "buckwheat cakes." English settlers brought with them the feast of Pancake Tuesday, an old name for Shrove Tuesday, the day before the Lenten fast begins. (In New Orleans this holiday was Mardi Gras.) Eating such rich, buttered cakes on this day was the last gasp of gourmandism before forty days of self-denial.

By 1745 Americans were also referring to "hoe cakes," perhaps because they were cooked on a flat hoe blade, and there were "rice cakes," "batter cakes," and "slapjacks" by the end of the eighteenth century. One of the most beloved versions of this simple cake is the JOHNNYCAKE, specifically associated with Rhode Island but well known throughout New England.

Meanwhile the rest of the country has gone on naming and renaming flat, griddle-fried cakes in all manner of ways. Thomas Jefferson served them at Monticello, and Benjamin Franklin called the Rhode Island variety "better than a Yorkshire muffin." By the nineteenth century northerners were referring to "flapjacks" and "griddle cakes," which by the 1830s and 1840s were being made with white flour rather than cornmeal. American versions of French crêpes sought refinement through names like "Quire-of-Paper Pancakes," a thin Virginia variety made with a little white wine. Another Virginia example, made with the coloring of beet juices and slathered with fruit preserves, was called "Pink-Colored Pancakes."

The word "pancake" itself was not in general usage until the 1870s, but afterward became the predominant American term for these traditional favorites. In mining camps and logging camps, they were called either "flannel cakes" (perhaps because they had the texture of the flannel shirts the workers wore), "a string of flats," or "flatcars" (after the flat, open cars used by the railroads to ship lumber). Still another name used by lumberjacks was "sweatpads," possibly after the round, perspiration-absorbent pads women wore under their dresses. Southerners called cornmeal cakes "Crispus Attucks," after the African-American patriot killed in the Boston Massacre in 1770.

Whatever they were called, pancakes became an American passion, and, as one English traveler wrote, "It is hard for an American to rise from his winter breakfast without his buckwheat cakes." American novelist James Fenimore Cooper made buckwheat cakes for Parisians in the 1820s. Buckwheat cakes are also called "ployes" among Acadians.

In 1889 Chris L. Rutt and Charles G. Underwood of St. Joseph, Missouri, introduced the first ready-mixed commercial food product at the New Era Exposition in St. Joseph when they began marketing "Self-Rising Pancake Flour," later renamed "Aunt Jemima," after a minstrel-show song.

So popular are they that nationwide chains of restaurants have opened up that specialize in pancakes in any number of forms, including "Silver Dollar" pancakes (small enough to be served in portions of six to a dozen), pancakes mixed with fruit, especially blueberries, or nuts, and pancakes topped with preserves, whipped cream, and often eggs. The first such restaurant was the International. House of Pancakes (called "IHOP" for short), opened in North Hollywood, California, in 1958.

The classic accompaniment to a stack of three or four pancakes (a "short stack" would be two or three) is either crisply fried bacon or link sausage. MAPLE syrup is poured over the top, and one is also likely to find hash-brown potatoes nearby, and, in the South, a side order of GRITS. Sometimes a garnish of orange slice is set on the plate.

PANCAKES

Sift together 1½ c. flour, ½ t. salt, and 2½ t. baking powder. In another bowl mix 1 well-beaten egg with 1 c. milk and 3 T. butter, then pour into flour mixture, and stir

---

just to moisten. Batter will be lumpy. Spoon out batter onto a hot buttered griddle in 4-in. rounds. When bubbles begin to show through top, flip over and cook until both sides are golden. Serve with butter and syrup.

FLANNEL CAKES

Cream ½ c. sugar with 1 T. butter, add 2 c. milk with ½ cake of yeast dissolved into it. Add 1 beaten egg and enough flour (about 1½ c.) to make a stiff, pancakelike batter. Let stand overnight. Batter will thicken still more. Stir and cook on buttered griddle, or, preferably, bake in muffin tins at 400° until brown.

---

pan drippings. The browned bits of fat and meat left in a pan after roasting or frying. Pan drippings are usually mixed with flour or cornstarch, water, and seasonings to make a GRAVY.

papaya (*Carica papaya*). Also, "papaw" and "tree melon." A tropical American tree bearing a sweet yellow fruit. The word, which is from Carib, *abadai,* was first recorded in English circa 1598. The papaya is sometimes called "pawpaw," but it is not the true PAWPAW.

The papaya was first noted by Christopher Columbus as a staple fruit of the West Indian diet, and other travelers soon brought its seeds to the Far East, including the Philippines and Nepal. In the United States it has only been grown successfully in Florida, Texas, and, predominantly, in Hawaii (where papayas have been cultivated since 1919). The main market varieties are the "Kapoho Solo" and "Sunrise." Usually eaten fresh as a fruit, papaya may also be boiled and served as a form of vegetable. Papaya's enzyme, "papain," is widely used in granular form as a tenderizer for meats.

New York City has a particular affinity for hot dogs and a drink made from the papaya, a combination said to have been started by Greek immigrant Constantine Poulos in 1928 when, having tasted papaya juice in Cuba, he began serving it at his hotdog stand on Eighty-sixth Street and Third Avenue. The stand was later christened "Papaya King," and soon similarly named competitors appeared around Manhattan.

parfait. A frozen dessert made from cream, eggs, sugar, and flavorings, or, as is more usual today, an ice-cream sundae of several different ice creams garnished with various syrups or crushed fruits. The word comes from the French, meaning "perfect," and first saw English print in 1890.

Parker House roll. A puffy yeast roll with a creased center, created at the Parker House Hotel in Boston soon after its opening in 1855 by the kitchen's German baker, whose name was Ward. One story holds that Ward, in a fit of pique over a guest's belligerence, merely threw some unfinished rolls into the oven and came up with the little bun that made his employer, Harvey Parker, famous. Such light, puffy rolls, sometimes called "pocketbook rolls" because of their purselike appearance, were a novelty in their day and became a standard item in American dining rooms and tables. The following recipe is from the Parker House kitchen and makes four dozen rolls.

PARKER HOUSE ROLL

Mix 2½ lb. flour with ¼ lb. shortening, 2½ oz. milk powder, ¼ lb. sugar, and ½ oz. salt. Melt ½ oz. dry yeast in ¾ qt. warm water, then add slowly to flour mixture. Beat until smooth. Let the dough rest for 1½ hr., then knead it. Cut dough into 1-sq.-in. pieces, stretch each piece, and fold over. Arrange on a greased baking pan, let rise for 45 min., then bake in a 400° oven for 10 min. until golden brown. Brush with melted butter and serve.

---

parsley (*Petroselinum crispum*). A green herb with a grassy taste. It is usually sprinkled on dishes as a garnish, though its flavor enhances stocks and sauces. The word is from the Greek, *petrosélinon* "rock parsley," which in Middle English became *persely*.

Waverley Root in *Food* (1980) notes that Giovanni da Verrazano reported seeing parsley when he landed in what is now Massachusetts in 1524, adding, "vigilant writers since have insisted that this could not have been true, since parsley is an Old World plant. The rectifiers were perhaps wrong. There were Norsemen not far from Massachusetts, if not actually there, five hundred years before Verrazano, to say nothing of the Basque fishermen who came from parsley country to the Grand Banks off Newfoundland before Columbus . . . where perhaps they let drop a seed or two [that] could easily have migrated from Newfoundland to Massachusetts in a couple of centuries." Root goes on to say, however, that no written record of parsley's presence in America occurs before 1806. Today two main varieties, the "Italian" (*P. c. neapolitanum*) and "Hamburg" or "turnip-rooted parsley" (*P. c. tuberoseum*), are

grown in the United States. The latter is the most readily available nationwide; the former, grown in southern Louisiana, is essential to Creole and Cajun cookery.

parsnip (*Pastinaca sativa*). A plant having a white root that is boiled and eaten as a vegetable. The word is from the Latin *pastināca*, which became in Middle English *pasnepe*.

The origins of the parsnip probably lie in northeastern Europe, though there is a wild parsnip found in the American West called "Indian celery" (*Hercaleum lanatum*). Europeans brought parsnips to North America in the seventeenth century, first to Virginia in 1608, where the Indians soon learned to enjoy them.

The vegetable has never been particularly popular with Americans, but a particularly hardy and early-maturing variety developed here is called the "All-American." Parsnips are usually boiled and buttered.

partridge. America has no true partridge (any of a variety of Old World game birds in the genera *Perdix* and *Alectoris*), but many birds are called by this name in America. The terminology is further confused by the use of other names, such as "quail" or "pheasant," for the same birds. The bobwhite (*Colinus virginianus*), a name first recorded in 1837, was erroneously called a "partridge" in print as of 1587. The "ruffed grouse" (*Bonasa umbellus*), so called as of 1752, was also termed a "partridge" in print as of 1630. (The ruffed grouse has also been called on occasion a PHEASANT or "mountain pheasant.") The "gray partridge" (*P. perdix*), which is a true partridge, was introduced from Eurasia into the northern United States, but, as noted in *Harper & Row's Complete Field Guide to North American Wildlife* (Eastern edition, 1981), has "generally [been] unsuccessful in becoming established."

passion fruit. Also, "passionfruit." Any of a variety of fruit of the genus *Passiflora*. The fruit was discovered in South America in the sixteenth century by Jesuit missionaries who gave it its name because the flower's parts appeared symbolic of the events and parts of Christ's passion, such as the crown of thorns, the nails, and the whip.

Passion fruit was introduced to Florida at the beginning of the twentieth century. The shell is usually coarse, the shape oval, and it has a pronounced tropical aroma. The "purple passion fruit" (*P. edulis*), called "lilikoi" in Hawaii, and "yellow passion fruit" (*P. edulis forma flavicarpa*) are among the most popular varieties.

pasta. A general term, from the Italian and in English print since 1874, for any spaghetti, macaroni, noodles, or other flour-and-water (sometimes with egg) preparations rolled, cut into myriad shapes and sizes, and boiled. Pasta is made from either fresh or dried dough, sometimes stuffed (as in Italian "manicotti," "ravioli," and "tortellini"), boiled, and sometimes baked (as in Italian *lasagne,* often spelled "lasagna" in American English).

While many of the world's cultures have long eaten various forms of boiled dough, it is most associated with the Italians and has become an Italian-American staple. The English brought recipes for macaroni to America. The first commercial pasta plant in the U.S. was set up in Brooklyn, New York in 1848, by Frenchman Antoine Zerega. By the Civil War pasta was well known and commonly available, usually baked with cheese. Italian immigrants made fresh pasta but, as was common in the south of Italy whence came most of the immigrants, dried pasta (preferably imported) made with hard durum wheat, which was not grown in the United States until the twentieth century, was preferred. Canned macaroni was first produced in the 1890s, by the Franco-American Company. In 1904 a group of Pittsburgh pasta makers formed the National Macaroni Manufacturers Association (since 1981 called the National Pasta Association).

The halt of pasta imports caused by World War I prompted the opening of hundreds of American pasta factories, and by the 1920s macaroni and spaghetti were promoted as highly nutritious items.

The term gained currency in the United States only in the 1960s, with the popularity of Italian food. Prior to that, pasta varieties were referred to by their specific names, like "spaghetti," "macaroni," or "egg noodles."

Americans eat about 19 pounds of pasta per person annually (4.8 billion pounds total). Seventy-seven percent of Americans eat pasta at least once a week, and the favorite shapes and preparations, in order of popularity, are spaghetti, macaroni (and cheese), fettuccine, linguine, elbow macaroni, pasta salad, and angel's hair. Ironically, Italian pasta makers import more than 165 million pounds of American durum wheat for grinding into semolina flour.

pasta fazool. An Italian-American colloquialism for the dish *pasta e fagioli* (Italian for "pasta and beans"), a bowl of pasta and white or red beans made into a thick soup.

pasta primavera. A dish of noodles, macaroni, or spaghetti, made with a sauce of quickly cooked vegetables. *Primavera* in Italian means "springtime," but there is no traditional or specific dish in Italian cuisine by this name. Pasta with vegetables in Italy would be referred to as *pasta al verdure,* or, as is more usual, according to the specific vegetables used—for example, *fettuccine con funghi e piselli* (fettuccine with mushrooms and peas). Pasta primavera became a very popular dish in America in the 1970s and 1980s, and, although there are other claimants for the invention of the dish, the version that gave it its name and spurred its popularity was created by Sirio Maccioni, owner of Le Cirque Restaurant in New York City, who while on a visit to Canada on October 2, 1975, made the dish from several vegetables he tossed together. Maccioni was encouraged by food writers to add it to his menu in New York, and the newly christened dish became an immediate favorite and had its instant imitators.

PASTA PRIMAVERA

Steam 1 c. sliced zucchini, 1 c. sliced broccoli, 1½ c. snow peas, 1 c. baby peas, 6 sliced asparagus stalks, and 10 sliced mushrooms. Rinse under cold water. Sauté in 1 T. olive oil, 2 coarsely chopped tomatoes, ¼ c. parsley, salt, and pepper for a few min. In another pan sauté ⅓ c. pine nuts and 2 t. minced garlic. Add to pan with garlic all vegetables except tomatoes. Simmer, add 1 lb. cooked spaghetti, ½ c. Parmesan cheese, ⅓ c. butter, 1 c. heavy cream, and ⅓ c. fresh basil. Toss, then pour tomatoes on top. Serves 6.

---

pastelles calientes. A Puerto Rican meat pie wrapped in plantains. The term, which means "hot pies" in Spanish, appears in print in 1953.

pastrami. Beef that has been cured in a brine of salt and other preservatives for one to three weeks, smoked over hardwood sawdust for two to twelve hours, then cooked by steaming for one to three hours (1920).

Pastrami is traditionally made from a forequarter cut of meat called the "deckle" or "plate," is usually served on sandwiches, and is a Jewish-American delicatessen item. Its name is derived from the Romanian word *păstra,* "to preserve."

"Pastrami dip" is a sandwich made with pastrami on a French roll dipped in gravy. It originated in Los Angeles in the 1940s or 1950s at hot-dog stands that dipped the pastrami in gravy as a way of keeping the meat from drying out.

pasty. Also, "Cornish pasty." A pastry turnover that may contain a variety of meats and fillings. Pronounced "PASS-tee," the dish has been known in England since the Middle Ages and is mentioned in Shakespeare's *Merry Wives of Windsor* (circa 1598–1600/1601). It has its variants in Scandinavian and Russian cookery.

Pasties became a staple midday meal for the Cornish miners who settled in Michigan's upper peninsula in the middle of the nineteenth century, and there have been attempts to have the pasty declared the state's official food. May 24 has been declared "Michigan Pasty Day," and people of the region will argue over every item that must go into a perfect pasty.

Cornish miners would wrap the hot pasty in a napkin, then in newspaper, and place it in their metal lunch pails so that by midday the pasty would still be warm. It was sometimes reheated on a shovel set over a miner's candle. There is some argument as to whether the pastry itself should be made with lard or suet. In *Heartland* (1991) Marcia Adams notes that "because the pasty was a portable meal, the dough was not known for its tender flakiness. It was said that a really good pasty should be tough enough to withstand being dropped down a mine shaft."

PASTY

Blend 3 c. flour with 1 c. suet and ¼ c. lard. Add 1 t. salt and about 7 T. cold water to make a dough. Divide in four pieces and roll into 9-in. circles. Stir together ¾ lb. coarsely ground beef chuck, ½ lb. coarsely chopped pork, 1 lb. diced peeled potatoes, 2 diced turnips, 1 chopped onion, 2 diced carrots, salt, pepper, and 2 t. butter. Spread on circles and fold the pastry together, crimping the top ridge. Bake at 350° on ungreased sheet for about 45–50 min., until browned.

---

pawpaw (*Asimina triloba*). Also "papaw" and "dog apple." A tree native to northern Central America bearing a soft fleshy fruit. The name, which is probably derived from the Spanish *papaya,* is often mistaken for the true PAPAYA, and the first recordings in English of the fruit are variations of "papaya." The word first appeared in print in 1624.

The pawpaw, with a taste that has been described as a cross between a banana and a pear, grows on stream banks from temperate regions of New York down to Florida and into the Midwest, where it is sometimes called the "Michigan banana" or "custard apple."

pea (*Pisum sativum*). A climbing plant having edible seeds enclosed in long pods. The word is from the Greek *pison,* which in Middle English became *pese* in the plural. There are many variant names for this species, including "field pea."

The pea is one of the oldest cultivated plants in the world. Peas were supposedly brought to the West Indies by Christopher Columbus in 1493 and planted on Isabela Island. By 1614 they were being cultivated at Jamestown, Virginia, and New England's first peas were planted by Captain Bartholomew Gosnold on the island of Cuttyhunk in 1602.

The most popular variety is called the "garden pea," also called the "English pea," the most popular forms being "Layton's Progress," the "Dwarf Telephone," "Gradus," and "Mammoth Melting Sugar," with the Great Lakes, Washington, and Oregon the highest producers. The "sugar pea" includes all edible pea pods, such as "snow peas" or "Chinese snow peas" and "sugar snap peas," developed as a cross breed by Calvin Lamborn in 1979. "Petit pois" (French for "little peas") are merely small greenhouse varieties, and "pea shoots" are the tendrils of pea plants, used as texture and garnish in hightly stylized restaurant cooking, while the COWPEA, "sweet pea," and CHICK-PEA are not peas, but plants in other genera.

"Split peas" are peas that have been dried so that the seeds split in two. They are customarily used to make split-pea soup. Whole peas, fresh or frozen or canned, are boiled or heated and served with butter, onion, or other seasonings.

peach (*Prunus persica*). A tree native to China that bears a sweet fruit with yellow flesh and a yellow-red, slightly fuzzy skin. The word is from the Latin plural of *Persicum* (*Persica*) *mālum,* "Persian apple," which in Middle English became *peche.*

The Romans imported the peach from the Persians, who got it from China and India. It was a popular, though rare, fruit in France and England through the seventeenth century. After the Spanish brought it to the New World in the sixteenth century, the peach thrived among the southern Indian tribes (the Natchez even named one of the months of the year after the fruit) and became just as popular with the northern tribes when they began planting it. In 1661

Philadelphia's William Penn told a friend that peaches proliferated in Pennsylvania "not an Indian plantation without them"—and Thomas Jefferson planted French varieties at Monticello in 1802.

Commercial plantings began in Virginia in the nineteenth century, led first by Maryland and Delaware, then by Georgia. "Peach brandy" was a specialty of the Ohio Valley. Today peaches, second only to the apple as an American crop, are produced in California, New Jersey, Pennsylvania, Virginia, North and South Carolina, Georgia, Alabama, Michigan, Arkansas, and Colorado.

Most peaches are eaten fresh or canned, often in a sweet syrup, and peach bread and peach pie are both long-standing southern specialties. The two main varieties of peaches are the "clingstone" (so called because the fruit's firm flesh clings to the pit) and the "freestone" (which has a softer flesh). The most popular yellow varieties include "Muir," "Lovell," "Rochester," "Blake," "Late Crawford," "Crosby," and the largest variety, the "Elberta." The most popular white peaches include the "Mountain Rose," "Alexander," "Champion," "Heath Cling," "Cling," "Old-mixon," "Summer Snow," "Iron Mountain," and "Belle of Georgia." The most successful crossbreeds include the "Golden Jubilee," "Halehaven," "Redhaven," "Dixieland," "Dixigem," "Southland," and "Goldeneats."

"Nectarines," mostly raised in California and Oregon, are a variety of peach having a firmer flesh.

peach melba. A dessert of peaches poached in vanilla syrup and served with vanilla ice cream and raspberry sauce. The dish was created by chef Georges Auguste Escoffier (1846–1935) and named after Australian opera singer Nellie Melba (born Helen Mitchell; 1861–1931), but it is not clear exactly when or where. Many stories printed during the principals' lifetimes only served to obscure the truth. André L. Simon and Robin Howe, in *A Dictionary of Gastronomy* (1978), state unequivocally that Escoffier served poached peaches with vanilla ice cream at a party given at the London Savoy Hotel to honor Melba on her Covent Garden opening in *Lohengrin*. The authors add that Escoffier later "improved [the dish] by adding a puree of fresh raspberries and a sprinkling of shredded green almonds," which appeared "on a menu of the Carlton Hotel on its first opening in London on July 15, 1899." In *Melba* (1909) the singer's biographer, A. G. Murphy, spoke of her 1898–99 tour and noted that "by this time innumerable soaps and sauces, ribbons and ruffles, had been named after her." But Escoffier himself

contended the dish was not created for Melba's *Lohengrin* debut; instead that he put it on the menu merely because she so often demanded peaches and ice cream for dessert. Escoffier says the dish was created at the Ritz-Carlton Hotel in London and that the peaches were from the Montreal suburb of Paris, while the raspberry puree was merely a rendition of sauce cardinal with Kirsch added. To make matters more confusing, Melba herself treats the subject of the dessert in her autobiography, *Melodies and Memories* (1925), in a chapter devoted to her activities during the years 1904-05, insisting that Escoffier made the dish for her at the Savoy Hotel, which Escoffier had left in 1898.

By 1905, however, the dessert must already have been fairly well known, for American author Edith Wharton mentioned the dish in her novel of that year, *The House of Mirth*. By 1906 the dish, called in French *pêches melba,* was on Escoffier's menus and given as a recipe, which appears below, a year later in his book, *A Guide to Modern Cooking.* (The version mentioned by Simon and Howe as the one appearing on the menu in 1899 is listed in Escoffier's book as "pêches cardinal.") The dish became a favorite in American hotel dining rooms, and an already mixed "melba sauce" was being bottled by 1951.

PEACH MELBA

Poach the skinned peaches in vanilla-flavored syrup. When very cold, arrange them in a timbale on a bed of vanilla ice-cream and coat with raspberry sauce.

---

peach schnapps. A cordial liqueur with a peach flavor, originally developed in the early 1980s by flavor scientist Earl LaRoe of National Distillers and sold as Peachtree Schnapps. The rights were later obtained by DeKuyper Liqueurs. Peach schnapps is most often used in the cocktail called the FUZZY NAVEL.

peachy. A CIDER made from peaches. It is quite possibly an American creation, since its first appearance in print was in S. Peter's *History of Connecticut* in 1781.

peanut. An edible, nutlike seed of the vine *Arachis hypogaea,* native to South America. Peanuts are widely enjoyed as a snack, as a sandwich spread called "peanut butter," and as an ingredient in candy. Peanut oil is often used in frying.

In *Food* (1980), Waverley Root points out that the seeds were found in Peruvian mummy tombs and pictured on Chimu pottery, but other authorities believe that the seeds came originally from Brazil. The Incas may have been the first to cultivate the plant. The Spaniard Hernando Cortés saw peanuts in Mexico; Columbus found them in Haiti. The Spanish and Portuguese took the peanuts to other parts of the world, including the Malay Peninsula, China, and Africa. In West Africa the Portuguese propagated the plant to feed the slaves bound for the New World, and the American colloquialisms "goober" and "pinder" (or "pindal") are derived from African words, brought by the slaves, either for the peanut itself or for an African underground species, *Voandgeia subterranea,* and other plants. These words soon appeared in print in America, the former in 1833, the latter first in Jamaica in 1707 and in South Carolina in 1848. Other names for the peanut include "monkey-nut," found in England and, to a certain extent, in America; "ground-nut," first recorded in 1602, and "ground-pea," in 1769; and others. Root says that Thomas Jefferson was propagating peanuts in the 1790s. The first appearance of the word "peanut" in print was in 1802.

Before the arrival of Europeans there were no peanuts on the North American continent. It was a locally propagated crop in the South, with Wilmington, North Carolina, the largest commercial market for the product. "Peanut boilings" were neighborhood get-togethers in the South. The peanut did not become a national food until after the Civil War, when Northern troops, having gotten used to the nut while fighting in the South, found them rare in the North. Virginia filled the void, and by 1869 more than six hundred thousand bushels were being produced. By the turn of the century vendors were selling peanuts on the streets of most major cities.

In the 1890s George Washington Carver of Alabama's Tuskegee Institute in Alabama, promoted the peanut as a replacement for the cotton crop destroyed by the boll weevil and as of 1903 had begun to develop hundreds of uses for the peanut, demonstrating its high nutritive value in dozens of recipes for appetizers, main dishes, soups, and desserts. His list of the most popular peanut varieties includes the "Spanish," "Georgia," and "Tennessee Red" and the "Virginia Running" peanuts, this last referred to as the typical "American peanut."

At the beginning of the twentieth century Italian immigrant Amedo Obici developed a process for commercially roasting shelled peanuts in oil, and, with Mario Peruzzi, began packaging their peanuts in air-tight bags under the "Planters" label. Meanwhile Russian immigrant Sam Fisher patented a "salted-in-the-shell" peanut cooker that made the snack much more widely available. In 1890 an unknown St. Louis physician created "peanut butter" as a protein substitute for those with poor teeth. A local food products manufacturer, George A. Bayle, Jr., mechanized the process, and in 1903 a patent was issued to Ambrose W. Straub for a peanut-butter machine. A year later peanut butter was being promoted as a health food at the St. Louis Universal Exposition by concessionaire C. H. Sumner. In 1922 J. L. Rosefield of the Rosefield Packing Company of Alameda, California, developed a process to prevent oil separation and spoilage in peanut butter, and in 1932 began marketing his product under the name "Skippy" as "churned" peanut butter. It soon became a favorite sandwich spread, usually layered with grape jelly, among American schoolchildren, and today more than half the American peanut crop goes into the making of peanut butter.

In the South peanut soup is very common, as is "peanut cream gravy." Peanuts are boiled or they are eaten roasted out of their shells, salted or unsalted. They are mixed into stuffings, salads, cakes, cookies, puddings, pies, and candies and are a versatile ingredient in many of the most popular commercial candy bars. "Peanut brittle" came along at the turn of the last century; "peanut stands" were known as early as the 1860s, and vendors selling peanuts in paper bags have been a fixture in sporting arenas and circus tents in America for decades.

By law any product labeled "peanut butter" must contain at least 90 percent peanuts, with the remaining 10 percent restricted to salt, sweeteners, and stabilizers. The majority of peanut butter is now imported. In 1997 U.S. per capita consumption of peanuts was 5.8 pounds and 2.8 pounds of peanut butter. In 1998 Americans consumed 700 million pounds of peanut butter.

The four principal peanut varieties raised commercially are the "Virginia," the "Runner," the "Spanish" and the "Valencia."

PEANUT PIE

Beat 3 eggs with ½ c. sugar. Add 1 c. white corn syrup, 1 t. vanilla, 1 t. butter, a pinch of salt, 2 T. peanut butter, and mix for 5 min. Pour into a 9-in. pie shell, sprinkle top with ¾ c. toasted peanuts, and bake for 45 min. at 300°.

PEANUT SOUP

(Also known as "Tuskegee soup," for its creator, George Washington Carver of the Tuskegee Institute.) Chop 5 scallions and sauté in 3 T. butter. Make a roux by blending in 3 T. flour, then add ½ c. peanut butter and 2 c. chicken stock, and stir until smooth. Add ½ c. cream and the juice from 1 qt. oysters. Add salt, cayenne pepper, and savory to taste, then finish with a dash of sherry, parsley, and shucked oysters.

---

pear (*Pyrus communis*). A tree bearing a fruit with a spherical bottom and tapered top. The word is from the Latin *pirum*. In Middle English it appeared as *pere*.

The pear originated in Asia, possibly China, and has been cultivated at least since 2000 B.C., with more than fifteen thousand species having since been developed from either the "Chinese pear" (*P. sinensis*) or the "European pear" (*P. communis*), Most American varieties have been developed from the latter, which was brought to the Colonies in the seventeenth century by Jesuit missionaries, English settlers in Massachusetts, and the Dutch in New Amsterdam. In the West the pear was introduced by Spanish missionaries.

By far the most widely cultivated variety in the United States is the "Bartlett," first mentioned in print in 1831. In Europe the Bartlett was called the "Williams' Bon Chrétien," because the fruit was supposedly brought to France in the fifteenth century by Saint Francis of Paola (*bon chrétien* in French means "good Christian") and was perhaps propagated in England and on the Continent by a horticulturist named Williams. Neither of these stories has been proven, but the pear acquired its American name thanks to Enoch Bartlett of Dorchester, Massachusetts, who promoted the variety in the United States. The Bartlett now accounts for three quarters of U.S. pear production.

Other important varieties include the "Seckel," the "Cornice," the "Bosc," the "Anjou," and the "Kieffer." Americans eat pears fresh or canned in syrup, with ice cream, and cooked in cream and sugar. The largest producers of pears are California, Washington, Oregon, New York, Michigan, Illinois, Pennsylvania, and New Jersey.

In Charleston, South Carolina, preserves of chopped pears (also pumpkins) are known as "chips," because the pears are "chipped" into pieces.

PEAR CHIPS

In a saucepan bring to a boil 4 c. sugar with 1 qt. water and cook for about 5 min. Add 4 lb. peeled, seeded, and chopped pears and 2 thinly sliced, seeded lemons. Cook until the pears are tender, then serve with the syrup over ice cream or store in vacuum jars.

---

pecan (*Carya illinoensis*). The nut of the tall hickory tree native to America, ranging from Illinois down to Mexico. After the peanut, the pecan is the most popular nut grown in this country, with an annual production of about 228 million pounds, led by Georgia, and is used in pies, PRALINES, candies, and ice cream. The name comes from various Indian words (Algonquian *paccan,* Cree *pakan,* and others) and was first mentioned in print in 1773. Thomas Jefferson introduced the tree to the eastern shores of Virginia, and he gave some to George Washington for planting at Mount Vernon. A Louisiana slave named Antoine was the first successfully to graft and cultivate pecan trees in 1846. "Pecan pie" is sometimes called "Karo, pie" after the brand name Karo corn syrup (introduced in 1902 by Corn Products Company of Edgewater, New Jersey), so often used in its preparation. The recipe below is adapted from *The Karo Cook Book* (1981).

The "pecan ball"—a dessert made by rolling a scoop of ice cream in chopped pecans and topping it with chocolate syrup—is a specialty of Pittsburgh, Ohio.

PECAN PIE

Beat 3 eggs until light in color. Beat in 1 c. Karo light or dark corn syrup, 1 c. sugar, 2 T. melted margarine, 1 t. vanilla, and ⅛ t. salt. Stir in 1 c. pecans and pour mixture into pastry shell. Bake at 350° for 55–65 min. or until inserted knife comes out clean. Serves 8.

---

pemmican. A Native American food made from buffalo meat or venison dried and compressed into small cakes also containing some form of melted fat, berries, and sometimes bone marrow. This highly nutritious food that kept well on long journeys was introduced to the early pioneers, though they did not take to it with any particular relish. The pioneers' version often did not contain the meat.

The word comes from Cree Indian *pemikān,* from *pimiy,* "grease," and was first used in print in 1791. A struggle between the hunters and fur traders of the Northwest Fur Company and the Hudson Bay Company, which lasted from 1812 to 1821, was referred to as the "Pemmican War," because it took place in the Native American country of the outer territories.

pepita. A word for a pumpkin seed, borrowed from the Spanish. Pepitas are usually sold raw or toasted or fried and salted as a snack in the Southwest. Ground up, they are added to sauces for texture and flavor.

pepper. Primarily this word refers to the peppercorn of the vine of the family Piperaceae, first domesticated in India and now used around the world as a seasoning, especially the peppercorn of the *Piper nigrum*, from which both black and white pepper are made. The word "pepper" is from the Greek *peperi*, ultimately from the Sanskrit *pippali*, "berry."

The distribution of pepper throughout the world was once fought over by several European countries that tried to monopolize the trade. For a while in the early nineteenth century, Salem, Massachusetts, was a dominant pepper-trading port of the Western Hemisphere, to which peppercorns from Sumatra were brought in the fast clipper ships developed in New England.

"Black pepper" is made from "peppercorn" berries that are picked prematurely, then dried. The major varieties of black pepper in the American market are "Malabar" (from the Malabar Coast), once called "Alleppey" after a major shipping port; "Tellicherry" (Malabar); "Lampong' (Indonesia); "Sarawak" (Malaysia); "Brazilian"; "Ceylon."

"White pepper" is produced from mature peppercorns by removing the dark skin and using only the cores, which are then dried. "Decorticated" black pepper or decorticated white pepper is a form of white pepper made by removing the skin from dried black pepper. The major varieties of white pepper are "Muntok" (Bangka, Sumatra); "Brazilian"; "Sarawak."

"Green peppercorns" are ripe peppercorns, mostly from Madagascar, used whole in cooking and in sauces rather than ground.

The term "pepper" is also, erroneously, applied to a wide range of fruits of the *Capiscum* plants, including the CHILE, CAYENNE, PIMIENTO, and "sweet" red and green peppers. These last two, *C. frutescens, grossum*, are far milder than the rest and are often eaten as a vegetable because they have a sweet, rather than a hot, flavor. In fact, the first mention of the "green pepper" in American print was as the "sweet pepper plant" in

1834. "Bell peppers," so called because of their bell-like shape, also have a sweet flavor and grow well in the southeastern United States, and in the Midwest are called mangoes. Bell peppers have commonly come in red and green varieties, but the "golden bell pepper" was only brought into the United States in 1981 by Moore Farming, Inc., of Salinas, California.

pepper steak. A dish of beef slices made with a sauce of onions, tomatoes, and green or red peppers.

PEPPER STEAK

Dip 4 slices of chuck or pot roast beef in flour and saute in 2 T. oil until browned. Add 2 T. oil, add 1 sliced onion and cook with meat for 4 min. Add 4 chopped, peeled, and seeded tomatoes, 1 T. parsley, salt and pepper to taste. In a separate pan in 2 T. oil, sauté 4 green or red sweet peppers for 2 min. Add to meat pan. Toss and serve.

---

perch. Any of a variety of fish in the family Percidae. Perch are freshwater inhabitants, although their name is also applied offhandedly to some marine fish of the families Percichthyidae and Scorpaenidae. The name goes back to the Greek *perké*. The main varieties of culinary interest in the United States are "yellow perch" (*Perca flavescens*); "white perch" (*Morone americana*), which is a temperate bass; and "ocean perch" (*Sebastes marinus*). U.S. commercial landings of perch totaled 42.6 million pounds in 1997.

perry. A pear CIDER made both still and sparkling. It is an ancient beverage in England and was very popular throughout the thirteen colonies in America.

persimmon (*Diospyros virginiana, D. texana*, and *D. kaki*). Also called "date plum." A tree chiefly of the tropics bearing a late-ripening orange-red fruit. The word is from the Algonquian, akin to the Cree word for dried fruit, *pasiminan*, first appearing in print as "putchamin" in 1612, then in its present form in 1709. *D. texana*, which grows in Texas, is called the "black persimmon," "chapote," "Mexican persimmon," "mustang persimmon," and "possum plum."

The earliest explorers and colonists of the New World were fascinated by the persimmon. Hernando de Soto, in about 1540, compared it with the Spanish red plum and preferred the persimmon. John Smith in Virginia at the beginning of the seventeenth century called it "one of the most palatable fruits of this land," something like an apricot. Not every settler agreed, for before the fruit is wholly ripe, it is acidic and astringent to the taste; it achieves its succulent ripeness only late in the fall. The Native Americans made it into beer, which the colonists soon adapted, and bread, which in Missouri was called "stanica." In the November 1981 issue of *Cuisine* magazine, Meryle Evans wrote, "In 1863 Logan Martin, an enterprising young southern Indiana farmer, took a gallon bucket of native persimmons to market in nearby Louisville, Kentucky, where they sold so quickly that he decided on the spot to raise the fruit commercially. Every autumn, for over forty years, 'Persimmon' Martin (as he came to be known) harvested and packed up over two thousand gallons for shipment by railroad from his hometown of Borden to city markets as far away as New York." Today, near Martin's hometown, the people of Indiana hold an annual persimmon festival the last week of September.

The native "American persimmon" was eventually pushed aside as a commercial crop in favor of the "Japanese persimmon" (*D. kaki*), which may have been introduced to the United States in 1855 by Commodore Matthew C. Perry.

In the South persimmon seeds are ground to be used as a coffee substitute, and throughout the Southeast and Midwest persimmon pudding is a Thanksgiving tradition. "Locust beer" is made from persimmons and locusts.

Petite Sirah. Also, "Petite Syrah." A red vinifera grape planted in California. The true identity of this grape has not yet been discovered, though some believe it derives from the Duriff variety of the Rhone Valley in southern France. Used both in blending wines and as a varietal, the Petite Sirah has an intense, spicy aroma and a range of colors from light to deep red.

petticoat tails. A shortbread cookie of Louisiana brought to America by Scottish immigrants. The term dates from the French-influenced court of Mary Stuart (1542–87), where the cookies were known as *petits gâtels* or *qâstels,* which later became *petits gâteaux,* "little cakes." The Scottish dialect transformed that sound into "petticoat tails," and the cookie is now made with scalloped edges that seem to resemble petticoat edges.

pheasant. Any of a variety of game birds in the family Phasianidae with characteristic long tails and colored plumage. Pheasants are native to the Old World, and there is some confusion in American terminology for the birds. The common term, "pheasant," is from the Greek *phasianos,* referring to the bird of the Phasis River in the Caucasus. In America, however, pheasant was applied by the early colonists to the "ruffed grouse" (*Bonasa umbellus*), which did not take this latter name until the middle of the eighteenth century. The Old World pheasant, specifically the "ring-necked pheasant" (*Phasianus colchicus*), also called the "English pheasant," was introduced from Europe and Asia, perhaps in the eighteenth century, but definitely by the nineteenth. L. Patrick Coyle, Jr., in *The World Encyclopedia of Food* (1982), writes that "George Washington imported pheasants from Europe in 1789 to stock his Mt. Vernon estate . . . [and] by the 1830s it was common enough to figure in cookbooks of the period." Waverley Root, in *Food* (1980), noted that Thomas Jefferson once proposed to raise French pheasants in Virginia, but it is not known if he succeeded. The usual date given for the introduction of the pheasant to America is 1881, when an American consul brought Shanghai pheasants home to his Oregon farm. Whenever the pheasant arrived in the United States, it proliferated so successfully that now it is found in more than thirty states.

The bird is usually roasted, and it can be bought frozen.

Philadelphia cheese-steak. A sandwich made with thin slices of beef topped with cheese and other condiments and served on a crisp Italian-style roll. It is a specialty of Philadelphia. Its origins have never been satisfactorily explained, although Pat and Harry Olivieri of Pat's Restaurant claim to have created the item in 1930 (although Pat Olivieri claimed to have added the cheese only in 1948). An order for "cheese with" means the dish should be made with sautéed onions. The cheese is usually, though not always, American, sometimes squirted from a plastic canister.

PHILADELPHIA CHEESE-STEAK

Slice several pieces of rare beef very thin and sauté quickly on a griddle. Place thin slices of cheese on top of meat to melt, place on Italian-style roll, and add ketchup, if desired.

Philadelphia eggs. A dish described by Oscar Tschirky in *The Cook Book by "Oscar of the Waldorf"* (1896) as two split muffins topped with cooked white chicken meat, poached eggs, and hollandaise sauce.

Philadelphia pepper pot. A dish of tripe, pepper, and seasonings supposedly created during the severe winter deprivations of George Washington's ragged army in 1777–78, when all the cook had to work with was tripe and pepper. The dish was named after the cook's hometown and was so well received by the starving troops that the dish became legendary and was later sold in the streets of Philadelphia by black women crying, "Peppery Pot! Nice and Hot! Makes backs strong, makes lives long!"

PHILADELPHIA PEPPER POT

Wash 3 lb. tripe thoroughly and bring to a boil in 4 qt. water. Cook on low heat for 6 hr., until tripe is soft, then allow to cool. Cut into small pieces. In another kettle place 1½ lb. veal knuckle, 3 sliced carrots, ½ c. chopped celery, 2 T. chopped parsley, 1 chopped onion, 1 t. each marjoram, bay leaf, summer savory, and basil, ½ t. thyme, ¾ t. whole black peppercorns, and 3 cloves. Cover with water and simmer for about 2 hr., until very tender. Strain, discard vegetables, cool and skim fat from broth. Add tripe and 2 chopped potatoes. Simmer until potatoes are tender. Serves 6.

Philadelphia sticky bun. A nineteenth-century Philadelphia yeast bun flavored with cinnamon and brown sugar. In Philadelphia these sweet rolls are called "cinnamon buns."

PHILADELPHIA STICKY BUN

Dissolve 1 pkg. yeast in ¼ c. lukewarm water. Scald 1 c. milk, then cool until lukewarm and add yeast and 1½ c. flour. Mix, cover, and let rise for 1 hr. Add 4 T. cooled melted butter, 2 beaten egg yolks, 4 T. sugar, 1 t. salt, the grated rind of 1 lemon, and 3 c. flour. Knead, then cover and let rise until doubled. Roll dough to 1-in.-thick long rectangle, brush with a mixture of melted butter, 2 T. brown sugar, 1 t. cinnamon, and 3 T. red currants (if desired). Roll and cut into 1-in. slices. Crumble ¾ c. brown sugar with 4 T. melted butter and spread in a skillet. Place dough slices in skillet, let rise for another 60 min., or until doubled, then bake at 350° for 30 min. Turn out onto cooling rack. Makes 12 buns.

philpy. A South Carolina rice bread. The name is of obscure origins.

PHILPY

To ½ c. flour add ½ c. milk and ½ t. salt. Mash ¾ c. cooked rice and add to flour mixture with 2 t. melted butter and 1 beaten egg. Pour into buttered 8-in. layer pan and bake 45 min. at 450° Cut into 6 wedges.

phosphoric acid. An acidifier and flavor enhancer used in soft drinks.

picadillo. A mincemeat stew of the Southwest whose name is taken from the Spanish word for "hash."

PICADILLO

Cook ½ lb. ground beef and ½ lb. ground pork, 1 minced onion, 1 c. canned tomatoes, 2 minced cloves of garlic, 1 T. vinegar, salt, pepper, 1 t. ground cinnamon cloves, ¼ t. ground cumin, 1 bay leaf, ½ c. seedless raisins, and ½ c. almonds. Add water if necessary to give a stew-like texture.

pickle. A food that has been preserved in a brine solution that has been flavored with herbs and seasonings. Although in America the word most often refers specifically to a cucumber preserved in this way, pickling may be done with fish and many other foods. Vinegar is most often the ingredient that defines the flavor of such items.

The word may derive from a Dutch fisherman named William Beukelz (died 1437), who is credited with inventing the pickling process. It was used in England as early as 1440 (*pekille* in Middle English) and by the eighteenth century any preserved food item could be called a "pickle." In America pickled food became the product most associated with Henry J. Heinz, who put up fifty-seven varieties for sale to groceries around Sharpsburg, Pennsylvania, beginning in 1869. Breaded, fried dill-pickle slices are a Mississippi specialty.

There are numerous varieties of cucumber pickles, including these main varieties in the United States: "dill pickles," flavored with dill leaves and seed heads; "kosher pickles," flavored with garlic; "overnight pickles," fermented for only two or three days; "sour pickles," fermented in a sour brine; "sour mixed pickles," cut into chunks and mixed with other vegetables like onion, cauliflower, carrots and peppers; "sour relish pickles," also called "piccalilli," made by finely chopping sour pickles with other vegetables; CHOW-CHOW; "sweet pickles," sugared as well as soaked in brine; "sweet mixed pickles," with other vegetables; "gherkins," miniature pickles used mainly as a garnish; "candied dills," sticks, chips, or strips of dill pickles packed in an extra sweet solution; "sliced sweet pickles" (also called "cross cuts"), cut crosswise in chips, which include "bread and butter pickles." "Ice-water pickles" or "cold water pickles" are initially treated with ice water.

"Fresh-packed pickles" are not cured by fermentation, but pasteurized and sealed in containers, although some cured pickles are also processed this way.

Americans eat about 9 pounds of pickles per person annually.

"Pickled peppers" are made with CHILE peppers much the same way as cucumber pickles. The most popular pickled peppers include jalapeños, cherry peppers, and banana peppers.

PICCALILLI

Chop 4 qt. green tomatoes, add salt to cover, and drain. Chop ¼ head of cabbage, 3 medium onions, and 3 green peppers and blend. Add 1 t. turmeric, 1 oz. mustard seed, 5 stalks celery, 1 c. brown sugar, and ½ oz. allspice. Cover with cider vinegar and cook for about 30 min. Put up in jars and seal.

pickled pork. Also, "sweet pickled pork." A Louisiana specialty made from pork shoulder marinated in brine. It used to be made at home by a lengthy, arduous process extending over two weeks, but today it is prepackaged and sold in markets. It is considered an important ingredient in making red beans and rice. The following recipe is from John Thorne's booklet *Rice & Beans: The Itinerary of a Recipe* (1981).

PICKLED PORK

Combine ½ c. mustard seeds, 1 T. celery, 1 dried hot pepper (or 2 T. Caribe chile powder or 2 T. Tabasco sauce), 1 qt. distilled white vinegar, 1 bay leaf, 1 T. kosher salt, 12 peppercorns, and 6 cloves garlic that have been peeled and flattened but left whole. Boil for 3 min. Let cool. Place ½ lb. boneless pork butt cut into 2-in. cubes (or 2½-3 lb. country-style spareribs individually cut) into pickling solution, stirring to remove all air bubbles. Completely submerge meat and refrigerate for 3 days, stirring occasionally.

picnic. A meal taken out of doors and away from home, often without benefit of tables, chairs, or other amenities. The word is borrowed from the French *piquenique*, meaning much the same thing, and entered the English language about 1748. In America picnickers usually pack a basket or hamper of cold foods, SANDWICHES, and cans or thermos bottles of beverages. Some people go to picnic areas specifically set up with outdoor tables in rural settings.

picnic ham. Also called "California ham." A shoulder cut of HAM, so called since about 1910. The meat is sometimes also referred to as CALAS.

pie. Any of a wide variety of desserts or savories baked in a pastry crust. The word is from Middle English and dates in print to the early thirteenth century. Pie fillings are made from fruits, vegetables, custards, fish, and meats. Some of the most popular American fruit pies include apple, blueberry, peach, and cherry. Common custard varieties include "custard pie," "banana cream pie," CHESS PIE, and "buttermilk pie." Pumpkin pie is particularly popular in autumn and winter, especially at Halloween and Thanksgiving. "Key lime pies" (see LIME) are Florida specialties, and MUD PIES are best known in the South. "Mock apple pie" is actually made with RITZ crackers.

American meat pies are better known as POTPIES (first in print about 1785), the most popular being filled with chicken or beef and vegetables. "Hartley's Pork Pie" is a specialty of Fall River, Massachusetts, created by Thomas Hartley. According to an article in *Yankee* magazine (October 1988), the pork pies of that region were sometimes called "Jickey wedding cakes" (originally a slur against low-class English immigrants called "Jickeys"), but Hartley's became locally famous. According to Hartley's grandson, Harold, the original recipe was sold to Don Setters, a pastry shop in Somerset, Massachusetts.

pie card. A union card used since the turn of this century by loggers to obtain lodging or a meal.

pie-washer. Bakers' term for the worker who paints the top crust of pastry with a wash of water, milk, or egg to give the finished baked item a glossy look.

pigeon. Any of a wide variety of birds in the family Columbidae. There are at least three hundred species, a half dozen of which are found in North American skies, including the "mourning dove" (*Zenaida macroura*), also called the "turtledove," and the "common ground dove" (*Columbina passerina*), but none is of much culinary interest to most Americans, who regard pigeons as anything from a pet to an urban nuisance. At one time, however, the native "passenger pigeon" (*Ectopistes migratorius*) was highly esteemed as a game bird, and it may have been the most numerous bird on earth, with an estimated population of 9 billion at its height. Almost immediately upon their arrival in the New World, European colonists hunted the passenger pigeon enthusiastically, and wholesale slaughter of the flocks continued unabated until well into the nineteenth century, when a shotgun could bring down a hundred of the birds in one burst. By 1900, however, only one wild bird was found, and the last passenger pigeon died in a Cincinnati zoo in 1914.

Today only young pigeons less than four weeks old, called "squabs," are of much culinary interest. They are raised on farms mostly for consumption in restaurants.

pig out. As a verb, a slang term from the 1970s meaning to overeat, usually without much discrimination. A "pig-out" refers to a binge of eating.

pigs' ears. Although this term may refer to a dish of pigs' ears, rarely served in the United States, it is more often used to describe a fried pastry popular in Louisiana, called by the French name LES OREILLES DE COCHONS, especially by Cajun cooks.

PIGS' EARS

Combine 2 c. flour, 1 t. baking powder, and ½ t. salt. Beat ½ c. melted cooled butter into 2 beaten eggs, stir into flour mixture, divide into 2 doz. balls, and roll out to 6-in. diameter. Deep-fry in hot oil. When the pastry rises to the surface of the oil, pierce center with a fork and turn pastry. Fry until golden brown, drain. Cook 1½ c. cane syrup to 230° on a candy thermometer, drizzle over pastries, and sprinkle with chopped pecans. Makes 24.

---

pike. Any of a variety of freshwater fish in the family Esox, five species of which are found in North America. The name is from Middle English, possibly referring to the spiked appearance of the fish. The pike has never been a popular eating fish in America, although it is highly praised by gastronomes as a fine food fish and is traditionally made into quenelles in French kitchens.

The main species in America include the "northern pike" (*Esox lucius*), and the "muskellunge" (*E.*

masquinongy), whose name derives from the Algonquian, *maskinonge*, "big pike," and is often called "muskie" for short.

piki bread. Also, "paper bread." A very thin cornmeal bread baked on a griddle and rolled up. It is of Hopi origins but has been adapted by various Pueblos and goes by other names such as *hewe* (Zuni) and *mowa* (Tewa). Often piki is flavored or colored. According to Carolyn Niethammer in *American Indian Food and Lore* (1974), piki bread making was considered an art and ritual, now fading, but "Years ago a young woman was required to demonstrate that she had mastered the art of piki-baking before she was considered a suitable bride."

The piki bread is made on a "pike stone" heated by a fire from cedar or juniper wood. Piki is made with a little ash left over from the burning of green plants such as bean vines, corncobs, or juniper.

PIKI BREAD

In a bowl mix 3 T. ash (or 1 T. baking soda) with about ½ c. cold water. In another bowl mix 4 c. blue cornmeal with 4 c. boiling water until well blended. Add 4 more c. boiling water and blend to make a thick dough. Strain the ash water through cheesecloth and blend into dough. Knead for a few minutes, then set aside to rest for about 10 min. Gradually add 4 c. cold water to make a creamlike batter. Grease a griddle, then brush on batter to make a thin film on the griddle. Cook for about 1 min., remove from griddle, and set aside. Spread another film of batter on the griddle. When it is dry, place the first piki on top, fold the first piki in thirds, and then roll into a cylinder. Continue to use all the batter this way to make about 50 piki.

---

pilau. Also, "plaw," "pilaw," "pilaf," and "pilaff." Any of a variety of steamed-rice dishes made of meat, chicken, fish, or vegetables in a broth.

The word comes from the Turkish *pilāw*, from the Persian *pilāw*, and from the Osmanli *pilav*, "rice porridge." The dish is known in numerous versions throughout the Middle East: The Greeks make *pilafi* with tomatoes, the Iraqis make a lentil version called *mejedrah* and the Iranians an apricot version called *geisi pelo,* the Poles cook *pilaw turecki,* and the dish found its way to France under the name *pilaff de crevettes,* made with shrimp.

The dish was spoken of by English writers in the seventeenth century, and by the eighteenth century it seemed to have taken hold in Britain, especially after the empire spread through the Middle East and into India. In America the dish became popular in the South because of the influence of the spice trade and the rice crop, and in Louisiana the French culinary influence was felt so strongly as to make *pilou français* or *pilaff de volaille* local delectables. Greek Americans adapted their native dish to *pilafi tou fournou,* baked in an oven. Most pilaus use a touch of curry powder, though the Louisiana versions more often do not. Marjorie Kinnan Rawlings, in *Cross Creek Cookery* (1942), called pilau "almost a sacred Florida dish. . . . A Florida church supper is unheard of without it." The word "pilau" is pronounced in a variety of ways, as in "PER-to," "PEE-Laf," or per-LO."

PILAU

In a Dutch oven cover 2½ lb. chicken with water, add salt and pepper, bring to a boil and simmer, covered, for ½ hr. Remove, cool, and cut chicken meat into strips about 3-in. long. To 3 c. of the cooking liquid add 1 t. curry powder, ½ t. parsley, 2 T. butter, and 1 c. raw rice. Bring to a boil, lower heat, cook 10 min., add chicken, and cook 10 min. more.

pilot pellets. Airline workers' slang for the peanuts served on board, so called because pilots eat so many of them. The term first appeared in print in 1990.

piña colada. A cocktail made from light rum, coconut cream, and pineapple juice. It is especially popular during warm weather with boating enthusiasts and at southern resort areas. The term was first printed in 1923.

The piña colada (which in Spanish means "strained pineapple") originated at the Caribe Hilton Hotel and Casino in San Juan, Puerto Rico. Back in 1952 bartender Ramón Monchito Marrero Pérez was introduced to a new product called Coco López cream of coconut (containing coconut, sugar, water, polysorbate 60, sorbitan monostearate, salt, propylene glycol alginate, mono- and diglycerides, citric acid, guar gum, and locust-bean gum). On August 15, 1954, after three months of trying out various liquors with the product, Marrero mixed pineapple juice and light rum with it, blended the mixture with crushed ice, and came up with a sweet, creamy drink that did not really catch on until 1954, when it was served to a group of government officials at a convention there.

Another Puerto Rican claimed to have invented the piña colada in 1963 at the bar called La Barrachina in San Juan's Old City, where there still hangs a plaque that announces "The House Where in 1963 THE PIÑA COLADA Was Created by Don Ramón Portas Mingot." But Mr. Marrero's 1952 claim seems clearly more authoritative, and, therefore, here is his original recipe.

PIÑA COLADA

Pour 2 oz. light Bacardi's rum, 1 oz. coconut cream, 1 oz. heavy cream, and 6 oz. unsweetened pineapple juice into a blender with a cup of crushed ice. Blend for about 15 sec. and serve in a large glass with a garnish of pineapple stick and maraschino cherry. (An almost identical drink, the Bahia, invented at Trader Vic's restaurant in San Francisco, substitutes 1 oz. white Jamaican rum and 1 oz. light Puerto Rican rum for the Bacardi rum in this recipe.)

pineapple (*Ananas comosus*). A tropical plant bearing a large ovular fruit with spiny skin and swordlike leaves. The word derives from its appearance, which resembles a pinecone, and its first appearance in print, in 1398, actually referred to a real pinecone. Not until 1664 did the fruit known by this name enter the printed language.

The pineapple is native to America and was first discovered by Christopher Columbus on the island of Guadeloupe in 1493, and called by him "*piña de Indes,*" "pine of the Indians." Indians of Paraguay and Brazil, especially the Guarani tribe, had domesticated the plant and called it *naná* ("excellent fruit"), from which the Latin term for the pineapple derived.

In 1519 Ferdinand Magellan found the pineapple in Brazil, and by 1555 the fruit was being exported from that country to England. It was also widely dispersed throughout Asia's tropics, growing in abundance in India by 1583, and it proliferated in the West Indies, where, in Barbados in 1751, George Washington tasted and preferred it to any other tropical fruit.

The pineapple was introduced to Hawaii by Captain James Cook in 1790, but it was not commercially cultivated there because of the difficulty of shipping between the islands and the United States. Throughout the nineteenth century the fruit was a rarity for most Americans, even though it was grown in Florida. In the 1880s, however, widespread cultivation was encouraged in Hawaii with the onset of the steamship trade in the Pacific, and in 1903 James

Drummond Dole began canning the pineapple at Wahiawa for shipment everywhere. Dole's Hawaiian Pineapple Company had by 1921 established the fruit as the largest crop in those islands. But by 1990 tourist dollars outstripped the profitability of raising the crop, and Hawaii's share of the world market has shrunk to 10 percent. Pineapple also comes into the U.S. from Honduras, Mexico, the Dominican Republic, and Costa Rica.

The most popular variety there is the "Smooth Cayenne," followed by the "Red Spanish." Americans eat pineapple fresh, as part of a salad or fruit cocktail, in sherbets, ice cream, and ices, in gelatin, in cocktails, and as a flavoring, including in cordials. Canned varieties include sliced rings, chunks, and crushed pieces. Pineapple juice is extremely popular and often used in mixed drinks like the MAI TAI and PIÑA COLADA. Dishes made with pineapple are often called "Hawaiian style."

pine nut. Also, "piñon," "pignoli," "pignotia," and "piñolos." Any of several pine tree nuts of the Southwest, especially *Pinus monophylla*, *P. edulis*, and *P. cembroides*. Pine nuts compose the largest uncultivated crop in North America, solely harvested from wild trees. About 3 to 5 million pounds are harvested each year in the Southwest and Mexico.

Pine nuts are eaten raw, toasted, used in soups, sauces, even candies.

pink lady. A cocktail, probably dating from the Prohibition era, with a recipe given in *The Savoy Cocktail Book* (1930), made by mixing 1 part grenadine, 2 parts lemon or lime juice, 2 parts apple brandy, 4 parts gin, and 1 egg white. Some recipes add cream.

pink sauce. A pink-colored sauce served with shrimp and dating probably from the 1950s.

PINK SAUCE

Blend ¾ c. mayonnaise, 1 c. ketchup, 1 t. horseradish, ¼ t. salt, 1 chopped onion, ¼ t. garlic, ¼ t. confectioners' sugar, ½ t. Worcestershire sauce, ¼ t. Tabasco, ½ t. paprika, and pepper to taste.

pinole. Dried, ground, spiced, and sweetened corn used in the Southwest, sometimes pronounced "panola." The term is Spanish American, from Nahuatl *pinolli*, and has been used north of Mexico at least since the 1840s.

Pinot Noir. A red vinifera grape that makes an intense, rich, tannic wine and that is also used to make champagne (1960). It is the principal grape used in France's Burgundy and in recent years has become an important grape in premium wines of California and the Northwest (although American Pinot Noirs have thus far lacked the finesse and complexity of the French examples).

pinwheel. Any of a wide variety of snacks or canapés cut from a stuffed or layered roll of bread or pastry into thick rounds whose centers form a pinwheel shape.

pipikaula. A Hawaiian dish made of beef jerky and soy sauce.

pistachio (*Pistacia vera*). A tree, native to Asia Minor, that bears green nuts within a pod that is often dyed a bright pinkish red for commercial purposes. The first commercial crop in California was grown in 1976 in the San Joaquin Valley, and today the United States is the second-largest producer of pistachios in the world. Pistachios are eaten as a snack or, very often, used as a flavoring for ice cream, the first example of which was created by confectioner James W. Parkinson of Philadelphia, Pennsylvania, about 1840.

English use of the word dates back to the early sixteenth century.

The dyeing of pistachios is not a Middle Eastern tradition but is said to have originated with a Brooklyn street vendor named Zaloom who colored his pistachios red to distinguish them from his competitors'. The idea caught on—especially in the East—that most pistachios used to be dyed red. This is no longer true, with only about 15 percent of those sold today so colored.

pita. A round, flat bread easily slit open to form a pocket that may hold everything from chicken salad to chili con carne to bean sprouts to cheese (1950). Its origins are in the Middle East, and it was first served in America in Greek, Turkish, Armenian, and other small restaurants. Pita became popular in the 1960s and 1970s as an ethnic bread, whereas today it is easily found in groceries throughout the country.

pizza. Also, "pizza pie." A flat pie made from a yeast dough topped with various cheeses, vegetables, meats, seasonings, and other ingredients. It is one of the most popular of all American meals and snacks, and it is made in restaurants called "pizzerias," sold frozen in groceries, or, occasionally, made at home. It is a $20 billion industry in the United States.

Contrary to some assertions, the pizza is not an American creation, but its acceptance in this country has made it a far more widespread food item here than in its country of origin, Italy. The American promotion of pizza has resulted in its becoming an international favorite, from Tuscaloosa to Tokyo.

The term "pizza" is clouded in some ambiguity, but etymologists believe it derives from an Old Italian word meaning "a point," which in turn led to the Italian word *pizzicare*, meaning "to pinch" or "pluck." The word shows up for the first time in a Neapolitan dialect word—*picea* or *piza*—about A.D. 1000, referring perhaps to the manner in which the hot pie is plucked from the oven.

Pizza has obvious analogues in Middle Eastern pita breads, and flat, seasoned yeast breads are known in many parts of the world (for example, Indian *naan*, Moroccan *Khboz Bishemar*, and Armenian *Lahma bi ajeen*), but it is useless to argue direct linkage to any such breads, because pizza is merely an elaboration of all these variants. The fact is that the pizza as we know it today could not have existed before the sixteenth century, when the tomato was brought to Italy from South America. Although the tomato was held in low esteem by most Europeans, the poor people of Naples, subsisting quite literally on their daily bread, added the new ingredient to their yeast dough, and created the first simple pizza, which by the seventeenth century had achieved a local notoriety among visitors who would go to the poor section to taste this peasant dish made by men called *pizzaioli*. By the next century pizza was known only as a curiosity outside of Naples (whose first pizzeria opened in 1830), and it was not until the nineteenth century that mozzarella cheese (usually made from buffalo milk) became a standard ingredient. Legend has it that Neapolitan *pizzaiolo* Raffaele Esposito of the Pizzeria di Pietro was the first to make a pie with tomato, basil, and mozzarella pizza (the colors of the Italian flag) to honor the visit of Queen Margherita, consort of King Umberto I, to Naples in 1889. This thereafter was called *pizza alla Margherita* and became very popular in that city.

But the pizza remained a local delicacy until the concept crossed the Atlantic in the memories of immigrants from Naples who settled in the cities along the Eastern Seaboard, especially in New York City. The ingredients these immigrants found in their new country differed from those in the old: In New York there was no buffalo-milk mozzarella, so cow's-milk mozzarella was used; oregano, a staple southern

Italian herb, was replaced in America by sweet marjoram; and American tomatoes, flour, even water, were different. Here the pizza evolved into a large, wheel-like pie, perhaps eighteen inches or more in diameter, reflecting the abundance of the new country.

These first American pizzas may have been made at home, but the baker's brick oven, preferably fueled with wood or coal, was (and still is) essential to making a true pizza, with its crispy crust, soft, bread-like middle, quickly seared topping, and bubbling cheese. The first record of a pizzeria in New York was Gennaro Lombardi's, opened in 1905 on Spring Street, but others quickly followed in the Italian communities around the city. Still, pizza and pizzerias and, later, "pizza parlors" were little known outside the large cities of the East until after World War II, when returning American GI's brought back a taste for the pizzas they had had in Naples along with the assumption that pizza, like spaghetti and meatballs, was a typical Italian dish, instead of a regional one.

Cookbooks of the early twentieth century that give recipes for Italian dishes do not list pizza, but by the 1950s they could be found in American collections as popular as Ford's *Treasury of Favorite Recipes from Famous Eating Places* (1954). In non-Italian communities in eastern states, pizza is often referred to as a "tomato pie," while the colloquial abbreviation "za" is particularly common among young people throughout the United States.

Pizza became very popular after World War II, especially as the fast-food business grew. Along with hamburger and hot-dog stands, the pizzeria became a fixture in many American cities and, later, part of commercial chains that expanded throughout the country in the 1960s and 1970s. The first frozen pizza was marketed by the Celentano Brothers in 1957. "Deep-dish pizza" or "Chicago-style pizza" created in 1943 by Ike Sewell and Ric Riccardo at the Pizzeria Uno in that city, is made with an inch-thick crust and cooked in a heavy skillet or pan. Chicago-style pizza, also called "pan pizza" and "thick crust pizza," now accounts for 22 percent of total pizza orders. The claim as to the invention of the tart-like "stuffed pizza," with fillings of cheese, meats, vegetables or other combinations of ingredients, in January of 1974 is made by Nancy's Pizzerias of Chicago, whose owners, Nancy and Rocco Palese, based the idea on an Italian Easter cake called *scarcidda*. "Sicilian-style" pizza has a thick crust and is usually cut into rectangles and has a thicker crust than standard, thin-crusted pizza, which is often called "Neapolitan-style." This standard pizza, cut into six or eight wedges, is usually made for more than one person and may be topped with ingredients as various as cheese and herbs, anchovies, onions,. mushrooms, sausage, pepperoni, small meatballs, mussels, and many others, in any combination. A "plain" or "cheese pie" is the standard mozzarella-and-tomato-sauce pizza. A "white pizza" is topped with mozzarella (sometimes with broccoli underneath) and not sauced. "Grilled pizzas" cooked right on an open grill were developed by Johanne Killeen and George Germon, owners of Al Forno restaurant in Providence, Rhode Island, in 1981 after seeing such a technique in Italy. "Designer" or "gourmet" pizzas were developed in California (they are sometimes called "California pizzas") with unusual and exotic toppings that might include goat's cheese, lamb sausage, smoked salmon, even caviar. The first commercial pizza-pie mix was produced in 1948 in Worcester, Massachusetts, by Frank A. Fiorello, who called it "Roman Pizza Mix."

Often pizza is ordered by the slice, which may be folded in half and held in the hand or cut up with a knife and fork on a plate. (In Italy pizza is usually served on a plate as an individual portion to be eaten with knife and fork.) By 1990 pizza was included in 13 percent of all restaurant orders, just behind hamburgers and cheeseburgers (17 percent). Americans' per capita consumption of pizza is 23 pounds, or about 10 pizzas per year. The most popular topping for pizza is pepperoni, followed by sausage and mushrooms.

The world's largest pizza was cooked by Lorenzo Amato, owner of Café di Lorenzo in Tallahassee, Florida, in 1991; it was ten thousand square feet.

PIZZA

Dissolve 1 pkg. yeast in ⅓ c. lukewarm water and let stand for 10 min. In a bowl mix 3 c. flour with 1 t. salt. Add the yeast mixture, blend, then add ⅔ c. lukewarm water to make a pliable, elastic dough. Form into a ball, cover with a clean cloth, and let rise until doubled in a warm place.

Meanwhile fry 2 cloves of garlic in 3 T. olive oil, add 1½ cans of Italian tomatoes, 1 t. salt, ¼ t. pepper, and ¼ t. oregano. Cook for about 20 min., until tomatoes have broken down and thickened.

Roll out the dough onto a flat pan, spread tomato sauce over the top, then add 1 lb. chopped mozzarella cheese. Bake at 450° for about 20 min., until crust is crisp and cheese is melted. To brown cheese, quickly place pizza under broiler flame.

pizza strip. A strip of thick dough topped with tomato sauce and Parmesan cheese. Pizza strips are usually bought in Italian bakeries in New England, especially Rhode Island, and are eaten hot or cold.

placebo bottle. Bartender's slang for liquor bottles filled with water and consumed by the bartender when someone insists on buying him a drink. The word "placebo" (from Latin) refers to the medical use of a pill or other substance given to a patient to satisfy a supposed need for medication. The slang term first saw print in 1991.

plantain. A variety of banana plant (*Musa paradisiaca*), especially popular among Latin-Americans. It is starchier and firmer than the banana enjoyed in North America, and must be ripened and then cooked.

plate lunch. In Hawaii, a lunch plate usually consisting of two scoops of rice, a macaroni and potato salad, and various meats or fish cooked in an Asian style, such as Korean barbecued ribs, *shoyu* chicken or beef *teriyaki*, as well as Filipino-style *adobo*. It is commonly sold from lunch wagons parked at the beach or near office buildings.

plum. Any of a variety of shrubs or trees in the genus *Prunus* bearing a smooth-skinned red, yellow, or purple fruit with a soft, pulpy flesh. The word is from Old English *plume*, ultimately from Latin *prunum*. The word in Latin once probably referred specifically to the fruit, but later many varieties in the genus were differentiated by various names, of which "plum" was one. There are hundreds of varieties of plum today, but those of culinary interest in the United States include the "European plum" (*P. domestica*), brought to America in Colonial times; the "native American plum" (*P. americana*); the "damson" (*P. damascena*), originally imported by the Romans from Damascus about the first century A.D.; and the "Japanese" (*P. salicina* or *triflora*), brought to the United States in 1870. Other varieties introduced from other countries include the "sloe" or "blackthorn" (*P. spinosa*), the "bullace" (*P. instituta*), the "gage" (*P. italica*), and the "cherry" (*P. cerasifera*). Other main species native to North America include the "Canada" (*P. nigra*), the "Chickasaw" (*P. anqustifolia*), the "Alleghany" or "American sloe" (*P. alleghaniensis*), and the "beach plum" (*P. maritima*), this last plum found in New England and most often made into jams and jellies.

Principal hybrids include the "Italian Prune," "Stanley," "Burbank," "Underwood," "Monitor," and many others.

Plums are usually eaten fresh. The traditional Anglo-American plum pudding (for recipe, see PUD-DING) contains no plums.

A "prune" is a plum that has been dried either in the sun or by artificial heat. The word "prune" comes from the Greek *proumnon,* which became in Middle English *prouynen.*

po'boy. Also "poor boy." A sandwich made from French bread loaves split in half and filled with a variety of ingredients like ham, beef, cheese, oysters, tomatoes, and gravy. Similar to a HERO, they are a specialty of New Orleans, where they were originally called "push" sandwiches because the meat was pushed along the length of bread to save the best part for last. The "po'boy" was created in the 1920s by Benny and Clovis Martin, owners of Martin Brothers Grocery, who served the sandwich to striking streetcar workers free of charge (other sources say for fifteen cents) until the strike ended. They used up more than a thousand loaves of bread in one day. Another story says that the term is related to the French for a gratuity, *pourboire.* Nonetheless, the term "poor boy" for a sandwich goes back to 1875. An "oyster loaf" (1893) is a form of po'boy made with oysters.

pocket soup. Also, "cake soup." A soup that was boiled down into a jellylike mass that could be put in a pouch and later reconstituted with hot water. A recipe in the *Lady's Companion* of 1753 calls for boiling a leg of veal until the liquid in the pot thickens to a jellied stage when cooled. This is strained and poured into cups, which are then placed in a pan of boiling water until jellied. The gel is then cooled and turned onto a piece of "new flannel," in order to absorb the moisture. The result was a very concentrated, strong jelly that was turned back into soup by the addition of hot water and salt.

poi. A pasty preparation of taro, breadfruit, sweet potato, or banana (1815). This staple of the Hawaiian diet, often referred to as the "staff of life" there, serves as the first solid food for infants and is recommended for everything from longevity to bee bites.

Today most poi is made with taro root, commercially produced and packaged in cellophane bags. In Hawaii's early days taro was washed and cooked (cooked taro was called *'aipa'a),* then peeled, scraped, and pounded laboriously into a paste by the men of

the tribe, who sat with taro on one side and water on the other, mashing the root into a firm mass called *pa'i'ai.* Poi was made by adding water to this mass and by kneading, usually followed by a period of a few days' fermentation, which imparted a sour taste to the paste.

Before World War II Hawaiians could purchase poi in white cotton bags, which had to be strained free of its fiber in a "poi strainer" hung on a clothesline. Today packaged poi has a more pliable texture, and it is scraped in a bowl with some water to achieve a consistency referred to as a thin "one-finger poi," a thicker "two-finger poi," or a still thicker "three-finger poi." As one can tell by these names, poi is eaten by dipping one's fingers into the paste and is served as a condiment with main dishes of meat or fish or as a breakfast food or dip for CANAPÉS. The longer the fermentation of the poi—"one-day," "two-day," and "three-day" poi—the more sour it becomes.

Breadfruit poi is called *poi 'ulu;* sweet-potato poi, *poi 'uala;* and banana poi, *poi mai'a.*

poke. A Hawaiian dish of diced fish marinated in various sauces. Hawaiian-style poke comes with chopped seaweed, "Korean-style" with chili, and "onion-style" with Maui onions.

"Poke" is also short for the salad herb "pokeweed" (*Phytolacca americana*), which dates in print to 1745, from the Algonquian *puccoon.* It is a wild field green and rarely planted. Some southerners even make wine from it.

"Pokeberries" are berries from the pokeweed.

poki. A Hawaiian dish made with ogo seaweed, Maui onions, scallions, and raw fish.

Polish sandwich. A sandwich of Polish-style sausage (such as KIELBASA) in a soft roll. It is particularly popular in and around Baltimore, Maryland.

pollock (*Pollachius virens*). Also, "Boston bluefish." A very widespread North Atlantic fish of the cod family that ranges from the North Atlantic south to Chesapeake Bay. The name is from the Scottish, *podlok.* The "walleye pollock" (*Theragra chalcogramma*), also called "Alaska pollock," ranges from Japan to central California, with 2.5 billion pounds landed in 1997, which made up 26 percent of all commercial landings in the U.S. "Walleye" refers to its whitish-gray eyes. This variety is usually sold salted rather than fresh and is the predominant fish used in the making of SURIMI.

Polynesian food. In American restaurants this term refers not to any specific foods or dishes of Polynesia but to a number of dishes and cocktails concocted to sound and taste as if they were of Polynesian origins. Many of the cocktails, like the ZOMBIE and the "vicious virgin" were created at a restaurant called Don the Beachcomber in Los Angeles, while many others, like the MAI TAI and the "Samoan Fog Cutter," were created by "Trader" Victor Bergeron, who began the Trader Vic's chain in San Francisco in 1937, where he used Pacific decor to enhance an atmosphere he said made people think of beaches and "moonlight and pretty girls without any clothes on." Bergeron based his Polynesian concoctions on food he had himself eaten in the South Pacific. Some of those items he made popular included BONGO BONGO SOUP, PU PU platters, barbecued spareribs, and "Indonesian lamb roast." Many such dishes have also become standards of Chinese-American restaurants, as have Polynesian cocktails, which are commonly served in ceramic mugs and glasses molded into fanciful shapes like skulls, rum kegs, and pineapples, and garnished with chunks of pineapple, maraschino cherries, and small paper umbrellas.

polysorbate 60. An emulsifier used in baked goods and other processed desserts to prevent spoilage. It also prevents oil and water from separating.

pomegranate (*Punica granatum*). Also, "Chinese apple." A tree native to Asia bearing a red tough-skinned fruit containing many seeds and a pulpy, sour-sweet flesh. The name derives from the Old French *pome* ("apple") plus *grenate* ("many-seeded").

The fruit has been highly esteemed ever since biblical times, when its many seeds symbolized fertility to the Jews. The pomegranate was brought to America by the Spanish and was quickly dispersed into the wild. It was found growing in Frederica, Georgia, in 1773 and earlier in California. Today California is the only state with significant production (160,000 trees bearing about 17 million pounds annually), with 80 percent of the crop from the "Wonderful" variety; the rest are "Granada," "Early Foothill" and "Early Wonderful."

pomfret. Any of various fish of the family Bramidae (1720), especially the Pacific "bigscale" or "sickle pomfret" (*Taractichthys steindachneri*), known in Hawaii as "monchong."

pommes de terre soufflées. Also, *pommes souf-flées* or "puffed potatoes." Potatoes that are sliced thin and deep-fried twice so as to give them a puffy, crisp texture. The term is French, and there are two stories as to the dish's origins.

Larousse Gastronomique attributes the dish to an unnamed chef at a restaurant in Saint-Germain-en-Laye near Paris, where in 1837 a new railway was being inaugurated. While waiting for the train to arrive for the meal ordered by the railway company, the chef prepared some fried potatoes, only to remove them from the hot oil on the news that the train was having difficulty getting up the hill. When the party finally arrived, the chef put the now-cold potatoes back into the hot oil and to his delight watched them puff up. "The famous analytical chemist Chevreul," *Larousse* explains, "who was informed of this phenomenon, studied it experimentally and established the conditions under which it occurred and could be reproduced at will."

But the man who brought these potatoes to America, Antoine Alciatore, owner of Antoine's Restaurant in New Orleans, told of how he came by the recipe from the man who created it, Chef Collinet, under whom Alciatore apprenticed at the Hôtel de Noailles in Marseilles. Collinet had waited for the train at Saint-German-en-Laye and for the arrival of King Louis-Philippe (1773–1850). Having cooked Louis's favorite potatoes, Collinet discovered that the king had been taken off the train as a precautionary measure and put on a carriage that would arrive late. When the king finally did arrive, the chef fried the cold potatoes again and produced the puffy crisps that became instantly popular.

POMMES DE TERRE SOUFFLÉES

Wash and peel 2 lb. potatoes, cut lengthwise into 1¼-in. slices about ⅛-in. thick. Soak in cold water, drain, and dry. Place a layer of potatoes in oil heated to 275°, moving the slices around until they begin to puff up. Remove potatoes, drain, and let cool for a few minutes. Replace the potatoes in 400° oil until puffed up and crispy. Remove, drain, salt, and serve.

---

pompano (*Trachinotus carolinus* and *Alectis crinitus*). A saltwater fish of the jack family (Carangidae). The pompano is esteemed as one of the favorite catches of the Gulf Coast and Florida, although it may be found as far north as Massachusetts. Most are taken at about four to five pounds.

The African pompano (*Alectis*) is also called the "threadfin" or "threadfish," but the "Florida pompano," sometimes called the "Irish pompano," is the more easily found at market. A similar fish, the "permit" (*T. falcatus*), which may run up to fifty pounds, is not a pompano and is rarely treated with the same culinary respect. The poppy fish (*Palometa simillima*) is sometimes called the "California pompano."

The name comes from the Spanish *pámpano*, and has been used at least since 1770. Mark Twain called the fish "delicious as the less criminal forms of sin." In New Orleans the fish is sometimes called "sole."

The most notable way to prepare the fish is as "pompano en papillote," created by Jules Alciatore, owner of Antoine's Restaurant in New Orleans, to honor Brazilian balloonist Alberto Santos-Dumont (1873–1932). According to Deirdre Stanforth in *The New Orleans Restaurant Cookbook* (1967), the dish was a version of one Alciatore's father, Antoine, had made in honor of the inventors of the balloon, Joseph-Michel (1740–1810) and Jacques-Étienne Montgolfier (1745–99), two brothers who inflated a linen bag with hot air in 1783. This dish was called "Pompano Montgolfier." The later dish became a specialty of Antoine's and, soon afterward, of other restaurants in New Orleans and America. Movie director Cecil B. DeMille enjoyed the dish so much while filming *The Pirate's Lady* in New Orleans in 1937 that he had it written into the script, even though the story took place long before Antoine's opened in 1840.

POMPANO EN PAPILLOTE

In 3 T. butter sauté 1 c. scallions until wilted, add 1 c. raw, peeled shrimp, and 1 c. white wine and bring to boil. Mix in 1 c. crabmeat and 2 c. fish velouté sauce, salt and pepper, and a dash of cayenne. Simmer for 10 min. and allow to cool. Poach 6 pompano fillets with water to cover, 1 sliced onion, 2 t. salt, 5 whole peppercorns, 1½ c. wine, 2 bay leaves, and the juice of 1 lemon. Cut 6 heart-shaped pieces of white parchment paper about 10 in. high and 14 in. wide. Spoon some of sauce into center of one half of a paper heart, top with a fillet, fold over the other half of the paper, and seal edges. Place on greased baking pan, bake for 15 min. at 400°, until paper begins to brown. Before serving, cut open top of paper. Serves 6.

Pompey's head. A roll of ground meat with a sauce of tomatoes and green pepper. In *The White House Cookbook* (1964) the dish is described as having been "popular before automatic ovens were invented because it could cook unattended for hours." The

name apparently refers to the broad head of Roman statesman and general Gnaeus Pompeius Magnus, called "Pompey the Great" (106–48 B.C.).

POMPEY'S HEAD

Mix 1 lb. sausage meat with 1 lb. ground beef, season with salt and pepper, and form into a roll. Dust with flour and brown in a 450° oven. Add 2 c. chopped tomatoes, 1 c. chopped celery, 1 T. chopped onion, ½ green pepper to pan, and bake, covered, for 1½ hr. at 350° basting occasionally. Serve with vegetables poured over it.

---

pony. A short bar glass shaped like a small sherry or brandy glass that is often used for cordials or for measuring one ounce of liquid. The term may also refer simply to a small drink of straight liquor, a meaning that dates back at least to 1849.

poor-man dishes. A very vague term for a wide variety of stews, pies, soups, desserts, and other foods, possibly because they are made with simple, inexpensive ingredients.

popcorn. Also, "popped corn." Corn kernels heated in oil until they burst open into white, fluffy textured balls.

Varieties of popping corn were known to Native Americans in both North and South America, with evidence of its cultivation dating back at least eighty thousand years. Native Americans believed that in the corn lived an angry demon who exploded when exposed to heat.

Popcorn was brought to the first Thanksgiving in 1621 by Chief Massasoit's brother, Quadequina. At first called by the early colonists "popped corn," "parching corn," or "rice corn," it became commonly known after 1820 as "popcorn," and was a popular treat for Americans, who not only ate it as a snack but strung it on Christmas trees. By the 1870s people were adding molasses to make crunchy "popcorn balls," and in 1896 the firm of F. W. Rueckheim and Brother of Chicago came up with a combination of popcorn, molasses, and peanuts that they called "Cracker Jack" (the confection had been sold without that name at Chicago's 1893 Columbian Exposition), which came from a contemporary slang term for anything considered excellent. Before long Cracker Jack was a staple food item at baseball games throughout America, and the cry "Getcha' peanuts, popcorn, and Cracker Jack'" is still heard at every circus, sporting event, and carnival in the land. Since 1912 Cracker Jack has placed a little "prize" in every box of their confection. In 1914 C. H. Smith of Sioux City, Iowa, developed a shelled popcorn whose kernels were guaranteed to pop every time. Before that, only about two thirds of the kernels would pop in most cases.

Popcorn machines, patented by C. Cretors & Company of Chicago, which opened in 1885, were soon fixtures on street corners and, particularly, in movie theaters, where popcorn became an absolute requisite for an enjoyable evening. By 1918 the Butter-Kist popcorn machine, which coated the popcorn with melted butter, was also common. In the 1920s Purdue University pioneered research into popcorn hybridization in order to improve taste and consistency of popping, and several popcorn varieties were specialty developed by Orville Redenbacher as of 1941. In 1945 James V. Blevins of the Blevins Popcorn Company in Nashville, Tennessee, developed a very fluffy, high volume popcorn that proved highly successful in movie theaters, which he later introduced to baseball stadiums in Japan.

Today popcorn is often made at home with nothing more than corn kernels and a pot, though electric popcorn poppers and cellophane packages of popcorn are sold too. Americans eat about 16.5 billion quarts of popcorn per year, i.e., 65 quarts per person. Seventy percent is eaten at home, with 90 percent of that made from unpopped corn.

pope's nose. Also, "parson's nose." The rump of a cooked fowl (1740). The phrase is a demeaning term for both parts of the anatomy, for it was originally meant as a slur against Catholics during the reign of James II of England, although "parson's nose" seems to predate it. In America "parson's nose" (called by New England poet Henry Wadsworth Longfellow an "epicurean morsel") was the more common slang term.

pop-out. A prepackaged frozen meal sold to many commercial airlines for use on their flights. The food pops out of the package and is then arranged on a tray to be heated aboard the aircraft.

popover. A light, hollow muffin made from an egg batter similar to that used in making YORKSHIRE PUDDING. The name comes from the fact that the batter rises and swells over the muffin tin while baking. The first appearance of the word in print was in 1875.

In *American Food* (1974), Evan Jones writes: "Settlers from Maine who founded Portland, Oregon, americanized the pudding from Yorkshire by cooking the batter in custard cups lubricated with drippings from the roasting beef (or sometimes pork); another modification was the use of garlic, and, frequently, herbs. The result is called Portland popover pudding, individual balloons of crusty meat-flavored pastry."

Most popovers, however, are not flavored but merely set in buttered muffin tins. They are served at breakfast or with meats at lunch and dinner.

POPOVER

Combine 1 c. sifted flour and ¼ t. salt. Beat until very smooth 2 eggs and 1 c. milk, then blend well with flour. Pour into buttered muffin tins and bake in 450° oven for about 20 min. Reduce heat to 350°, bake 10–15 min. until puffy and brown.

pop wine. A term of recent years used to describe a sweet, fruit-flavored wine that is usually quite inexpensive.

porgy. Any of a variety of marine fishes of the family Sparidae. Porgies are small-mouthed, have strong teeth, and inhabit sandy bottoms both inshore and offshore. The name, according to the *American Heritage Dictionary*, derives from the Spanish *pargo*, which goes back to the Greek *phágros*, "sea bream," by which the porgy is known outside the United States. A. J. McClane, however, in his *Encyclopedia of Fish Cookery* (1977), asserts that the name is "strictly American, derived from the Narraganset Indian word *mishcuppauog. Pauog* meant fertilizer, for which the fish was widely used." But the first instances of the word in English print were in 1671, and in Sir Hans Sloane's 1725 book, *A Voyage to the Islands Madera, Barbados, Nieves, S. Christophers, and Jamaica, with the Natural History . . . of the Last.* Since the Narragansets were a tribe of North America, and specifically of what is now Rhode Island, the appearance of the word in a text on the Caribbean throws McClane's contention into doubt. The fish has always been enjoyed in the South, with more than 20 million pounds marketed annually along the Atlantic coast, and in the nineteenth century they were hawked on the streets of southern cities like Charleston, South Carolina, the setting for the American opera *Porgy and Bess* (1935), about a crippled black man named Porgy.

The main species of culinary interest in the United States include the "scup" (*Stenotomus chrysops*), whose name derives from the Narraganset word *mishcùp;*

"jolthead porgy" (*Calamus bajonado*); "Pacific porgy" (*C. brachysomus*); and "sheepshead" (*Archosargus probatocephalus*).

pork. The edible flesh of a pig or hog. The word derives from the Latin *porcus*.

Pork is the most widely eaten meat in the world, and from the time the first settlers came to the New World, it was the predominant meat in the American diet. Pigs have been domesticated since the Stone Age, and wild pigs, called "peccaries" or "javelinas" (*Tayassu tajacu* or *T. peccari*), may have crossed the Bering Strait from Russia to disperse throughout North and South America.

Hernando Cortés (1485–1547) found pigs in Mexico, but the first domesticated pigs were a herd of thirteen brought from Spain to Tampa, Florida, in 1539 by Hernando de Soto (circa 1500–42), and from these all North American domesticated pigs are descended. Some of these Spanish pigs escaped into the forests and turned wild. They are called RAZOR-BACKS and are not related to the peccaries.

English, French, and all other Colonists found pigs easy to raise, for they foraged on their own and lived off scraps. By 1640 Massachusetts had already built a small salt-pork trade. Salting and smoking was the standard method of treating a butchered hog, and salt pork became the dominant meat in the in Colonial diet; it was used for its oil and its meat as bacon, in stews, as flavoring, in pies, roasted, boiled, barbecued, and in all manner of preparations. The HAMS of Virginia became famous for their succulent flavor, especially those of Smithfield, where the pigs forage in the peanut fields.

Southerners ate every part of the hog, saving some pieces for some special dish like RED BEANS AND RICE, a Louisiana delicacy traditionally made on Monday with the ham bone left over from Sunday's dinner. Families had pork barrels in their cellars, and the term "pork-barrel legislation" came to mean laws passed by a region's congressman designed specifically to help his local constituency. To be living "high on the hog" meant that one was eating the best meat on the pig, while others had to subsist on belly BACON meat.

Thomas Jefferson, with his usual curiosity, experimented with new breeds by crossing Virginia hogs with Calcutta varieties, soon cornering the local market and overcharging his neighbors, who began calling him the "hog governor" and in defiance hung his Monticello fence with pig entrails.

By the 1830s the streets of major cities were criss-crossed with hog tracks, for they were allowed to feed on the garbage, and English traveler Francis Marryat noted of a Fourth of July in New York that the three-mile-long stretch of Broadway was lined on both sides of the street with booths selling roast pig. During the same era Cincinnati became the major pork-packing center, earning its nickname "Porkopolis." Pork itself was sometimes called in slang "Cincinnati olive."

The demand for pork increased during the Civil War, when hog production doubled to provide meat for the Union troops while soldiers of the Confederacy starved for lack of it. After the war a new industry arose in meat-packing, led by Gustavus Franklin Swift and Philip Danforth Armour, who independently set up companies in Chicago in 1875. Chicago soon became the center of the industry for the entire United States, which was served with pork in abundance, thanks to the newly developed refrigerated railroad cars. (Long into the present century "Chicago" was a slang term for pork.) Still, those pioneers who set out for California after the Civil War always packed a full load of salt pork, which they usually cursed for its monotonous appearance in their diet as they crossed the Great Plains.

The introduction of pigs (many of which ran wild) to Hawaii made this one of the favorite meats of the populace, especially pit-roasted or barbecued pork and "kalua pig," which is roasted in ti leaves.

With the increase in available beef in the late nineteenth century, pork began to recede in popularity, tied as it was to a coarse and boring diet of the poor. By the twentieth century beef began to compete favorably in price and was preferred at the table, so that Americans ate less and less pork as the decades wore on. Today, though pork consumption is again on the rise, 40 percent of Americans eat little or no pork at all, but Americans consume about 47.8 pounds per person per year, compared with 66.4 pounds of beef.

In order to counter American dietary fears about excessive fat, the pork industry now produces hogs 50 percent leaner than they were in the 1950s.

Iowa leads the U.S. in pork production, followed by North Carolina, Minnesota, Illinois and Indiana.

Today pork is served in a wide variety of ways, as roast pork or ham, as spareribs, chopped up in a southern-style BARBECUE, in sausages, in stews, as chops, and in a wide range of ethnic foods. Roast suckling pig in Louisiana is called "cochon de lait," from the French for suckling pig. The innards, especially the intestines, called CHITTERLINGS, are an important part of SOUL FOOD. The Department of

Agriculture grades pork No. 1, No. 2, and No. 3. The various cuts of pork are listed below:

primal Boston (or shoulder) butt. This section comprises the Boston butt and the picnic ham.

primal leg. From this section is cut the meat to make fresh ham—that is, pork roasted as is—and the ham that is to be cured and smoked, which is cut into the butt end and shank end.

primal loin. This cut runs along the pig's back and is the preferred meat. It includes the sections from which come Canadian bacon and the best spareribs, as well as the tenderloin, sirloin, center loin, blade (or rib) loin, and the finest chops. The chops from this section are often called "country style."

primal picnic shoulder. A cut from the foreleg that is usually sold cured and smoked, though some of the meat is sold as an arm roast.

primal side pork. Also called "pork belly." This section provides bacon.

primal spareribs. These lie under the primal side pork. A slab of between two and five pounds is cut into spareribs.

For information on HAM, see main entry.

port. A fortified wine usually made in America with ZINFANDEL and other grape varieties. The name comes from the city of Oporto, Portugal, where the original port was made. In the United States Portuguese ports are labeled "Porto" to distinguish them from American bottlings. Port wines began to be fortified with brandy in the eighteenth century, after which their distribution became dominated by the British shipping trade.

American ports generally contain between 18 and 20 percent alcohol and 5 to 10 percent residual sugar. Most are produced in California, and some, since the 1970s, are marketed as vintage ports.

Port is traditionally served with the cheese course or after dinner, although some light ports are enjoyed as apéritifs.

porterhouse. Also, "porterhouse steak." A beefsteak cut from the thick end of the short loin, containing a T-bone and part of the tenderloin. The name derives from the taverns or alehouses of the eighteenth cen-

tury that were called "porterhouses" (because porters in London's Covent Garden market drank ale in such places). The steak itself was popularized around 1814 by a New York City porterhouse keeper named Martin Morrison. It soon became the most popular form and cut of steak in America.

Portuguese sweet bread. A white loaf of bread sweetened with sugar and sometimes baked with slices of sausage. The Portuguese, who call it *pao doce*, brought it to American communities on the East Coast, where it is called *massa suvada*, as well as to the Hawaiian Islands in the nineteenth century.

PORTUGUESE SWEET BREAD

Combine ⅓ c. sugar, I t. salt, 2 pkgs. yeast, and I c. flour. In saucepan over very low heat combine ¼ c. butter in ⅔ c. milk until warm, then gradually beat into flour mixture, increasing speed of mixer. Beat in 6 eggs and I½ c. more flour to make a thick batter, then stir in about 2½ c. more flour to make a soft dough. Turn onto floured surface and knead until elastic, about 10 min., using more flour as necessary. Shape into ball, turn into greased bowl, cover, and let double. Punch down dough, cut in half, shape into 2 loaves, and place on buttered cookie sheet. Let double again, brush tops with milk, and bake 35 min. at 350°. Cool.

Porty Reek long-lick. A New England sailor's slang term for molasses. Porty Reek refers to Puerto Rico, where sugar was produced. Long-lick probably referred to its dense, viscous texture and was also used by westerners. Long-tailed sugar was a variant of the phrase.

posset. A drink of sweetened hot milk, wine, or ale. The word is from Middle English *poshet* or *possot*. It was a popular drink in the fifteenth century and continued to be well into the nineteenth, though it is rarely seen today. Sometimes posset contains egg, in which case it is called an "egg posset."

potato (*Solanum tuberosum*). A native South American plant having a rough-skinned, starchy tuber that is widely propagated and eaten in a great variety of ways as a vegetable. The word comes from the Spanish *patata,* which derives from the Taino word *batata,* but this is only the beginning of the many confusions surrounding the potato and its history. When Christopher Columbus explored the

West Indies, he found a tuber, which is now called the SWEET POTATO (*Ipomoea batatas*), called in the Taino language *batata*. This tuber was immediately transported back to Spain and propagated there. The confusion arose when John Gerard's *Herball* in 1597 listed the white potato as a North American plant, and for a good while afterward it was assumed that there were white potatoes in North America. This, however, was not the case. The white potato is native to South America and was cultivated perhaps five thousand years ago in Peru. It was this plant that the Spanish found in 1537 cultivated by the Incas, who called it *papa* (the Quecha language has more than a thousand names for the potato), in the Andean village of Sorocota and which the conquistadores believed was a form of truffle thought to be an aphrodisiac that might cause both syphilis and leprosy. Potatoes were very important to the Indian diet, and the Incas even measured time by how long it took to cook potatoes.

Potatoes were sent back to Spain from Ecuador in the 1530s, may have reached France about 1540, and were mentioned in print in 1553 by Pedro de Cieza León in his *Crónica del Perú*.

Legend has it that Sir Walter Raleigh's men brought the white potato back from Virginia in 1586, but there is no evidence of the white potato's existence in North America at that time. Waverley Root in *Food* (1980) suggests a plausible explanation of the legend by noting that Sir Francis Drake picked up Raleigh's disgruntled colonists in 1586 on his way back from Cartagena, Colombia, from where he had taken some white potatoes. These were of considerable interest to Thomas Hariot, one of Raleigh's men, and it was Hariot who gave the tubers to John Gerard, who thereupon planted them in his own garden and ten years later reported that this white potato had come from Virginia.

Whatever happened in Virginia and England, Raleigh has been credited with planting the first white potatoes in Ireland soon afterward, where they were grown to prevent famine, as they were in Germany and elsewhere.

The white potato finally entered North America at least as early as the middle of the 17th century, for the first printed reference to its being planted is 1685, clearly distinguished from the sweet potato. By 1762 it was a field crop in Salem, Massachusetts, and by 1770 it was grown for commercial sale back in England. It was not even eaten in Spain until the middle of the eighteenth century. By then Americans had learned to distinguish the white potato from the

orange tuber that originally took its name. The latter variety was by the 1740s called the "sweet potato."

Still, the white potato had few admirers well into the nineteenth century. Although praised by Shakespeare's Falstaff and Byron's Don Juan as an aphrodisiac, the tuber was considered poisonous and a cause of everything from leprosy to birth defects. In Sicily some believed you could cause someone's untimely death merely by writing the person's name on a paper pinned to a potato. The potato was considered fit only for the poor and largely associated with the Irish, who in their own country had staved off starvation with the potato in 1740 and continued to live on it almost to the exclusion of every other food. In fact, the potato was so closely associated with the Irish that the slang term for the tuber became the same as the slur word for an Irishman—"mickey." When the Irish Potato Famine hit in 1845, owing to a failure of the crop, the only solution for the poor was to emigrate to America, which more than a million did in the decades to follow.

By the mid-nineteenth century the potato was no longer feared for its poisonous properties, having been widely promoted by French agriculturist Antoine-Augustin Parmentier as of the 1770s, and cookbooks began carrying a few recipes for potatoes as vegetables. Even fried potatoes were called by Sarah J. Hale, in the 1857 *Mrs. Hale's New Cook Book*, "an admirable way of dressing potatoes," and fried potato slices, called SARATOGA CHIPS, had become popular in that same decade. FRENCH-FRIED POTATOES came along near the end of the century, by which time Americans consumed great quantities of the tuber—two hundred pounds per person per year by 1900. Cookbooks listed scores of ways to prepare them—boiled, baked in their skins, cooked in the fat of a roast beef, and sliced up to be baked in cream, called "scalloped potatoes." "Mashed potatoes" (first in print in 1896) are boiled and mashed, usually with butter and milk. In large eastern cities street vendors would roast potatoes over coals, and children would cook them on a stick over an open fire. They were boiled and made part of hot or cold "German POTATO SALAD," and the idea of Swiss *roesti* became American or "hash browns" or "hashed browns"—potatoes that are shredded or chopped and cooked with butter and bacon and onion in a skillet. Hash browns go by several other names, including "haystack potatoes" in the Midwest. "Homefried potatoes" (in restaurants called "house fried" or "cottage fried") are similar—first boiled, then chopped or sliced and cooked in fat in a skillet. "Potato skins" are a dish of baked potatoes whose insides have been scooped out, mixed with other ingredients like butter, cheese, and seasonings, and replaced in the skins and heated through, supposedly first sold by the Prime Rib restaurant in Baltimore, Maryland, about 1965. Frozen potato skins were first marketed in 1978 by Frederic D. Starret, Jr., of the Penobscot Frozen Food Company in Belfast, Maine.

During World War II dehydrated potatoes became a staple part of the serviceman's diet. Later these were a commercial success in the grocery. After the war frozen french-fried potatoes supplanted freshly made french fries in most homes and restaurants, especially at FAST-FOOD stands, where thinly cut shoestring potatoes are generally sold. Today Americans eat 46 pounds of potatoes per person, but only about one third that amount is made fresh. Potatoes are served in some form at 60 percent of the main meals of the day.

Most potatoes are harvested from September to November and then stored, although potatoes harvested and shipped directly to the market are called "early" or "new" potatoes.

The main varieties produced in the United States may be broken into four groups: "Round White," which includes the "Kennebec" (usually used for potato chips or for baking and boiling), "Katahdin" (used mostly for boiling and canning), "Superior," "Nor-chip," "Irish Cobbler," "Monona," "Sebago," "Ontario," and "Chippewa"; the "Russet" (mostly long), which includes the "Russet Burbank" and the "Norgold Russet"; the "Round Red Group," which includes the "Norland," "Red Pontiac," "Red La Soda," "La Rouge," and "Red McClure"; and the "Long White Group," mainly the "White Rose." The buttery-tasting "Yukon gold" variety, first marketed in America by Michigan farmer Jim Huston as of 1996, became very popular, especially in restaurants.

The most important potato-producing states include Idaho, Washington, Maine, California, North Dakota, Oregon, Minnesota, Wisconsin, Michigan, Colorado, and New York. Despite its popularity, the so-called "Idaho" potato is actually a Russet Burbank that is grown in Idaho.

potato salad. A cold or hot side dish made with potatoes, mayonnaise, and seasonings. It became very popular in the second half of the nineteenth century and is a staple of both home and food-store kitchens. Hot potato salad, usually made with bacon, onion, and vinegar dressing, was associated with German immigrants and therefore often called "German potato salad."

COLD POTATO SALAD

In a bowl stir together ½ c. mayonnaise, 2 T. milk, ½ t. salt, ¼ t. pepper, 2 ½ c. cooked cubed potatoes, and ½ c. chopped celery and mix thoroughly. Chill for 2 hr. Makes 3 c.

HOT POTATO SALAD

Cook 6 potatoes in salted boiling water, peel, and slice. In a large skillet sauté 4 strips bacon, ¼ c. chopped celery, and ⅓ c. chopped onion until browned. In a saucepan heat to boiling ¼ c. chicken stock, ½ c. vinegar, ⅓ t. sugar, salt and pepper, and ⅛ t. sweet paprika. Pour into skillet, add potatoes, and stir thoroughly. Cook until well blended and slightly thickened. Serve with chopped parsley. Serves 6.

---

potato snow. Described by Eliza Leslie in *Directions for Cookery* (1837) as potatoes that have been boiled, thoroughly dried, then pushed through a sieve but afterward not mixed in any way.

poticia. A jelly and walnut-filled coffee cake popular in Minnesota. The confection derives from Yugoslavian and Slovenian immigrants. "It could not be a Slovenian wedding without poticia (pronounced po-TEET-tsa) and cabbage rolls," wrote Marcia Adams in *Heartland* (1991).

potlikker. Southerners, particularly African-Americans, call the liquid left over from a meal of greens, field pea, pork, or other items "potlikker." Often served on its own as a vitamin-rich broth, potlikker was a staple among the field hands of the South and is now an essential ingredient of modern SOUL FOOD.

A passion for potlikker (the term "pot liquor" was first in print in 1744) is a requisite for political office in the South, for, as Marjorie Kinnan Rawlings observed, "a man addicted to the combination [of potlikker and corn bread could] claim himself a man of the people." Governor Huey Long of Louisiana, in an all-night filibuster on the subject of authentically made potlikker, once claimed that fried corn pone must be dunked into the broth for the best results, although opponents countered that the corn pone should be crumbled into the potlikker. Franklin D. Roosevelt jokingly suggested that the issue be referred to the Platform Committee at the 1932 Democratic National Convention.

As for the spelling of the word, Lieutenant Governor Zell Miller of Georgia corrected a 1982 article in *The New York Times* with the following blast:

I always thought The New York Times *knew everything, but obviously your editor knows as little about spelling as he or she does about Appalachian cooking and soul food. Only a culinarily-illiterate damnyankee (one word) who can't tell the difference between beans and greens would call the liquid left in the pot after cooking greens "pot liquor" (two words) instead of "potlikker" (one word) as yours did. And don't cite Webster as a defense because he didn't know any better either.*

potluck. A meal composed of whatever is available or a meal (also called a "carry-in" or "covered dish meal") whereby different people bring different dishes to a social gathering. In the West "potluck" meant food brought by a cowboy guest to put in the communal pot. The term dates in print to 1585.

potpie. Also, "pot pie." A crusted pie made with poultry or meat and, usually, chopped vegetables. The term, which first appeared in American print in 1785, probably refers to the deep pie pans or pots used to bake the pies in, and it has remained primarily an Americanism. The most popular pot pies have been chicken, beef, and pork. The first frozen pot pie was made with chicken in 1951 by the C. A. Swanson company.

CHICKEN POT PIE

In a kettle cook 1 quartered chicken in 2 c. chicken broth for 30 min. Cool, reserve broth. In another pot cook 1 doz. small onions in 1 c. chicken broth for 10 min., add 4 chopped carrots, 1 c. peas, and ½ c. chopped celery. Cook 20 min., then remove from heat. In a saucepan make a roux of 6 T. butter with 6 T. flour, stirring about 1 min. Stir in reserved chicken broth, season with salt and pepper, cook about 7–10 min., until thickened, and remove from heat. Remove chicken meat from bones, place in vegetable mixture, and blend in roux. Pour into pastry-lined deep-dish pan, cover with top crust, slit air vents for steam to escape, and bake 10 min. at 450° then lower heat to 350° and cook another 20 min., until crust is golden brown.

---

pot roast. A meat that is browned and cooked with vegetables and gravy in a deep pot or saucepan, usually covered. The term dates in print to 1881. Pot roast was once an appetizing way to cook beef from beasts that had been work animals rather than food animals or other inferior cuts of meat. Today, the availability of good beef makes pot roast a delicious hearty dish, though lesser cuts of meat are still used for the cooking. Beef brisket, bottom and top round, and chuck are the usual choices.

poultry. Defined by the United States Department of Agriculture as "all domesticated birds (chickens, turkeys, ducks, geese, guineas)."

poultry by-product. Any edible part of a domesticated bird other than the sex glands and POULTRY MEAT.

poultry food product. Also called "poultry product." Any food suitable for human consumption made from any domesticated bird and containing more than 2 percent poultry meat.

poultry meat. The white and dark meat portions of deboned poultry, excluding fat, skin, and other edible poultry parts.

pound cake. A plain white-cake loaf whose name derives from the traditional weight of the ingredients—one pound of flour, one pound of butter, one pound of sugar, and one pound of eggs—although these measurements are generally not followed in most modern recipes. Its first printed mention was in 1740 according to *Webster's Ninth,* and it has remained a popular and simple cake to make to this day.

POUND CAKE

Cream ½ c. butter with 1 c. sugar until light and fluffy. Add 1¾ c. flour, 3 egg yolks, a pinch of salt, and 1 t. vanilla extract. Pour into loaf pan and bake at 350° for about 45 min.

---

pousse-café. A drink made by pouring successive layers of cordials on top of one another, creating a rainbow effect of color. The term is French, meaning "push down the coffee," and in France a pousse-café is merely a cordial, brandy, or other digestive alcohol. In America, however, it is a bibulous tour de force, its success depending upon the specific densities of the cordials, with the heaviest going on the bottom and the lighter ones toward the top. A tall, slender cordial glass (or special pousse-café glass) is needed, and care must be taken in pouring each cordial so as not to disturb the one under it. A typical pousse-café might be layered in the following order: Kirsch, grenadine, orange curaçao, green crème de menthe, purple crème de cassis, and yellow crème de bananes. The word was first printed in English in 1875.

power lunch. A business lunch attended by the most powerful people within an industry. The term was coined in an article by Lee Eisenberg entitled "America's Most Powerful Lunch" in *Esquire* magazine (October 1979) to describe the number of powerful business people who dined at The Four Seasons restaurant in New York City.

The "power breakfast" was begun unofficially (and not under that name) in March 1976 at the Regency Hotel's 540 Park Restaurant in New York by Preston Robert Tisch, president of the Loews Corporation, which owns the hotel, as a way for businesspeople to fit in an early meeting before the regular business day began. ("Power breakfast" was being used by the end of 1980.) The idea had evolved out of breakfast meetings held by various Manhattan power brokers who had been meeting since the early 1970s to discuss ways to improve their city's image and fortunes. Currently the average price for breakfast of juice, muffins, and coffee at that restaurant is between $25 and $30. "But you can't really complain about the price," said one habitué, "because it's cheaper than office space."

prairie chicken. The "greater prairie chicken" (*Tympanuchus cupido*) and the "lesser prairie chicken" (*Tympanuchus pallidicinctus*) are grouse of the open plains of the West. The bird was named as early as 1685, and the Lewis and Clark Expedition of 1804 referred to it as the "prairie hen" or "prairie fowl." Later they were also called "prairie grouse." They are roasted, fried, or stewed.

prairie oyster. A cocktail made by dropping 1 unbroken egg yolk into a tumbler, adding 2 t. Worcestershire sauce, 2 dashes Tabasco sauce, a pinch of salt and pepper, and 1 t. malt vinegar. It is considered by bartenders to be a good cure for the hiccups. The term (also, sometimes, prairie cocktail) has been part of western lingo since the late nineteenth century.

praline. A confection made from almonds or pecans and caramel. It is a great favorite in the South, especially in New Orleans, and derives from the French preparation of *pralin*, caramelized almonds or hazelnuts and sugar pounded into a fine, crumblike

texture. Both terms come from the name of French diplomat César du Plessis-Praslin, later duc de Choiseul (1598–1675), whose cook suggested that almonds and sugar aided digestion. The American Creoles substituted pecans for the almonds.

The confection is first mentioned in print in 1715, and part of Louisiana food culture as early as 1762. The term had various meanings by 1809, when one chronicler told of pralines made from corn and sugar.

> ### PRALINE
>
> Combine 3 c. light brown sugar with ¼ c. water and 1 T. butter. Heat to a temperature of 238° on a candy thermometer, add 1 c. pecan meats, remove from heat, and stir until mixture loses glossiness. Drop in spoonfuls on waxed paper.

prawn (*Macrobrachium acanthurus*). A crustacean similar to a SHRIMP but with a more slender body and longer legs. The name is from Middle English *prayne*. At market the term prawn is often used to describe a wide variety of shrimp that are not prawns at all. The only native American species is found in the South, ranging from North Carolina to Texas. Prawns are cultivated in Hawaii.

pressure cooker. A saucepan with a locking lid that creates within intense steam heat to cook foods in a shorter period of time than in a conventional saucepan. The term dates in print to 1910. The commercial pressure cooker was introduced in the United States at the 1939 New York World's Fair by National Presto Industries.

pretzel. A crisp, salted biscuit usually twisted into a loose knot, though often made in sticks. The word is from the German, and some believe it refers to the Latin word *pretium*, "reward," as in a little gift to a child. Others trace the roots to the Latin *brachium*, arm.

Pretzels can be traced back to Roman times, and they have long been traditional in Alsace and Germany. Legend has it that a monk of France or northern Italy first twisted the pretzel into its unusual shape about A.D. 610 in order to imitate the folded arms of someone praying. The Dutch probably brought the pretzel to America, and there is a story that in 1652 a settler named Jochem Wessel was arrested for using good flour to make pretzels to sell to the Indians at a time when his white neighbors were eating bran flour. The first mention of the word "pretzel" in American print was about 1824, and the first commercial pretzel bakery in the United States was set up in 1861 by Julius Sturgis and Ambrose Rauch in Lititz, Pennsylvania. Most pretzels are twisted by machine, introduced in 1933.

Today pretzels come in a variety of shapes and sizes, from sticks, called "thins," to rings and saltless, hard, thick teething pretzels called "Baldies" (because there is no surface salt and it appears "bald"), a registered trademark of the Anderson Bakery Company (the world's largest pretzel producer) in Lancaster, Pennsylvania. Especially popular in New York and the eastern cities are soft, puffy yeast pretzels sold by street vendors and at candy stores. In Philadelphia these same pretzels are usually eaten with a squirt of yellow mustard or slathered with melted butter. So famous are Philadelphia's pretzels that the city is nick-named the "Big Pretzel" and Pennsylvania manufactures more than half the 400 million pounds of pretzels made in the United States annually.

prickly pear. Also called "prickly cactus." Any of a variety of cacti in the genus *Opuntia* bearing an ovular fruit with a spiny skin—hence its name, first recorded in print in 1605. It is native to the New World tropics and is grown in the southeastern United States, where it is eaten in salads or made into jams, jellies, and pickles. Mexican Americans called the plant *nopal*.

progressive dinner. A meal in which each different course is eaten at a different neighbor's house. The practice became popular in the 1950s with the expansion of suburban housing developments.

Prohibition. An era lasting from 1920 to 1933 during which the United States government forbade the manufacture, sale, or transportation of intoxicating liquors. Prohibition began with passage of the Eighteenth Amendment to the federal Constitution on January 16, 1919, which went into effect one year later, and was repealed by the Twenty-first Amendment on December 5, 1933.

The Prohibition era (called by President Herbert Hoover [1874–1964; in office 1929–33] the "Noble Experiment") was the result of intense pressure by temperance groups across the country, especially the Women's Christian Temperance Union, founded in 1874 in Cleveland, Ohio, and a Washington, D.C., lobbying organization called the Anti-Saloon League, founded in 1893. Continuous political challenges were mounted by the Prohibition party, founded in 1869, which ran candidates in several presidential elections but failed ever to receive a large percentage of the popular vote.

The temperance advocates, whose main argument was against the deleterious effects of alcohol on the drinker and, by extension, on the family, the society, and the nation itself, sought to turn America "dry." Maine had already gone "dry" as of June 6, 1851, and Oklahoma followed in 1880, then most of the South, and, by the First World War, most of the Midwest, which argued that precious grain be reserved for the war effort rather than for distilleries. There was also a deliberate anti-German sentiment against the beer-brewery owners, most of whom had German backgrounds. Finally, bowing to temperance pressures or drawing support from temperance funds, the House of Representatives and the Senate passed a joint resolution on December 5, 1917, to propose the ratification by at least thirty-six states of the Eighteenth Amendment. By January 16, 1919, the amendment was ratified and was put into effect one year later (after Congress had overridden President Woodrow Wilson's veto), with additional legislation under the Volstead Act (named after its sponsor, Minnesota Representative Andrew J. Volstead [1860–1947]) to enforce it.

The law was stringent: An intoxicating liquor was defined as "any beverage containing ½ of 1% alcohol," which effectively put an end to the legal manufacture and sale of beer and wine as well as hard liquor. This aspect of the law crippled the hopes of building a great wine industry in America just when it seemed possible to do so. California and New York grape growers shifted to selling their fruit to home winemakers (allowed under the law originally to placate Virginia apple farmers who sold their fruit to make cider), leading to an enormous two-thirds increase in wine consumption. Beer consumption, however, declined drastically to three tenths of what it had been before Prohibition.

Alcohol could still be sold for medicinal purposes under the Act Supplemental of 1921. But the Treasury Department issued only ten special permits for the storage and transport of whiskey to wholesale druggists. And many people found sympathetic pharmacists who were willing to sell alcohol or alcohol-based tonics to those who sought to drink them for more convivial purposes. Sacramental wine was also allowed to be used in Catholic and Jewish services, and a good deal of New York State's wine production shifted to reaching this market.

The sale of illegal spirits soared, and the sale of bad spirits kept pace, causing 11,700 deaths in 1927 alone. The bootlegger, a smuggler of whiskey, became a kind of folk hero to those who found evasion of an unpopular law to be in the tradition of American individuality and resourcefulness. A most fashionable spot in the major cities was the SPEAKEASY, selling illicit liquor, often to prominent people in society and politics who publicly denounced the abuses of alcohol. In New York alone there were thirty-two thousand speakeasies, many of them horrid places, others clubbish and genteel, where "café society" congregated. It has been estimated that Americans drank $32 billion of illicit liquor during the Prohibition era.

The same law that kept such speakeasies thriving throughout the 1920s drove many legitimate restaurants out of business, including some of the famous opulent dining establishments of the pre-Prohibition era, such as Delmonico's, and the development of fine cuisine suffered accordingly because of the lack of fine wines to accompany it.

Prohibition led immediately to opposition, mostly in the form of gangsters who controlled the importation of illegal spirits and the manufacture of the same. By also controlling distribution and many of the establishments that sold these spirits, the criminal underworld was able to coerce public officials, police, and the common people into maintaining a vicious circle of lawlessness, bloodshed, and corruption at every level of society.

Clearly the Noble Experiment was a failure, and small concessions, such as allowing in 1932 the public to buy beer and wine containing 3.2 percent alcohol (called "McAdoo wine" after the bill's sponsor, Senator William Gibbs McAdoo of California), did nothing to modify the wrongs that Prohibition had unwittingly wrought. Finally, on December 5, 1933, the Twenty-first Amendment repealed the Eighteenth and the Volstead Act, although it was not until 1966 that all statewide prohibition laws were finally repealed. Today there are still many counties, particularly in the South and Midwest, that are dry.

prole food. Short for "proletarian food," meaning food enjoyed by the working class. The abbreviation "prole" has been in use at least since the last quarter of the nineteenth century, but seems to have been applied to food in America only in the 1960s. It was used as the title of an article in *Esquire* magazine for July 1968.

proof. A term that describes the alcoholic strength of a spirit. The word originates in its meaning "to pass a test," as described in *Grossman's Guide to Wines, Beers,*

and Spirits, by Harold J. Grossman, revised by Harriet Lembeck (1977):

Before making distilled spirits became a science, the primitive distillers had a very simple method for determining the potable strength of the distillate. Equal quantities of spirit and gunpowder were mixed and a flame applied. If the gunpowder failed to burn, the spirit was too weak; if it burned too brightly, it was too strong. But if the mixture burned evenly, with a blue flame, it was said to have been proved.

In America approximately one half the proof listed on the label of a spirit indicates its alcoholic content at a temperature of 60 degrees Fahrenheit. One proof gallon equals one measured wine gallon at 100 proof. Since each degree of proof equals one half percent alcohol, an 80-proof spirit would contain 40 percent alcohol.

propyl gallate. An antioxidant used in vegetable oils, meat products, chewing gum, and other foods.

prosciutto. An air-cured or dry-cured ham that originated in Italy (1935). Prosciutto is sliced paper-thin and eaten raw, usually with ripe melon. Since an embargo prohibited the importation of Italian prosciutto until 1989, American companies have manufactured a similar product under the name "prosciutto," which is made according to the same method. The word is Italian, derived from the Latin *petaso,* and first appeared in print in the 1920s.

protose steak. A steak substitute made from vegetable protein. It was eaten by Jewish Americans prohibited by kosher dietary laws from eating meat at certain times.

prune. A PLUM that dries without spoiling, resulting in a very sweet fruit eaten as a snack or used in desserts and other dishes. The word is from the Middle English *pruna.* Most prunes—about 200,000 tons—are grown in California, where the predominant variety is made from the plum "La Petite d'Agen," brought from France in 1856 by French horticulturist Louis Pellier.

Americans consume about ¾ lb. of prunes per capita annually, 70 percent of them at breakfast.

ptarmigan. A bird of the genus *Lagopus* that inhabits the arctic and subarctic regions (1590). The name is originally from the Scottish Gaelic *tarmachan,* which was transformed into a specious Greek form derived from *pteron,* "wing." The bird is hunted and roasted by the Alaskans.

pudding. A term describing several different desserts, usually cooked, including cakelike confections such as plum pudding; or a dish of suet crust containing fruits and sugar; or a spongy steamed dish; or a pastry crust filled with chopped meats, like kidney; or YORKSHIRE PUDDING, a crisp, breadlike side dish made from a flour-and-egg batter cooked in pan drippings; or, as is most usual in contemporary usage, milk-based dessert made with flavorings like chocolate or vanilla cooked with a starch until thickened and then cooled until well set.

Eighteenth- and nineteenth-century cookbooks refer to any and all of these as puddings. The word seems to derive from the Old French *boudin,* "sausage," and, ultimately, from the Latin *botelīnus,* for many puddings were a form of encased meat or innards. The earliest examples of the word in English refer to such dishes. Dr. Johnson's *Dictionary* (1755) defines the word as "a kind of food very variously compounded, but generally made of meal, milk, and eggs." One of the earliest American desserts was a quickly thrown-together mixture of cornmeal, milk, and molasses called "cornmeal mush" or "hasty pudding," known at least since 1691. (Harvard's literary society has been called the "Hasty Pudding Club" since 1795.) "Plum pudding" did not contain plums ("plum" in the seventeenth century referred to raisins or other fruits).

In the present century a pudding almost always means a soft-textured, milk-based dessert, the most popular being those packaged commercially and a large number of which, called "instant puddings," require no cooking at all. "Tapioca pudding" (or "tapioca," from the Tupi word *tipioca,* "residue") is made with a starch from the cassava root. A Hawaiian pudding called HAUPIA is made with coconut milk. "Indian pudding" is an old Colonial dessert based on cornmeal, which used to be called "Indian meal." "Noodle pudding" is particularly savored by Jewish Americans, and "sweet potato pudding" is beloved in the South.

BREAD PUDDING

Combine 4 eggs, 2 c. sugar, and ¾ c. vanilla extract until light in color. Melt ¾ lb. butter in 1½ qt. milk, beat in with egg mixture, and pour over 4 c. cubed stale bread. Add ¾ c. raisins and let soak for ½ hr. Pour into buttered dish, place in hot water bath, and bake for 1 hr. at 350° Serve with custard sauce or whipped cream.

INDIAN PUDDING

Scald 5 c. milk and pour slowly over ⅓ c. cornmeal. Cook in double boiler until slightly thickened, then add 1 t. salt, ½ c. molasses, and a pinch of grated nutmeg. Pour into buttered dish and bake at 300° for about 2 hr. or until set. Serve with whipped cream or ice cream.

---

pueblo bread. A white flour bread made by Native Americans of the Southwest, specifically the Pueblo of New Mexico. The dough, made with flour, salt, yeast, and water (and sometimes eggs), is allowed to rise overnight in a metal washtub or large basin. The loaves are shaped by the women of the tribe into various forms of animals or sunbursts. The hot embers from the fire of pine branches are cleared out of the adobe oven so the bread may be put in to bake for about an hour.

Pullman car. A dining car on a railroad train, named and invented by George Mortimer Pullman of Palmyra, New York, in 1868. The first, rudimentary railroad dining cars had been put in service in 1863 on the Philadelphia, Wilmington, and Baltimore Railroad, with only stand-up buffets for food service. Pullman constructed elaborate dining cars with full-service signature china and silverware, and impeccable service. The first Pullman car was named the "Delmonico," after the fashionable New York restaurant.

Pullman loaf. A square loaf of bread served on the PULLMAN CARS.

pumpernickel. A dark bread made from rye flour. Pumpernickel was originally made in Westphalia, Germany, and in that country is called *Schwarzbrot,* "black bread." It is firm, slightly acidic in flavor, and of varying densities and textures. The word was first printed in 1750.

The term is of somewhat obscure etymology. The *American Heritage Dictionary* cites "German *Pumpernickel:* early New High German *Pumpern,* a fart (imitative) + *Nickel,* 'devil,' general pejorative; so named from being hard to digest." The *Morris Dictionary of Word and Phrase Origins* states the word was a combination of *Pumper,* the sound "made by a person falling," and *Nickel,* a "dwarf" or "goblin." A "pumpernickel," therefore, was a dolt or fool. Theodora FitzGibbon, in her *Food of the Western World,* cited a story that the word is a corruption of the phrase *"pain pour Nicole"* ("bread for Nicole"), after Napoléon's horse Nicole's fondness for black bread.

Pumpernickel was brought by German immigrants to America and is now found in most supermarkets, though the best is usually found in German or Jewish neighborhood bakeries.

pumpkin (*Cucurbita pepo*). A trailing vine and its fruit, having a yellow-orange rind and flesh. The name is from the Greek *pepōn,* for a large melon. An English word for the pumpkin, pompion or pumpion, had been in use at least since 1545, whereas in America pumpkin did not make an appearance in print until 1640.

Pumpkins were among many squashes eaten by the Indians and introduced early on to the European settlers. In fact, pumpkin pie, still one of the country's favorite desserts, was served at the Pilgrims' second Thanksgiving in 1623 and has become a traditional Thanksgiving food. The colonists made pumpkin beer, and pumpkin soup was also popular. Pumpkin seeds are roasted and eaten as a snack. Indeed, it was such a frequent and important item in their diet that a seventeenth-century rhyme went, "We have pumpkin at morning and pumpkin at noon. If it were not for pumpkin, we should be undoon."

Pumpkins may be cooked like other squashes, roasted with butter and brown sugar, or boiled as a side dish. Most Americans today use canned pumpkin filling for their pies.

The sugar pumpkin is also used as a Halloween jack-o'-lantern.

PUMPKIN PIE

Combine 2 c. cooked pumpkin with ⅔ c. sugar, 1½ t. cinnamon, ½ t. nutmeg, ¼ t. ground cloves, and ½ t. salt. Blend 3 eggs with ½ c. heavy cream and ½ c. milk, then mix in pumpkin. Pour into pastry crust and bake for about 45 min. at 400° until inserted knife comes out clean. Serve with whipped cream.

---

punch. An alcoholic beverage mixture of various ingredients (1625). Today the term usually refers to a bowl of citrus- or fruit-based party drink containing any number of liquors, sparkling wine, or champagne.

The word originally came from the Hindi *panch,* meaning "five," in reference to the five original ingredients used—lime, sugar, spices, water, and a fermented sap called "arrack." British sailors had picked up the drink and spoken of punch as of the early seventeenth century. It soon became a popular beverage in the West Indies and North American colonies, where it might be mixed with wine, milk, hot water, and, most often, rum. At the large Caribbean plantations enormous bowls of punch—described by one onlooker as big enough "for a goose to swim in"—were served at lavish social gatherings, and people of the day already were arguing as to what made a perfect punch. An advertisement in the *Salem Gazette* for 1741 by a West Indies trader proclaimed that his orange juice was preferred by many punch enthusiasts to lemon. Few would agree on the exact proportions of "planter's punch," which was created at The Planter Hotel in St. Louis in the 1840s.

FISH HOUSE PUNCH, created at the State in Schuylkill, founded in 1732, is another punch hotly debated as to its original ingredients. Many other punches became associated with specific regiments, navy crews, and Ivy League universities. "Sangaree" (from the French *sang,* "blood"), also spelled "Sangaree," was a Colonial punch made with red wine and fruits (sometimes ale), an early version of Spanish SANGRIA, which became popular in the 1960s as a party punch. In the 1920s many colleges lent their names to punches, such as "Yale punch," "Harvard punch" and "Columbia punch."

"Pisco Punch," created in the 1870s by Duncan Nichol of the Bank Exchange bar in San Francisco, is made with Pisco muscat brandy from Pisco, Peru.

Nonalcoholic punches, usually made with club soda or ginger ale and various fruits, are still popular at children's parties in America.

NAVY PUNCH

Mix 6 oz. lime juice, 2 pt. liquid sugar, and 3 pt. dark rum and blend over an ice chunk. Garnish with fruit and a sprinkle of nutmeg.

---

pupu. Also, "pu pu." A Hawaiian term for various appetizers, such as macadamia nuts, barbecued meats, coconut chips, and wonton. In Chinese-American or Polynesian-American restaurants a "pu pu platter" is usually a plate of appetizers spread around a lighted burner, into which one sticks the morsels for heating.

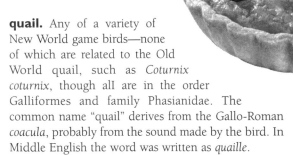

quail. Any of a variety of
New World game birds—none
of which are related to the Old
World quail, such as *Coturnix
coturnix*, though all are in the order
Galliformes and family Phasianidae. The
common name "quail" derives from the Gallo-Roman
coacula, probably from the sound made by the bird. In
Middle English the word was written as *quaille*.

There is some confusion in American terminology
for quail, especially since the most familiar variety, the
"bobwhite" (*Colinus virginianus*), is called "quail" in the
North and "partridge" in the South. (For further information, see PARTRIDGE.) "Quail" was first applied to
this fowl in print in 1625; "bobwhite" is first recorded
in 1837 and "bobwhite quail" in 1920. The term "bobwhite" derives from the sound the bird makes, as
Americans perceive it. This same bird has also been
called the "blue quail" in the Southwest.

Other American quails include the "mountain
quail" (*Oreortyx pictus*), "Montezuma quail" (*Cyrtonyx
montezumae*), "gambel's quail" (*Lophortyx gambelii*),
also called "redhead," "California quail" (*L. californicus*), and "scaled quail" (*Callipepla squamata*).

Other varieties of quail are raised on farms in the
United States, primarily the "Pharaoh," "Egyptian," or
"Japanese quail," most of which are grown now for
food rather than as game birds. Quails are usually
roasted or grilled and are often served with wild rice.

quaking custard. A cream custard of New England
around which are garnished egg whites. The name
refers to the quivering texture of the dish.

quiche. A pie or tart
having an egg filling and
a variety of other ingredients (1945). The word is
French, probably from a German
dialect word *Küche*, "cake." Quiche is
certainly a dish of French origins, especially of
Lorraine. In fact, the first quiche recipes to become
popular in America were those for the egg-
onion-and-bacon tart called "quiche Lorraine,"
which was extremely fashionable in the 1970s as a
luncheon, brunch, or appetizer dish in the United
States. Since then quiches have been adapted to contain all manner of ingredients, from peppers and
cheese to vegetables, sausage, and other meats.
There are even retail stores specializing in a variety
of quiches, which may be cooked as a large tart or as
individual tarts.

quick bread. A bread, biscuit, muffin, or other
baked good without yeast or too much sweetness. The
term was first printed in 1918.

quinoa (*Chenopodium quinoa*). Also, "quinua."
Pronounced "KEEN-wah," this grain was central to the
Incas' diet (they called it "the mother grain") but not
raised in the United States until recently (first in
Colorado). The word was first mentioned in print in
the 1620s. There are about eighteen hundred varieties
of quinoa in many different colors, and it has been
termed the "supergrain" because of its high nutritional
benefits. It is used as a cereal, stuffing, bread grain,
and in salads.

R

rabbit. A herbivorous, long-eared mammal of the Leporidae family that is found both wild and domesticated in America. Wild rabbits are up to sixteen inches long and weigh two to three pounds. The New World genus *Sylvilagus* includes the "cottontail," the "marsh," and the "swamp rabbit." The "Idaho pygmy rabbit" (*S. idahoensis*) is found in the Great Basin of the United States. The "jackrabbit" and "snowshoe rabbit" are actually hares, though of the same family. The word in Middle English was *rabet*.

The rabbit was in America long before Europeans arrived, and the Aztecs worshiped a rabbit god; the North American Indians certainly ate them. Although Americans have always eaten rabbits, their association in the present century with pets and the image of the anthropomorphic Easter Bunny have made many people squeamish about cooking such beloved animals. Nevertheless, they are still hunted and valued for their meat, which should be taken young. The best domesticated rabbits for eating are about two months old and can be roasted whole, sautéed, fried, or broiled. Mature rabbits should be stewed and are best marinated before cooking. Americans consume about 50 million pounds of rabbit meat each year.

RABBIT STEW

Disjoint a young rabbit and season inside and outside with salt and pepper. Melt 1 T. butter in pan and brown rabbit meat. Add 1 T. flour and simmer for 2 min. Add ½ c. red wine and ½ qt. chicken stock to cover the rabbit. Boil, then add 2 cloves of garlic, 2 cloves, 1 bay leaf, and a pinch of thyme. Cover and bake at 350° for 45 min. Add white onions and ½ c. mushrooms and return to oven for 15 min. Serves 4.

rabbit food. A slang term to describe vegetables or vegetarian diets, so called because it is the kind of food eaten by rabbits, a usage dating in print to 1905, but as a condescending slang term to the 1960s.

raccoon (*Procyon lotor*). Also, "coon," "'coon," "racoon." A grayish-brown furred mammal with black, masklike markings found throughout North America. The name comes from the Virginian Algonquian Indian *aroughcoune, arathkone,* and is first noted in English as early as 1600. Raccoons also go by the very old name of "chaoui," derived from Choctaw or Mobilian *shaui.*

Raccoon was once enjoyed by the early Colonial settlers of the East and South as a matter of course and continued to be enjoyed regularly by westerners. Today it is something of a delicacy among hunters and is almost never found commercially. Louisiana African-Americans used to call a dish of raccoon sprinkled with gin and served with mashed potatoes "drunk coon."

radicchio (*Cichorium intybus*). A bitter salad vegetable, with favored varieties having a deep red-and-white coloring (1968). *Radicchio* is the Italian word for the vegetable, but it was first cultivated in the United States in 1981 by Moore Farming, Inc., of Salinas Valley, California, and is now grown as well in New Jersey.

radish. Any of a variety of plants in the genus *Raphanus*, especially *R. sativus*, bearing pungent roots usually eaten raw in salads. The word is from the Latin *radix*, "root."

The "wild radish" (*R. raphanistrum*) is common in both Europe and North America, but the origins of the cultivated species, *R. sativus*, is unknown. An Oriental radish, the "daikon," is sometimes seen at market in the United States and is grown privately by Asian immigrants.

railroad cookie. A cookie swirled on the inside with cinnamon and brown sugar. The origin of the name may derive from the dark tracks of filling that look like railroad tracks. The cookies were mentioned in a Missouri recipe book as early as 1875.

RAILROAD COOKIE

Cream 1 c. butter with 2 c. brown sugar. Beat in 2 eggs, 1 t. baking soda, ¼ t. salt, 1 t. cinnamon, and 2 c. flour. Add 2 more c. flour (dough will be stiff), divide dough, roll out to ⅛-in. thickness, spread with date filling, roll up, and slice to ¼-in. thickness. Bake 15 min. at 350°.

---

raisin. A sweet, dried grape. Raisins are eaten plain, mixed with nuts, cooked in cakes, pastries, breads, and puddings, and mixed with cereals, especially bran flakes, as a breakfast dish.

The word comes from the Latin *racémus,* which became *raisin* in Middle English.

California produces the most raisins of any region in the world, mostly from THOMPSON SEEDLESS and Muscat of Alexandria grapes. The industry began there in September 1873, when a heat wave dried out much of the grape harvest, causing one San Francisco grocer to market the shriveled grapes as "Peruvian Delicacies."

Raisins are sun-dried in the vineyards, then graded, cleaned, and packed, sometimes lightened in color with sulfur dioxide.

Ramos Gin Fizz. A cocktail made from cream, gin, lemon juice, orange-flower water, and egg whites. It was first made by Henry C. Ramos, a New Orleans bar owner who had purchased the Imperial Cabinet (or Cabaret?) soon after he had arrived in the city in 1888. The drink became famous for its preparation at the hands of the Imperial's squad of bartenders, who during Mardi Gras of 1915 numbered thirty-five. (Rima and Richard Collin in *The New Orleans Cookbook* [1975] cite Meyer's Restaurant as the place where Ramos concocted the drink, although since 1935 the Roosevelt Hotel, now the Fairmont Hotel, has held the trademark on the name "Ramos Gin Fizz.")

Most authorities on the cocktail recommend a long shaking time for the ingredients to achieve the proper texture.

RAMOS GIN FIZZ

Shake with crushed ice 1 T. confectioners' sugar, the juice of half a lemon, the juice of half a lime, 1 egg white, ½ oz. heavy cream, 1½ oz. gin, a dash vanilla extract, a dash seltzer, and 3 drops orange-flower water. Continue shaking until foamy and of a consistent texture—about 5 min. Pour into a highball glass. (The ingredients may be mixed in an electric blender for 1½ min.)

---

ramp (*Allium tricoccum*). A wild onion native to North America with a long green leaf and slender white bulbs resembling the scallion. The word is an Elizabethan dialect rendering of the wild garlic, *rams* or *ramson,* and is first mentioned in English print in 1530, though it was used earlier by the English immigrants of America's southern Appalachian Mountains.

Ramps grow from South Carolina to Canada. "To many West Virginians," according to E. Kemp Miles in an article in *Gourmet* magazine (April 1983), "ramps are the harbingers of spring. The first appearance of the flat green leaves of this wild leek jutting through the snow signals the beginning of feasts and festivals where bushels of the pungent stalks are consumed, both raw and cooked, along with quantities of ham, eggs, and potatoes."

Ramps have a somewhat stronger flavor than scallions, but are eaten raw, as well as in preparations where onions, scallions, or shallots would be called for.

ranch dressing. A dressing made with mayonnaise, onion, garlic, buttermilk, and various seasonings. There are two claims as to the origin of the term "ranch dressing." The Todds Food Company of Glendale, Arizona, claims that part-owner David Bears of Todds created the dressing for Bobby McGee's Restaurants in 1980 as a dipping sauce for breaded, fried zucchini.

According to the Clorox Company of Oakland, California, however, "ranch-style dressing" was originated by the Henson family, owners of Hidden Valley Ranch near Santa Barbara, California, who began marketing a packaged dry mix after World War II. In October 1972 the Clorox Company purchased the trademark rights from the Henson family for "Hidden Valley Ranch Original Ranch" salad dressing, which is sold as a dry mix, one made with buttermilk, the other with regular milk.

rankins. A nineteenth-century cheese pudding.

RANKINS

Combine 1 c. buttermilk, 6 T. grated cheese, 3 T. bread crumbs, 3 T. butter, ⅓ t. salt, ⅓ t. dry mustard, a pinch of cayenne pepper, and a pinch of ground pepper. Bring to a boil, cool, then add 2 beaten egg yolks and fold in two stiffly beaten egg whites. Bake 15 min. in a 375° oven.

---

raspberry. Any of a variety of plants in the genus *Rubus* bearing fleshy dark-purple or red berries. The name derives from an earlier word, *raspis,* and was first recorded as "raspberry" in the early seventeenth century.

America offered a wide variety of wild raspberries to the early Colonists, who nevertheless imported their European variety, *R. idaeus,* for cultivation. The American red raspberry (*R. i. strigosus*) was known in Massachusetts and first listed as of 1621 among the region's wild fruits. The black raspberries (*R. occidentalis* of the East and *R. leucodermis* of the West) are the other major varieties grown in the United States, chiefly in Michigan, Oregon, New York, and Washington.

Americans eat raspberries fresh or frozen, in pies, ice cream, sherbets, and ices, and make them into sweet dessert sauces, such as "melba sauce" (see PEACH MELBA).

ratafia. A sweet cordial made from the infusion of fruit kernels in alcohol. The word is from the French, via West Indian Creole, and in France ratafia more specifically refers to sweetened apéritifs made from wines such as Burgundy and champagne. It first appeared in print in English in 1690 to describe a cherry brandy made with peach and apricot pits. (By 1845 there was also a "ratafia biscuit" to be eaten with the cordial.) "It is claimed," *Alexis Lichine's New Encyclopedia of Wines and Spirits* (1981) notes, "that the name was applied to any liqueur at the ratification of a treaty or agreement," but this seems highly unlikely.

Ratafia was a popular nineteenth-century home-made cordial, but it is now rarely seen. There have been some efforts in California wineries to produce a French-style ratafia apéritif.

ration. Generally a fixed allotment of food, but more commonly referring to the food served to the armed forces in the field (1540). Long a subject of griping and jokes among military personnel, rations have played a great part in the success of various campaigns, for as Napoléon Bonaparte is said to have observed, "An army marches on its stomach" (also attributed to Frederick the Great).

The set rations of the American Revolutionary War were established in 1775, with daily provisions including one pound of beef or one-quarter pound of pork or one pound of salt fish, one pound of bread or flour, three pints of peas or beans, one pint of milk, one-half pint of rice or one pint of cornmeal, one quart of spruce beer or cider. Nine gallons of molasses was provided per company of one hundred men per week.

When these were not able to be provided, soldiers had to live off a diet of HARDTACK and JERKY, especially in the navy, where fresh food was difficult to preserve.

By the time of the Civil War soldiers also carried coffee, tea, potatoes, and seasonings (the cost of rations then was about fifteen cents per day per man), and strides in preserving foods through canning, vacuum packing, and heating gave the Union Army a pronounced advantage over Confederate forces that often went hungry for lack of set rations.

By World War I one pound of hard bread and one pound of canned meat, along with coffee, sugar, and a cube of condensed soup, were provided. There were basically four types of ration: "garrison ration"—perishable food; "reserve ration"—non perishable canned food; "emergency ration"—dried compressed meat and cereal bar; and "trench ration"—designed to protect against gas-chemical-attack contamination, these were rations placed in large steel cans for about twenty-five troops.

In the mid-1930s the Quartermaster Corps began researching rations more scientifically and developed a wide range of products for use in the field and at home base. By 1940 the term "trench ration" was done away with, "garrison ration" was called "A" ration, "reserve ration" became "B" ration, then "C" ration, and "emergency" ration was called "D" ration.

"C" ration (or "combat ration") was the most commonly used, consisting of six cans weighing 4.3 pounds and containing three different meals. Three cans were called "M units" for "meat units." "M-1" was meat and beans, "M-2" was meat and vegetable hash, and "M-3" was meat and vegetable stew. "B units" ("bread unit") contained bread, coffee, a sugar packet, soluble coffee, and sundry items. "C" rations cost about sixty cents per piece.

A big breakthrough came in 1940 with the "K" ration, a light, sealed ration for easy potability on paratroopers and other light infantry. Developed at the University of Minnesota by Ancel Keys (and possibly deriving its name from the first letter of his last name), this was originally called a "para-ration," until General George Patton asked for the name change because he wanted it for use with his tank troops.

The "Logan bar" was a chocolate and oat-flour bar developed by Capt. Paul P. Logan and made by the Hershey Chocolate Company that contained six hundred calories, to provide quick energy.

A few enhancements of the World War II products were made during the war in Vietnam around 1965. "Long-range patrol packets" were developed to be carried in soft packets that wouldn't tear. Some further developments were made for the NASA astronaut programs, and experiments were done with irradiated foods in the early 1980s.

By the 1980s the goal was to provide personnel with two hot meals a day when possible. These fell under "Group" rations and "Individual" rations. The former included "B" rations designed for use in organized dining facilities and Individual Rations, and "'T' rations," which stands for "Tray Pack," intended to be boiled and served to twelve to eighteen people. These had a three-year shelf life. "Individual" rations have been where the most strides have been made in recent years. In 1975 the "'MRE' ration" (short for "Meal, Ready to Eat") was developed—a range of meals packed entirely in pouches and containing a complete thirteen-hundred-calorie meal that includes an eight-ounce entrée and items like cake, peanut butter, hot sauce, and candy. They are designed to be eaten cold, but MREs usually include a "flameless ration heater," a water-activated exothermic chemical heating pad containing magnesium iron and polyethylene powder, and salt. The food is placed in the bag, then placed in the soldier's pocket. Within twelve minutes of the soldier's walking, the food is heated to 100° Fahrenheit. MREs may also contain "pouch bread"—fresh bread seated in a soft pouch and having a three-year shelf life. Responding to troops' complaints about the quality and variety of MREs served during the Gulf War in Iraq, the Pentagon introduced a new array of 24 different MREs that included Jamaican-spiced pork chops, vegetable pasta with cream sauce, beef teriyaki, chili and macaroni, and a number of brand name items like M&M's candy and bottles of TABASCO sauce.

In addition to MREs, the military now uses "'MORE' rations" (for "Meal, Operational, Ready to Eat"), which come packed on plastic trays as a ready-to-eat meal and often contain many commercial items favored by personnel off base.

rattlesnake (genera *Sistrurus* and *Crotalus*). Any of a number of venomous snakes, found in North America, whose tails have interlocking links that make a rattling sound when shaken by disturbed vipers (1620). Rattlesnakes are found throughout the country and include such species as the "massasauga," "timber," "pygmy," "Eastern and Western diamondback," "red diamond," "sidewinder," "rock," "speckled," "blacktailed," "twin-spotted," "tiger," "Mojave," and "western" rattlesnake.

Although they have never been particularly relished as food by most Americans, rattlesnakes have held a certain gastronomic interest among hunters,

woodsmen, trappers, and cowboys, who usually put them in a stewpot or grill them.

In Mooresfield, West Virginia, the people hold an annual Hardy County Rattlesnake Hunters' Rattlesnake Feed featuring a variety of rattlesnake recipes.

BARBECUED RATTLESNAKE

Remove head and skin snake, cut into 2-in. pieces, and parboil for ½ hr. in a broth seasoned with salt, pepper, and herbs. Combine juice of 1 lemon, ½ c. honey, 2 T. Worcestershire sauce, 2 T. red-wine vinegar, 1 chopped chile pepper, 1 clove chopped garlic, salt, and pepper. Baste snake with mixture and cook on grill.

---

ravigote. The word, from the French, "to refresh," applies to both a spicy sauce of butter cooked with flour, wine, and white stock, and a cold sauce made with vinegar, oil, capers, parsley, tarragon, chervil, and onion. As the former, it is widely used in Louisiana Creole cooking, especially with crabmeat. The word was first recorded in 1820.

CRABMEAT RAVIGOTE

In a sauté pan melt 1 stick butter and sauté 1 cup chopped bell peppers, ½ c. chopped pimientos, ½ c. sliced mushrooms, ½ c. chopped scallions, ⅛ c. chopped parsley, ⅛ c. chopped chervil, 2 T. capers, ⅛ t. cayenne pepper, salt and pepper to taste. Mix well, add 1 lb. lump crabmeat, and cook for about 10 min. Place equal portions into individual buttered ramekins, sprinkle with bread crumbs and melted butter, and brown under a broiler. Serves 4.

---

raw bar. A food stand or bar serving uncooked shellfish. They are quite often attached to a somewhat more formal restaurant, especially those specializing in seafood.

razorback. A wild hog of the southeastern United States that is descended from domesticated hogs brought over by the Spanish in 1539. The razorback was again domesticated by the American pioneers, who made bacon from its meat. It is not the same animal as the American wild pig—the "peccary" or "javelina." "Razorback" was first printed in 1815.

Recognized Viticultural Regions. Grape-growing areas recognized by the Federal Bureau of Alcohol, Tobacco and Firearms. Such areas must meet the following guidelines: (1) That a named viticultural area is locally and/or nationally known as a grape-producing area. (2) That the geographical features of the region (climate, soil, elevation, physical features, etc.) are distinctly different from surrounding regions.

The currently approved Recognized Viticultural Regions are:

ARIZONA
Sonoita

ARKANSAS
Altus
Arkansas Mountain
Ozark Mountain

CALIFORNIA
Alexander Valley
Anderson Valley
Arroyo Grande Valley
Arroyo Seco
Atlas Peak
Ben Lomond Mountain
Benmore Valley
California Shenandoah Valley
Carmel Valley
Central Coast
Chalk Hill
Chalone
Chiles Valley
Cienega Valley
Clarksburg
Clear Lake
Cole Ranch
Cucamongo Valley
Diablo Grande
Dry Creek Valley
Dunnigan Hills
Edna Valley
El Dorado
Fiddletown
Guenoc Valley
Hames Valley
Howell Mountain
Knights Valley
Lime Kiln Valley
Livermore Valley
Lodi
Los Carneros
McDowell Valley

Madera
Malibu-Newton Canyon
Mendocino
Mendocino Ridge
Merritt Island
Monterey
Mt. Harlan
Mt. Veeder
Napa Valley
North Coast
Northern Sonoma
North Yuba
Oakville
Pacheco Pass
Paicines
Paso Robles
Potter Valley
Redwood Valley
Russian River Valley
Rutherford
Saint Helena
San Benito
San Francisco Bay
San Lucas
San Pasqual Valley
San Ysidro District
Santa Clara Valley
Santa Cruz Mountains
Santa Lucia Highlands
Santa Maria Valley
Santa Ynez Valley
Seiad Valley
Shenandoah Valley
Sierra Foothills
Solano County Green Valley
Sonoma Coast
Sonoma County Green Valley
Sonoma Mountain
Sonoma Valley
South Coast
Spring Mountain Disirict
Stags Leap District
Suisun Valley
Temecula
Wild Horse Valley
Willow Creek
Yorkville Highlands
Yountville
York Mountain

COLORADO
Grand Valley

CONNECTICUT
Southeastern New England
Western Connecticut Highlands

INDIANA
Ohio River Valley

KENTUCKY
Ohio River Valley

LOUISIANA
Mississippi Delta

MARYLAND
Catoctin
Cumberland Valley
Linganore

MASSACHUSETTS
Martha's Vineyard
Southeastern New England

MICHIGAN
Fennville
Lake Michigan Shore
Leelanau Peninsula
Old Mission Peninsula

MISSISSIPPI
Mississippi Delta

MISSOURI
Augusta
Hermann
Ozark Highlands
Ozark Mountain

NEW JERSEY
Central Delaware Valley
Warren Hills

NEW MEXICO
Mesilla Valley
Middle Rio Grande Valley
Mimbres Valley

NEW YORK
Cayuga Lake
Finger Lakes
The Hamptons
Hudson River Region
Lake Erie

Long Island
North Fork of Long Island
North Fork of Roanoke

OHIO
Grand River Valley
Isle St. George
Kanawha River Valley
Lake Erie
Loramie Creek
Ohio River Valley

OKLAHOMA
Ozark Mountain

OREGON
Columbia Valley
Rogue Valley
Umpqua Valley
Walla Walla Valley
Willamette Valley

PENNSYLVANIA
Central Delaware Valley
Cumberland Valley
Lake Erie
Lancaster Valley

RHODE ISLAND
Southeastern New England

TENNESSEE
Mississippi Delta

TEXAS
Bell Mountain
Escondido Valley
Fredericksburg in the Texas Hill Country
Mesilla Valley
Mississippi Delta
Texas Davis Mountains
Texas High Plains
Texas Hill Country

VIRGINIA
Monticello
Northern Neck
    George Washington birthplace
North Fork of Roanoke
Rocky Knob
Shenandoah Valley
Virginia's Eastern Shore

WASHINGTON
Columbia Valley
Puget Sound
Walla Walla Valley
Yakima Valley

WEST VIRGINIA
Kanawha River Valley
Ohio River Valley
Shenandoah Valley

WISCONSIN
Lake Wisconsin

Recommended Daily Allowance. Offically
known as the "United States Recommended Daily
Allowance," this term refers to federal regulations for
the minimum amount of nutrients needed by people
over the age of four. It is usually included on food
labels as a list of nutrients like vitamins and minerals.
The "Recommended Dietary Allowance" (RDA) refers
to the estimated amount of various nutrients needed
each day to maintain good health, which varies
slightly depending on age and sex.

red beans and rice. A Louisiana dish of kidney
beans and rice flavored with a ham bone and traditionally served on Monday after a Sunday dinner of ham.
The dish originated with Louisiana's African-American
cooks, who call it "red and white," but it has also
became associated with the Creoles and can be found in
numerous New Orleans restaurants and homes on
Mondays. As John Thorne notes in *Rice & Beans. The
Itinerary of a Recipe* (1981), "Although red kidney beans
are often used in making red beans and rice, strict
purists aver that they have too strong a flavor for the
dish, and that the small South Louisiana red bean is
preferred." Similarly purists insist on using Louisiana
PICKLED PORK (or sweet pickled pork), a packaged seasoning made from pork shoulder marinated in brine.
There is also considerable debate as to whether the
beans and rice should be cooked together or separately.
The *Picayune's Creole Cook Book* (1900), from which the
following recipe is taken, prefers the latter method.

RED BEANS AND RICE

Wash 1 qt. dried red beans and soak overnight in
cold water. Drain off water, place beans in a pot and
cover with at least 2 qt. fresh water, and heat slowly. Add
1 lb. ham or salt pork, 1 chopped carrot, 1 minced onion,
1 bay leaf, salt, and pepper, and boil for at least 2 hr.
When tender, mash beans, place meat and vegetables on
top, and serve on a bed of white boiled rice. May be
served as an entree or side dish.

redeye gravy. Also, "red-eye gravy," "red ham
gravy," "frog-eye gravy," and other terms. A gravy
made from ham drippings, often flavored with coffee.
It is a traditional southern gravy served with ham, biscuits, and grits and takes its name from the
appearance of a "red eye" in the middle of the reduced
gravy. It has been popular at least since the 1930s, and
the term was in print by 1945.

REDEYE GRAVY

Remove ham steak from skillet in which it has fried
and add ½ c. water (some insist on ice water) or ½ c.
strong black coffee. Scrape up ham drippings and cook
about 3 min., stirring constantly. Pour over ham, biscuits,
or grits.

redhorse (genus *Moxostoma*). Any of a variety of reddish-brown fishes of which eighteen species inhabit
the eastern rivers, including the "river redhorse" (*M.
carinatum*), "silver redhorse" (*M. anisurum*), "short-
head redhorse" (*M. macrolepidotum*), "torrent sucker"
(*M. rhothoecum*), "rustyside sucker" (*M. hamiltoni*),
"golden redhorse" (*M. erythrurum*), and "black redhorse" (*M. duquesnei*). It is a popular food fish, and
South Carolinians make a "redhorse bread" with cornmeal and redhorse. "Redhorse" first saw print in 1790.

red ink. Slang term used to describe the Italian-
American wine sold at delicatessens in New York
during Prohibition. The term appears in print in 1906.
Also called "dago red."

red rice. Also, "Spanish rice." A southern seasoned
rice dish made with tomato to give it color. It is often
served with shrimp.

red sauce. This term may refer either to an Italian-
style tomato sauce or to a tomato-flavored clam sauce,
also a standard item in Italian-American cookery. Both
terms have become common since the end of World
War II. See also WHITE SAUCE.

red snapper Veracruz. Red snapper cooked with
chile peppers, tomatoes, and other seasonings. In

Mexico this dish is called *huachinango a la veracruzana,* but it has also become a popular item in Mexican-American restaurants across the country.

RED SNAPPER VERACRUZ

Salt and pepper 4 red snapper fillets and sauté in 3 T. olive oil. Remove from pan and keep warm. Add 1 T. olive oil to pan and sauté 1 chopped onion, 2 chopped garlic cloves, 4 peeled, seeded, and chopped tomatoes, the juice of 1 lime, a pinch of oregano, and 2 red or green chile peppers that have been seeded. Cook for 10 min., return fish to pan and simmer, covered, for 10 min. Serve with rice. Serves 4.

refried beans. A Mexican-American dish of mashed cooked pinto beans, usually served as a side dish or as a filling for various tortilla preparations. The term "refried" is actually a mistranslation from the Mexican *frijoles refritos,* which means "well-fried beans," a distinction first mentioned in Erna Fergusson's *Mexican Cookbook* (1934), but "refried" has remained in common parlance with regard to this dish.

REFRIED BEANS

Cook 4 c. pinto beans in water to cover until tender, and place in a skillet with 4 T. lard or bacon fat. Mash down the beans, adding a little of the bean liquid. Add 2 minced garlic cloves, salt, and pepper. Cook over medium heat for about 30 min., until edges are crispy. Turn out onto a warm plate. Serves 6.

relish. Any of a variety of spicy, often PICKLE-based condiments served as a side dish or spread on a food item. The word, which first appears in English in 1798, is from the Middle English for a "taste" and is derived from Old French *reles,* "something remaining." As Theodora FitzGibbon noted in *The Food of the Western World* (1976), "In Britain ["relish"] usually means a thin pickle or sauce with a vinegar base. In the United States the term also embraces finely chopped fruits or vegetables with a dressing of sugar, salt, and vinegar; this is not only served as an adjunct to a main course, but may also constitute the first course of a meal, as apple relish, garden relish, and salad relish."

American relishes would include CHOW-CHOW, piccalilli, KETCHUP, watermelon rind, chutneys, and the many pickle-based bottled varieties that are customarily spread on hot dogs and hamburgers.

rémoulade. Also, "remoulade," "rémolade." A mayonnaise dressing or sauce of French origin flavored with mustard and other seasonings. The word is a variant of the Picard dialect *ramolas,* "horseradish." In New Orleans cookery the sauce is made spicier than the French version and often contains hard-boiled eggs. If chopped parsley is added, it may be called a "green rémoulade" or "rémoulade verte." Different versions will include different ingredients.

RÉMOULADE

Mix 2 C. mayonnaise with ¼ c. hot mustard, ¼ c. horseradish, ½ t. cayenne, 2 chopped shallots, and 2 T. Worcestershire sauce. Chill and serve over fish, meat, or shrimp.

restaurant. A dining room or other eatery where one pays for a meal. The concept of a public place selling full meals is of rather recent origins, for although inns and taverns of one form or another have long histories, the main business of such places was either as a dispenser of spirits or as a travelers' waystop that sold food only incidentally. The word "restaurant" is French, from the verb *restaurer,* "to restore." But the word *restaurant* in France referred specifically to a restorative kind of soup, according to the guild guidelines for cookshops called *traiteurs.* Therefore, when an upstart Parisian *traiteur* named Boulanger in 1765 served a soup of sheep's foot in white sauce and called it a *restaurant,* his colleagues took him to court to refute the service of such a dish. Boulanger won, and his *restaurant* became fashionable. Then, in 1782, a *traiteur* named Beauvilliers began serving guests at separate tables, and the term *restaurant* came to describe such establishments.

The first appearance of the word in American print was in 1920 and there is an early reference in the novel *The Prairie* (1827), by James Fenimore Cooper, to "the most renowned of Parisian restaurants."

The taverns and inns of England and America had since the sixteenth century served food, usually one set meal each day called the "ordinary," which also came to mean the establishments themselves. These were common in Colonial America too, as were the coffeehouses and men's clubs first set up in London in the seventeenth and eighteenth centuries. The White Horse Tavern in Newport, Rhode Island, established in 1673, claims to be the oldest continuously operating tavern in America. Hotel dining rooms began to improve after 1800, and the opening of the Tremont House in Boston in 1829 was heralded for its two-hundred-seat dining room and its use of the new four-tined forks.

After the Revolution in France, many chefs once attached to the homes of the aristocrats opened public restaurants there, and before long the concept caught on in the United States, where in 1794 French chef Jean "Julien" Baptiste Gilbert Payplat, former cook for the archbishop of Bordeaux, opened a French-style restaurant in Boston where one might sit at a separate table, order from a menu, and pay one's bill for what was consumed. But the idea of a public restaurant not attached to a hotel was given its true impetus by John and Peter Delmonico, two Swiss brothers, the first a former sea captain, the second a pastry-shop manager, who in 1827 opened up a small, six-table coffee-and-pastry shop called Delmonico's on William Street in New York City. In 1831 the brothers opened a full-fledged restaurant with a French chef and a number of then-exotic dishes that included salad and green vegetables served in the French manner.

Delmonico's became the beacon of good taste and lavish meals, and the brothers' success begat ten more restaurants under their family name, each one more grandiose than the last, usually run by a relative imported for the purpose of maintaining tradition.

Everyone of importance went to Delmonico's, where the finest wines and the greatest array of game were offered on a daily basis. The menu (a term first recorded in America in 1830) went on for several pages, with nearly thirty poultry dishes, eleven beef dishes, and sixteen pastries listed. The influence of French cooking on the Delmonico's menus set a mold for American deluxe dining rooms that has been maintained ever since. Delmonico's lent its name to many dishes, like DELMONICO POTATOES, "Delmonico bombe," and "Delmonico steak."

Delmonico's had its imitators in New York, like Rector's, Lüchow's, and Louis Sherry, and other cities followed suit, especially New Orleans, whose own French heritage enabled Antoine Alciatore to succeed immediately when he opened Antoine's in that city in 1840. Elsewhere the best restaurants were those opened in hotels, like Boston's Parker House. Niagara's International Hotel (where waiters served to the sound of a full band), Denver's Brown Palace, and many others around the country. In such establishments the food was served course by course, and with military efficiency.

In lesser public dining rooms meals were served at a furious pace and with all courses set on the table at once. English traveler Basil Hall noted that at one New York City lunchroom in 1827 two complete dinners were served to two sets of customers within twenty minutes. Crucial to the development of American hotel dining-room service was the idea of the "American Plan," initiated around 1830, by which guests at hotels had to pay for their meals whether they ate them in the hotel or not. Guests on such a plan enjoyed four large meals a day at set hours, served by waiters tottering under huge platters of food and served in cavernous dining halls that were often segregated by sex. Little of the food was prepared with much sophistication, and it was consumed by the hundreds of guests present with amazing speed.

The "European Plan," introduced at New York's Tammany Hall Hotel in the 1830s, allowed guests to dine at whatever hour they pleased and to choose what they wanted from the menu—an idea that at the time was regarded as something unacceptably aristocratic.

Eating out in America was an exercise of one's capacity to consume enormous amounts of food, whether it was at a restaurant like Delmonico's (where twelve-course meals were rather ordinary affairs) or at "lobster palaces" and "beer halls" of the post-Civil War era, where customers ate and drank their fill very cheaply. Dickens once commented on the American passion for shellfish, saying he saw "at every supper at least two mighty bowls of hot stewed oysters, in any one of which a half-grown Duke of Clarence might be smothered easily." Game was equally relished by the gastronomes of the day, and a typically lavish meal, like the one served to President Ulysses S. Grant at Chicago's Parker House, might include young bear, Maryland coon, leg of elk, and loin of buffalo.

Women were not admitted to all dining rooms, and until the 1870s separate rooms were provided for them to take their meals at eastern hotels. All-male establishments like saloons and barrooms often gave away a FREE LUNCH in order to attract customers, and the fare might have included anything from crackers and cheese to caviar (then a very inexpensive item).

Cheap, low establishments went by slang terms like "hole in the wall," "mulligan joint," "slop joint," "slop chute," and "hash house."

"Coffee shops" were prevalent as early as the 1830s, and LUNCH COUNTERS as of the 1820s. "Snack bars" came in about 1895, while CAFETERIAS began in the Midwest about the same time. The first AUTOMAT was opened in Philadelphia in 1902.

Americans have always prided themselves on their mobile eateries, from the chuck wagons used on the range to the urban lunch wagon and food-purveying street vendors of the post-Civil War period. Steamboats were especially lavish in their dining-room decor and offered extensive menus of fashionable foods. The first dining cars on American trains were known as of 1838, but the truly lavish and impeccably appointed dining car (later called the "club car") was the creation, in 1868, of George Pullman, who named his first mobile restaurant after Delmonico's. DINERS were modeled after the design of railroad dining cars, though rarely adapted from an actual car. These stationary lunchrooms became representative symbols of American roadside hospitality after the automobile became part of most people's lives and traveling the highways part of the national destiny. In the East diners were often bought and run by Greek immigrants who had previously run inexpensive hash houses or coffee shops, and some of the lunch-counter slang and jargon was once referred to as "hash-house Greek."

Mining towns like Denver and San Francisco grew rich overnight, and saloons and taverns were immediately followed by elegant restaurants to serve a newly affluent clientele who wanted to spend their wealth on the finest foods, wines, and amenities they could afford. Much more important to the establishing of culinary standards, however, were the contributions of Englishman Frederick Henry Harvey, who in 1876 in Topeka, Kansas, set up the first of hundreds of "Harvey restaurants" along the route of the Atchison, Topeka & Santa Fe Railway. Harvey not only brought cleanliness, good food, changing menus, and reasonable prices to small towns in the West, but also brought out more than a hundred thousand young women from the East to become waitresses in his restaurants, the effect of which was to bring a modicum of civilization to some rough-and-tumble new townships as well as providing prospective brides to an overwhelmingly male population in the West.

Immigrant food culture both influenced and was adapted to American gastronomy in remarkably diverse ways. Immigrants found that opening up foodservice establishments—from Jewish DELICATESSENS to Italian "pizzerias," from German rathskellers to JAPANESE STEAK-HOUSES—was a relatively easy way to make money and to draw Americans into their neighborhoods like Little Italy and Chinatown. In most cases these immigrant restaurant owners had to adapt their traditional recipes to American products and to the American palate, so that dishes and foods like LOX, CHICKEN TETRAZZINI, LIEDERKRANZ, CHOP SUEY, EGG FOO YUNG, NEGIMAKI,

LONDON BROIL, SWEDISH MEATBALLS, JANSSEN'S TEMPTATION, and others were actually American immigrant creations rather than traditional Old Country foods. These foods and restaurants greatly enriched American food culture, so that dishes like pizza, bagels, and tacos now rank with hot dogs, steaks, and turkey as some of Americans' favorite foods.

Prohibition effectively put a brake on the evolution of fine dining at restaurants in America, and many of the old-fashioned establishments of the Gilded Age were forced to close, including Delmonico's itself, which went out of business in 1923. Speakeasies took up the slack, ranging from terrible "dives" to society saloons like New York City's "21" Club, which after Prohibition went on to become a serious restaurant.

But throughout the United States roadside eateries and FAST-FOOD restaurants proliferated during Prohibition and afterward. The cheap, fast restaurant in America might well be understood by the straightforward emblem (often in neon lights) reading EATS, which was set on many such establishments. This might apply to "chili" or "taco stands," "night-owl" restaurants (places open late at night), or "burger joints." The idea of serving customers in their cars by "carhops" who jumped up on the running board of cars to take customers' orders was begun at the first "drive-in"—the Pig Stand barbecue stand set up by J. G. Kirby in September 1921 on the Dallas-Fort Worth Highway. The drive-in flourished along the public highways and was widespread throughout the United States by the 1930s, when one would go to a drive-in for hamburgers, hot dogs, milk shakes, and other quickly prepared dishes, called "FAST FOOD" in the 1960s. The Pig Stand also pioneered the "drive-through," whereby the customer drives up to a window where a worker takes the order and money and hands it to the customer.

The possibilities for expansion rose to a new level when Howard Dearing Johnson of Wollaston, Massachusetts, began franchising his Howard Johnson's restaurants to other entrepreneurs as of 1935. The hamburger stand itself took on a new allure when franchised chains like White Castle, opened in 1921 in Wichita, Kansas, by Walter Anderson and Edgar Waldo "Billy" Ingram, began selling a standardized product. Another concept for rushed customers was the "one-arm lunchroom" (started about 1912), at which the eater sat at a chair with armrests on which the food was placed.

In the 1930s restaurants again started to acquire an affluent clientele, although the tastes of such people were either basic or informed only by the amount of money something on a menu cost. At the other end of the scale were the cheap immigrant restaurants that catered to Americans' idea of what Italian, Greek, Chinese, German, and other cuisines were, resulting in standard dishes, like chow mein, spaghetti and meatballs, and goulash, that had little to do with the traditions of the cooking of the countries from which these dishes were supposedly "imported."

New York still dominated the rest of the country for the sheer number and variety of restaurants, although New Orleans had developed its own Creole-Cajun-French cuisine and restaurants that resembled few that could be found elsewhere. San Francisco, which had enjoyed something of a gastronomic reputation before the 1906 earthquake, slowly built up its renown for good American food after that disaster. It was not until the 1970s that Los Angeles began to diverge from its self-perpetuated image as the capital of FAST FOOD.

The 1939 World's Fair in New York City had an enormous effect on American restaurants, for it brought in excellent chefs from all over the world who served imaginative cuisine to a public generally ignorant of authentic European dishes. The manager of the French Pavilion restaurant, Henri Soulé, opened his own restaurant in New York called Le Pavillon, which became the bellwether of French classic dining rooms for the entire country, although the restaurant's influence was not significant outside New York until the 1960s.

In that same decade a new gimmick became popular—"theme restaurants," in which the style, design, decor, and food itself was all made to coalesce around a central idea, such as the Wild West, a Roman garden, or a pirate's cove. A company called Restaurant Associates, begun in 1945 by Abraham F. Wechsler, opened sleek, well-thought-out dining rooms with names like the Forum of the Twelve Caesars, the Trattoria, and The Four Seasons, all wed to motifs that were carried through from menu items to ashtrays. Such restaurants were widely imitated around the country, often by franchise chains. The "singles' bar" also became a genre of its own during this period, with New York's T.G.I. Friday's, which opened in 1965, the first example of a place where the postwar "baby boomers" could congregate for a good meal and fellowship.

Concomitant with the growth of such mainstream and glamorous restaurants was a growing counterculture food movement spurred by the dissension over civil rights and the Vietnam War in the 1960s and 1970s. As a reaction against the fat-rich, excessive diet of traditional American restaurants, counterculturists showed renewed interest in "ethnic restaurants"—Indian, Thai, Korean, Mexican, and a variety of Chinese restaurants featuring regional cuisines—as well as "health-food restaurants" specializing in salads, vegetables, and, often, amateur cooks. One of these, Alice Waters of Berkeley, California, came out of the protest movement of the 1960s to open a little restaurant called Chez Panisse in 1971 based on her love of French country food and organic produce, which she gathered from local California farmers. The success of Chez Panisse helped focus the iconoclasm of the counterculture into a far more productive, positive approach to food and cooking in America, so that virtues like freshness, local ingredients, and careful cooking techniques were exalted and became the basis of the so-called "California Cuisine movement," ironically itself an extrapolation of the very fussy, very elaborate new French style of cooking called la NOUVELLE CUISINE, which was a deliberate reaction against the staid clichés of the classic menu as interpreted by kitchens in French and American hotel dining rooms for decades. This, in turn, led to a so-called NEW AMERICAN CUISINE, promoted by young American chefs and glossy magazines as using American ingredients in new, often startling combinations and with French techniques.

By the 1980s new restaurants of every stripe—from the deluxe to the fast-food chains—were soaring in the United States, driven by a heated economy that helped make gourmandism into another form of social climbing. Cities that previously had little in the way of fine dining suddenly had a slew of new, expensive establishments to cater to an affluent new clientele who demanded the very best in ingredients, wine, and decor.

The recession of the 1990s restricted this growth and led to a good deal of "downscaling" of restaurants, so that instead of more posh dining rooms serving caviar and truffles with abandon, restaurateurs opened more bistros, trattorias, and cafés serving a wider range of less-expensive foods from around the world. When the recession ended in the mid-1990s and a boom economy fueled new restaurant growth, the industry grew to sales of $354 billion in 1999, with 50 billion meals eaten away from home each year. In fact, on any single day in the U.S. almost half of all Americans eat at some form of restaurant, and about 44 percent of the U.S. food dollar is spent at restaurants, compared with only 25 percent in 1955 and 33 percent in 1981. In 1999 there were more than 815,000 restaurants in the U.S.

restaurant row. A street, sometimes comprising several blocks, known for its extensive number of restaurants. The term originally referred to the block of Forty-sixth Street between Eighth and Ninth avenues in New York City, where many Theater District restaurants are located.

Reuben sandwich. Also, "Reuben." A sandwich made with corned beef, Swiss cheese, and sauerkraut on rye bread that is then fried like a grilled-cheese sandwich. Although there have been various claims as to the creation of the Reuben, the most probable is that of Arnold Reuben (1883–1970), owner of Reuben's Restaurant in New York City at 6 East Fifty-eighth Street. According to *Craig Claiborne's The New York Times Food Encyclopedia* (1985), Reuben's daughter, Patricia R. Taylor, contended that the sandwich was created in 1914 by her father for an actress named Annette Seelos. Arnold had a habit of naming dishes and sandwiches after the showbusiness celebrities who ate at his restaurant, but in this case he instead gave it his own name—the "Reuben Special," and G. Selmer Foughner, in his book *Dining in New York* (1939), made reference to a dish at Reuben's called the "Reubenola" but did not describe its contents.

It has also been asserted that Reuben Kolakofsky, a grocer, claimed to have invented the sandwich in 1922 during a poker game with friends at the Blackstone Hotel in Omaha, Nebraska. The recipe was later submitted by Fern Snider (a waitress at the Blackstone Hotel) and won first prize at the National Sandwich Contest in 1956, held by the Wheat Flour Institute in 1956 and later revived by Pepperidge Farm.

rhubarb. Any of a variety of plants with long stalks in the genus *Rheum,* although the leaf stem of *Rheum rhaponticum* is the species of culinary interest. The etymology of the word goes back to the Greek *rha,* which probably derived from the former name for the Volga River, Rha, where rhubarb was grown. In Middle English *rha* became *rubarbe,* possibly through an alteration of the Latin term *rha barbarum,* meaning "barbarian rhubarb."

Rhubarb is of Asian origins, and, although it had been cultivated at monasteries for its medicinal values, Europeans showed little culinary interest in the plant. It was not until the nineteenth century that the plant began showing up in London markets. At that time in the United States its pouch of unopened flowers, which the Alaskan Eskimos customarily ate raw, was of some gastronomic interest. Rhubarb pie, first mentioned in print in 1855, was to become one of the two most popular preparations of the food; the other was stewed, sweetened rhubarb served as a dessert. So

popular was rhubarb pie that the plant is often called the "pie plant." It has been particularly relished by the Pennsylvania Dutch.

In the United States rhubarb is grown either as a hothouse or field variety, the latter more flavorful and more deeply pink in color. A pie made with rhubarb and strawberries of angelica is a traditional American dish.

RHUBARB PIE

Combine 4 c. chopped rhubarb, 1⅓ c. honey, 7 T. flour, 4 T. angelica, and ½ t. salt. Pour into pastry crust, dot with butter, cover with another crust, bake at 450° for 10 min. Reduce to 350° and cook another 50 min.

---

rice (*Oryza sativa*). A cultivated cereal grass that is one of the most important foods of the world, especially in Asia, where it forms a large part of the diet. The word is from the Greek *óruzon,* which in Middle English appears as *rys.*

Although rice was a popular food in Italy, Spain, and France by the Renaissance, it did not make much of a stir in England, which nevertheless encouraged experiments to grow the crop in its American colonies, the first in 1622. In 1647 William Berkeley sowed half a bushel of rice in Virginia and reaped thirty times that amount in his first harvest. But the crop eventually failed. South Carolina is generally credited as the birthplace of the rice industry in America, based on a legend concerning the arrival in 1685 at Charleston of a Captain John Thurber, who had been blown off course. Thurber gave some Madagascar rice to one of the city's foremost citizens, Henry Woodward, who planted it in his garden. Some stories tell of the rice dying, others of it flourishing. Another tale credits a Dutch captain with bringing the grain to Charleston in 1694, while still another gives the honor to Anthony Ashley Cooper, first earl of Shaftesbury, who planted one hundred pounds of seed in South Carolina and sent back sixty tons to England in 1698.

However rice got to South Carolina, the state remained the leading rice-producing region for two hundred years, exporting about forty-five hundred metric tons annually as of 1726. During the American Revolution the British captured Charleston and shipped the entire rice crop home, leaving no seed behind. Thomas Jefferson smuggled some Italian rice seed out of Europe in 1787 and brought it back to the Carolinas. The industry eventually revived, and a favorable trade was established with England in the early nineteenth century, during which time every southern state east of the Mississippi began growing rice, the exception being Louisiana, which did not produce a rice crop until 1889, although it had been introduced there as early as 1718. California also produced rice as early as 1760, although it did not produce its first commercial crop of short-grain rice until 1912, and the territory between the Pacific and the Mississippi took on the crop slowly: Texas was not cultivating the grain until 1850, and ten years later referred to the crop as "providence rice," because low-lying regions depended wholly on collected rainwater for irrigation.

By 1905 Arkansas was growing rice, and the industry took off quickly in the Sacramento Valley in California. Missouri followed in 1920 and Mississippi in 1949. Today very little rice is grown in the original delta lands of the southern Atlantic states, with Arkansas, California, Louisiana, and Texas the major producing states. South Carolina, ironically, is no longer a major producer, having picked its last commercial crop in 1927. Today the United States rice growers' total crop is about 10 billion pounds, and the United States is the world's leading exporter of rice, even though America produces less than 2 percent of the world's crop which totaled 563 million tons in 1996, with 57 percent of the crop produced by China and India. The U.S. crop totaled 171.3 million hundredweight.

In the 1940s Texan Gordon Harwell, using a British process of treating rice with pressurized steam to drive minerals and vitamins into the kernel and out of the discarded bran layer, marketed "converted rice" under the name "Uncle Ben's," whose name was based on a renowned African-American rice farmer in Houston known for the high quality of his rice.

"Minute Rice" was a product developed by Ataull K. Ozai Durrani and sold to General Foods that allowed precooked rice to be cooked at home in only ten minutes. The product was introduced in 1949.

Americans' consumption of rice has more than doubled in the past twenty years, with 26.29 pounds consumed per person in 1998. Americans of the South and Southwest eat the most rice in the United States, for it is a staple food of Hispanic-American, Creole, and Delta cookeries although Hawaiians consume the most of all, 105.8 pounds per capita annually. In Charleston, South Carolina, rice is part of a long tradition. Samuel Gaillard Stoney, in *Charleston: Azaleas and Old Bricks* (1937), records that "on every proper Charleston dinner table [there is] a spoon that is peculiar to the town. Of massive silver, about fifteen inches long and broad in proportions, it is laid on the cloth with some-

thing of the reverential distinction that surrounds the mace in the House of Commons at Westminster. . . . If you take away the rice-spoon from the Charleston dinner table, the meal that follows is not really a meal."

Rice is combined into seafood and meat preparations, in pancakes called "rice cakes" (see CALA), in breads, puddings, breakfast cereals, and dumplings, or served simply boiled and buttered. It is the basis of many American dishes, like DIRTY RICE, PILAU, JAMBALAYA, and RED BEANS AND RICE, and is used in the making of beer.

So-called "Carolina rice" is a long-grain variety, which accounts for nearly 69 percent of American rice. (Medium-grain totals about 27 percent and short-grain, also called "pearl white rice," about 4 percent.) "Brown rice" (3 percent) is the unpolished grain of rice containing the wheat germ and outer layer of bran, which gives the seed a brownish coloring. WILD RICE is discussed under its main entry. "Rough" or "paddy" rice is rice as it comes straight from the field, with hull intact. "Brewers rice" is taken from the smallest size of broken rice fragments and used in brewing and in pet foods.

"Converted," "conditioned," or "parboiled" rice is precooked (a process going back to ancient India), which improves nutritional value and inhibits rancidity. "Precooked," "quick-cooking," or "instant rice" has been cooked then dehydrated to cut down on cooking time. "Sticky," "sweet," "waxy," "mochigome," or "glutinous" rice has a sticky texture and is used primarily in Asian cooking.

"Arborio" rice is a plump, starchy rice used in the making of the Italian dish called "risotto," with the most favored varieties coming from around the Po Valley in Italy.

Various "aromatic" rices like "Basmati" from India and Pakistan and "Thai jasmine" (or "Thai fragrant") from Thailand are imported, although there is an American "basmati-type" rice that came to the United States at the turn of the century and recently some American "jasmine-type" rices have been grown.

"Puffed rice" is a cereal introduced at the 1904 St. Louis World's Fair by Dr. Alexander P. Anderson by shooting them from guns.

RICE PUDDING

Combine 2 T. cooked rice with 1 T. raisins, and place in buttered pudding pan. Beat 2 egg yolks, add ½ c. sugar, 2 c. milk, and 1 t. vanilla. Pour over rice and bake for 40 min. at 325°. When done sprinkle with cinnamon.

Rice Krispies Treats. Registered trademark by the Kellogg Company for a confection developed in the 1930s using Rice Krispies cereal and marshmallows. It is a cross between a cake and a candy.

RICE KRISPIES TREATS

🥄 Melt ¼ butter or margarine in a saucepan over low heat, add one 10-ounce package of marshmallows and blend well. Remove from heat, then add 6 cups Kellogg's Rice Krispies cereal, stir until coated with marshmallow. Press mixture into a buttered square cake pan 13" x 9" x 2", then cut into two-inch squares.

---

rickey. A drink whose basic ingredients are lime juice and soda water (1890). In its nonalcoholic form, a sweet syrup is usually added. In its alcoholic form, sugar is traditionally forbidden, and a spirit is added, usually gin, though bourbon, blended whiskey, or applejack are sometimes used. Adding sugar would make the drink a TOM COLLINS.

In his abridged edition of Mencken's *American Language* (1963), Raven I. McDavid, Jr., notes that "authorities agree that the drink was named after a distinguished Washington guzzler of the period, but his identity is disputed, as is the original form of the rickey." One attribution is to a "Colonel" Rickey from Kentucky, with no further information on the subject; another names him "Joe Rickey."

The "lime rickey" is a Boston soda-fountain drink made with a sweet lime syrup, the juice of a lime, the crushed lime skin, and seltzer.

RICKEY

🥄 In an old-fashioned glass mix with 1 ice cube 2 oz. gin, 1 oz. fresh lime juice, club soda, and a twist of lime.

LIME RICKEY

🥄 Place 3 T. cherry syrup in a tall glass, add 1½ T. lime juice, 1 T. bar sugar, and ice cubes. Fill with club soda or seltzer and garnish with a slice of lime.

---

rivel. A small dumpling added to soups. Betty Groff in *Betty Groff's Pennsylvania Dutch Cookbook* (1990) wrote that "chowders and soups may be considered the main course when rivels are added," and rivels are usually considered to be a Pennsylvania-Dutch dish.

The Random House Dictionary, however, says the item is "Chiefly Western Canadian" and lists the origins as "uncertain."

RIVEL

🥄 Combine 2 c. sifted flour with ½ t. salt and 1 beaten egg. Rub the mixture between your fingers to create very small droplets of dough. Drop into boiling water or broth and cook for 3 min.

---

riz. A Southern baker's term for biscuits or other confections made with yeast and therefore "riz'd" ("risen").

roach coach. Slang for mobile catering trucks.

roadhouse. An inexpensive restaurant, saloon, nightclub, or inn located along a highway. The term dates in print to 1855.

Rob Roy. Also, "Scotch Manhattan." A cocktail made with Scotch, sweet vermouth, and bitters. According to William Grimes in *Straight Up or On the Rocks* (1993), the cocktail was named after a Broadway play about the legendary Robert MacGregor (1671–1734), hero of a Sir Walter Scott novel entitled *Rob Roy* (1817). The drink's name was first printed in 1865.

ROB ROY

🥄 Shake ¾ oz. Scotch whiskey, ¾ oz. sweet vermouth, and 2 dashes bitters with cracked ice. Strain and pour into chilled glass. In a dry Rob Roy dry vermouth is substituted for sweet.

---

rock and rye. A liqueur with a blended-whiskey base, to which is added rock-candy syrup and sometimes fruits, and having a proof of 60 to 70 (1875). It was used in the nineteenth century as a digestive aid.

ROCK AND RYE

🥄 Combine 1 pt. whiskey, ½ pt. glycerine, and ½ lb. powdered rock candy. Bottle and seal.

---

rock candy. A hard candy made by cooling a concentrated sugar syrup (1715). It is often sold crystallized around a piece of string or a stick. It is sometimes used to make rock and rye, the liqueur.

Dryden & Palmer of Norwalk, Connecticut, has manufactured rock candy since 1880 and claims to be the only company still doing so.

rockfish (genus *Sebastes*). A family of fish that inhabit rocky regions of the sea and that go by many names. The name dates in print to 1590. In his book *Seafood: A Connoisseur's Guide and Cookbook* (1989), Alan Davidson describes the confusion over the various species that go under the name "rockfish," noting that in California more than fifty species of so-called "rock cod" fall under the general group known as "rockfish." Among the most popular rockfish are the "bolina" (*S. auriculatus*) and the "goldeneye rockfish" (*S. ruberrimus*), the "cowfish" or "cowcod" (*S. levis*), and the "chili pepper" (*S. goodei*). Members of the genus *Scorpaena* are also called "rockfish," though they are more commonly known as "scorpionfish" or "sea scorpion" because of their venomous dorsal fins.

rocky road. A confection of milk or dark chocolate mixed with marshmallows and nuts. Its name derives from the texture of the finished product. Culinary historian Jean Anderson has found a recipe for the candy dating to *Young American's Cookbook* (1938). It is also the familiar name of a similarly flavored ice cream.

ROCKY ROAD

In a saucepan mix 2 c. milk chocolate or dark chocolate morsels, one 14-oz. can sweetened condensed milk and 2 T. butter. Heat until chocolate is melted. Remove from heat. Combine 5½ c. small marshmallows with 1½ c. unsalted roasted peanuts or chopped almonds, then fold into chocolate mixture. Spread into a pan lined with waxed paper and chili for about 2 hr., until firm. Remove from pan, peel off waxed paper, and cut into squares. Makes 8 doz.

Roffignac. A cocktail made with whiskey, grenadine, or raspberry syrup, and soda water. It is a New Orleans beverage named after an early mayor of that city, Louis-Philippe Joseph de Roffignac.

An oyster dish made with mushrooms, red wine shrimp, and scallions also goes by this same name.

rollmops. A marinated herring fillet that is stuffed and rolled and served as an hors d'oeuvre (1910). The name comes from Germany, a combination of *rollen,* "to roll," and *mops,* "pug dog"—perhaps so called because of its stubby appearance.

ROLLMOPS

Spread individual herring fillets with mustard, then place chopped onion, a slice of pickle, and some capers on top. Roll into snug packages and tie with a string or secure with a toothpick. Marinate the rollmops in a boiled solution of 1 c. vinegar, 1 c. water, 1 t. sugar, 2 bay leaves, and 1 T. pickling spices.

Romano. A cow's-milk cheese that originated in Italy but is made in several American dairy states. The name derives from the city of Rome, and there are several varieties, including "Pecorino Romano" (which is quite sharp and salty) and a Wisconsin-made flattened ball of cheese called "Piccolo Romano" ("Little Roman"). Romano is fairly firm and is usually used as a grating cheese for pasta, salads, and other dishes.

rooster-spur pepper (*Capiscum frutescens fasciculatum*). A hot red CHILE pepper, sometimes called the "bird pepper," whose name derives from its resemblance to the spur of a rooster's claw. These peppers are not commercially grown but raised in home gardens in the South.

The rooster-spur pepper took on some political clout in 1978, when Attorney General Griffin Bell snuck some sausages seasoned with the pepper past Secret Service officers and into the White House, to the delight of President Jimmy Carter (1924–; held office 1977–1981), who asked Bell for more. As a result the Justice Department was deluged with requests for the recipe, which came from a farmer named H. S. Williams in Haralson, Georgia.

Sending rooster-spur pepper condiments to politicians has been something of a small tradition in the South, maintained in Mississippi for half a century by J. C. Luter, Sr., of Walthall County, whose pepper sauce was famous as of the 1920s.

ROOSTER-SPUR PEPPER SAUCE

Clip several rooster-spur peppers from a bush, leaving short stems. Wash, drain, and pack tightly in bottles. Pour boiling water over the peppers and into the bottles and let stand until scalded. Drain water, add a pinch of sugar and salt, then pour hot vinegar over peppers to fill the bottles. Seal tightly.

Roquefort dressing. A salad dressing made with Roquefort or blue cheese.

ROQUEFORT DRESSING

Combine 1 lb. Roquefort, 2 T. lemon juice, ½ c. heavy cream or sour cream, 1 T. chopped chives, Worcestershire sauce, and Tabasco sauce to taste, and a dash of garlic salt.

---

roux. A mixture of a starch (flour, cornstarch, or arrowroot) and a fat that is browned in a saucepan until thickened and that serves as the base of a sauce or gravy (1805). The word is French, via Latin *russus*, "red."

Roux has a particular fascination for Louisiana cooks, who contend it is the ingredient that distinguishes their finest preparations. Creole roux are made with butter or bacon fat and are cooked far longer than most French roux and achieve a deep honey color (although there is also a white roux, which is pale in color because it is cooked quickly and not allowed to brown).

Cajun roux are made with vegetable oil or lard and cooked to a caramel color, although Cajuns also use lighter roux.

ROUX

Combine 4 T. butter or lard with 4 T. flour in a skillet and cook, stirring constantly, over a very low flame until it is a rich brown color throughout. This may take 20–45 min.

---

rubber-chicken dinner. A slang term for the kind of unsavory, mass-produced food commonly served at a banquet dinner. It is most often associated with political fund-raisers. The "rubber-chicken circuit" (1955) is a series of such dinners a speaker or political candidate is often forced to attend. The reference to a rubber chicken, dating back at least to the 1950s, is to the rubbery kind of meat served at such functions but, more specifically, to an actual rubber-chicken gag item sold at novelty stores.

Ruby Cabernet. A red vinifera grape used to make a medium-bodied red wine. It was developed in 1946 by Harold Paul Olmo at the University of California at Davis from crossing CABERNET SAUVIGNON and Carignane. Most Ruby Cabernet wine is produced in California's Central Valley.

rugelach. Also, "rugalach" and "rogelach." Jewish-American cookies, usually made with a cream cheese

dough and stuffed with nuts, fruits and raisins. The word is Yiddish. According to Joan Nathan in her *Jewish Cooking in America* (1994), "The American addition to *rugelach* was cream cheese and the myriad of fillings used today," suggesting that the cream cheese dough may have been developed by the Philadelphia Cream Cheese Company and that one of the earliest references to such dough was in *The Perfect Hostess* (1950) by Mildred Knopf, who said the recipe came from Nela Rubinstein, wife of pianist Arthur Rubinstein. Nathan also contends it was a rugelach recipe by Florida dessert expert Maida Heatter that "put *rugelach* on the culinary map . . . and is the *rugelach* recipe most often found in upscale bakeries nationwide."

rugola (*Eruca vesicaria sativa*). Also, "arugola," "arugula," and others. An herb, known in England as "rockets." The name is derived from Italian regional words for the herb, *rucola* or *ruccetta,* and first appeared in English print as "arugala" in 1965. The herb is native to Eurasia but was brought to America by the Italian immigrants of the late nineteenth century, and it is still very much localized in this country within cities with large Italian populations. It is eaten with salad dressing and often with tomatoes. It should not be confused with "rocket salad," an American winter cress.

rum. A spirit distilled from fermented sugarcane, principally molasses. There are several types of rum, ranging from light to full-bodied, most produced in the islands of the Caribbean but also on Java in Indonesia (called "Batavia Arak") and in Guyana along the Demerara River. Although some heavy rums may be distilled at 190 proof, federal regulations require a minimum of 80 proof.

Rum was first made in the Caribbean, possibly in Barbados, around 1600, after Christopher Columbus brought sugarcane to the West Indies from the Azores. These first rums were made by the Spanish, but the rum trade was quickly picked up by various Europeans. By 1639 the spirit was called "kill-devil." The word rum is of somewhat obscure origins: Some believe it may derive from the Latin *saccharum,* sugar. The *Oxford English Dictionary* suggests "rumbustion" and "rumbullion" are earlier forms. The first use of the word was in 1645, long before the date of another story sometimes cited to explain the origin of the name, the legend that in 1745 British admiral Edward Vernon (also credited with providing the word GROG) tried to cure his crew's scurvy by switching their beer ration to the molasses-based spirit. The grateful seamen nicknamed their captain "Old Rummy," for rum was then a slang term for "the best."

The rum trade was exceptionally important in the Colonial era, and by 1657 rum was even being produced in New England. The spirit was shipped to Europe and sold or traded in Africa for slaves to work the American plantations, which produced the molasses to make more rum.

Until gin replaced it as a cheap drink in the eighteenth century, rum was the predominant alcohol of the poor and a subject of frequent jeremiads from the pulpit. It was often drunk at breakfast or mixed with other ingredients to make early forms of cocktails, such as shrub, flip, punch, and grog. "Bombo" (possibly named after British admiral John Benbow [1653–1702]), made from rum, hot water, and molasses, was popular in North Carolina, while "blackstrap," a mixture of rum and molasses, was favored in New England, where pungent rums were called "stink-a-bus." "Samson," referring to the most powerful of biblical heroes, was rum mixed with cider.

Rum was given out at political rallies; in fact, George Washington gave out seventy-five gallons of rum to voters during his successful campaign in 1758 for representative in the Virginia House of Burgesses. By 1775 Americans were drinking four gallons of rum per person per year, but this was soon to change. The British had passed in 1733 the Molasses Act, which imposed high duties on the colonists; this was followed by the Sugar Act in 1764, which cut the duties on molasses but made the importation of sugar, wine, and coffee very expensive. Both acts were strictly enforced against smugglers. These laws had a crippling effect on the New England distilleries and further hastened the general dissent that led to revolution in the next decade. One story has it that Paul Revere fortified himself with two drafts of Medford rum at Isaac Hall's distillery before beginning his famous ride to warn the colonists of a British invasion on the night of April 18, 1775.

After the war America's favorable trade relations with the British West Indies were disrupted, and the price of rum rose. Also, a strong temperance movement was building in the new country that effectively prevented the recovery of the New England distilleries. Domestic production was further impaired by war between France and England and America's own War of 1812 with England. The abolition of the slave trade in 1808 destroyed any possibility for economic viability in United States rum production, although a low-grade drink made from molasses, called "tafia," was produced in New Orleans during the nineteenth century.

Rum continued to be very popular, however, and, after the reestablishment of the United States Navy in 1794, an act of Congress decreed that every sailor's ration should include "one half pint of distilled spirits per day, or in lieu thereof, one quart of beer per day." Rum was preferred, usually drunk in the form of grog and mixed with water. The Navy Department tried to substitute whiskey for rum as an economic measure, but it was years before the latter spirit was accepted by most sailors. The grog ration was reduced throughout the nineteenth century, after a panel of surgeons in 1829 had found it inexpedient and demoralizing. Finally, after urging from Assistant Secretary of the Navy Gustavus V. Fox, Congress resolved on July 14, 1862, that the "spirit ration shall forever cease and thereafter no distilled spiritous liquor shall be admitted onboard vessels of war, except as medicine." The grog ration ended when President Abraham Lincoln signed the resolution on September 1, 1862, though the Confederate Navy kept up the ration throughout the Civil War. (The British Admiralty did not abolish the ration until August 1, 1970.)

Today Americans obtain most of their rum from the Virgin Islands, where rum has been made since the repeal of Prohibition in 1933. Seventy percent of the rum comes, however, from Puerto Rico, which makes light White or Silver rums and more flavorful Amber or Gold rums, all hovering around 80 proof, and "liqueur rums," which are dry and robust. There is still some rum made in Massachusetts, but the Bureau of Alcohol, Tobacco and Firearms of the United States Treasury dropped the appellation "New England rum" from the United States Standards of Identity list in 1968. Nevertheless, New Englanders continue to consume more rum than any other Americans. Currently Americans drink about 30 million gallons of rum, mostly light. The spirit constitutes about 7½ percent of the liquor market. Today rum is usually mixed with other ingredients to make cocktails like the DAIQUIRI, the PIÑA COLADA, EL PRESIDENTE, and the CUBA LIBRE. Rum and Coke (rum mixed with Coca-Cola) is particularly popular among young Americans, and hot buttered rum is consumed in winter.

By federal law rum proof must be at least 60 (30 percent alcohol by volume). Total U.S. production (including Puerto Rico and the Virgin Islands) of rum in 1997 was 11.5 million 9-liter cases.

between the sheets. The name probably refers to the cocktail's supposed ability to force one to bed, but see THREE SHEETS IN THE WIND for another alternative.

BETWEEN THE SHEETS

Shake with crushed ice 1 part Triple Sec, 2 parts lime juice, 3 parts brandy, and 3 parts Gold rum. Serve with lemon twist.

---

hot buttered rum. In Kenneth Robert's novel, *Northwest Passage* (1937), a character says of this old New England favorite.

And it ain't a temporary drink. . . . No matter how much you drink of anything else, it'll wear off in a day or so, but you take enough hot buttered rum and it'll last you pretty near as long as a coonskin cap. . . . After a man's had two-three drinks of hot buttered rum, he don't shoot a catamount; all he's got to do is walk up to him, kiss him just once; then put him in his bag, all limp.

Robert's recipe is as follows:

HOT BUTTERED RUM

Heat a tumbler, add ½ in. hot water, and dissolve 1 t. sugar in it. Add a jigger of New England rum, ½ t. cinnamon, a pat of butter, and more hot water.

---

rumrousal. A New England milk punch made by combining 1 qt. Jamaican rum, 3 qt. milk, 1½ c. honey, and ½ pt. bourbon. The origin of the name is unknown.

rumaki. A canape or appetizer made by wrapping bacon slices around around chestnuts and chicken livers that have been marinated with soy sauce and Chinese spices (1961). The item became popular in so-called "polynesian" restaurants like Trader Vic's in San Francisco, whose owner said rumaki was of Chinese origin but with a Japanese name. Etymologists suggest the word may derive from the Japanese *harumaki*, which itself derives from the Chinese *chunjuan* for "spring roll."

rum tum tiddy. Also, "rinkum-dity." A New England blend of tomato soup or tomatoes, eggs, and Cheddar cheese served on toast.

RUM TUM TIDDY

To 2 c. of tomato soup add ½ lb. sharp Cheddar cheese and cook in a double boiler until cheese is melted.

Add ¼ t. dry mustard and 1 beaten egg. Stir briefly, then serve on buttered toast.

running south. A term dating from the turn of the last century to describe cheeses so overripe and runny that they may be eaten with a spoon.

Runza. Also, "runsa." Trademark name for a Nebraska drive-in restaurant chain's oblong bun filled with ground meat, cabbage, and onions. Similar to a PASTY, it was at first called a "kraut runsa," and it was first made after World War II by Sally Everett of Lincoln, Nebraska, as a picnic item. By changing the *s* to a *z*, she was able to trademark the name "Runza," which in the 1960s her son Don expanded into a chain of drive-ins, later adding an "Italian-style Runza" to the menu.

Russian dressing. A salad dressing made from mayonnaise, pimiento, chile sauce, green pepper, and chives. It is so called possibly because the mixture was thought to resemble those found in Russian salads, but it is American in origin, first found in print in 1922.

RUSSIAN DRESSING

Combine ½ c. mayonnaise with ¼ c. chile sauce, 1 T. chopped pimiento, 1 T. chopped green pepper, and 1 t. chopped chives.

---

rye 'n' Injun bread. Also, "Rhineinjun bread." A New York Dutch bread made from 1 qt. unbolted Rhode Island rye meal and 2 qt. Narraganset cornmeal. According to Alice Morse Earle's *Colonial Recipes in Old New York* (1926), the bread was cooked in a fireplace and covered with hot ashes. Its first mention in print was in 1805.

rye whiskey. One of the first whiskeys made in America, rye must be made from at least 51 percent rye grain, which can be mixed with corn and barley, and must be aged in barrels for at least a year. The word "rye" is often casually used for blended whiskeys that do not have the legal 51 percent rye grain, but to print such an appellation on the label would be forbidden by law.

The first distilleries to make rye whiskey were set up in the eighteenth century by Scots and Irish settlers in western Pennsylvania. The first appearance of the term in print was in 1775.

sablefish (*Anoplopoma fimbria*). A rich, oily Northern Pacific fish (1800). The name derives from its blackish skin, and the fish is commonly called "black cod." It is usually sold frozen or smoked, and market size is usually about two feet long and ten pounds. U.S. commercial landings of sablefish totaled 52.9 million pounds in 1997.

saccharin. An artificial sweetener that is 350 times sweeter than sugar. Saccharin is used in processed foods and as a substitute for sugar. Created in 1879 at John Hopkins University by chemistry student Constantine Fahlberg (who refused to share credit with his teacher Ira Remsen), saccharin is now manufactured by the Sherwin-Williams Companies and currently accounts for about 70 percent of the artificial-sweetener market in America, packaged in familiar pink packets under the name Sweet 'N' Low and now ubiquitous on restaurant tables. The chemical makeup of saccharin is $C_7H_5NO_3S$, and the name derives from Latin, Greek, Pali, and Sanskrit root words meaning "sugar."

sad cake. A pecan-coconut-raisin cake so called because it sinks in the middle after baking and has a "sad" look to it. The confection is best known in the South. The following recipe is adapted from one printed in 1984 in the Louisville *Courier-Journal*.

SAD CAKE

Mix 1 lb. brown sugar with 4 beaten eggs. Add ½ c. vegetable oil, 2 c. packaged biscuit mix, 1 t. vanilla, 1 c. chopped pecans, 7 oz. flaked coconut, and ½ c. raisins. Bake in an ungreased 9-by-13-in. pan at 325° for 45 mins. The middle should fall when almost done. Cut into squares.

---

sago. A starch from the sago palm (*Metroxylon, Arenga,* and *Caryota*) used as a thickener for puddings and other desserts (1545). The word is from the Malay *sagu,* and first appears in English print in 1580.

salad. A dish of leafy vegetables dressed with various seasonings, sauces, and other vegetables or fruits. The word is from the Latin *sāl,* salt, because the first salads of Rome were dressed with little more than simple salt. In Middle English the word became *salade,* and throughout the nineteenth century "salat" is often used in American cookbooks. In England a salad composed of lettuce or other leafy vegetable only is called a "green salad" and is served as an accompaniment to cooked meats or poultry, whereas a "green salad" in America has, at least since 1891, meant a separate salad course, usually served before the main course, with a simple dressing of oil and vinegar. In France and elsewhere in Europe salads are customarily served after the main course and before the cheese.

Americans had very little interest in salad for most of their history, and more often than not after the Civil War a salad was largely composed of poultry or seafood and vegetables surrounded by only a few lettuce leaves. The wealthy, however, began enjoying European-style salads in the new restaurants opening in the large cities, especially in New York, where Delmonico's Restaurant specialized in novel salad dressings and the WALDORF SALAD of the Waldorf-Astoria Hotel was an instant sensation.

"Molded" or "congealed" salads, made with gelatin or aspic and sugar or sweet fruits, were common in the late nineteenth century. The Shakers had long made "fruit salads," which might not have had any greens at all, and these became a popular luncheon dish in place of a first course. The Germans brought POTATO SALAD, and the Italians made tomatoes the most popular ingredient of all in twentieth-century salads, especially with the availability of excellent fruit and vegetables from California then entering the market. California was also the inspiration for a great number of famous salads, such as the GREEN GODDESS, PALACE COURT, and (via Tijuana, Mexico) CAESAR SALAD. So pervasive was the California influence that a salad has become a common main-course item in itself, called "chef's salad" and including ham and hard-boiled eggs, on many menus as well as at many hosts' tables.

In 1971 Chicago restaurateurs Rich Melman and Jerry Orzoff opened a place called R. J. Grunts, which featured a "salad bar," a long counter of greens, seasonings, vegetables, and condiments at which the customer arranges his own salad on whim; this became a fixture of medium-priced and family restaurants throughout the United States.

Some sandwich fillings made with mayonnaise are also called salads, as, for example, tuna salad, chicken salad, or egg salad. In the 1970s and 1980s cold pasta salads, particularly those made with tortellini, mayonnaise, and dill, became fashionable.

Dressings have ranged from the very simple oil and vinegar, called FRENCH DRESSING since 1900, to elaborate sauces that might contain orange slices and marshmallows. Only in the recent past have endive, escarole, rugola, and other European greens become popular.

For individual salads or dressings see main entries.

Salad Savoy. Trademark name for a vegetable in the Cruciferae family with a flavor resembling cauliflower, broccoli, and cabbage. The leafy heads have either white or violet centers. Salad Savoy was created by John Moore of Moore Farming, Inc., in Salinas, California, in 1983 and began production a year later, when the trademark took effect.

salami. A well-seasoned, often smoked sausage of various kinds most often used as a cold cut or sandwich meat. The name is from the Italian *salame,* "salted pork," and Vulgar Latin *salāre,* dating in English print at least to 1850. Since foreign sausages are not allowed to be brought into the United States for health reasons, many varieties of Italian salami have been reproduced here, although usually somewhat less spicy. Most are made from a combination of pork and beef, the best known being "Genoa salami," which derives its name from the kind of sausage made in Genoa, Italy. "Mortadella" is a BOLOGNA-style sausage that is larded with pork fat. The name is from the Latin *murtātum,* a sausage made with myrtle and berries, first appearing in English in 1613.

saleratus. An early-nineteenth-century form of BAKING POWDER (1830). Used as a leavening agent, it was an improvement over pearlash (used in the eighteenth century) and predated baking soda, which came along in the 1870s. Saleratus (which in Latin means "aerated salt") was first made from potassium bicarbonate, then sodium bicarbonate, and it imparted an undesirable bitterness. One may still hear of old-fashioned saleratus bread and biscuits, although one will no longer find saleratus in a grocery store.

Salisbury steak. A patty made of ground beef and seasonings that is usually broiled. The dish was named after Dr. James Henry Salisbury, who devised a "meat cure" for Civil War soldiers suffering from "camp diarrhea." Salisbury insisted they be fed a diet of chopped beef patties cut from disease-free animals' muscle fibers, with no connective tissue, fat, or cartilage. He went on to advocate this same diet for all Americans, advising them to eat beef three times a day for health benefits. The term dates in print to 1895. The Salisbury steak is often cited as an early example of what was soon to become the HAMBURGER.

SALISBURY STEAK

Combine 1 lb. chopped beef with 1 minced onion, 1 T. chopped parsley, salt, and pepper. Shape into ovals about 1¼-in. thick and broil on one side. Press in fried bacon bits on the other, and then broil that side until bacon is crisp and the inside is cooked as desired. May be served with a pan gravy. Serves 2.

Sally Lunn. Also, "Sally Lunn bread." A bread, made from flour, yeast, eggs, and sugar, of English origins and usually associated with the city of Bath, where a woman named Sally Lunn is supposed to have sold these tea cakes in the eighteenth century. Others suggest the name derives from the French *soleil* and *lune,* "sun and moon," or *soleil* and *une,* "sun-one," because of their golden bright, puffy appearance. The first appearance of the name in English print was in 1770. In 1827, William Hone's *Everyday Book* remarked that Sally Lunn was a Bath woman who sold the bread "about thirty years ago" on the streets and whose business was bought by a local banker and musician who made up a song about her.

Sally Lunn bread recipes are found throughout American cookbooks of the nineteenth century.

SALLY LUNN

Scald 1 c. milk, cool until warm, dissolve 1 pkg. yeast in the milk, and set aside. Cream ½ c. butter with ⅓ c. sugar until light. Beat 3 eggs into butter and add 4 c. sifted flour and 1 t. salt, alternating with the milk mixture. Cover and let rise to double. Beat again and pour into a 10-in. tube pan. Let rise to double again, then bake at 350° for 45 min.

salmagundi. Also, "salmagundy." A dish of chopped meat, eggs, anchovies, onions, and vinegar served on lettuce. The word is from the French *salmigondis,* for a "hodgepodge," and first appears in English print about 1665. Salmagundi was a popular English and American Colonial dish.

SALMAGUNDI

In boiling water cook 12 white onions until tender. Drain and cool. Mix together 3 c. cooked chicken cut into strips, 4 chopped hard-boiled eggs, 8 anchovies, 1 T. chopped parsley, ½ c. salad oil, ¼ c. white wine vinegar, salt, and pepper. Add white onions and mix together well, then pour over lettuce leaves. Serves 6.

---

salmon. Any of a variety of fish of the genera Salmo and Oncorhynchus having eight species in United States waters. The name is from Latin *salmō,* which became the Middle English *samoun.*

As with many of America's fishes, the salmon was noted for its size and abundance by the first white settlers, only to be fished out or driven out by pollution.

The salmon was extremely important to the Native American diet, and as Waverley Root pointed out in *Food* (1980), "in several of the Indian languages the word for 'salmon' was also the word for 'fish.'" The great majority of the fish consumed by the Northwest Native Americans was salmon, cooked in scores of ways, including planking the fish on driftwood or alderwood and allowing the embers of a fire to cook the flesh. Salmon was also dried and smoked, then stored in seal bladders, a preparation white settlers called "Siwash cheese."

The superstitions about salmon that abounded among the Chinook were based on the fear that if the salmon disappeared, the tribes would starve to death. They removed the heart and burned it, lest it be eaten by dogs, who would defile the fish's spirit; menstruating women and girls could not eat salmon. In *American Cooking: The Northwest* (1970), Dale Brown wrote that "the Chinook Indians believed . . . that anyone involved in preparing a corpse for burial could drive the fish away, and to avert this danger went so far as to bury the infirm alive."

Viking seafarer Eric the Red was amazed at the size of the Atlantic salmon he found when he sailed American waters in the tenth century, and early European settlers bemoaned the constant diet of salmon they endured, even to the point of having a clause written into indentured servants' contracts that forbade the serving of salmon more than once a week.

The waters of the East and West swarmed with salmon. When Lewis and Clark made their way through the Columbia River in the Northwest Territory, they found their boats blocked by thousands of enormous salmon that had died spawning. In New England it was not considered a true celebration of the Fourth of July if steamed salmon was not part of the feast. In Hawaii, LOMI-LOMI salmon is equally beloved. By 1840 salmon was being canned in New England and shipped across the country, and then the Californians reversed the transport about 1864. By the end of the nineteenth century salting plants had proliferated on the Columbia River. "Alaskan turkey" is a slang term for salmon.

By 1889 the Maine coast salmon catch totaled 150,000 pounds, but by the First World War overfishing and pollution had reduced the Northeast's salmon fisheries so severely that in New York one might find only cod and trout sold fresh at market. The salmon became fewer in number in the East and began to dwindle in the West, too, so that by 1950 only about a thousand pounds—about eighty-two fish—were taken in Maine. In 1964 fishermen discovered a large salmon feeding ground off Greenland. This revived hopes of a resurgence, but domestic fisheries do not produce nearly enough salmon for the market, with only about 17 million pounds landed in the Columbia River in recent years. Today all Atlantic salmon come from Canada or Europe.

The main species of salmon in American waters include the "Atlantic salmon" (*Salmo salar*); the "Chinook salmon" (*Oncorhynchus tshawytscha*), also called "spring," "king salmon," and "quinnat salmon"; the "Pink salmon" (*O. gorbuscha*), which is the smallest salmon; the "chum salmon" (*O. keta),* also called "silver brite," "keta" and "dog salmon," because the Athabascan Indians of the Yukon fed it to their dogs. (The word "chum" derives from Chinook jargon *cam,* "mixed colors"); the "coho" (*O. kisutch),* also called "silver salmon," "coho salmon," "blue jack," and "cohoe" (the origin of the word "coho" possibly derives from a Halkomelem word for the fish); and the "sockeye salmon" (*O. nerka*), also called "blueback" or "red salmon" (the word "sockeye" is from dialectical Salish *suk-kegh*).

Domestic smoked salmon comes from the Pacific and is often labeled "Nova," "Novy," or "Novie" in imitation of true Nova Scotia salmon, which is rarely seen in United States markets. The Pacific fish is wet-cured, that is, it is placed in a salt brine, while the Atlantic, which is almost never encountered at market anymore (except if the salmon is from Canadian or European waters), is dry-cured with salt and sugar. "Indian cure" or Indian hard cure is a process of brining and cold-smoking Pacific salmon once used by the northwest Native Americans. "Kippered salmon" is mildly brined and hot-smoked. "Squaw candy" is a colloquial term for strips of Pacific salmon salt-brined and hot-smoked. "Kennebec salmon" (the name derives from the Kennebec River in Maine) merely refers to a preparation of poached salmon steaks.

The entire salmon market totals over a billion pounds annually (third in commercial landings) with about 10–12 million pounds harvested through aquaculture, constituting about 70 percent of the salmon brought to market today. Per capita U.S. consumption is just under one pound annually.

In New England poached salmon with egg sauce and a side dish of steamed peas is traditionally served on Independence Day. "Salmon-burgers" were created in March 1985 by the Alaska Seafood Marketing Institute's test kitchens, made from canned salmon, mayonnaise, bread crumbs, and Parmesan cheese, served on a buttered bun.

See also LOX.

saloon. A place where alcoholic drinks are sold by the glass and drunk either at a bar or a table (1720). The term comes from the French *salon*, "room," and in England for a long while it meant just that, especially a large, public room. But in America the term had come to mean a bar or tavern by the 1840s and saloon keeper was an acceptable term by 1860. Following the Civil War, New York saw the opening of scores of "concert saloons," which were somewhat more savory than ordinary saloons and employed "waitergirls." Concert saloons pretty much vanished by 1905. By the time of Prohibition the word "saloon" had taken on a particularly unsavory connotation, so that after the repeal of Prohibition in 1933 Americans continued to use other terms, like bar, tavern, lounge, and others. By the 1960s "saloon" had a distinctly antique ring to it, and establishments that used the word in their names often were trying to convey a certain "turn-of-the-century" connotation about the barroom.

salsa. A general term for seasoned sauces, usually made with chile pepper and tomatoes, in Mexican-American and Tex-Mex cookery. Salsa is used for dipping or as a condiment to main courses. The word is Spanish, dating in English print to 1962.

Though traditionally associated with Hispanic food culture, by 1991 salsa sales surpassed those of ketchup in the United States.

SALSA

Chop up 1 tomato with 1 onion, 4 green or red chiles, and 2 cloves garlic. Add salt to taste and let marinate for ½ hr.

salsify (*Tragopogon porrifolius*). Also "vegetable oyster" or "oyster plant." A native European plant with an edible taproot (1690). The name is derived from the French *salsifis*, and Italian *salsifica*. Some believe the root has a faint oysterlike flavor (nineteenth-century cookbook author Mrs. Sarah Tyson Rorer wrote that vegetarians would make a mock-oyster soup from it), and it was once very popular as a vegetable. Recently there has been a resurgence of interest in the plant.

salt. Sodium chloride, widely used as a seasoning, a curing medium for meat and fish, and the basis for pickling brine. Salt appears in a wide range of foods, from cheese to applesauce, and in many foods where one would not expect to find it, such as in sweet desserts. The food-processing industry in America adds salt indiscriminately to food items that home cooks would rarely salt. As a result, one fourth to one half of Americans' salt intake comes from processed food; only one third is added directly at home in cooking or serving. The rest is ingested through some foods and some drinking water in which salt is naturally found. Americans consume an average of about two teaspoons per day, or eight-and-a-half pounds per year, an amount that has raised some concern among health officials and led in recent years to a reduction by some food processors of the salt added to their products.

Salt (Old English *sealt*; Latin *sāl*) is an ancient seasoning and a valued one, having at certain times in history been used as money and barter. It is obtained from the evaporation of seawater (called "sea salt") and is also dug out of the earth in crystalline form, commonly called "rock salt" and, in Hawaii, *limu*.

The early settlers in America brought salt with them, as well as salted meat and pork called "salt horse." Importing salt from England, France, Spain, the Canary Islands, and the West Indies was preferred to early attempts at domestic salt making. "Bay salt," from seawater evaporation, was preferred for curing meat and fish, while the salt used for seasoning at home was generally referred to as "table salt." Later, salt was obtained from the Great Salt Lake in Utah, but during the Civil War the seizure by Northern troops of the saltworks in the Great Kanawha and Holston valleys cut off the South's supply, causing widespread spoilage of meats and other foods for the Confederacy and forcing some Southerners to scrape the floors of smokehouses for the residue dripped from ham and bacon cured with the substance.

In 1912 the Morton Salt Company added magnesium carbonate to its salt, allowing it to pour freely rather than stick together.

A "salt cellar" was not only a treasured repository at an American dinner table of the eighteenth and nineteenth centuries, but also functioned as a centerpiece and social "borderline," with honored guests sitting above it with the host and lesser guests positioned below it.

A "salt lick" is a natural deposit of salt licked by animals in the wild.

"Salt rising bread" is a bread of the 1830s and 1840s made from flour, water, or milk, and salt, which had a leavening effect.

Salt is packaged and sold in a variety of ways. Seasoned salts are those flavored by onion, garlic, celery, pepper, monosodium glutamate, and other substances. "Kosher salt" is a large-grained, coarsely crushed salt used by Orthodox Jews according to kosher food laws. "Iodized salt" contains cuprous iodide or potassium iodide, added as a public-health measure to prevent goiter due to insufficient iodine in the American diet.

salteur liquor. Diluted spirits given to the native Americans by early fur traders.

salt potato. A small new potato that has been soaked or boiled in a brine solution. It is a specialty of Syracuse, New York, once a great salt-producing center. Originally the potatoes were soaked in the residue of the brine used in the production of sodium carbonate (washing soda) by the Solvay process. Today the potatoes may be boiled in heavily salted water at home or purchased already packaged at a grocery.

sand dab (*Citharichthys sordidus*). Also, "Pacific sand dab." A flounderlike flatfish found from the Bering Sea to Cape San Lucas, Baja California. It is a delicacy of the Pacific, usually dredged in flour, salt, and pepper, sautéed in butter, and served with a dip of vinegar, parsley, and garlic or merely sprinkled with lemon. The first mention of the fish by this name in print was in 1830.

sandwich. A dish of sliced bread and any variety of meats, cheese, relishes, jellies, vegetables, lettuce, and condiments. It is primarily a LUNCH item for most Americans and is far more popular here than in its country of origin, England, where it was named after a notorious gambler in the court of George III named John Montagu ("Jemmy Twitcher"), fourth earl of Sandwich (1718–92), who during a twenty-four-hour betting marathon in 1762 ordered bread-and-meat dishes that he could eat while continuing to gamble. The combination came to be named after him, but it was not known in America until some time later. Eliza Leslie's *Directions for Cookery* (1837) listed ham sandwiches as a supper dish, but it was not until much later in the century, when soft white bread loaves became a staple of the American diet, that the sandwich became extremely popular and serviceable. By the 1920s white loaf bread was referred to as "sandwich bread" or "sandwich loaf."

Most American sandwiches are made with this type of presliced bread, sometimes toasted, sometimes trimmed of its crusts to make "tea sandwiches" for afternoon teas. There are also toasted sandwiches, often made with melted cheese, and "open-faced" sandwiches, usually made with one slice of toast, slices of meat or poultry, and a gravy. These are also called "hot sandwiches." "Brain sandwiches" are a delicacy specific to St. Louis saloons, made with fried calf's brains (either in slices or chopped up), commonly served with pickles and onions on rye bread. They originated in the Depression, when poor people ate all parts of the animal. Brains were usually eaten with eggs.

Sandwiches are usually made on buttered bread. The most popular sandwich among Americans is the ham sandwich, followed by bacon, lettuce, and tomato (called a "BLT" for short), corned beef, and PASTRAMI. Among schoolchildren one of the most popular is the "peanut butter and jelly" (sometimes called by the abbreviation "PBJ" by schoolchildren) sandwich and the tuna-fish sandwich, invariably made from canned tuna and mayonnaise. See also CANAPÉ, CLUB SANDWICH, HERO, PHILADELPHIA CHEESE STEAK, REUBEN, SLOPPY JOE, and STROMBOLI. Fifty-nine percent of all sandwiches eaten in the U.S. are HAMBURGERS.

sangría. A drink made from red wine, fruits, and, sometimes, brandy (1960). The word is Spanish for "bleeding" and refers to the drink's blood-red color. Sangría originated in Spain, where it is made in batches and often served in a pitcher, a practice that has become just as popular in the United States.

The drink took on a certain faddishness after being introduced by Alberto Heras, supervisor of the Spanish Pavilion at the 1964 New York World's Fair (his recipe is given below). It was a very popular party drink throughout the 1960s and 1970s.

SANGRÍA

Empty bottle of red Spanish wine into a pitcher, add 2 t. sugar, and mix until dissolved. Add 1 lemon cut in slices, ½ orange cut in slices, 1½ oz. Cointreau, 1½ oz. Spanish brandy, ice, and one 12-oz. bottle of club soda. Stir, then let chill for 15 min. Pour sangría into wineglasses without the fruit.

sapsis. A porridge flavored with beans. It was made by Native Americans on the eastern coast of North America and may still be found in New England states.

Saratoga potatoes. Also, "Saratoga chips." Thinly sliced deep-fried potatoes. "Potato chips" have been known since the 1840s, but they were sliced fairly thick in those days. According to most authorities the thin potato chip was created in 1853 at the Moon's Lake Lodge in Saratoga, New York (another story places it at the Montgomery Hall Hotel in the same town), when chef George Crum supposedly sliced his potatoes as thin as possible to placate the request of a particularly stubborn customer for thinner potatoes. (Legend has it that the customer was transportation tycoon Cornelius Vanderbilt, whose great-great-grandson's wife, Marylou Whitney, went so far as to write *The Potato Chip Cookbook*.) The next day the chips were given out free in paper cones to customers, and a sign was put on the bar reading HELP YOURSELF. They became very popular across the country (especially after automatic potato-peelers were introduced in 1925), and after a while the term "potato chip" meant a very thin, fried potato, usually served cold as a snack and most often purchased at a food store, usually from a large barrel or display case. (In England french-fried potatoes are called "potato chips," a usage first referred to in a letter of Oscar Wilde, dated March 1876.)

In 1926 a potato-chip maker named Laura Scudder of Monterey Park, California, had women workers iron sheets of waxed paper into bags that were thereupon filled with chips and sealed to maintain freshness. This was refined by the Dixie Wax Paper Company of Dallas, Texas, in 1933, whose "preprint" waxed glassine bags allowed companies to print their names on them and shop them more easily.

Except at restaurants, potato chips are rarely prepared fresh. Potato chips grew into a major SNACK business in the twentieth century, with about three hundred potato-chip factories currently producing the item. The largest, Frito-Lay, begun by Herman Lay and Elmer Doolin in 1945 (though not called by that corporate name until 1961), uses 4.2 percent of all potatoes produced in the United States.

Potato chips are made from specially grown varieties of potatoes called "chipping potatoes," with 25 percent coming from the Red River Valley of Minnesota and North Dakota.

Today potato chips come in a wide variety of styles and thicknesses, some with the skin still attached, others flavored with cheese, chile pepper, and other condiments. The first flavored potato chips were "barbecue-flavored," introduced in the late 1940s. Sour-cream-flavored potato chips came out soon after. One popular form is the ridged potato chip. Some potato chips are not made from sliced potatoes but are produced from mashed-up potatoes that are molded into uniform shapes.

sardine. Any of a variety of small species of fish in the HERRING family. The name derives from the Greek *sardinos*, which became the Middle English *sardeyn*.

Canning of the fish began on the island of Sardinia. Today sardines are air-dried and coated with oil, then canned, occasionally with other seasonings such as mustard or chile.

Most American sardines now come from Maine, after a long period during which the industry was dominated by Pacific companies. The "Pacific sardine" (*Sardinops sagax*) population has declined significantly since the 1930s, however.

sarsaparilla. Also, "sassparilla." A carbonated beverage, which first appeared in the 1840s, made from the smilax plant or ginger flavors. The name comes from the Spanish words for a bramble (*zarza*) and a small vine (*parrilla*). The soft drink is still found today, though it is not as popular as it once was.

sassafras (*Sassafras albidum*). An aromatic tree of the laurel family, native to North America. The bark of the root is dried and used as a flavoring for root beer and as a brew called "sass tea" (also "grub hyson," from the words *grub* plus Chinese *hyson*, a type of green tea). The leaves were pounded by the Choctaw Native Americans to make filé powder, an essential ingredient in the Creole stew called "filé gumbo."

The tree was given the name *sasafrás* by the Spaniards, who may have taken it from a Native American word or confused it with the *Saxifrage* genus of plant. By 1602 it had taken on its English spelling, though it had been mentioned in print as of 1570.

The Food and Drug Administration banned the sale of sassafras tea when it was found to have carcinogenic properties, and the leaves may no longer be used as a flavoring for root beer or other beverages, although extracts of the plant are considered safe.

sauce piquante. A spicy Louisiana tomato-based sauce customarily cooked with shellfish, turtle, or frogs' legs. The term is from the French *piquante*, "sharp" or "tart."

SAUCE PIQUANTE

In 2 T. oil sauté 2 chopped onions, 2 chopped cloves garlic, and 1 chopped bell pepper. Then add 1 stalk chopped celery, 1 can tomato paste, 2 chopped scallions, salt and pepper, and ¼ c. vinegar. Bring to a boil, then lower to a simmer. Add meat from shellfish, turtle, or frogs' legs and enough water to cover meat. Cook until meat is tender and sauce is reduced. Serve over rice.

---

sauerkraut. Also, "sourcrout." A chopped cabbage that is salted and then fermented in its own juice. The word, which in German means "sour cabbage," was first mentioned in American English in 1776 (though dates in English to 1610), and the dish was long associated with German communities in the United States. It is still widely enjoyed, especially with pork dishes and as a condiment on hot dogs. It is usually bought in groceries rather than made at home. Americans consume about 359 million pounds of sauerkraut per year, or 1.5 pounds per person.

sausage. Any of a wide variety of chopped or ground meat blended with herbs and spices and molded into a casing, usually made from animal intestines. The word is from Middle English *sausige*.

Sausages have been common throughout the world for millennia, and the idea was brought to America by European settlers who used it as a way to preserve meat, especially the lesser cuts.

Sausages are divided into six major categories:

Fresh sausage—made from meats that are neither cured nor smoked. They must be cooked before serving.

Cooked sausage—made from uncured meats that are cooked but not smoked.

Cooked, smoked sausage—made from cured meats that are lightly smoked, then cooked. They do not require further cooking. These include BOLOGNA and HOT DOGS.

Uncooked, smoked sausage—either cooked or cured meats that are smoked and then later cooked before serving.

Dry Sausage—also called "summer sausage" (because it can be kept in warm weather without refrigeration) and "seminary sausage" (because it is associated with the type of sausages made at monasteries), made from cured sausage that is air-dried under controlled time-temperature-humidity conditions. They may or may not be smoked. Lebanon bologna, salami, KOSHER sausage, and Spanish chorizo are examples of such sausages.

Specialty meats—a wide range of products made from cured or noncured chopped or comminuted meats, usually baked or cooked rather than smoked and formed into loaves to be sliced and served cold in salads or sandwiches or as a breakfast meat, like SCRAPPLE.

The United States is home to twenty-one thousand sausage processors who produce more than 6.3 billion pounds of sausage each year and more than two hundred different varieties.

Sauvignon Blanc. Also, "Fumé Blanc." A white vinifera grape that makes a fruity, spicy wine (1940). It is used extensively in the white wines of Graves in Bordeaux and in the Loire Valley. In California it has achieved great success in the last ten years, especially after the Robert Mondavi Winery of the Napa Valley introduced the name "Fumé Blanc" for a somewhat drier version in the late 1960s in order to make it sound more attractive to American ears.

saxifrage. Any of a variety of plants in the genus *Saxifraga* bearing a leafy, lettuce-like green. The word is from the Latin *saxifragus*, "rock-breaking," because the plant grows in the crevices of rocks. The main North American variety is the "mountain lettuce" (*S. micranthidifolia*), also called "branch lettuce" and "deer-tongue." Two other varieties, *S. virginiensis* and *S. pennsylvanica*, proliferate along the eastern coast.

Saxifrage is cooked as a vegetable and added to soups. In the South it is often fried with bacon and onions.

Sazerac. Trademark name for a cocktail made with whiskey, sugar, bitters, and an anise-flavored cordial. It is a famous drink of New Orleans and took its name from a French brandy of the firm Sazerac-de-Forgeet et Fils that was imported to the city by John Schiller, who opened his Sazerac Coffee House in 1859 at No. 13 Exchange Alley in the French Quarter. In 1870 Schiller's bookkeeper, Thomas Handy, bought the establishment and changed the name to the Sazerac House. About the same time Handy changed the original recipe for the cocktail to include a slight taste of ABSINTHE, a dash of red Peychaud BITTERS (introduced to New Orleans by pharmacist A. A. Peychaud in the 1790s), and, ironically, replaced the Sazerac brandy with American blended whiskey. (Leon Lamothe, another importer, has been mentioned as the man who added the absinthe back in 1857, but this seems rather early.)

The recipe was further changed when absinthe was banned from sale in the United States in 1912 because of its harmful effects on the body and anise-flavored liqueurs like Spanish Ojen or Louisiana "Herbsaint" were substituted. Some bartenders made the drink with bourbon instead of blended whiskey, and it is rarely made with brandy anymore.

The name "Sazerac" became a trademark of the Sazerac Company, Inc., and the "original" recipe is still served at the Sazerac Bar in the Fairmont Hotel (formerly the Roosevelt). Following is a substitute recipe:

SAZERAC

Combine 1½ oz. rye or bourbon, 4 t. bar sugar, ½ t. Peychaud bitters, and ice cubes. Pour 3 dashes of Herbsaint into a chilled old-fashioned glass, coat the sides, then pour out. Pour the mixed ingredients into the glass and garnish with a lemon twist.

scallion. A general term for any of a variety of onions, including the shallot, the leek, and the white onion. The name comes from the Latin *Ascalōnia*, referring to Ascalon, where a certain onion was grown. The word shows up in English in the fourteenth century.

In the United States the word scallion usually refers to *Allium fistolosum*, a bulbless onion also called the "spring onion," "bunch onion," or "green onion." In Creole and Cajun cookery, however, the word is used to describe a young shallot, as explained in the recipe book of *American Cooking: Creole and Acadian* (1971) by Peter S. Feibleman:

In Louisiana, which produces about 90 percent of the shallots grown in the United States, the shallot crop is sold and used in its green form. For this reason, perhaps, a special problem of terminology has developed there. Since the green shallot is the most readily available form of scallion in Louisiana, the term scallion is usually restricted to that vegetable in Creole and Acadian cooking. Elsewhere in the United States, the term scallion usually refers to a green or bunching onion, while a shallot is the mature vegetable, usually reddish brown, clove-shaped, and dried.

scallop. Any of a variety of marine mollusks of the family Pectinidae. Scallops are usually sold in American markets dead and without their coral.

The name derives from Old French *escalope*, "shell," which refers to the shell in which the mollusk lives.

In the eastern United States there are four species: the "deep-sea scallop" (*Placopecten magellanicus*); the "lion's paw" (*Nodipecten nodosus*); the "calico scallop" (*Argopecten gibbus*); and the "bay scallop" (*A. irradians*). The first and last in this group are the most often encountered at market in the East, with the latter generally preferred for its delicacy of taste.

In the western United States one finds the "pink scallop" (*Chlamys herica* or *C. rubida*); the "hinds' scallop" (*C. rubida*); the "Iceland scallop" (*C. islandica*); the "speckled scallop" (*A. circularis aequisulcatus*); the "kelp-weed scallop" (*Leptopecten latiauratus*); and the "giant rock scallop" (*Hinnites giganteus*), which may measure up to six inches.

In American kitchens scallops are either breaded and deep-fried or cooked according to French recipes such as *coquilles Saint-Jacques*, with cream and seasonings. U.S. commercial landings of scallops was 15.5 million pounds of meats in 1997.

scampi. A Venetian term, dating in English print to 1920, that in America refers to shrimp cooked in garlic, butter, lemon juice, and white wine, commonly listed on menus as "shrimp scampi." The true *scampo* (*scampi* is the plural) of Italy is a small lobster or prawn, of the family Nephropidae, which in America is called a "lobsterette." These shellfish are available in United States waters, first introduced in

1962 by deepwater-shrimp fishermen of Florida, but are not generally found in markets. The term "scampi," then, has come to mean any shrimp—usually of medium size—cooked in butter, to which is added finely chopped garlic and a dash of dry white wine. It is a staple feature of Italian-American restaurants.

schichtkuche. A Pennsylvania-Dutch layer cake, typical examples of which are the king's cake and the queen's cake. The word *Schichte* in German means "layer." See also KING CAKE.

KING'S CAKE

Add 16 egg yolks and 1 lb. sugar to 1 lb. whipped cream. Stir for 1 hr., then add 1 lb. fine flour and stir for ½ hr. Add 1 lb. Sultana raisins, 1 lb. dried currants, and 3 oz. finely cut citron shell. Add 9 stiffly beaten egg whites. Bake 1 hr.

QUEEN'S CAKE

Mix together 1 lb. sugar, 1 lb. flour, 1 lb. butter, and 8 eggs that have been separated and beaten separately, the whites until they are of a thick consistency that holds to the whisk. Add ½ lb. currants, 1 ground nutmeg, and an equal amount cinnamon and bake.

---

schmaltz. A Yiddish-American term for rendered fat, most often chicken fat, first printed in 1930. The word is of German origin.

schmear. A Yiddish term for a daub or smear of a condiment, like cream cheese spread on a bagel or sandwich, dating in print to 1960.

schnitz und kneppe. Also, "schnitz un knepp" and "Schnitz-und-Gnepp." A Pennsylvania-Dutch dish made from the butt of an Easter ham with dried apples and dumplings (1869). "Schnitz" (often spelled "snitz") refers to "slices" of dried apples, while "knepp" refers to the small dumplings pinched off from a mass of dough, derived from the Dutch *kneep*, meaning a "pinch." According to William Woys Weaver in *America Eats* (1989), the dish is a descendant of another Pennsylvania-Dutch dish called "gumbis" (derived from the Latin *compositum*, "compositions") that also included cabbage and meat along with various fruits.

SCHNITZ UND KNEPPE

Soak 1 qt. dried apples overnight in water, then drain and set aside. Place a 3-lb. ham butt in a large casserole and pour in enough water to cover the ham. Bring to a boil, reduce to a simmer, and cook for about two hours or more, until tender. Pour off the water, remove the ham from the casserole, and cut into small cubes. Return the ham to the casserole, add the apples, 2 T. brown sugar, and about 6 c. chicken stock. Bring to a boil and cook for 20 minutes.

Meanwhile make a dumpling batter by sifting together 2 c. flour, 4 t. baking powder, 1 t. salt, and ½ t. ground black pepper. Add 1 beaten egg and 1½ c. milk. Blend well, then add 3 T. melted butter, and blend completely. Drop the batter by spoonfuls into the boiling ham liquid, cover, and cook for about 15 minutes. Serve hot on a large platter.

---

school breakfast program. A federally sponsored program to provide income assistance to impoverished families, whereby children are fed breakfast at school at no or little charge.

school lunch program. Formally called the National School Lunch program. A federally sponsored program (begun in 1946) of the United States Department of Agriculture in 1990 that provides free lunches to 24.4 million school children at 91,400 schools each day. The federal school breakfast program, begun in 1969, provides breakfast to 4.5 million children in 47,627 schools.

In 1994 the Department of Agriculture was instructed to set limits on the fat, cholesterol, and sodium content of school lunches.

schooner. A drinking glass popular in the last half of the nineteenth century (1705). It held a pint or more of beer. The word probably derives from the large size of a type of ship of the same name.

scoff-law cocktail. A drink made of Canadian whiskey, dry vermouth, and grenadine. According to the *Chicago Tribune* for January 27, 1924, "Hardly has Boston added to the gaiety of nations by adding to Webster's Dictionary the opprobrious term of 'scoff-law,' when Jock, the genial manager of Harry's Bar in Paris, yesterday invented the Scoff-Law Cocktail, and it has already become exceedingly popular among American prohibition dodgers."

SCOFF-LAW COCKTAIL

Shake together with ice 1 dash orange bitters to a mixture made up of ⅓ Canadian whiskey, ⅓ dry vermouth, ⅙ lemon juice, and ⅙ grenadine. Strain and pour into cocktail glass.

scrapple. Also, "Philadelphia scrapple." A porridge-and-pork breakfast or brunch dish that is chilled and served in slices (1810). It is an old Pennsylvania-Dutch dish often served with apple slices and brown sugar, the name being a diminutive of "scrap." The Pennsylvania Dutch also called it "pawnhaus" (finely chopped food) and, later, "poor-do," since it was made often from leftovers. It was introduced at least as early as 1817 to the city of Philadelphia, where it became an immediate favorite, especially among the upper-class gentry. In the Midwest a similar dish made by German immigrants was called "gritz" (also "grits wurst," "breakfast grits," and "knipp"). In the area of Cincinnati, Ohio, a similar dish is called GOETTA.

SCRAPPLE

Cover 1½ lb. boneless pork with water, bring to boil, and simmer for 2 hr. Remove and slice and then mince meat. To 3 c. of the cooking liquid add ½ t. pepper, 1 t. sage, and ½ t. salt. Return meat to broth. Mix 1½ c. cornmeal with 1 c. water, stir into meat mixture, and cook on low heat until thickened, then 10 min. more. Rinse a 9-by-5-in. loaf pan with cold water, put in meat mixture, and chill. Unmold and slice. Brown in bacon fat. Serves 6–8.

screwdriver. A drink made with vodka and orange juice. It has been popular since the 1950s but origins are obscure. According to one story the name came about when an orange-juice salesman in Bakersfield, California, asked a bartender to mix orange juice with vodka and to serve the drink to six customers, five of whom liked the concoction, but one of whom tasted it and said, "I'd just as soon swallow a screwdriver."

A more frequently cited story—though with no more evidence to back it up—contends the drink was created by American oil-rig workers in the Middle East who mixed vodka with orange juice packed in cans that they opened with screwdrivers, which were also used to stir the drink's ingredients. In a glass with ice cubes pour 1½ oz. vodka and 3 oz. orange juice. Stir.

scripture cake. A cake made with ingredients as listed in certain verses of the Bible. Though known throughout the American Colonies, it was a traditional confection among the Baptists. The recipe below is from a Pennsylvania woman, as published in *Famous Old Receipts* (1908):

SCRIPTURE CAKE

Combine 1 c. butter (Judg. 5:25), 3½ c. flour (1 Kings 4:22), 3 c. sugar (Jer. 6:20), 2 c. raisins (1 Sam. 30:12), 2 c. figs (1 Sam. 30:12), 1 c. water (Gen. 24:17), 1 c. almonds (Gen. 43:11), 6 eggs (Isa. 10:14), 1 T. honey (Gen. 43:11), a pinch of salt (Lev. 16:13), spices to taste (1 Kings 10:10), and 2 T. baking powder (1 Cor. 5:6). [It is interesting to note that, since baking powder was only invented in the 1850s, the biblical reference uses the verse "Your boasting is unseemly. Do you not know that a little leaven ferments the whole lump?"] Follow Prov. 23:14, Solomon's advice for making good boys: "Thou shalt beat him with a rod."

scrod. Also, "scrode." A young COD or a young haddock, specifically one that has been split and prepared for cooking. The word may derive from obsolete Dutch *schrood*, "slice" or "shred," but the sometimes-encountered variant *escrod* is more obscure. The Parker House Hotel in Boston, famous for its simple preparation of the dish (see recipe below), calls it "schrod." There seems no evidence to support the contention that "scrod" is an acronym for "serving catch reeled on the day."

Although cod was a staple fish of old New England, this term for a young example seems to be of rather recent origins, appearing in print, according to the *Dictionary of Americanisms*, for the first time in 1835. Today it is still a specialty of New England.

SCROD

Marinate a 12-oz. fillet of cod (or haddock) in ½ pt. milk, 1 t. lemon, ½ t. Worcestershire sauce, salt, and pepper for about 1 hr. Mix 3 T. vegetable oil with ½ t. paprika, dip the fish into this mixture and then in ½ c. bread crumbs. Place in a baking dish with a little white wine and 2 T. butter. Bake for about 12 min.

scuppernong. A species of Muscadine grape used to make wines and jellies, or the wine made from such a grape (1805). The Scuppernong is grown throughout the South, particularly in North Carolina, where the name covers almost all wines made from various Muscadine grapes.

The origins of the word scuppernong are given in Leon D. Adams's *Wines of America* (2nd ed., rev., 1978):

> *Scuppernong was named for a town, which was named for a river, which was named for a tree. Ascopo was the Algonquian Indian name for the sweet bay tree. Ascuponung, meaning place of the Ascopo, appeared on old maps of North Carolina as the name of the river in Washington County, near Albermarle Sound. Later maps spelled it* Cuscopung, *then* Cusponung, *next* Scuponing *and by 1800 the spelling of the river had become* Scuppernong. *The grape, however, was merely called the White Grape until James Blount of the town of Scuppernong took the census of Washington County in 1810 and reported 1,368 gallons of wine made there in "this small but very interesting branch of our infant manufactures." An article in the* Raleigh (North Carolina) Star *for January 11, 1811, commenting on Blount's report, was the first to call it "The Scuppernong Grape."*

Wine has been made from the Scuppernong since the 1560s, when the French Huguenots who settled in Florida fermented the grapes, which were exceptionally abundant and needed only to be knocked to the ground from the high, prolific vines. Sir Walter Raleigh's men discovered the vine growing in Virginia's Roanoke Island in 1584 and introduced it elsewhere. (Supposedly the original vine Raleigh's men propagated still exists on Roanoke and is called the "Mother" or "Raleigh vine.")

The fame of the Scuppernong wines was fostered by a North Carolinian named Captain Paul Garrett (1863–1940), who, after working as a salesman for his uncle Charles Garrett's winery, established his own winery called Garrett & Company in 1900. By 1903 he had four more and was becoming rich selling Scuppernong, which he first called "Escapernog," then "Minnehaha" and "Pocahontas," and, finally, "Virginia Dare," after the first child born of English parents in America. (Dare, born in 1587 of Ananias and Elenor Dare, vanished with the rest of Raleigh's settlers on Roanoke after four years of deprivation.) Garrett's wines became the most popular in the country until certain states and then the country went dry with Prohibition. Garrett had plantings of Scuppernong in other states, but after Prohibition the grapes were scarce in the East, and

Virginia Dare no longer tasted the same. By 1966 propagation of the Scuppernong had fallen to a few hundred acres in North Carolina. Since then, with the help of the state legislature and State University in Raleigh, there has been renewed interest in the Scuppernong, in addition to several other Muscadine varieties that now go under the name Scuppernong.

The original Scuppernong is a greenish-bronze grape grown in bunches that produces a distinctive, amber-colored wine that is most often sweetened. If blended with other labrusca grapes, it tends to mute the foxy taste of the finished wine.

sea foam. Any of a variety of desserts or sweet confections whose texture or appearance resembles sea foam. They are usually made with some form of beaten egg whites.

sea pie. A stew of pork, veal, or fowl mixed with sweet dried apples, molasses, and dumplings. The dish is served in New England and so called, according to Josephine H. Pierce in *Coast to Coast Cookery* (1951), "because a sea captain told how to make it." A recipe may be found in Mary Randolph's *Virginia Housewife, or Methodical Cook* (1836).

sea urchin. Any of a variety of marine echinoderms of the class Echinoidea having a soft flesh encased in a spiny shell (1585). The name derives from its resemblance to a hedgehog, which in Middle English was (h)irchon, and Latin (h)ēricius.

Sea urchins are unappreciated by most Americans, and in fact are called "whore's eggs" by fishermen whose bait they steal and swimmers who brush up against the animal's sharp, painful thorns. But Mediterranean immigrants buy most of the catch at market, and Maine ships more than 10 million pounds (especially the "green sea urchin" [*Strongylocentrotus droebachiensis*]), to Japan. The reproductive organs (called the "roe") of the animal are considered great delicacies in Japan.

The "giant red urchin" (*S. franciscanus*) of California is considered one of the best for eating. Other main species of sea urchin for consumption include: "purple sea urchin" (*Arbacia punctulata*), "keyhole urchin" (*Mellita quinquiesper forata*), "purple sea urchin" (*S. purpuratus*, a Pacific species different from the eastern variety above), "white sea urchin" (*Lytechinus vari egatus*), and "heart urchin" (*Moira atropos*). U.S commercial landings of sea urchins totaled 44,568 pounds in 1997.

seed cake. A nineteenth-century cake made from caraway seeds. The following recipe dates from *Mrs. Winslow's Domestic Receipt Book* for 1865:

SEED CAKE

Combine 4 c. flour, 1½ c. cream, ½ c. butter, 3 eggs, ½ c. caraway seeds, 1 t. baking soda, and 1 t. rosewater and make a dough. Cut with biscuit cutter and bake at 350° for about 20 min.

seltzer. A plain, naturally or man-made carbonated water with no taste of its own, drunk plain or as a mixer in everything from soda-fountain confections to alcoholic drinks. The word was first printed in English in 1735.

Carbonated waters have been known for hundreds of years. The word "seltzer" comes from a bottled mineral water called *"Selterser Wasser,"* made from the waters of the Prussian town, Nieder Selters.

Man-made carbonated water was created by Joseph Priestly in 1767, and Swedish chemist Torbern Bergman produced commercial quantities of carbonic gas in 1770. By 1807 such man-made sodas were sold around New York by Yale University's Professor Benjamin Silliman, and in 1832 an English immigrant to New York named John Matthews crafted a practical small machine to carbonate water for use in pharmacies. It was called a "soda fountain," and its use in drugstores was evidence of the era's belief in seltzer's medicinal and curative value. By the end of the century soda fountains ranged from elaborate marble-and-silver salons that served as significant social-gathering spots in many communities to small, unadorned neighborhood stores with counters (often part of a "candy store") in large cities. In New York's predominantly Jewish Lower East Side, there were no fewer than seventy-three soda fountains located within a one-third-square-mile area.

Flavors were soon added to seltzers, and such mixtures were called "soda pop" by the 1840s, but the word seltzer has continued to mean an unflavored carbonated water to this day. Seltzer was served both at fountains and in siphon bottles that became standard items at the home bar, a practice that has all but disappeared. Today seltzer is distinguished from club soda by having less or no salt added. The term "club soda," and also "sparkling water," came into use after the repeal of Prohibition in 1933, when the association with elegant supper or private clubs deliberately removed the drink's medicinal connotations.

In New York seltzer was sometimes humorously called "Jewish champagne" because of its popularity among Jews, who in Yiddish called it *grepsvasser,* "belch water," and who drank it to help the digestion of their fatty diet and to adhere to kosher rules against mixing meats with milk. In the early part of this century in New York one would go to a candy store and order "for-two-cents-plain," a glass of seltzer for two pennies.

semmel. A Pennsylvania-Dutch yeast roll, whose name is borrowed from the German for "roll."

SEMMEL

Mix ½ pkg. yeast in ¼ c. warm water. Add to ½ c. cooled, cooked mashed potatoes and stir in ½ c. sugar. Let stand 4 hr. Add ½ c. butter to 2 c. scalded milk. Cool, add 2 beaten eggs, ½ c. sugar, and ½ t. salt. Beat into yeast mixture, add 6 c. flour, cover, and let rise 8 hr. Roll dough into a square ¼-in. thick. Brush with melted butter and cut into 2-in. squares, then turn up corners. Place on buttered baking sheet and let rise to double. Bake at 450° for 20 min. Brush with butter and sprinkle with confectioners' sugar and cinnamon. Makes about 30.

Senate bean soup. A white-bean soup served for half a century in the United States Senate restaurant, which is operated for the senators and their guests. Credit for the soup's creation has gone to Senator Fred T. Dubois of Idaho in the 1890s, but its association with the Senate restaurant began in 1907 when Senator Knute Nelson of Minnesota, chairman of the Senate Committee on Rules, decreed that the soup must be served every day in the dining room. Congressman Joe Cannon later decreed it should also be served in the House of Representatives' dining room, while Bob Traxler of Michigan further decreed that the soup must be made only with Michigan white navy beans.

SENATE BEAN SOUP

Wash 2 c. dried white navy beans, then (according to Senate directions) "run them through hot water until they are white again." Drain, place in a large pot with 3 qt. water and 1 lb. smoked ham hocks. Bring to a boil, lower to a simmer for 2 hr. until beans are tender. Add 3 cooked mashed potatoes, 3 chopped onions, 2 chopped garlic cloves, and 3 chopped stalks of celery. Cover, simmer for 1 hr., remove ham bone, and scrape off meat into soup. Stir in ¼ c. parsley. Serves 12.

sesame (*Sesamum indicum*). A tropical Asian plant whose small, flat seeds are used to make oil and cookies and as a garnish for some breads and rolls. The name is from the Greek. In the South the seeds are called *benne,* from an African word, and are much used in SOUL FOOD. Benne cookies or cakes are sometimes called "good luck cookies" in South Carolina.

BENNE COOKIES

Combine 2 c. flour, 1½ t. baking powder, ¼ t. salt, and ¼ t. nutmeg. Cream ½ c. butter with ¼ c. sugar until light, then add the grated rind of 1 orange or lemon. Beat 1 egg with ⅓ c. milk and blend into butter and flour mixtures. Place by tablespoons on a greased cookie sheet and bake for 10 min. at 350° Combine in a saucepan ½ c. honey, 1 T. butter, and 2 T. sesame seeds, and cook until the mixture reaches 290° on a candy thermometer. Dip cookies in glaze or brush glaze over tops of cookies. Makes about 3 doz.

---

seven sweets and seven sours. Side dishes of sweet, spiced fruits and sour pickles served as accompaniments to main dishes in Pennsylvania-Dutch meals. They do not strictly have to be seven in number; more is better, and less is quite all right, as long as there are several from which to pick and choose, such as spiced apples, cantaloupe, CHOW-CHOW, peppers, and COLESLAW.

sex on the beach. A cocktail made by mixing vodka, peach schnapps, cranberry juice, and orange juice. It is a drink from the 1980s, and its name suggests its association with college students who annually took their spring vacation in warm climates.

Seyval Blanc. A white French hybrid grape officially named "Seyve-Villard 5-276" after its creator, Bertrand Seyve (1895–1959), whose father owned a nursery with Victor Villard, whose daughter married the younger Seyve. It has become a notable wine grape in New York's Hudson Valley and elsewhere.

shad. Any of a variety of fishes of the herring family in the genus *Alosa*. The name is from the Old English *sceadd.* The "American shad" (*A. sapidissima*) is the most important shad from a culinary standpoint, although early in this country's history the common availability of the fish was such that settlers considered it a fish of last resort, and it is thought that the native Americans used the fish for fertilizer. But by the time of the American Revolution shad was much appreciated, and Washington's troops had the fish as part of their rations in 1776.

Parties were held by the native Americans to celebrate shad time, which occurred in spring. The Indians dried the shad and may have "planked" it on wood to cook it slowly. But specific credit for this method of cooking has been given to the State in Schuykill, a fishing and cooking society formed in 1732. The fish fillets are seasoned and wrapped with bacon, then nailed to greased hardwood planks set at an angle near a hot ash fire made from charcoals. Shad roe, traditionally served with lemon, sorrel, and boiled potatoes, is particularly appreciated by gourmets, who cook it in a variety of ways.

By the nineteenth century shad was a popular fish, and, after several attempts, the American shad was successfully introduced in 1871 to the Sacramento and Columbia rivers by aquaculturist Seth Green. So plentiful were shad in the Connecticut River that they were colloquially referred to as "Connecticut River Pork" in the nineteenth century. By 1889 4.5 million pounds of shad were taken, although some, like Henry David Thoreau, noticed a decline in the quality of the fish in certain waters. The pollution caused by industries on the rivers drove out or killed the large fish, but, as Thoreau wrote, "Perchance, after a few thousands of years, if the fishes will be patient and pass their summers elsewhere meanwhile, Nature will have leveled the Billerica dam and the Lowell factories, and the Grassground River run clear again, to be explored by new migratory shoals."

The shad have rebounded since their nadir in the years that followed the end of the nineteenth century and are now found in eastern markets, though often they are imported from western fisheries. Boned, filleted shad was introduced in 1922 to New York's Fulton Fish Market after Peter Andreotti sold deboned shad to the J. P. Morgan Company restaurant at $1.50 per fish. U.S commercial landings of shad totaled 3.2 million pounds in 1997.

SHAD ROE WITH BACON

Boil 4 shad roe for 5 min., remove and drain. Brush roe with melted butter and broil until golden brown. Serve on toast with strips of bacon.

---

shake-up whiskey. Prohibition slang for corn or rye whiskey sold in speakeasies. According to an interview with Naomi Washington in *You Must Remember This: An Oral History of Manhattan from the 1890s to World War II,* compiled by Jeff Kisseloff (1989), "If you want to go to a house [i.e., a speakeasy], never mind everybody's drinking. You want a drink? Take that bottle. Shake it up. If it don't hold a head, pass it up. You don't need it. That was called shakeup whiskey. If it had good bubbles after you shook it, it was good."

shallot (*Allium ascalonicum*). An onionlike plant of the lily family used to flavor a wide variety of dishes and having a more delicate flavor than onion. The word is from the Latin *Ascalōnia,* referring to a kind of onion grown in Ascalon. The herb was first mentioned in English print in 1655, then also called "Spanish garlick."

The shallot is a native of Central Asia, possibly introduced to England in the thirteenth century, though long known to the Romans. It is now widely planted in the United States and is an essential part of most European immigrant cookeries.

In Creole and Cajun cookery, however, the term SCALLION is often applied to the green shallot, that is, the shoots of the shallot before it matures.

Most of the mature shallots found in the American market are grown in New Jersey and New York, with others imported from Mexico and France.

shark. Any of a variety of voracious marine fishes under the order *Squaliformes* or *Selachii.* The origin of the name is obscure. Feared for their legendary attacks on man (which in truth are exceptionally rare), the shark has not garnered much attention as a food fish in America, although the United States government in 1916 tried to promote the "dogfish shark" species (*Squalus acanthias* and *Somniosus microcephalus*) as a nourishing fish having large amounts of protein. After World War I this momentary infatuation with the shark died out, although another peak of favor was reached just before World War II, when the liver of the shark was especially sought for its nutrients. Some fishermen have tried to pass off meat from the "mako" (*Isurus oxyrhynchus*) and "blue shark" (*Prionace glauca*) as SWORDFISH steaks, and "soupfin shark" (*Galeorhinus zyopterus*) is often used to make the Chinese dish shark's fin soup. Many other sharks are poor eating and may in fact cause sickness. U.S commercial landings of sharks totaled 61.2 million pounds in 1997.

she-crab soup. A soup made from blue crabs, crab roe, sherry, and vegetables. It is a specialty of Charleston, South Carolina, and Savannah, Georgia, both of which claim credit for the dish's creation,

probably at the beginning of the nineteenth century. The female crab's roe gives the soup a slightly sour, tangy flavor that marks it as distinct from other crab soups. State law, however, forbids taking she-crabs with mature eggs, so cooks often use male crabs and immature females and then add eggs from unfertilized females (which are allowed to be caught). Crumbled egg yolk is sometimes used to give the traditional orange color of the roe to the soup.

SHE-CRAB SOUP

In a saucepan cook 1 grated onion, ½ t. mace, 2 grated celery stalks, salt, and pepper in 2 T. butter. Add 1 c. crabmeat and heat through thoroughly. Heat 2 c. milk and add to crab mixture. Stir and add ½ c. cream, 2 T. Worcestershire sauce, and 2 T. flour dissolved in water. Add 3 T. sherry and cook for 30 min. Serves 4.

---

sheeny destroyer. Slang for pork, derived from the derogatory word for Jews, "sheeny" (or "sheenie"), probably from the German *schin,* "a cheat" or "miser." Since Jews are not allowed under religious law to eat pork, serving them such a dish would "destroy" them. The term probably dates from the period 1910 to 1930. In a similar vein, an order of two pork chops was sometimes called "a couple of Hebrew enemies."

shelf-stable. Food that has been cooked at high temperatures so as to kill bacteria, thereby rendering it less likely to spoil over a longer period of time than foods not so treated. This period of time when the product remains safe to eat is called "shelf life," first used in print about 1925.

sherry. A fortified wine originally made in Spain and now produced in the United States most often by a process of "baking" that gives the drink its characteristic burnt flavor.

Sherry was first made in and around the town of Jerez in Spain's Andalusia, and the word sherry is an Anglicized rendition of the town's name, for the British were major shippers of Spanish wines. By the sixteenth century the wine was called "sherris-sack," the word "sack" perhaps having been derived from Old French *sec,* "dry." H. Warner Allen in *A History of Wine* (1961), however, suggests that it comes from the Spanish *sacar,* meaning "to take out" or "export," an opinion shared by Pauline and Sheldon Wasserman in their *Guide to Fortified Wines* (1982). Sack was the wine beloved by Shakespeare's Falstaff, who attributed his own "excellent wit" to the wine's powers. But by the beginning of the seventeenth century sherry was fast replacing sack (which is today a registered trademark of sherry shippers William & Humbert).

Americans of the Colonial era much preferred Madeira and port to sherry, and the sherries that later became favored were the sweeter Spanish varieties like *olorosos* and "creams," whose high alcohol content also coincided with Americans' tastes after the end of Prohibition in 1933. American sherries are made by three basic methods. The most frequently used is the baker's method, by which dry or sweet white wine is fortified with brandy and then heated to between 120° and 140° for between 45 and 120 days. (A variation on this method, called "weathering," exposes the wine and brandy to outdoor weather conditions.) The second process is the traditional Spanish solera system, by which the wines are constantly blended with other, older wines in a complex tier system involving stacked barrels, with the newest and freshest wines on top. The third method is the "submerged flor" process, by which new wine is continuously pumped over the yeast (*flor* in Spanish) that develops on the top of the wine, thereby giving the sherry a yeasty, tangy flavor without the benefits of aging.

American sherries are made from a variety of grapes, including Mission, Malaga, Palomino, Concord, and others, while traditional Spanish sherries are made with Palomino Blanco and Pedro Ximénez varieties, with some producers using Mantuo Castellano and others to a lesser degree.

Americans usually drink sweet sherries, either as an apéritif, on the rocks, or after dinner as a cordial.

Shirley Temple. A nonalcoholic beverage usually made for children who enjoy the idea of drinking an "adult" cocktail before dinner. It is named after child actor Shirley Temple, who began making movies in 1932 and three years later had attained the position of the number-one box-office star in the United States. Her curly-haired image was world famous, and hundreds of products, from dolls to clothes, appeared with her name or face on them. She was held up to children as a model of good behavior, and, thus, a cocktail called a "Shirley Temple" was considered the very essence of innocence. The drink was invented in the 1930s at the Brown Derby Restaurant in Hollywood.

In 1988 Shirley Temple herself sued to have her name dropped from two bottled soft drinks called "Shirley T Sparkling Soda" and "Original Shirley Temple Soft Drink."

Such a non-alcoholic cocktail was sometimes called a "Roy Rogers," after an equally wholesome movie cowboy of that name.

Occasionally one will hear such nonalcoholic cocktails referred to as "pussyfoots." A term of some derision in its meaning of an indecisive or weak person, this word may have been coined by President Theodore Roosevelt (1858–1919), appearing in print for the first time in 1893 as a verb, later, in 1934, as a noun. One of the greatest enforcers of temperance laws in the 1890s, William Eugene Smith, was called "Pussyfoot" for his zeal in sending offenders to jail, especially in Oklahoma.

SHIRLEY TEMPLE

In a cocktail or champagne glass pour ½ oz. Grenadine syrup, fill with lemon-lime soda, and garnish with a maraschino cherry.

shit on a shingle. Also, "S.O.S." A GI term for creamed CHIPPED BEEF. Civilians often refer specifically to SALISBURY STEAK by this term. See also SPAM.

shoofly pie. Also, "shoo-fly pie" and "Montgomery pie." A pie made of molasses and brown sugar, so called supposedly because one had to "shoo away the flies" from this sweet dessert. It is of Pennsylvania-Dutch origins, but was not mentioned in American print until 1926. Shoofly pies are made with either a "wet bottom" (soft filling and crumb topping) or "dry bottom" (crumb topping is mixed into the filling), which is commonly served for breakfast.

SHOOFLY PIE

Line a pie plate with a pastry crust. Combine 1½ c. sifted flour, 1 c. brown sugar, ⅛ t. salt, and ¼ c. cold butter to make a crumbly blend. Dissolve ½ t. baking soda in ½ c. molasses, then add ¾ of the crumb mixture. Pour into pie pan, top with the rest of the crumbs, and bake in a 350° oven for about 30 min., until firm.

shore dinner. A large meal based mostly on fresh, locally caught seafood (1890). The term is most readily associated with the eastern coastline cities from New York to Maine, where restaurants featured lavish spreads of steamed clams in clam broth, mussels, lobsters, and corn on the cob. In New York the offerings might include shrimp or crabmeat cocktail and broiled fish as well.

shortnin' bread. A southern quick bread made with a shortening like butter or lard.

SHORTNIN' BREAD

Mix 2 C. flour with ½ c. brown sugar and blend until crumbly. Work in ¼ lb. butter until dough is smooth. Divide, pat into a circle ½ in. thick, prick the top, and cook in ungreased pan at 350° for about 30 min.

---

shot. A jigger of alcohol, about one to one and a half ounces.

shot-and-a-beer. Bartender's term for a quick drink of alcohol followed by a glass of beer. By extension, a "shot-and-a-beer town" is a slang term for a blue-collar industrial town like Pittsburgh, Ohio.

shrapnel. Bartender's slang for a tip consisting of loose change. The word refers to the fragments of bullet or cannon shells in a bursting charge thrown in all directions, a weapon designed by English army officer Henry Shrapnel and dating in print to 1800, although the slang term only dates to 1991.

shrimp. Any of a wide variety of ten-legged crustaceans of the suborder Natantia. It is the most popular shellfish in the United States, with U.S. commercial landings totaling 290.3 million pounds in 1997. U.S. annual consumption is about 850 million pounds.

The word shrimp derives from Middle English *shrimpe,* meaning "pygmy" or the crustacean itself.

Shrimp harvesting was known as early as the seventeenth century in Louisiana, whose bayou inhabitants used seine nets up to two thousand feet in circumference. Only after 1917 did mechanized boats utilize trawl nets to catch shrimp. Americans have always eaten shrimp, but its tendency to spoil quickly has for most of our history confined its availability to regions having access to the sea or rivers. Fresh shrimp are available in the South, but almost all the shrimp Americans buy at market or in restaurants is in fact frozen. Only in the twentieth century, with advances in refrigeration on-board trawlers (which began plying the waters for lengthy voyages only in 1917), did shrimp become readily available in American markets, with New York City consuming the lion's share of the catch—about a million and a half pounds a week.

Most shrimp come from Atlantic waters, though there are some from Alaska and from the rivers of the South. The main species for culinary use include seven species in the Atlantic—the "edible shrimp" (*Pevaeus aztecus, setiferus,* and *duorarum*), also called, respectively, "brown," "pink," and "white" shrimp; the "Caribbean shrimp" (*P. schmitti*); the "sea bob" (*Xiphopeneus kroyeri*); the "royal red shrimp" (*Hymenopenaeus robustus*); and the "rock shrimp" (*Sicyonia brevirostris*)—and in the Pacific the "side-stripe shrimp" (*Pandalopsis dispar*); the "pink shrimp" (*P. borealis* and *P. jordoni*); the "coon-stripe shrimp" (*P. danae*); and the spot shrimp" (*P. platyceros*).

Shrimp are graded by size or "count," which indicates the number of shrimp likely to be in a pound, so that the smaller the number in the count, the larger the shrimp. A pound of "small" would therefore number 50-plus shrimp; "medium," 43–50; medium large," 36–42; "large," 31–35; "extra large," 26–30; "Jumbo," 21–25; "extra jumbo," 16–20; "colossal," 10–15; "extra colossal," under 10.

Per capita U.S. consumption of shrimp is 2.4 lbs. Americans eat shrimp boiled and served plain or with a ketchup sauce seasoned with chili pepper and horseradish (called a "shrimp cocktail"), deep-fried, grilled, baked in various sauces, and in many other forms. In New Orleans shrimp RÉMOULADE is a traditional dish and "shrimp boils" popular social affairs. "Barbecued shrimp" is also a specialty of New Orleans, having originated at Pascal's Manale Restaurant in 1952, although the shrimp are not actually barbecued but baked with butter and seasoning.

Many preparations originally made with lobsters are adapted for shrimp. Shrimp SCAMPI, rarely made with true scampi, is a dish of shrimp sautéed in garlic and oil or butter.

BARBECUED SHRIMP

In a blender mix 2 peeled, sliced onions, 2 cloves garlic, ½ t. oregano, ½ t. marjoram, ½ t. salt, ¼ t. black pepper, 3 T. white vinegar, 1 T. cayenne pepper, 2 t. lemon juice. In a casserole dish, melt 2 sticks butter and blend in other seasonings. Coat 2 lb. of peeled shrimp with the sauce and bake in a 375° oven from about 15 min. Serves 4.

SHRIMP CREOLE

In a sauté pan pour 3 T. vegetable oil. Sauté ½ c. chopped celery, ½ c. chopped onion, 2 cloves chopped garlic for 2–3 min., then add 1 lb. peeled tomatoes and 8 oz. tomato sauce. Add 2 t. salt, ¾ t. pepper, ½ t. cayenne pepper, 1 t. sugar, 1 T. Worcestershire sauce, and *a dash bottled hot sauce. Cook over low heat for about 40 min. Mix 1 t. cornstarch with 2 t. water and add to mixture to thicken. Add 1 lb. peeled shrimp and ½ c. chopped bell pepper. Cook just until shrimp are tender and pink. Serves 4.*

shrimp and grits. A Low Country dish made with sautéed shrimp served with GRITS. Because it is commonly served for breakfast during the shrimp season, the dish is sometimes called "breakfast shrimp." Often seasonings and bell peppers are added, as in the recipe below.

SHRIMP AND GRITS

In a skillet heat 3 T. butter and sauté 1 chopped onion and ½ chopped green bell pepper for about 10 min. Sprinkle vegetables with 2 T. flour and brown slightly. Add 1 lb. peeled shrimp, season with salt and a pinch of cayenne, and add 1 c. chicken or shrimp stock. Cook for about 3 min., add the juice of one lemon, cook until sauce reduces. Serve over freshly made grits.

shrimper's sauce. A tomato sauce made by the shrimp fishermen of the South. The following recipe is given in the Federal Writers Project American Guides volume on the *Mississippi Gulf Coast* (1939).

SHRIMPER'S SAUCE

Fry 1 c. chopped salt pork in 1 c. oil, add 3 French onions, 1 can tomato sauce, 3 c. boiling water, 1 t. chile powder, 2 cloves minced garlic, 1 sprig of thyme, 1 t. celery salt, salt, and pepper, and cook about 30 min.

shrimps de Jonghe. A dish of baked shrimp topped with seasoned bread crumbs. It originated around 1900 at Chicago's de Jonghe's Hotel and Restaurant, run by Belgian immigrant Henri de Jonghe. It is not known whether the dish was created by de Jonghe or by his chef, Emil Zehr.

SHRIMPS DE JONGHE

Cream ¾ c. butter with 1 t. salt, 1 mashed clove of garlic, 1 c. bread crumbs, ¼ c. parsley, ½ c. sherry, and a dash of cayenne and paprika. Shell and devein 3 lb. shrimp, then boil until half-cooked. In 8 small cooking tins

place some of the bread-crumb mixture, top with the shrimp, layer on more of the bread crumbs, and bake at 375° for 20–25 min.

shrimp wiggle. A dish of creamed shrimp especially popular in New England and the Midwest. The reason for the name is not known, though it may refer to the ease and quickness with which the dish is made. It dates in print at least to 1949. In *American Cookery* (1972), James Beard comments, "For many years this was in the repertoire of every coed with a chafing dish and every girl who had a beau to cook for."

SHRIMP WIGGLE

Combine 1 T. butter, 1 T. chopped onion, 1 c. boiled rice, and ½ can tomato soup in a double boiler. Add a dash of red pepper, salt and pepper to taste, 1 c. cream, 2 c. shelled, deveined shrimp, and 2 c. peas. Heat through and serve on crackers, toast, or in pastry shells.

Siberia. A section of a restaurant dining room that is considered either socially inferior or merely poor seating. While not all American restaurants have such undesirable sections or tables, much fuss is made over those that do, and some people would rather not sit down at all than to be escorted to Siberia.

The term is said to have originated in the 1930s, when a society woman named Peggy Hopkins Joyce entered the class-conscious El Morocco nightclub in New York and found herself being led to a less than desirable table. "Where are you taking me," she asked the maître d'hôtel, "Siberia?"

In most society restaurants the most treasured tables are usually situated along the banquettes that line the room as one enters, though in other restaurants a good table, called an "A" table, may be a corner table or one that is regularly occupied by a person of some celebrity.

An alternate term for Siberia is the "doghouse," used by those who frequented New York City's Colony Restaurant, opened in 1926, to describe the least desirable of its three rooms.

sidecar. A cocktail made from brandy, orange-flavored liqueur, and lemon juice. The drink seems to have originated at Harry's New York Bar in Paris, but the date and inspiration of the invention are uncertain. The bar's owner, Harry MacElhone, claimed the drink was concocted in 1931 for a customer who always arrived in a motorcycle sidecar. But the sidecar appears in several places in Carl Van Vechten's 1931 short story collection, *Parties*. But David A. Embury, in *The Fine Art of Mixing Drinks* (3rd American ed., 1958), says it was invented by a friend of his during World War I and was "named after the motorcycle sidecar in which the good captain customarily was driven to and from the little bistro where the drink was born and christened." The drink was apparently well known by 1934, however, when a recipe for it was printed in *Dining in New York, an Intimate Guide* by Rian James.

Embury recommends a blend of one part Cointreau or Triple Sec, two parts lemon juice, and eight parts cognac or Armagnac. But the more usual mix is as follows:

SIDECAR

Shake together with ice 1 part orange liqueur, 1 part cognac, and 1 part lemon juice. Strain and serve in cocktail glass.

Singapore sling. A cocktail of gin, cherry brandy, Cointreau, Benedictine, and citrus juices. It was supposedly created by bartender Ngiam Tong Boon of the Long Bar in Singapore's Raffles Hotel in 1915 and is sometimes called the "Singapore Raffles gin sling" or the "Raffles bar gin sling." There are many variants; one admirer of the drink has said the original was topped off with club soda, but the official Raffles version given below is without any such additive.

SINGAPORE SLING

Into a shaker with 4 ice cubes put 1 oz. gin, ¾ oz. cherry brandy, a "few drops" Cointreau, the juice of ½ a medium-size lemon, 2 oz. fresh pineapple juice, 1 or 2 drops bitters, and 1 dash grenadine. Cover and shake for 10 sec., pour into a 10-oz. glass with 2 ice cubes. Garnish with a wedge of pineapple and maraschino cherry.

singles' bar. A bar or lounge dispensing alcoholic beverages and frequented by single—that is, unmarried—people who go to such places specifically to meet other single people of the opposite sex (1965). Although bars have long been social centers, it was not until the 1960s that working women in large cities began to visit such establishments without worrying about public opinion. By the 1970s, however, the term "singles' bar" had taken on a pejorative connotation.

The first singles' bar was "T.G.I. Friday's" (short for "Thank God It's Friday"), opened by Alan Stillman in New York City on March 15, 1965.

sirloin. A cut of beef from the upper part of the loin between the rump and the porterhouse. Between six and eight one-inch-thick sirloins may be taken from the hip, though many Americans prefer a two-inch steak. If aged correctly, sirloin is one of the best steak cuts for tenderness and flavor.

Depending on the way a butcher cuts the meat, different kinds of sirloin may be produced. When cut across the grain, the steaks will be called "pinbone," "flat bone," "round bone," and "wedge bone," from the shape of the hipbone they contain. By cutting with the grain, the butcher produces boneless roasts called "tenderloin," "top sirloin," and "bottom sirloin." A whole, uncut sirloin is called a "king-sized roast," weighing between twelve and twenty pounds.

Sirloins are usually broiled or grilled, though they can be pan-fried.

The origin of the word is from Old French *surlonge* (*sur*, "above" and *longe*, "loin"). A cherished but wholly inaccurate legend attached to the name has to do with an English king who knighted a piece of beef "Sir Loin." Thomas Fuller's *Church History* (1655) maintained that the monarch in question was Henry VIII, but Jonathan Swift vouched for James I.

There are references to the word "sirloin" as far back as 1515. In many parts of the United States a sirloin is called a "New York cut."

six-pack. Slang term for six bottles or cans of beer or other beverage sold in a package. The term has been in print since 1950.

sizzling platter. A service of meats on a heated platter so as to create an audible sizzle when brought to the table. The idea was introduced in New York City at the Longchamps Restaurant chain in the 1930s. A "sizzle platter" is a shallow, aluminum platter set into a removable wooden or plastic tray.

skate. Also, "ray" and "ray fish." Any of a variety of fishes in the family Rajidae, especially the genus *Raja* whose radiating pectoral fins give it a flat, diamond shape. In eastern waters of the U.S. the "smooth butterfly ray" (*Gymnura micrura*) and "winter skate" (*Raja ocellata*) are popular edible species, whose flesh was once cut into circles and sold dishonestly as scallops. Western species of culinary interest include the "California skate" (*R. inorata*), "big skate" (*R. binocu-*

lata), and "longnose skate" *(R. rhina)*. Skate is best when poached before any preparation, and its most popular culinary form is to serve it with a French *buerre noir* sauce. The U.S. commercial landings of skate totaled 27.9 million pounds in 1997.

skipjack. Any of a variety of species of fish (mostly tuna and mackerel) whose members "skip" out of the water. The term dates in print to the middle of the sixteenth century. The species *Katsuwonus pelamis* (also called "oceanic BONITO" and "striped bonito") and *Sarda sarda* (also called "Atlantic bonito") are commonly called "skipjack."

skirt. Ice-cream maker's term for the rim of ice cream created when a scoop is pushed down onto an ice-cream cone.

skully-jo. A dish made by the Portuguese settlers in Provincetown, Massachusetts, from dried cod or haddock cured in the sun until, in the opinion of one observer, "it's hard enough to bend lead pipe around." The children of the region would chew it instead of candy. It is rarely made anymore.

slinger. A southerner's term for someone who takes a drink of spirits upon awakening in the morning.

sloppy Joe. A dish of ground beef, onions, green peppers, and ketchup made in a skillet and often served on a hamburger roll. It is sometimes called a "skilletburger."

The origins of this dish are unknown, but recipes for the dish date back at least to the 1940s. It dates in print to 1935. There is probably no Joe after whom it is named—but its rather messy appearance and tendency to drip off plate or roll makes "sloppy" an adequate description, and "Joe" is an American name of proletarian character and unassailable genuineness. There are many individual and regional variations on the dish. In Sioux City, Iowa, a dish of this type is called a "loosemeat sandwich," created in 1934 at Ye Olde Tavern Inn by Abraham and Bertha Kaled.

SLOPPY JOE

Cook 1 lb. ground beef in a skillet with 2 T. butter. Mix in ¼ c. flour, 1 T. chopped onion, ¼ c. chopped green pepper, 1 c. chopped celery, ¼ c. ketchup (or canned tomato soup), 2 t. salt, ½ t. pepper, and 3 c. water. Boil together until tender and well blended.

slumgullion. Also, "slum." A term from the California Gold Rush days used by miners for any disgusting or makeshift food or drink. It first appears in print in 1840 (and as "slum" in 1874), and in *Roughing It* (1872) Mark Twain wrote of being offered a drink of slumgullion by a station keeper in Nebraska who said it was like tea. But, Twain remarked, "there was too much dish rag, and sand, and old bacon-rind in it to deceive the intelligent traveller." Nevertheless, Twain admired whoever it was who named it.

slump. A dish of cooked fruit and raised dough known since the middle of the eighteenth century and probably so called because it is a somewhat misshapen dish that "slumps" on the plate. Louisa May Alcott, author of *Little Women,* named her Concord, Massachusetts, home "Apple Slump" and recorded this recipe:

SLUMP

Pare, core, and slice 6 apples and combine with 1 c. sugar, 1 t. cinnamon, and ½ c. water in a saucepan. Cover and beat to boiling point. Meanwhile sift together 1½ c. flour, 1¼ t. salt, and 1½ t. baking powder and add ½ c. milk to make a soft dough. Drop pieces of the dough from a tablespoon onto apple mixture, cover, and cook over low heat for 30 min. Serve with cream.

small beer. A beer of low alcoholic content. The term is more widely used in England, where it first saw print in 1560, than in the United States.

smelt (family Osmeridae). A silvery, small, slender fish found in North American oceans, rivers, and lakes. The name is from the Anglo-Saxon *smoelt,* meaning "smooth" or "shining." U.S. commercial landings of smelt totaled 27.8 million pounds in 1997.

In the Great Lake regions spring is marked by the arrival of smelt, which are cause for many nighttime fishing parties. Although the fish is not native to the Great Lakes, they were introduced there in the early 1900s. Smelts are a very perishable fish and are often sold frozen. They are best coated with seasoned flour and beaten egg and pan-fried in butter or oil. It requires about a dozen to make a pound. The main North American species are:

eulachon (*Thaleichythys pacificus*). Also, "candle-fish" (because its oiliness made it a good candle when dried by Native Americans, who inserted a bark wick through the fish). Found from the Bering Sea to central California at lengths up to twelve inches, the eulachon is often marketed as "Columbia River smelt" in the Northwest. The name "eulachon" is from a Chinook Indian dialect word, *vlâkân,* for the fish, and one encounters renderings such as "uIchen" and the colloquial American "hooligan" (which itself is a word for a ruffian). Because of their fattiness, eulachon are sometimes dried out in a warm oven after being fried.

rainbow smelt (*Osmerus mordax*). Also, "ice fish." A smelt found along the Atlantic coast, measuring about seven to eight inches long and having a silver band. It was introduced to the Great Lakes drainage in 1912, where it has proliferated.

surf smelt (*Hypomesus pretiosus*). Also, "silver smelt." Found from Alaska to southern California, the surf smelt grows to about ten inches and is netted on sandy beaches of the outer coast.

Other, less well known smelts include: "night smelt" (*Sprinchus starski*), found from Alaska to central California; "delta smelt" (*Hypomesus transpacificus*), in the San Joaquin and Sacramento river systems; "longfin smelt" (*S. thaleichthys*), similar to the night smelt; "Pacific smoothtongue" (*Leuroglossus stilbius*), a Pacific species; "whitebait smelt" (*Allosmerus elongatus*); and "pond smelt" (*Hypomesus olidus*), found in Alaska and Canada. The "top smelt" and the "Jack smelt" are "Pacific silversides" of the family Atheriniclae, of a different order from other smelts, and "deep-sea smelts" are of the family Bathylagidae, but closely related to true smelts.

smoothie. A drink with a thick, smooth consistency made from pureeing fruit with yogurt, ice cream, or milk. The term dates to the 1970s.

s'mores. A confection made from graham crackers, marshmallow, and chocolate heated until the contents melt. The word "s'mores"—always used in the plural—is short for "some mores," referring to one's appetite for more than just one. It is a cookie said to be particularly popular at Girl Scouts' campfire cookouts. According to Jane and Michael Stern in *Square Meals* (1984), s'mores are also known as "Princess Pats," "Perfection Crisps," and "Slapsticks."

S'MORES

Toast 1 large marshmallow and place on a graham cracker. Add a layer of chocolate-bar candy and place another graham cracker on top. S'mores may also be made by making a sandwich of graham crackers, chocolate bar, and marshmallow heated in an oven or microwave oven.

---

smorgasbord. A buffet meal of Swedish origins that has become in this century a very popular party spread. The word comes from the Swedish *smörgåsbord,* a "bread and butter table," and first appeared in American print in 1893. The idea soon caught on, so that by 1941 the *West Hartford Ladies Aid Society Swedish American Cook Book* listed several suggestions for a smorgasbord, including the following items: butter balls, Swedish rye bread, pumpernickel, hardtack, pickled herring, baked ham, smoked tongue, lingonberries, radish roses, omelets, "Rulle Pulse" (rolled pressed lamb), "liver pastej" (liver pâté), jellied veal, head cheese, hot SWEDISH MEATBALLS, Swedish pork sausage, brown beans, Swedish fish pudding, smoked salmon, stuffed eggs, potato salad, "sill salad" (herring salad), meat and potato sausage, fruit salad, Swedish apple cake, and coffee with cream.

Today smorgasbords may still contain many of these same items, as well as dishes from other countries.

smothered. A word used to describe any of a variety of dishes in which the meat, poultry, or fish is "smothered" with a gravy and/or vegetables while baked, braised, or cooked in a covered skillet. One authority, Craig Claiborne, believes the term may derive from the use of a weighted-down plate to cover the dish as it cooks.

SMOTHERED CHICKEN

Cut a 3-lb. chicken into pieces and dredge in a mixture of ¾ c. flour, 1½ t. salt, and ¼ t. pepper. Brown chicken in 4 T. butter, add ½ c. water, cover, and simmer for about 1 hr. until very tender. During the last 20 min. of cooking, add 1 c. green peas, 2 T. pimiento strips, and ½ c. onions. Reduce sauce and spoon over chicken. Serves 4.

---

snack. A meal or food item eaten hurriedly or casually, which might include anything from a candy bar to a hamburger. The word, also used as a verb, "to snack," derives from the Dutch *snacken*, "to bite," and in English (dating in print to 1757 as a noun; to 1807 as a verb) first meant a small portion of liquor. By the eighteenth century it had acquired its present meaning. Snack bars, where one bought a snack, were known as of 1895, though this term was more popular in England than in America until well into the twentieth century.

Americans buy about 4.3 billion pounds of snack food annually (a $13.4 billion market) and consume more than 17 pounds per person. The most popular snack food among Americans is potato chips (6.1 pounds per person), followed by tortilla chips (3.9), snack nuts (1.6), pretzels (1.4), microwave popcorn (1.3), and corn chips (0.9).

snapper. A bony fish of the Lutjanidae family. There are 250 species in the world, of which fifteen are found in United States waters from North Carolina to the Gulf of Mexico. Snappers are usually panfried. The most popular American species for eating are:

gray snapper (*Lutjanus griseus*). Also called "mangrove snapper." Found in southern United States waters, the gray snapper may weigh from under a pound up to ten pounds.

mutton snapper (*L. analis*). Also, "muttonfish." The mutton snapper, found from south Florida to the tropical Atlantic, is olive green and has range-red sides and brick-red fins. Though it is rarely seen in American markets, it is good baked.

red snapper (*L. campechanus*). By far the most popular of the species in America, the red snapper is found from North Carolina down through the Gulf of Mexico, and although it can grow to thirty-five pounds, the typical specimens found in markets weigh between four and six pounds. This beautiful red-pink fish takes well to most forms of cooking. It is quite similar to the "silk snapper" (*L. vivanus*), which is often called "red snapper" at market. The "Creole rouget" is red snapper, not kin to the French *rouget*, which is a "red mullet." In Hawaii the "onaga" (*Etelis coruscans*) is a fish often called "red snapper," while the "uku" (*Aprion virescens*), also called a "jobfish," is a pale pink color, considered excellent for making sashimi.

RED SNAPPER

A red-snapper recipe popular in Florida calls for the fillets to be marinated in a baking dish with ½ c. chopped onions, ¼ c. fresh orange juice, 2 t. grated orange peel, and 1 t. salt for about 30 min. Sprinkle a pinch of nutmeg and black pepper on the fish, then bake for about 10 min. in a 400° oven.

---

yellowtail snapper (*Ocyurus chrysurus*). This yellow-striped, shallow-water snapper is usually about one-and-a-half pounds in size and rarely weighs over five pounds. Its main popularity has traditionally been around Key West, where it was long considered a breakfast fish because it was sold early in the morning after the catch. It is excellent pan-fried with a squeeze of Key lime over it. The yellowtail snapper is not to be confused with a form of TILEFISH, found in American waters further north, that goes by the name "yellow snapper."

kalikali. Hawaiian name fro a speicies of snapper (either *Pristipomoides sieboldii* or *Rooseveltia brighami*) of the Pacific (1926).

snickerdoodle. A New England cookie made with flour, nuts, and dried fruits. The name is simply a nineteenth-century nonsense word for a quickly made confection.

SNICKERDOODLE

Sift 3½ c. flour with ½ t. salt, 1 t. baking soda, 1 t. cinnamon, and ⅛ t. nutmeg. Cream 1 c. butter, add 1¼ c. sugar slowly, beat in 3 beaten eggs, stir in flour, then add 1 c. chopped nuts, ½ c. currants, and ½ c. raisins. Drop in spoonfuls onto buttered cookie sheet, and bake at 350° for 12–15 min. Makes about 10 doz.

---

snow ball. Also, "sno' ball." A scoop of vanilla or other flavor of ice cream rolled in shredded, sweetened coconut that is chilled and served with a topping of chocolate syrup, or a ball of shaved ice with fruit syrup.

Also, "snow ball" refers to a pastry-wrapped apple topped with a white icing to resemble snow.

snow cone. A confection of crushed ice or freshly fallen snow drizzled with a fruit syrup and usually served in a paper cone (1960). It is a traditional treat of summer, especially among Hispanic Americans, who call them *raspas,* from the Spanish *raspar,* "to scrape." In New Orleans this confection is called a "snowball."

snow cream. A southern confection especially popular with African-Americans, snow cream is nothing more than freshly fallen snow that is scooped up and mixed with a variety of flavorings like vanilla, sugar, and cinnamon. Some devotees claim that only the first snow of the season should be used, though some claim that it is the third snow of the season that is the purest.

In New England children pour cooked maple syrup over snow and let it harden. This is called "sugar-in-snow."

sober side of the bar. The bartender's side.

soda. Also, "soda pop" and "soft drink." Carbonated water or a flavored juice drink, usually flavored and colored. The first carbonated waters were from natural sources and sold at the end of the eighteenth century as "soda water" at "soda fountains." By 1809 the drink was being sweetened and flavored to make items like "ginger pop," also called "ginger beer" (which once had a slight alcoholic content), and, later, "ginger champagne" or "ginger ale" (which does not). "Belfast Style Ginger Ale" was produced by Toronto pharmacist John J. McLaughlin in 1890, though in 1907 he changed the name to "Canada Dry Pale Ginger Ale" and began producing it in New York City in 1922. See main entry on SELTZER.

In 1812 English author Robert Southey commented on the new word "pop" as deriving its meaning from the sound made when the cork is drawn from the bottle.

By 1819 a patent was issued for "carbonated mead," and in 1824 one for SARSAPARILLA. In the 1830s the first man-made carbonated waters became available, and lemon, strawberry, vanilla, and other flavors were popular. By 1854 "cream soda" was vanilla flavored. In 1889 a cream soda was cited as ice cream in soda water—"a favorite drink of American women." "Birch beer" came along in the 1880s to compete with Philadelphian druggist Charles E. Hires's "Herb Tea," later changed to "Root Beer" (a previously common term for a soda flavored with various roots and herbs). Hires had first made the beverage in 1875, advertised it as "the National Temperance Drink" and first served it at the 1876 Philadelphia Centennial Exposition.

In 1881 there appeared "Imperial Inca Coca,"

made from extracts of the cola, or kola nut, and the leaf of the coca plant. Five years later, on May 8, 1886, an Atlanta, Georgia, pharmacist named John Styth Pemberton made a cola syrup that he brought to Jacob's Pharmacy, where it was mixed with carbonated water to make the first cola drink. Pemberton's bookkeeper, Frank M. Robinson, named the drink Coca-Cola, which was registered as a trademark in 1893, and Atlanta businessman Asa G. Candler bought total rights to the soda syrup in 1891 for $2,300 and immediately began promoting the drink as a refreshment, whereas it had previously been sold as a medicinal aid to cure hangovers and headaches.

Early batches of Coca-Cola (since 1909 called "Coke" for short) may once have contained trace elements of cocaine but these were removed at the turn of the century. "Cherry Coke" is a cherry-flavored version of Coca-Cola sold in cans, though it was once customarily mixed by soda jerks.

Another pharmacist, Caleb Bradham of New Bern, North Carolina, came up with a similar concoction in 1896, which he sold as "Brad's drink" to his local customers. He changed the name in 1903 to "Pepsi-Cola" and began bottling the beverage in 1904; three years later the Pepsi-Cola Company had forty franchises, and the drink, usually sold by horse-drawn cart, began to be purveyed by motor vehicles, and auto racer Barney Oldfield was enlisted as a spokesman for the drink.

Coca-Cola and Pepsi-Cola went on to become great American success stories after World War I, thanks to a developing taste for such drinks and a drop in the price of sugar (although Pepsi-Cola had several difficult years because Bradham had overbought sugar when it was at its most expensive). Both companies also used advertising and marketing with amazing results. Pepsi-Cola was the first company to broadcast a jingle on radio, and every American was soon able to sing along with the words,

> *Pepsi-Cola hits the spot.*
> *Twelve full ounces,*
> *That's a lot.*
> *Twice as much for a nickel, too,*
> *Pepsi-Cola is the drink for you.*

(The lyrics indicated that "Pepsi," as it was called for short, sold twelve ounces for the same price Coca-Cola charged for six ounces, then the standard of the industry.)

Both products became among the best-known American food items in the world, and one or the other, or both, can be found around the globe, including, in Pepsi-Cola's case, as a franchise in the Soviet Union. The formulas for these drinks are considered to be among the world's best-kept industrial secrets, with only a handful of people knowing different parts of the formulas. Coca-Cola sells about 265 million eight-ounce servings of their product per day. Pepsi-Cola sold 1.1 billion cases in 1981.

Another soda that became a national favorite was created in 1885 by pharmacist Charles C. Alderton at the Wade B. Morrison Old Corner Drugstore in Waco, Texas. The drink was named "Dr Pepper" after Dr. Charles K. Pepper of Rural Retreat, Virginia, whose daughter Morrison had once fallen in love with (but never married). The drink was first bottled in Waco and by Sam Houston Prim in Dublin, Texas, as of 1891. The original formula for Dr Pepper, using sugar rather than corn syrup, is available only from one bottling plant in Dublin, owned by W. P. "Bill" Kloster, who refused to modify the formula when the national Dr Pepper Company (based in Dallas) changed to corn syrup. A popular way to drink Dr Pepper among Texas schoolchildren is to pour peanuts into the drink, drink the soda, and eat the peanuts.

Other significant soda drinks in the American market would include: "7 UP," a lemon-lime-flavored drink originally marketed in St. Louis, Missouri, by Charles L. Grigg in 1929 under the name "Bib-Label Lithiated Lemon-Lime Soda." The reason for 7 UP's name was never divulged by Grigg, but Stuart Berg Flexner in *I Hear America Talking* (1976) noted that a card game by that name was known since the 1820s. Others have suggested the number referred to the seven-ounce bottle size. But in *I'm a Spam Fan: The Stories Behind America's Favorite Foods* (1992), Carolyn Wyman wrote that

> . . . recent 7-Up scholarship reveals the name had more to do with Grigg's long admiration for cattle brands as a simple and clear method of identification. Reading a newspaper article about several cattle brands, Griggs saw a reference to one that consisted of the numeral 7 with an adjacent letter u. So cattle were the real inspiration for the 7-Up name.

In New York a coffee-flavored soda called "Passaro's Famous Manhattan Special" was created in 1895 by Dr. Teresa Cimino.

The first sugar-free soda was sold in March 1953 by Morris Kirsch of Kirsch Beverages in Brooklyn, New York, who, with Dr. S. S. Epstein, came up with "No-Cal soda" (short for "no calories") for diabetics,

although it was soon marketed for those trying to cut calories from their diet. In 1964 Pepsi-Cola introduced one of the first diet sodas, "diet Pepsi." Other diet drinks named "Tab," (later "diet Coke"), "Diet 7 UP," "Fresca," and others were developed, and they now represent about 13 percent of the $25 billion soda industry business. In the 1970s, led by Pepsi-Cola, plastic bottles (invented by Nathaniel C. Wyeth of the Du Pont chemical company) began to replace the traditional glass ones.

By 1984 Americans were actually drinking more soft drinks (11.5 billion gallons) than they did water (11.2 billion). Current U.S. per capita consumption of carbonated soft drinks 53 gallons..

soda beer. A nineteenth-century substitute for real beer.

SODA BEER

For 5 min. boil together 2 oz. cream of tartar, 2 lb. sugar, the juice of ½ lemon, and 3 pt. water. Cool and add 3 stiffly beaten egg whites and ½ c. flour, ½ oz. wintergreen essence, and ½ oz. lemon essence. Stir to blend and bottle. Use 1 T. of soda beer for each glass of water or soda.

---

soda jerk. Also, "soda jerker." A person who prepares sodas and other confections behind the counter at a soda fountain. The word dates back at least to the 1880s and comes from the jerking motion the hand has to make on the soda spigots then in use in order to fill glasses.

sodium nitrite ($NaNO_2$). A preservative used in bacon and other cured meats. It is made by the transformation of sodium nitrate ($NaNO_3$) by sodium carbonate. Questions raised about nitrites that can combine with secondary amines to form compounds known as "nitrosamines" (which can cause certain types of cancer in laboratory animals) in some bacon as a result of severe frying caused a reassessment of the necessity of sodium nitrite in curing meats. In May 1978 the USDA announced regulations requiring bacon to be made using 120 ppm of sodium nitrite or the equivalent amount of potassium nitrite plus 550 ppm sodium ascorbate or sodium erythorbate, and that cooked bacon may not contain nitrosamines.

sole. Any of a variety of flatfish of the family Soleidae. Some confusion has been created by the use of the name "sole" for other species, and restaurant terminology does not always adhere strictly to the rigors of taxonomic nomenclature. The word comes from Old French *sole,* referring to the shape of the foot, which the fish's flat form resembles.

The true soles of American waters—four species—are rarely sold as food fish, while American flounders of various species are often called "sole." These include "butter sole" (*Isopsetta isolepsis*); "English sole," also called "lemon sole" (*Parophrys vetulus*); "petrale sole" (*Eopsetta jordani*); "rex sole" (*Glyptocephalus zachirus*); "sand sole" (*Psettichthys melanostictus*); and the best known, "Dover sole" (*Microstomus pacificus*), which is a common name for the major fish of the sole market, but it is not the true "Dover sole" (*Solea vulgaris*) of Europe.

Americans enjoy sole sautéed or grilled with BUTTER, sometimes breaded, and very often prepared according to classic French recipes, such as SOLE MARGUERY, SOLE MEUNIÈRE (with butter and fines herbes), and "sole amandine" (with slivers of blanched almonds).

sole Marguery. Or, "filets de sole Marguery." Fillets of sole served in a sauce made with egg yolks, butter, and white wine and cooked with mussels and shrimp.

Although it is decidedly a French creation—by chef M. Mangin of the Café de Marguery in Paris—and is listed in Escoffier's *Le Guide Culinaire* and in *Larousse Gastronomique,* sole Marguery is far more popular in the United States than in France, and much of its celebrity derives from the story of how it came to these shores.

Diamond Jim Brady, one of the most flamboyant American gourmands at the turn of the century, returned from Paris to his favorite New York restaurant, Rector's, with the news that he had enjoyed a remarkable dish called "filets de sole Marguery." George Rector thereupon withdrew his son from Cornell Law School and sent him off to Paris to get the recipe by working in the kitchens of the Café de Marguery, where he labored for more than a year before he was able to "get the hang of the famous sauce." The young Rector worked fifteen hours a day until he produced a version of the dish that seven master chefs pronounced perfect. He immediately quit his Parisian post, sailed for America, and was greeted in New York Harbor by Rector's Russian Orchestra, his father, and Brady, whose first words were "Have you got the sauce?" Rector made the sauce that night at a fabulous banquet, and Brady pronounced the dish "so good I could eat it on a Turkish towel," and proceeded to down nine portions.

The dish immediately became a sensation and a standard item on American deluxe restaurants' menus.

Ironically the recipe given by the originator, M. Mangin, to *Larousse Gastronomique* differs from that published by George Rector, Jr., in his book, *The Girl from Rector's* (1927). Here is the recipe from Mangin:

MANGIN'S SOLE MARGUERY

Fillet two fine soles. Use the bones and trimmings to make a white wine fumet, flavored with a little chopped onion, a sprig of thyme, quarter of a bay leaf and a little parsley. Season with salt and pepper. Simmer for 15 minutes. Add to this fumet, which should be strained and concentrated, the strained cooking liquor of a quart of mussels cooked in the usual way (using white wine). Place the fillets of sole, seasoned and lightly flattened, on a buttered baking dish. Sprinkle over a few tablespoons of the aforesaid fumet. Cover with buttered grease-proof paper and poach gently. Drain the fillets well. Set them in an oval dish and surround with a double row of shelled mussels and shrimps. Keep hot, if covered, while the sauce is prepared.

The sauce. Strain the fumet to which will have been added the cooking juices of the soles. Boil down by two-thirds. Remove from heat, allow the sauce to cool a little, then add 6 egg yolks. Whisk the sauce over a gentle heat, like a hollandaise, incorporating about ¾ pound of the finest butter, slightly melted. Season the sauce and strain. Coat with it the fillets and garnish. Glaze in a hot oven.

Here is Rector's recipe:

RECTOR'S SOLE MARGUERY

Cut the fillet with a very sharp knife. There are four fillets to a fish. Take the rest of the fish and put them into a big boiler with plenty of leeks, onions, carrots, turnips, lettuce, romaine, parsley, and similar vegetables. The whole mass is reduced by boiling from eight to twelve hours. This leaves a very small quantity of a jellylike substance, which is the essence of the fish. If properly prepared, only a handful of jelly will be obtained from two hundred fish.

In another pan we place the yolks of four dozen eggs. Work a gallon of melted butter into this, stopping every ten minutes to pour in a pint of dry white wine of good Bordeaux quality. Add from time to time a spoonful of the essence of fish. This is stirred in and cooked in a double boiler in the same way as you would make a hollandaise sauce.

Strain the sauce through a very fine sieve. Season with a dash of cayenne salt. At no time in the preparation of the sauce should it be allowed to come to a boil.

Now we take the fillets, which should be kept on ice to retain their freshness until the sauce is ready. Place them in a pan with just sufficient water to float them a little. About half an inch of water should be sufficient to cover them. After they simmer for ten minutes or less, remove and place on a silver platter. Garnish the dish on one end with small shrimp and on the other with imported mussels from northern France.

Pour a liberal amount of the sauce over the whole platter. Sprinkle with chopped parsley and place under the grill for the purpose of allowing it to glaze to a golden brown. Then serve.

son-of-a-bitch stew. Also, "son-of-a-gun stew" and "cowboy stew." A slang term among cowboys, loggers, miners, and other westerners for a stew made pretty much from whatever was available at the moment or from kitchen scraps. Larry Ross, in *Nanny's Texas Table* (1987), contended that " 'Son of a Gun Stew' can mean just about anything in the Lone Star State, and it doesn't always relate to food. 'Rich as . . .' or 'More full of . . .' . . . the possibilities are just as varied and equally questionable. Some say it's a stew of heart, lungs, and other organs, you name it. Others claim it's what the cowboys called what the cook couldn't identify."

sop. Gravy. A colloquialism of the West, "sop" may also refer to a habitual drunkard.

sopaipilla. A deep-fried fritter usually served with honey (1935). Sopaipillas, whose name is from the Spanish, are a staple of Mexican-American menus. Yet in Jane Butel's *Tex-Mex Cookbook* (1980), the author notes that "history reveals they originated in Old Town, Albuquerque, [New Mexico,] about 300 years ago." Diana Kennedy, in her *Recipes from the Regional Cooks of Mexico* (1978), writes, "For years I have been denying to aficionados of the sopaipillas of New Mexico that they have a Mexican counterpart. I have now discovered that they can be found, though rarely, in the state of Chihuahua. . . . I have yet to see them on any restaurant menus in the north." A good sopaipilla is supposed to resemble a puffed-up pillow; if cut into a round shape, it is called a "buñuelo." "Sopaipilla" was first found in American print circa 1940.

SOPAIPILLA

Mix 2 c. flour, 1 T. baking powder, and ½ t. salt. Cut in 1 T. lard until of a crumbly texture, then gradually add ⅔ c. lukewarm water. Knead in to smooth ball and let rest for 10 min. Divide in two, then roll into thin sheets. Cut into 2½-in. squares and fry in hot oil until golden brown. Drain and serve with honey, cinnamon, or powdered sugar. Makes about 3 doz.

---

sorbic acid. A preservative that prevents the growth of mold. Taken from the berries of the mountain-ash tree, sorbic acid is used, often in cheese, syrup, wine, and dried fruits.

sorbitan monostearate. An emulsifier that prevents water and oil from separating and prevents discoloration in heated chocolate. It is found in many dessert products.

sorbitol. A sweetener and thickener added to diet drinks, candy, chewing gum, and other foods (1890).

sorghum. Any of a variety of Old World grasses in the genus *Sorghum* that is grown both for animal forage and for a sweet syrup. The word is from Vulgar Latin *syricum (grānum),* "Syrian grain," although the grain may have originated in Africa. It is first mentioned in English print in 1590.

Sorghum may have been brought to the United States from Africa, probably around 1700, but it was not an important crop until settlers moved west of the Mississippi, where forage for cattle and sheep was needed in the Great Plains. Sweet sorghum (*S. vulgare saccharatum*), also called "sorgos," was made into "sorghum molasses," first recorded in print as of 1860. This was an important sweetener throughout the nineteenth century, but it decreased in popularity as refined cane sugar became cheaper and more available after World War I. The grain is still grown in the southeastern United States to some degree. The variety known as "Chinese sugar" (*S. v. drummondii*) is in the South called "chicken corn."

sorrel. Any of a variety of plants in the genus *Rumex,* especially the French sorrel (*R. scutatus),* whose leaves are used in salads and as a seasoning for soups, sauces, and other preparations.

The word is from Old French *surele,* from *sur,* "sour," because of its tangy taste, and in Middle English appeared as sorel. Wild sorrel in the United

States is rare, but the plant is widely cultivated in many states, often as a pasture fodder.

soul food. Although this term applies to traditional foods eaten by African-Americans, especially in the South, it is of rather recent vintage, first in print in 1960, when it became associated with the growth of ethnic pride in African-American culture, of which food was a significant part. The term dates in print to 1964 and comes from the fraternal spirit among African-Americans that their culture, heritage, and cooking gives them an essential "soulfulness" that helps define the African-American experience.

Soul food dishes include CHITTERLINGS, blackeyed peas, collard greens, HOMINY, GRITS, ham hocks, and more. As Bob Jeffries, in his *Soul Food Cookbook* (1969), notes, "While all soul food is southern food, not all southern food is soul."

soup-en-famille. A vegetable-and-beef-brisket soup served in Louisiana. The term is from the French for "family soup."

soup kitchen. Originally an army term for a MESS kitchen, used since 1850; during the Great Depression it was used to describe a charitable organization's kitchen, where free soup and bread were served to the poor and unemployed. Today they are officially called "emergency food programs."

sour. A drink made with liquor, sugar, and citrus juice and usually shaken with cracked ice. Sours first became popular in the middle of the nineteenth century, at first made with brandy and by the end of the century with whiskey. The bar at the "21" Club in New York City began mixing sours with bourbon and honey in the 1950s, in homage to society woman Princess "Honey Child" Wilder. A sour glass is a squat bar glass that holds six ounces.

WHISKEY SOUR

Over cracked ice, shake together ¾ oz. lemon or lime juice, 1 t. powdered sugar, and 1½ oz. bourbon or blended whiskey. Strain into sour glass, add cocktail cherry and slice of orange. Scotch, gin, brandy, rum, vodka, or other spirits may be used instead of bourbon or blended whiskey.

---

sourdough. A white bread made with a sour starter made from flour, water, and sugar (1725). The use of a sour starter is a method of bread baking that goes back at least six thousand years, for yeast had to be sustained from bread batch to bread batch. Legend has it that Columbus brought a starter with him to America, and the technique was certainly a standard method of baking in the early days of this country. With the advent of commercially available yeast and baking powder in the nineteenth century, the use of such starters was confined to those pioneers who moved farther and farther from settlements. These included the gold prospectors of northern California in the 1850s and the Yukon in the 1890s. The first sourdough purveyor in San Francisco, called the French Bakery, opened the year the Gold Rush began—1849—and it was because of the bread's popularity among miners that "sourdough" became a slang term for the prospectors themselves, and, later, by extension, all Alaskans.

Because many of these prospectors set out by boat from San Francisco, sourdough bread is often associated with that city to this day, and it is still a San Francisco specialty.

Although sourdough starter can be purchased, it can be made by mixing together 1 c. flour, 1 c. water (Alaskans often use potato water), and 1 T. sugar, and letting it stand in a warm place for 2 or 3 days. It will begin to ferment and have a sour smell. This starter can be continued and preserved by each week adding a bit more flour and water to the mixture and storing it in the refrigerator.

Sourdough starter may also be made by combining a package of dry yeast with 1 c. lukewarm water. Stir to dissolve completely, then blend in 1 c. flour and 1 T. sugar. Cover and let stand for 2 to 3 days in a warm place. A sourdough yeast made from apples or pumpkins is called a "ferment," a term that dates back to seventeenth-century Long Island, New York.

In the West some starters are said to have been handed down from one generation to another. In the Midwest a popular starter is called HERMAN.

SOURDOUGH BREAD

Mix 1½ c. starter with 1 c. warm milk, 1½ T. sugar, 2 t. salt, and 3 T. butter or shortening. Knead well with 4½ c. flour. Place in greased bowl and let rise in a warm place until doubled in bulk. Punch down and let rise again for 45 min. more. Shape into two loaves and bake on greased pan at 375° for about 45 min.

Southern Comfort. A trademark for a cordial made from freshly pitted peeled peaches and bourbon, which is bottled at 100 proof. It was supposedly made and named by Louis Herron, a bartender at The Planter's Hotel in St. Louis, Missouri, about 1875, when it was originally called "Cuff and Buttons," then a phrase that meant the equivalent of "white tie and tails," or formal dress.

southern fried chicken. Chicken parts that are floured or battered and then fried in hot fat. The term "southern fried" first appeared in print in 1925. This description does little justice to what is perhaps the best-known and best-loved southern dish of all. There are hundreds of recipes for southern fried chicken that may deviate in any or every variable, from the seasoning to the skillet to the fat to the cooking time, and significant debates may be heard in the South (where it may be called "country fried chicken," as noted in Lafcadio Hearn's *La Cuisine Créole* [1885]) over the best accompaniment for this simple but delectable dish. Some will use Tabasco or lemon or garlic in the seasonings; some swear by lard, others by shortening; some insist gravy should never be served with the chicken, while others wouldn't serve the dish without it; some will swear it is best eaten hot from the skillet, while others prefer it cold the next day; some will argue that the best fried chicken is not fried at all, but battered or bread-crumbed and then baked in an oven.

Southerners were not the first people in the world to fry chickens, of course. Almost every country has its own version, from Vietnam's *Gà Xaò* to Italy's *pollo fritto* and Austria's *Wiener Backhendl*, and numerous fricassees fill the cookbooks of Europe. And fried chicken did not become particularly poplar in the northern United States until well into the nineteenth century: Miss Leslie did not mention it in her 1857 Philadelphia cookbook, and Fannie Merritt Farmer's 1896 cookbook refers only to "Fried Chicken" as a fricassee served with "Brown Sauce" or as oven-baked "Maryland Chicken." But by the first quarter of this century southern fried chicken was well known and appreciated throughout the country, as Lettie Gay, editor of *200 Years of Charleston Cooking* (1930), bears witness: "If you say the words 'south' and 'chicken' to most northerners they think of fried chicken. But in Charleston chicken is cooked in many ways."

The Scottish, who enjoyed frying their chickens rather than boiling or baking them as the English did, may have brought the method with them when they settled in the South. The efficient and simple cooking process was very well adapted to the plantation life of the southern African-American slaves, who were often allowed to raise their own chickens. Louisiana

African-Americans called a breakfast of fried chicken and grits a "Sunday breakdown."

The idea of making a sauce to go with fried chicken must have occurred early on, at least in Maryland, where such a match came to be known as "Maryland fried chicken." By 1878 a dish by this name was listed on the menu of the Grand Union Hotel in Saratoga, New York, and, Richard J. Hooker notes, "In B. C. Howard, *Fifty Years in a Maryland Kitchen* (Baltimore, 1873), p. 52, the only fried chicken recipe calls for a sauce made of butter, cream, parsley, salt and pepper." Except for the sauce, Marylanders make their fried chicken in as many different ways as do the rest of the cooks in the South—dusted with flour, rolled in cornmeal, patted with bread crumbs, or even dipped in an egg batter. This last method was harshly criticized by novelist and Virginian William Styron, who wrote, "There is a school, developed mainly in the State of Maryland, which holds that, before cooking, the chicken parts should be immersed in some sort of 'batter.' This is absolute rubbish. Southern fried chicken should have after cooking a firm, well-developed crust—this is one of its glories—but the 'batter' principle simply won't hold up after pragmatic examination."

The cooking oil itself is of significance in such debates, with most authorities supporting the idea that a certain amount of bacon fat is advisable to give the chicken full flavor. Some, like Styron, demand undiluted bacon fat, while others, like James Villas, suggest a few tablespoons mixed in with some Crisco shortening. Peanut or other vegetable oils are also popular.

Most southerners would argue that southern fried chicken is never "deep-fried," but, rather, fried in just enough oil to reach halfway up the sides of the chicken parts. Some suggest frequent turning, while others advise one side be completely cooked at a time. Some prefer to cover the skillet in order to keep in the moistness, while others believe this will make the chicken steamy. Almost everyone agrees the frying pan itself should be a black, well-seasoned iron skillet.

However southern fried chicken is cooked, it is always eaten with the fingers—a habit that is obviously practical but that probably kept the dish out of the more delicate ladies' cookbooks of the nineteenth century. It is to southern fried chicken that the colloquial phrase "finger lickin' good" (adopted by one commercial fried-chicken company as its slogan) is most often applied.

Once a recipe has been decided upon, next comes the matter of what southern fried chicken demands as an accompaniment. Coleslaw is often cited, as is corn on the cob in season. There is one sect that likes it with rice, but most southerners would feel more comfortable with mashed potatoes and gravy made from the giblets and pan drippings of the chicken.

Southern fried chicken has been known to get dipped into honey as well, and biscuits are often found within reach.

After all this debate one would think it is a difficult dish to prepare well, and many Americans have avoided the problem (and the mess of frying) by buying their fried chicken in groceries, where it is most often found frozen, or at restaurant chains that specialize in cooking the dish.

SOUTHERN FRIED CHICKEN

In a paper bag put 1 c. flour, grind a generous amount of black pepper, and add 2 t. salt. Cut a tender chicken into pieces and soak in cold milk for ½ hr. Place the chicken pieces in the paper bag and shake until they are all coated. In a skillet of hot oil, fry the chicken pieces on one side until golden brown. Turn and brown the other side. Drain on paper bags and serve hot.

---

southern style. A colloquial expression used in reference to chicken cut in uniform pieces for eating with the fingers.

Southside. A cocktail made by shaking over crushed ice the juice of 1 lemon, 2 t. sugar syrup, and 2 oz. Jamaican rum. A "Northside" substitutes orange juice for the lemon juice. The drink may have originated in Chicago, possibly in the 1950s.

soybean (*Glycine max*). Also, "soya bean" and "soypea." Any of more than one thousand varieties of beans that come in a wide range of colors, though the yellow and black soybeans are the best known in the United States, where, until World War II, it was used mainly for fodder and soil improvement. The soybean, whose name is derived from the Japanese *shoyu* and dates in English print to the 1690s, has for millennia been part of Oriental cookery but did not make its way to Europe until the seventeenth century. Today it is popular in Oriental dishes as well as an ingredient in many processed foods for its high nutritive value. "Tofu" (from the Japanese) is a creamy cheese-like food made from "soybean milk" that has been curdled. It is eaten on its own and in a variety of dishes, including as "Tofutti," an ice-cream substitute first sold in 1982 in New York City by David Mintz, who

originally created the product as a kosher substitute for dairy products.

soy protein. A substance made from soybeans that is often used as a binder or extender in meat and poultry products like sausages, luncheon meats, soups, sauces, and gravies. According to the United States Department of Agriculture, "Soybeans are processed into three basic soy protein products: soy flour, soy protein concentrate, and isolated soy protein, each of which may be converted to textured vegetable protein. Whenever soy protein is added to a meat or poultry product, its presence is noted in the ingredients statement on the label."

spacer. Bartender's term for a drink of nonalcoholic brew served between regular beers or other alcoholic beverages as a way to space out the intake of alcohol over an evening. According to brewer Brooks Firestone in November 1989, he first heard the term in an English pub: "A friend of mine asked the publican to give him a 'spacer' and the man automatically gave him a nonalcoholic beer instead of the regular beer he'd been drinking."

Spa Cuisine. Trademark name for dishes served at the Four Seasons Restaurant in New York City created to be lower in calories, fat, cholesterol, and sodium than most other dishes on the menu. It was developed by chef Seppi Renggli in concert with Dr. Myron Winnick of the Institute for Human Nutrition at Columbia University's College of Physicians and Surgeons. Although introduced in 1983, the term was registered for a trademark February 26, 1985.

spaghetti alla Caruso. Also, "spaghetti Caruso." An Italian-American dish of spaghetti with chicken livers and tomato. The dish was named after opera singer Enrico Caruso, but there are several versions as to the dish's origins. One newspaper account reprinted in the book *Spaghetti Dinner* (1955) by Giuseppe Prezzolini contended that the dish was actually created for a reporter by Caruso himself while living at the York Hotel in New York City. The sauce for this dish was made without chicken livers, using instead tomatoes, basil, parsley, red pepper, garlic, and olive oil, then "dusted with Parmesan cheese and decorated with coins of fried zucchini squash."

In Craig Claiborne's *The New York Times Food Encyclopedia* (1985), the author noted that a recipe for "Spaghetti alla Caruso" appeared in Louis P. De Gouy's *The Gold Cook Book* (no date given), with the remark

"Original recipe as prepared by this writer." Claiborne also cited a book entitled *The 60 Minute Chef* (no date given) by Lillian Bueno McCue and Carol Truax, who contended that Caruso would visit Truax's house, where he once "slapped on a high chef's cap and created an enormous platter of his own very special spaghetti, with chicken livers." The earliest recipes date to 1939, including in Diana Ashley's *Where to Dine in '39*, where it is attributed to chef Antonio With of the Caruso chain of New York restaurants.

Spam. Trademark name for a canned ground-pork shoulder and ground-ham product seasoned with salt, sugar, water, and sodium nitrite. It was introduced in 1937 by the Geo. A. Hormel Company and was a staple of army RATIONS during World War II, when soldiers sometimes referred to it as S.O.S.—short for SHIT ON A SHINGLE (a term also applied to creamed chipped beef). Spam has been tremendously popular as a breakfast item and sandwich meat, with Hawaii consuming the most per capita, 12 cans per household per year. In Hawaii Japanese Americans enjoy a dish called *Spam musubi* made with sushi and sautéed Spam.

speakeasy. Also, "speak." A term popular during PROHIBITION to describe an establishment selling illegal alcoholic beverages. In order to gain entrance, you had to speak in a low voice through a small opening in the back door and tell the attendant inside who it was who sent you to the place.

The term itself (which dates in print to 1889) may derive from the English "speak-softly-shop," an underworld term for a smuggler's house where one might get liquor cheaply, its usage in this sense having been traced back to 1823. But with the onset of Prohibition in America, speakeasies sprang up overnight, sometimes in shabby sections of town, but often in the best neighborhoods, and many of these establishments were actually fine restaurants in their own right. New York's "21" Club was a speakeasy during this period and had two bars, a dance floor, an orchestra, and dining rooms on two floors. The term "café society" was coined in February 1919 by gossip columnist Maury Paul ("Cholly Knickerbocker") right after Prohibition's onset to describe a new, chic crowd in New York that, in the words of Lucius Beebe, "found itself living frankly, unabashedly, and almost entirely in saloons."

Not all speakeasies enjoyed such favorable notoriety.

French diplomat Paul Morande, visiting New York for the first time in 1925, reported his experience at a speakeasy:

> There is a truly New York atmosphere of humbug in the whole thing. The interior is that of a criminal house; shutters are closed in full daylight, and one is caught in the smell of a cremation furnace. Italians with a too familiar manner, or plump, blue jowled pseudo-butlers, carrying bunches of monastic keys, guide you through the deserted rooms of the abandoned house. Facetious inscriptions grimace from the walls. There are a few very flushed diners. At one table some habitués are asleep, their heads sunk on their arms; behind a screen somebody is trying to restore a young woman who has had an attack of hysteria. . . . The food is almost always poor, the service deplorable.

Designed to shut down all saloons, the Volstead Act instead spurred more illicit ones, to open, so that, thanks to a thoroughly entrenched system of graft and police corruption, New York had more than thirty-two thousand speakeasies within its boroughs—twice the number of saloons closed.

spiedie. A sandwich of Italian bread enclosing grilled, skewered cubes of marinated beef or lamb, it is a specialty of Binghamton, New York. The name—pronounced as "speedy"—probably derives from the Italian word *spiedo*, "kitchen spit." Credit for the introduction of the item to the Binghamton area has gone to Augustino Iacovelli, who opened Augie's Restaurant in 1939 in nearby Endicott, New York, and began selling skewered meats reminiscent of those he'd enjoyed in his native Abruzzi section of Italy.

spinach (*Spinacia oleracea*). A dark green plant with rippling leaves eaten raw in a salad or boiled as a vegetable. The plant is native to Asia, and the name derives from the Arabic *isfānākh*, appearing in English print about 1530.

Of the two main groups of spinach, the prickly-seeded and the smooth-seeded, the former is the most widely cultivated in the United States, with about half the production coming from California. The Spanish brought spinach to the New World.

"New Zealand spinach" (*Tetragonia implexicoma*) is not a true spinach and is grown only to a small extent on the West Coast.

The bitter taste of spinach has made the plant a particular anathema to American children, who have long been coaxed into eating it as a vegetable by reminding them that the cartoon character "Popeye," created by Elzie Crisler Segar in 1919, derived his extraordinary strength from spinach. Nevertheless Americans still eat only half a pound of spinach per capita each year.

split. A bottle half the size of a regular bottle of soda or liquor, a usage dating in print to 1884.

spoon bread. Also, "spoonbread" or "spoon corn-bread." A soft, custardlike dish usually made with cornmeal. The term may come from a Native American word for porridge, *suppawn,* or from the fact that the dish is usually eaten with a spoon. Its first mention in print was in 1905.

SPOON BREAD

Sift together 1 c. cornmeal, ½ c. flour, 2 T. sugar, sift 1½ t. salt, and 2 t. baking powder, then mix in 2 beaten eggs and 2 c. milk. Blend well. In a baking pan melt 4 T. butter and pour in the cornmeal batter. Pour 1 c. milk over top, then bake for 45 min. at 375°.

---

sports bar. A bar where people congregate to watch televised sporting events or, more commonly, a bar owned by a celebrity sports figure. Although there is a long tradition of sports figures owning such establishments, the term "sports bar" itself only gained currency in the 1980s. A true sports bar is a place where sports is the principal topic of conversation. One of the common features at such a place is a large-screen TV broadcasting sporting events.

spot (*Leiostomus xanthurus*). Also, "spot fish," "red drum," "Lafayette," and "Cape May goody." An eastern freshwater fish that ranges from Maine to Texas. Its black spot behind the gill cover gives it its name, which has been in use at least since 1875. Spot is a favorite fish in Virginia and the South. U.S. commercial landings of spots totaled 6,775,000 pounds in 1997.

spotted sea trout (*Cynoscion nebulosus*). A variety of WEAKFISH found in southern waters. It is not a true TROUT, but its black spots give it a similar appearance, and it is sometimes marketed as "gray trout."

Springfield horseshoe. A sandwich made of various fillings topped with a Cheddar-cheese sauce. According to food writer Susan Costner in *Susan Costner's Great Sandwiches* (1990):

Created by Steve Tomko and Joseph Schweska at the Leland Hotel in Springfield, Illinois, in 1928, this regional specialty starts with a slice of toast and can have a filling of ham, egg, hamburger, and chicken, just chicken, just ham, just egg, bacon, shrimp, or turkey and corned beef—but the sauce is the star of the show. This should be of sharp, creamy, slightly spicy Cheddar cheese; a classic Welsh rabbit sauce is a good choice. When the filling has been doused with sauce, the horse-shoe is topped with a second slice of toast. The name "horseshoe" was derived from the shape of the cut of ham used on the hotel's original sandwich. So far this local gem has gained no wider acceptance, but to Springfield residents it clearly ranks as that city's fore-most contribution to gastronomy.

spring house. A house built over a cold spring to keep dairy foods cool, the term dating back at least to 1755.

spring roll. An Asian-American appetizer made of crisp dough wrapped around a filling of various ingredients such as vegetables, meat, shrimp, and seasonings. Sometimes synonymous with the "egg roll," it is considered somewhat more "authentic" and delicate than the latter. The name, which dates in English print to 1943, comes from the Chinese tradition of serving them on the first day of the Chinese New Year, which is also the first day of the lunar year's spring.

sprinkle the infield. A Chicago bar-goer's colloquialism, meaning "to order another round of drinks."

spritzer. Originally a drink made with Rhine wine and club soda or seltzer, but today a spritzer may be made with almost any dry white wine. The name comes from the German, for a "squirt." The drink dates in print to 1940 but became very popular in America in the 1960s, at a time when many people were just being introduced to wine. Often it is ordered as a "wine spritzer."

spud. A colloquial name for a potato. The word comes from a Middle English word for a short knife, and, later, a spade with which to dig up a tuber such as the potato. The term as used in England in the nineteenth century was a slur against Irishmen, as it was later in America, because of Ireland's dependence on the potato for food. Americans also called a person who picked potatoes a "spud-glommer," especially in Idaho, one of the biggest potato-producing states.

There is no truth to the story that the term comes from a nineteenth-century organization formed to discourage the growing and eating of potatoes—"the Society for the Prevention of Unwholesome Diet," whose initials were "S.P.U.D."

squash. Any of a variety of plants and their fruits of the genus *Cucurbita.* This term includes the native American "summer" and "winter" squashes as well as PUMPKINS, gourds, and ZUCCHINI. The name is from the Narraganset *asquatasquash,* meaning "eaten raw, green," and refers specifically to the summer varieties (*C. pepo*). The word "squash" first appeared in print in 1634.

The European settlers were introduced to squashes by the Indians, and John Smith, who traveled through Virginia in 1607, commented that the fruits, called by the Native Americans there *macocks,* were similar to English muskmelons.

Squashes were a staple of the Native American diet throughout the continent. The oldest evidence of their being used as food, dating back to between 7000 and 5500 B.C., was found at the Ocampo Caves in Mexico, whence they were carried to North America, where evidence of squash has been found in the burial mounds of Ohio, Kentucky, and Virginia from two thousand years ago.

Early botanists disagreed on or confused the terminology of squashes, so that one may find some varieties described with various overlapping Latin names for three basic species: *C. Pepo, C. maxima,* and *C. moschata.* The English, meanwhile, call them "vegetable marrow." In America squashes are generally separated at market into winter and summer varieties, as noted below.

"Summer squashes" include the "yellow" or "orange crookneck," "turban squash," "zucchini," "spaghetti squash" (so called because its fibers took like strands of spaghetti), and "pattypan" (also called "cymling" and "scalloped squash"). The "winter squashes" include the HUBBARD SQUASH, "winter crookneck," "butternut," "buttercup," "acorn squash," and "sugar pumpkin."

squid. Any of a variety of marine cephalopod mollusks of the genera *Loligo, Rossia,* and others, which is similar to the OCTOPUS but has instead ten legs. The origin of the word is unknown. In Hawaiian the squid is called *muhe'e.* In the United States squid consumption is largely confined to ethnic restaurants and Mediterranean immigrants' homes. The most important species for food is the "common Pacific squid" (*L.

opalescens) found in California waters. The best-known Atlantic species are the "longfinned squid" (*L. pealei*), also called "white squid" and "winter squid," and the "short-finned squid" (*Illex illecebrosus*), also known as "red squid" and "summer squid." Most Americans know squid better by their Italian name, *calamari.* U.S. commercial landings of squid were 223.8 million pounds in 1997.

squirt. A drink of liquor or wine, fresh fruit or fruit syrup, and seltzer or club soda, made deliberately sweet.

WHISKEY SQUIRT

Crush half a peach with 1 T. sugar syrup, 1 t. curaçao, and 1½ oz. bourbon or blended whiskey. Shake with crushed ice and fill glass with seltzer or club soda.

---

stack cake. A six-layer (sometimes more) ginger cake filled with a cooked paste of apples. It is a specialty of Appalachia.

stack pie. A caramel-covered pie made of several layers of pie crust and custard filling.

state doin's. Trappers' term for food.

states' eggs. In the early days of the western frontier eggs had to be shipped from eastern states to those cow-country territories not then part of the Union.

steam beer. A beverage produced on the West Coast in the mid-nineteenth century by a process that circumvented the shortage of ice needed to make lagers. In *The Great American Beer Book* (1978), James D. Robertson describes the process:

Fermentation proceeds at a relatively high temperature (60°–68°F.) and barley malt is used exclusively. Within twelve to eighteen hours after the yeast has been added to the wort in the fermenting tubs, the beer comes into "krausening," where it is kept from six to eight hours. It is then run into the clarifier for two to three days . . . for completion of fermentation. If fermentation has been proper, at the end of this stage the beer shall have undergone a reduction of fifty to sixty percent and be quite clear in appearance. From the clarifier, the beer is racked directly into barrels, where it receives an addition of about twenty percent of krausen, together with some fining. In four to six days the beer has raised a sufficient amount of "steam" in the barrels (some fifty pounds per square inch), and some bleeding of pressure must be done. In olden days these barrels were shipped to saloons, rested a few days, and then tapped for the trade. Steam beer is made today by only one West Coast firm [The Anchor Brewing Company of San Francisco, begun in 1896] and the product is bottled. . . . Steam beer has a golden brown color, sharp hoppy taste, full body, and a lingering malt finish.

sticky. A sweet pastry popular in South Carolina.

STICKY

Make pastry dough for 2 pies, roll out thin, cut into 12 squares about 3½ in. in size. Divide ½ lb. butter into 12 pieces, place on squares, and pour 1 c. sugar on pastry. Fold corners into center, close edges, place closely together on a greased pan, and bake at 350° until browned.

---

sticky bun. Also, "honey bun." A yeast pastry topped with melted brown sugar or honey, cinnamon, and raisins, so called because they have a very sticky texture when eaten with the fingers. Although they are popular throughout the United States, they are often associated with Philadelphia and sometimes called "Philadelphia sticky buns," although in Philadelphia itself, they are called " cinnamon buns."

STICKY BUN

Dissolve 1 pkg. yeast in ¼ c. lukewarm water. Scald 1 c. milk, then cool until lukewarm and add yeast and 1½ c. flour. Mix, cover, and let rise for 1 hr. Add 4 T. cooled melted butter, 2 beaten egg yolks, 4 T. sugar, 1 t. salt, the grated rind of 1 lemon, and 3 c. flour. Knead, then cover and let rise until doubled. Roll dough to 1-in.-thick long rectangle, brush with a mixture of melted butter, 2 T. brown sugar, 1 t. cinnamon, and 3 T. red currants (if desired). Roll and cut into 1-in. slices. Crumble ¾ c. brown sugar with 4 T. melted butter and spread in skillet. Place dough slices in skillet, let rise for another 60 min., or until doubled, then bake at 350° for 30 min. Turn out onto cooling rack. Makes 12 buns.

---

stifle. Also, "stiffle." A New England stew made with salt pork and vegetables or seafood. The word probably suggests the "stifling"—that is, smothering of the ingredients—in the cooking process. "Eel stiffle" is described by Josephine H. Pierce in *Coast to Coast Cookery* (1951) as "a scalloped dish made with eels, onions, potatoes and salt pork. A favorite on Martha's Vineyard [in Massachusetts]." Pierce also notes that a similar stew without the eel is known on Cape Cod as "Halieluia," the biblical exclamation for good news, though this may be a bit of hyperbole or sarcasm.

stirabout. A form of porridge whose name is formed from the words "stir" and "about." The Pennsylvania Dutch of the nineteenth century made this dish with vegetables, saffron, and chicken broth, but in the mining towns of the Northwest it was a simpler affair, no more than a breakfast of oatmeal mush thinned with milk and salt. In the Federal Writers Project volume entitled *Copper Camp: Stories of the Greatest Mining Town, Butte, Montana* (1943), the authors report that stirabout was brought to that locale by Irish miners and dished out at the Clarence Hotel and Florence Hotel, where servings were "computed in tons," and every boarder ate two to three bowls each morning and carried more to the mines for lunch.

STIRABOUT

To a kettle of 6 c. boiling chicken broth add 4 c. sliced peeled potatoes, 2 T. chopped parsley, 1 c. chopped celery, salt, pepper, and ⅛ t. saffron. Reduce heat, and then simmer for 20 min. Beat 2 eggs with ½ c. flour, drop into simmering broth by teaspoonfuls, then cover and boil another 7 min. Serves 6.

---

stone boiling. A Pueblo method of cooking by placing hot stones into a basket with food.

stone crab (*Menippe mercenaria*, although *Lithodes maja* is also called by this name). Also, "moro" or "morro" crab. A crab with very hard claws filled with sweet white meat. "Stone crab" first appeared in print in 1700. The stone crab is one of the delicacies of the southern United States and particularly of Florida, where the main harvesting areas include Marathon Island, Crystal River, Biscayne Bay, and Naples.

Damon Runyon said of the crustacean, "The stone crab is much larger than the northern crab and has a shell harder than a landlord's heart." Before 1920 the crab was eaten only by Miamians and others in the Florida and Gulf Coast communities. The stone crab has become especially associated with a restaurant in Miami Beach that popularized the dish in the 1920s—Joe's Stone Crab Restaurant, opened in 1913 by Joe

Weiss and designated a historical landmark in 1975.

Since only the claws are eaten, fishermen twist them off and throw back the crab (usually only one claw is taken so that the creature can defend itself), which grows new claws (called "retreads") within eighteen months. By law, the claws must then be boiled for seven minutes, then either put on ice or frozen, because cooks have found that freezing removes the unpleasant taste of iodine frequently noticed in the meat. Chilled claws are then "floated" in a tank of water to determine which have the most meat ("lights" are unmeaty claws that float to the top). When served, the claws are cracked with a mallet and eaten with dipping sauces of either melted butter or mustard-mayonnaise. They are usually eaten cold.

The season lasts from October 15 through May 15. More than 2.5 million pounds are harvested yearly. The minimum size for selling claws is 2-2.75 ounces, called "mediums." "Large" claws are three to six ounces, and "jumbos" over six ounces.

JOE'S STONE CRAB MUSTARD-MAYONNAISE

Beat together 3½ t. dry mustard, I c. mayonnaise, 2 t. Worcestershire sauce, I t. A.I steak sauce, I ½ T. light cream, and ⅛ t. salt. Chill and serve with stone crabs or other seafood. Makes ⅔ c.

stone fence. Also, "stonewall." An alcoholic drink made from apple cider or applejack and a whiskey such as rum. *The Dictionary of Americanisms* traces "stone fence" to 1843, but Washington Irving mentions the drink in his *History of New York... by Diedrich Knickerbocker* (1809). According to the *Better Homes and Gardens Heritage Cook Book* (1975), "stonewall was the favorite drink of Ethan Allen and his Green Mountain Boys."

STONE FENCE

Combine I ½ oz. applejack with ½ oz. dark rum. It may be poured over crushed ice.

straight. An alcoholic spirit of any kind drunk with no other ingredients, except, in some cases, ice. Americans have used this word at least since the middle of the nineteenth century. In England a drinker would say "neat" instead.

strawberry. Any of a variety of plants in the genus *Fragaria* bearing a red berry with a soft, pulpy flesh. The word is from Old English *strēawberige,* possibly because the low-lying plant's runners resemble straw.

Strawberries have been eaten by man for thousands of years, but little trouble was taken to cultivate them before the Renaissance in Europe. In the New World strawberries were abundant, and the Indians made them into bread and held feasts at the harvest of the fruit. Jacques Cartier mentioned seeing wild strawberries along the banks of the St. Lawrence River in Canada in 1534, and a white strawberry was noted in 1536 to be growing in Massachusetts and New York.

The "native American strawberry," called the "Virginia strawberry," "meadow strawberry," or "scarlet strawberry" (*F. virginiana*) by the white settlers and *wuttahimneash* by the tribes of the eastern coast of America, was admired by the first colonists and plants were soon sent back to Europe, perhaps as early as 1600. (France had samples as of 1624.) In 1607 Captain John Smith reported, "Captain Newport and my selfe with divers others, to the number of twenty-two persons, set forward to discover the [James] River, some fiftie or sixtie miles, finding it in some places broader, and in some narrower . . . the people in all places kindly treating us, daunsing and feasting us with strawberries, Mulberries, Bread, Fish, and other their Countrie provisions. . . ." Roger Williams of Rhode Island marveled at the great size of his region's strawberries—"four times bigger than ours in England," he wrote.

A second American berry was discovered by the Spanish explorers of Central and South America, where they found Indians cultivating a very large berry the conquistadores called *frutilla*. This strawberry was of little interest until French navy engineer André François Frézier rediscovered it while exploring Peru and Chile in 1712 and sent some back to the royal gardens in France and some to Brittany. This strawberry was widely proliferated throughout the Pacific coast, as far as Alaska, and also in Hawaii, and in English took the name "beach" or "Chilean strawberry" (*F. chiloensis*). Frézier's plants did not bear fruit in France because he had unknowingly brought only female examples of a species that needed a separate male in order to breed. Thirty years later an accidental crossing of these same berries with the already established Virginia strawberries in France resulted in an excellent hybrid that became known as the "pine" or "pineapple strawberry" (*F. ovalis*), now one of the major cultivated varieties.

In the United States few people bothered to cultivate berries because they were so plentiful in the wild.

After Englishman William Cobbett visited the United States, he reported in *A Year's Residence in America* (1818) that "strawberries grow wild in abundance; but no one will take the trouble to get them." By one estimate there were only fourteen hundred acres of cultivated strawberries in America at the beginning of the nineteenth century, and the wild strawberry patch was a well-established fixture in rural areas and home gardens. Cultivation did begin, however, in the early years of the nineteenth century, and strawberries became something of a luxury, especially when served with cream. President Martin Van Buren (1782–1862; held office, 1837–41), who was often accused of trying to turn the White House into a highfalutin palace, was criticized before his election for using public money to grow strawberries for his delectation.

New York became a strawberry market after the Erie Railroad brought in eighty thousand baskets in a single night in June of 1847, and wide-scale cultivation began in America four years later, with the development by Albany, New York, horticulturist James Wilson of the hardy Wilson variety. By the 1880s more than one hundred thousand acres were under cultivation for the fruit, and the refrigerated railroad cars perfected in that era meant that the perishable strawberry could be shipped to the Midwest. A strawberry industry began to grow in Arkansas, Louisiana, northern Florida, and Tennessee, and today strawberries are grown in all fifty states, with 75 percent coming from California, which has a year-round harvest. Per capita U.S. consumption of strawberries in 1997 was about 4 pounds.

The main species is the hybrid *F. ovalis*, the main varieties of which include the "Aroma," the "Beaver," the "Blakemore," the "Catskill," the "Dorset," the "Fairfax," the "Howard 17," the "Klondike," the "Klonmore," the "Lupton," the "Marshall," the "Massey," the "Missionary," the "Redheart," the "Fairpeake," the "Swanee," the "Tennessee Beauty," the "Florida Ninety," and the "Tioga."

Americans eat strawberries fresh or frozen in syrups, particularly on strawberry sundaes (first recorded in 1904), and STRAWBERRY SHORTCAKE, as well as a flavoring for various desserts, especially ice cream. There are many strawberry festivals held throughout the United States each year, a tradition dating back to the 1850s.

strawberry shortcake. A dessert made with a biscuit pastry, strawberries, and whipped cream. The name derives from its being made "short," that is, crisp, by the use of lard or another fat, a meaning of the word that dates back to the fifteenth century. In England shortcake, mentioned in Shakespeare's *Merry Wives of Windsor* (1598), is usually synonymous with shortbread, which is crisp and a traditional speciality of Scotland. In America, however, shortcake meant a rich pastry enclosing fruits, to which Washington Irving in his story "The Legend of Sleepy Hollow" (1821) may have referred when he wrote of a table laid with "sweet cakes and short cakes, ginger cakes and crumbling cruller, and the whole family of cakes." By the 1830s strawberry shortcake was known and soon became one of the best-loved American desserts, especially after the popularity of strawberries rose to the point in the 1850s when people spoke of "strawberry fever."

The recipe below is adapted from Marjorie Kinnan Rawlings's *Cross Creek Cookery* (1942).

STRAWBERRY SHORTCAKE

Sift twice 2 c. flour, 1/4 c. sugar, 4 t. baking powder, and 1/2 t. salt. (Add a few grains of ground nutmeg if desired.) Work mixture with 5 1/3 T. butter until coarse and crumbly. Add 1 well-beaten egg, then 1/3 c. milk, and blend to make a dough. Turn into buttered pan and pat into shape. Bake 15–20 min. at 400°. An hour before serving cut up 1 qt. fresh strawberries, saving about 1 doz. whole. Add 1/4 c. brown sugar. Let stand in a warm place for 1 hr. Split the shortcake hot from the oven into 2 layers, butter each side, lay on strawberries and juice, cover with other shortcake layer, and top with whole strawberries and whipped cream.

---

streak-of-lean. Also, "streak-o-lean." A southern African-American term for salt pork.

streeted. Restaurant workers' slang for the act of being thrown out into the street. In *The Girl from Rector's* (1927), restaurateur George Rector described the action thus: "The process of being streeted meant that you were grasped by the slack of the trousers and the back of the neck and tossed out into the street."

streusel. A crumb topping of flour, butter, and spices that is sprinkled and baked on breads, cakes, and muffins (1925). The term is from the German, for "something strewn together," and these toppings are certainly of German origin, although they are sometimes referred to as "Danish" or "Swedish."

string bean (*Phaseolus vulgaris*). Also called "snap bean" or "green bean." A long, slender green bean, so called because of its stringy tendrils. The term is first recorded in 1750, and "snap bean" (because of its crisp sound when cracked) is first recorded in 1770. String beans are widely eaten in the United States, usually boiled and buttered.

The yellow variety of string bean is called the "wax bean," which dates in print to 1888.

striped bass (*Morone saxatilis*). Also, "rockfish" and "striper." A North American fish whose name derives from the dark stripes along the length of its body (1810). They are considered one of the principal game fish of the world. (For distinctions among BASS, see main entry.)

The striped bass was one of the many fish early European settlers marveled at for its size and abundance, and Captain John Smith, who sailed into Chesapeake Bay in 1607, wrote enthusiastically of striped bass "so large, the head of one will give a good eater a dinner, and for the daintinesse of diet they excell the Marybones of Beefe." The Pilgrims were nourished on striped bass heads and salted the bodies for winter, also using the fish for fertilizer to such an extent that the Massachusetts Bay Colony General Court put a stop to the practice in 1639, because the fishes were quickly dwindling in number. In those days the striped bass grew to an enormous size, sometimes six feet long and well over a hundred pounds. By the nineteenth century the bass had become one of the sportsmen's favorite fishes, and waters of both coasts were full of this elusive challenger to the talents of the best fishermen. (The fish had been introduced to the Pacific in 1879.)

About 6 million pounds of striped bass were brought to market in 1997.

stromboli. A sandwich made with pizza dough folded over a variety of ingredients, most often mozzarella and sliced pepperoni. The stromboli is a specialty of Philadelphia, though similar to an Italian confection called the CALZONE (which is far more commonly sold at pizzerias in the United States than the stromboli), whose dough pocket is somewhat puffier. The name may derive from the Italian island of Stromboli, but more probably refers to a very big, strong character in the fairy tale *The Adventures of Pinocchio* (1882) by Carlo Lorenzini, whose pen name was "Collodi." The association with such a character may play off another Italian-American sandwich, the HERO.

strudel. A rolled pastry filled with nuts, STREUSEL mixture, fruit, or cheese, brought to America by German immigrants. The name is from Middle High German, meaning a "whirlpool." "Apple strudel" is the most common form of the pastry. The word was first printed in English circa 1893.

stuffing. A packed combination of meats, vegetables, grains, fats, or other ingredients inserted in the cavity of meat, poultry, or fish. The word comes from the verb to stuff and first appears in English print in 1538, displacing the customary forcemeat (from the French *farcir*, "to stuff") used in the English tradition. After the 1880s, however, Victorian propriety in America made the term "dressing" more acceptable; both stuffing and dressing are still used interchangeably today, with the former finding more adherents in the East and South.

Turkeys and most roast poultry and game are stuffed, usually with bread or cornmeal crumbs and various seasonings. Oysters were a very popular nineteenth-century stuffing, and pecan or rice stuffings were often used in the South. Italian-Americans may use a stuffing of sausage, onion, and mozzarella cheese, while dried fruit, potatoes, and apples are customary among German Americans.

OYSTER STUFFING

Drain 1 pt. oysters and retain liquid. Cut oysters in half. Sauté in 8 T. butter, 2 c. chopped onion, 1½ c. chopped celery, 1 cup chopped green pepper, 1 T. minced garlic, ½ t. thyme, ½ t. rosemary, 1 crushed bay leaf, and 1 c. chopped parsley. Cook with onion for about 5 min. Add oyster liquid, cook for 5 sec., remove from heat, and add 5 c. bread crumbs, salt and pepper, and 2 beaten eggs. Blend well, adding water if necessary for texture.

---

sturgeon. Any of a variety of fishes in the family Acipenseridae. It is a very large fish particularly known for its roe, which is turned into CAVIAR. The name is from Germanic *sturjōn*, and has been used in English at least since the thirteenth century.

The sturgeon in North American waters amazed the early European settlers, who found two-hundred-pound examples in the Hudson River, and Captain John Smith, who explored the Virginia coastline in 1607, wrote, "We had more Sturgeon, than could be devoured by Dog and Man." Sturgeon was an everyday food for southerners: "The supplies seemed limitless," wrote Richard J. Hooker in *Food and Drink in America* (1981). "Stories were told of men becoming physically tired from pulling fish from the rivers, of catches with hooks of 600 sturgeon, and of immense takes on the rivers with seines, eelpots, weirs, and fish pots."

In the nineteenth century the sturgeon became the source of a booming American caviar business, but by 1900 supplies of both the Atlantic and Pacific sturgeon were almost totally depleted. So far the resurgence of the fish has been modest but encouraging, with most coming from the Northwest, though the "Atlantic sturgeon" (*A. oxyrhynchus*) is taken in the waters of South Carolina and Georgia. The main species marketed for consumption are the "white sturgeon" (*A. transmontanus*), the "green sturgeon" (*A. medirostris*), and the "lake sturgeon" (*A. fulvescens*). The white sturgeon is now being farm-raised. The largest sturgeon farm in the world is Sierra AquaFarms, begun in 1980 in Elverta, California, which now produces about 100,000 pounds of white sturgeon per month. Farm-raised sturgeon average about ten to twenty-five pounds, while wild sturgeon average between fifteen and eighty, but may grow much larger.

Today most sturgeon that comes to market is smoked, frozen, or packed in jars with pickling spices.

succotash. A cooked dish of corn and lima beans. More popular in the South these days than elsewhere, it is still often found in cafeterias.

The term first made its appearance in print in 1745, an Americanism formed from the Narraganset word *misickquatash* (and other Native American words, for example, *sukquttahash* and *msakwitash*), referring to various ingredients in a stew pot, and, more specifically in the Narraganset, to an ear of corn.

So American is the term that President Ronald Reagan once lumped "South Succotash" in with "Podunk" as epithets for an out-of-the-way, insignificant small town, which immediately got up the dander of the six hundred people who actually live in a place called Succotash Point, Rhode Island, on Narragansett Bay.

SUCCOTASH

Cook 1 c. fresh corn kernels until tender in boiling water. Do the same with 1 c. lima beans. Mix together with ½ t. salt, ⅛ t. pepper, 1 T. salt pork or butter, and ¼ c. milk, and cook together until hot but not boiling. Serves 4.

A recipe for "Delaware succotash," appearing in *The American Heritage Cookbook* (1980), contains tomato and nutmeg.

sucker. Any of a variety of fish in the family Catostomidae. These fishes derive their name from the sucking, protractile mouth that attaches itself to whales, sharks, other fish and boats. The freshwater varieties of sucker are so called because their method of eating is to suck up the algae and crustaceans of their diet. The first mention of such fish in print was in 1772, referring to species in the Hudson River.

The principal suckers of culinary interest include: "blue sucker" (*Cycleptus elongatus*), ranging throughout the Midwest and South; the "bigmouth buffalo" (*Ictiobus cyprinellus*), also called "redmouth" and "gourdhead buffalo"; "black buffalo" (*I. niger*), also called "bugler," "Prairie buffalo," and "rooter"; "smallmouth buffalo" (*I. bubalus*), also called "highback," "channel buffalo" and "razorback"; "black redhorse" (*Moxostoma duguesnei*); "golden red-horse" (*M. erythrurum*), "spotted sucker" (*Minytrema melanops*); and "white sucker" (*Catostomos commersoni*).

Not related to these species is a marine fish of the family Echeneidae, the "remora," also called "suckerfish." The remora takes its name from the Latin word *re-*, back, and *mora*, delay, because they held back and delayed a ship's passage.

suckling pig. A pig six to eight weeks old that is usually roasted on a spit or in the oven. In Louisiana this dish goes by the name *cochon de lait* or *cochon du lait* (French for suckling pig), a term that dates in print to 1968 but is much older. The pig is usually seasoned inside and out and then stuffed with apples or other ingredients.

suffering bastard. A name used for two entirely different cocktails. An American drink of this name was created by a Los Angeles restaurateur of the 1930s named Don the Beachcomber (born Don Richard Beaumont-Gantt), who specialized in creating rum drinks like the "missionary's downfall," the "vicious virgin," and the ZOMBIE. His "suffering bastard" was made with lime juice, ½ oz. curaçao, ¼ oz. sugar syrup, ¼ oz. orgeat syrup, 1 oz. light rum, and 1 oz. medium rum, all shaken with crushed ice and garnished with cucumber peel, fresh mint, lime shell, and a fruit stick.

The other "suffering bastard" is attributed to the bar at the Shepheard Hotel in Cairo, Egypt, where it was originally called the "suffering bar steward." The name changed when it became associated with the hard-pressed World War II British and Australian defenders of Tobruk in 1941 in North Africa. In this drink 2 oz. cognac or brandy, 2 oz. dry sherry, and ginger ale are poured over ice in a tall tumbler and decorated with fresh mint.

sugar. There are more than a hundred substances that may be described as "sugars"—including honey, dextrose, CORN SYRUP, levulose, lactose, sorbitol, mannitol, maltitol, xylitol, total invert sugar, turbinado sugar, and scores of others—but common white sugar, called "sucrose," is the one most used in the American home. The word "sugar" (which derives ultimately from Sanskrit *sárkarā*) refers to sweet, water-soluble carbohydrates extracted from plants such as cane and sugar beets, maple sap, fruits, sorghum, and other sources.

Until the Middle Ages honey was the only sweetener known in Europe, but sugarcane products, including molasses, were used in Asia at least as early as 800 B.C. The Arabs brought sugarcane to the West, and the Crusaders may have brought some back too. By the fifteenth century Venice was importing it from Alexandria, and sugar became a sensation throughout Italy, where it was used to sweeten not only desserts but hors d'oeuvres, meats, and macaroni as well. In 1498 the Portuguese explorer Vasco da Gama brought back sugarcane from his voyage to India, heralding an expansion of sugarcane production into the Cape Verde and Canary islands and Madeira. But four years before that Christopher Columbus had planted pieces of cane in the New World that were to flourish and change the course of Caribbean history, for soon the Spanish introduced the plant to Hispaniola, Cuba, and other islands, the Portuguese to Brazil, the English to Barbados, and the French to Martinique, establishing both a profitable sugar trade and a slave trade to support it. As Reay Tannahill points out in *The Fine Art of Food* (1968), "Sugar became so important to trade that in the 1670s the Dutch yielded New York to England in exchange for the captured sugar lands of Surinam, and in 1763 France was prepared to leave England with the whole of Canada, provided she had Guadeloupe returned to her." By 1520 there were at least sixty sugar factories on the island of Saint Thomas alone. Whole native populations, such as the Caribs and Arawaks of the Greater Antilles, were forced into slavery on the sugar plantations, causing the virtual extermination of these tribes. The Europeans then turned to Africa for slave labor, bringing more than 10 million wretched souls to work the New World's plantations. Soon a reciprocal trade

network was set up between the islands, the North American Colonies, and Europe, with New England selling codfish (with which to feed the slaves) to the islands, the islands shipping sugar and molasses to New England and Europe, and New England sending cod and rum made from molasses to Africa in return for a fresh supply of slaves. "King Sugar" ruled an empire of human misery. Many abolitionists urged people to refrain from using sugar, and some sugar vendors advertised their product as "East India sugar not made by slaves."

France's loss of the Sugar Islands of the West Indies to England after 1761 severely crippled Louis XV's prosperity and was one of the significant reasons his successor entered America's War of Independence on the Colonists' side. Despite the outcome of the war, however, France never did regain much of the Caribbean sugar trade.

Sugarcane never brought North American farmers much profit, though it was grown in the South in Louisiana, Alabama, Mississippi, Florida, and Georgia until competition from the Caribbean and the Far East after the Civil War pretty much wiped out the domestic industry. Today only Florida, Hawaii, Louisiana, and Texas have a sugarcane industry, producing only a small percentage of the world's output. Some cane is still grown in other southern states to make sugar syrup.

Although white sugar was always popular with Americans, it was often more expensive than alternatives like molasses, maple syrup in the Northeast, and "muscovado" (from Portuguese *mascavado,* unrefined sugar), an unrefined product derived from sugarcane juice that was considerably cheaper than white sugar. In 1868 Claus Spreckels of San Francisco patented a method of refining sugar in eight hours, rather than the usual three weeks, and, after opening his "California Sugar Refinery," became known as the "Sugar King."

After the lifting of sugar tariffs in the 1880s sugar came down in price and afterward became a cheap commodity all Americans could easily afford. Consumption doubled between 1880 and 1915.

Today Americans ingest about 9 million pounds of sugar per year (66.5 pounds per capita), of which about half is cane sugar.

The following list includes the most common sugars and sweeteners:

brown sugar. Less refined than white sugar, brown sugar consists of sugar crystals contained in molasses syrup with natural color and flavor. It may also be made by adding syrup to white sugar and blending. It may be found in groceries in either a light or dark brown shade, the latter having a somewhat stronger taste.

colored sugar. Also, "confetti sugar." Any sugar variously colored for cake and dessert decoration.

confectioners' sugar. A highly ground form of powdered sugar (which would be labeled "XXX") that is labeled "XXXX," ideal for making icings and other confections.

corn syrup. See main entry.

dextrose. Also, "glucose" or "corn sugar." A commercial sugar made from the action of heat and acids, or enzymes, on starch. Dextrose is often blended with regular sugar.

flavored sugar. Any sugar scented with aromatics such as lemon, vanilla, or cinnamon, often added to tea or coffee.

fructose. Also, "levulose." A commercial fruit sugar sweeter than sucrose and used in cooking.

honey. See main entry.

lactose. Also, "milk sugar." Made from skim and whey milk for commercial purposes, lactose is found in mammals' milk and is used mainly by the pharmaceutical industry.

maple sugar. See MAPLE.

raw sugar. A coarse light brown granulated sugar evaporated from cane juice. Only purified raw sugar may be sold.

sucrose. Obtained from cane or sugar beets, sucrose is a compound of glucose and fructose, is 99.9 percent pure, and is sold granulated or powdered.

sugar alcohol. Also, "polyol." Any of the natural fruit sugars like sorbitol, mannitol, maltitol, and xylitol that are commercially produced from sources like dextrose.

total invert sugar. A mixture of glucose and fructose, made by a process called "inversion," by which acids or enzymes split sucrose. Total invert sugar is sweeter than sucrose and comes in liquid form; it helps to prolong the freshness of baked goods.

turbinado sugar. Produced by separating raw sugar crystals and washing them with steam, turbinado sugar must be refined to remove impurities.

sukiyaki. A Japanese dish of meat and vegetables simmered together. Sukiyaki is a standard item in Japanese-American restaurants. The word, which dates in print to 1920, translates as "broiled on the blade of a plow," from the practice of Japanese farmers who often cooked their meals in the fields on such a utensil. Today, however, the dish is not broiled but stir-fried and simmered.

sunfish. Any of a variety of North American freshwater fishes in the family Centrarchidae or marine fishes in the family Molidae. Their brightly colored bodies give these fishes their name, which was first mentioned in print in 1629 referring to the sea species, and in 1685 (by William Penn) referring to the North American freshwater variety. The most important sunfish for culinary reasons include: the "bluegill" (*Lepomis macrochirus*); the "black crappie" (*Pomoxis nigromaculatus*) and "white crappie" (*P. annularis*), also called "speckled perch," "calico bass," "strawberry bass," "bachelor perch," "bachelor," "papermouth," and, in Louisiana, "sac à lait" (Creole French for "milk sack"); "crappie" is from a Canadian French name for another fish, *crapet*; the "flier" (*Centrarchus macropterus*); the "green sunfish" (*L. cyanellus*); the "longer sunfish" (*L. megalotis*); the "pumpkinseed" (*L. gibbosus*); the "redbreast sunfish" (*L. auritus*), also called the "robin," "sun perch," and "yellow-belly sunfish"; the "redear sunfish" (*L. microlophus*), also called the "shellcracker"; the "rock bass" (*Ambloplites rupestris*), also called the "redeye bass" or "goggle-eye"; and the "warmouth" (*L. qulosus*), also called the "stump knocker."

sunflower. Any of a variety of plants in the genus Helianthus, especially the "common sunflower" (*H. annuus*), native to the New World, bearing seeds that are dried or roasted to be eaten as a snack or pressed to make an oil. The word derives from its bright yellow flowers surrounding a dark center and was first recorded in English in 1555. "Sunflower oil" is first mentioned in print in 1819.

Sunflowers were cultivated by the Native Americans long before the arrival of the Europeans, but Russia became the world's largest producer. Although the sunflower is the official state flower of Kansas, the states producing the largest sunflower crops are North Dakota, Minnesota, and California.

supermarket. A large self-service food market that also sells many nonfood items (1920). The supermarket is the principal retail food store for Americans. The various items and brands are arranged on open shelves along long aisles, and customers line up at cash registers near the exit to unload their purchases from a rolling metal gridwork basket. The items are totaled up by a cashier as they move along a conveyor belt and then placed in brown paper or plastic bags by a store attendant called a "packer." Often the bags will be placed on another conveyor belt that brings them outside to a spot where customers can easily stop their cars to pick up the bags.

The supermarket is a specifically American notion built on the ideas that efficiency is increased by self-service, that variety is a tempting and competitive manner of advertising on the spot, and that the mobile nature of the American consumer is conducive to shopping in large retail stores with easy access by automobiles. In the last fifteen years such stores have become popular in Europe, too, often under the same term, "supermarket," in various languages.

The first self-service market was opened in 1916 by Clarence Saunders on Jefferson Avenue in Memphis, Tennessee, and a patent for a "self-service store" was issued to him on October 9, 1917. Items were prepackaged, labeled, and priced, and the store was kept impeccably clean, in contrast to the traditional rustic grocery store where many items were sold loose, priced according to how much one bought, and often delivered to one's home.

The self-service idea did not really catch on, however, until the 1930s, when such stores were sometimes referred to as "cafeteria-type" markets. In August 1930 a grocery-chain manager named Michael Cullen opened the King Kullen Grocery in an abandoned garage in Jamaica, New York, that was ten times the size of the average grocery and cut prices radically by doing high-volume business, making it the first true "supermarket." By 1936 there were more than twelve hundred supermarkets under different names in eighty-four cities. In 1937 Sylvan N. Goldman of Standard Food Stores in Oklahoma City, Oklahoma, debuted the first "shopping cart."

The first printed mentions of the word "supermarket"

in America were in the 1920s, and the term became as firmly entrenched as the concept, so that by 1950 America had more than ten thousand supermarkets, their growth encouraged by the postwar "baby boom" and the movement of the middle class to the suburbs.

The average supermarket was by then more than thirty thousand square feet, with chains like A&P, Safeway, Grand Union, and others dominating the food-buying habits of the country. In significant ways these large chains influenced what Americans ate to the extent that pretty much the same offerings in the West were enjoyed by those in the East, North, and South. By the 1960s supermarkets were carrying everything from imported foods to lawn furniture, and many had sections selling delicatessen-style items, fresh bread, and cooked foods.

But by the 1970s competition and overexpansion caused the supermarkets to lose money, even though sales in 1981 totaled $150 billion. Profit margins, never very high, fell to half what they had been in the 1950s and 1960s, and some chains went bankrupt.

To some extent many Americans began to regard the supermarket as depersonalized and lacking the nostalgic charm of the older neighborhood groceries, and in cities increasing numbers of "gourmet" or delicacy shops opened, carrying better-quality (and higher-priced) merchandise. Supermarkets in the 1980s and 1990s thereupon tried to meet this challenge by creating small delicacy shops, butchers, seafood sections, and take-out counters within the walls of the traditional supermarket structure. Many others started to carry HEALTH FOOD and more organically grown produce. The size of supermarkets grew so large in the 1980s that many were called "hypermarkets" or "superstores." While many of these were dazzling in design and elaborateness, other supermarkets, called "warehouse stores," shed all but the most rudimentary amenities and decor, offering lower prices and volume. These began in the Midwest in the 1960s when wholesalers tried to unload excess merchandise, but their popularity rose during the recession of 1974–75. A "club store" is a form of supermarket offering wholesale prices to members, with as many as 35 percent of such members being consumers, the rest wholesale business members.

suption. A southern African-American word for "flavor" in food, perhaps a variant of the word "sup," "to eat."

surf-n'-turf. A dish of meat and seafood served on the same plate. The meat is usually beef, the seafood lobster. This combination has led to several colloquial variants, including "pier-n'-steer," "lobsteer," "beef-n'-reef," and others, used as menu listings or restaurant names. These began to appear in the 1960s and 1970s.

surimi. A minced fish paste that can be molded and flavored to taste like higher-priced seafood such as crab, scallops, shrimp, or lobster. The term *surimi*, for the process of preserving fish this way, has long been used in Japan (though sometimes referred to as *kamaboko,* which is more specifically a form of surimi crab cake), where records mentioning the process date back to A.D. 720. Surimi was introduced into the United States in the early 1980s, and today between 160–175 million pounds are produced for the domestic market each year.

Surimi usually begins with an inexpensive fish, mostly Alaska pollock, which is skinned, filleted, minced, washed with water, then flash-frozen before shipping to processors who add flavorings, natural binders and stabilizers (including starch, salt, egg white, or sugar), and natural coloring. The resulting paste is shaped into various analogs marketed under different brand names. Surimi is also sold in chunks and flakes (called "salad style"). One of the most popular forms of surimi is in imitation crab legs.

In the United States "surimi" is used to describe the raw material used in making "surimi seafood," which is the final product.

sweaty saddles. Winemakers' slang term for wine spoiled by *Bretanomyces* yeast. See also BRET.

Swedish meatballs. A dish of seasoned pork or beef meatballs covered with a brown gravy. There are endless variations on this dish, which is most popular in the Midwest and derives from Swedish origins. Swedish meatballs are usually served at buffets and SMORGASBORDS, a custom that reflects their Swedish origins. Buttered noodles are the traditional accompaniment. Swedish meatballs date in print to the 1920s.

SWEDISH MEATBALLS

Grind together ¾ lb. beef, ¼ lb. pork, and ¼ lb. veal. Soak 1½ c. soft bread cubes in 1 c. light cream for several min., then mash into meat with ½ c. mashed potatoes, ½ c. chopped onion, 1 beaten egg, salt, pepper, ¼ c. chopped parsley, and a dash of ginger and nutmeg. Form into meatballs about 1 in. in diameter. Sauté meatballs in

---

3 T. butter until browned, then remove. Melt 2 T. butter in same skillet, scrape meat drippings, stir in 2 T. flour, cook briefly, and add 1⅓ c. beef bouillon. Cook until thickened, return meatballs to skillet and cook, basting often, for about 30 min. Serve with buttered noodles or rice.

---

sweet and sour. Any dish that combines the flavors of sweet and sour, usually achieved by the use of a sweetener, like sugar, corn syrup, or jelly, and a vinegar-based ingredient.

SWEET AND SOUR MEATBALLS

In a bowl combine 1 lb. ground beef, 1 beaten egg, 1 c. bread crumbs, 2 T. minced onions, 1 clove minced garlic, 1 t. salt, ½ t. black or white pepper, 2 T. milk, and 1 T. vegetable oil. Mix well and form into small meatballs. Brown meatballs in a pan with 3 T. vegetable oil, drain excess fat. Blend together ½ c. fruit jelly with ⅔ c. chile sauce and pour over meatballs. Simmer for about 10 minutes.

---

sweet potato (*Ipomoea batatas*). A vine native to the New World tropics, the yellow or orange tuber of which is eaten as a side dish in various forms. Sweet potatoes may be baked, boiled, candied, mixed in a pie or in biscuits, and topped with marshmallows. They are an important crop of the American South, though grown elsewhere in the United States, too, with two types being dominant—the "pale" sweet potato and another, darker-fleshed type called, erroneously, "yam." The true yam (*Dioscorea bulbifera*) is a different tropical vine, whose tuber may grow to lengths over seven feet and which is generally sweeter than the sweet potato. It is rarely seen in the United States, except, perhaps, in Latin-American markets, although it is called in regional English the "air potato." The confusion with the true yam came from the habit of slaves calling the American sweet potato by an African word (either Gullah, *njam,* Senegal, *nyami,* or Vai, *djambi*) meaning "to eat." The word was first recorded in America in 1676.

The earliest records of the cultivation of the sweet potato, dated to around 750 B.C., come from Peru, but it was grown throughout South and Central America by the time Christopher Columbus arrived in the New World. He found the tuber in Saint Thomas, where it was called *aje* or *axi*; on Hispaniola (*ages*); in the Yucatán (*camote*); and in Arawak (*batatas*).

The Taino word *batata* was soon transformed into

several European words, including the Spanish *patata,* French *patate,* and English "potato." These words first meant specifically the sweet potato, not the white potato that was introduced much later to the North American colonies. John Gerard in his *Herball* (1597) called sweet potatoes "common Potatoes," and, according to the *Oxford English Dictionary,* he termed white potatoes "Virginia Potatoes," and, later, "Bastard Potatoes." But as Waverley Root points out in *Food* (1980), Gerard could not have meant the white potato, for "not only did [it] not exist in Virginia, it did not exist anywhere in North America." (For further information on the white potato, see POTATO.)

The sweet potato, meanwhile, had already been shipped back to the Old World, perhaps as early as 1493 in Columbus's ship, and was cultivated in Spain by the middle of the sixteenth century. England got its first taste of the tuber in 1564, when Sir John Hawkins brought it back from "the Indies of Nova Hispania," although Henry VII might have sampled some Spanish varieties earlier. By the turn of the century Shakespeare wrote of them in *Merry Wives of Windsor,* and "sweet potato pie" had become an English delicacy.

But the term "sweet potato" was not in use in America until the 1740s, by then distinguished from the white potato that had come to Boston about 1719 with Irish immigrants. Long before then the sweet potato was being shipped to ports in Massachusetts from as far away as Bermuda. Root said earliest evidence for the cultivation of the tuber in North America dates to 1648, and probably back to 1610. It was in cultivation in New England by 1764 and much earlier in Virginia. In the South it was also called the "Carolina potato" or "dolley."

In the nineteenth century George Washington Carver devised more than a hundred uses for the sweet potato, which he noted was also called the "Indian potato," the "Tuckahoc," and the "hog potato," and listed table varieties that included the "Dooley yam," "Triumph," "Pumpkin yam," "Porto Rico," and "Nancy Hall." By the 1880s Americans were enjoying candied sweet potatoes, along with less lavish preparations of boiled, roasted, or mashed tubers. Today some of the most popular market varieties include the "Centennial," "Goldrush," "Georgia Red," "Puerto Rico," "New Jersey," and "Velvet." The sweet potato has long been associated with southern and soul cooking, and it is still traditional to serve it with the Thanksgiving meal. Per capita U.S. consumption of sweet potatoes in 1997 was 4.1 pounds.

In *Invisible Man* (1952) Ralph Ellison reminisced about the sweet potatoes of his childhood:

At home we'd bake them in the hot coals of the fireplace, had carried them cold to school for lunch; munched them secretly, squeezing the sweet pulp from the soft peel as we hid from the teacher behind the largest book, the World's Geography. *Yes, and we'd loved them candied, or baked in a cobbler, deep-fat fried in a pocket of dough, or roasted with pork and glazed with the well-browned fat; had chewed them raw—yams and years ago. More yams than years ago, though the time seemed endlessly expanded, stretched thin as the spiraling smoke beyond all recall.*

SWEET POTATO PIE

Boil 1 lb. sweet potatoes, remove the skins, mash, and beat. Blend with ¾ c. brown sugar, ¼ t. salt, and 1 t. ground cinnamon. Beat in 3 eggs, ¾ c. milk, ¾ c. heavy cream, and 1 T. butter. Spoon into pie plate lined with a pastry crust and bake at 400° for about 45 min.

CANDIED SWEET POTATOES

Boil, peel, and cut up 6 sweet potatoes. Place in a buttered pan, sprinkle with ¾ c. brown sugar, ½ t. grated lemon rind, and 1½ T. lemon juice, and bake in 375° oven for about 20 min. Serves 4.

sweetsop. (*Annona squamosa*) Also called "sugar apple." A tropical American tree bearing a yellow-green fruit with sweet yellow pulp, which is grown to some extent in Florida. The word first appeared in print in 1696.

swellfish (family Tetraodontidae). Any of a variety of fish that can inflate themselves with air or water, which gives them their name, as well as others, like "puffer," "blowfish," "globefish," and "sea squab." Swellfish are often poisonous to eat. The two main American species are the "smooth puffer" (*Lagocephalus laevigatus*) and the "northern puffer" (*Sphoeroides maculatus*).

Swiss steak. Sliced BEEF rump or round baked with tomatoes, onions, peppers, and sometimes seasonings such as thyme, rosemary, basil, or chile. In England it would be called "SMOTHERED steak," but there is really no direct corollary for the dish in Switzerland, the closest being carbonades. The name may derive instead from an English term, "swissing," which refers to a method of smoothing out cloth between a set of rollers, because Swiss steak is usually pounded and flattened before cooking. According to food historian Jean Anderson, the first known recipe for the dish appeared in 1915.

SWISS STEAK

Rub 2 lb. sliced round steak with ½ t. sugar and ½ lemon. Mix ½ c. flour, salt, and pepper, and pound into the meat. Sear the slices, then place in casserole. Sauté 2 sliced onions, 1 chopped green pepper, and 3 chopped celery stalks in 3 T. oil until tender. Add a 1-lb. can of stewed tomatoes, ¼ t. rosemary, and ¼ t. basil. Cook until tomatoes break down. Spoon over the meat, cover, and cook at 300° for 1½-2 hr. Serves 4.

---

switchel. A Colonial drink made from molasses, vinegar, and water. It is sometimes called "haymaker's punch." Brandy, cider, or rum was often added.

SWITCHEL

Combine 1 c. light brown sugar, 1 c. wine vinegar, ½ c. light molasses, 1 T. ground ginger, and 1 qt. cold water. Stir.

---

swizzle. A tall drink, usually made with rum (1805). Its origins are unknown, but the term perhaps is onomatopoeia that refers to the sound of mixing the drink in a glass. Swizzle has been used to describe a drink since the early nineteenth century, and it also came to mean drunkenness. A "swizzle stick," first mentioned in 1875 in print, is a kind of small paddle used to stir a drink.

swordfish. Any of a variety of large marine fish in the family Xiphiidae. Swordfish is one of the great game fishes and is found throughout the world. The name refers to the fish's swordlike upper jaw and has been used in English at least since 1400. The fish usually referred to under this name is *Xiphias gladius*, which is found in the waters of both the Atlantic and Pacific coasts and is called *shutome* in Hawaii. Although expensive because of the difficulty in landing the large fish, the swordfish has always been enjoyed by Americans, even though in the 1960s the Food and Drug Administration announced that it found dangerously high levels of mercury in the majority of speci-

mens it examined. This is no longer believed to be of major concern. U.S. commercial landings of swordfish totaled 13.6 million pounds in 1997.

Sydney Smith's Salad Dressing. A salad dressing of potatoes, mustard, olive oil, egg yolks, onions, and anchovies. The recipe—which came from a doggerel poem by English clergyman and founder of the *Edinburgh Review*, Sydney Smith (1771–1845)—was quite popular among American cooks in the nineteenth century.

> Two boiled potatoes strained through a
>   kitchen sieve,
> Softness and smoothness to the salad give,
> Of mordant mustard take a single spoon,
> Distrust the condiment that bites too soon!
> Yet deem it not, thou man of taste, a fault
> To add a double quantity of salt.
> Four times the spoon with oil of Lucca crown,
> And twice with vinegar procured from town;
> True taste requires it and your poet begs
> The pounded yellow of two well-boiled eggs.
> Let onion's atoms lurk within the bowl
> And, scarce suspected, animate the whole,
> And lastly in the flavored compound toss
> A magic spoonful of anchovy sauce.
> Oh, great and glorious! Oh, herbaceous meat!
> 'Twould tempt the dying Anchorite to eat,
> Back to the world he'd turn his weary soul
> And plunge his fingers in the salad bowl.

syllabub. An eggnog made with wine. It was once a popular drink at American Christmas parties, though it is rarely seen today. *The American Heritage Cookbook* (1980) contends the name "is derived from wine that came from Sillery in the Champagne region of France, and from 'bub,' an Elizabethan slang word for bubbling drink." The term first appears in print about 1530.

SYLLABUB

Combine 2 c. white wine, 5 T. grated lemon rind, 1 c. sugar, and ⅓ c. lemon juice. When sugar is dissolved, add to a blend of 3 c. milk and 2 c. light cream, then beat until frothy. Beat 4 egg whites with ½ c. sugar until stiff. Pour wine mixture into bowl and top with mounds of egg white. Sprinkle with nutmeg.

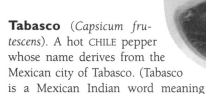

Tabasco (*Capsicum frutescens*). A hot CHILE pepper whose name derives from the Mexican city of Tabasco. (Tabasco is a Mexican Indian word meaning "damp earth.") The chile was first cultivated in Louisiana by banker Maunsell White, who brought the seeds from Tabasco and gave them to Edmund McIlhenny, who in turn planted them on a hillock named Avery Island. In 1859 McIlhenny began producing a bottled HOT SAUCE made by aging mashed chile peppers with salt and vinegar in casks for three years and sold it (in used perfume bottles) under the trademark name "Tabasco sauce," which has become the most famous hot sauce in the world. Tabasco sauce is so thoroughly identified with hot sauces that many recipes specifically refer to this brand, and it is commonly set on tables in the South along with the salt and pepper shakers so that people can season their food according to their own taste. Today the McIlhennys ship 50 million bottles of Tabasco each year to more than a hundred countries.

tablecloth restaurant. Also, "tableclother" and "white tablecloth restaurant." A restaurant industry term for a full-service restaurant, usually set with tablecloths, offering a wide variety of foods and some level of formal dining. Such a restaurant would be distinguished from a LUNCH COUNTER, diner, or other common eatery.

taco. In Mexico this refers to a stuffed and folded TORTILLA, but in the United States a "taco" is more commonly a crisp fried tortilla shaped into a U and filled with various stuffings. The word was first printed in English in 1930. Tacos are often served as a snack but also as a main course when served with refried beans, rice, and chili sauce. The word is Mexican-Spanish, meaning a "wad" or "plug," but colloquially refers to a light meal or snack. Small Mexican-American restaurants, especially those found along the road, are often called "taco stands," which are usually fast food restaurants in the United States. A national chain of taco stands under the name 'Taco Bell' was begun in 1962 by Glen Bell in Downey, California. It is now owned by PepsiCo, Inc., of Purchase, New York, and has more than thirty-five hundred outlets.

Tacos are usually bought in packages at a grocery and are quite crisp, though in Mexico they are generally more pliable. The various fillings for a taco, usually doused with a hot chili sauce, include ground beef, chicken, pork, chorizo sausage, tomato, cheese, lettuce, guacamole, onion, and refried beans.

taffy. A confection made from sugar, butter, and flavorings that has a chewy texture obtained by twisting and pulling the cooked ingredients into elasticity.

The British term for such candy is "toffee" or "toffy," possibly from "tafia," a cheap West Indian rum made from molasses and used originally to flavor candy. The *Oxford English Dictionary* notes that "taffy" (the preferred word in Scotland, Northern England, and America) seems to refer to an older form of the candy. By the 1870s "taffy bakes" and "taffy pulls," at which young people would gather to stretch the candy between them, had become social occasions.

English toffees are often harder than American taffies. "Saltwater taffy," which actually contained a small amount of saltwater, was popularized as "Fralinger's Original Salt Water Taffy," established as a confectionery stand by Joseph Fralinger in 1885 on the Boardwalk in Atlantic City, New Jersey. The story of how the taffy got its name dates back a couple of years earlier when one taffy stand was hit by an ocean wave, drenching the stock with saltwater. According to legend, the next day a little girl tasted the candy and asked, "Is this saltwater taffy?"

tailgate picnic. A meal served outdoors off the folded-down rear door, or tailgate, of a station wagon, an American car designed to carry several family members or a large load. The term dates in print at least to 1941, although a photo in a spring 1936 English magazine and an illustration in a November 1936 New York City clothing advertisement both depict tailgate picnics.

The food is varied and of a kind found at any picnic—salads, sandwiches, fried chicken, beer, soft drinks, coffee, cakes, and anything else that strikes the fancy.

take-out. A term for food that is bought at a restaurant but taken elsewhere to be eaten. The term has been in use at least since the 1940s, and is shown on the sign of the "Tail o' the Pup" hot dog stand in a 1949 photo. Synonyms would be "carryout," "take-home," and "to go." While the majority of restaurants in the United States provide some form of take-out food, it is those restaurants with average checks of under twenty-five dollars that most widely offer the service.

take the pledge. An alcoholic's phrase for abstaining completely from alcohol.

tamale. A term describing a wide range of dishes based on a cornmeal-flour dough that is placed inside cornhusks (sometimes a banana leaf) and then steamed. Tamales are of Mexican origin and were enjoyed by the Aztecs (the word comes from the Nahuatl *tamalli)* in several versions, from appetizer to sweet dessert. In Mexico they are traditionally served in restaurants on Sunday nights and as ceremonial food on All Saints' Day. As early as 1612 Englishman Captain John Smith mentioned a kind of tamale made by the Indians of Virginia, and by 1691 note was made by others of a bean-filled tamale of the Southwest. By 1854 the dish had been described in *Bartlett's Personal Narratives.*

TAMALE

Coarsely chop 2 lb. pork and cover with water, bring to boil, then simmer until tender. Drain, reserving 1½ c. stock. Shred the pork and sauté in 4 T. oil until brown, then stir in 2 T. flour until brown. Stir in a sauce made from 1 chopped tomato, 1 chopped garlic clove, 1 chopped red or green chile pepper, 1 chopped onion, salt, and pepper pureed in a blender. Add 3 chopped green or red chile peppers, ¼ t. oregano, salt, and pepper, and simmer for about 30 min. Make a dough of 1½ c. lard creamed with 1½ t. salt. Mix 4½ c. masa with 2½ c. warm water. Beat into lard. Place portions of the dough into a dozen cornhusks, spread portions of meat mixture on dough, and fold opposite sides of husks toward center. Peel dough from husks and seal, then close husks around dough to seat into a packet. Steam for 1½ hr. Serves 12.

---

tamale pie. A dish of cornmeal mush filled with chopped meat and a hot chili sauce. The term first appeared in 1911.

tangelo *(Citrus tangelo).* A hybrid fruit obtained by crossing a grapefruit with a tangerine. The word entered English print in 1900 as a portmanteau from *tangerine* and *pomelo.* The main varieties grown in the United States are the "K Early," the "Nova," and the "Mineola" (called "honey belles" in Florida).

tansy. Also, "tansey." A pudding made from the juice of the tansy plant (of the genus *Tanacetum,* especially *T. vulgare),* or any such confection made with a tart fruit. The word is from Middle English, derived from Old French *tanesie,* and, ultimately Greek *athanasía,* "immortality."

"Tansy cake" was known in England at least since the fifteenth century. As a pudding, tansy was first mentioned circa 1450, said to be eaten at Easter to commemorate the "bitter herbs" of the Passover.

In America the dish often lacked the ingredient that gave it its name, a tart fruit such as the cherry being substituted. It was a popular dessert at George Washington's Mount Vernon home in Virginia.

Taos lightnin'. Also, "Touse." A variety of distilled spirits originally made at San Fernández de Taos, now Taos, in New Mexico. The Spanish called it *aquardiente,* or "burning water," and it was enjoyed by the early trappers in that region.

taro *(Colocasia esculenta,* family Araceae). Also, "dasheen," "eddo," and many other regional names. A tropical plant with broad leaves and a starchy, edible root (1770). The name comes from the Tahitian and Maori and was mentioned by Captain James Cook in 1779 after finding the plant in the Sandwich Islands of the Pacific. The plant is cultivated in the southern United States, and there are at least one thousand varieties in the world.

Taro was a staple of the high islands of Polynesia and Hawaii, where it is called *kalo,* and treated with the respect that made it the islands' most important food. The corm of the plant was used for food, with some of the leaves and stalks occasionally cooked as greens. Taro's most important use in Hawaii to this day is in the preparation of POI, and it is also made into cakes and biscuits and fried in butter.

tarragon *(Artemisia dracunculus).* A Eurasian herb used as a seasoning in soups, sauces, salads, and other foods. The name is from the Greek *drákōntion*, "adderwort," which became in Middle English *tragonia* or *tarchon*.

Although tarragon is used as a seasoning in the United States, it is little grown here except in home gardens, where it was first reported in 1806. In many home gardens the variety grown may actually be the "false" or "Russian tarragon" (*A. dracunculoides*), which has a less pungent flavor.

tarte à la bouie. A Creole or Cajun custard tart. The name is from the French for "boiled tart."

tasso. A Cajun and Creole smoked, pickled pork that is usually added to flavor GUMBO, JAMBALAYA, and other dishes. The word may derive from the French *tasser*, "to shrink," because the pickled pork shrinks in size when it is dried, or the Spanish *tasajo*, for dried, cured beef. To make tasso, pickled pork is rubbed with a blend of herbs and spices, then air-dried and cold-smoked over an aromatic wood.

tassy. According to Nathalie Dupree in *New Southern Cooking* (1987), "Tassies are tiny tarts frequently served at weddings and special occasions which may require a finger-food dessert treat."

tautog (*Tautoga onitis*). Also, "blackfish." A fish of the wrasse family (Labridae), found on the Atlantic coast. It is of little commercial value. The name comes from the Narraganset, tautauog, and appears in print as early as 1635.

tea. A beverage made by steeping the leaves of various shrubs or herbs, but specifically of the shrub *Thea sinensis* (or *Camellia sinensis*). The word derives from the Ancient Chinese *d'a*, as transmuted by the early Dutch traders in that region. The word first appears in English print in 1598.

The first canisters of tea were brought from Bantam in Java to England in 1669 by the East India Company, but they were merely a novelty until 1678, when larger quantities began to be imported. Thomas Twining, who already owned one coffeehouse in London, opened a second (called the Golden Lyon) in 1717 that also featured tea, which soon exceeded coffee in popularity.

Tea drinking caught on quickly in America soon afterward and became a convenient product for the English to tax heavily. The passage of the Townshend Acts in 1767, which levied a three pence-per-pound tax on tea imported to the Colonies, and in 1773 the

Tea Act, which nearly gave the British East India Company a monopoly on the selling of tea, was cause for great dissent and opposition to British policies. Protests erupted in Boston on the night of December 16, 1773, when a group of colonists dressed in Indian outfits boarded three English ships and threw the tea shipments into the harbor. By the 1830s, this became known as the Boston Tea Party. Patriots took to drinking "liberty tea," made from loosestrife leaves, or turned to coffee.

After the Revolutionary War United States shippers established a trade with China in 1784 and had shipped more than a billion pounds of tea three years later. The British still dominated the tea trade, however, until 1859, when Americans George Huntington Hartford and George Gilman eliminated the wholesaler and bought tea directly from ships and sold it directly to their customers for one-third the price charged by their competitors. They established the "Great Atlantic and Pacific Tea Company," later to grow into a chain of supermarkets under the name "A&P."

By the 1860s Americans were enjoying "iced tea," which was popularized at the 1903 St. Louis World's Fair by Richard Blechynden after finding he couldn't sell much hot tea in the summer's heat. Iced tea is especially popular in the South, where it is often presweetened before being iced and where hot tea is often prepared by heating up iced tea for those few who want a cup of the beverage. Sun tea is tea steeped in cold water and then left to stand in the hot sun for several hours. It is thereafter iced. Instant iced tea was introduced in 1953 under the label "White Rose Redi-Tea" by the Seeman Brothers of New York City.

The "tea bag" was first marketed in 1904 by Thomas Sullivan of New York City and quickly replaced loose tea in the decoction of the leaves. Although few Americans adopted the British custom of having "afternoon tea," first enjoyed in the 1840s, by 1915 young women attended "tea dances" (see THÉ DANSANT) during World War I and afterward many women invited their friends for "tea parties," often as part of a fashion show at a club.

By the 1930s Americans could buy instant tea, made from processed granules (and often containing sugar) that needed only water from the tap to produce the beverage.

Tea leaves have never been successfully cultivated in the United States (more than 50 percent is now imported from China, 30 percent each from Argentina and Indonesia), the last significant attempt having been made by C. U. Shepard and the Department of

Agriculture at Summerville, South Carolina, from 1890 to 1916.

Herb (or herbal) teas made from sassafras, ginger, and other herbs have long been a part of American history. They received a great boost in popularity during the "natural foods" movement of the 1960s when such decoctions were thought to be soothing and beneficial to one's health (for more information see HEALTH FOOD). About 50 percent of Americans drink tea—80 percent of which is iced tea, about 1.9 billion gallons. U.S. per capita consumption of tea in 1997 was 7.4 gallons.

Teas are generally named after their type and size of leaf or their region of origin; most are blends of several varieties. Some of the most common teas consumed in the United States include:

Darjeeling tea. A costly Indian tea. The name comes from a Bengali town in Northeast India.

Earl Grey tea. A blend of China teas whose name derives from Charles, the second Earl Grey, prime minister of England from 1830–34 under William IV. The blend was supposedly presented to Earl Grey and originally made by the Twinings tea company but never trademarked, so that various "Earl Grey" blends are now made by several tea companies.

English breakfast tea. A blend of Ceylon and India teas, whose "brisk" flavor is considered especially bracing at breakfast.

jasmine tea. Chinese tea scented with jasmine petals.

orange pekoe. A blend of Ceylon teas, whose name refers only to the color of the leaf. It is the largest-selling tea in the United States.

tenderizer. A substance used to make meat more tender, usually taken from an enzyme, papain, of the papaya plant. As a powder, this substance will partly digest up to three hundred times its weight in lean meat with which it comes in contact, but it is deactivated when heated. Although it is considered no substitute for proper aging, a powdered tenderizer can improve inferior cuts of meat.

tenderloin. The most tender fillet of beef cut from the hindquarter in the primal short loin. Tenderloin is almost entirely free from fat, marbling, or bone, and sometimes is sold as part of the "porterhouse steak."

Butchers may also refer to this cut as "filet mignon," "chateaubriand," and "tournedos." "Tenderloin" has been in print since the 1820s.

Colloquially the term has long been associated with sections of cities where vice and graft run rampant, originally referring to the Twenty-ninth Precinct of Manhattan, which extended from Seventh Avenue to Park and Fourth avenues and from Fourteenth to Forty-second streets. According to a deposition given to a committee investigating police corruption in 1894, police captain Alexander S. Williams testified that the term had been picked up by a reporter for the *New York Sun* from an interview with Williams, who, on being transferred to the Twenty-ninth in 1876, said, "I have been living on rump steak in the Fourth District, I will have some tenderloin now."

Tennessee whiskey. A straight whiskey that must be made from at least 51 percent of a single grain, usually corn, and made by a sour-mash process similar to that used for bourbon. The term has been in use at least since the 1840s.

The most famous name in Tennessee whiskey is "Jack Daniel's," the name of a distillery set up in Lynchburg's Cave Spring Hollow by Jasper Newton "Jack" Daniel. Registered with the government in 1866, Jack Daniel Distillery claims to be the oldest registered distillery in the United States.

tepary (*Phaseolus acutifolius latifolius*). A New World vine bearing a bean that is particularly grown in the Southwest and Mexico. The origin of the word is obscure, mentioned in Spanish as of 1716, in English since 1910. It has been suggested that the name is from a Papago word, *'stäte päve,* "wild pave."

tequila. A liquor distilled from the Central American blue AGAVE (*Agave Rigidae tequilana weber, var. azul*) plant (1840). The name comes from the Tequila district of Mexico, where the best tequila traditionally is made. The word was first printed in English in 1849, and the Bureau of Alcohol, Tobacco and Firearms recognized tequila as a distinctive product of Mexico in September 1975.

The agave plant contains a sweet sap at its heart called *aquamiel* ("honey water") that is made into a brandy called *vino mezcal,* which is tequila. The fermented and double-distilled spirit is drawn off at 104 to 106 proof and reduced to 80 to 86 proof when shipped to the United States, most of it unaged. The Mexican government allows a spirit to be labeled "tequila" if it has a minimum of 51 percent agave-derived sugar (the rest may be cane or corn sugar). Tequila at this level of agave sugar is called "white tequila," and is the most common variety used for mixed drinks. Tequila made from 100 percent agave is generally sipped on its own.

Tax records of the town of Tequila show that Don Cenobio Sauza shipped barrels of "mezcal wine" to the U.S. in 1873, and American troops brought it back from their campaign against Pancho Villa in 1916. During a gin shortage in 1944 in this country tequila enjoyed a brief popularity, but it was not until the 1960s, when it became a faddish drink among California university students, that the sales of the spirit really grew, especially as the basis for the MARGARITA cocktail. By 1990 shipments had soared to 4 million gallons (about 5.1 million cases), making it the tenth-largest-selling spirit type in the United States.

The "classic" way (sometimes called the "Mexican Itch") to drink straight tequila, which required dried crushed worms from the agave plant in a shaker of salt, was described by Green Peyton in his book *San Antonio: City in the Sun* (1946): "You gulp the Tequila, sprinkle the mummified condiment on the back of your hand, swallow it, suck on a small piece of lime, and then sit down for a while to recover your senses." The "worm" Peyton speaks of is a caterpillar or larva sometimes placed as a gimmick in a bottle of mezcal and drunk down as a show of bravado.

tequila sunrise. A cocktail made from tequila, orange juice, and grenadine. According to *The Tequila Book* (1976), by Marion Gorman and Felipé de Alba, the drink may have originated at the Agua Caliente racetrack bar in Mexico during the Prohibition era, when Californians would drive there to play the horses and have a few drinks. After a night of carousing, the visitors would need a pick-me-up at sunrise, and the addition of one's morning orange juice to tequila seemed appropriate.

Another tequila drink, the "tequila sunset," must have come some time afterward.

TEQUILA SUNRISE

In a shaker with crushed ice combine 1½ oz. tequila, 1 oz. grenadine, and 3 oz. orange juice. Shake, strain into a wineglass that has been chilled, and garnish with lime slice.

TEQUILA SUNSET

In a blender with crushed ice combine 1½ oz. orange juice, 1½ oz. pineapple juice, and 1 oz. tequila. Blend for about 30 sec. Pour, without straining, into a chilled wineglass whose rim has been sugared.

Texas toast. Toast that is cut about one inch in thickness, so called because of the popular mythology that everything in Texas is bigger than anywhere else. It may be spread with a cheese topping and baked in the oven.

Tex-Mex. A combination of the words "Texan" and "Mexican," first printed in 1945, that refers to an adaptation of Mexican dishes by Texas cooks. It is difficult to be precise as to what distinguishes Tex-Mex from true Mexican food, except to say that the variety of the latter is wider and more regional, whereas Tex-Mex is a more standardized cookery popular throughout the state and, now, throughout the entire United States. The best-known Tex-Mex dishes might be found at a roadside taco stand or at a fine home, and they might include TACOS, TORTILLAS, CHALUPAS, BURRITOS, corn bread, TAMALES, TOSTADAS, NACHOS, ENCHILADAS, and various forms of CHILE, the most specific Tex-Mex version being CHILI CON CARNE, or, as Texans call it, "a bowl of red." Central to Tex-Mex cooking is the CHILE pepper, which may go into anything from bread to jelly.

Thanksgiving. A national American holiday centered around a family feast commemorating the first harvest of the Plymouth Colony in 1621 after a winter of great suffering and near starvation. The fifty-odd members of the colony had been established the year before, and, in thanks to God for their survival, Governor William Bradford declared a feast be held between the settlers and the Native Americans of the region, led by Chief Massasoit of the Wampanoag tribe, which had signed a treaty with the Pilgrims. It is not known exactly when the feast was held, but it was most probably between September 21 and November 9. (It should be noted, however, that a year before the Pilgrims landed at Plymouth, a band of 38 settlers arrived in Virginia at what is now the Berkeley Plantation on the James River, where, on December 4, 1619, Captain John Woodlief ordered that the day of the ship's arrival be "yearly and perpetually kept holy as a day of Thanksgiving to Almighty God," a commemoration President John F. Kennedy in 1961 declared the first Thanksgiving. In addition, other Virginia claims as to the first Thansgiving have been made for 1584, 1607 and 1610.)

Massasoit arrived at the feast, which probably lasted several days, with ninety braves, bringing many of the dishes, including a form of flint corn that popped a bit when roasted. Governor Bradford sent out four men to catch game, but it is not known for sure whether the fowl consumed on the first Thanksgiving included turkey, which has since become the traditional main course of Thanksgiving celebrations. It is known that oysters, cod, eel, corn bread, goose, venison, watercress, leeks, berries, and plums were eaten, all accompanied by sweet wine.

The next recorded Thanksgiving in the Plymouth Colony was on July 30, 1623, at which turkey was definitely served, along with cranberries and pumpkin pie.

Thanksgiving was not held as a regular feast, but it became traditional in New England to give thanks on a day set aside for that purpose; Connecticut had its first Thanksgiving in 1649, the Massachusetts Bay Colony in 1669, and by the 1780s the feast day was popular throughout the region. President George Washington proclaimed the first nationally observed Thanksgiving for November 26, 1789.

In her 1827 novel *Northwood* Mrs. Sarah Joseph Hall (also author of the nursery rhyme "Mary Had a Little Lamb") expressed the hope that Thanksgiving would soon become a "national festival . . . [and] a grand spectacle of moral power and human happiness, such as the world has never witnessed." As editor of Philadelphia's *Godey's Lady's Book* Hall campaigned as of 1846 to turn Thanksgiving into a national holiday. President Abraham Lincoln declared August 6 the appropriate day in 1863, but a few months later changed the date to the last Thursday of November. This tradition was maintained until 1939, when president Franklin Delano Roosevelt changed the date to the third Thursday in November in an effort to stimulate sales in retail stores by heralding the advent of Christmas a week earlier. In December 1941 Congress changed it back again to the last Thursday in November.

The traditional Thanksgiving meal for most Americans is eaten at home (45 percent at one's own, 42 percent at someone else's) and includes many of the same dishes enjoyed at the first Thanksgiving—the turkey having been well established as the feast's main course by the 1820s.

thé dansant. A term from the French, "tea dance," to describe a fad in American hotels from 1914–16 wherein young women would attend tea dances in the afternoon. The practice originated in England, where the dances were often charity affairs, but in the United States, more often than not, these became what restaurateur George Rector called "booze dansants," because liquor and cocktails were served in teacups.

Thompson Seedless. A white vinifera grape used as a blending grape in sparkling wine and brandy, as well as a popular table grape. It was introduced in 1872 by farmer William Thompson of Yuba City, California, and it became the most widely planted variety of grape in the state.

Thousand Island dressing. A salad dressing based on RUSSIAN DRESSING with various additions of pickles, cream, green peppers, and other seasonings. The term dates in print to 1920, probably derived from the Thousand Islands in the St. Lawrence River that cuts between New York and Ontario, where the dressing may have first been concocted. But Craig Claiborne in *Craig Claiborne's Southern Cooking* (1987) wrote: "Legend has it that it was created many years ago by the executive chef at the Drake Hotel in Chicago . . . and when his wife saw it she remarked that it looked like the Thousand Islands, near Ontario, New York, that they had recently visited." The current management at the Drake Hotel cannot confirm this, however.

It has also been suggested that the bits and pieces of seasonings and ingredients resemble a multitude of islands in a sea of dressing.

THOUSAND ISLAND DRESSING

Fold 1 qt. mayonnaise into 1 qt. chile sauce, add 1 chopped pimiento, 5 chopped hard-boiled eggs, 1 pt. chopped sweet pickles, and 2 chopped green peppers. Mix well.

---

three sheets in the wind. Also, "three sheets to the wind." An expression meaning to be drunk. It derives from a sailor's tacking of the sails by means of a chain or rope called a "sheet" attached to the lower corner of the sail. If the sail fluttered freely, it was said to be "in the wind." If three sheets were thus free, the sail would not be under control, causing the ship to weave and sway in the wind. The phrase "three sheets" dates in print to 1857; "sheet in the wind" to 1862.

thyme. Any of a variety of herbs grown in New England in the genus *Thymus*, of the mint family, especially the "garden" or "black thyme" (*T. vulgaris*), the "lemon thyme" (*T. citriodorus*), and the "wild thyme" (*T. serpyllum*). The word is from the Greek *thýmon*. Thyme is used as a seasoning in soups, sauces, salads, and other dishes. It is customarily added to chowder.

ti. Polynesian name for the tropical plant *Cordyline terminalis* (1830), whose leathery leaves are used to steam foods in the IMU pit.

tilapia. Also, "St. Peter's fish." Any of a variety of cichlids from the genus *Tilapia* (the origins of the word are New Latin, in English print since 1849) from African waters. In recent years they have become an important food fish in the American market and aquaculturists have high hopes that the species can be successfully farmed. Market varieties are usually about ten to twenty ounces in weight, and are usually broiled, steamed, or sautéed.

tilefish. Any of a variety of marine fish in the family Branchiostegidae, with four species in the United States. The name is actually short for a species known in taxonomic Latin as *Lopholatilus chamaeleonticeps*, although the tilelike spots on the fish probably also influenced the name, which first appeared in print in 1849. This species is found from Chesapeake Bay to Maine and was first noted off the New England coast in May 1879. In 1882 the fish had totally disappeared, possibly as a result of a climatic change in the water temperature, but it came back in abundance five years later and is readily available at market today. The main species of culinary interest include the common tilefish named above, the "blackline tilefish" (*Caulolatilus cyanops*), the "sand tilefish" (*Malacanthus plumieri*), and the "ocean whitefish" (*C. princeps*). U.S. commercial landings of tilefish totaled 4.2 million pounds in 1997.

tipsy. Also, "tipsy parson" in the South. A sponge cake spread with almonds, soaked in sherry, and served with custard (1570). It was a dish of the late nineteenth century. The name apparently refers to the alcohol content, which if taken in large doses would make the imbiber "tipsy" or slightly drunk.

TIPSY

Moisten a sponge cake with 1 c. sherry. Beat 3 egg yolks until light yellow and stir in 2 c. milk. In a saucepan heat the liquid until it coats the spoon and becomes a custard. Pour over the sponge cake. Sprinkle with ½ c. blanched almonds. Whip 3 egg whites with 2 T. powdered sugar, then blend in 1 c. cream and ¼ c. candied fruit. Pour over the sponge cake and spoon a little currant jelly in the center.

tiswin. A fermented beverage made by the Apache Indians (1875). The name comes from the Spanish *tesquino*, derived from Cahita, the language spoken by the Yaqui and Maya Indians of Sonora. Is also spelled *tiswino* or *tesquino* by the New Mexican Indians. Tiswin is made by fermenting dried corn with water, PILONCILLO cones of brown sugar, and spices such as cinnamon and orange peel.

toasted ravioli. A St. Louis, Missouri, specialty of meat-filled pasta dough that is deep-fried golden brown. Italian ravioli are boiled and served with a sauce, but toasted ravioli was supposedly first made in the 1930s[?] at a St. Louis restaurant named Angelo Oldani's when a German employee named Fritz accidentally threw freshly made ravioli into a pan of boiling oil. Owner Oldani tried to salvage them, brushed them with grated cheese, and served them to his customers, who loved them.

TOASTED RAVIOLI

In a shallow pan sprinkle a thin layer of bread crumbs. Dip meat ravioli into milk, place on top of the crumbs, dust the tops of the ravioli with more bread crumbs and pat down to coat evenly. Heat oil to 375° and fry ravioli for about 3–4 min. until golden brown. Drain, sprinkle with Parmesan cheese, and serve plain or with tomato sauce or melted butter.

toddy. Although there are many variations, a toddy is usually a heated mug of whiskey flavored with citrus fruits and spices. The word comes from the Hindi *tāri*, for the fermented or fresh sap of a palm tree, and the English traders picked up the word in India. Originally the drink was made cold, but cold days at sea made the idea of a hot toddy more convivial on board. Scottish poet Robert Burns was the first to note the drink in print, in 1600.

TODDY

Dissolve 1 lump of sugar in a glass half-filled with boiling water, add 1½ oz. rum or whiskey, 2 cloves, a stick of cinnamon, and lemon rind.

togue. A Maine term for a large lake trout, first noted in print in 1830. The name is from the Canadian French, via Algonquian.

togus. A New England dish of the nineteenth century made from milk, cornmeal, and molasses, whose name possibly derives from an Indian word. *The Pentucket Housewife* (1882) lists the ingredients as 3 c. milk, 1 c. sour milk, 3 c. cornmeal, 1 c. flour, ½ c. molasses, and 1 t. baking soda. The dish is steamed for 3 hr. and eaten with butter and sugar.

Toll House cookie. A cookie made from flour, semisweet chocolate chips, brown sugar, and nuts. It is by far the most popular of all-American cookies. In 1930 Mrs. Ruth Wakefield and her husband purchased a 1709 tollhouse on the outskirts of Whitman, Massachusetts, a halfway point for travelers between Boston and New Bedford. Mrs. Wakefield turned the house into the Toll House Inn, and one day in her kitchen, while experimenting with an old American recipe for "Butter Drop-Do" cookies, she happened to cut up a bar of Nestlé semisweet chocolate into small chips and added them to the batter. Instead of melting, the chocolate bits retained their texture in the baking and gave the cookie a flavor that soon was to make her famous. The Toll House cookie was born (Wakefield originally called it the "chocolate crunch cookie" or "chocolate crispies"), and, after the recipe appeared in a Boston newspaper, people began writing to her for the recipe, and sales of Nestlé's chocolate bar increased dramatically. With Wakefield's permission the Nestlé Company began printing the recipe on its semisweet chocolate-bar wrappers, and in 1939 it began packaging bits of uniformly shaped chocolate chips called "Nestlé Semi-Sweet Chocolate Morsels." Today Nestlé produces 250 million morsels a day in three factories, and it has been estimated that half the cookies baked at home in America are chocolate chip, making them as famous as the proverbial apple pie. In fact, after Canadian diplomats had secretly helped six Americans to escape from Iran during the hostage crisis of 1980, the grateful people of America sent a large bag of chocolate-chip cookies to the Canadian embassy in Washington. The recipe is still printed on the Nestlé Semisweet Chocolate Morsels package.

TOLL HOUSE COOKIE

Combine in a bowl 2¼ c. unsifted flour, 1 t. baking soda, and 1 t. salt. In another bowl combine 1 c. butter, ¾ c. sugar, ¾ c. brown sugar, and 1 t. vanilla extract. Beat until creamy, then add 2 eggs. Gradually add the flour mixture and blend in well. Stir in 12 oz. Nestlé semisweet chocolate morsels (2 c.) and 1 c. chopped nuts. Drop by rounded teaspoons onto ungreased cookie sheet. Bake in 375° preheated oven for 8 to 10 min. Makes 100 2-in. cookies.

BLONDIES

A variation in the shape of Toll House cookies achieved by spreading the dough into a greased 15-by-10-in. baking pan. Bake at 375° for 20 min., then cut into thirty-five 2-in. squares.

Tom and Jerry. A beverage made from eggs, sugar, brandy or bourbon, and whiskey, topped with milk or boiling water. Some believe the name comes from *Pierce Egan's Life in London, or the Days and Nights of Jerry Hawthorne and his Elegant Friend Corinthian Tom* (1821), which did help connote rowdy, drunken behavior known as "Tom-and-Jerrying," and a "Tom and Jerry shop" was a low beerhouse of the day. But the first printed reference, 1861, predates that publication date. It was not until 1862 that American bartender "Professor" Jerry Thomas gave the first recipe for a Tom and Jerry in his *The Bon Vivant's Companion, or How to Mix Drinks,* and Thomas has been credited for first serving the drink at St. Louis's the Planter's Hotel. Thomas is said to have refused to make the drink in warm weather and refused to serve it before the first snowfall.

"Tom and Jerry mugs" were ceramic cups with handles.

TOM AND JERRY

Separate 6 eggs. Beat ¼ lb. sugar into yolks until the mixture is light yellow, then pour in 2 oz. whiskey. Beat egg whites until stiff and fold into mixture. Ladle into a cup, add 2 oz. brandy or bourbon to each mug, and fill with boiling milk or water. Stir and sprinkle on nutmeg and a dash of brandy, if desired.

---

tomatillo. A berry of the family Physalis that resembles a small unripe tomato. It is known under various names in Mexico—*tomate verde, tomate de cáscara,* and *fresadilla*—and canned in the United States as "tomatillo enter" or "tomatito verde" and "peeled green tomato."

(There is also a shrub in Chile [genus *Solanaceous*] called "tomatillo.") When ripe, tomatillos turn yellow, but the green fruit is preferred for coloring sauces. The term has been in English print since about 1910.

tomato. The fleshy, juicy, usually bright red fruit of the plant *Lycopersicon esculentum*. Tomatoes are used in a wide variety of ways—including fresh, in salads, in sauces, as juice, and in other preparations. The word is from the Nahuatl *tomatl*, and first appears in English print about 1595, though then the tomato was also referred to as a "love apple." (The Italian name for the fruit is *pomodoro*, "golden apple," because the first examples to reach Europe were yellow varieties.)

The tomato is probably native to Peru and Ecuador, but it was widely established throughout Central America by the time the Spanish arrived in the early sixteenth century. Because the tomato is taxonomically a member of the deadly nightshade family, *Solanaceae*, Europeans approached the idea of eating the fruit with extreme caution. The Spaniards had brought the tomato back to their own country early in the century, and from there to Italy (though some authorities posit that the fruit may have gotten to Italy via Neapolitan sailors). M. Pietro Andrea Mattioli Sanese's 1544 translation of a botany text described the tomato as a kind of eggplant, but later changed his description to *mala insana*, "unhealthy apple." Indeed, most Europeans continued to believe the tomato was poisonous—or at the very least an exotic fruit or vegetable to be cooked cautiously and eaten sparingly.

Tomatoes were not cultivated in North America until the 1700s, and then only in home gardens. Thomas Jefferson was raising tomatoes by 1782 and noted that others in Virginia grew them for private consumption. Nevertheless, most people of that century paid little heed to tomatoes, and only in the next century did they make their way into American cookbooks, always with instructions that they be cooked for at least three hours or else, as Eliza Leslie wrote in her *Directions for Cookery* (1848 ed.), they "will not lose their raw taste." Nineteenth-century cooks used them in KETCHUPS or in sauces, but did not recommend eating them raw. Waverley Root, in *Food* (1980), notes that "the Thorbun seed catalog gave directions for growing tomatoes in 1817, but offered only one variety; by 1881 it would be selling thirty-one." By 1865 northern markets offered tomatoes year-round. In 1893 the Supreme Court decreed that, for trade purposes, the tomato could be classified as a vegetable, though it is in reality a fruit.

Tomato sauces became popular with the arrival of Italian immigrants in the late nineteenth and early twentieth centuries, and after 1900 the tomato itself finally gained credibility as a flavorful, healthy food, aided by southern farmers who began propagating the fruit on a widespread basis. By 1929 Americans were eating thirty-six pounds of tomatoes per capita per year. The tomato has become the most widely planted of all home-garden fruits or vegetables and is now grown in every state in the Union.

Fresh tomatoes are grown in every state, though market varieties are most likely to come from Florida, California, New Jersey, Texas, or Alabama, with the principal varieties being "Fireball," "Big Boy," "Manapal," "Floradel," and "Pinkshipper."

Tomatoes grown primarily for canning are raised in California and include the "Bouncer," "New Yorker," "Red Top," "Campbell 1327," and "San Marzano." Homegrown varieties include the "Red Cherry," "Bonney Best," "Marglobe," "Jubilee," "Rutgers," and "Beefsteak."

Many Americans who have grown their own tomatoes or who remember the tomatoes of other decades believe that the various hybrids and commercially cultivated tomatoes marketed today have lost a great deal of their natural flavor in return for easy availability on a year-round basis and a high yield. As John L. and Karen Hess observed in *The Taste of America* (1977):

> *More and more of the produce grown in those far-off factories of the soil is harvested by machine. It is bred for rough handling, which it gets. A chemical is sprayed on trees to force all the fruit to "'ripen"—that is, change color—at once, in time for a monster harvester to strike the tree and catch the fruit in its canvas maw. Tomatoes are picked hard green and gassed with ethylene in trucks or in chambers at the market, whereupon they turn a sort of neon red. Of course, they taste like nothing at all, but the taste of real tomatoes has so far faded from memory that, even for local markets, farmers now pick tomatoes that are just turning pink. This avoids the spoilage that occurred when they used to pick tomatoes red-ripe.*

Industry terms for the ripening process of tomatoes includes "green" (the surface of the tomato is completely green); "breakers" (a break in the color from green to yellow-pink or red on 10 percent of the surface); "turning" (at least 10 but not more than 30 percent has changed color); and "pink" (30 to 60 percent has changed color). "Vine ripened" actually means that the tomato was harvested when it was turning pink, although greenhouse-grown tomatoes may well be shipped red. Tomatoes are also one of the most successful crops grown hydroponically. U.S. per capita consumption of tomatoes in 1997 was 16.1 pounds.

Green tomatoes are particularly popular in the South and Midwest, where they are often fried or made into relishes or "green tomato pie."

GREEN TOMATO PIE

Chop up 8 peeled green tomatoes and place in a saucepan with 2 T. cider vinegar and 2 T. butter and cook on medium heat about 10 min. In a bowl combine 1 c. sugar, 2 T. cornstarch, and ½ t. cinnamon, then add to tomato mixture. Heat through, stirring, remove from heat, and pour into a pie crust. Layer over a top crust, slash the pastry a few times to release steam, and bake at 425° for 10 min. Reduce heat to 350° and bake for another 20 min. or until the crust is light brown.

Tom Collins. A cocktail made with gin, citrus juice, and soda water, customarily served in a tall glass called a 'Tom Collins glass" or "Collins glass." The drink is supposedly named after the bartender who created it, though the moment of creation is highly speculative. The first American reference to the drink is in 1909, but H. L. Mencken, in *The American Language,* Supplement I (1945), guessed that it came out of the post-Civil War era. The original Tom Collins was supposedly made with Old Tom gin, which was slightly sweet, but another drink, the "John Collins," was customarily made with Holland gin, with its more pronounced, aromatic flavor. The problem is that the first printed reference to a John Collins is in 1865, and, suggests the *Oxford English Dictionary,* it may be of American origins. Mencken writes of the John Collins, "Who John Collins was I do not know. Sidney J. Baker, author of A *Popular Dictionary of Australian Slang* (Melbourne, n.d.) tells me that the John Collins was known in Australia so long ago as 1865, but he does not list it in his dictionary." The "fizz" is a similar drink made with crushed ice in the blend and dates back at least to the 1860s.

Whichever cocktail came first, American bartenders at the beginning of the twentieth century mixed both, making a John Collins with dry London gin and a Tom Collins with Old Tom gin. This latter gin gradually disappeared from the American market, however, and the dry London gin replaced it. After a while both drinks went by the name "Tom Collins," and today the cocktail is made with dry gin.

Still later a carbonated citrus soda appeared called "Tom Collins mix," which most bartenders use instead of fresh citrus juice and sugar.

TOM COLLINS

In a glass with ice cubes stir 1 T. sugar syrup, the juice of 1 lemon, and 3–4 oz. gin. Fill glass with soda water or seltzer.

Tom Fuller. A dish of cooked corn, peas, beans, and dried venison similar to succotash. It was originally a Native American dish of the Mississippi region called *sofkee.* The reason for the name "Tom Fuller" is unknown, but the dish was popular in the beginning of the nineteenth century in the southern Appalachian Mountains.

tortilla. A flat, unleavened cake made of cornmeal or white flour cooked on a griddle and used in a variety of dishes of Mexican origin, including as a bread, in a casserole, or as a sandwichlike holder for other foods. Tortillas are a staple of Mexican-American and TEX-MEX cookery. The word comes from the Spanish-American diminutive for the Spanish *torta,* "round cake." (In Spain, the *tortilla española* is more like an omelet.) The word was first printed in English circa 1690.

In the United States tortillas are usually bought in groceries and are rarely made at home, except in the Southwest. In Arizona, where a great deal of wheat is grown, they are often made from white flour and are called *tortillas de harina de trigo,* as opposed to those made with cornmeal flour, *tortillas de masa harina.* When a tortilla is filled with meat and sauce and rolled, it is called a TACO, which is often fried in hot lard. An ENCHILADA. is somewhat more elaborate, with CHILE peppers and cheese as well as other ingredients in the stuffing. Tortillas now outsell bagels and English muffins in the United States.

"Tortilla soup" is a southwestern dish made with chicken soup and seasonings with a base of fried tortilla strips.

"Tortilla chips" (or "taco chips") are cut-up fried pieces of tortilla, the first commercial example being "Doritos," which appeared in 1966 and are now produced by Frito-Lay, Inc.

TORTILLA SOUP

In a large pot heat 4 T. corn oil. Sauté 1 chopped large onion and 3 cloves chopped garlic for about 1 min. Cut 4 tortillas into ½-in. strips and fry in oil until crisp.

Pour in 8 c. chicken broth, add 4 skinned, seeded, chopped tomatoes, ½ t. salt, ¼ t. black pepper, ¼ t. ground cumin, ¼ c. chopped cilantro, and 1 seeded jalapeño or serrano chile pepper. Bring to a boil and simmer for about 20–30 min. Serve in bowls with garnishes of shredded Monterey Jack cheese and more fried tortilla strips. Serves 6.

tortoni. Also, "biscuit tortoni." An Italian-American ice cream with crushed almonds or macaroons sprinkled on top (1940). The confection originated in the eighteenth century at the Café Napolitain in Paris, and was named after the owner, Tortoni. After the arrival of Italian immigrants in New York, the ice cream became featured in every Italian-American restaurant (and often called "biscuit tortoni"). The word was first printed in English in 1922.

Tortoni can be made simply by mixing finely chopped almonds into vanilla ice cream and topping the cup with more chopped almonds before freezing. Macaroons may be substituted for the almonds.

tostada. A deep-fried corn chip popular as a snack in Mexican-American and Tex-Mex cooking. The name is from the Spanish for "toasted," and first appears in English print in 1935.

TOSTADA

Cut corn tortillas into wedges, fry in hot oil, drain, and sprinkle with salt, and, if desired, minced garlic. Serve with guacamole and other appetizer dips or sauces.

trade whiskey. Whiskey traded to the Indians in the nineteenth century. The term later became associated with any cheap, inferior spirit.

transparent pie. Also, "transparent pudding." A nineteenth-century midwestern custard-style dessert made with a smooth filling, without nuts or fruits, giving the pie a semitranslucent appearance.

TRANSPARENT PIE

Beat 3 eggs until frothy, add 2 T. sugar and 1½ c. heavy cream until well blended. Add 3 T. fruit jelly, stir in the zest of one lemon and 1 T. lemon juice. Pour the filling into a pastry crust and bake at 350° for 30–35 min. until set. Let cool on rack.

trappers' butter. Trappers' term for bone marrow of a killed animal, which was often made into a thickened broth.

trash fish. A fishermen's term (dating in print to 1940) for any fish that has no commercial value. The species of such fish may change whenever one comes into favor and another goes out. Trash fish are usually sold for animal fodder or manufactured products.

Treasure Cave. A blue-veined cheese, also called "Minnesota Blue," ripened in sandstone caves. It is produced by the Treasure Cave Blue Cheese Company in Faribault, Minnesota.

Trenton cracker. A light, puffy round cracker made from wheat flour, vegetable shortening, salt, and yeast. It is a traditional eastern cracker used in oyster stews.

The Trenton cracker was first made in 1848 by Adam and John Exton, two English immigrants who created the item in their Trenton, New Jersey, bakery. They called it the "Exton Oyster and Butter Cracker and Wine Scroll Biscuit." Within a short time more than thirty competitors were making imitations, including Ezekiel Pullen, owner of the Pullen Cracker Company in Trenton. This company was later sold and in 1887 became the Original Trenton Cracker Company, which in 1962 bought exclusive rights to the Exton products. Today the crackers are stamped before baking with the company's initials, "O.T.C.," which is a trademark of the company, now located in Lambertville, New Jersey.

The crackers are still served in chowders and stews or eaten buttered with a small bit of horseradish. They are called "Trentons" for short.

trevally. Any of a variety of Pacific fish in the genus *Caranx,* but especially *C. georgianus.* The origins of its name are obscure, dating in print to 1880. In Hawaii the fish is known as the *ulua.*

triggerfish. Also, "leatherjacket." Any of a variety of fishes of the family Balistidae that is found in Atlantic waters and is enjoyed in the South as fillets. Triggerfish have a second, "trigger" spine that releases the first spine—hence, the name (1880).

tripe. The stomach of a cow, sheep, or pig. Its name is from the Old French *tripe,* and first appears in English in the fourteenth century.

Owing to its perishable nature and the difficulty of cleaning it, tripe has never been a popular meat with most Americans, although it has some ethnic interest among Mediterranean immigrants and Chinese in this country. The only American recipe of note, given below, was developed at Boston's Parker House Hotel.

TRIPE

Boil a piece of tripe (about 8 oz.) until tender, cool, then soak in milk for 2 hr. Sprinkle with 2 T. white wine, 1 T. oil, ½ c. bread crumbs, 1 t. vinegar, a dash of paprika, and salt, pepper, and thyme to taste. Broil until golden brown. Serve with a mustard sauce made by combining 1 cup demiglaze, 2 t. Dijon mustard , 1 oz. white wine, ½ oz. white vinegar, 1 small shallot finely minced, peppercorns, and 2 T. heavy cream.

---

trout. Any of a variety of fishes of the genera *Salvelinus* and *Salmo* cultured throughout the world both for sport and for food. The name derives from the Latin *tructa*.

As did sturgeon and salmon in the Colonial era, trout became an everyday food for the first settlers, and there seemed little reason to imitate the efforts of the French, which culminated in 1852 with the construction of the first public-owned trout hatchery, to propagate fish commercially. American anglers merely had to dip their lines in the rivers and come up with large, beautiful fish perfect for pan-frying on the spot; America's first great fishing author, Frank Forester, complained in his *Fish and Fishing* (1849) that Americans did not take their flyfishing with all due seriousness. A hatchery was set up in 1864 at Mumford, New York, by Seth Green, for the days when anglers filled their baskets with forty trout in an afternoon were almost over. When the end came—as a result of industrial pollution and invasion of the trout streams, as well as overfishing—it came quickly, and after the Civil War the trout population decreased at a depressing rate. It was the introduction of the "German brown trout" (*Salmo trutta*) to North America in 1883, and Seth Green's stocking of his own hatcheries with that fish in 1886, that caused a comeback of the trout in America, and before long the native rainbow trout (*S. gairdneri*) was being introduced as far away as New Zealand and South Africa.

Protective measures also helped restore the trout populations, and, since American anglers had by then become serious about their sport, efforts were made to maintain the balance of nature in trout streams. U.S.

commercial landings of trout totaled only 303,000 pounds in 1997.

Some of the finest literature on trout has come from American authors, from specialists like George Michel Lucien La Branche, Charles Zebulon Southard, Arthur Flick, Sparse Grey Hackle, and Ernest Schwiebert to outdoorsmen like Zane Grey (who wrote mostly fishing books in his later life), John Steinbeck, and Ernest Hemingway, whose "Big Two-Hearted River" is a classic short story for its description of the challenge and beauty of the sport.

The trout species of the most culinary interest include: the "brook trout" (*Salvelinus fontinalis*), also called a "brookie" and other names, and the "brown trout," both found in nearly every state in the Union; the "cutthroat trout" (*Salmo clarki*), so called because of slash marks on the throat; the DOLLY VARDEN (*Salvelinus malma*); the "golden trout" (*Salmo aquabonita*); the "lake trout" (*Salvelinus namaycush*), in Maine called the TOGUE or the "mackinaw" (possibly from its coloring, which resembles a plaid mackinaw coat or cloth, which itself refers to an island in Michigan called Mackinac) or the "gray trout" (in Canada); "salmon trout," and the "rainbow trout."

Trout in America is prepared in a variety of ways, from simple pan-frying or grilling to French recipes such as *amandine* (with almonds) and *meunière* (with browned butter) to the Swiss *truite au bleu*, by which a freshly caught trout is cooked in a court bouillon that turns the skin blue.

truck farm. Also, "truck garden." A garden producing vegetables intended for sale in the market. Today there is a double meaning to the word. Originally the word "truck," derived from an Old French word, *trogue*, for "barter," referred to the vegetables themselves. By the eighteenth century in America people referred to "market truck," meaning fresh produce brought to the market, and "truck farm" dates to 1865 in print.

Truck farms became very important to the agricultural economy of the South, so that seasonal crops decreased small farmers' dependency on cash crops and agribusiness.

Much later, when motorized trucks began carrying fresh produce to city markets, it was quite natural for "truck farm" to take on a double meaning, both for the vegetables themselves and for the means of conveyance.

truffle. Any of a variety of subterranean ascomycetous fungi in the genus *Tuber*, from Middle French.

The term has been used in English since the sixteenth century.

Truffles have long been a delicacy in Europe, where they are found by specially trained dogs and pigs under oak trees. The most famous truffles are the black variety (*T. melanosporum*) grown in France's Périgord region, and it is this truffle that American scientists have experimented with growing in a laboratory, first successfully done by Dr. Moshe Shifrine and Dr. Randy Dorian in Woodland, California, in the late 1980s.

"Chocolate truffles" are chocolate candies (sometimes with a filling of chocolate ganache or other flavors) molded and dusted with powdered chocolate to look like black truffles.

tuckahoe. A starchy root vegetable of the arum family (Araceae) commonly used in Colonial times as a flour additive or as a flour itself. The term dates in print to 1605, derives from a Virginia Native American word (*tockawoughe*), and came to have a perjorative reference to poor Virginians who could not afford wheat flour, although tuckahoe was also used as a starch in puddings and blancmange.

tuna. Also, "tuna fish." Any of a variety of marine fishes of the genus *Thunnus*, although the name is also applied to some related species. The name is derived from the Latin *thunnus*, and is a variation on the English name for the fish, "tunny." The *Oxford English Dictionary* says tuna is "Spanish American" and a "name in California for the tunny." The word dates only to 1880 in print.

The tuna is a member of the mackerel family (Scombridae), with six species available at market in the United States, where most of the catch has been from Pacific waters. Not until 1960 were significant commercial catches made in the Atlantic, and the industry continues to be centered in California.

The most important species for culinary interest include: the "albacore" (*T. alalunga*), called the "tombo" in Hawaii, the most desirable tuna for the canning industry, which labels its product "white-meat" tuna; the "bluefin tuna" (*T. thynnus*), the largest tuna, weighing up to sixteen hundred pounds; the "bonito" (*Sarda sarda* in the Atlantic and *S. chiliensis* in the Pacific), which cannot legally be labeled "tuna" and must be put in brine before cooking (its name is from the Spanish for "beautiful"); the "false albacore" (*Euthynnus alletteratus*), also called the "little tunny" or "bonito"; the "kawakawa" (*E. yaito*); the "skipjack tuna" (*E. pelamis*), also called "oceanic bonito," "water-melon," "oceanic skipjack," "Arctic bonito," and, in Hawaii, *aku*; and the "yellowfin tuna" (*T. albacares*), which in Hawaii is called *ahi* and which is the principal fish of the California tuna industry.

Canned tuna is designated as "solid" or "fancy" (with several large pieces), "chunk" (smaller pieces), and "flaked" or "grated."

The FDA Standards of Identity require that "white" tuna must be limited to albacore; "light," any tuna not darker than the Munsell color value 5.3; "dark," all tuna darker than the value 5.3. "Blended" applies to a blend of tuna flakes.

Tuna may be canned in oil or water and may be seasoned.

Americans have, since the 1980s, eaten an increasing amount of fresh tuna (3.6 pounds per capita), with about 456 million pounds (373.8 million from U.S. vessels) brought to market in 1997. It is usually grilled or sautéed as steaks, but most often it is served from a can as a filling for a tunafish sandwich or a tuna-fish salad, in both cases mixed with mayonnaise. A "tuna melt" is a grilled sandwich made with tuna fish and American cheese. The "tuna casserole" has long been a staple of the American dinner table, and the recipe given by the Campbell's Soup Company on the back of its cans is considered a "classic."

TUNA CASSEROLE

In a casserole mix 1 can Campbell's Condensed Cream of Celery Soup with ½ c. milk. Add 1 c. peas, 2 T. chopped pimiento, and 2 seven-ounce cans drained, flaked tuna. Add 2 c. cooked egg noodles, if desired. Bake for 25 minutes at 425° until hot. In a saucepan combine 1 T. butter or margarine and 2 T. bread crumbs and sauté until brown. Top casserole with bread crumbs and bake for 5 more minutes.

turkey (*Meleagris gallopavo*). A large native North American game bird widely domesticated here and abroad. With its brownish feathers and wattled head and neck, the turkey is certainly an unattractive fowl, but its associations with Colonial American history and its indigenous character throughout the United States caused Benjamin Franklin to remark, "I wish the Bald Eagle had not been chosen as the representation of our country. . . . The turkey is . . . a much more respectable bird, and withal a true original native of America."

The turkey proliferated throughout Mexico, the Southwest, and the East. The Plains Indians and New England tribes caught the bird in the wild with little trouble, whereas the Aztecs and others of the Southwest had domesticated the birds very early so that by the time the Spaniards arrived in Mexico, the turkey was a staple part of the Native American diet.

It is not known who first brought the turkey back to Europe (according to Waverley Root, there is a turkeylike bird woven into the Bayeux tapestries of 1087), but by the first quarter of the sixteenth century Spanish explorers had brought the bird home. One English chronicler of the seventeenth century noted that turkeys were brought to England about 1524, giving rise to the ditty, "Turkeys, Carps, Hoppes, Piccarell, and Beer, Came into England in one year." By 1570 Englishman Thomas Trusser could vouch that the domesticated turkey already formed part of the common farmer's "Christmas husbandlie fare," and across the channel the bird was highly esteemed.

It is not entirely clear how the bird got its name. The *American Heritage Cookbook* suggests "turkey" is a corruption of *furkee*, a Native American name for the bird. But most authorities believe the name was the result of the bird's being confused with the guinea fowl, which the Portuguese had brought to Europe from Guinea, through the dominion of Turkey, so that both birds were called "turkeys" in the sixteenth century. Even after the confusion was cleared up and the American fowl took the name "turkey," the Linnaean system devised in the eighteenth century christened it with the Latin word for the guinea fowl, *Meleagris*.

The turkey throve in Europe under various names: The French called it *d'inde* (later *dinde*), "of India"; the Germans called it *calecutische Hahn*, "Calcutta hen"; the Native Americans themselves called it *peru*, with no reference to the country of that name.

Captain John Smith, who explored the Virginia territory during the first two decades of the seventeenth century, spoke of turkeys brought to feasts by the Native Americans, but at least one authority doubts that they brought turkeys to the famous 1621 feast that initiated the tradition of THANKSGIVING in the Plymouth Colony. It is curious that the colony's governor, William Bradford, did not mention the bird in his transcript of the feast's menu (which probably extended over days), but another attendant, Governor Edward Winslow, described how the settlers brought in their harvest and sent out "foure men on fowling," who "killed as much fowle as, with a little helpe beside [possibly from the Indians], served the Company almost a weeke." It is a safe assumption that these fowl included wild turkeys.

Turkey was certainly served at the Pilgrims' next Thanksgiving, on July 30, 1623. The term "Thanks-giving turkey" was in circulation by 1829, and Thanksgiving itself was referred to as "Turkey Day" by 1916.

In the early days turkey was a frequently served dish, usually a wild bird, sometimes weighing up to forty pounds, and by 1820 turkeys were cheaper than chickens in Kentucky. In other parts of the Colonies, however, the wild turkey was nearly wiped out by hunters, so that by the end of the eighteenth century the bird had virtually disappeared east of the Connecticut River. After World War II the federal government began protecting the wild turkey, so that by 1991 the bird's population had risen from thirty thousand in the 1930s to more than 4 million today, and they are now found in forty-nine states. A small, seven-to ten-pound breed called the "Bronze" is, however, marketed as "wild," even though it is, in fact, farm raised. It tends to have a gamier taste but drier flesh than the more common farm-raised breeds.

Domesticated turkeys filled the void rapidly, and turkey was readily available to most people year-round. But the bird's association with Thanksgiving became so distinct after President Abraham Lincoln proclaimed the last Thursday in November as the official holiday that most Americans ate turkey only on that day and perhaps on Christmas. In 1935 the per capita consumption of turkey in the United States was only 1.7 pounds. But increased interest in turkey as a nutritious meat and the selling of various turkey products and parts not requiring the cooking of a whole bird have now raised the consumption figure to 18 pounds per person, with 300 million turkeys produced in 1998.

Today turkeys are raised on more than seven thousand farms (North Carolina leads the nation in turkey production), inspected by the USDA and sold both fresh-killed or frozen, their average weight being between eight and sixteen pounds. Most of these are young hens of the White Holland breed (first used for commercial production in the late 1950s), for mature "tom turkeys" are increasingly rare. Breast meat is the most valued part of the turkey by Americans, and one may buy such meat separately, sometimes smoked. Other turkey meat may be compressed into turkey roll, used for sandwiches. There is even a "self-basting turkey," injected with oils beneath the skin. In some instances, the poultry producer also inserts a small plastic thermometer in the bird's skin that pops out when the turkey is cooked to the right temperature.

Ninety-two percent of the turkeys consumed are eaten at home. Of the 3 percent consumed in restaurants, 74 percent are prepared as sandwiches, 26 percent as entrées.

American recipe writers have over the years come up with all manner of methods of cooking a turkey, from covering it with foil to placing it on a rack, from turning the bird on its back to cooking it in a very slow oven. The simplest way to cook a turkey is to wash and clean the bird, stuff it, baste it with butter, place it in a large roasting pan, and set it in a 450° oven for fifteen minutes. Turn down the heat to 350° and continue cooking and basting until a fork inserted in the leg joints shows the juices running clear.

In Cajun country turkeys are often deep-fried.

Any number of side dishes are traditionally served with turkey—cranberry sauce, sweet potatoes, turnips, and, of course, the stuffing.

Turkey Devonshire. A dish of turkey breast and bacon on toast with a Cheddar cheese sauce, created in 1934 by Frank Blandi, a restaurateur in Pitsburg, Ohio. The sauce itself became so popular that it is often used on other dishes.

turnip (*Brassica rapa*). An Old World plant bearing a large yellow or white root that is usually boiled and served as a vegetable. The word comes from the Latin *nāpus,* which in Middle English became *nepe,* and is first recorded as "turnip" in 1533.

The turnip, native to Asia Minor, was eaten in Europe in the Middle Ages and cultivated in England by the seventeenth century. The French and English brought the plant to America, though the root was of little culinary interest until the eighteenth century. The "common turnip" (*B. rapa*), also called the "white turnip" for its coloring, is the most available variety in United States markets, though in the South the "rutabaga" (*B. napus rutabaga*), also called the "big yellow" or "Canadian turnip," is particularly well liked, often mashed and served with butter. (The name "rutabaga" comes from dialectical Swedish *rotabagge,* "baggy root.")

There are records of turnip cultivation in Canada as of 1540, and Virginia had them by 1609, but it took another century and more before they found their way into southern soil. They were very successful with the Native Americans, who preferred them to their native "Indian turnip" (*Arisaema dracontium,* also called "green dragon" or "dragonroot," and *A. triphyllum,* also called "Jack-in-the-pulpit," "starchwort," and "bog onion"). Today the turnip is widely planted throughout the United States.

"Turnip greens" are often cooked with bacon as a vegetable.

turnover. A pastry filled with fruit preserves, chopped meat, or cooked sauce (1605).

turtle (order Testudinate). Any of a large number of fresh- or saltwater reptiles having a shell, a horny beak, and a wide array of colorings. There are about 225 species in the world, found at sea, in lakes, rivers, ponds, woodlands, fields, and pastures. The most treasured—and today one of the rarest—for the American connoisseur has always been the "diamond-back terrapin" (*Malaclemys terrapin*), whose name comes from a Virginian Algonquian name, *toolepeiwa,* and its diamond-shaped polygonal *scutes* with concentric ridges on its back. The "green turtle" (*Chelonia mydas*) of the Caribbean is also eaten in the South with great favor, while other species—such as the southeastern "alligator snapping turtle" (*Macroclemys temminckii*), the "common snapping turtle" (*Chelydra serpentina*), the "caouane" (*M. lacertina*), and the "loggerhead" (*Caretta caretta*)—are also considered good food turtles. The eggs from various species, too, are of culinary interest.

The word "turtle" may derive from the French *tortues,* from which we also get "tortoise." "Cooter" (also "slider" in the Mississippi Valley) is a southern term derived from the African *kuta* (dating in print to 1832) for a variety of freshwater species of the genus *Chrysemys* found mainly in the eastern United States. In *Hoppin' John's Lowcountry Cooking* (1992) John Martin Taylor notes that in the South the word "turtle" is reserved for sea turtles. Europeans have depended on the West Indies, South America, Africa, and Australia for these delicacies.

The earliest explorers of North America commented on the variety and numbers of turtles here, and Thomas Harriot, who wrote *A Briefe and True Report of the New Found Land of Virginia* (1588), spoke of turtles a yard in breadth and found the meat and eggs good eating. By the seventeenth century turtle meat was being exported back to England, where it became an expensive item of exotica. But in America turtle was cooked by most coastal settlers, who used the meat as steaks, in stews, or in soups. So popular was the turtle that Eliza Leslie, in her *Directions for Cookery,* published in Philadelphia in 1837, noted that turtle soup was a time-consuming, difficult process best left to a "first-rate cook" or ordered in a "turtle-soup house." This appetite for turtle led quickly to the near extinction of several species, including the diamondback terrapin, and before the middle of the nineteenth century the American rich had joined their European peers in the consumption of the few turtles that were caught. As a result, turtle dishes became the pride of the elite social clubs in cities like Baltimore and Philadelphia, whose wealthy citizens argued over the correct way to treat a tortoise. Marylanders insisted a turtle should be the base for a sherry-tinged clear consommé, while their northern neighbors preferred the turtle meat in a cream sauce. According to Evan Jones, members of Philadelphia's Rittenhouse Club and Baltimore's Maryland Club met with an impartial jury in 1893 to decide the matter of taste: The turtle consommé won.

By 1920 the prices for terrapin had grown so high that even the wealthy found them too much, and, fortunately, the species has since then been restored to a certain extent.

In other parts of the country other species have been consumed; in Florida and the South the green sea turtle has been prized as steak meat or used for turtle soup. Today sea turtles are being commercially raised, especially in the Cayman Islands. Turtle eggs are also a southern delicacy.

"Snapper soup," a specialty of Old Original Bookbinder's Restaurant in Philadelphia, where it was introduced in 1941, is made from farm-grown snapping turtles.

Turtle is today found frozen, canned, or in prepared soups.

TURTLE SOUP

Brown 1 lb. chopped turtle meat in a kettle, add 1 c. water, bring to a boil, then simmer, covered, until tender. In a saucepan mix 2 stalks chopped celery, 2 chopped carrots, 1 chopped onion, 2 c. chopped cabbage, 8 peppercorns, 3 sprigs parsley, 2 bay leaves, 2 cloves garlic, 1 ½ t. salt, and 5 c. water. Bring to boil, cover, simmer for 1 hr., then strain. Stir in turtle meat, add ½ c. dry sherry, heat, and serve. Serves 6.

---

tutti-frutti. A maceration of fruits and brandy especially popular in the South, where ladies would add one of each fruit of the season to one pint brandy along with an amount of sugar equal to a quart of fruit. The mixture would be stirred each morning and kept for the season.

Tutti-frutti is also an ice cream flavored with various fruits. The term is from the Italian, meaning "all fruits," and in America dates to 1875 in print.. There was also a gum-ball candy called by this name in New York City in the 1880s.

TV dinner. A meal of meat, poultry, or fish, together with vegetables and dessert, all precooked and packed on an aluminum plate, frozen, and sold in groceries and supermarkets (1950). The meal has simply to be heated in the oven, and its self-contained character makes it easy to eat it away from the dining-room table while watching television. After World War II many frozen foods appeared on the market, but the concept of a frozen, fully prepared meal under the name "TV Dinner" was marketed most successfully by Clarke and Gilbert Swanson of the C. A. Swanson Company, of Omaha, Nebraska, who marketed a turkey-and-mashed-potatoes meal under the trademark "TV Dinner" in 1952. The name was later dropped in favor of "Frozen Dinner" by the end of the 1960s.

Twinkies. Trademark name for a confection of small oblong sponge cakes with a cream filling. They were the creation of James A. Dewar, manager of Chicago's Continental Bakery, and named after a billboard ad for Twinkle Toe Shoes he'd seen in St. Louis. They were sold under the Hostess baked goods line. The first filling (originally done by hand) was a "banana creme," but was changed in the 1940s to vanilla creme. Hostess today produces about fifty-two thousand Twinkies per hour.

So associated with JUNK FOOD were Twinkies that, in 1978, a San Francisco man named Dan White, who shot and killed the city's mayor, used what became known as the "Twinkie defense," meaning that White's consumption of Twinkies and candy bars before the shooting radically altered his frame of mind and made him momentarily insane. (White was convicted on a lesser charge and later committed suicide.)

tzimmes. Also, "tzimmis" and "tsimmes." Any of a wide variety of Jewish-American casserole dishes made of various sweetened vegetables, fruits, and, sometimes, meats. The word is from the Yiddish, *tsimes*, meaning something complicated and fussy, and dates in print to 1890.

U

Universal Product Code.
A printed series of symbols on a prepackaged food item in a retail store that identifies the type of product, manufacturer or distributor, contents, and price. The symbols are printed in binary forms that are scanned by a low-powered laser beam near the cash register. The laser converts these symbols into an electronic code that is then imprinted and tallied on the cash register's tape. This allows for fewer mistakes for the customer, higher efficiency for the store, and an automatic record of sales and inventory. There is even one Universal Product Code (UPC) scanner, called "Positalker," that enunciates in a female voice the price of each item as it passes by the laser beam.

The UPC was devised by a committee formed in 1970 by manufacturers and grocers and began to appear on food products as of 1973.

upside-down cake. A cake that is baked with its filling or flavoring on the bottom and then inverted before serving. The first mention in print of such a cake was in 1920, and was so listed in the 1936 Sears, Roebuck Catalog, but the cake is somewhat older.

Sometimes, the cake is cooked in a skillet.

u'u (*Myripristis murdjan*). A popular Hawaiian fish of the Pacific reefs.

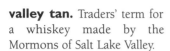

valley tan. Traders' term for a whiskey made by the Mormons of Salt Lake Valley.

vanilla (*Vanilla planifolia*). Also called "vanilla bean." The seed pod of a tropical American orchid. It is frequently used as a flavoring, especially in desserts.

The word is from the Spanish *vainilla*, "little sheath." Vanilla was brought to Europe by the Spanish conquistadores returning from Mexico. The word is first mentioned in English in 1662 as a flavoring used by the Native Americans with their chocolate, but although it became a highly desirable substance in France and England, Americans were not much familiar with vanilla until ice cream became popular in the late eighteenth century. Thomas Jefferson discovered its virtues in France and on arriving back in the United States in 1789 sent for some pods from Paris, which must have come from Central America in the first place.

By the nineteenth century Americans developed a passion for vanilla, especially as an ice-cream flavoring (by 1932 it was estimated that 75–80 percent of all ice cream was vanilla) and today America uses more vanilla than any other country. The supply of vanilla beans, however, has never met demand, so substitutes, especially "vanilla extract," were developed. Vanilla extract (or "vanilla essence"), created by Joseph Burnett in 1847, was made by soaking vanilla beans in grain alcohol and water (requirements stipulate that bottled extract must contain at least 35 percent alcohol; "vanilla flavoring" may contain less than 35 percent alcohol). There is also a concentrated vanilla extract that may be used as a flavoring for regular vanilla extract. During Prohibition, some producers removed the alcohol from their product as a temperance precaution.

"Vanillin" is a flavoring obtained either from vanilla itself or from various balsams and resins; it is chemically a crystalline compound, $C_8H_8O_3$.

veal. The meat of a slaughtered calf. The word is from the Latin *vitellus*, which became, in Middle English, *veel*.

Esteemed as a delicate meat since biblical times, veal achieved its greatest popularity in Italy. By the Renaissance it was valued in France, Germany, Austria, Holland, and elsewhere in Europe, where the high price of the meat never dissuaded connoisseurs from enjoying it. In America, where beef cattle were not plentiful until the middle of the nineteenth century, veal was not much appreciated. Also, the abundance of grass and fodder in America's Midwest promoted the growing of cattle to their full size for BEEF, while in Europe the availability of pastureland was severely restricted, thereby making the slaughter of an unweaned calf more the norm.

Veal was eaten, especially in the South and Midwest, but it was often ill treated by overcooking. It was only with the arrival of Italian and German immigrants in the late nineteenth and early twentieth centuries that an appetite for veal developed in the eastern cities, with schnitzels and veal scallopine showing up on restaurant menus. Consumption of veal by Americans in the 1940s was nearly ten pounds per capita per year, but, largely owing to the high cost of the meat, consumption had fallen to 1.4 pounds by 1992 (254.7 million pounds total) and to less than a pound by 1998. It is still mostly eaten in Italian and French restaurants, where adaptations of Old World recipes have resulted in dishes like VEAL PARMESAN and VEAL FRANCESE, whose names are unknown abroad.

The three basic categories of veal are "bob veal," usually the meat of a calf up to one month old; "veal," between one and three months; and "baby beef" or "calves' meat," between three and twelve months. These categories are not strict, however, and the terminology is inexact. A colloquial expression for a very young calf, especially a weakling, is a *deacon*.

The best veal, called "milk-fed veal," is usually considered that from unweaned calves. A feeding system called the "Dutch method" (because it was developed in Holland) raises the calves on a special formula of milk solids, water, and nutrients, producing an anemic animal.

The main cuts of veal include the "primal leg" (for veal scallops), the "primal loin" (for chops), the "primal rib" (for chops and roasts), the "primal shoulder" (for veal rolls or blade roasts), the "primal shank" (for braised dishes like the Italian menu item *osso buco),* the "primal breast" (for riblets and veal breast), and the "primal flank" (for stew meat).

veal francese. A dish of pounded veal scallops cooked in butter and white wine. The cutlets are often dipped in egg and flour before cooking.

The name is Italian, meaning "veal French style," which seems to indicate nothing more than the use of white wine in the recipe and a lighter treatment than in many Italian-American recipes for veal scallops, which are often covered with tomato sauce and cheese. There is no specific or traditional dish in Italy by this name.

VEAL FRANCESE

Pound 4 veal scallops until thin and tender, sauté in 2 t. butter until browned, then remove from skillet. Add to skillet 1 T. butter and ½ c. dry white wine, scraping brown bits from skillet. Reduce, burn off alcohol, pour sauce over veal scallops, and serve with a slice of lemon and a bit of chopped parsley.

veal Parmesan. Also, "veal parmigiana" and "veal alla parmigiana." A dish of pounded veal scallops that are breaded, sautéed, topped with mozzarella cheese and tomato sauce, and heated until the cheese is melted. Although it is a dish in the Italian style and a staple of Italian-American restaurants, there is no dish specifically by this name in Italy. The name probably derives from Parmesan cheese, a grating cheese originally made in Parma, Italy, and now made there and in the United States, though the dish does not necessarily contain Parmesan cheese.

VEAL PARMESAN

Dip veal scallops in an egg-and-milk mixture, then in a plate of bread crumbs. Sauté in butter or olive oil until browned. Top with a thin slice of mozzarella cheese and some tomato sauce, and either bake in a 400° oven or put under broiler until cheese is melted.

vegetable liver. A Jewish-American dish made of eggplant and seasonings as a substitute for chopped

chicken liver, which is forbidden at certain times under KOSHER dietary laws.

vegetable oil. Any oil made from various vegetables and seeds, such as sesame, safflower, corn, peanut, soy, and olive, used both for cooking and for salad dressings. These oils are pressed in large cylinders that squeeze out 95 percent of the oil in the seed or are extracted through a method invented in Germany in 1870 by which the seed is treated with a bath of solvent such as hexane. The often seen term "cold-pressed" has no real authority, though it is often used by the food-processing industry to indicate a superior method of oil extraction. The fact is that all oils reach at least 130–150° F. during pressing.

The usual distinction between an "oil" and a "fat" is that the former is liquid and the latter solid. Saturated oils are those in which each of the molecule's carbon atoms is paired with two attached hydrogen atoms; if there are fewer than two hydrogens per carbon, the oil is unsaturated, in which case adjacent carbon atoms make a double bond. If there is one double bond in the oil molecule, the oil is monounsaturated; if there are two or more double bonds, it is polyunsaturated. These differences are mainly the concerns of nutritionists who fear that the more saturated the oil, the greater the likelihood that it will be turned into cholesterol by the body. Generally speaking, most vegetable oils are polyunsaturated. A "hydrogenated oil" is one in which the polyunsaturated oils are saturated with hydrogen in order to stabilize them.

"Crude" or "virgin" oils are not processed after pressing.

vegetable (plant) protein. According to the United States Department of Agriculture guidelines, "Vegetable protein products derived from soybeans may be used as binders or extenders in such meat and poultry products as sausages, luncheon meats, soups, sauces and gravies. Sometimes, they are the main ingredients in meat and poultry product substitutes."

veggies. A slang term for vegetables. It has been in use only in the last two decades and derives from the maternal admonishment to "eat your veggies" (1965).

vending machine. A coin-operated dispenser of various items, but especially food like candy, snacks, soda, and coffee. The idea actually dates back to Hero of Alexandria, who in the first century introduced a holy water-dispenser that required five drachmas. But the first modern food-vending machines were called Tutti Frutti machines, set up on New York City train platforms by the Adams gum company in 1897. The AUTOMAT was a restaurant that offered customers a wide range of foods set behind glass windows that opened when a coin was inserted in the slot. When candy rationing began in America during World War II, the Austin Baking Company created the peanut-butter-and-cheese cracker for vending machines. Today vending machines dispense hot, cooked, microwaved foods like popcorn, pizza, and french-fried potatoes.

Today the National Automatic Merchandising Association has more than two thousand members.

venison. The flesh of the deer, which is usually marinated and cooked as a steak, a stew, or a barbecue. The word is from the Latin *venatio*, "hunting."

Venison was eaten by Native Americans, who stored it for the winter, as Captain John Smith noted on his travels in Virginia in 1607. The woods were filled with deer, and the early Colonists followed the Native Americans' example of drying the meat by grilling it over fires. By the nineteenth century venison was a common meat in large cities' markets, but few could vouch for its freshness and so treated the meat with marinades and heavy, highly seasoned sauces that lessened its gaminess. Venison with a pronounced gamy taste is colloquially called "balsam steak."

Today venison is readily available in restaurants during the season, but it is illegal to sell a deer freshly killed by a private hunter unless it has been inspected by government inspectors.

vermouth. An aromatized wine flavored with various herbs and spices and made in either dry or sweet varieties. The word comes from the German, *Wermut*, "wormwood," which was once customarily used in the manufacture of vermouth, though it is now considered poisonous. Today's vermouths are made with herbs and spices like cinnamon, gentian, cloves, artemisia, quinine, orange peel, camomile, and angelica root.

France and Italy are generally conceded to make the best vermouths, but some are made in the United States, including some under license from European companies. The word "vermouth" was first printed in 1800.

veto. A beverage of the 1840s. It was mentioned in the New Orleans *Picayune* in 1841, though it is not known precisely what the ingredients were, or the origin of the name.

vichyssoise. A potato-and-leek cream soup served cold. Vichyssoise was created by Chef Louis Diat at the Ritz-Carlton Hotel in New York City. In *American Food* (1975) Evan Jones said the soup was first served in 1910, while *The American Heritage Cookbook* (1980) adds, "[The soup] was served for the first time to Charles Schwab, the steel magnate" for the opening of the hotel's roof garden. But there are several things wrong with these assertions: Diat did come to work at the Ritz-Carlton sometime in 19 10, but the restaurant did not open until December 14 of that year, and this was not the roof-garden restaurant in any case. Nor was Charles M. Schwab (1862–1939) present. Also, the menu for that opening night's meal was listed in *The New York Times* the next day; the soup served was a turtle soup, not leek and potato. The *Times* also noted that the meal was overseen not by Diat but by Auguste Escoffier, the renowned chef who had opened Ritz hotels in Paris and elsewhere. Finally, Diat himself remarked, in his book *Louis Diat's Cookbook* (1946), that "one of my earliest food memories is of my mother's good Leek and Potato soup made with plump, tender leeks I pulled myself from the garden. . . . When I first came to this country I actually couldn't find any [leeks]. I finally persuaded one of my vegetable suppliers to find someone who would grow leeks for me." It is unlikely that Diat found someone to grow leeks quickly enough to have them in time for the opening in 1910.

Curiously enough, Diat does not mention his famous soup by name in his 1946 cookbook, published at a time when many French chefs in New York had tried to change the name to *crème gauloise* because of their hatred for the wartime government established at the city of Vichy, after which Diat had named the soup because he had grown up nearby. Nor did he give the date he created the soup in his earlier book, *Diat's Cooking à la Ritz* (1941). Elizabeth David, however, in her *French Provincial Cooking* (1960), gave, without comment, the date 1917 as the year of the soup's creation.

The recipe below is from Diat's 1941 volume, in which the full, formal name of the soup is "crème vichyssoise glacée":

VICHYSSOISE

Finely slice the white parts of 4 leeks and 1 medium onion, brown very gently in 2 oz. sweet butter, then add 5 medium potatoes, also finely sliced. Add 1 qt. water or chicken broth and 1 T. salt. Boil for 35–40 min.

Crush and rub through a fine strainer. Return to fire and add 2 c. milk and 2 c. medium cream. Season to taste and bring to a boil. Cool, then rub through a very fine strainer. When soup is cold, add 1 c. heavy cream. Chill before serving. Finely chopped chives may be added when serving. Serves 6.

victuals. Also, "vittles," so spelled because of the usual pronunciation of the word, meaning "food or provisions" (1275). It is from the Latin *victualia.*

vinegar. A pungent, sour, acidic solution of fermented wine, apple cider, or other substances. Vinegar is the result of a conversion by bacteria of alcoholic solutions into acetic acid. The word is from the Latin *vīnum,* "wine," plus *acer,* "sharp," which in Middle English became *vinegre.*

Vinegar is used as a flavoring, especially in salad dressings, and as a pickling solution. It is made by any of three methods, called the "slow process," the "generator process," or the "submerged process" (this last developed since World War II). Homemade vinegar must utilize a starter known as "mother of vinegar."

In Europe most vinegars are based on wine, and the United States produces this kind, too, sometimes by winemakers who age the vinegar in oak casks. "Distilled white vinegar" (also called "white vinegar," "grain vinegar," or "spirit vinegar") is made from grain alcohol diluted with water to a strength of about 5 percent acidity. The H. J. Heinz Company, established in 1869, claims to have produced the first bottled distilled white vinegar, which is today the largest selling of its type in the United States. The most commonly produced vinegar in this country, however, is "apple cider vinegar," diluted with water to a table strength of 5 percent acidity.

VINEGAR CANDY

A popular nineteenth-century confection made by combining 1 c. sugar, ½ c. water, 2 T. white vinegar, 1 T. molasses, 2 T. butter, and 1 T. chocolate. Boil for about 20 min. and turn out on buttered sheet. Cut up into small candy pieces.

vinegar pie. A spiced pie made with vinegar, common in the North and Midwest since the nineteenth century. In *America Eats,* written in the 1930s for the WPA Illinois Writers Project but not published until 1992, Nelson Algren noted that as winter wore on midwestern settlers' systems craved fruit and tart flavors:

> To satisfy their craving, ingenious housewives invented the vinegar pie. . . . When baked in a pie tin, the resulting product was much relished and remained a favorite springtime dessert until young orchards coming into bearing provided real fruit pies to take its place.

VINEGAR PIE

Mix 1 beaten egg, 1 t. flour, 1 t. sugar, 1 T. white vinegar, 1 c. cold water, and a pinch of ground nutmeg. Pour into a pie crust, top with another pie crust, brush with cold water, and bake at 375° until filling is set and the crust is browned.

vodka. A distilled spirit made from potatoes, corn, or other grains (1795). It is usually neutral in flavor and, in America, bottled at proofs between 80 and 100, although 60 is the legal minimum.

The word "vodka" is from a Russian diminutive, *vodka,* meaning "little water," and although some claim the spirit originated in Russia, other authorities believe its birthplace was Poland, at the end of the tenth century. *Zhizennia voda* ("water of life") is first mentioned in Russian records in the twelfth century, but the spirit was also being made in Finland, Czechoslovakia, and other regions of Eastern Europe. Its prominence in the czarist Russian courts was legendary, and in the sixteenth century Ivan the Terrible opened taverns where the general populace could enjoy vodka. Western Europeans became familiar with the spirit during the Crimean War (1854–56), but vodka was still a rarity in the West until well into the twentieth century.

Vodka first came to America with Russian émigré Rudolph Kunnetchansky, son of a Ukrainian plantation owner who supplied the P. A. Smirnoff Company (which supplied the czar's vodka) with grain-neutral spirits. Kunnetchansky fled Russia during the Revolution of 1917 and settled in the United States where he changed his name to Kunett and became a salesman for Standard Oil, then a manager for Helena Rubinstein Cosmetics. He also bought the rights from Vladimir Smirnoff, then in Paris, for $2,500 to produce and sell Smirnoff vodka in the United States and with Smirnoff's help set up the first American vodka distillery in Bethel, Connecticut, in 1934. In 1939, after years of low sales, the Smirnoff Company was sold to G. F. Heublein and Brothers for $14,000 plus royalties.

Still there was little interest in vodka among Americans, even though the BLOODY MARY cocktail had achieved some success after the end of Prohibition. It was not until well after the Second World War that interest in the spirit picked up, and cocktails like the MOSCOW MULE helped spur a taste for vodka. By the 1960s vodka sales soared, buoyed by a new generation of young Americans who found the lack of a distinct flavor in the spirit perfectly suited to their taste, mixing vodka with all sorts of fruit juices and tonic waters. Even the vodka martini became faddish, especially after the success of Ian Fleming's series of spy books in the 1960s about James "007" Bond, a suave British agent who preferred vodka to gin in his MARTINIS.

By 1975 vodka had become the best-selling spirit in the United States (a position it has held ever since), with about 32 million cases sold each year, less than 2 percent of it imported.

American vodkas are distilled to be odorless, colorless, and nearly tasteless, although a few flavored vodkas are made in small quantities. American vodkas are unaged, distilled from a fermented mash, and highly purified. If a vodka is colored, that fact must be noted on the bottle's label. There are today more than three hundred brands of vodka, both foreign and domestic, available on the United States market.

Volstead cocktail. According to Harry MacElhone's *ABC of Mixing Drinks* (reprinted in various editions from 1919 to 1939), "This cocktail was invented at Harry's Bar, Paris, in honour of Mr. Andrew J. Volstead (who brought out the Dry Act in the U.S.A.) and was the reason for sending such a large number of Americans to Europe to quench their thirst." (See PROHIBITION.) The drink is made with "⅓ Rye Whiskey, ⅓ Swedish Punch, ⅙ Orange Juice, ⅙ Raspberry Syrup, 1 dash of Anisette."

W

waffle. A light batter cake cooked on a griddle with a special weblike pattern. Waffles are a popular breakfast dish served with butter and maple syrup. The word is from the Dutch *wafel,* and first appeared in English print in 1735. The item was known to the Pilgrims, who had spent time in Holland before sailing to America in 1620, and "waffle parties" became popular in the latter part of the eighteenth century. Thomas Jefferson returned from France with a waffle iron, a long-handled patterned griddle that encloses the batter and gives it its characteristic crispness and shape. A century later vendors on city streets sold waffles hot and slathered with molasses or maple syrup.

Waffles continued to be extremely popular breakfast items in the twentieth century, and electric waffle irons made the timing of the cooking easier. Then, in 1953 Frank Dorsa introduced frozen waffles into supermarkets, calling them Eggo Waffles. At the 1964 World's Fair "Belgian waffles," made with yeast and thicker than the usual waffle, were an immediate sensation, and they are sold today at stands, county fairs, carnivals, and other fast-food outlets. In the South waffles are also made with rice or cornmeal (sometimes called "Virginia waffles"). In Baltimore, Maryland, kidney stew on waffles is a traditional Sunday specialty.

WAFFLE

Combine 1 c. flour, 1½ t. baking powder, a pinch of salt, ½ c. milk, and 1 beaten egg yolk. Mix in 1 T. melted, cooled butter, then fold in 1 stiffly beaten egg white. Pour onto a well-buttered waffle iron and cook until golden brown. Serve with butter and maple syrup.

Waldorf salad. A salad with a mayonnaise dressing, apples, and celery, though walnuts are traditional too. The dish was supposedly created by maître d'hôtel Oscar Tschirky of the Waldorf-Astoria Hotel in New York City, which opened in 1893. By 1896, when Tschirky compiled *The Cook Book by "Oscar of the Waldorf,"* the recipe—given without comment—called for only apples, celery, and mayonnaise, and the salad later became a staple item in most hotel dining rooms

and other restaurants. At some point in the next two decades chopped walnuts were added, for they are listed by George Rector in the ingredients for the salad in *The Rector Cook Book,* which appeared in 1928, after which walnuts became standard in the recipe, including the one given in *The Waldorf-Astoria Cookbook* (1981), by Ted James and Rosalind Cole.

OSCAR'S ORIGINAL WALDORF RECIPE

Peel 2 raw apples, cut into small pieces about ½-in. square, cut some celery the same way, and mix with the apple. Add "a good mayonnaise."

---

walleye (*Stizostedion vitreum*). A North American freshwater fish whose wide, bright eyes give it its name, from the Middle English, *wawil-eghed*. It is sometimes called "yellow pike," "dory," and "pike perch," although it is not a pike or a John Dory. According to A. J. McClane *in The Encyclopedia of Fish Cookery* (1977), the walleye was apparently introduced into the Chemung River, a tributary to the north branch of the Susquehanna at Elmira, New York, in 1812 by a Jesuit priest. "The reproduction of these walleyes," wrote McClane, "was so successful that they literally swarmed in the pools and eddies of the entire river system, and 'Susquehanna salmon' were soon in greater favor than shad." For a long while afterward the walleye was called a "salmon."

walnut. Any of a variety of trees in the genus *Juglans* bearing a nut that is eaten on its own, in pastries and desserts, in stuffings, and as a flavoring for ice cream, syrups, and other foods. Cordials and oils are also made from walnuts.

The word is from the Latin *nux Gallia,* "Gaulish nut" (referring to a nut from Gaul), which in Middle English became *walnot.*

The native "American black walnut" (*J. nigra*) was eaten by the Native Americans three thousand years ago, about the same time that the "Persian walnut" (*J. regia*) was being consumed in Babylon. Other native American varieties include the "butternut" or "white walnut" (*J. cinerea*), the "little walnut" (*J. microcarpa*), the "Arizona walnut" (*J. magor*), the "California walnut" (*J. californica*), and the "Hinds" (*J. hindsi*). Eleven other species are native to Central and South America. Nevertheless, nearly 100 percent of the walnuts produced in the United States come from California, where Spanish Franciscans brought the plant during the missionary period, with first commercial planting in the state done by Joseph Sexton in Santa Barbara in 1867. Today about 217,000 tons are produced annually, but most of those are of the Persian variety, also called the "English walnut" because of its wide propagation by the English.

Walnuts are often combined with maple syrup or flavoring to make maple-walnut ice cream. Walnut fudge appeared just after World War I.

wanigan. The cook's boat that followed a river drive of logs. Wanigan was also used by sheepherders to mean the supply wagon. The word comes from the Ojibwa Indian *wannikan*, "man-made hole," because it originally referred to a large supply chest. The word was first printed in 1848.

Washington pie. Also, "Martha Washington pie," "Washington cake," and other variants. A cake of several layers spread with fruit jelly or marmalade. The name derives from Martha Washington (1732–1802), who in her day was a prominent hostess and fine cook, basing many of her preparations on two old recipe collections, *A Booke of Cookery* and *Booke of Sweetmeats*, given to her by her first husband, Daniel Custis, in 1749. These collections, passed on to her granddaughter, Nelly Custis, in 1799, were reprinted by Karen Hess as *Martha Washington's Booke of Cookery* (1981) and contain several cake recipes, none of which much resembles the Washington cakes of the nineteenth century that supposedly were variants of a cake Martha Washington was said to have made for her granddaughter's wedding in 1799. The following recipe is adapted from one of these nineteenth-century preparations.

WASHINGTON PIE

Beat together ½ lb. butter with ¾ lb. sugar until light. Add the rind of half a lemon, then beat in 6 eggs, one at a time. Mix 3 t. baking powder with ¾ c. cream, stir into batter, then add 4 c. flour and blend well. Pour into 4 cake pans and bake at 350° until an inserted knife comes out clean, about 30 min. Cool, then spread layers with fruit jelly or marmalade.

Another kind of Washington pie was described by H. L. Mencken as being "about two inches thick and [sold] in blocks about two inches square. It was made of stale pies, gingercakes, etc., ground up and rebaked." The dish is mentioned in the Ladies of the First Baptist Church's *Pentucket Housewife* (1882).

water. The most basic of drinks, H_2O, clean, pure water was one of the potables early colonists found in America in what seemed unlimited quantities. This was not true in European cities, where water was often contaminated, and in Colonial America cities' water supplies were primitive, although one European traveler pronounced the waterworks of Bethlehem, Pennsylvania, "excellently contrived" as of 1783. For the most part city water in the eighteenth century was supplied by hand pumps, and in New York City tank carts sold water from the so-called "Tea Water Pump," noted for its purity. The first major city to provide its citizens with fresh, pure water was Philadelphia, when Benjamin Henry Latrobe installed a marble pumping station in Center Square in 1801. Fifty years later more than eighty American cities had public water supplies, and New York's Croton System of aqueducts was one of the marvels of the age. Modern American water supplies are often treated with fluoride to help prevent tooth decay.

As concerns about the purity of American water grew in the 1970s, BOTTLED WATER grew enormously popular, both "flat" and carbonated waters. (See also SELTZER.) "Distilled water" is usually plain water from the tap that has had all minerals removed. "Mineral water" has 500 parts per million of dissolved mineral salts and is taken from underground water sources. Bottled waters must meet the federal standards set by the Safe Drinking Water Act of 1974. Americans now consume more than a billion gallons of bottled water annually. Twenty-five percent of sales is from purified water from municipal sources, with 75 percent from private springs or wells.

watermelon (*Citrullus vulgaris*). A vine native to Africa bearing a large, green-skinned fruit with bright pink flesh and black seeds. The name derives from the great amount of watery juice in the fruit and first appears in English in 1605.

Cultivated for thousands of years in the Middle East and Russia, the watermelon was brought to America by the African slaves. In fact, watermelons have long been associated with African-Americans, not always in a complimentary way, for much of the graphic and cartoon art of the nineteenth century pictured African-Americans as docile people content to walk barefoot and eat watermelon. The word itself has sometimes been used as a slur word for African-Americans, and one slang term for the fruit is "nigger special." A colloquial name for the fruit is "August ham," because of its size and time of appearance. An "icebox melon" is a small watermelon that may be easily stored in the refrigerator.

Watermelons were grown in Massachusetts as of 1629, and there is some evidence that in Florida Native Americans cultivated the watermelon as early as 1664. The watermelon has been widely cultivated in California, Indiana, and Texas. It is usually eaten fresh in the summertime, although pickled watermelon rind is a traditional American relish. Per capita U.S. consumption of watermelons in 1997 was 14.5 pounds.

WATERMELON RIND OR PICKLE

Cut away 1 lb. of watermelon rind and cut into chunks. Cover with cold salted water and boil until softened. Drain, cover again with cold water, and cook until very tender. Dissolve ¾ lb. sugar in 1 c. hot water, add rind and 1 sliced lemon, bring to a rapid boil, and cook until rind turns clear. Add 2 T. vinegar, ½ oz. whole cloves, and cook until clear. Chill.

weakfish (*Cynoscion regalis*). Also, "sea trout" and "squeteague" (the latter from the Narraganset). A variety of marine fish found in the Atlantic (1790). It seemed to have vanished from American waters after 1800 and did not reappear in force until 1870, with remarkable numbers swarming off New York City's Rockaway Beach in 1881. The fish again disappeared in the 1950s and came back in 1972. It has since made progress as a desirable food fish in eastern restaurants. U.S. commercial landings of weakfish totaled only 62,000 pounds in 1997.

The name is from Obsolete Dutch *weekvische,* probably referring to the soft mouth of the fish, although an English encyclopedia of the 1830s suggested that Americans called the fish by that name because it was "considered by some as a debilitating food."

weeper. Vinicultural slang for a bottle whose wine has leaked out from the cork to form a sticky substance around the neck. It is usually caused by keeping wines at too warm a temperature.

western. A sandwich composed of an omelet with green pepper, chopped ham, and onions on white bread or toast. It is sometimes called a "western omelet" (which first appeared in print in 1935; "western" in 1951) or, in Utah, a "Denver omelet" or "Denver sandwich" (in print since 1925).

wet bar. A small bar equipped to make drinks and cocktails at home or in a hotel room. The term dates in print to 1965.

wheat. One of the most important grains of man, with several varieties in the genus *Triticum.* The word is from Old English *hwaete.*

There is no evidence that wheat existed in the New World before Columbus brought it to Isabela on Hispaniola in 1493, and it was introduced to Mexico by Hernando Cortés as of 1519. The Spanish missionaries brought the grain to Arizona and California in the eighteenth century. In the East wheat was sown unsuccessfully by the Pilgrims, who made do with corn, and in Virginia tobacco was a more profitable crop, so wheat was relegated to a minor role in that colony. It was not until it was planted in the Mississippi Valley in 1718 by the Company of the West that wheat became an important American crop, increasingly so during the Civil War, when the mechanized Northern harvesters brought in far more wheat for their troops than the Southerners could with manual labor. The North was even able to export wheat and flour to Europe during the hostilities.

Today the countries of the former Soviet Union are the world's leading producers of wheat, followed by the United States, which in recent years has exported a great deal of wheat to these countries.

Wheat is turned into flour, cereals, pasta, and enough kinds of food to provide one quarter of the total food requirements of man. Americans' consumption of wheat flour in 1998 was 148 pounds, with a total U.S. production of wheat at 2.5 billion bushels.

The principal varieties of United States wheat include:

durum wheat. High in gluten, durum wheat is ground to make semolina for pasta.

hard red spring wheat. High in protein and gluten, this is excellent for making bread flour.

hard red winter wheat. A thinner kernel than hard red spring wheat, also good for bread flour.

soft red winter wheat. Starchier than hard wheat, this is good for pastry flour.

Commercial forms of wheat include:

bran. The outer covering of the wheat kernel, used to make cereals.

bulgur. Also called "wheat pilaf," bulgur is the ground whole kernel, often used in Middle Eastern dishes.

cracked wheat. Another form of crushed whole-wheat kernels.

wheat germ. The embryo of the wheat kernel, often used as a nutritional supplement for cereal and other foods. The word first saw print around 1903, when Charles Kretschmer and his son Charles, Jr., began toasting wheat germ that was then bottled and sold as a cereal and nutritious food additive.

whelk. Any of a variety of marine snails in the family Buccinidae having a thick turreted shell and a large foot that is used as food. The name is from Old English *weoloc*. The two species of culinary interest are the "waved whelk" (*Buccinum undatum*) and the "channeled whelk" (*Busycon canaliculatum*).

Whelk is usually prepared with garlic and tomato sauce or served with lemon, oil, and vinegar as part of a cold salad.

whip. A dessert of whipped cream to which has been added sugar and lemon juice.

WHIP

Combine 1 c. sugar with the juice of 3 lemons. Add 1 pt. heavy cream and whip until stiff. Serve in glasses.

---

whiskey. An alcoholic distilled spirit from grains such as corn, barley, or rye. In the United States several grain spirits are produced, but the only true American whiskeys (that is, those that are produced only within the United States) are BOURBON, TENNESSEE WHISKEY, and BLENDED WHISKEY (often erroneously called RYE), each of which should be consulted under those names. Minimum proof for whiskey is 60.

The word "whiskey" comes from the Gaelic *uisqebeatha*, "water of life." When it specifically refers to scotch (produced only in Scotland), the word is spelled without the *e*, although this spelling has been adopted as standard for all domestic whiskeys by the Bureau of

Alcohol, Tobacco and Firearms. Still, Americans continue to spell domestic and Irish grain spirits whiskey. The earliest European settlers in America brought distilled spirits with them, and rum was commercially produced in New England very early. By 1640 there was a distillery on New York's Staten Island, but the industry grew rather slowly, with rye and barley the principal grains used. Many farmers used their excess grain to this end, and during the Revolutionary War whiskey was used as a medium of exchange.

In 1791 Alexander Hamilton passed a federal excise tax on whiskey that resulted, three years later, in an uprising of mostly Scottish-Irish farmers in western Pennsylvania who opposed this incursion into their livelihood. President George Washington was forced to call out the militia to quell the revolt, called the "Whisky Rebellion," thereby demonstrating the federal government's resolve in enforcing the new laws of the land.

Today the best American whiskeys continue to come from those regions where the water passes through layers of limestone, as it does in the principal whiskey-producing states of Pennsylvania, Indiana, Tennessee, Maryland, and Kentucky.

The principal types of American whiskey are defined as:

straight whiskey. Whiskey distilled at 160 PROOF or less, aged at least two years in new white, charred oak barrels. The addition of water brings the alcohol down to no lower than 80 proof, with a minimum of 51 percent of the volume being the grain. A spirit that has reached a proof above 160 is called a "neutral spirit" and should not possess any discernible flavor, aroma, or body. About half the whiskey consumed in the United States is straight whiskey.

bottled-in-Bond. Only straight whiskeys are thus called, a term that has nothing to do with guaranteeing quality but is instead a means of aging whiskey without having to pay tax on it until the spirit is ready for sale. The Bottled in Bond Act of 1894 required that the whiskey be aged at least four years (usually higher in practice), bottled at a minimum of 100 proof, and kept under the supervision of the Internal Revenue Service in a "bonded warehouse." When the distiller removes the whiskey from the warehouse, he then pays the tax.

light whiskey. Whiskey distilled at 161 to 189 proof, stored in used or uncharred new oak containers. This category was established in 1972. Most light whiskey is made from corn, and it may be called a "blended light whiskey" if mixed with less than 20 percent straight whiskey on a proof-gallon basis.

whiskey mill. A frontier saloon.

white bass (*Morone chrysops*). A freshwater fish similar to the STRIPED BASS. White bass are particularly popular in lakes and rivers of the Midwest, where pan-frying is the most usual preparation.

white chocolate mousse. A dessert made from white chocolate, cream, egg whites, and sugar. It was created by chef Michel Fitoussi in 1977 on the occasion of the second anniversary of the Palace Restaurant in New York City and quickly became popular in other restaurants around the United States; it also began an interest in white chocolate (actually a form of flavored cocoa butter) as a confectionary ingredient.

WHITE CHOCOLATE MOUSSE

Whip 1 qt. heavy cream until stiff. Chill in refrigerator. Cook 1 lb. sugar with 1 c. water to 250° on a candy thermometer. Beat 1 c. egg whites until almost stiff, pour in sugar syrup, and blend until almost cool. Cut 2 lb. white chocolate into small cubes, fold in egg whites and whipped cream. Puree 4 pt. strawberries with sugar to taste and a little Kirsch. Spoon sauce onto plate, spoon mousse onto sauce, and top with strawberry or raspberry. Serves 10.

whitefish. Any of a variety of freshwater fishes in the genus *Coregonus*, although other related species are usually called by this name. Whitefish are members of the salmon family, and the most important species gastronomically include the cisco, whose name derives from the Ojibwa *pemitewiskawet*, "oilyskinned fish" and of which there are several species—the "cisco" (*C. artedii*), also called "lake herring"; the "deepwater cisco" (*C. johannae*); the "longjaw cisco" (*C. alpenae*); the "shortjaw cisco" (*C. zenithicus*); the "shortnose cisco" (*C. reighardi*); and the "blackfin cisco" (*C. nigripinnis*); the "lake whitefish" (*C. culpeaformis*); the "mountain whitefish" (*Prosopium williamsoni*), also called the "Rocky Mountain whitefish"; and the "round whitefish" (*P. cylindraceum*), also called "Menominee whitefish" (after the Menominee River in Michigan). U.S. commercial landings of whitefish totaled 12.8 million pounds in 1997.

white lady. A drink of equal parts lemon juice, white crème de menthe, and Cointreau, shaken over ice and strained into a cocktail glass. The original was created by bartender Harry MacElhone in 1919 at London's Ciro's Club, but he changed the formula in 1929 at Harry's New York Bar in Paris to substitute gin, which is more readily found today, for the white crème de menthe. Sometimes the drink is made with the addition of half an egg white.

whites. Restaurant workers' slang for the white jackets traditionally worn by chefs and cooks.

white sauce. This term may refer to a sauce made from a roux of flour, butter, and milk or cream or to a light, clear sauce made with clams and clam broth that goes with spaghetti, usually LINGUINE. The former usage is far older than the latter, which has been heard in Italian-American restaurants only since World War II. See also RED SAUCE.

WHITE CLAM SAUCE

In 1/4 c. olive sauté 1 sliced clove garlic for 1 min. Add 1/4 c. water, stir in 1/2 t. chopped parsley, salt and pepper, 1/2 c. minced clams, and 1 c. clam broth. Simmer until tender.

whoopie pie. A Pennsylvania-Dutch confection resembling a cupcake. It is usually made with chocolate batter and a white icing filling, though there are many flavor variations. According to cookbook author and Pennsylvania restaurateur Betty Groff, whoopie pies may have originated with mothers who used leftover batter from more traditional cakes to make little cakes on cookie sheets for their children. The origin of the name is obscure, perhaps simply related to the whoop of joy uttered by children on receiving such an unexpected sweet.

wild boar (*Sus scrofa*). A Eurasian swine with a thick, short, powerful body and upcurved tusks. It was domesticated in Europe about 1500 B.C. and introduced in its wild state to the United States by sportsmen. Waverley Root and Richard de Rochemont noted in *Eating in America* (1976) that Hernando de Soto "landed near what is now Tampa [Florida] in 1542 with thirteen porkers in his supply train, and although other explorers and settlers of the American South brought pigs which eventually ran wild, Louisianans like to think of their wild boar as having a true Creole ancestry, that is to say, in this case, Spanish, with no native intermixture." Yet de Soto's swine were obviously domesticated boars or, more probably, simple hogs.

Wild boars proliferated throughout New Hampshire, North Carolina, and the Southwest (where they are called "javelinas") and are still hunted and, when taken, cooked in a stew or as a roast.

wild rice (*Zizania aquatica*). Also called "Indian rice," "Tuscarora rice," and "Canadian rice." Not a true rice, but the grain of a tall aquatic grass grown in the northern part of the United States. The Native Americans of that region called it *manomin* or *Meneninee*. It was called "crazy oats" by the French and "wild rice" by Americans as of 1748. Later it was also referred to as "water oats" or "water rice."

Wild rice is now cultivated in rice paddies, mostly in Minnesota, though increasingly in California since 1986, where it is most often cooked by the following method:

WILD RICE

Cover 1 c. wild rice with boiling water, cover the pot, and let stand for 20 min. Drain, repeat process three more times. Add salt to taste, drain, then dry briefly over a low heat. It is usually served with butter, but sliced almonds, mushrooms, or onions may be added also.

wine. Fermented grape juice, although wine may also be made from other fruits. The word is from the Latin *vinum*.

The story of wine in most wine-producing countries is the history of a culture, but in America the story of wine is a spotty narrative of fits and starts, blind alleys, and intermittent, slow progress. Viticulture in this country has been a series of vignettes rather than a saga. Only within the last twenty years have Americans begun to appreciate wine as an ordinary beverage with some extraordinary characteristics.

The earliest settlers in this country set about making wine almost as soon as they arrived. These were wines made from wild American grapes, the MUSCADINE (*Vitis rotundifolia*) and "labrusca," strong-flavored wines that were unfamiliar to the Europeans' taste. But the French Huguenots made wine from these grapes in the 1560s near Jacksonville, Florida, and Captain John Hawkins noted in 1565 that the Spanish settlers in Florida had made their own wine there. By the early 1600s Captain John Smith of Virginia could report "a great abundance [of vines] in many parts, that climbe the toppes of highest trees in some places. . . . Of these hedge grapes we made neere twentie gallons of wine, which was like our British wine, but certainly they would prove good were they well manured."

There was certainly wine at the first Thanksgiving feast in 1621. Lord Delaware brought French vines to Virginia in 1619, and the Virginia Assembly required landowners to plant ten vines and offered prizes for the best wines.

In the seventeenth century there were several failed attempts throughout the eastern colonies to grow wine grapes—in Maryland, in Massachusetts, in Pennsylvania, in Rhode Island, in New York, and throughout the South. Thomas Jefferson's wine-producing attempts at Monticello in 1773 were unsuccessful, too, largely because he, like the other farmers of the day, tried to plant European vinifera grapes that were not resistant to American disease, pests, and cold winters.

Meanwhile, wines were being successfully introduced in the West, particularly in California. As early as 1518 the Spanish explorer Hernando Cortés ordered grapes to be grown for wine in Mexico, a program so swiftly successful that the Spanish wine producers feared the competition and decreed that New World wines would be considered contraband. Nevertheless, the wines prospered. Franciscan friar Augustin Rodriguez is said to have brought grape vines to southern New Mexico about 1580, and by 1662 sacramental wine was being produced in that territory's Mesilla Valley.

Legend has it that wine vines were introduced into California by a Franciscan priest named Junipero, Serra in 1769, when he founded the Mission San Diego. Research now shows that this was probably too early. In an article in *New West* magazine (September 24, 1979), Roy Brady showed that Father Serra did not choose the San Diego site until July 16, 1769, too late in the year to plant vines for successful propagation, and by 1772 Serra lamented the lack of wine at the mission in his letters to his superior. By 1777 Serra was certain that wine could be made at the mission, and in a letter of March 15, 1779, Father Pablo de Mugártegui refers to "vine cuttings which at your request were sent to us from the lower country" having been planted. Brady surmised that the first vines actually arrived in 1778, brought aboard Don José Camacho's ship, the *San Antonio*, and were planted at San Juan Capistrano and that the first wines were ready for drinking in 1783, from a year-old vintage.

The grape the Spanish used in California was a type of vinifera called "Mission" or "Criolla." Leon D. Adams noted in *The Wines of America* (1978) that "ampelographers say it probably grew from a seed brought from Spain via Mexico by the conquistadores," since there is no precise counterpart for the grape in Europe.

Until the late nineteenth century New Mexico continued to produce more wine than California, but a series of natural and man-made disasters killed off the industry. After the devastating flood of 1897 and a bad drought that followed, many vintners switched to the more profitable cotton crop. When Prohibition arrived, New Mexico's wine industry which had been producing nearly a million gallons per year as of 1880—all but disappeared.

Native American grapes were propagated back East, with the first plantings of an indigenous grape made by James Alexander of Pennsylvania, and named after him, in the 1730s. By 1793 the first commercial wine producing was being done northwest of Philadelphia along the Susquehanna River by the Pennsylvania Vine Company. Grape growing for wine expanded into the Midwest by 1804, when Jean Jacques Dufour planted Alexander grapes at Vevay, Indiana. By the 1820s there were vineyards in Ohio, the Hudson Valley of New York, Missouri, and North Carolina.

All these were wines made from varieties of labrusca, which possess a very grapey flavor Americans called "foxy." This term, considered derogatory by growers of labrusca, refers to the fox grape, *Vitis labrusca*, of the eastern United States. (Actually all eastern wine grapes are by now crossbreeds, more properly called *Vitis labruscana*.) Purplish and large, the fox grape was first mentioned in 1657 and was described in 1682 by William Penn as "the great red grape (now ripe) called by ignorance, 'The foxgrape,' (because of the relish it hath with unskilful palates)." By 1864 Webster defined "foxy" as having the coarse flavor of the fox grape.

Vinifera grapes had failed consistently in the East, but in 1833 Jean Louis Vignes brought French vines to Los Angeles and grew them successfully, spurring more farmers to plant such varieties. After the Gold Rush of 1849, many failed miners stayed on in California to plant grapes, so that by 1863 there were more than 12 million vines in the state. There was even an industry bust in 1858 and 1859, and another in 1876, owing to an overproduction of wine.

American wines by then were being shipped abroad in increasing numbers, and the French even feared United States competition in viticulture.

A great deal of credit for improving the California wine industry has been given to Hungarian-born Ágoston Haraszthy, who in 1857 opened a successful winery (still in operation) called the Buena Vista Winery in California's Sonoma County, then returned to Europe, with the approval of the state legislature, to bring back one hundred thousand vine cuttings. It has often been charged that the legislature reneged on a promise to reimburse Haraszthy (who called himself "Count" with no documentation to back up the title) for his trip and cuttings, but Charles L. Sullivan showed in his article "Viticultural Mystery Solved: The Historical Origins of Zinfandel in California," in *California History* (Summer 1978), not only that Haraszthy did not bring back the Green Hungarian and ZINFANDEL grapes that would eventually become important varieties in California viticulture, but that he guaranteed the legislature his trip would not cost them a cent. Haraszthy's contributions to viticulture in the state were considerable in terms of technical methods and improved propagation, but there seems little reason now to christen him the "Father of California's Wine Industry," as some have in the past.

Sometime between 1858 and 1863 American vines were imported by Europeans for experimental purposes. These labrusca vines carried with them a louse, the *Phylloxera vastatrix*, that attacked the susceptible European vines, almost completely destroying the vineyards over the next fifty years and eventually affecting the vines of Russia and Australia as well. Ironically the vines of the eastern United States were resistant to the phylloxera, but those of California had never built up such a resistance, and in 1873 the lice attacked the vines in Sonoma and devastated many vineyards throughout northern California before it was checked at the turn of the century.

The phylloxera was stopped in Europe by grafting European vines onto resistant American roots, principally from the Midwest, so California vineyards began replantings with these same roots, halting the ravages of the lice. (Another infestation began in the California vineyards in 1985, with the arrival of a strain called Biotype B, and it is estimated that more than 75 percent of Napa and Sonoma Valley vineyards will have to be replanted over the next decade.)

In 1880 the California state legislature ordered the University of California to undertake a continuing program of intensive research in viticulture, a tradition that has made the school preeminent in the world today. California surpassed Ohio and Missouri as the largest wine-producing state in 1870, but wineries were thriving in the South, the Midwest, the Northwest, and even in Utah. After 1860 New York State's Finger Lakes became an important wine-producing region, and by 1876 American wines were winning medals in international expositions. American CHAMPAGNE was first made in Ohio in 1842, and a sparkling wine made from Catawba grapes by New York's Pleasant Valley Winery in 1865 won an honorable mention at the Paris Exposition two years later.

American wines had earned international respect, but Americans themselves drank very little wine, and what was available was usually sold in bulk. Italian immigrants set up wineries in New York and California and made wine according to Old World methods, which sometimes included pressing the grapes with their feet, leading to appellations that were sometimes facetious, such as calling the harsh red wines of northern California "Château La Feet" (a pun on the prestigious French Bordeaux wine, Château Lafite) or, with a somewhat more belittling tone, "dago red" (from the ethnic slur "dago," which originally derived from the common Spanish name "Diego" but which by 1887 referred to an Italian). "Dago red" (used in print at least as early as 1906) was used as a general term for red wines made from Zinfandel and other grapes and often marketed under the name "Chianti" (a red wine made in Italy's Tuscany region from Sangiovese and other grapes).

It was not the low reputation of more ordinary American wines that kept Americans from building a palate for table wine, but instead the growing temperance movement of the early twentieth century that first demonstrated its power in individual counties, then states, with Kansas having declared itself "dry" as early as 1880. By the First World War thirty-three of the forty-eight states forbade the sale of spirits and wine, and the passage of the Volstead Act in 1919 effectively crippled the rapidly developing wine industry, causing growers to switch to the production of "sacramental wine," used for religious rituals, or supplying home winemakers (as well as bootleggers) with grapes. One provision of the Volstead Act (Section 29), added at the behest of Virginia apple farmers, allowed private citizens to make up to two hundred gallons a year of home made cider or nonintoxicating fruit juice, and the Department of Agriculture even amended its own crop reports to read "juice grapes" instead of "wine grapes." The popularity of homemade wine was so great that the California grape growers suddenly found what they thought was a disaster had turned into an astounding boom for their industry. By the end of PROHIBITION grape acreage in California was 35 percent greater than it had been when the Volstead Act was passed, and more than 90 million gallons of "nonintoxicating fruit juice" were being made at home each year, though the majority was made from inferior grapes the industry had been quick to provide.

Owing to an oversupply, there was a collapse of the California grape market in 1925, and many growers switched to other fruits, like apricots. But most wineries went out of business during Prohibition, with only a hundred or so surviving the Great Experiment,

During this period wineries sold sacramental wine, wine bricks (compressed grapes), grape juice, and "Vine-Glow," a syrupy concentrate marketed in 1931 for the home winemaker (this last product was denounced in public forums and removed from the market soon afterward). In 1932, on the verge of repeal, Senator William Gibbs McAdoo of California proposed to allow wine and beer to be sold at 3.2 percent alcohol, and the little wine that was made according to this formula was scornfully called "McAdoo wine."

Even after repeal, the wine industry took a long while to recover, largely because the growers had already switched to other crops or to inferior grapes. Sweet dessert wines gained in popularity, as did high-alcohol "fortified wines," with a 20 percent alcoholic content boosted by brandy. And, too, the legacy of Prohibition was still manifest in many states that chose to remain "dry" after repeal.

In 1935, however, Philip Wagner of Baltimore began bringing in hybrid grapes from France. A home winemaker himself, Wagner could not obtain his preferred Zinfandel and Carignane grapes from California after 1933, and he did not care for the labrusca flavors of eastern grapes. He therefore imported the new French hybrids and began making wines that did indeed taste more like European wines. Wagner's first hybrids, created by Maurice Baco and Albert Seibel, became the basis for wideranging experimentation in New York during the 1960s, revitalizing the industry in that state, where sweet labrusca wines had been made almost exclusively.

A small but ultimately significant boost was given American wines when New York journalist Frank Musselman Schoonmaker began importing the best wines of California, Ohio, and New York and labeling them not with imitative and misleading names like "Burgundy," "Chianti," and "Sauterne" (American winemakers commonly spell the French wine *Sauternes* without the final *s*), but with varietal names based on the principal grape used—"CABERNET," "Catawba," "Riesling," "Grenache Rosé," and others, sold at premium prices to the best restaurants and wine stores. Together with Tom Marvel, Schoonmaker also published *American Wines* in 1941, which tried to interest more Americans in drinking wine by removing the pompous snobbism of connoisseurship—what they called "Wine Hokum."

In 1934 the California Wine Institute was formed to work toward national standards for winemaking in the United States. In 1938 the word "fortified" (which had a connotation of alcohol abuse) was banned from labels and advertising, and by 1954 the term was removed completely from federal regulations regarding wine. By the 1950s the prestige of the University of California's enology school at Davis was unparalleled in the world, and, thanks to its efforts, American wines improved year by year.

Still, Americans continued to drink more dessert wines than table wines, and by the mid-1950s per capita consumption was less than a gallon per year, much of that being softer versions of red wine called "vino" with an attempt to imbue such wines with an Italian cachet. Flavored wines with high alcohol and strange proprietary names like "Pagan Pink Ripple" and "Thunderbird" seemed ideal for the soda-pop palate of the postwar generation. Dozens of "pop wines" made from fruit juices and other flavorings became extremely popular in the 1960s. WINE COOLERS, made with fruit juices, became popular in the 1980s, especially among young drinkers.

It was during the same decade, however, that American wines took an astonishing leap in quality and reputation. In California established wine producing families and individuals like Sam Sebastiani, Robert Mondavi, André Tchelistcheff, Joe Heitz, and others pioneered the new technologies that utterly transformed the industry into a modern, efficient system capable of turning out varietal vinifera wines of great character, long-livedness, and prices competitive with the best French wines. Indeed, the taste for European varietals grew so much in the 1980s that native American varieties fell in popularity and were often replaced by European varietals, with CHARDONNAY and CABERNET SAUVIGNON now accounting for 50 percent of the total vinifera grapes crushed in 1991.

This rise in quality, coupled with a growing interest on the part of American consumers in their own wines, boosted the sales of table wines over dessert

wines for the first time in 1968, and by 1972 per capita consumption had risen to a gallon and a half per year. Land prices in the Napa and Sonoma valleys soared, investors bought up farms in an increasing number of wine regions in California, Washington, Idaho, and elsewhere, and there was increased activity in wine culture along the Hudson Valley in New York, as well as renewed efforts in Maryland, Virginia, Connecticut, Texas, and other states that had all but abandoned winemaking on a commercial scale. Even on the island of Maui in Hawaii a winery was opened by Emil Tedeschi, who used a hybrid called "Carnelian" made from Grenache, Cabernet Sauvignon, and Carignane grapes that flourished in the Pacific heat.

By the mid-1980s, however, many California winemakers showed a renewed interest in blending grapes to achieve more multidimensional wines and formed a group called the MERITAGE association to develop wines made with a mix of traditional Bordeaux wine grapes rather than depend on a single varietal.

Today almost every state in the Union produces wine, although California's nearly 800 bonded wineries (up from 540 in 1981) produce more than 90 percent (375 million gallons) of the wine made in America. The leading producer (60 million cases annually) of American wines and the largest ine producer in the world is the firm of E. & J. Gallo of Modesto, California, which began making wine right after Prohibition ended. New York is the next largest producer, with about 20 million gallons annually, most of that from the Finger Lakes and the Hudson Valley. Washington, South Carolina, Georgia, Oregon, Texas, Florida, Ohio, and Virginia follow, for a total of nearly 413 million gallons of wine produced in the United States in 1992.

An increasing number of Americans are buying "light wines," which may have one-third fewer calories than regular wine. Light wines are produced in various ways, but most winemakers pick their grapes earlier, when the sugar level is lower than that at full ripening, thereby decreasing the alcohol content before fermentation. Other producers remove the alcohol after fermentation is completed. Light wines have been made commercially since December 1979, when California laws permitted a reduction of alcohol from a previous minimum of 10 percent down to as low as 7 percent, and in February 1981 vintners won the right in federal court to use the term "light" on their labels. "Nonalcoholic," "alcohol-free" or "de-alcoholized" wines may contain no more than 0.5 percent alcohol (about the same as orange juice).

Varietal wines must contain, under federal regulations that went into effect on January 1, 1983, a minimum of 75 percent of the grape variety named on the label, although premium varietals have often been made using 100 percent of the grape named. Multivarietal labels listing two different grapes are also allowed, as long as the exact percentages appear on the label. "Fighting varietal" is a wine producer's term from the 1980s for a varietal wine that can be produced in sufficient volume to sell at a price considerably cheaper than such varietals usually do.

"Estate bottled" may be printed on wine labels when both the vineyard and the winery are in the same RECOGNIZED VITICULTURAL REGIONS, according to federal regulations; furthermore, the winery must own its own vineyard or have it under long-term lease, and all winemaking activities must occur on the premises. A specific geographical region—for instance, "Napa Valley" or "Western Connecticut Highlands"—may be listed on the label only if 85 percent of the grapes have been grown in that region. If a county is named—for instance, "Mendocino"—85 percent of the grapes must be grown in that county. The same percentage applies to state names appearing on labels (although California law mandates that 100 percent of the grapes come from the state for a California appellation).

"Chaptalization" (after a Napoleonic minister named Chaptal), a process of adding sugar to wine in order to increase its alcohol content through fermentation, has been forbidden in California since 1887 but is permitted in New York.

Home winemaking is allowed by the federal government if no more than one hundred gallons per year per adult, or two hundred gallons per household with two or more adults, are produced. In 1991 Americans made 2.5 million cases of wine at home.

In 1998 sales of U.S. wines totalled 531 million gallons, with a sales total of $17 million. Ninety percent of the wine produced was from California. Sparkling wine consumption accounted for 22 million gallons. One-hundred twenty-five American wineries exported a total of 72 million gallons abroad in 1998, the principal importers being th United Kingdom, Japan, and Canada.

Americans still do not drink much wine compared to other countries: 2 gallons per capita (compared to 54 gallons of soft drinks), while the French consume about 60 gallons per capita. Indeed the U.S. is 30th in terms of consumption among wine-drinking countries. The U.S. is the fourth largest market for French-produced Champagne.

The most popular varietals of Amrican wines are Chardonnay, White Zinfandel, Merlot and Cabernet Sauvignon.

The following is a list of the principal grape varieties grown in the United States for making wine. Those printed in small capital letters are major varieties having main entries elsewhere in this book. A name preceding numerals indicates the creator of the hybrid.

Aleatico (red vinifera)

Alicante Bouschet (red vinifera)

Aligoté (white vinifera)

Aurora (also, "Aurore"; white hybrid; Seibel 5279)

Baco Noir (red hybrid; Baco No. 1)

Barbera (red vinifera)

Cabernet Franc (red vinifera)

CABERNET SAUVIGNON (red vinifera)

Carignane (red vinifera)

Cascade (red hybrid; Seibel 13053)

CATAWBA (native red labrusca American hybrid)

Cayuga White (white hybrid)

Chancellor (also, "Chancellor Noir"; red hybrid; Seibel 7053)

Charbono (red hybrid)

CHARDONEL (white vinifera hybrid)

CHARDONNAY (white vinifera)

Chelois (red hybrid)

CHENIN BLANC (white vinifera)

CONCORD (red labrusca hybrid)

Cynthiana (also, "Norton" and "Virginia Seedling"; red hybrid)

De Chaunac (red hybrid; Seibel 9549)

DELAWARE (red labrusca hybrid)

Diamond (white labrusca hybrid)

Dutchess (white labrusca hybrid)

Emerald Riesling (white vinifera)

Flora (white vinifera)

Foch (also, "Maréchal Foch"; red hybrid; Kuhlmann 188–2)

Folle Blanche (white vinifera)

FRENCH COLOMBARD, (also, "Colombard"; white vinifera)

Gamay (also, "Napa Gamay"; red vinifera)

Gamay Beaujolais (red vinifera)

Gewürztraminer (white vinifera)

Green Hungarian (white vinifera)

Grenache (red vinifera)

Grey Riesling (white vinifera)

Grignolino (red vinifera)

JOHANNISBERG RIESLING (also, "White Riesling"; white vinifera)

Leon Millot (red hybrid; Kulhmann 192–2)

Malbec (red vinifera)

Merlot (red vinifera)

Mission (red vinifera)

Moscato (white vinifera)

Müller-Thurgau (white vinifera)

MUSCADINE (gold or reddish black labrusca)

Napa Gamay (red vinifera)

Nebbiolo (red vinifera)

Niagara (white hybrid)

Palomino (also, "Golden Chasselas"; white vinifera)

PETITE SIRAH (also, "Petite Syrah"; red vinifera)

Pinot Blanc (white vinifera)

Pinot Gris (white vinifera)

PINOT NOIR (red vinifera)

RUBY CABERNET (red vinifera)

SAUVIGNON BLANC (white vinifera)

Sémillon (white vinifera)

SEYVAL BLANC (also, "Seyval"; white hybrid; Seyve-Villard 5–276)

Sylvaner (also, "Sylvaner Riesling" or Franken Riesling"; white vinifera)

THOMPSON SEEDLESS (white vinifera)

Tinta Madeira (red vinifera)

Vidal Blanc (white hybrid; Vidal 256)

Villard Blanc (white hybrid; Seyve-Villard 12–375)

ZINFANDEL (red vinifera)

wine brick. Dehydrated grapes pressed into a brick and later put in water for homemade wine, used during Prohibition.

wine cooler. Beverages made from wine and citrus-fruit juices. The first wine cooler was called "California Cooler," introduced in 1981. The popularity of wine coolers soared, especially among Americans under thirty years of age, during the 1980s, reaching a peak of 71 million cases sold in 1986, but interest in the category has declined since then.

Wisconsin cake. A popular nineteenth-century MUFFIN baked in cast-iron "Wisconsin cake pans" made by Nathaniel Waterman of Boston as of 1859.

WISCONSIN CAKE

Sift together 1 c. whole-wheat flour with ½ c. white flour, 1 t. baking powder, and ½ t. salt. In a bowl beat 2 egg yolks, add 1 c. milk, and 2 T. maple syrup, then add to dry ingredients. Beat 2 egg whites until stiff, fold into batter, fill greased cast-iron muffin cups to two thirds and bake at 350° for about 20 min.

---

witch. A nineteenth-century New England cookie described in *The Pentucket Housewife* (1882) as containing 2 eggs, 1½ c. sugar, ½ c. butter, 1 T. milk, ½ t. baking soda, and 1 t. each of cinnamon, cloves, and allspice.

wohaw. Native-American term for the cattle native Americans first saw with the white men. The story goes that the native Americans combined the trail calls "Whoa!" and "Haw!" into a general name for the beasts.

wolf fish. Also, "wolffish." Any of a variety of marine fishes in the genus *Anarhichas* having sharp teeth and an ugly appearance that has kept it from becoming a popular food fish. The name, derived from its appearance, is sometimes changed at the market to "ocean catfish." The first appearance in print of the wolf fish was in 1569.

In the United States the "Atlantic wolffish" (*A. lupus*) is found from Labrador to Nantucket. It is sometimes called the "ocean catfish."

wop salad. A salad of lettuce made with olives, oregano, capers, anchovies, garlic, and oil. It is a Louisiana specialty whose name derives from the ethnic slur "wop," from a Neapolitan word *guappo*, "handsome man," used since the 1890s.

wrass. Any of a large variety of tropical, large-scaled fish in the family Labridae (1672), including the "cunner" (*Tautogolabrus adspersus*) and the TAUTOG in eastern waters and the "señorita" (*Oxyjulis californica*), the "Pacific sandfish" (*Trichoden trichodon*), the "kelpfish" (*Halichoeres semicinctus*) and "California sheephead" (*Semicossyphus pulcher*).

Y

yakitori. A Japanese dish of skewered broiled chicken pieces that have been dipped in a soy-sauce marinade (1960). Yakitori is a staple of Japanese-American restaurants. The word in Japanese means "grilled chicken."

Yale boat pie. A dish made with layers of meat, poultry, and shellfish set in a pastry crust. The name comes from Yale University in New Haven, Connecticut, and the recipe below is from *Jennie June's American Cookery Book* (1866) by J. C. Croly, who says, "This pie is excellent for a picnic or water excursion."

YALE BOAT PIE

Season with salt and pepper 3-4 lb. beef steak, then place in a large baking dish. Cut 2 chickens into pieces and place on top of steak, add 1½ doz. oysters (without their liquid) and 6 sliced hard-boiled eggs. Dampen the bottom of the dish with ale, cover with mushrooms and ½ lb. meat glaze. Top with a pastry crust, bake at 400° until bubbling inside.

Yale cocktail. A drink made by mixing 3 dashes orange bitters, 1 dash Angostura bitters, and 2 oz. gin with ice and garnished with lemon peel. Named after Yale University in New Haven, Connecticut, though its origins are unknown; it probably dates from the post-Prohibition era of the 1930s.

yeast. Any of a number of fungi in the phylum Ascomycota that may be fermented into alcohol and carbon dioxide, or any number of fungi of the genus *Saccharomyces* that may be used as a leavening agent in making bread and brewing. The word is from Middle English *yest*, and Old English *gist*. The term also refers to commercial products of dried yeast cells pressed into "yeast cakes" or "moist yeast," which was first produced in the United States by Charles and Maximilian Fleischmann and James E. Gaff of Cincinnati, Ohio, in 1868. The Fleishmanns also introduced packages of dry yeast in 1942 for use in the military, and in 1984 introduced RapidRise Yeast that acted quickly to leaven dough. SOURDOUGH yeast is made from *Lactobacillus sanfrancisco*, named after the city where sourdough starters were extensively used during the gold Rush.

"Turnpike Cakes" or "hard yeast" were described by Lafcadio Hearn in *La Cuisine Créole* (1885) as a dried cake made by mixing hops with water, boiling, straining, and pouring over cornmeal to which is added baker's yeast.

In the Midwest generations of families have used a yeast called HERMAN for sweet confections, and in Central Texas a yeast that is passed on by saving a remnant for a new batch is called "everlasting yeast."

Wild yeasts are often used in the production of wine and beer.

yogurt. A creamy food made from MILK curdled with bacteria such as *Lactobacillus bulgaricus* and *Streptococcus thermophilus*. The word is Turkish, first mentioned in English in 1625.

Yogurt is a very old food, probably of Middle Eastern origins. Turkish immigrants are said to have brought yogurt to the United States in 1784, but its popularity dates only from the 1940s, when Daniel Carasso emigrated to the United States and took over a small yogurt factory in the Bronx, New York. He was soon joined by Juan Metzger, and the two sold their yogurt under the name Dannon (originally Danone, after Daniel Carasso, whose father was a Barcelona yogurt maker). In 1947 the company added strawberry fruit preserves to make the first "sundae-style yogurt." When nutrition promoter Benjamin Gayelord Hauser published an excerpt from his book *Look Younger, Live Longer* (1950), in the October 1950 issue of *Reader's Digest* magazine extolling the health virtues of yogurt, the product's sales soared. They leaped again—500 percent from 1958 to 1968—when so-called health foods were popularized by the counterculture of the 1960s. Aside from the obvious nutritive values of the milk used, the health benefits of yogurt have not been conclusively proven, and in 1962 the FDA forbade claims that yogurt had any therapeutic or weight-reducing value.

Today Americans eat about a billion cups of yogurt a year, (or 5.1 pounds per person) often as a light lunch or dessert, and increasingly as frozen yogurt. Yogurt is also made at home, usually with a simple yogurt machine that uses already made commercial yogurt as a culture starter. "Swiss" or "French-style" yogurts usually have the fruit flavors already mixed in, rather than in a separate layer at the bottom of the cup. Strawberry yogurt is the most popular of all flavors.

Yorkshire pudding. A puffy, breadlike side dish made by cooking an egg-and-milk batter in the hot fat and pan drippings from a roast beef. It is a traditional English dish named after a northern county in England. The first recipe for Yorkshire pudding appears in Mrs. Hannah Glasse's *Art of Cookery,* printed in England in 1740 and widely circulated in America. The dish is now a traditional accompaniment to roast beef in this country as well.

YORKSHIRE PUDDING

Combine 1 c. flour, ¼ t. salt, and 1 c. milk. Add 2 beaten eggs, make a smooth batter, and let stand until roast beef is done. Pour off the hot fat, retaining about ½ in. in the pan. Pour in the batter evenly, bake at 450° until browned and puffy. Cut into wedges and serve with beef.

---

yucca. Also "yuca," "Indian cabbage," "Our Lord's candle," and "Joshua palm." Any of a wide variety of plants in the genus *Yucca* of the AGAVE family. The word is from the Spanish and first appeared in English print about 1655. It has a bananalike fruit and is eaten raw, dried, or cooked. It is most appreciated in the Southwest, where the "banana yucca" (*Y. baccata*), also called "soap plant" and "Spanish bayonet," is widely used. The "cassava" (*Manihot esculenta*) is also made into meal and sweet desserts and is very popular in South America.

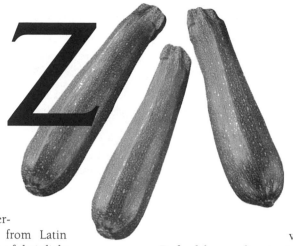

zephrina. A North Carolina cookie baked by both the Native Americans and the early settlers of the territory. The name derives from Latin *zephyrus*, for "wind," because of their light, airy quality.

Zinfandel. Also, "Zin" for short. A red vinifera grape that is usually made into a robust, fruity, tannic wine. It is the most widely propagated grape in California, growing in nearly every wine region in the state, and one of American viticulture's most distinctive wines.

There has been a great deal of speculation as to the origins of the Zinfandel. Once thought to be indigenous to the United States, it is now generally believed to have been brought to this country. There is a record of William Robert Prince growing a "Black Zinfandel" grape on Long Island, New York, as early as 1830, and he said the grape had come from Hungary. Four years later a Zinfandel grape was exhibited by Samuel J. Perkins of Boston. In California, where the grape thrived, it was generally classified as a claret.

It has long been legend that Hungarian viticulturist Ágoston Haraszthy brought the grape with him to San Diego, California, where he supposedly planted vines in 1852. But in his own *Report on Grapes and Wine* six years later he did not mention Zinfandel at all, nor did he include it in his 1861 list of 156 imported Hungarian wines. Nevertheless, Miles Lambert-Gocs, in his article "On the Trail of Zinfandel" in *The Journal of Gastronomy* (1986), contended that Zinfandel was indeed a Hungarian name for a grape better known as the "Blaufrankisch/Kekfrankos," and that Haraszthy did receive Zinfandel from Dalmatia. In 1854 Antoine Delmas was said to have brought "Black St. Peter's" vines to California from France, which Lambert-Gocs believed must have been Blaufrankisch. Other historians believe Black St. Peter's may have been Zinfandel brought from New England vineyards. But the eastern Zinfandel, according to John W. McConnell of the University of California Davis Shields Library, was a table grape, not a wine grape. Even if Zinfandel wine grapes had been grown in the East, it is still not known how or when they arrived there from Europe. In separate opinions on the origin of the name zinfandel, wine writer Gerald Asher and etymologist David L. Gold believe the word derives from the Czech *cinifádl* (Gold also mentions the possiblility of the German *Zinifal*), though those may not be the same grape as the American varietal. The assertion that the precursor of the American zinfandel is a clone of a Croatioan grape name Plavač Mali or Mali Plaveč by Croatian-born California winemaker Miljenko Grgich was made in an article in *Wine Enthusiast* (August 1996) by Terry Robards. Meanwhile David Darlington in his book *Angels' Visits, An Inquiry into the Mystery of Zinfandel* (1991) notes that when Haraszthy lived in Hungary, Dalmatia was part of Hungary and may well have provided the grapes he brought to America.

In 1967 ampelographer Austin Goheen identified Zinfandel as being identical to a grape known in Italy's Puglia region as Primitivo di Gioia (also called Zingarello), believed to have come originally from Greece. But wine writer Sheldon Wasserman later showed that Zinfandel was introduced to Italy forty or fifty years after its first appearances in the United States. Today some Italian and other European winemakers produce a wine they call "Zinfandel," but it has been banned from importation by the BATF.

While the mystery of Zinfandel's origins may never be known, the variety has flourished and attained great popularity in northern California, which has medium-to-warm coastal climates. The grape, grown for decades in California by Italian immigrants, was sometimes characterized as undistinguished "dago red," but today Zinfandels are among the most sought-after and respected California bottlings. Zinfandel is also blended with other grapes to make a PORT or rosé, or, as "blanc de noir," made into a rosé itself. The first varietally labeled "rosé" was a Zinfandel introduced in 1958 by J. Pedroncelli Winery in Sonoma. So-called "White Zinfandel," made with little skin contact and therefore a very pale rose color, was first made by George West in California in 1869 but not successfully marketed until the 1980s (by Sutter Home Winery of St. Helena, California). Occasionally one finds a "Late-Harvest Zinfandel" that is a sweet dessert wine. Some light varieties are made in a fruitier style.

zip-code wine. A wine-industry term to describe a French wine made from grapes not grown in a prestigious region like Burgundy but whose shipper's office is in such a region. Under French law only the regional zip code may be used on the label, not the region's name.

zombie. A drink made from various rums and citrus juices. It was created in the late 1930s by Don the Beachcomber (born Don Richard Beaumont-Gantt), whose restaurant in Los Angeles was known for its rum-based concoctions. The story goes that the zombie was created to cure a customer of his hangover. Several weeks later the customer showed up again, and, when asked how he'd enjoyed the drink, replied, "I felt like the living dead." The cocktail was thereafter called the zombie, after the legendary spirits that reanimate the bodies of dead people in voodoo mythology. The word is from Kongo *zumbi*, "fetish."

ZOMBIE

Shake together ¾ oz. limejuice, 1 oz. pineapple juice, 1 t. sugar syrup, 1 oz. light rum, 2 oz. medium rum, 1 oz. Jamaican rum, ½ oz. 151-proof Demeraran rum, and ½ oz. apricot liqueur. Pour into a tall glass with shaved ice, garnish with a slice of orange and sprigs of mint. Serve with straw.

---

zoo. Hotel workers' slang word for the place where the help eats.

zucchini. Also, "Italian squash." A summer SQUASH of the species *Cucurbita pepo*, which measures from four to six inches in length, has a smooth green skin, and grows from flowers that themselves are sometimes battered and fried (1925). The word is derived from the Italian *zucchino*, for a small squash. Zucchini became known to Americans only in the 1920s. By the 1950s it was a staple of Italian-American restaurant menus and served either stewed with tomatoes, battered and fried in olive oil, or cut into salads. A dip made with eggplant and anchovies is sometimes referred to as "poor man's caviar."

zwieback. Dry toasted bread slices, long popular for their digestibility and often served to young children. The word is from the German for "twice baked" and first appears in English print in 1890. Zwieback is usually bought at the grocery.

A BIBLIOGRAPHIC GUIDE

Since bibliographic items of specific interest or particular scholarship are cited and credited in the text of this book, it would be repetitious to list all references again in a complete bibliography of everything I have read or looked at during my research. I have decided, therefore, to provide both the scholar and the general reader with a brief guide to the best and most important sources for my research, giving credit where it is heavily due while establishing a working bibliography for future scholarship in the field of American studies.

Etymology

For standard definitions and etymology, I relied first on *The American Heritage Dictionary of the English Language,* first published in 1969. Words were checked for their first appearance in English in the *Oxford English Dictionary, The Random House Dictionary of the English Language* (second edition, unabridged, 1987), which added to and altered much of the material found in *A Dictionary of Americanisms* (1951), and *Merriam Webster's Collegiate Dictionary* (tenth edition, 1993). *The Dictionary of American English,* which appeared from 1936 to 1944, and *The Oxford Dictionary of New Words* (1991) were used to a lesser degree in my research. For slang I found invaluable Eric Partridge's *Dictionary of Slang and Unconventional English* (eighth edition, 1984), Harold Wentworth and Stuart Berg Flexner's *Dictionary of American Slang* (second supplemented edition, 1975) and its revision, the *New Dictionary of American Slang,* edited by Robert L. Chapman (1986). Also of interest was *The American Thesaurus of Slang,* edited by Lester V. Berrey and Melvin Van den Bark (second edition, 1953).

The publication of the first three volumes of the *Dictionary of American Regional English,* edited by Frederic G. Cassidy (1985, 1991 and 1996), was of signal importance in American studies.

In addition, the first two volumes of the *Random House Historical Dictionary of American Slang,* edited by J. E. Lighter (1994 and 1997) have enriched this book on American linguistic studies immeasurably.

Every lover of words is equally a lover of H. L. Mencken's *The American Language,* first published in 1919, followed by a greatly expanded fourth edition in 1936 and two massive supplements in 1945 and 1948. All of this material was revised, brought up to date, and abridged by Raven I. McDavid, Jr., in a one-volume edition that appeared in 1963.

Mencken made American linguistic studies exciting for the student and fascinating for the general reader, a tradition that was admirably maintained by Stuart Berg Flexner in two remarkable works on Americana—*I Hear America Talking* (1976) and *Listening to America* (1982)—which in both narrative and illustration, with scrupulous attention to detail and a fine eye for anecdote, make the study of the American language as much a social history as an analysis of word origins. And, of course, there is much pleasure and information found nowhere else to be derived from perusing various numbers, of *American Speech.*

The Morris Dictionary of Word and Phrase Origins, by William and Mary Morris (1977), has the same delight in it for the general reader, as does *The Merriam-Webster Book of Word Histories* (1976).

There is real delight and solid information to be gleaned by Martha Barnett's *Ladyfingers & Nun's Tummies* (1997), appropriately subtitled "A Lighthearted Look at How Foods Got Their Names."

For the language of cowboys, miners, trappers, loggers, and other westerners I turned most often to Ramon F. Adams's *Western Words: A Dictionary of the American West* (1968), and for the language of African Americans I consulted Clarence Major's *Dictionary of Afro-American Slang* (1970). For Jewish-American words *The Joys of Yiddish*, by Leo Rosten (1968), wholly lives up to its title.

Encyclopedias, Dictionaries, Etc.

One general encyclopedia was used extensively, the *Encyclopaedia Britannica* (1992). For information on animals, birds, and fish, I relied first on *Harper & Row's Complete Field Guide to North American Wildlife* (two volumes, 1981). *The Oxford Book of Food Plants,* by G. B. Masefield, M. Wallis, S. G. Harrison, and B. E. Nicholson, was consulted for fruits and vegetables, while A. J. McClane's *Encyclopedia of Fish Cookery* (1977) was an inexhaustible source of information on edible marine life. For the beauty of its illustrations by Charlotte Knox alone, but also for its superb scholarship by Alan Davidson, *Seafood: A Connoisseur's Guide and Cookbook* (1989) is a joy to read.

I constantly turned to the following books for general information on cooking, ingredients, and origins of dishes: Theodora FitzGibbon's *Food of the Western World* (1976); André L. Simon's *Concise Encyclopedia of Gastronomy* (1952) and its revision by Robin Howe, *A Dictionary of Gastronomy* (1962). The American edition of *Larousse Gastronomique,* edited by Jenifer Harvey Lang (1988), was a standard source, and I relied often on the *World Encyclopedia of Food,* by Patrick L. Coyle, Jr. (1982); Tom Stopart's *Cook's Encyclopedia* (1980); *Craig Claiborne's The New York Times Food Encyclopedia* (1985), compiled by Joan Whitman; Harold McGee's *On Food and Cooking* (1984) and *The Curious Cook* (1990); and Howard Hillman's *Cook's Book* (1981). Special credit must be given to the late Waverley Root, who not only published excellent studies of the cuisines of France and Italy, but whose beautifully written and lavishly illustrated *Food* (1980) is an example to all food writers for style, wit, personality, and breathtaking scholarship. Sadly and ironically, Root's greatest work was cut by two thirds for publication, and its glaring omissions make the reader wonder what fascinating information he or she is missing by having only such an abridgment of what was clearly Root's masterwork.

There is also much good information to be dug out of a quirky hodgepodge entitled *The Enriched, Fortified, Concentrated, Country-Fresh, Lip-Smacking, Finger-Licking, International, Unexpurgated Foodbook,* by James Trager (1970), as is the same author's *The Food Chronology* (1995).

Individual Topics

The value of Elizabeth Schneider's *Uncommon Fruits & Vegetables: A Commonsense Guide* (1986) cannot be overstressed when it comes to puzzling out the vagaries of botanical edibles, and *The Encyclopedia of Herbs, Spices & Flavorings,* by Elisabeth Lambert Ortiz (1992), is equally rewarding. For cheese history and description of types throughout the world, I consulted most often Steven Jenkins's *Cheese Primer* (1996), Evan Jones's *World of Cheese* (1979), and the same author's *Book of Bread,* written with his wife Judith Jones (1982), is just as good on the subject of baked goods. H.E. Jacob's *Six Thousand Years of Bread* (1944) is a profound study of the importance of this human staple. The subject of ice cream confections is lovingly covered in Paul Dickson's *The Great American Ice Cream Book* (1972), while Ray Broekel's *Great American Candy Bar Book* (1982) is just as important and just as much fun on the subject of the Milky Way, the Tootsie Roll, and Hershey's chocolate.

The best source of basic information on wines and spirits is still *Grossman's Guide to Wines, Beers, and Spirits* (seventh revised edition, 1983), by Harriet Lembeck, while for individual histories of American viticulture, *American Vineyards,* by Barbara Ensrud (1988), is superb. The whole story of American viticulture is comprehensively told in Leon D. Adams's *Wines of America* (second revised edition, 1978), and Matt Kramer has proven himself one of our foremost wine reporters and essayists with his *Making Sense of California Wine* (1992) and for its comprehensiveness *The Connoisseurs' Handbook of the Wines of California and the Pacific Northwest* by Norman S. Roby and Charles E. Olken (4th edition, 1998) is essential. The publication of *The Oxford Companion to Wine*, edited by Jancis Robinson (1994) pulls together all the most up-to-date information on wines and wine-making around the world.

For cocktails and mixed drinks, I found the following extremely helpful for information and recipes: *Straight Up or On the Rocks* by William Grimes (1993), *The Fine Art of Mixing Drinks,* by David A. Embury (third American edition, 1958), and *Trader Vic's Bartender Guide,* by Victor J. Bergeron (revised, 1972), and for current data on the U.S. spirits industry, the *Impact* newsletter.

Histories, Reminiscences, and Essays

Little academic attention has been paid until recently to American gastronomy, and few history texts spend any time at all on the subject, the exception being Daniel J. Boorstin's *The Americans: The Colonial Experience* (1958), *The Americans: The National Experience* (1965), and *The Americans: The Democratic Experience* (1973). I consider it a serious omission that the *Harvard Encyclopedia of American Ethnic Groups*, edited by Stephan Thernstrom (1980), barely mentions the foods and culinary traditions of the immigrants to this country.

The full history of American gastronomy is told admirably in *Eating in America*, by Waverley Root and Richard de Rochemont (1976). Evan Jones's *American Food: The Gastronomic Story* (second edition, 1981) is eminently readable and full of fine recipes. Often overlooked but extremely valuable is Richard J. Hooker's *Food and Drink in America: A History* (1981), and there is much useful information in *The American Heritage Cookbook*, by Helen McCully and Helen Duprey Bullock (1964), and in *The Better Homes and Gardens Heritage Cook Book* (1975), both of which have excellent historical recipes. For an idiosyncratic but fascinating study of the role of food in human civilization, Maguelonne Toussaint-Samat's *History of Food*, translated from the French by Anthea Bell (1992), is not to be ignored nor is Reay Tannahill's *Food in History* (1988). The sheer delight in reading Margaret Visser's *Much Depends on Dinner* (1986) is balanced by some of the most erudite scholarship in the field. The same might be said of *Good to Eat*, by Marvin Harris (1985). There's worthwhile cogent social history to be found in Donna R. Gabaccia's *We Are What We Eat* (1998), about the influence and interchange of ethnic foods in America, and Richard Pillsbury's *No Foreign Food: The American Diet in Time and Place* (1998).

The Time-Life series *American Cooking* (seven volumes, 1970-1973) was a landmark in American studies of our food and our culture. Various numbers of John Thorne's intermittently published booklets collected in *Simple Cooking* (1987), on subjects like chili, chowder, and the English muffin, are exhaustive commentaries on those items. Raymond Sokolov's *Fading Feast* (1981), originally commissioned as a series of articles for *Natural*

History magazine, has much of the same flavor and treats many dishes and traditions that are indeed fast fading in this country for a variety of reasons. Jane and Michael Stern's *Roadfood and Goodfood* (1986) and its revisions, *Roadfood* (1992), and *Eat Your Way Across the U.S.A.* (1997), constitute a rich store of Americana and anecdote along with serving the practical object of pointing the reader to the best American regional restaurants.

The Taste of America, by John L. and Karen Hess (1977), is an instructive and disturbing jeremiad aimed at those who would corrupt the traditions of American cookery, and it includes an excellent bibliography of eighteenth- and nineteenth-century works on cookery.

A book with a similar name but a more engaging author is *American Taste*, by James Villas (1982), one of a number of southern writers who have fondly kept alive the lore and traditions of southern cooking. This group would also include Craig Claiborne, whose *A Feast Made for Laughter* (1982) is an excellent memoir of a Mississippi childhood; Edna Lewis, who in *The Taste of Country Cooking* (1976) recalls Virginia; and Norma Jean and Carole Darden, who write of North Carolina in *Spoonbread and Strawberry Wine* (1978). Most comprehensive of all is John Egerton's evocative *Southern Food* (1987).

What these southerners lovingly did for their region's culinary heritage, James Beard did for Oregon in *Delights and Prejudices* (1964), E. Mae Fritz for Nebraska in *Prairie Kitchen Sampler* (1988), and Nelson Algren for Illinois in a work compiled for the Illinois Writers' Project under the Works Progress Administration of the 1930s, but not published until 1992 under the title *America Eats*. An excellent study of New York's culinary and social history will be found in Michael and Ariane Batterberry's *On the Town in New York* (1973 and 1999).

For some of the best and most affectionate writing on American regional dishes, I turn to Calvin Trillin's *American Fried* (1974) and *Third Helpings* (1983) as well as to Jean Anderson's *American Century Cookbook* (1997). Readers may also find of interest my own *America Eats Out: An Illustrated History of Restaurants, Taverns, Coffee Shops, Speakeasies, and Other Establishments That Have Fed Us for 350 Years* (1991).

Other Books

The scholar may wish to consult Eleanor Lowenstein's *Bibliography of American Cookery Books, 1742-1860* (1972) and Katherine Golden Bitting's *Gastronomic Bibliography* (1939) for long lists of American recipe books, but the printed, bound catalogs of the Library of Congress and the New York Public Library are the most rewarding for their inclusiveness.

I shall list only some of the hundreds of cookbooks and recipe collections I found most useful in my own research; this list is more for the general reader's interest than for the scholar's. I have not listed here very old or rare cookbooks, and most of the books below are still in print or readily available at libraries.

Adams, Marcia. *Heartland: The Best of the Old and the New from Midwest Kitchens,* (1991).
Aidells, Bruce, and Denis Kelly. *Hot Links and Country Flavors* (1990).
Anderson, Jean. *The American Century Cookbook* (1997).
Andrews, Glenn. *Food from the Heartland* (1991).
Barr, Nancy Verde. *We Called It Macaroni* (1992).
Beard, James. *James Beard's American Cookery* (1972).
Belk, Sarah. *Around the Southern Table* (1991).
Bjornskov, Elizabeth. *The Complete Book of American Fish and Shellfish Cookery* (1984).
Blue, Anthony Dias. *American Wine* (1988).
Braun, Lionel, and Marion Gorman. *The Drink Directory* (1982).

Brown, Ellen. *Cooking with the New American Chefs.* (1985).

Brown, Helen Evans. *The West Coast Cook Book* (1952).

Buckeye Publishing Company. *The Buckeye Cookbook* (1883; facsimile edition, 1975).

Burton, Nathaniel, and Rudy Lombard. *Creole Feast* (1978).

Butel, Jane. *Tex-Mex Cookbook* (1980).

Cameron, Angus, and Judith Jones. *The L.L. Bean Game & Fish Cookbook* (1983).

Carr, Sandy. *The Simon & Schuster Pocket Guide to Cheese* (1992).

Chalmers, Irena. *Great American Food Almanac* (1986).

Claiborne, Craig. *The New York Times Cook Book* (revised edition, 1990).

——. *Craig Claiborne's Southern Cooking* (1987).

Collin, Rima, and Richard Collin. *The New Orleans Cookbook* (1980).

Copage, Eric V. *Kwanzaa: An African-American Celebration of Culture and Cooking* (1991).

Costner, Susan. *Great Sandwiches* (1990).

DeWitt, Dave. *The Chile Pepper Encyclopedia* (1999)

DeWitt, Dave, and Nancy Gerlach. *The Whole Chile Pepper Book* (1990).

DeWitt, Dave, and Mary Jane Wilan. *The Food Lover's Handbook to the South West* (1992).

Dupree, Nathalie. *New Southern Cooking* (1987).

Early, Eleanor. *New England Cookbook* (1954).

Engel, Allison, and Margaret Engel. *Food Finds* (1984).

Engle, Fannie, and Gertrude Blair. *The Jewish Festival Cookbook* (1954).

Farmer, Fannie Merritt. *The Boston Cooking-School Cook Book* (1896; Facsimile edition, 1973).

Folse, John D. *The Evolution of Cajun & Creole Cuisine* (1989).

Frank, Lois Ellen. *Native American Cooking* (1991).

Fussell, Betty. *I Hear America Cooking* (1986).

Gault, Lila. *The Northwest Cookbook* (1978).

Gay, Lettie, ed. *200 Years of Charleston Cooking* (1930).

Gerras, Charles, ed. *Rodale's Basic Natural Foods Cookbook* (1989).

Good, Phyllis Pellman. *The Best of Amish Cooking* (1988).

Groff, Betty. *Betty Groff's Pennsylvania Dutch Cookbook* (1990).

Guste, Roy F., Jr. *Antoine's Restaurant Since* 1840 *Cookbook* (1979).

Hazelton, Nika. *American Home Cooking* (1980).

Hibler, Janie. *Dungeness Crabs and Blackberry Cobblers* (1991).

Hooker, Richard J. *The Book of Chowder* (1978).

Hunter, Ethel Farmer. *Secrets of Southern Cooking* (1956).

Ingle, Schuyler, and Sharon Kramis. *Northwest Bounty* (1988).

Jeffries, Bob. Soul *Food Cookbook* (1969).

Jones, Judith, and Evan Jones. *The L.L. Bean Book of New New England Cookery* (1987).

Kander, Mrs. Simon. *The Settlement* Cookbook (originally published in 1901, with several revisions, the latest being *The New Settlement* Cookbook, edited by Charles Pierce, 1991).

Kennedy, Diana. *The Cuisines of Mexico* (1972).

Kurlansky, Mark. *Cod* (1997).

Lassiter, William Lawrence. *Shaker Recipes and Formulas for Cooks and Homemakers* (1959).

Lobel, Leon, and Stanley Lobel. *All About Meat* (1975).

London, Anne, and Bertha Kahn Bishov. *The Complete American-Jewish Cookbook* (1971).

London, Sheryl, and Mel London. *The Versatile Grain and the Elegant Bean* (1992).

Loomis, Susan Herrmann. *Farm House Cookbook* (1991).

Lovegren, Sylvia. *Fashionable Food* (1995).

McClane, A. J. *McClane's North American Fish Cookery* (1981).

Muscatine, Doris. *A Cook's Tour of San Francisco* (1963).

Naj, Amal. *Peppers: A Short History of Hot Pursuits* (1992).

Nathan, Joan. *An American Folklife Cookbook* (1984).

Nathan, Joan. *Jewish Cooking in America* (1998).

Neal, Bill. *Southern Cooking* (1985).

Niethammer, Carolyn. *American Indian Food and Lore* (1974).

O'Neill, Molly. *New York Cookbook* (1992).

Parents' Club of Ursiline Academy. *Recipes and Reminiscences of New Orleans*, Vol. II (1981).

Picayune's Creole Cook Book, The (1901; facsimile edition, 1971).

Plotch, Batia, and Patricia Cobe, eds. *The International Kosher Cookbook* (1992).

Porterfield, James D. *Dining by Rail* (1993).

Prudhomme, Paul. *Chef Paul Prudhomme's Louisiana Kitchen* (1984).

Puckett, Susan. *A Cook's Tour of Mississippi* (1980).

Rombauer, Irma S., and Marion Rombauer Becker. *The Joy of Cooking* (1931).

Ross, Larry. *Nanny's Texas Table* (1987).

Rosso, Julee, and Sheila Lukins. *The Silver Palate Cookbook* (1982).

Rozin, Elizabeth. *Blue Corn and Chocolate* (1992).

Sarlin, Janeen Aletta. *Food from an American Farm* (1991).

Sarvis, Shirley. *Crab and Abalone* (1968).

Schultz, Phillip Stephen. *As American as Apple Pie* (1990).

Shindler, Merrill. *El Cholo Cookbook* (1998).

Sokolov, Raymond. *Why We Eat What We Eat* (1991).

Stallworth, Lyn, and Rod Kennedy, Jr. *The Brooklyn Cookbook* (1991).

Stern, Jane and Michael. *American Gourmet* (1991).

——. *A Taste of America* (1988).

——. *Jane & Michael Stern's Coast-to-Coast Cookbook* (1986).

——. *Square Meals* (1984).

Taylor, Demetria. *Apple Kitchen Cook Book* (1979).

Taylor, John Martin. *Hoppin' John's Lowcountry Cooking* (1992).

Voltz, Jeanne A. *The Flavor of the South* (1977).

Weaver, William Woys. *America Eats* (1989).

Yardly, Maili. *Hawaii Cooks* (1970).

INDEX

The following index contains main entries and subentries. Principle edible species of flora and fauna are listed as well as numerous colloquial and regional names for various animals, vegetables, fruits, and dishes. If the reader does not find a particular name in this index, it would be wise to consult the main entry for its possible inclusion.

abalone, 1
Aberdeen angus, 1, 23
absinthe, 1
absinthe frappé, 1
absinthe suissesse, 1
AC, 190
achiote, 1
acidophilus milk, 205
acorn, 1–2
acorn squash, 2, 309
Adam and Eve on a raft, 190
Adam's ale, 2, 191
adderwort, 323
additive, 2–3, 153, 168
Adirondack Special, 224
Adirondack steak, 141
adobe bread, 3
afternoon tea, 323
after-theater supper, 112
agave, 3–4
aged ice, 162
aglomerization, 90
aguardiente, 4
ahi, 4
ahole, 4
airline food, 4
aku, 4
akule, 4
Alabama slarnmer, 4
Alaska, Florida, 17
Alaska king crab, 102
Alaskan turkey, 281
Alaska pollock, 246
albacore, 333
Albany beef, 4
Albermarle, 9
albóndiga, 4
alcohol-free beer, 27
alcohol-free wine, 351–352
ale, 25, 27
Aleatico, 352
alewife, 155
algin, 5
Alicante Bouschet, 352
Aligoté, 352
alive, 191
alligator, 5
alligator bread, 5
alligator corn, 5
alligator gar, 137
alligator pear, 14
alligator snapping turtle, 335
allmouth, 209
all-purpose flour, 129
all the way, 191

Almeria, 143
almond, 5
alphabet soup, 5
amaretto, 5
amberjack, 169
ambrosia (cocktail), 5
ambrosia (dessert), 5
American black currant, 108
American bullfrog, 134
American Cheddar, 64–65
American cheese, 66
American coffee, 90
American fried potato, 133
American hazelnut, 153
American persimmon, 238
American raw fry, 133
American shad, 291
American sturgeon caviar, 60
American Sweet, 8
Amish Baby Swiss, 66
Amish preaching soup, 5
ammonia chicken, 5–6
Anadama bread, 6
Anaheim chile, 75
ancho, 75
anchovy, 6
andouille, 6
angel-food cake, angel cake, 6, 111
Angel-food cake and wine, 191
angeliquor, 6
angels on horseback, 54
angel's tit, 6
anglerfish, 209
angostura bitters, 30
Animal Crackers, 104
antelope, 6
antifogmatick, 6
apee, 6–7
A-pie, 191
Aplet, 7
apple, 7–10
Apple Annie, 10
apple bees, 8
apple brown betty, 10
apple butter, 10
apple charlotte, 10–11
apple cider vinegar, 341
apple crisp, 10
apple crust, 10
apple duff, 117
apple dumpling, 11
apple float, 11
apple fritter, 11
applejack, 11
apple john, 11

apple knocker, 11
apple pandowdy, 11
apple pie, 11
applesauce, apple sass, 1
apple slump, 297
apple snow, 11
apricot, cots, 12
apron string, 218
aquaculture, 12
Arab, street arab, 12
A ration, 263
arborio rice, 273
Arbuckle's, 99
Arctic grayling, 144
arctic wine, 12
Arizona, 191
Arizona walnut, 344
Arkansas traveler, 12
Arkansas water, 12
Arkansas wedding cake, 12
armadillo, 12
army chicken, 12
aromatic rice, 273
arrowroot flour, 129
arroz con polio, 12
artichoke, 12
artillery, 151
arugala, arugola, arugula, 276
ascorbic acid, 13
aseptic packaging, 13
Ashley bread, 13
asparagus, 13
asparagus lettuce, 183
aspartame, 13
Atlantic bonito, 35, 297
Atlantic cod, 89
Atlantic croaker, 116
Atlantic halibut, 128
Atlantic herring, 155
Atlantic octopus, 220
Atlantic salmon, 281
Atlantic sturgeon, 60, 314
atole, 13
August ham, 345
Aurora, 352
automat, 13 51, 269
avocado, 14
awa, 14
Awenda bread, 14
axle grease, 191

baby, 191
baby beef, 15, 338
baby food, 15
baby lamb, 180

Baby Ruth, 55–56
baby vegetable, 15
Bacardi cocktail, 15
Bacardi rum, 15
bachelor's button, 15
back bacon, 16
backdaag, 15
Back fin meat, 103
back of the house, 15
bacon, 15–16
bacon bit, 16
Baco Noir, 352
Bac.Os, 16
bagel, 16, 106
Bagel Dog, 16
bagoong, 16
Bahamian, 75
bait can, 188
Baked Alaska, 16–17
baked Boston brown bread, 36–37
baker's cheese, 66
Baker's Chocolate, 79
Baker's German Sweet Chocolate, 79
bake sale, 17
Baking Day, 15
baking powder, 2, 17, 41
baking soda, 40
bald face, 17
baldface dish, 100
Baldwin, 8
Baldy, 256
balkenbry, 17
ballie, 102
ballpark mustard, 214
ballpark nacho, 215
bally, 102
Baltimore crab cake, 102
bamboche, 17
bamboo cocktail, 17
banana, 17–18
banana bread, 18
banana cream pie, 240
banana fish, 35
banana pepper, 75
banana republic, 18
bananas Foster, 18
banana split, 165
banana yucca, 356
banded croaker, 116
Bandon, 66
banket, 18
bannock , 18, 97
Baptist cake, 18
bar, 18–19
Barbary duck, 117

barbecue, Bar-B-Q, 19–20
barbecued rattlesnake, 264
barbecued shrimp, 294
barbecue-flavored potato chip, 284
barbecue pit, 19
barbecue sauce, 19–20
Barbera, 352
bar chum, 20
bar clam, 86
bar counter, 18
bar dog, 100
barfly, 20
bargirls, B-girls, 18–19
bar glass, 20–21
bar jack, 169
bar keep, 18
barley, 21
barley meal, 129
barracuda, 21
bar room, 18–19
barstools, 18–19
bartender, 18
Bartlett pear, 236
basmati rice, 273
basmati-type rice, 273
Basque barbecue, 100
bass, 21, 30
bastard bread, 21
Bastard Potato, 319
bath towel, 21
bathtub gin, 21, 140
batter bread, 21
batter cake, 229
battery acid, 21
bayou blue, 21
bay salt, 282
bay scallop, 286
Bazooka, 71
BBQ, 19–20
beach plum, 21
beach strawberry, 311
beaked hazelnut, 153
bean, 22
bean eater, 22, 100
beanery, 22
bean-hole cookery, 22
bean supper, 22
bear, 22
bearberry, 104
bear claw, 168
bear sign, 100
beautiful bean, 216
beech wheat, 45
beef, 22–24
beefalo, 46
beef bacon, 16
beef barbecue, 19
beefburger, 149
beef club, 23
beef flank, 128
beef-on-weck, 24
been to Barbados, 116
beer, 24–27
beer blast, 27
beer chaser, 64
beer cheese, 66
beer hall, 25, 269
beer up, 27
beet, 27–28
beggar's purse, 28
behind the stick, 28
beignet, 28
belch water, 191, 290

Belfast Style Ginger Ale, 300
Belgian endive, 74
Belgian waffle, 343
bell pepper, 237
belly bacon, 16
belly bomb, 149
belly-button orange, 223
belly-wash (coffee), 100
belly wash (soft drink), 188
belon, 227
Bel Paese, 66
belt, 28, 185
bend an elbow, 28
bender, 28
Benedictine sandwich spread, 28
benne cookie, 291
bent, 116
Berliner, 30
Bermuda onion, 222
beta carotene, 28
between the sheets, 277–278
BHA, 2
BHT, 2
bialy, 28
Bibb lettuce, 183
bière douce, 28
bierkäse, 66
big antelope, 100
bigeye scad, 4
bigmouth buffalo, 314
big pike, 241
Big Pretzel, 256
big yellow, 335
billi-bi, 28
billy-goat date cake, 28
binder, 28–29
Bing cherry, 69
birch beer, 300
bird pepper, 75, 275
birdseed, 191
birds-nest pudding, 29, 87
biscuit, 29, 40, 41, 104
biscuit roller, 100
biscuit tortoni, 331
bishop, 29
bishop's bread, 29–30
bismarck, 30
Bismarck castle cheese, 183
Bismarck herring, 155
Bisquick, 29
bite-and-stir box, 30
Bit-O-Honey, 56
bitter orange, 223
bitters, 30
black and fat, 30
black-and-white, 30
blackback flounder, 129
black bass, 21, 30
black bean, 22, 30
black bean soup, 30
blackberry, 30–31, 111
blackberry vinegar, 31
blackberry winter, 31
black Betty, 31
black-bottom, 31
black-bottom pie, 31
black-bottom sundae, 31
black brant, 142
black bread, 258
black buffalo, 314
black cake, 31
black cod, 279
black coffee, 91

black cow, 31
black drink, 31, 36
black drum, 116
black duck, 117
blackened, 31–32
blackened redfish, 31, 52
black-eyed pea, 101–102
blackfish, 32, 39, 323
Black Forest mushroom, 213
black fruitcake, 31
black grouper, 146
black harry, 32
black huckleberry, 160
blackjack, 32
blackline tilefish, 327
black Mike, 188
black mullet, 212
black mustard, 213
black pepper, 237
black redhorse, 314
black sea bass, 21, 32
black skillet, 32
black stick, 191
blackstrap, 32, 146, 207, 277
blackstripe, 146
black thunder, 210
black thyme, 327
black velvet, 32
black water, 100
blended oils, 222
blended whiskey, 32, 44
Blenheim apricot, 12
Blibber Blubber, 71
blind pig, 32
blind tiger, 32
blintz, 32
bloater, 155
blonde, 191
blondies, 328
blood orange, 224
Bloody Bronx, 43
Bloody Mary, 32–33, 45
Bloody Mary Quite Contrary, 33
Bloody Shame, 33
blowfish, 319
blow foam, 33
BLT, 190, 283
blueback, 281
blueback flounder, 129
blueberry, 33
blueberry rake, 33
blue blazer, 33
blue-bottle, 191
blue catfish, 60
blue cheese, 66
blue corn, 97
blue crab, 102
bluefish, 33–34
blue jack, 281
blue john, 205
blue lagoon, 34
blue meat, 34
blue mussel, 213
blue-plate special, 191
blue runner, 169
blue sailors, 73
blue sucker, 314
bluff lettuce, 34
Blush Wine, 34
boardinghouse man, 188
boardinghouse meat, 34
boardinghouse potato, 34
boardinghouse reach, 34

boat steerer, 86
bob veal, 338
bobwhite, 260
bock beer, 27
bodega, 34
boeren jongens, 34
bog, 34
boiled dressing, 115
boiled grits, 145
boiler, 188
boilermaker, 34
boiling fowl, 71
Bok choy, 78
bolichi roast, 34
bollo, 34
bologna, 34–35
bolted meat, 35
bombed, 116
bomber, 154
bombo, 35, 269
bonbon, 54
bonefish, 35
bone-in ham, 148
boneless ham, 148
bongo bongo soup, 35
bonito, 35, 333
bootleg, 35
boova shenkel, 35
booya, 35
bop, 36
borscht, 36
Borscht Belt, 36
bosk, 36
Bossy in a bowl, 191
Boston baked beans, 22, 36
Boston bluefish, 246
Boston brown bread, 36–37, 40
Boston butt, 37
Boston coffee, 90
Boston cooler, 31
Boston cracker, 37, 92
Boston cream pie, 37
Boston lettuce, 183
Boston mackerel, 195
Boston strawberries, 36
botanza, 125
bottle baby, 37
bottle club, 37
bottled-in-Bond, 346
bottled water, 37–38
bottom, 191
bottom sirloin, 296
bottoms up!, 38
boucherie, 38, 52
boudin, 38, 52
boula, 38
bounce, 38
bounce berry, 105
bouncer, 38
bourbon, 38–39, 44
bourbon ball, 38
bourbon cakes, 38
bowfin, 39
bowl of red, 191
bowwow, 191
boysenberry, 31
Brad's drink, 300
brain sandwich, 283
brake fern, 126
bramble, 31
bramble jelly, 39
bran, 346
branch lettuce, 285

branch water, 39
Brandon puff, 39
brandy, 39–40
brandy alexander, 40
brandy smash, 40
brannigan, 40
brant, 142
brasserie, 40
brat, 40
B ration, 263
Braunschweiger, 185
brawn, 153
Brazilian pepper, 237
bread, 40–41
bread and butter pickle, 240
bread and with it, 41
bread line, 41
bread pudding, 258
breakfast, 41–42, 43
breakfast cereal, 61–62
breakfast club, 42
breakfast cream, 42
breakfast dance, 42
breakfast shrimp, 294
break it and shake it, 191
Breakstone's Downsville Cream
    Cheese, 106
breath, 191
brekkie, 41
bret, 42
brew, 43
brewers rice, 273
brewery, 25
brewpub, 26
brick cheese, 42, 66
bridge, 191
bridge mix, 42
bridge party, 191
Brie, 66
broccoflower, 43
broccoli, 43, 50
broccoli rabe, 43
broiler, 71
broken victual, 43
Bronx cocktail, 43
Bronx vanilla, 137
Brooklyn cake, 43
brook trout, 332
Brother Jonathan's hat, 43, 110
brown-and-serve bread, 41
brown bag, 44
brown coffee, 100
brown goods, 44
brownie, 44
Brown Leghorn chicken, 71
brown mustard, 214
brown rice, 273
brown shrimp, 294
brownstone front cake, 44
brown sugar, 315–316
brown-sugar pie, 70
brown trout, 332
bruiss, 44
brûlot bowl, 51
brunch, 32, 42, 44
Brunswick stew, 44
brush roast, 44
Brussels sprouts, 44–45, 50
brut, 63
bubble gum, 71
bubbly, 62–64
buccaneer crab, 187
buck, 45, 102

buck and breck, 45
bucket candy, 45
bucket of blood, 33, 45
bucket of hail, 191
bucket shop, 45
buckeye, 45
buckle, 45
buckler, 102
buckram, 102
buckwheat, 45
buckwheat cake, 45, 230
buckwheat pudding, 45
buffalo, 46
Buffalo chicken wing, 46–47
buffalo cider, 46
buffet, 47
Buford stew, 134
bug juice, 47
bugler, 314
bulgur, 346
bulk process, 63
Bullace grape, 212
bull and bear, 47
bull and bear cocktail, 47
bull cheese, 47
bullets, 191
bullneck, 117
bullshot, 47
bull trout, 113
bumper scallop, 47
bumper to bumper, 47
bunch onion, 286
bun pup, 191
Bundt cake, 47
buñuelo, 47
Burbank plum, 246
burbot, 48
burger, 149
burger and fries, 150
burger joint, 270
burgoo, 48
burn it and let it swim, 191
burn one, 191
burn one all the way, 191
burnt brandy, 51
burnt cream, 106–107
burn the British, 191
burrito, 48
busboy, 48
busgirl, 48
bush huckleberry, 160
business lunch, 48, 190
busing, 48
butter, 48–49
butter bean, 184
buttercup squash, 309
butterfish, 49
Butter Flavor Crisco, 107
buttermilk, 49, 205
buttermilk pie, 49, 240
butternut, 49
butternut squash, 309
butterscotch, 49
butterscotch brownie, 44
butterscotch sauce, 49
butter sole, 302
butter substitute, 49
buttery, 49
butt halves, 148
button onion, 222
buyback, 49
BX, 49
B.Y.O.B., BYOB, BYO, 49

cabbage, 50
cabbage lettuce, 183
cabbage salad, 92
cabbage sprout, 43
Cabernet Franc, 352
Cabernet Sauvignon, 50, 352
cabinet, 50, 206
cab joint, 50
cackleberry, 188
cackler, 188
cactus, 50
Caesar salad, 50–51
café, 51
café au lait, 51, 74
café brûlot, 51
café filtré, 90
cafeteria, 51–52, 269
Cajun, 52
Cajun popcorn, 52, 105
Cajun Power, 159
cake, 52–53
cake flour, 52–53, 129
cake social, 52
cake soup, 246
cakewalk, 52–53
cala, 53
calabasate, 53
calabash, 53
calcium (or sodium) propionate, 53
calcium (or sodium) stearyl lactylate,
    53
Calcutta pepper, 74
calf fry, 211
calibougas, 53
calico scallop, 286
California Dip, 112
California halibut, 128, 148
California ham, 53, 240
California hazelnut, 153
California mussel, 213
California oyster, 227
California pizza, 245
California pompano, 248
California roll, 53
California-style restaurant, 51
call liquor, 53
Calmeria, 143
calves' meat, 338
calzone, 53
cambric tea, 53
Camembert, 66
camper, 53
Canada Dry Pale Ginger Ale, 300
Canada goose, 142
Canadian coffee, 90
Canadian rice, 348
Canadian-style bacon, 16
Canadian turnip, 335
canaigre, 53
canal boater, 60
canapé, 53–54
Canary Island special, 191
candied dill, 240
candied pumpkin, 53
candied sweet potato, 319
candlefish, 297
candy, 54–55
candy apple, 55
candy bar, 55–57
candy boiling, 57
candy heart, 94
candy shop, 55
candy stew, 57

candy store, 55, 290
cane beer, 57
cane corn, 57
canned cow, 100
canned fruit, 42
canoe race, 57
cantaloupe, 57
cantina, 57
canvasback duck, 57, 116
caouane, 335
Cape Cod turkey, 57–58
Cape May goody, 308
caper, 58
capon, 71
cappuccino, 58
carambola, 58
caramel, 54, 58
caramel custard, 107
carbo-load, 58
carbonated mead, 300
card cheese, 98
Cardinal, 143
Cardini's Original Caesar dressing mix,
    51
Carignane, 352
carne seca, 47
carob, 58
Carolina rice, 273
Carolina tea, 31
carp, 58
carpetbag steak, 58–59
carrageenan, 59
carrot, 59
carrot stick, 59
carry-in meal, 254
carry-out, 322
casaba, 59
Cascade, 352
cassabanana, 59
cassava, 356
casserole, 59
casserole cookery, 59
Castlebrite apricot, 12
Catawba, 59, 64, 352
cat beer, 59
catchup, catsup, 174
catfish, 60
Catfish Friday, 60
catfish row, 60
cat's eyes, 191
cattalo, 46
cauliflower, 43, 50, 60
caviar, 60–61
caviarteria, 52
Cayenne, 75
cayenne pepper, 61
Cayuga white, 352
CB, 191
celery, 61
celery cabbage, 50
celery salt, 61
celtuce, 183
cellar kitchen, 61
century plant, 3
cèpe, 213
cereal, 42, 61–62
cereal crop, 96–97
cero, 195
challa, challah, challeh, 62
chalupa, 62
champagne, 62–64
champagne cocktail, 88
champagne glass, 21

champagne process, 63
Chancellor, 352
channel bass redfish, 116
channel buffalo, 314
channel catfish, 60
chanterelle, 213
chapote, 237
chaptalization, 352
character lunch box, 190
Charbono, 352
chardonel, 64, 352
Chardonnay, 64, 352
charge account, 106
charge plate, 106
Charleston Chew, 56
Charlie Taylor, 64
charlotte russe, 10, 64
Charmat, 63
chaser, 34, 64
chateaubriand, 24, 324
chaudin, 52, 64
chaurice, 64
chayote, 64
Cheddar, 64–65
Cheddar cheese soup, 65
Cheerios, 62
cheese, 65–68
cheesecake, 68–69
cheese crock, 66
cheese food, 66
cheese pie, 240
Chelois, 352
Chenin Blanc, 69, 352
cherimoya, 69
cherries jubilee, 69
cherry, 69
cherrybarb, 69
Cherry Coke, 300
cherry soup, 69
cherrystone, 85
chervil, 70
chess pie, chess-cake pie, chess tart, 70, 240
chestnut, 70
cheval du diable, 105
chewing gum, 70–71
Chicago, 250
Chicago (doughnut), 114
Chicago (pineapple), 71
chicago onion, 222
Chicago-style dog, 158
Chicago-style pizza, 244
Chicago sundae, 71
Chickalona, 71
chicken, 71–72
chicken à la king, 71–72
chicken bog, 72
chickenburger, 72
chicken cacciatore, 72
chicken coffee, 74
chicken corn, 303
chicken divan, 43, 72
chicken fajita, 125
chicken fixings, 72
chicken francese, 72
chicken-fried steak, 72–73
chicken hash, 152
chicken-in-the-shell, 73
chicken lobster, 186
chicken mushroom, 213
chicken of the woods, 213
chicken pot pie, 254
Chicken Raphael Weill, 73

chicken steak, 83
chicken tetrazzini, 73
chicken Vesuvio, 73
Chicken Wing Day, 46
chick-pea, 73–74
chicle, 70
chicory, 73–74
chicory coffee, 74, 90
chief cook and bottle washer, 74
chiffon, 74
chiffon cake, 74
chiffon pie, 74
chilaca, 75
children's menu, 125
Childs brothers, 51
chile, 74–76
Chilean sea bass, 76
Chilean strawberry, 311
chile bravo, 75
chile colorado, 75
chile mesquito, 75
chile negro, 75
chile pepper, 74
chile powder, 74
chile size, 77
chiles rellenos, 74, 76
chili, 76–77
chili chaser, 76
chili con carne, 76–77
chili con queso, 78
chili eater, 76
chili joint, 76, 77
chili parlor, 77
chili pie, 134
chili powder, 74, 76
chili queen, 77–78
chili sauce, 78
chili stand, 270
chili water, 218
chiltepin, 75
chimichanga, 48, 78
China, 191
Chinese cabbage, 50, 78
Chinese chestnut, 70
Chinese date, 173
Chinese gooseberry, 176
Chinese grits, 78
Chinese parsley, 84
Chinese pear, 236
Chinese restaurant syndrome, 209
Chinese star fruit, 58
Chinese sugar, 303
Chinook salmon, 281
chipotle, 75
chipped beef, 78
chipped ham, 78
chipped ice, 163
chipping potato, 284
chips, 133
Chipwich, 165
chitlins, 78–79
chitterlings, 78–79
choc, 79
chocoholic, 79
chocolate, 31, 79–80
chocolate baby, 80
chocolate belt, 80
chocolate Easter bunnies and Easter eggs, 80
chocolate fondue, 130
chocolate fudge, 135
chocolate kiss, 80
chocolate liquor, 80

chocolate milk, 79
chocolateria, 52
chocolate Santa, 80
chocolate sauce, 30
chocolate truffle, 333
chocolate velvet cake, 80
cholesterol free, 131
chop house, 80–81
chopper, 191
chop suey, 81
chorizo 64, 81
choupique, 39, 61
chow, 81
chow-chow 45, 82, 240
chowder, 82–83
chowder clam, 85
chowhound, 81
chow mein, 83
chow time, 81
Christy Girl, 83
chubby mya, 110
chub mackerel, 195
chuck, 83
chuck box, 83
chuck eye, 24
chuck habit, 83
Chuckles, 56
chuck steak, 24
chuck wagon, 83–84
chuck-wagon chicken, 84
chug, 84
chug-a-lug, 84
chum salmon, 281
Chunky, 56
church key, 84
cibola, 100
cider, 8, 84
ciderkin, 84
cider molasses, 84
cider royal, 84
cider sauce, 84
cider wine, 84
cigar store, 55
cilantro, 84
cinci, 84
Cincinnati chili, 77
Cincinnati Five-way Chile, 77
Cincinnati olive, 250
Cincinnati oyster, 84
cinderella, 84
cinnamon bun, 239, 310
cinnamon fern, 126
cioppino, 84–85
cisco, 347
citric acid, 85
citron, 182
city juice, 191
CJ, 191
clabber, 85
clabber biscuit, 85
clabber cheese, 85
clabbered milk, 98
clam, 85–86
clambake, 85, 86, 117
clam belly, 85
clam chowder, 82–83
clam fritter, 86
clams casino, 86
clams posillipo, 86
clarified butter, 49
Clark bar, 56
clay eater, 112
clean, 177

clean up the kitchen, 191
Clementine, 224
clingstone, 234
club, 87
club car, 270
club sandwich, clubhouse sandwich, 87
club soda, 290
club steak, 24
club store, 317
cluck and grunt, 146
coal juice, 210
cobbler, 87
cobbler's punch, 87
Cobb salad, 87
cobia, 87
Coca-Cola, Coke, 300–301
cochon de lait, 250, 314
cocktail, 87–88
cocktail dress, 88
cocktail glass, 20
cocktail hour, 88
cocktail lounge, 88
cocktail party, 88
cocktail pianist, 88
cocktail shaker, 88
cocktail table, 88
cocoa, 80
cocoa butter, 80
cocoa powder, 80
Coco Lopez, 88
coconut, cocoanut, 88
cod, codfish, 88–89
codde, codfish ball, coddy, 89
coddle, 89
coddled apple, 89
codfish, 88–89
coffee, 89–91
coffee and (doughnuts, pastries, cake, etc.), 91
coffee break, 91
coffee cream, 106
coffee filter, 91
coffee gossip, 91
coffeehouse, 51, 90
coffee klatch, 91
coffee milk, 91
coffee shops, 269
coffee with milk, 91
coffin, 91
coffin varnish, 100, 185
c.o. highball, 192
coho, cohoe, coho salmon, 281
Coke, Coca-Cola, 300–301
coke pie, 192
cola cake, 91
cola roast, 91
Colby, 66
colcannon, 91
cold cut, 91
Cold Duck, 91–92
cold ending, 91–92
coldpack cheese, 67
cold potato salad, 253
cold-pressed, 339
cold spot, 192
coleslaw, 47, 50, 92
colewort, 92
collard greens, 92
collation, 92
Collins glass, 20
colored sugar, 316
Columbia punch, 259

Columbia River smelt, 297
combination platter, combo platter, 92
comfort food, 92
common artichoke, 12
common cracker, 92–93, 104
common doings, 93
common huckleberry, 160
common meal, 93
common onion, 222
common Pacific octopus, 220
common Pacific squid, 309
commons, 93
common snapping turtle, 335
common storages, 8
common sunflower, 316
common turnip, 335
complimentary drink, 49
compounding, 140
conch, 93
Concord, 93, 143, 352
condensed milk, 100, 205
conditioned rice, 273
coney, 93
Coney Island, 93, 192
Coney Island chicken, 192
confectioners' sugar, 316
confetti sugar, 316
congealed salad, 279
Connecticut River pork, 291
conscience joint, 51
convenience store (C-store), 93
conversation heart, 94
converted rice, 273
cookbook, cookerie book, 94–95
cooked sausage, 285
cooked smoked sausage, 285
cookhouse, 100
cookie (cook), 100
cookie (small cake), 95
cookie pusher, 100
cooking wine, 95
coon, 66, 261
Coon cheese, 66
cooney, 83
coon oyster, 227
coon-stripe shrimp, 294
cooter, 95
cooter stew, 95
coot, 117
copra, 88
coquina soup, 95–96
cordial, 96
coriander, 84
corn, 96–97
cornbeef Willie, 152
Corn Belt, 97
corn bread, 40, 97
Corn Chex, 62
corn chip, 98
corn chip chili pie, 134
corn chowder, 97
corncracker, 97
corn dodger, 97
corn dog, 98, 158
corned beef, 98
Cornell bread, 98
corner saloon, 19
cornflakes, 97
corn flour, 129
corn fritter, 97
Cornhusker cheese, 66
Cornish game hen, 71
Cornish pasty, 233

cornmeal, 14
cornmeal mush, 258
corn mush, 156
corn on the cob, 97
corn oyster, 97
corn pone, 40, 97
corn popper, 97
corn roast, 97
cornstarch, 129
corn sugar, 316
corn syrup, 2, 97, 98, 316
Cornucopias, 164
corn whiskey, 57, 98
Cortland, 8
Cos lettuce, 183
cotlet, 7
cottage cheese, 66, 85, 97–98
cottage-fried potatoes, cottage fries,
    country fries, 99
cottage pudding, 99
cotton candy, 55, 99
cottontail rabbit, 261
Cougar Gold, 66
Count Chocula, 62
country captain, 99
country-cured ham, 148
country fried chicken, 305
country pie, 99
country-style bacon, 15
country-style chop, 251
country-style ham, 148
court-bouillon, 99
couscous, 108
coush-coush caille, 108
covered dish meal, 254
cowboy, 192
cowboy cocktail, 100
cowboy coffee, 100
cowboy slang, 99–100
cowboy stew, 303
cowboy toast, 100
cowcumber, 101
cow feed, 192
cow grease, 101
cow juice, 192
cow parsnip, 36
cowpea, 101–102
cowpuncher's sandwich, 102
cow salve, 101
crab, 102–103
crabapple, crab apple, 8, 103
crab boil, 117
crabburger, 103
crab butter, 103, 117
crab cake, 103, 128
crab feed, 117
crab house, 103
crab imperial, 167
crab lantern, 103
crab Louis, 103
crabmeat, 103
crabmeat à la Dewey, 103
crabmeat ravigote, 264
crabmeat Remick, 103
crab Norfolk, 104
cracked wheat, 346
cracker, 104
cracker barrel, 104
Crackerjack, 54, 248
cracker pudding, 104
crackling, cracklins, chicharrons, 15,
    16, 104
crackling bread, 104

crackseed, 104
cranberry, 104–105
cranberry sauce, 105
crane berry, 105
C ration, 263
crawdad, crawdaddy, 105
crawfish, 105–106, 186
crawfish boil, 105
crawfish éouffée, 105, 124
crayfish, 105–106, 186
crayfish tail, 52, 105
cream, 106
cream cheese, 66, 99, 106
cream doughnut, 114
creamed chipped Beef, 78
creamed corn, 97
creamery butter, 49
Cream of Wheat, 61
creams, 293
cream soda, 300
cream toast, 106
credit card, 106
creekcrab, 105
creep, 192
crème brûlée, 106–107
Crenshaw, 59
creole caviar, 30
Creole cheese, 66
Creole mustard, 107
Creole rouget, 299
crevalle, 169
crevalle jack, 169
crib, 188
Crimini mushroom, 213
Crisco, 107
crisp head lettuce, 183
Crispus Attucks, 230
crockery cooker, 107
Crockpot, 107
Crocus, 116
croque-cignole, 114
Cross cracker, 93
cross cut, 240
cross-rib roast, 24
crouton, 50
crowd, 192
crow's-nest pudding, 87
crude oil, 339
cruller, 114
crumb bun, 107
crumb coffee, 90
crummin, 107
crushed ice, 163
crust coffee, 107
Cruvinet, 107
Cuba libre, 107–108
Cuban-Chinese food, 108
Cuban sandwich, 154
cucumber, 108
cuitlacoche, 108
cull, 108
Cup, 67
currant, 108
cush, 108
cushaw, 108
custard apple, 7, 69, 233
custard pie, 240
cut straw and molasses, 108
cutthroat trout, 332
cyclone candy, 108
cymling, 309
Cynthiana, 352

cypress trout, 39
czarnina, czarina, 108

dab, 128
dago red, 267, 350, 357
Dagwood sandwich, 109
daikon, 261
daiquiri, 109
dairy farm, 205
daisy, 109
damson plum, 245
Dancy orange, 224
dandelion, 109
dandelion wine, 109
dandy funk, 151
dangleberry, 160
Danish bowl cocktail, 47
Danish pastry, 109
Darjeeling tea, 324
dark fruitcake, 31
dasheen, 322
date, 109–110
date fish, 110
date milk shake, 110
date shake, 206
Deacon Porter's hat, 43, 110
deadeye, 192
dead marine, dead soldier, 110
dead to the world, 116
de-alcoholized wine, 351–352
de arbol, 75
De Chaunac, 353
decorator crab, 103
Deedie, 71
deep-dish pizza, 244
deep-fried frogs' legs, 134
deep-sea scallop, 286
dehydrated milk, 205
Delaware, 110, 353
Delaware succotash, 314
deli, 110
delicatessen, 16, 110, 270
Delicious apple, 8
Delmonico potato, 110
Delmonico's Restaurant, 269
Delmonico steak, 24, 269
demi-sec, 63
Democrat, 110
Dentyne chewing gum, 71
depth charge, 110
Derby pie, 110
designated driver, 110
designer pizza, 245
Des Moines squash, 2
deviled, 110–111
devilfish, 220
devil's food, 111
Devils on horseback, 54
dewberry, 31, 111
dextrose, 111, 316
diamondback terrapin, 335
Diamond grape, 353
diastoid, 196
Dick Smith, 111
diet Coke, 301
diet Pepsi, 301
Diet 7UP, 301
dill, 111
dill pickle, 239
dime-a-dip dinner, 111
diner, 111–112, 190, 270
dining saloon, 80
dinner, 112

dinner bucket, 190
dinnerhouse, 112
dinner pail, 190
dip, 112
dirt, 112
dirty rice, 112
dish night, 113
dishwater, 113
Disney School Bus, 190
distilled water, 344
dive, 270
divinity fudge, 135
Dixie Cup, 113
Dixie wine, 113
dodger, 97
dog, 113
dog and maggot, 192
dog apple, 233
dog biscuit, 151, 192
dogfish, 39, 113
dogfish shark, 292
doggie bag, 113
doghouse, 295
dog-in-a-blanket, 113
dog's body, 192
dog wagon, 111
Dolly Varden, 113, 332
Dolly Varden cake, 113
dolphin, 113–114
donut, doughnut, 114– 115
dope, 114
dorado, 113
dory, 343
doughboy, doughgod, 114
doughnut hole, 115
dough well done with cow to cover,
    192
doux, 63
Dover sole, 302
downhome, 115
draft beer, 26
Dram shop, 19
D ration, 263
draw one, 192
Dr. Brown's Cel-Ray Soda, 115
Dresden dressing, 115
dressing, 115, 313
dried apple, 115
dried milk, 205
drink box, 115
drinking straw, 116
drinking water, 38
drip pot, 90
drive-in, 270
drive-through, 270
driving while under the influence
    (DWI), 110
dropped egg, 116, 120
drown the miller, 116
Dr Pepper, 301
drum, 31, 116
drunk, 116
drunk and disorderly (D and D), 116
drunk coon, 261
dry, 63
dry beer, 27
dry bottom, 293
dry ice, 162
Dry Manhattan, 197
dryness, 201
dry sausage, 285
Dubble Bubble, 71
dubie, 111

duck, 116–117
duff, 117
du jour, 117
dulse, 117
dump cake, 117
dunfish, 89
Dungeness crab, 102, 117
Dungeness Crab Louie, 117
dunking, 114
durum wheat, 345
dusty miller, 117
Dutch bake oven, 118
Dutch courage, 117, 140
Dutchess, 353
Dutch grocery, 118
Dutch lunch, 118
Dutch oven, 118
Dutch salad, 118
DWI, 110
dyspepsia coffee, 118

Earl Grey tea, 324
early-bird special, 119
early potato, 253
Easter bunny, 80
Easter egg, 80
easy over, 192
eatin' iron, 100
eau sucrée, 119
echo, 192
Edam cheese, 67
eddo, 322
edible mussel, 213
edible seaweed, 185
edible shrimp, 294
EDTA, 2, 119
eel, 119
eel time, 119
egg, 119–120
egg bread, 120
egg butter, 120
egg coffee, 120
egg cook, 120
egg cream, 120–121
egg foo yung, 121
egg mushroom, 213
eggnog, 121, 205
egg noodle, 218, 232
eggplant, 121
eggplant caviar, 121
eggplant parmigiana, 121
egg pop, 118
egg posset, 251
egg roll, 308
eggs Benedict, 121
eggs ranchera, 160
eggs Sardou, 122
egg substitute, 119
egg toast, 134
Egyptian onion, 222
Egyptian quail, 260
eighty-one, 192
eighty-six, 192
election cake, 122
Elena Ruiz, 154
elephant garlic, 138
elevener, 122
Elijah's Manna, 61
el presidente, 122
Emerald Riesling, 353
emergency food program, 304
Emmaline sauce, 122
empanada, 122

Emperor grape, 143
emperor goose, 142
empty calorie, 125
enchilada, 123, 330
English breakfast tea, 324
English fly, 156
English fruitcake, 31
English monkey, 123
English muffin, 123
English muffin pizza, 123
English pheasant, 238
English sole, 302
enriched bread, 41
entrée, 123
Epsicle, 165
escarole, 74
Eskimo ice cream, 123
Eskimo Pie, 165
espresso, 90, 123–124
estate bottled, 352
estomacs mulâtres, 124
ethnic restaurant, 271
étouffée, 52, 124
eulachon, 297
European pear, 236
European plum, 245
evaporated milk, 205
Eve with a lid on, 192
expiration date, 223
extender, 28
extra dry, 63
extra lean, 184
extra sec, 63
extra virgin olive oil, 222

Fairy Floss Candy, 99
fajita, 125
fake bacon, 42
false morel, 213
family restaurant, 125
family soup, 304
fannie daddy, 86
farina, 129
farkleberry, 125
farmer cheese, 67
fast food, 13, 42, 112, 125, 133
fast-food restaurant, 125, 271
fat free, 131
FDA, 131, 142
feed bag, 100
feed trough, 100
feeling no pain, 116
fenberry, 105
fennel, 125–126
fermented mash, 45
fern bar, 126
feta, 67
fettuccine Alfredo, 126
fettuccine alla crema, 126
fettuccine alla panna, 126
fiambre, 126
fiddlehead fern, 126
fiddleneck, 126
field corn, 97
field pea, 233
5th Avenue candy bar, 56
fifty-five, 192
fifty-one, 192
fig, 126–127
fighting varietal, 352
Fig Newton, 95, 127
filbert, 153
filé gumbo, 147

filet, 192
filet mignon, 127, 324
filled cookie, 95
filling, 127
fill-of-container standards, 131
finger food, 127
Finnan haddie, 89
fire, 127
fireball, 158
fire cake, 127
firewater, 185
first lady, 192
fish boil, 127
fish camp, 127
fish chowder, 82–83
Fish House punch, 127, 259
fishing frog, 209
fish muddle, 127–128
fish stick, 128
five, 192
flake meat, 103
flameless ration heater, 264
flanken, 128
flanker, 128
flannel cake, 230
flapjack, 229
flat bone, 296
flatbread, 128
flatcar (pancake), 230
flat car (pork chop), 128
flatfish, 128
flauta, 128
flavored sugar, 316
fletcherism, 128
fletcherizing, 128
Fletcher's Original State Fair Corny
    Dog, 98
flint, 97
flip, 128
flitch, 16
floating island, 128
Flora, 353
Florida, 223
Florida lobster, 105
Florida pompano, 247–248
Floridita, 109
flounder, 128–129
flour, 129–130
Fluffernutter, 130
fluke, 128
flummery, 130
fly cake, 192
fly pie, 160
Foch, Maréchal Foch grape, 353
foie gras, 130
Folle Blanche, 353
fonda, 130
fondant, 130
fondue, 130
Food and Drug Administration, 2, 131
food court, 131
foodie, 131
food stamp, 131
food wine, 131–132
foo-foo, 132
fool, 132
forbidden fruit, 188
fortified wine, 350
fortune cookie, 132
freestone, 234
for-two-cents-plain, 290
forty-five-ninety, 188
forty-one, 192

Fox's u-bet Chocolate Flavor Syrup, 120
foxy, 349
Franconia potato, 132
Frankenberry, 62
franks and beans, 158
frappe, 164, 206
free, 184
free lunch, 60, 132, 269
free-range, 132
freestone, 234
freeze-dried instant, 90
French, 90, 133
French bread, 41
French cheesecake, 68
French Colombard, 132–133, 353
French cruller, 133
French dip sandwich, 133
French dressing, 133
french fry, 133
frenching, 133
Frenchman's delight, 192
French-style yogurt, 356
French toast, 133–134
Fresca, 301
freshman fifteen, 135
freshness date, 223
fresh-packed pickle, 240
fresh sausage, 285
freshwater cod, 48
freshwater lobster, 105
Fresno chile, 75
fress, 134
fried chicken, 134
fries, 133
frito pie, 98, 134
Fritos Corn Chips, 98
frizzled hot dog, 158
frog-eye gravy, 267
Frogmore stew, 134
frogs' legs, 134
fromage de tête de porc, 153
from the well, 134
frosted, 134, 206
frostfish, 148
frosting, 166
frozen daiquiri, 109
Frozen Dinner, 336
frozen margarita, 199
frozen waffle, 42
frozen yogurt, 166
fructose, 316
fruit cocktail, fruit cup, 135
fruiteria, 52
fruit salad, 135, 279
fruit soup, 135
fry bread, 135
fryer, 71
frying-pan bread, 135
fudge, 135
fudge brownie, 135
fudge candy, 54
fudge frosting, 135
fumaric acid, 135
Fumé Blanc, 285
funeral pie, 135–136
funnel cake, 136
funny cake, 136
furmenty, 130
fusion cuisine, 136
fuzzy navel, 136
fuzzy pucker, 136

GAC, 192
galley queen, 137
Gamay, 353
Gamay Beaujolais, 353
gap 'n' swallow, 137
gar, 137
garbanzo, 137
Garbo, 137
garden pea, 233
garden vegetable, 137
garlic, 137–138
garlic bread, 138
gaspergu, 116
Gatorade, 138
gavage, 130
gazpacho, gaspacho, 138
gazpacho salad, 138
gefilte fish, 58, 138
gelatin, 138
gelatin dessert, 170
gem, 138
generally recognized as safe, 2
Genoa salami, 280
gentleman will take a chance, 192
geoduck, 86
George Eddy, 192
Georgia peanut, 235
Gerber's, 15
German mustard, 158
German potato salad, 252
German puffs, 84
German's Sweet Chocolate cake, 139
Gewürztraminer, 353
gherkin, 240
giant red urchin, 289
giant rock scallop, 286
giant sea bass, 171
gibraltar, 139
Gibson, 139
gimlet, 139
gin, 43, 139–140
gin buck, 45
ginger, 140–141
ginger ale, 300
ginger beer, 141, 300
gingerbread, 140, 141
gingerbread man, 140, 141
ginger champagne, 141, 300
ginger pop, 300
gingersnap, 141
gingivere, 140
gin mill, 19, 141
Girl Scout Cookies, 141
globe artichoke, 12
globefish, 319
glucose, 111, 316
gluten flour, 129
glycerin, glycerol, 141
goat, 141
goat cheese, 67
goatfish, 141, 212
goat's milk Cheddar, 64–65
goetta, 141
go for a walk, 192
gohan, 142
golden bell pepper, 237
golden Cadillac, 142
Golden Delicious apple, 8–9
golden-finned trout, 113
golden red-horse, 314
golden trout, 113, 332
golden whitefish caviar, 60
Gold'N'Rich cheese, 67

gollipop, 187
goober, 235
Good Humor man, 165
good luck cookies, 291
goody-bread, 104
Gooey Butter Cake, 142
googlum, 142
Goo Goo Cluster, 54, 55
goose, 142
goosefish, 209
goosefoot, 181
goozlum, 142
gopherberry, 160
gorditas, 142
gordos, gordas, 142
Gorgonzola cheese, 67
gorp, 142
go south, 143
Gouda cheese, 67
goulash, 142
gourdhead buffalo, 314
gourmet pizza, 244–245
grab joint, 51
Graham bread, 143
graham cracker, 104, 143
graham-cracker crust, 143
graham flour, 129, 143
grain vinegar, 341
Granny Smith, 9
Granola, 62
grape, 143
grapefruit, 143–144
Grape-Nuts, 61
grape pie, 144
grape sugar, 111
GRAS, 2
grasshopper pie, 144
grattons, 104
gravel train, 192
Gravenstein, 9
graveyard stew, 144, 192
grayfish, 113
Gray Grunt, 146
grayling, 144
gray mullet, 212
gray partridge, 231
gray snapper, 299
gray trout, 308, 332
grazing, 144
grazing restaurant, 144
greasy spoon, 144
greater prairie chicken, 255
great hominy, 156
Great Molasses Flood, 208
green bean, 312
green corn, 96
green corn dance, 36
green frog, 134
green garlic, 138
Green Goddess, 144–145
Green Hungarian, 353
green lamb, 145
greenling, 145
green meat, 145
green onion, 286
green pepper, 237
green peppercorn, 237
green rémoulade, 268
green ripe olive, 221
greens, greenings, 92, 145
green salad, 279

green sea urchin, 289
green sturgeon, 60, 314
green tomato pie, 330
green turtle, 335
Grenache, 353
grenadine, 145
Grey Riesling, 353
griddle cake, 229
Grignolino, 353
grill, 32
grillade, 145
grillades and grits, 145
grilled pizza, 245
grinder, 154
grindle, 39
grits, 42, 145, 156
grits soufflé, 145
gritz, 288
grocery, 208
grocery bag, 44
grog, 145–146
grog blossom, 146
grog ration, 277
ground artichoke, 171
ground beef, 24
ground chuck, 24
groundhog, 192
ground meat, 24
ground-nut, 235
ground-pea, 235
ground round, 24
ground sirloin, 24
grouper, 21, 146, 171
group rations, 264
growler, 83, 146
grub, 146
grub hyson, 284
grunt, 146
guacamole, 14, 146–147
Guajillo chile, 75
guinea grinder, 154
guinea squash, 121
Guinness Stout, 32
gum, 147
gumball machine, 71
gumbis, 287
gumbo, 52, 102, 147
Gumbo aux Herbes, 147
gumbo filé 147
gumbo Ya-Ya, 147
gumbo z'herbes, 147
gumdrop, 54
gundinga, 147
gun-wadding bread, 100
gut-eater, 100
gut grenades, 149
gyro, 147
gyromitra, 213

habanero pepper, 75
haddock, 89
hake, 148
half-and-half, 106
halibut, 148
halitosis, 137
halvah, halavah, 148
ham, 42, 148–149
hamburger, 93, 149–150
hamburger meat, 24
hamburger stand, 149
Hamburg parsley, 231
Hamburg steak, 149
hamlette, 192

Hamlin orange, 224
hand-packed ice cream, 165
hangtown fry, 119, 150
hannahill, 32
happy hour, 150
hard-boiled egg, 120
hard candy, 54
hard cider, 84
hardhead, 195
hard maple, 197
hard red spring wheat, 345
hard red winter wheat, 345
hard roll, 174
hard-salted or hard-cured herring, 155
hard sauce, 150
hard-shell, 85
hardtack, hard Tommy, 150–151, 263
hard-wheat flour, 129
Harlem, 192
Harlem midget, 192
Harlem soda, 192
hartshorn, 151
hartshorn jelly, 151
Harvard beet 151
Harvard cocktail, 151
Harvard punch, 259
Harvey diner, 151
Harvey Girls, 151
Harvey restaurants, 151, 270
Harvey Wallbanger, 151–152
Harwich hermit, 154
hash, 152
hash browns, hashed browns, 252
hasherie, 152
hash house, 152, 190, 269
hash house Greek, 152
hash slinger, 152
hasty pudding, 42, 137, 167, 258
haupia, 152
have a glass eye, 116
Hawaiian Food, 152
Hawaiian haystack, 153
Hawaiian Passion, 159
haymaker's punch, 320
haystack potato, 252
hazelnut, 153
headcheese, 153
head lettuce, 183
health bar, 55
health food, 153, 215–216
health food movement, 41
health food restaurant, 271
health food store, 153
heart urchin, 289
heat-and-serve bread, 41
heat-and-serve eggs, 42
HeatH Bar, 56
heavenly hash, 153
heavy cream, 106
hemorrhage, 192
hen, 71
hen of the woods, 213
Herkimer Cheddar, 67
Herman, 153–154
hermit, 154
hero, 93, 154
hero boy, 154
herring, 155
Hershey Almond Bar, 55
Hershey Bar, 79
Hershey Milk Chocolate Bar, 55
Hershey's Kiss, 56
hibachi, 20, 155

hickory, 155
higdom, 155
high, yellow, black and white, 192
high and dry, 192
highback, 314
highball, 155
highball glass, 20
high muckamuck, 211
high on the hog, 250
hill dirt, 112
hinds' scallop, 286
hip flask, 155
historical flask, 155–156
hoagie, 154
hoarhound candy, 54, 156
hobo egg, 156
Hoboken special, 156
hockey puck, 156
hoe cake, 229
hogfish, 156
hogs and hominy, 156
hog snapper, 156
hokey-pokey, 154, 165
hokey-pokey man, 154, 165
hold the hail, 192
hole in the wall, 269
holiskes, 156
holy poke, 18
homard à l'américaine, 187
home brew, 26
home-fried potato, 252
home meal replacement, 156
hominy, 97, 145, 156
hominy grits, 14, 145, 156
honey, 156–157
honeybell, 224
honey bun, 310
honeycomb, 157
honeydew, 157
honeymoon, 24
hooch, hootch, 157
hooligan, 297
Hoosier bait, 157
Hoosier cake, 157
hooted, 116
hopping John, 102, 157, 185
hops, 192
horehound, 156
Horlick's Malted Milk, 196
hors d'oeuvre, 54
horse, 157–158
horse mackerel, 35, 169
horsemeat, 158
horseradish, 158
horse's neck, 158
hot ball, 158
hot bird and a cold bottle, 158
hot bricks, 158
hot brown, 158
hot buttered rum, 278
hot cha, 193
hot chocolate, 79
hot dog, 93, 158–159
hot dog stand, 159
hot dollar, 158
hot fudge, 159
hothouse lamb, 180
hot potato salad, 253
hot rock, 101
hot sandwich, 283
hot sauce, 159
hot sausage, 64
hot scotch, 159

hot slaw, 92
hot spot, 193
hot water, 159
hot-water tea, 53
houseboat, 193
house fried potato, 252
house pie, 159
houska, 159
Hubbard squash, 159, 309
huckleberry, 33, 160
huevos rancheros, 160
huff juff, 18
hukilau, 160
hulled corn, 156
humble pie, 160
humbo, 198
Humboldt dressing, 160
humbug, 160–161
humbug pie, 161
hummer, 161
humpback, 32
Hungarian goulash, 142
hurricane, 161
hush puppy, 161
hustler, 18
HVP, 161
hydraulic sandwich, 161
hydrogenated oil, 339
hydrogenation, 107
hydrolyzed vegetable protein, 161
hypermarket, 317

ice, 162
iceberg lettuce, 183
icebox, 162
icebox cookie, 162
icebox melon, 345
icebox pie, 162
ice bucket, 162
ice cream, 163–166
ice-cream cake, 165
ice-cream cone, 164
ice-cream fountain, 164
ice-cream parlor, 164
ice-cream sandwich, 165
ice cream soda, 55, 164
ice-cream stand, 164
iced coffee, 90
iced tea, 323
ice fish, 298
ice house, 93, 166
Iceland scallop, 286
ice man, 162
ice the rice, 193
ice wagon, 162
icing, 127, 166
I.D., 166
Idaho potato, 253
Idaho pygmy rabbit, 261
IHOP, 230
imitation, 167
imitation cream, 42
imitation cream cheese, 106
immigrant butter, 101
imperial crab, 167
Imperial Inca Coca, 300
Imperial lettuce, 183
Imp 'n' Ahrn, 167
imu, 167
inamona, 167
Indian, 167
Indian bread, 167
Indian cake, 229

Indian corn, 96
Indian cure, 282
Indian flour, 97
Indian lemonade, 167
Indian mustard, 213
Indian potato, 319
Indian pudding, 167, 258
Indian rice, 348
Indian River orange, 223
Indian whisky, 167–168
individual ration, 264
ingredients statement, 168
Inner Beauty, 159
instant coffee, 90
instant rice, 273
in the alley, 193
in the hay, 193
in the weeds, 168
invert sugar, 168
iodized salt, 283
Irish coffee, 168
Irish moss, 168
Irish pompano, 248
Irish turkey, 193
I-Scream Bar, 165
isinglass, 168
isleta bread, 168
Italia, 143
Italian beef sandwich, 154
Italian beef stand, 168
Italian bread, 41
Italian brown mushroom, 213
Italian cheesecake, 68, 69
Italian deli, 110
Italian grinder, 154
Italian hero sandwich, 154
Italian ice, 166
Italian ice cream, 165
Italian parsley, 231
Italian perfume, 137
Italian prune plum, 246
Italian sandwich, 154
It's It, 168
izer cookie, 168

jack, 169, 192
Jack Benny, 192
Jack Daniel's, 324
jack mackerel, 169
jackrabbit, 261
Jack Rose, 169
jake, 169
jalapeño, 75
jam, 171
Jamaican Hellfire, 159
jambalaya, jambolail, 52, 169
jamoka, 100
jamoke, 91
Jansson's Temptation, 169–170
Japanese crab, 102
Japanese oyster, 227
Japanese persimmon, 238
Japanese plum, 245
Japanese quail, 260
Japanese steakhouse, 170, 270
jasmine tea, 324
jasmine-type rice, 273
java, 90, 193
javelina, 250, 264
jawbreaker (candy), 54, 170
jawbreaker (hardtack), 151
Jeff Davis, 170
Jeff Davis coffee, 170

Jeff Davis pie, 170
Jeff Davis pudding, 170
Jell-O, 170–171
jelly, 171
jelly bean, 54, 171
jelly cake, 171
jelly roll, 171
jerk, 193
jerky, 46, 171, 263
Jersey lightning, 185
Jerusalem artichoke, 171
jewelhead, 116
jewfish, 21, 146, 171
Jewish champagne, 290
Jewish cheesecake, 68
Jewish delicatessen, 110
Jewish fillet, 24
Jewish penicillin, 171
jicama, 172
Jickey wedding cake, 240
jigger, 20
Jim Hill mustard, 172
jimmies, 172
joe, 193
Joe Frogger, 172
Joe's stone crab mustard mayonnaise,
  311
Johannisberg Riesling, 172, 353
John Chinaman, 101
johnnycake, 172, 229, 230
Johnny Marzetti, 173, 185
jojoba, 173
jolly boy, 173
jolthead porgy, 250
Jonah crab, 102
Jonathan, 9
jook, 173
jook house, 173
Juicyfruits, 55
jujube, 173
Jujubes, 55, 173
juke, 173
juke house, 173
juke joint, 19
julekake, 173
julep, 206
jumble, jumbal, 173
junior club, 87
Junior Mints, 56
juniper berry, 139
junk food, 125, 173

Kairomel, 98
kaiser roll, 174
kale, 50
kalua pig, 174, 250
kamikaze, 174
Kansas City fish, 101
Kansas City strip, 24
Kansas dog, 158
Karo, 98
Karo pie, 98, 236
kasha, 45
Katy apricot, 12
kaukau, 174
kedgeree, 174
keech cake, 174
Keitt, 197
Kellogg's Toasted Corn Flakes, 61
kelp greenling, 145
kelp-weed scallop, 286
Kennebec salmon, 282
Kentucky bourbon, 39

Kentucky breakfast, 174
Kentucky oyster, 78
ketchup, 174–175
kettle meat, 175
keyhole urchin, 289
Key lime, 184
Key lime pie, 184, 240
Kickapoo Indian Medicine, 175
Kickapoo Joy Juice, 175
kidney bean, 22, 175
kielbasa, kolbasa, kolbasy, 175
killer bar, 175
kinaalda, 40
King Boletus, 213
King cake, 175–176
King cake party, 175
king crab, 102
kingfish, 176, 195
king mackerel, 195
King orange, 224
King Ranch chicken, 176
king's cake, 287
king-sized roast, 296
kipper, 155
kippered salmon, 282
kishka, 176
kiwifruit, 176
Kix, 62
klatch, 176
knickknack, 217
knipp, 288
knish, 176
Knish Alley, 176
knockout drops, 204
knockwurst, 176
know your cans, 101
kolache, 177
Kool-Aid, 47
Korean-style poke, 246
kosher, 93, 177
kosher pickle, 239
kosher salt, 283
kosher-style, 177
Kossuth cake, 177
Kraft Dinner, 195
K ration, 264
kräusening, 27
kreplach, 177
kringle, 177–178
kringle cookie, 177–178
kugel, 178
kulolo, 178
kumiss, koumyss, koumiss, 178
kummelweck, 24
Kwanzaa, 178

L.A., 193
lab, 215
laban, 178
labrusca grape, 59, 110
labskaus, 186
lactic acid, 179
lactose, 316
la cuite, 179
ladies' night, 179
Lady Baltimore cake, 179
ladyfinger, 179
ladyfish, 35
lady lock, 179
Lafayette, 116, 308
Lafayette gingerbread, 140, 179–180
lager, 25
lagniappe, 180

lake lawyer, 39
lake sturgeon, 314
lake trout, 332
Lalla Rookh, 180
lamb, 180
lamb's lettuce, 181
lambs'-quarters, 181
la médiatrice, 154
land crab, 102–103
Lane cake, 181
la nouvelle cuisine, 271
lap lunch, 181
largemouth bass, 30
larrup, 101
lasagna, 232
last call, 181
Late Harvest, 181
lath-open bread, 181
Latin-American deli, 110
latke, 181
laulau, 181
LBA culture, 205
leaf lettuce, 183
leaf mustard, 214
lean, 183
leather, 181–182
leather or feather, 182
Lebanon bologna, 34
Lebkuchen, 182
lecithin, 182
Lee cake, 182
leek, 182
Lee orange, 224
lefse, 182
lemon, 182–183
lemonade, 182
lemon-belly, 103
lemon-meringue pie, 182–183
lemon sole, 129
lemon thyme, 327
Leon Millot, 353
lesser prairie chicken, 255
lettuce, 183
levulose, 316
liberty cabbage, 183
liberty garden, 137
liberty tea, 323
Liederkranz, 67, 183
Life Savers, 54
light, 27, 131, 183–184
light beer, 183
light coffee, 91
light cream, 106
lighter, 183
light in sodium, 183
lightnin' bread, 41
light whipping cream, 106
light whiskey, 346–347
light wine, 351
lima bean, 22, 184
Limburger, 67
lime, 184
lime rickey, 274
limpa, 185
limpin' Suzan, 185
limu, 185
Lindy's cheesecake, 68–69
lingonberry, 104
linguine, 185
lion's paw, 286
liqueur glass, 20
liqueur rum, 277
liquor, 185

liquor sock, 185
lite, 183–184
little, few, 184
little cake, 238
Little Joe's, 184
littleneck clam, 85
little roncador, 185
liver pie, 99
liverwurst, 185–186
lobscouse, 186
lobster, 186–187
lobster à l'américaine, 187
lobsterette, 187, 286
lobster fajita, 125
lobster fra diavolo, 187
lobster Newburg, 187–188
lobster palace, 186, 269
lobster roll, 188
lobster shack, 188
lobster Thermidor, 186
loco moco, 188
Logan bar, 263
loganberry, 31
Log Cabin Syrup, 198
loggerhead, 335
logger slang, 188
lollipop, 54, 188
lomi-lomi salmon, 188, 281
London broil, 189
London Dry Gin, 140
long-finned squid, 309
longhorn, 22, 23
Longhorn Cheddar, 67
Long Island duckling, 117
Long Island iced tea, 189
Long Island lobster roll, 188
long-john, 30, 114
long-life milk, 205
longneck, 189
long-necked clam, 85
long-range patrol packet, 263
long sauce, 189
looped, 116
loose in the hilt, 116
loose meat, 189
loosemeat sandwich, 297
looseners, 193
Lord's Supper, 191
lost bread, 133
lotte, 209
Louisburg pie, 189
Louisiana Kitchen, 52
love and tangle, 189
love apple, 189, 329
love knot, 114
low (fat, calorie, cholesterol content),
  183–184
low-alcohol beer, 27, 215
low calorie, 183
low cholesterol, 183–184
lower fat, 183–184
lower-salt bacon, 16
low fat, 183–184
low-fat cottage cheese, 66
Low Grade Hash, 152
low mull, 189
low saturated fat, 184
low sodium, 183
lox, 16, 189, 282
luau, 152, 190
lumber, 193
lumberjack pie, 188
lump meat, 103

lunch, 44, 190
lunch box, 190
lunch counter, 2, 190, 269
luncheon, 190
luncheonette, 190
lunch pail, 190
lunchroom, 190
lunch stand, 190
lushed 116
lutefisk, 194

macadamia nut, 195
McAdoo wine, 257
macaroni, 195, 232
McGinty pie, 202
McIntosh apple, 9
mackerel, 195
mackinaw, 332
made dish, 123
Madeira nut, 195
mademoiselle, 195–196
mahimahi, 114
maiden's delight, 193
maid of honor, 196
Maine lobster, 186
Maine Pure Spruce Gum, 70
mai tai, 196
maître d'hôtel butter, 196
maize, 96
make it virtue, 193
mako, 292
makoola, 196
malasado, 196
Malbec, 353
mallard, 117
malted, 164, 196–197, 206
Maltex, 62
malt liquor, 27
malt shop, 206
mama, 193
man-about-town, 197
manapua, 197
man at the pot!, 101
mandarin orange, 224
M & M's Plain Chocolate Candies, 56
mandrake, 7
manini, 197
mango, 197
mangrove snapper, 299
Manhattan, Manhattan cocktail, 87, 197
Manhattan Clam Chowder, 82
manicotti, 232
Manila clam, 86
mannitol, 197
maple syrup, 197–198
maquechou, maque choux, 198
maraschino, 198–199
marchpane, 54
Mardi Gras, 175
margarine, 49, 199
margarita, 199
marinara, 199
Marlborough pie, Marlborough pudding, Marlborough tart, 199–200
marlin, 200
marmalade, 200
marshmallow, 200
marsh rabbit, 261
Marsh Seedless, 143
Martha Washington pie, 344
martini, 87, 200–201
martini sandwich, 201

marvels, 225
Mary Ball Washington's ginger bread, 179
Mary Jane, 54, 56
Maryland fried chicken, 305
Maryland stuffed ham, 201
Mary Washington, (asparagus), 13
marzipan, 54
masa, 201
Masa Harina, 201
mashed potato, 252
mashu, 201
Mason jar, 201
matrimony knot, 114
matzo, 202
Matzo brei, 202
mawmouth, 202
mayapple, 7
mayfish, 202
mayhaw, 202
Maylay Hen, 71
mayonnaise, mayo, 193, 202
Maytag Blue, 202
M.D., 193
meadow strawberry, 311
meadow tea, 203
Meal, Operational, Ready-to-Eat, 264
Meal, Ready to Eat, 264
meat, 203
meat by-product, 203
meateria, 52
meat loaf, 203
meat product, 203
medianoche, 154
meeting seeds, 203
melba sauce, 263
melba toast, 203
menudo, 203
merganser, 117
Meritage, 203
Merlot, 353
Merry Christmas cake, 31
mescal, mezcal, 3
mess, 203
mess crew, 203
mess hall, 203
mess sergeant, 203
mess tent, 203
mess wagon, 83
metal money, 106
metate, 204
metzel soup, 204
Mexican-American cuisine, 74
Mexican breakfast, 204
Mexican lime, 184
Mexican parsley, 84
Mexican strawberry, 101
Miami grill, 204
Michigan banana, 233
mickey, 204, 252
Mickey Finn, 204
microbrewery, 26
microwave oven, 204
middling bread, 41
migas, 204
Mike and Ike, 193
mile-high cake, 204
milk, 204–205
milk bottle, 205
milk can, 205
milk cap, 213
milk chocolate, 80
Milk Duds, 56

milk-fed veal, 338
milkmen, 205
milk punch, 205
milk ranch, 205
milk sherbet, 164
milk shake, 31, 50, 134, 164, 206
milk sugar, 316
milk wagon, 205
Milky Way, 54, 56, 205
mince, mincemeat, 206
Mineola orange, 224
mineral water, 37, 344
ming-mang, 206
miniature marshmallow, 200
minimum drained weight, 131
Minnehaha, 206
Minnesota Blue, 331
Minnesota Slim cheese, 67
mint, 206
mint jelly, 206
mint julep, 206
Minute Rice, 273
miracle, 207
mirasol chile, 75
mirliton, 64
Mission, 353
missionary's downfall, 314
Mission bell, 207
Mississippi catfish, 60
Mississippi mud cake, Mississippi mud pie, 207
Mississippi paddlefish, 61
Mixed grill, 207
Mix-in, 166
mock apple pie, 207, 240
mocktail, 207
mock-turtle soup, 207
Modesto apricot, 12
modular eating, 144
moi, 207
molasses, 101, 207–208
molded salad, 279
mom-and-pop, 208
mongole soup, 208
Monitor plum, 246
monkey bread, 208
monkey food, 208
monkey gland, 209
monkey-nut, 235
monkey rum, 209
monkfish, 209
monoglyceride, 209
monosodium glutamate, 2, 209
Monte Cristo sandwich, 209
Monterey Jack, 65, 67
Montgomery, 201
Montpelier cracker, 92
moo juice, 191
moon, 210
mooneye, 209
moon-eyed, 116
moonfish, 209
Moon Pie, 209
moonshine, moonshiner, 209–210
moonshine whiskey, 45, 98
Moors and Christians, 157
moose, 210
Moravian Christmas cookie, 210
morel, 213
MORE ration, 264
Mormon dip, 101
moro crab, 310
Moro orange, 224

Mortadella, 280
Moscato, 353
Moscow mule, 141, 210
Mossholder's, 67
mother liquor, 208
Mounds candy bars, 56
mountain dew, 210–211
mountain lamb, 141
mountain lettuce, 285
mountain oyster, 211
mountain tea, 211
mourning dove, 240
Moxie, 211
mozzarella, 66, 67
MRE ration, 264
Mr. Goodbar, 56
Mrs. Washington's pie, 37
MSG, 3, 209
muckamuck, 211
Mud, 193
mudbug, 105
muddle, 211
muddler, 211
mudfish, 39
mud hen cake, 44
mudjack, 39
mud pie, 240
Muenster, 67
muffin, 211
muffuletta, muffaletta, 154, 211–213
mulacolong, 212
mulatto crab, 102
mulberry, 212
Müller-Thurgau, 353
mullet, 212
mulligan, 212
mulligan car, 188
mulligan joint, 269
mulligan-mixer, 212
mulligan stew, 212
mulligatawny, 212
multiple offender bar, 175
munchies, 212
Muntok pepper, 237
Murcott, 224
Murphy, 193
Muscadine, 143, 212–213, 353
Muscat of Alexandria, 143, 262
Muscovy duck, 117
mush, 213
mushroom, 213
Music Hall Influence, 213
musk duck, 117
muskellunge, 241
muskie, 241
musk melon, 57
mussel, 213
mustang, 157
mustard, 213–214
mustard greens, 214
mutton, 180
muttonfish, 299
mutton snapper, 299
mystery meat, 214

nab, nablabs, 215
nacho, 215
naked martini, 201
'nana 'n' pudding, 215
Napa Gamay, 353
Naples biscuit, 215
Nassau grouper, 146
native American strawberry, 311

native beef, 215
natural, 193
natural food, 137, 153, 215–216
natural water, 38
navel orange, 223
navy bean, 22, 216
Navy punch, 259
Neapolitan flip, 90
Neapolitan ice cream, 163
Neapolitan-style pizza, 244
near beer, 26
neat, 311
Nebbiolo, 353
NECCO wafer, 55, 94
ned, 216
needle beer, 26
needlefish, 137, 216
negative reservation, 216
negimaki, 216
negro coffee, 216
negus, 216
nene, 216
Nescafé, 90
netted melon, 57
New American cuisine, 216–217, 219, 271
New Bedford pudding, 217
New England boiled dinner, 217
New England Clam Chowder, 82
New England hake, 148
New England hardscrapple, 217
New Jersey tea, 217
New Mexico chile, 75
new potato, 253
Newton's cakes, 127
Newtown Pippin, 9
New York Cheddar, 65
New York cheesecake, 68
New York Nick, 85
New York strip, 24
New York System, 217
Niagara grape, 353
nicknack, nic-nac, 217
nigger babies, 80
niggers-in-a-blanket, 101
nigger special, 345
nightcap, 217
night-owl restaurant, 270
nimtopsical, 116
nioi, 218
Nipku, 58
nitrosamines, 301
Noah's boy, 193
no-alcohol beer, 215
nocake, 218
No-Cal soda, 301
no cow, 193
nonalcohol, 27
nonalcoholic wine, 351
nonkosher, 177
nonsparkling, 37
noodle, 218
noodle pudding, 258
nooning, 218
nooning shed, 218
nopall, 218
Norfolk aluminum pan, 104
northern leopard frog, 134
northern pike, 241
northern puffer, 319
Northern Spy, 9
nosh, 218
nosher, 218

Nosh restaurant, 218
nougat, 218
nouvelle cuisine, 176, 218–219
Nova, Novie, Novy, 281
Nova orange, 224
Nova Scotia salmon, 16, 281
Nuevo Latino, 219
nun's toast, 134
nutmeg melon, 57
NutraSweet, 13
nutrition labeling, 219
Nuworld cheese, 67

oat, 220
oat flour, 129
oatmeal, 220
oceanic bonito, 297
ocean whitefish, 347
octopus, 220
O.D. gravy, 220
Ogeechee lime, 220
ohelo, 220
ohelo-kai, 220
Oh Henry! candy bar, 56
ohia, 220
Ohio pudding, 220
Ohio squash, 159
oiled, 116
O.J., 193
oke, 220
okolehao, 220
okra, 179, 220–221
old-fashioned cocktail, 221
old-fashioned cocktail glass, 20
old ham, 148
old maid, 221
Old Ned, 221
Old Tom, 140
oleomargarine, 199
olestra, 221
olive, 221–222
olive drab gravy, 220
olive oil, 222
omelette, 120
one-arm lunchroom, 270
one-dish meal, 59
one-finger poi, 246
onion, 222
onion fish, 222
onion ring, 133
onion-style poke, 246
ono, 222
on scholarship, 222
on the hoof, 193
on the rocks, 222
on wheels, 193
oopu, 222
opah, 222
opaka-paka, 222–223
opaleye, 223
opelu, 223
open dating, 223
open-faced sandwich, 283
opihi, 223
opossum, 223
orange, 223–224
orange blossom, 224
orange crookneck, squash, 309
Orange Julius, 224
orange pekoe, 324
orange roughy, 224
Oregano, 224–225
Oregon tea, 225

oreilles; de cochon, les, 225
OREO, 225
organic, 225
organic food, 137, 153
orgeat, 225
Original Shirley Temple Soft Drink, 293
Orlando orange, 224
ortolan, 225
Oscar's original Waldorf recipe, 343
Osceoloa orange, 224
Osgood pie, 70
ostkaka, 225
ostrich fern, 126
Oswego tea, 225
OTW, 225
overnight pickle, 239
ox dung gravy, 220
Oxford John, 226
oyster, 226–227
oysters Bienville, 227–228
oyster cellar, 226
oyster cocktail, 226
oyster cracker, 104, 226
oyster house, 226
oysters Kirkpatrick, 228
Oyster Line, 226
oyster mushroom, 213
oyster plant, 282
oysters Rockefeller, 228
oyster room, 80
oyster saloon, 226
oyster shooter, 228
oyster stew, 227
oyster stuffing, 313
oyster war, 226

Pacific halibut, 148
Pacific herring, 155
pacific porgy, 250
Pacific sand dab, 128, 283
Pacific sardine, 284
pack, 229
packaged pancake batter, 42
package-goods store, package store, 229
pack date, 223
paddy rice, 273
Pagan Pink Ripple, 351
Page orange, 224
painted greenling, 145
painted mackerel, 195
pair of drawers, 193
pair of overalls, 101
Palace Court salad, 229
palmetto, 229
palm heart, 229
Palomino, 353
pancake, 42, 229–230
pancake syrup, 198
pan drippings, 230
pan pizza, 244
panther sweat, 185
pantile, 151
papain, 230
papaw, 230
papaya, 230
paper bread, 241
papershell, 102
paralyzed, 116
para-ration, 263
parboiled rice, 273
parched corn, 156

parching corn, 248
parfait, 230–231
Parker House roll, 231
Parmesan, 68
parsley, 231
parsnip, 231
parson's nose, 249
partridge, 231
party dip, 112
pasilla, 75
Passaro's Famous Manhattan Special, 301
passenger pigeon, 241
passion fruit, 231–232
pasta, 232
pasta fazool, pasta and beans, pasta e fagiole, 232
pasta primavera, 232
pastelles calientes, 232
pastrami, 232–233
pastry flour, 129
pasty, 233
Patterson apricot, 12
pattypan, 309
paw bread, 168
pawnhaus, 288
pawpaw, 233
PBJ, 283
pea, 233
pea bean, 216
peacemaker, 154
peach, 233–234
peach brandy, 234
peach melba, 234
peach schnapps, 234
peachy, 234
peanut, 234–236
peanut boilings, 235
peanut brittle, 235
peanut butter, 225
peanut butter and jelly, 283
peanut cream gravy, 235
peanut pie, 235
peanut soup, 236
peanut stand, 235
pear, 236
pear chip, 236
pear cider, 237
pearl corn, 97
pearl hominy, 156
pearl onion, 222
pearl white rice, 273
pecan, 236
pecan ball, 236
pecan pie, 236
peccary, 250, 264
pecorino, 68
Pecorino Romano, 275
peeled green tomato, 329
Peerless Wafers, 55
Peking duck, 117
pemmican, 46, 104, 171, 236–237
penny candy, 54, 55
penny restaurant, 51
pepita, 237
pepper, 237
peppercorn, 237
peppermint, 206
peppermint stick, 54
peppermint-stick ice cream, 206
pepper steak, 237
Pepsi-Cola, Pepsi, 300, 301
pequin pepper, 75

perch, 21, 237
Perfection Crisps, 298
Perfect Manhattan, 197
perry, 237
persimmon, 237–238
Petite Sirah, 238, 353
petrale sole, 302
petsai, 50
petticoat tail, 238
Peychaud's bitters, 30, 286
Pharaoh quail, 260
pheasant, 238
Philadelphia Brand Cream Cheese, 106
Philadelphia cheese-steak, 238
Philadelphia eggs, 238
Philadelphia Nick, 85
Philadelphia pepper pot, 239
Philadelphia scrapple, 288
Philadelphia sticky bun, 239, 310
philpy, 239
phlegm cutter, 185
phosphoric acid, 239
Phylloxera vastatrix, 349
picadillo, 239
piccalilli, 239
Piccolo Romano, 275
pickle, 239–240
pickle cured, 15
pickled, 116
pickled herring, 155
pickled lox, 189
pickled pepper, 240
pickled pork, 240, 267
pick me up, 185
picnic, 240
picnic ham, 53, 240
pie, 240
pie card, 240
pie plant, 272
pie-washer, 240
pigeon, 240–241
pigeon pea, 157
pigfish, 146, 156
pignoli, pignolia, 243
pig out, 241
pigs' ear, 225, 241
pigs-in-a-blanket, 54, 158
Pig Stand, 270
pigs vest with buttons, 101
pigweed, 181
pike, 241
piked dogfish, 113
pike perch, 343
pike stone, 241
piki bread, 241
pilaf, pilaff, pilau, pilaw, plaw, 72, 241–242
piloncillo, 101
pilot bread, 150
pilot pellet, 242
pilsener, 25
pilsner glass, 20
pimiento, 76
piña colada, 88, 242
pinbone, 296
pinder, pindal, 235
pineapple, 242–243
pineapple Cheddar, 65
pineapple cheese, 68
Pineapple orange, 224
pineapple strawberry, pine strawberry, 311

pine nut, 243
Pink-Colored Pancakes, 229–230
pink lady, 243
pink salmon, 281
pink sauce, 235
pink scallop, 286
pink shrimp, 294
pinole, 243
piñolos, piñon, 243
Pinot Blanc, 353
Pinot Chardonnay, 64
Pinot Gris, 353
Pinot Noir, 243, 353
pinwheel, 243
pipikaula, 171, 243
pistachio, 243
pita, 243
Pittsburgh, 193
pixillated, 116
pizza, pizza pie, 243–245
pizza strip, 245
pizzeria, pizza parlor, 52, 243–245, 270
placebo bottle, 245
plain pizza, 245
planked, 291
plantain, 17, 245
planter's punch, 259
plastered, 116
plate lunch, 245
ployes, 230
plum, 245–246
plum duff, 117
plum pudding, 246, 258
Plymouth Rock chicken, 71
poblano pepper, 76
po'boy, 154, 246
pocket bread, 41
pocket soup, 246
poi, 246
poke, 246
pokeberry, 246
pokeweed, 246
poki, 246
Polish sandwich, 246
Polish sausage, 175
pollock, 246
Polynesian food, 246
polysorbate 60, 247
pomegranate, 247
pomelo, 143–144
pomfret, 247
pommes de terre soufflées, pommes soufflées, puffed potato, 247
pommes frites, 133
pompano, 49, 169, 247–248
pompano en papillote, 248
pompano Montgolfier, 248
Pompey's head, 248
pone, 42, 96
Ponkan, 224
pony, 248
pony glass, 20
pooch, 101
poor boy, 246
poor doe, 101
Poor Knights of Windsor, 133
poor-man dishes, 248
popcorn, popped corn, 96, 97, 248–249
popcorn ball, 248
pope's nose, 249
pop-out, 249

popover, 249
poppy fish, 248
Popsicle, 165–166
pop wine, 249, 351
porgy, 249–250
pork, 250–251
pork barbecue, 19
pork belly, 251
port, 251
porter, 25
porterhouse, 251
porterhouse steak, 24, 25, 251, 324
Porto, 251
Portuguese sweet bread, 251
Porty Reek long-lick, 251
Positalker, 337
posset, 251
possum, 223
possum plum, 237
Post Toasties, 61
Postum Cereal Food Coffee, 61
potato, 251–253
potato chip, 133, 284
potato flour, 129
potato salad, 253
potato skin, 252
potato snow, 253
pot cheese, 98
poticia, 253
potlikker, 92, 253–254
potluck, 254
pot marjoram, 224
potpie, 240, 254
pot roast, 254
potted, 116
pouch bread, 264
poultry, 254
poultry by-product, 254
poultry food product, poultry product, 254
poultry meat, 254
pound cake, 49, 254
pouring cream, 104
pousse-café, 254–255
powdered egg, 42
powdered milk, 205
power breakfast, 255
power lunch, 190, 255
prairie bass, 39
prairie beeve, 101
prairie bitters, 101
prairie buffalo, 314
prairie chicken, 255
prairie fowl, 255
prairie grouse, 255
prairie hen, 255
prairie oyster, 255
praline, 54, 255
prawn, 255
precooked rice, 273
preserves, 171
pressure cooker, 255
pre-theater dinner, 112
pretzel, 255–256
pretzel thins, 256
prickly cactus, prickly pear, 256
primal Boston (or shoulder) butt, 251
primal brisket, 24
primal chuck, 24
primal flank, 24
primal leg, 251
primal loin, 251
primal picnic shoulder, 251

primal plate, 24
primal rib, 24
primal round, 24
primal shank, 24
primal short loin, 24
primal side pork, 251
primal sirloin, 24
primal sparerib, 251
Princess Pats, 298
Prize Cake, 181
Prizetaker onion, 222
processed cheese, processed cheese food, processed cheese spread, 68
progressive dinner, 256
Prohibition, 256–257
prole food, proletarian food, 257
pronghorn, 6
proof, 257
propylene glycol alginate, 5
propyl gallate, 257
prosciutto, 149, 257
protose steak, 257
prune, 246, 257
PT, 193
ptarmigan, 257–258
pudding, 258
pudding cake pie, 37
pueblo bread, 258
puffed potato, 247
puffer, 319
pug dog, 275
Pullman car, 258
Pullman loaf, 258
pummelo, 143
pumpernickel, 258–259
pumpkin, 259
pumpkin pie, 240, 259
punch, 259
punk, 102, 103
pupu, pu pu platter, 259
pure olive oil, 222
purified water, 38
purple passion fruit, 232
purple sea urchin, 289
push sandwich, 246
pussyfoot, 293
put out the lights and cry, 193

quahog, 85
quail, 260
Quaker Oats, 61
quaking custard, 260
queen's cake, 287
Queensland nut, 195
quiche, 260
quiche Lorraine, 260
quick bread, 40, 260
quick-cooking rice, 273
quinoa, 260
Quire-of-Paper Pancakes, 229

rabbit, 261
rabbit food, 261
rabbit stew, 261
raccoon, 261
raccoon oyster, 227
Radar range, 204
radicchio, 261
radio, 193
radish, 261
Raffles bar gin sling, 296
railroad cookie, 261–262
rainbow runner, 169

rainbow smelt, 298
rainbow trout, 332
raised doughnut, 114
raisin, 262
raisin bread, 41
raisin pie, 135–136
Ramos Gin Fizz, 262
ramp, 262
ranch dressing, 262
ranch eggs, 160
rankins, 262
rapini, 43
raspberry, 31, 263
ratafia, 263
ration, 263–264
rattlesnake, 264
ravigote, 264
ravioli, 232
raw bar, 264
raw sugar, 316
razorback, 250, 264, 314
razor clam, 85
recipe book, receipt book, 94
Recognized Viticultural Regions, 264–267
Recommended Daily Allowances (RDAs), 219, 267
recooked cheese, 68
red and white, 267
red beans and rice, 157, 267
red cap, 213
red drum, 116
red eye, 185
redeye bass, 30
redeye gravy, 149, 267
redfish, 31, 116
red grouper, 146
red ham gravy, 267
redhead, 117, 260
redhorse, 267
red hot, 159
red ink, 267
Red Italian onion, 222
redmouth, 314
red mullet, 212
red rice 267
red salmon, 281
red salmon caviar, 60
red sauce, 267
red snapper, 299
red snapper Veracruz, 267–268
Red Spanish pineapple, 243
red squid, 309
red tangelo, 224
reduced, 183–184
Reese's Peanut Butter Cups, 57
refried beans, 268
regular, 158
regular bacon, 15
regular doughnut, 114
relish, 268
rémoulade, 268
rennet, 96
restaurant, 268–271
restaurant row, 271–272
Reubenola, 272
Reuben sandwich, Reuben, 272
Reuben Special, 272
revenooer, 210
rex sole, 302
Rhineinjun bread, 278
Rhode Island Greening, 10
Rhode Island Red chicken, 71

Rhode Island White chicken, 71
rhubarb, 272
rhubarb pie, 272
Ribier, 143
rice, 272–273
rice cake, 228, 273
Rice Chex, 62
rice corn, 97, 248
rice flour, 129
Rice Krispies Treats, 274
rice pudding, 273
rickey, 274
ricotta, 68
riddling, 63
ring-necked duck, 117
ring-necked pheasant, 238
rinkum-dity, 278
ripe olive, 221
risotto, 273
rivel, 274
riz, 274
roach cake, 192
roach coach, 274
roadhouse, 274
roaster, 71
roasting corn, 97
Robinson orange, 224
Rob Roy, 197, 274
rock and rye, 274
rock bass, 32
rock candy, 274–275
rock crab, 102–103
rockets, 276
rockfish, 146, 275, 313
rock lobster, 187
rock maple, 197
rock parsley, 231
rock salt, 282
rock shrimp, 294
Rocky Mountain oyster, 210–211
rocky road, 275
Roffignac, 275
rollmops, 155, 275
romaine lettuce, 50, 183
romainian, 24
Romano, 68, 275
Rome Beauty, 10
rooster-spur pepper, rooster-spur pepper sauce, 275
root beer, 31, 300
rooter, 314
Roquefort dressing, 275–276
rosé, 353
Rose's Lime Juice, 139
rosina, 135–136
Ross's goose, 142
rotgut, 185
rough rice, 273
round bone, 296
round clam, 85
roux, 276
royal red shrimp, 294
rubber-chicken dinner, 276
Ruby Blood orange, 224
Ruby Cabernet, 276, 353
Ruby Red, 144
rugelach, 276
rugola, 276
rum, 276–278
rumaki, 278
rum and Coke, 277
rumrousal, 278
rum tum tiddy, 278

Rhode Island White chicken, 71
running south, 278
Runza, runsa, 278
Russian caviar, 60
Russian charlotte, 64
Russian crab, 102
Russian dressing, 47, 278
rusty flounder, 129
rutabaga, 335
rye, 32
rye flour, 129
rye 'n' injun bread, 40, 278
rye whiskey, 278

sablefish, 279
saccharin, 2, 279
sacramental wine, 350
sad cake, 279
sago, 279
St. Peter's fish, 327
salad, 279–280
salad bar, 280
Salad Savoy, 280
salamander, 32
salami, 280
saleratus, 280
Salisbury steak, 280
Sally Lunn, Sally Lunn bread, 280
salmagundi, salmagundy, 281
salmon, 281–282
salmon berry, 123
salmon-burger, 282
saloon, 282
salsa, 98, 112, 282
salsify, 282
salt, 282–283
salt cellar, 283
salteur liquor, 283
salt horse, salt hoss, 101, 282
Saltines, 104
salt lick, 283
saltpeter, 98
salt pork, 16
salt potato, 283
salt rising bread, 283
saltwater taffy, 321
samp, 156
Samson, 277
sand, 193
sand crab, 103
sand dab, 128–129, 283
sand-lapper, 112
sand lobster, 187
sand sole, 302
sand tilefish, 327
sandwich, 283
sandwich bread, 283
sandwich loaf, 40, 283
sangaree, 259
sangría, 259, 283–284
Sanka, 90
sapsis, 284
Saratoga potato, Saratoga chip, 252, 284
Sarawak pepper, 237
sardine, 284
sargo, 146
sarsaparilla, sassparilla, 31, 284
sassafras, 284–285
sass tea, 284
Saturday nights, 191
sauce, 144
sauce piquante, 285
saucer glass, 21

sauerkraut, sourcrout, 183, 285
sausage, 285
sausage shop, 177
Sauvignon Blanc, 285, 353
savoy cabbage, 50
saxifrage, 285
Sazerac, 87, 286
scaled ling, 39
scallion, 285
scallop, 286
scalloped potato, 252
scalloped squash, 309
scampi, 286–287, 294
scared whiskey, 210
scarlet strawberry, 311
schichtkuche, 287
schmaltz, 287
schmaltz herring, 155
schmear, 287
schnitz und kneppe, Schnitz-und-Gnepp, schnitz un knepp, 287
school breakfast program, 287
school lunch program, 287
schooner, 287
scoff-law cocktail, 287–288
scorpionfish, 275
scotch, 44
Scotch bonnet, 75
Scotch ham, 149
Scotch Manhattan, 274
scoter, 117
scrambled egg, 120
scrap johnycake, 104
scrapple, 141, 288
screwdriver, 87, 288
scripture cake, 288
scrod, scrode, 89, 288
scup, 249
Scuppernong, 212, 288–289
sea biscuit, sea bread, 150
seaboard, 193
sea bob, 294
sea dust, 193
sea foam, 289
sea herring, 155
sea pie, 289
sea plum, 101
sea scorpion, 275
sea squab, 319
sea sturgeon, 60
sea trout, 145, 345
sea urchin, 289
seal oil, 123
sec, 63
seed cake, 7, 290
seed onion, 222
self-basting turkey, 334
self-service store, 317
sell date, 223
seltzer, 290
semiboneless ham, 148
Sémillon, 353
seminary sausage, 285
semisweet chocolate, 80
semmel, 290
semolina, 129
Senate bean soup, 290
serrano chile, 76
sesame, 291
seven sweets and seven sours, 291
7UP, 301
Seville orange, 223

sex on the beach, 291
Seyval Blanc grape, 291, 353
Seyve-Villard 5–276 grape, 291
shad, 291
shaddock, 143
shad roe with bacon, 291
Shaker lemon pie, 182
shake-up whiskey, 291–292
shallot, 292
shark, 292
shaved ice,162
she-crab soup, 292
sheeny destroyer, 292
sheep dip, 185
sheepshead, 116, 250
shelf date, 223
shelf life, 223, 292
shelf-stable, 292
shells, 188
shell steak, 24
shenkbeer, 26
sherry, 292–293
sherry-cobbler, 87
sherry glass, 21
shiitake mushroom, 213
shine, 209–210
ship biscuit, 150
Shirley Temple, 293
Shirley T Sparkling Soda, 293
shirred egg, 120
shish kebab, 127
shit-faced, 116
shit on a shingle, 78, 293, 307
shoestring potato, 133
shoofly pie, 293
shoot it yellow, 193
shoot one from the south, 193
shopping cart, 317
shore dinner, 293
short broth, 99
shortening, 107
short-finned squid, 309
shortnin' bread, 293–294
short-order restaurant, 190
shot, 185, 294
shot-and-a-beer, 294
shot-and-a-beer town, 294
shot glass, 21
shoulder bacon, 53
shovel-nosed lobster, 187
shrapnel, 294
Shredded Ralston, 62
Shredded Wheat, 62
shrimp, 294–295
shrimp and grits, 145, 295
shrimp cocktail, 88, 294
shrimp Creole, 294
shrimper's sauce, 295
shrimp scampi, 287
shrimps de Jonge, 295
shrimp wiggle, 295
shrink-wrapping, 55
Siberia, 295
Sicilian-style pizza, 244
sidecar, 295–296
side-stripe shrimp, 294
silk snapper, 299
sill salad, 298
silver Bronx, 43
silver hake, 148
silver salmon, 281
silver smelt, 297

Singapore sling, Singapore Raffles gin sling, 296
singles' bar, 271, 296
sinker, 115
sinkers and suds, 193
sippin' whiskey, 39
sirloin, 296
Siwash cheese, 281
six-pack, 296
six-shooter coffee, 100
sizzling platter, 296
skate, 196–197
skilletburger, 297
skim milk, 205
skipjack, 35, 297
skirt, 24, 297
skully-jo, 297
skunk egg, 101
Sky Bar, 57
slapjack, 229
Slapsticks, 298
sliced sweet pickle, 240
sliders, 149
slinger, 297
slip go down, 45
slipperdowns, 211
slipper lobster, 187
sloe gin, 140
slop chute, 269
slop joint, 269
sloppy Joe, 185, 297
sloshed, 116
slug, 156
slumgullion, 297
slump, 297
small beer, 297
smallmouth bass, 30
smallmouth buffalo, 314
smart bar, 19
smear case, 99
smelt, 297–298
Smith College Fudge, 135
Smithfield ham, 148–149
Smooth Cayenne pineapple, 243
smooth dog, smooth dogfish, 113
smoothie, 298
smooth puffer, 319
s'mores, some mores, 298
smorgasbord, 298
smothered, 298
smothered chicken, 298
smut, 108
snack, 298–299
snack bar, 190
snack food, 20
snail, 109
snake-head whiskey, 101
snap bean, 312
snapper, 298–299
snapper soup, 336
snickerdoodle, 299
Snickers, 54, 57
snitz, 287
snoots, 19
snow, 103, 123
snow ball, sno' ball, 299
snow cone, 299–300
snow cream, 300
snow egg, 128
snow goose, 142
snowshoe rabbit, 261
soap plant, 356
sober side of the bar, 300

society saloon, 270
sockeye salmon, 281
soda, 31, 300–301
soda beer, 301
soda cracker, 104
soda fountain, 2, 55, 290, 300
soda-fountain confection, 50
soda jerk, soda jerker, 301
soda pop, 290, 300
soda water, 300
sodium (or calcium) propionate, 53
sodium nitrite, 301
sodium (or calcium) stearyl lactylate, 53
soft drink, 300
soft red winter wheat, 345
soft-shell clam, 85
soft-shell crab, 102
soft-wheat flour, 129
sole, 301–302
sole Marguery, 303
son-of-a-bitch stew, son-of-a-gun stew, 303
sook, 102
sop, 144, 303
sopaipilla, 303
sorbic acid, 303
sorbitan monostearate, 303
sorbitol, 303
sorghum, 303
sorghum molasses, 303
sorgos, 303
sorrel, 303–304
S.O.S., 293, 307
sotol, 3
soul food, 19, 102
soup-en-famille, 304
soupfin shark, 292
soup kitchen, 304
sour, 304
sourball, 54
sour cabbage, 285
sour cream, 106
sourdough, 41, 304
sourdough bullet, 101
sour glass, 21
sour mash whiskey, 39
sour mixed pickle, 239
sour pickle, 239
sour relish pickle, 239
Southern Comfort, 304–305
Southern flounder, 128
southern fried chicken, 107, 304–306
southern style, 306
Southside, 306
soybean, soya bean, soypea, 22, 306
soybean milk, 306
soy protein, 16, 306
spacer, 306
Spa Cuisine, 306
spaghetti, 232
spaghetti alla Caruso, 306–307
spaghetti squash, 309
Spam, 307
Spanish bayonet, 356
Spanish chestnut, 70
Spanish garlick, 292
Spanish lobster, 187
Spanish mackerel, 195
Spanish omelet, 120
Spanish onion, 222
Spanish peanut, 235
Spanish rice, 273

Spanish-style olive, 221
sparkling, 37
sparkling Burgundy, 63
sparkling Moscato, 63
sparkling water, 290
speakeasy, speak, 47, 270, 307
spear leek, 137
spearmint, 206
special, 176
special meal, 4
specialty meat, 285
speckled cat, 39
speckled scallop, 286
spider crab, 102
spiedie, 307
spinach, 307–308
spinach beet, 28
spiny dogfish, 13
spiny lobster, 186
spirit vinegar, 341
split, 308
split peas, 233
sponge, 102
spoon bread, spoon cornbread, 308
sports bar, 308
spot, spot fish, 308
spot shrimp, 294
spot-tail, 39
spotted bass, 30
spotted cabrilla, 146
spotted pup, 101
spotted sea trout, 308
spotted sucker, 314
spray-dried instant, 90
Springfield horseshoe, 308
spring herring, 155
spring house, 308
spring lamb, 180
spring onion, 286
spring roll, 308
spring water, 38
sprinkle the infield, 308
spritzer, 308
spud, 308–309
spud with the bark on, 188
spur dog, 113
squab, 241
squab chicken, 71
squash, 309
squaw candy, 282
squeeze one, 193
squid, 309
squirrel stew, 44
squirt, 309
stack, 190
stack cake, 208, 309
stack pie, 309
standards of identity, 131
standard of quality, 131
standing rib roast, 24
stanica, 238
Stanley plum, 246
star fruit, 58
starry flounder, 128
state doin's, 309
states' eggs, 309
Stayman, 10
steak fries, 133
steam beer, 26, 309–310
steamer, 85
steer joint, 50
stewed, 116
sticky, 310

sticky bun, 310
sticky rice, 273
stifle, stiffle, 310
stink-a-bus, 277
stinking, 116
stirabout, 310
stirrup, 158
stone boiling, 310
stone crab, 310–311
stone fence, stonewall, 311
stone-ground flour, 129
store cheese, 65
stout, 25
straight, 311
straight whiskey, 346
strawberry, 311–312
strawberry fever, 312
strawberry shortcake, 312
streak-of-lean, streak-o-lean, 312
streeted, 312
stretch one, 193
streusel, 312
string bean, 22, 312–313
striped bass, striper, 21, 313
striped bonito, 297
striped mullet, 212
strip steak, 24
stromboli, 313
strudel, 313
stuffing, 115, 313
sturgeon, 60, 313–314
submarine, 154
subway, 191
succory, 73
succotash, 96, 184, 314
sucker, 314
suckerfish, 314
suckling pig, 314
sucrose, 315, 317
suffering bar steward, 314
suffering bastard, 314–315
sugar, 2, 315–316
sugar alcohol, 316
sugar bush, 198
sugar cone, 165
sugar corn, 97
sugar-cured ham, 148
sugar house, 198
sugaring, 197
sugar-in-snow, 300
sugar pea, 233
sugar pie, 70
sugar plum, 54
sugar pumpkin, 309
sugar snow, 198
sukiyaki, 316
summer flounder, 128
summer sausage, 285
summer squash, 309
summer squid, 309
sunchoke, 171
sundae, Sunday, 164
Sunday dinner, 112
sunfish, 30, 316
sunflower, 316–317
sunflower oil, 317
sun tea, 323
supermarket, 317
superstore, 317
supper, 112
suption, 317
surf-n'-turf, 317–318
surf smelt, 298

surimi, 317–318
swamp cabbage, 229
swamper, 101
swamp rabbit, 261
swamp seed, 101
sweatpads, 230
sweaty saddles, 318
Swedish meatball, 318
Sweet Alice, 191
sweet and sour, 318
sweet and sour meatball, 318
sweet banana pepper, 75
sweet butter, 49
sweet chocolate, 80
sweet cider, 84
sweet corn, 97
Sweet Fire, 159
sweet marjoram, 224
sweetmeats, 54
sweet mixed pickle, 240
sweet orange, 223
sweet pepper, 197
sweet pepper plant, 237
sweet pickle, 240
sweet pickled pork, 240
sweet potato, 252, 318–319
sweet potato pie, 319
sweet potato pudding, 258
sweet rice, 273
sweetsop, 319
swellfish, 319
Swiss cheese, 65, 68
Swiss steak, 319–320
Swiss-style yogurt, 356
switchel, 320
swizzle, 320
swizzled, 116
swizzle stick, 320
swordfish, 320
Sydney Smith's salad dressing, 320
syllabub, 320
Sylvaner, 353
Syrian grain, 303

Tab, 301
tabasco, 159, 321
tablecloth restaurant, tablecolther, 321
table salt, 282
taco, 321, 330
Taco Bell, 321
taco chip, 330
tacos al carbon, 125
taco stand, 270, 321
taffy, 54, 321
taffy bake, 321
taffy pull, 321
tafia, 277, 321
tailgate picnic, 321–322
take-out, take-home, 322
take the pledge, 322
tallywag, 32
tamale, 322
tamale pie, 322
tangelo, 224, 322
tangerine, 224
tanglefoot, 185
tanked, 116
tanner's dock, 53
tansy, tansey, 322
tansy cake, 322
Taos lightnin', 322
tapioca flour, 129
tapioca pudding, 258

tarantula juice, 185
taro, 322
tarragon, 322–323
tarte à la bouie, 323
tasso, 323
tassy, 323
tautog, 32, 323
tavern, 19
TBHQ, 3
T-bone, 24
tea, 323–324
tea bag, 323
tea-cake, 211
tea dance, 323
tea party, 323
tea sandwich, 283
Teleme Jack, 68
Temple orange, 224
ten-cents-a-dip, 111
tenderizer, 324
tenderloin, 296, 324
Tennessee Red peanut, 235
Tennessee whiskey, 324
tepary, 324
tequila, 3, 324–325
tequila sunrise, 325
tequila sunset, 325
Texas cake, 139
Texas Caviar, 102
Texas fries, 133
Texas Gunpowder, 159
Texas sheet cake, 139
Texas toast, 325
Tex Mex, 75, 76, 325
Thai fragrant rice, 273
Thanksgiving, 96, 325–326
Thanksgiving turkey, 326
thé dansant, 326
The fox-grape, 349
theme restaurant, 271
thick crust pizza, 244
thick shake, 206
Thin Mints Girl Scout cookies, 141
Thompson Seedless, 144, 262, 326, 353
Thousand Island dressing, 47, 326
threadfin pompano, threadfish pompano, 247–248
three-finger poi, 246
three-martini lunch, 190
3 Musketeers, 57
3.2 beer, 26
three sheets in (or to) the wind, 326
through Georgia, 193–194
Thunderbird, 351
thyme, 326–327
tight, 116
tilapia, 327
tilefish, 327
Tillamook, 65, 68
Tilton apricot, 12
Tinta Madeira, 353
Tiny Conversation Hearts, 94
tipsy, tipsy parson, 327
tiswin, 327
toasted ravioli, 327
Tobacco onion, 222
toddy, 327
toffee, toffy, 321
tofu, 306
Tofutti, 306
to go, 322
togue, 322, 328

togus, 328
Tokay grape, 143
Toll House cookies, 95, 328
Tom and Jerry, 328
Tom and Jerry mug, 328
tomatillo, 328–329
tomatillo enter, 328
tomatito verde, 328
tomato, 329–330
tomato pie, 244
Tom Collins, 330
Tom Collins glass, 330
Tom Fuller, 330
Tommy Atkins, 197
Tootsie Roll, 57
Tootsie Roll Pop, 188
top heavy, 116
toppings, 166
top Sirloin, 296
torriga, 133
tortellini, 232
tortilla, 40, 48, 96, 123, 330
tortilla chip, 330
tortilla soup, 330–331
tortoni, 331
tostada, 331
total invert sugar, 316
to the left, 194
to the right, 194
totuava, 116
tournedos, 324
Touse, 322
trade whiskey, 331
trading card, 71
training cake, 122
transfer process, 63
transparent pie, transparent pudding, 331
trappers' butter, 331
Trappist cheese, 68
trash fish, 331
T ration, 264
Treasure Cave, 331
tree melon, 230
tree onion, 222
Trenton cracker, 104, 331
trevally, 331
triggerfish, 331
tripe, 331–332
trout, 332
truck farm, truck garden, 332
truffle, 213, 332–333
Trumanburger, 150
Tuckahoc, 319
tuckahoe, 333
tuna, tuna fish, 333
tuna casserole, 59, 333
tuna melt, 333
turban squash, 309
turbinado sugar, 316
turkey, 333–335
turkey bacon, 16
Turkey Devonshire, 335
turnip, 335
turnip greens, 335
turnip-rooted parsley, 231
turnover, 335
Turnpike Cake, 355
turtle, 335–336
turtledove, 240
turtle soup, 336
Tuscarora rice, 348
tutti-frutti, 336

TV dinner, 336
Twelfth Night cake, 175
twenty-one, 194
Twinkie defense, 336
Twinkies, 336
two-finger poi, 246
tzimmes, tsimmes, tzimmis, 327

ultra-pasteurization, 205
unclean, 177
uncooked smoked sausage, 285
Underwood plum, 246
Universal Product Code, 337
Universal Product Code (UPC)
    scanner, 337
unsalted butter, 49
upside-down cake, 337
u'u, 337

Valencia orange, 224
valley tan, 338
vanilla, vanilla bean, 31, 338
vanilla extract, 338
vanilla flavoring, 338
vanilla ice cream, 31
vanillin, 338
variety meat, 203
Vassar Fudge, 135
veal, 15, 338–339
veal francese, 339
veal Parmesan, 339
vegetable liver, 339
vegetable marrow, 309
vegetable oil, 339
vegetable oyster, 282
vegetable pear, 64
vegetable (plant) protein, 339
veggie burger, 150
veggies, 339
vending machine, 70, 339–340
venison, 340
Vermont, 194
Vermont Cheddar, 65
vermouth, 340
very low sodium, 184
veto, 340
vichyssoise, 340–341
vicious virgin, 314
victory garden, 137
victuals, vittles, 341
Vidal Blanc, 353
Vidalia onion, 222
Vienna roll, 174
Villard Blanc, 353
vinegar, 341
vinegar candy, 54, 341
vinegar pie, 341
vine ripened, 329
vinifera, grape, 50
Virginia ham, 149
Virginia opossum, 223

Virginia oyster, 226–227
Virginia Potato, 319
Virginia Running peanut, 235
Virginia strawberry, 311
Virgin Mary, 33
virgin oil, 339
vitamin C, 2
vodka, 44, 341–342
vodka martini, 201
Volstead cocktail, 342

waffle, 343
waffle cone, 165
Waldorf salad, 343
walleye, 343
walleye pollock, 246
walnut, 343–344
wanigan, 344
warehouse store, 317
wart, 194
Washington Navel orange, 223–224
Washington pie, Washington cake,
    344
wasp nest, 101
water, 344
water chinquapin, 5
watermelon, 344–345
watermelon rind or pickle, 345
wax bean, 313
waxy corn, 97
waxy rice, 273
weakfish, 345
wedge, 154
wedge bone, 296
weeper, 345
Weisswurst, 93
Welch's Grape Juice, 143
Wellesley Fudge, 135
well water, 38
western, 345
Western New York chicken wings, 46
western omelet, 120, 345
West's White Pacific, 132
wet bar, 345
wet bottom, 293
wheat, 345–346
Wheat Chex, 62
wheat germ, 346
Wheaties, 62
wheat pilaf, 346
whelk, 346
whey, 98
whip, 346
whipped butter, 49
whiskey, 346–347
whiskey mill, 347
whiskey sour, 304
whiskey squirt, 309
Whisky Rebellion, 346
whistleberry,101, 191
white bass, 347

White Castle, 270
White Castle hamburger, 149
white catfish, 60
white chocolate mousse, 347
white clam sauce, 347
white crab, 102
whitefish, 347
white-fronted goose, 142
white goods, 44
white hake, 148
white lady, 347
white legger, 102
white lightning, 210
white man's fly, 156
white mullet, 212
white mustard, 213
white pepper, 237
white perch, 237
white Pinot, 69
white pizza, 245
whites, 347
white sauce, 347
white sea urchin, 289
white shortening, 107
white shrimp, 294
white squid, 309
white sturgeon, 60, 314
white sucker, 314
white sugar, 315
white tablecloth restaurant, 321
white turnip, 335
white vinegar, 341
white Zinfandel, 69
whiting, 148
whole hominy, 156
whole wheat bread, 41
whole-wheat flour, 129
whoopie pie, 347
whortleberry, 160
wiener, 158
wienie roast, 158
Wilbur Buds, 80
wild boar, 347–348
wild garlic, 137–138
wild marjoram, 224
wild pave, 324
wild radish, 261
wild rhubarb, 53
wild rice, 273, 348
wild spinach, 181
wild thyme, 327
Wimpy burger, 149
wine, 348–353
wine brick, 353
wine cellar, 57
wine cooler, 353
wine glass, 21
wine in a bag, 13
wine in a box, 13
Winesap, 10
Winkler, 132–133

winter crookneck squash, 309
winter flounder, 128
winter melon, 59
winter squash, 309
winter squid, 309
Wisconsin cake, 353–354
Wisconsin cake pan, 353
Wisconsin Cheddar, 65
witch, 354
witloof, 74
wohaw, 354
wolf fish, 354
wonder, 114
Wonder Bread, 41
woodear mushroom, 213
woosher, 101
woozy, 116
wop salad, 354
Worcestershire sauce, 51
wreath, 194
wrass, 354
wreck pan, 83
Wrigley chewing gum, 71
wrinkled steak, 78
Wyandotte chicken, 71

yabbie, 105
yakitori, 355
Yale beet, 151
Yale boat pie, 355
Yale cocktail, 355
yeast, 355
yeast cake, 355
yellowfin croaker, 116
yellow jack, 169
yellowmouth grouper, 146
yellow mustard, 214
yellow passion fruit, 231–232
yellow perch, 237
yellow pike, 343
yellow squash, 309
yellowtail, 169
yellowtail flounder, 128
yellowtail snapper, 299
yogurt, 355–356
York Imperial, 10
Yorkshire pudding, 249, 258, 356
yucca, yuca, 356
yum-yum, 194

za, 244
zephrina, 358
zeppelins in a fog, 194
Zinfandel, 353, 357–358
zip-code wine, 358
zombie, 314, 358
zone fractionalization, 162
zonked, 116
zoo, 358
zucchini, 309, 358
zwieback, 358